Sixth Edition

Family and Intimate Partner Violence

Heavy Hands

Denise Kindschi Gosselin
Professor Emerita, Criminal Justice and Sociology
Western New England University

330 Hudson Street, NY NY 10013

Vice President, Portfolio Management: Andrew Gilfillan
Portfolio Manager: Gary Bauer
Editorial Assistant: Lynda Cramer
Field Marketing Manager: Bob Nisbet
Product Marketing Manager: Heather Taylor
Director, Digital Studio and Content Production: Brian Hyland
Managing Producer: Jennifer Sargunar
Content Producer: Rinki Kaur
Manager, Rights Management: Johanna Burke
Operations Specialist: Deidra Smith

Creative Digital Lead: Mary Siener
Managing Producer, Digital Studio: Autumn Benson
Content Producer, Digital Studio: Maura Barclay
Full-Service Management and Composition: Integra Software Services Pvt. Ltd.
Full-Service Project Manager: Kiran Kumar
Cover Designer: Studio Montage
Cover Art (or Cover Photo): adl21/ Vetta/Getty images
Printer/Binder: LSC Communications Kendallville
Cover Printer: Phoenix Color/Hagerstown
Text Font: Times LT Pro

Library of Congress Cataloging-in-Publication Data
Names: Gosselin, Denise Kindschi, 1954- author.
Title: Family and intimate partner violence : heavy hands / Denise Kindschi
    Gosselin, Professor Emerita, Western New England University.
Other titles: Heavy hands
Description: Sixth edition. | Boston : Pearson, [2019] | Earlier editions
    published as: Heavy hands : an introduction to the crimes of intimate and
    family violence.
Identifiers: LCCN 2017054406| ISBN 9780134868219 | ISBN 0134868218
Subjects: LCSH: Family violence—Philosophy. | Family violence—Government
    policy. | Victims of family violence—Services for.
Classification: LCC HV6626 .G67 2018 | DDC 362.82/92—dc23 LC record available at
https://lccn.loc.gov/2017054406

ISBN 10:   0-13-486821-8
ISBN 13: 978-0-13-486821-9

*This edition is dedicated with love to Dr. Richard and Mrs. Allyson Gosselin, &
Lillian for the joy and inspiration that you bring to me.*

CONTENTS

Chapter 14 THE COURT RESPONSE TO INTIMATE PARTNER VIOLENCE   347

PREFACE

NEW TO THIS EDITION

- To address the changing protections available under the VAWA for immigrants seeking asylum as domestic violence victims, NEW to Chapter 1 is a discussion on asylum law with information on the U & T visas.
- Chapter 3 is revised to update the theoretical perspectives in family violence. Having gained prominence in domestic violence theory, the perspective of *Coercive Control Theory* is NEW.
- NEW to Chapter 4 is the cooperative nature of child abuse investigation with information on the role of the first responders, in addition to the investigation processes of both the police and child protective services.
- Noting the current emphasis on multidisciplinary team child abuse investigations, a NEW section on the *Children's Advocacy Center Model* is included in Chapter 5.
- Chapter 6 is entirely NEW. To address adolescent and young adult victimization this new chapter discusses human trafficking, teen dating violence, college dating violence, rape, and more. This new chapter reflects the most current concerns in the field of family violence with survey results and research from prominent academics.
- NEW information on *survival sex* and *couch surfing* among homeless youth is included in Chapter 7 on adolescent perpetrators and consequences of abuse.
- Changes in the field of intimate partner violence influenced the NEW sections in Chapter 8 on economic control, *gaslighting*, male partner reproductive coercion, IPV victimization of men with disabilities, and the domestic violence green card.
- Chapter 9 is now appropriately entitled LGBTI Partner Abuse and updated to reflect the legitimacy and domestic status of the community due to the Supreme Court decision in *Obergefell v. Hodges* (2015).
- Assignments with links to Internet research at the end of each chapter have been tested and updated. The wealth of information available to our students from legitimate Web sites can be daunting. Encouraging the use of these resources is recommended.

It has been over a decade since the first edition of *Heavy Hands* was published. The first edition was called "groundbreaking." It was the first text for a course not then taught in college classrooms. This classic has been tried and found true for hundreds of courses. It is used in the United States and abroad. Over a decade later, *Heavy Hands* has grown up and kept pace with the fast-changing field of family violence.

There have been so many important changes in family violence practice, policy, and research. We have seen its criminalization and the resulting controversy. Domestic violence protection orders are now a common source of protection for the survivors of intimate partner violence. Offenders are routinely referred to treatment programs. We now recognize that abuse in later life may come from a spouse or close family member and not merely from stressed caregivers. Child abuse has gained recognition as an important criminal justice and police investigation focus. Rates of intimate partner violence and homicide have declined. Violence against males and LGBTI populations is now acknowledged. No longer is there an expectation for the one-size-fits-all response. Things have changed.

Criminal justice has evolved as a profession that values higher education and research. This sixth edition has evolved as well. It includes current information on numerous topics of interest within the field of family violence. While it cannot cover everything, this text provides all of the essential information for a course on family violence. It is comprehensive, yet easy to understand. The text has been reorganized so that each chapter stands alone, as part of the larger issue of family violence. This should allow students and instructors to more easily find the information of interest to them. Each chapter ends with a practical scenario that poses a question for students to consider. The answer will be provided within that chapter. This will allow students to test their knowledge through a real-life situation.

INSTRUCTOR SUPPLEMENTS

Instructor's Manual with Test Bank. Includes content outlines for classroom discusion, teaching suggestions, and answers to selected end-of-chapter questions from the text. This also contains a Word document version of the test bank.

TestGen. This computerized test generation system gives you maximum flexibility in creating and administering tests on paper, electronically, or online. It provides state-of-the-art features for viewing and editing test bank questions, dragging a selected question into a test you are creating, and printing sleek, formatted tests in a variety of layouts. Select test items from test banks included with TestGen for quick test creation, or write your own questions from scratch. TestGen's random generator provides the option to display different text or calculated number values each time questions are used.

PowerPoint Presentations. Our presentations are clear and straightforward. Photos, illustrations, charts, and tables from the book are included in the presentations when applicable.

To access supplementary materials online, instructors need to request an instructor access code. Go to **www.pearsonhighered.com/irc,** where you can register for an instructor access code. Within 48 hours after registering, you will receive a confirming e-mail, including an instructor access code. Once you have received your code, go to the site and log on for full instructions on downloading the materials you wish to use.

ALTERNATE VERSIONS

eBooks. This text is also available in multiple eBook formats. These are an exciting new choice for students looking to save money. As an alternative to purchasing the printed textbook, students can purchase an electronic version of the same content. With an eTextbook, students can search the text, make notes online, print out reading assignments that incorporate lecture notes, and bookmark important passages for later review. For more information, visit your favorite online eBook reseller or visit **www.mypearsonstore.com**.

ACKNOWLEDGMENTS

My appreciation to the following reviewers for their helpful comments on the chapters:

Kim Mac Innis, Bridgewater State University
Melinda Roberts, University of Southern Indiana
Sheryl Van Horne, Arcadia University

Thank you to the many victims who have confided in me about atrocities too horrible to recount. I STILL remember you. You taught me the value of dignity and the importance of equal enforcement of the law. To the women, men, boys, and girls who have suffered from domestic crimes, I marvel at your resilience and applaud your survival.

Austin Provost of Western New England University contributed to the end-of-chapter questions for the fifth edition. In the third edition, Melissa Kliesch and Jeffrey Huguenor assisted. I owe a debt of gratitude to Kathy Arenstam, whose contribution in the first edition provided consistency. Thank you, Danielle D. McIntosh, for the research on elder law. To my friends and colleagues at Western New England University, who encouraged my efforts, thank you. In particular, Professor Janet Bowdan whose reading and editing on the first edition was invaluable.

ABOUT THE AUTHOR

 A pioneer in law enforcement, the author was the first uniformed female officer in her hometown, Lunenburg, Massachusetts, and the first female campus police officer at the community college she attended. The Massachusetts Senate honored her in 1978 as the first woman appointed constable for the City of Fitchburg. In 2011, Dr. Gosselin received accolades as *Alumna of the Year* at Mt. Wachusett Community College where she now serves on its Board of Trustees.

Dr. Denise Gosselin graduated in the 61st Recruit Training Troop of the Massachusetts State Police in January 1980. During the years that followed she served as a uniformed officer performing route patrol activities, as an instructor at the Massachusetts State Police Academy, and as a detective in major crime investigations. Recognized as a local expert in child abuse investigation, she has spoken on cable television and radio. She appeared on the *America's Most Wanted* television show in connection with a fugitive in a case she was investigating. She has made many presentations at professional meetings with the Department of Social Services, Department of Mental Health, and Office of the District Attorney. She has testified in numerous major crime cases in both criminal and civil hearings.

Dr. Gosselin served as a faculty member and Department Chair in the Criminal Justice and Sociology Department at Western New England University until her retirement as Professor Emerita in 2017. Her other publications include *Interviewing and Interrogation: Smart Talk,* currently in its second edition and *Crimes and Mental Disorders: The Criminal Justice Response.* Dr. Gosselin has contributed to the *Encyclopedia of Police Science,* the *Encyclopedia of Juvenile Justice,* and the *Encyclopedia of Domestic Violence,* as well as chapters to *Women, Law, & Social Control* and *Policing & Victims*.

Dr. Gosselin is an experienced Criminal Justice Program Reviewer. Her major presentations and invited lectures have been at the 12th United Nations Congress on Crime and Criminal Justice in Salvador, Brazil; the Massachusetts State Police Academy, at West Point Military Academy, Campbell University, NC, and at Gwynedd-Mercy College, PA.

As a life-time member of the *Academy of Criminal Justice Sciences* (ACJS), Dr. Gosselin has served as Region One Trustee 2013–2016 and ACJS Trustee-at-Large 2009–2012. As a member of the *Northeastern Association of Criminal Justice Sciences,* she has served as President, Vice President, and Secretary. She is also a member of the European Society of Criminal Justice and is a co-founding member of the Everywoman Everywhere Workgroup, from the Harvard Kennedy School project of the International Commission on Violence Against Women and Girls.

Global Violence Against Women

CHAPTER OBJECTIVES

After reviewing this chapter, you should be able to:

1. Describe the forms of violence against women and its definition.
2. Discuss the scope of *violence against women*.
3. Explain the three forms of immigration relief established by the VAWA.
4. Discuss the status of female genital mutilation as a global concern.
5. Differentiate between female feticide and femicide.

KEY TERMS

Bride burning	Honor killing
Female genital mutilation	Refugee
Female feticide	Trafficking in Persons
Femicide	Violence against women

INTRODUCTION

Even without an exact count of the numbers of victims, it can be easily said that family violence affects millions of women, men, and children across the United States and around the world. It is not simply a problem for the family experiencing the violence, but, as you will note throughout this text, it is a crisis that will affect us all. The manner in which we respond depends on the nature of the violence as well as the cultural, economic, social, and political contexts. The consequences of this violence affect society as a whole, the community, and its children. Additional costs beyond the human toll include lowered economic production as well as political and social instability through intergenerational transmission of violence.

Women are the most frequent targets of intimate partner violence, a significant form of violence against women (refer to the photo in Figure 1-1). This chapter looks at the larger picture of violence against women to prepare students for the subsequent chapters on violence in the family. This chapter outlines the prevalence of violence against women in 15 countries around the world; most of the violence occurs behind closed doors at the hands of an intimate partner. From this chapter, it is possible to understand the current global concern

FIGURE 1-1   Eliminating violence against women begins with an examination of patriarchal attitudes.   Jason Stitt/Shutterstock

over the treatment of women within the home and outside. Later in this text, various forms of violence will be defined, along with response options available in the United States. Theoretical explanations are included. An in-depth examination of the criminal justice response to family violence will follow.

The United Nations (UN) Secretary-General's in-depth study on all forms of violence against women reported that the most common form of violence that women experience globally is intimate partner violence, commonly referred to as spousal abuse (UN, 2006). Violence against women within families is a pervasive and long-standing problem, although it was not considered as such until quite recently. Violence against women is recognized as a global crisis of staggering proportion.

VIOLENCE AGAINST WOMEN: A GLOBAL CONCERN

Violence against women is an international epidemic of global concern. Women are not safe from brutality in any country of the world. Acts of violence include threats of violence, coercion, or arbitrary deprivation of liberty, whether occurring in public or private life. Any definition of violence against women includes, but is not limited to, the following forms:

- Physical, sexual, and psychological violence occurring in the family, including battering, sexual abuse of children in the household, dowry-related violence, marital rape, female genital mutilation (FGM), and other traditional practices harmful to women, and violence related to exploitation.
- Physical, sexual, and psychological violence occurring within the general community, including rape, sexual abuse, sexual harassment and intimidation at work and educational institutions and elsewhere, trafficking in women, and forced prostitution.
- Physical, sexual, and psychological violence perpetrated or condoned by the state, wherever it occurs.

Advocates recognize that the violence against women in the United States affects a staggering one in four American women. The rates are even more astonishing for women and girls globally. On average, the World Health Organization (WHO) estimates that 18 women suffer death due to gender-related violence every day (WHO, 2013). Globally, WHO estimates that an intimate partner commits more than 35 percent of female murders.

Out of 10 countries surveyed in a 2005 study by the WHO, more than 50 percent of women in Bangladesh, Ethiopia, Peru, and Tanzania reported experiencing physical or sexual violence by intimate partners (García-Moreno, Jansen, Ellsberg, Heise, & Watts, 2005). The authors found figures reaching a staggering 71 percent in rural Ethiopia. Only in one country (Japan) did less than 20 percent of women report incidents of intimate partner violence. Among women ages 15 to 44, violence against women accounts for more death and disability than cancer, malaria, traffic injuries, and war put together. The Council of Europe has stated that intimate partner violence is the primary cause of death and disability for women ages 16 to 44 in Europe—more than cancer or traffic accidents (Love, 2005). The 2014 European Union survey found that one in three women has experienced a form of physical and/or sexual violence by intimate partners (Bonewit, 2016).

The United States is committed to combating violence against women around the world. In 2012, the United States released its first-ever strategy to prevent and respond to gender-based violence globally (U.S. Department of State, 2012a). Efforts to raise the status of women and girls around the world are the cornerstone of the government's commitment to preventing and responding to gender-based violence. The strategy outlines four key objectives: (1) to increase coordination of gender-based violence prevention and response efforts among U.S. government agencies and with other stakeholders; (2) to enhance integration of gender-based violence prevention and response efforts into existing U.S. government work; (3) to improve collection, analysis, and use of data and research to enhance gender-based violence prevention and response efforts; and (4) to enhance or expand U.S. government programming that addresses gender-based violence.

Included in this heightened effort is the integration of gender-based violence prevention for police and military training outside of the United States. For example, the U.S. Police Training and Advisory Team, assisted by four interpreters, teaches practical, hands-on training to Afghanistan police trainees in the spirit of our leadership role. Refer to the illustration in Figure 1-2 (Myers, 2008). During the training, police officers learn to investigate intimate partner violence in addition to techniques

FIGURE 1-2   Navy Petty Officer 2nd Class Jovener R. Mironchik of the Kunar Provincial Reconstruction Team gets handcuffed while Navy Seaman Brian L. Boyd Jr. watches during a training session with Afghan National Auxiliary Police students at the Kunar PRT's training facility near Asadabad, Afghanistan.
U.S. Navy Permissions Department, Academic Publishing

for traffic accident investigation, weapons familiarization, vehicle searches, community policing, explosives detection, the penal code, baton training, handcuffing, and a variety of other law enforcement skills.

Istanbul Convention

The 2011 Council of Europe Convention on preventing and combatting violence against women and domestic violence, commonly referred to as the Istanbul Convention, defines the term "**violence against women**" as a violation of human rights and a form of discrimination against women and shall mean all acts of gender-based violence that result in, or are likely to result in, physical, sexual, psychological, or economic harm or suffering to women, including threats of such acts, coercion, or arbitrary deprivation of liberty, whether occurring in public or in private life (Council of Europe, 2011). The economic costs of violence against women in the European Union in 2011 were estimated to be 228 billion euro each year, roughly 247 billion in U.S. dollars (Bonewit, 2016). Of this total, 45 billion euro is needed for services for victims, 24 billion for the loss of economic output, and 159 billion on pain and suffering.

REFUGEE AND ASYLUM PROTECTIONS

The international refugee protection response followed atrocities from World War II and the failure to protect Jews and other victims of the Holocaust (Musalo, 2014). The treaty known as the 1951 Convention Relating to the Status of Refugees and its

1967 Protocol defined the international **refugee** as an individual with a "well-founded fear of being persecuted for reasons of race, religion, nationality, membership in a particular social group, or political opinion." This protocol pre-dated the UN concerns of women's rights; therefore, its application to gender violence in the United States is still evolving. The 1996 *Illegal Immigration Reform and Immigrant Responsibility Act* expanded this definition to include persons who have been forced to abort a pregnancy, undergo a forced sterilization, or have been prosecuted for their resistance to coercive population controls (Burt & Batalova, 2014). There are currently 147 countries, including the United States, which are parties to the Refugee Convention, its Protocol, or both (Musalo, 2014).

Asylum seekers must also show that one of the refugee grounds was, or will be, at least one central reason for their persecution (Matter of ARCG, B.I.A. 2014). The primary difference in the United States between refugees and asylum seekers is the location of the person at the time of application. Refugee status applies to persons who are outside of the United States when considered for entry. Asylum status applies to someone who is already in the United States or at a U.S. port of entry.

Immigration authorities in the United States have long struggled with the question of whether victims of domestic violence qualify for asylum under the 1951 Refugee Convention. No official statistics exist in the United States regarding the number of individuals who seek asylum with claims for protection involving domestic violence (Bookey, 2013). In an examination of the Center for Gender and Refugee Studies (CGRS) database at the University of California, Bookey found claims coded under domestic violence to include child abuse, threats of forced marriage, threats of sale into human trafficking by family members, female genital cutting, and intimate partner violence. Narrowing the focus to 206 cases that involve intimate partners, Bookey notes different and arbitrary outcomes to applications of asylum across the nation. Until recently, there has been a lack of guidance from U.S. courts on the necessary elements for asylum to be granted when relief is sought due to a claim of domestic violence.

In 2014, the first case to find that women who are victims of severe domestic violence in their home countries might be eligible for asylum was decided by the U.S. Board of Immigration Appeals in the *Matter of ARCG* (B.I.A. 2014). Asylum was granted to a Guatemalan woman who had been severely beaten and raped by her husband for more than 10 years, and that the abuse occurred in a country where society failed to protect victims of intimate partner violence. The Board held that an asylum seeker might qualify as a "member of a particular social group," in this case, of married women in Guatemala who are unable to leave their relationship (Matter of ARCG, B.I.A. 2014). While *ARCG* clarifies how the law of asylum applies to applicants within the domestic violence context, it fails to analyze the extent of harm amounting to persecution (Harv. L. Rev., 2015). Claims for asylum in the United States due to domestic violence are still expected to be difficult as no general rules exist on when domestic violence rises to the level of persecution (Chow, 2016).

VIOLENCE AGAINST WOMEN ACT (VAWA)

U.S. federal law provides numerous forms of protection for vulnerable immigrant women and men. According to the American Immigration Council (2012), the Violence Against Women Act (VAWA) established three forms of immigration relief. Protections are available under a "self-petitioning" option for survivors of family violence: for victims of violent crime the "U" visa, and for victims of sexual assault or trafficking the "T" visa. The *Violence Against Women Reauthorization Act of 2013* (VAWA) amends the Immigration and Nationality Act (INA) regarding noncitizen family members in cases of domestic violence.

The first form of immigration relief established by the VAWA of 1994 is a process called "self-petitioning." Abused spouses, children, and parents of U.S. citizens (and certain permanent residents) can now self-file a petition for an immigrant visa without the abuser's knowledge (U.S. Citizenship and Immigration Services, 2016). The self-petitioning option recognizes that abusive spouses who file immigration petitions often delay or revoke petitions for their family members and may threaten to report them to immigration authorities. Qualifying family members who have suffered extreme cruelty or harm by a U.S. citizen-family member (spouse, child, or parent) may apply for eligibility to work in the United States and to file for green card. The VAWA equally applies to men and women, and is dependent on a good faith marriage and residence with the abusive family member.

The U Visa

The U visa is the second form of relief, created by VAWA under the Victims of Trafficking and Violence Prevention Act of 2000, effective in 2007. To qualify for a U visa, a noncitizen must have suffered substantial physical or mental abuse as the result of certain criminal activity and be willing to cooperate with a government official in the investigation or prosecution of the criminal activity. Examples of criminal activities covered under the U visa provisions include domestic violence, torture, trafficking, female genital cutting, incest, rape, and any substantially similar crime. There is no requirement that the survivor be legally married to her abuser or that the abuser be a U.S. citizen or permanent resident. The U visa is valid for up to four years and may be extended. After three years of continuous presence in the United States an individual may apply for lawful permanent resident status.

The T Visa

In 2000, Congress created the T visa to provide immigration relief to victims of severe forms of human trafficking, the third form of immigration relief under VAWA. U.S. Immigration and Customs Enforcement (ICE) defines **Trafficking in Persons** as a commercial sex act induced by fraud, force, coercion, or in which the victim is younger than 18 years of age, or the recruitment, harboring, transportation, provision, or obtaining of a person for labor or services, through use of force, fraud, or coercion for the purpose of subjection to involuntary servitude or slavery. A T visa protects victims from removal and permits them to work in the United States. Applicants have access to the same benefits as refugees, including cash assistance, food stamps, and job training. Victims over the age of 18 are required to assist law enforcement in the investigation or prosecution of the traffickers. The T visa lasts for four years and may lead to lawful permanent resident status after three years of continuous physical presence in the United States under specific circumstances.

THE UNITED NATIONS

The UN leads the effort to protect vulnerable women and girls worldwide. One of the most important actions in this field consists of the adopting of the 1979 Convention on the Elimination of All Forms of Discrimination Against Women (CEDAW) (A/34/46), which provides that state parties will perform the following:

- Embody the principle of the equality of men and women in their national constitutions and ensure the practical realization of this principle (Art.2 (a)).
- Adopt appropriate legislative measures prohibiting all discrimination against women (Art. 2 (b)).
- Establish legal protection of the rights of women on an equal basis with men (Art. 2 (c)).
- Modify or abolish existing laws, regulations, customs, and practices that constitute discrimination against women (Art 2 (f)).
- Repeal all national penal provisions that discriminate against women (Art. 2 (g)).
- Accord women equality with men before the law, a legal capacity identical to that of men and the same opportunity to exercise that capacity (Art. 15).

Also, the UN General Assembly adopted the Declaration on the Elimination of Violence Against Women in 1993. This declaration emphasizes that violence against women is a violation of human rights and recommends strategies to be employed by member states and specialized agencies to eliminate it. The UN's Fourth World Conference on Women took place in Beijing in 1995. Highlighting the problems of violence against women, the UN conference signified a worldwide effort toward ending intimate partner violence.

The active movement by the UN toward eliminating female violence has prompted action toward that goal. The UN Development Fund for Women (UNIFEM) was created to provide financial and technical assistance for innovative programs and strategies that promote women's human rights, political participation, and economic security. UNIFEM promotes gender equality and links women's issues and concerns to national, regional, and global agendas by fostering collaboration and providing technical expertise on gender mainstreaming and women's empowerment strategies. As a result of UNIFEM-supported training, police throughout Cambodia work more closely with village chiefs, and men who exhibit violence toward their wives are required to sign a contract stating they will discontinue their threatening behavior. The contract is used as evidence against the man in court if the violent behavior continues.

One initiative that resulted from the 1995 UN Fourth World Conference on Women in Beijing was the formation of Women Against Violence Europe (WAVE).

More About It: Female Genital Mutilation

The term "**female genital mutilation**" (FGM) refers to all procedures involving partial or total removal of the external female genitalia or other injury to the female genital organs for nonmedical reasons. Almost exclusively, the term is used to describe a procedure for which parents must give consent due to the age of the minor. The practice is harmful to women and girls in many ways. In addition to the pain involved, the procedure interferes with normal functioning of the body and causes several immediate and long-term health consequences. FGM has been reported to occur in all parts of the world. More than 90 percent of women ages 15 to 49 have been mutilated in Djibouti, Egypt, Guinea, and Somalia (UNICEF, 2013). Prevalence of FGM/C among women ages 15 to 49 varies widely, from 98 percent in Somalia to 1 percent in Cameroon, Uganda, and Zambia. The United States is not immune to this human rights issue. An estimated 507,000 women and girls in the United States are at risk or have been subjected to FGM (Mather & Feldmann-Jacobs, 2016). Although FGM is illegal in the United States, a few have been mutilated in the United States or sent abroad to undergo this procedure.

In the News: First U.S. Federal Case Involving FGM

In April 2017, CNN reported that the first federal case involving FGM in the United States was filed against two Michigan doctors and the wife of one doctor charging them with performing FGM on two 7-year-old girls (Cuevas, 2017). Assistant U.S. Attorney Sarah Woodward has stated in court that it is possible that Dr. Nagarwala performed nearly 100 procedures over the 12-year period between 2005 and 2017. Currently, the federal penalty for the charge is five years. U.S. Representatives David Trott and Carolyn Maloney have introduced the *Stopping Abusive Female Exploitation* (SAFE) Act, which would increase the penalty to 15 years in prison and require public education on the topic.

Do you think that the government has the right to interfere with this "religious practice"?

Read more at http://www.cnn.com/2017/04/26/health/fgm-indictment-michigan/index.html.

National membership of WAVE now stands at 46 countries and over 4,000 women's help organizations. Operating from its office in Vienna, Austria, the organization participates in the UN study on violence against women and other research projects. In addition to collecting and disseminating data on violence against women and children, it manages the European Info Centre Against Violence, acting as a point of contact between organizations that aid women in Europe.

In December 2012, the UN General Assembly accepted a resolution on the elimination of FGM (World Health Organization [WHO], 2013). FGM procedures that intentionally alter or cause injury to the female genital organs of girls and women for nonmedical reasons without any health benefits are banned. The UN acknowledged that FGM nonmedical procedures typically occur between infancy and age 15, causing severe bleeding and problems urinating, infections, infertility, as well as complications in childbirth and increased risk of newborn deaths.

In 2016, the United Nations Children's Fund (UNICEF) estimated that over 200 million women and girls had been subjected to FGM worldwide. The U.S. Congress passed laws making it illegal to perform FGM or for families to knowingly transport a girl outside of the United States for mutilation in their home countries (Mather & Feldmann-Jacobs, 2016). The practice has gained attention in the United States in part because of the rising number of immigrants from countries where FGM is prevalent. In 2017, Michigan became the 26th state to officially ban the practice of FGM, making it a 15-year felony (Eggert, 2017). Surgery performed for custom or religion is not a defense to the illegal practice.

VIOLENCE AGAINST WOMEN: AROUND THE WORLD

A legal analysis by the American Bar Association reveals that European countries have initiated legislative reforms to prevent intimate partner violence (Crohn, 2007). Two common points of law appear in the study:

1. All acts of intimate partner violence are recognized as crimes and fall under the provisions of the penal code. However, only two European countries—Spain and Sweden—criminalize intimate partner violence acts as specific offenses, whereas in other countries such as the United Kingdom, Germany, Austria, Belgium, Bulgaria, and Turkey, a relationship between the victim and the abuser aggravates the offense. In France, such a relationship can be either an aggravating factor or an element of the offense.

2. Victims can request measures of protection from the state. Such measures vary from financial assistance to the victim in Sweden to restraining orders issued against the abuser in the United Kingdom and Austria. In Canada, the violation of a restraining order can be an aggravating circumstance.

According to the Report of the Secretary-General of the UN in 2006, 89 states have some form of legislative prohibition on intimate partner violence, including 60 with specific intimate partner violence laws, and a growing number of countries have instituted national plans of action to end violence against women (UN, 2006). This is an evident increase in comparison to 2003 when UNIFEM did a scan of anti-violence legislation and found that only 45 countries had specific laws on intimate partner violence. There are still 102 states that have no specific legal provisions against intimate partner violence. Only 93 states (of 191 reviewed) have some legislative provision prohibiting trafficking in human beings.

For cases of marital rape, the UN study found that perpetrators may be prosecuted in at least 104 states, and 90 states have some form of legislative provision against sexual harassment. Marital rape is not a prosecutable offense in at least 53 states. In many places, laws contain loopholes that allow perpetrators to act with impunity. In some countries, a rapist can go free under the penal code if he marries the victim.

Afghanistan

Considerable legal reforms are evident in recent years in Afghanistan, despite the reality of life for women there. The Constitution of the Islamic Republic of Afghanistan (2004) and the ratification of the Elimination of Violence Against Women (EVAW) law in 2009 are touted as major achievements toward defining violence as a major crime and for the advancement of human rights, including women's rights (Hasrat & Pfefferle, 2012). No formal reporting on intimate partner violence occurs in Afghanistan; therefore, prevalence rates are nonexistent. Amnesty International's research indicates that country custom or tradition is used to legitimize the violent deaths and injury of women by family members.

Violence against women in Afghanistan is a dramatic problem that includes forced child marriages, physical and sexual abuse, public execution, and girls burning themselves to death out of despair due to impunity for abusers. Economic abuses in addition to practices such as forced divorce, high dowry requirements, denial of education, and expulsion from home make the country unique in its cruel treatment of women. The victim's husband commits 70 percent of all violent acts against women in Afghanistan (Hasrat & Pfefferle, 2012). Strangers commit approximately 10 percent of violence against women; an additional 20 percent is perpetrated by other family members of the victim, including parents, brothers, mothers, sisters, sons, and in-laws.

In the News: Honor Killings: When the Ancient and the Modern Collide

According to a story in the *San Francisco Chronicle* (Stillwell, 2008), throughout the United States, Canada, and Europe, young Muslim women are being targeted for violence. It might be thought that hate crimes are to blame, but it is, in fact, their own relatives who are the perpetrators. While statistics are notoriously hard to come by due to the private nature of such crimes and the fact that very few are reported, the UN Population Fund approximates that as many as 5,000 women are murdered in honor killings each year worldwide.

Honor killing is the traditional practice in which men kill a female relative who is believed to have brought dishonor upon the family or community for forced or suspected sexual activity outside of marriage. While fathers are commonly responsible for honor killings, they often act in concert with their family members, even female relatives. Honor crimes occur worldwide and are based on a variety of cultural and religious practices, including Christians and Jews; however, most honor crimes are associated with the Islam (Bonewit, 2016). Article 42 of the Istanbul Convention states that honor cannot serve as an acceptable justification for committing violence against women. Infringements upon a Muslim daughter's "honor" constitute the greatest humiliation possible to the religious and tribal tradition from which many such immigrant families emerged. Acts that demand "punishment" include refusing to wear a hijab (or headscarf), having non-Muslim boyfriends or male friends of any origin, being sexually active, rejecting arranged marriages, aggressively seeking employment and education, and, more than anything else, attempting to assimilate into Western culture.

Amnesty International reports alarming numbers of Afghan women and girls attempt suicide by dousing themselves with gasoline and setting themselves on fire (Amnesty International, 2005). Some have died while others suffer horrific burns for life. From 2003 to 2004, more than 380 burning cases were documented by Amnesty International. Some of the cases were attempted suicides while others resulted in death. Family violence accounted for 80 percent of the female burnings, but it is not clear whether family members are setting the women on fire or whether the victims have committed the act independently. The overwhelming majority of suicide survivors report that they had attempted suicide as a result of violence in the family.

Australia

The Western Australian Police responded to 30,933 incidents of family and domestic violence over a 12-month period between 2008 and 2009 (Western Australia, 2013). In the other states and territories of Australia, approximately 22,000 female victims of assault identified a family member as the offender during 2011, according to the Australian National Crime Victimization Survey (Linacre, 2012). The Northern Territory of Australia had the largest proportion of female victims identifying the offender as a family member (62 percent). In New South Wales, 49 percent of female victims identified the offender as a family member; in South Australia, 44 percent of female victims; and in the Australian Capital Territory, 43 percent of victims. Similarly, in the United States, women are more likely than men to be assaulted by a partner or family member than by a stranger.

Relationship information for homicides is incomplete for some of the states and territories of Australia and therefore does not represent the entire nation. According to the Australian Personal Safety Survey, 17 people lost their lives in Western Australia as a direct result of family and domestic violence from May 2008 to April 2009 (Western Australia, 2013). The Australian National Crime Victimization Survey reveals that the victims were killed by a partner in 6.9 percent to 17.0 percent of all homicides (Linacre, 2012). Similarly to the United States, Australian homicide victims are predominately male and typically know the offender.

In response to the problems of family violence, some legislative changes that affect the police response in Australia have occurred (Australian Government Solicitor [AGS], 2009). The legislative changes give stronger powers to police, assigning officers a legal obligation to investigate if they have a reasonable suspicion that an act of family and intimate partner violence has occurred. Police are now allowed to enter and search premises without a warrant (but with the approval of a senior officer at the level of Inspector or above) to establish whether intimate partner violence has occurred, and to provide protection.

Police may now remain on the premises for as long as necessary to investigate or ensure the safety of a person. Under the legislation, if the police investigate or enter a premise, they must either take action (apply for a VRO or make a police order) or write a report explaining why no action was taken. Police are also now able to issue on-the-spot police orders. These orders can last for 24 hours without victim consent or up to 72 hours with victim consent. A police order can effectively remove from a residence a person suspected of posing a risk to another, without the requirement of evidence to lay charges. Police orders are particularly useful to police if they do not have sufficient evidence to charge a person but recognize that there is a substantial risk of the escalation of violence if suspected perpetrators (who are most commonly male) remain near their partners.

The police in Australia recognize and respond to a diverse population. The Australian Aboriginal people are made up of 700 traditional societies that speak over 200 languages who live in Western Australia alone (Western Australia, 2013). Aboriginal women are overrepresented as victims of violence. In 2011, Aboriginal and Torres Strait Islanders in the Northern Territory, Queensland, and South Australia were victims of sexual assault at up to four times the rate of nonindigenous persons (Linacre, 2012).

Culturally sensitive responses to the family violence experienced by indigenous people have led to a balanced approach focusing on prevention, protection, and provision. Intervention models appropriate to indigenous communities include a preference for "cooling off" rather than criminalization. Suspicion of first response agencies such as women's refuges, welfare, and police services is common. Cultural appropriateness of services attempts to reduce the unease about using the criminal justice approach. Appropriate intervention designed to improve access to legal services for indigenous women is accomplished through the *Aboriginal Family Violence Prevention Legal Services* in Australia.

Canada

Similar to that in other countries, violence against women is a persistent and ongoing problem in Canada. The Canadian Criminal Code has no specific offense of violence against women or spousal assault. Code provisions that most commonly apply to cases of violence against women include the offenses of assault, sexual assault, criminal harassment, threats of violence, forcible confinement, and homicide. *Measuring Violence Against Women: Statistical Trends* reveals the following information on family violence in Canada (Sinha, 2013):

- The rate of spousal homicide has declined in recent years for both women and men, and survey data suggest that the severity of nonlethal assaults against women has also declined.
- Perpetrators of six in ten spousal homicides against women have had a history of family violence.

- Rates of sexual assault increased in 2010 and remained stable in 2011.
- Women are more likely than men to be the victims of the most severe forms of intimate partner assault, as well as intimate partner homicide, sexual assault, and criminal harassment (stalking).
- Common assaults account for about half of all police-reported violent crimes against women. They were followed by uttering threats, which represented another 13 percent; serious physical assaults, 10 percent; sexual assaults involving little to no physical injury, 7 percent; and stalking, 7 percent.
- The economic costs of violence against women and men to victims and society in health, criminal justice, social services, and lost productivity are estimated to be about 7 billion dollars.
- Between 2001 and 2011, there were 26 female and 36 male infants killed per million in the population.

India

Violence against women in this country takes on an added twist because of "dowry death," a form of intimate partner violence practiced due to an inadequate dowry. Although law strictly forbids the practice of insisting on a dowry, it is still a common practice (Asian Centre for Human Rights [ACHR], 2012). According to the New Delhi Supreme Court, dowry is payment of money or articles during, before, or after marriage by the girl's parent to her in-laws; the cash and presents given must be linked to the actual marriage to be considered illegal dowry (Mahapatra, 2008). More than 6,000 women are killed each year because their in-laws consider their dowries inadequate; **bride burning** is an example of dowry death. In bride-burning cases, a man, or a family member, douses his wife with kerosene, gasoline, or other flammable liquid, and sets the woman on fire, leading to her death. Between 2008 and 2010, over 24,946 dowry deaths were reported in violation of the Dowry Prohibition Act of 1961 (ACHR, 2012).

In a country where hundreds and perhaps thousands of newborn girls are murdered each year merely because they are female, little value is given to adult women. A British medical journal reported in early 2006 that up to 10 million female fetuses had been aborted in India over the past 20 years and about 500,000 female fetuses continue to be aborted annually (Jha, 2006). This practice of **female feticide** is the act of aborting a fetus because it is female. In 2008, the Indian prime minister described the widespread practice of aborting female fetuses as a "national shame," calling for stricter enforcement of laws devised to prevent doctors from helping parents to avoid the birth of unwanted daughters (Gentleman, 2008). According to the provisional census of 2011, the sex ratio (the number of females per 1,000 males) continues to fall. For the 0 to 6 age group, the ratio dropped to 914 from 927 in the 2011 census (ACHR, 2012).

India has been proactive in passing laws to protect women from intimate partner violence. The major problem is that these laws are often in conflict with social practices and seldom enforced (ACHR, 2012). In 1983, intimate partner violence was first recognized as a specific criminal offense by the introduction of Section 498-A into the Indian Penal Code and had been revised since. This section deals with cruelty by a husband or his family toward a married woman. The punishment is imprisonment for up to three years and a fine. The complaint against cruelty does not have to be lodged by the victim herself. Any relative may also make the complaint on her behalf. Four types of cruelty are covered under the law:

1. Conduct that is likely to drive a woman to suicide.
2. Conduct that is likely to cause grave injury to the life, limb, or health of the woman.
3. Harassment with the purpose of forcing the woman or her relatives to give some property.
4. Harassment because the woman or her relatives are unable to yield to demands for more money or do not give some property.

What are the forms of "cruelty" recognized by the courts?

- Persistent denial of food.
- Insisting on perverse sexual conduct.
- Continually locking a woman out of the house.
- Denying the woman access to children, thereby causing mental torture.
- Physical violence.
- Taunting, demoralizing, and putting down the woman with the intention of causing mental torture.
- Confining the woman to home and not allowing her ordinary social intercourse.
- Abusing children in their mother's presence with the intention of causing her mental torture.
- Denying the paternity of the children with the intention of inflicting mental pain upon the mother.
- Threatening divorce unless dowry is given.

According to the National Crime Records Bureau (NCRB), crime against women in India continues on an upward trend (NCRB, 2012). The overall rate of crimes against women increased by 7 percent from 2011 to 2012. Increases were notable for rape, kidnapping (abduction), dowry deaths, and torture by husband and relatives over the previous year. Overall, 35 percent of women in India have experienced physical or sexual violence, including 40 percent of ever-married women (International Institute for Population Sciences, 2007). One in three ever-married women reports having been slapped by their husband. Between 12 percent and 15 percent report having their arms twisted; being pushed, shaken, kicked, dragged, or beaten up; or having something thrown at them. Ten percent report that their husbands have physically forced them to have sex. One in seven ever-married women has suffered physical injuries as a result of spousal violence.

Women whose mothers were beaten by their fathers are twice as likely to be in abusive marriages themselves. For most women who have ever experienced spousal violence, the violence first occurred within the first two years of their marriage. Only one in four women who have ever experienced violence has sought help to end the violence. Two out of three women have neither sought help nor told anyone about the violence. Among women who experienced only sexual violence, only 12 percent have ever told anyone or sought help. Abused women most often seek help from their own families. Very few women seek help from any institutional source such as the police or social service organizations.

Malaysia

The country of Malaysia is unique in that it has a dual legal system of Sharia law and civil law (Figure 1-3). The two systems act independently to protect the diverse population that is 60 percent Muslim. The Malaysian *Domestic Violence Act 1994* defines domestic partners as married or previously married men and women, children under the age of 18, and incapacitated adults who share the home. Abuse protection involves physical, sexual, emotional, and psychological abuse and intimidation (including harassment and stalking). Complaints of abuse are lodged with the social welfare department. Police have the power to detain the perpetrator for 24 hours, and the court may grant a restraining order. The police hold the right to determine whether a report or prosecution is appropriate (The Malaysian Bar, 2006).

According to an annual report of the Malaysian Women's Aid Organisation, approximately 75 percent of women seeking its shelter are survivors of domestic violence; over 90 percent of the women were physically assaulted by an intimate partner (Ghani, 2011). The organization provides education and advocacy through shelter, counseling, and hotline services for women and children. There are at least 28 shelters in Malaysia, which are referred to as "Rumah Nur," or House of Light (Ja'afar, Rahim, Ahmad, & Ismail, 2006).

The Women's Development Research Centre (KANITA) at the Universiti Sains Malaysia (USM) recently identified a gap in gender research in the country of Malaysia. It found that no large-scale government study has been conducted on violence against women in Malaysia since 1995. The sources of information on domestic violence are police reports and hospital reports. Experts believe that the vast majority of abused women do not come forward due to beliefs that the police will not do anything to

FIGURE 1-3   Malaysia is a unique country in that it has a dual legal system of Sharia law and civil law, which work independently to protect victims of violence. Zou Zou/Shutterstock

help them. In a rare report concerning domestic violence in Malaysia, police statistics showed that the reports of domestic violence cases rose from 3,264 in 2006 to 3,769 in 2008 ("Violence against women on the rise in Malaysia," 2009).

In 1994, Malaysia was at the forefront of domestic violence response through the establishment of the One Stop Crisis Centre (OSCC) in the Hospital Kuala Lumpur. The OSCC model requires an interagency response to medical examination and treatment in coordination with counseling and support services in each state hospital. When women report to a hospital with a complaint of domestic violence, they receive prompt medical attention with referrals for counseling and support services at the same facility. As mandated by the Ministry of Health, the OSCC was established in 90 percent of government hospitals across the country by 1997. However, the subsequent lack of funding has resulted in a gradual withdrawal of counseling and support services (Colombini, Ali, Watts, & Mayhew, 2011). The lack of financial commitment to the model has called into question its current effectiveness and future existence.

Mexico

Of the top 20 major economies of the world, Mexico ranks among the top five worst places for women to live (Baldwin, 2012). The TrustLaw survey cited extreme levels of violence against women living in Mexico, social and economic disparity, and limited access to health care among the reasons for the dismal rating. The country is plagued with hundreds of unsolved killings and abductions of women and girls, many of whom are tortured or raped. During 2011 alone, over 300 women were murdered in the city of Ciudad Juárez (Baldwin, 2012). Societal acceptance of violence against women is a pervasive problem in Mexico.

The Mexican government acknowledges the unfavorable conditions under which its women live, including high levels of violence in the home (INEGI, 2011). Actively seeking ways to combat its social problem, the government has developed the National Institute of Statistics, Geography and Informatics (*Instituto Nacional de Estadística y Geografía e Informática*—INEGI) to gather information to drive future policies oriented toward eliminating discrimination between women and men. According to the INEGI 2011 *National Survey on the Dynamics of Relationships in Homes*, over 49 percent of women reported currently experiencing intimate partner violence, having experienced it in the past from a former spouse or partner (INEGI, 2011). Women ages 15 to 49 are at the highest risk of abuse in the home. One in every five women in Mexico lives in a relationship of physical and sexual abuse where domestic abuse is considered to be the most prevalent form of violence in the country (INEGI, 2011).

Advocates of reform claim that while the documented levels of violence against women are not good news, data from the INEGI survey in 2003 and 2006 have contributed to public policy change and legal protections for women in Mexico (Instituto Nacional de Estadística y Geografía, 2009). Notable legal changes include passage of the *General Act for Equality between Women and Men* (August 2006). The 2007 *General Act on Women's Access to a Life Free of Violence* became Mexico's first federal law to explicitly combat domestic violence and other abuse against women, though similar statutes already existed at the state and local level. The measure provides for emergency protection orders to help victims of violence, with provisions to remove aggressors from homes in domestic violence cases, suspending perpetrators' visits to children, and freezing assets to guarantee alimony payments. Due to Mexico's federated government system, however, nonpayment of child support is punishable in some states while not in others (Mexico, 2012).

Opponents of recent legislation suggest that the family violence laws passed in Mexico do little to challenge the patriarchal structure of its society (Frias, 2010). One controversial provision of Mexican family violence legislation is a mediation process called *conciliación*. It involves a face-to-face meeting between the victim and the offender as the first response to domestic violence disputes. The goal of this process is a reconciliation of the couple as the means to end the abuse. There are concerns that this approach may not provide protection to the victim and may even add to her frustration because the violence is not considered a criminal matter. Agency response is burdened with official red tape, insufficient resources, and bias against women who are victimized by partner abuse (Frias, 2010). The president of the National Women's Institute of Mexico (INMUJERES) reports to the UN that much progress has been made toward the legal protection of women in Mexico since the institute was developed (Gaytan, 2012). As of 2011, 26 out of Mexico's 32 states had passed laws for equality between women and men, 18 had published laws to combat human trafficking, and all 32 were covered under federal law. The federal government in Mexico classifies trafficking of people as a crime, and 10 states have passed laws classifying **femicide**, the killing of women because of their gender, as a crime. The legal definition of femicide has been established to include the mutilation or other harm to the body of the murdered woman, a history of harassment by her attacker, and the dumping of her body in a public place (Mexico, 2012). Mexico's patriarchal, macho, and misogynistic culture is acknowledged as the worst enemy of women's equality. The implementation and enforcement of laws aimed at protecting women is among the challenges Mexico faces, as illustrated in Figure 1-4.

FIGURE 1-4   Mexico's patriarchal, macho, and misogynistic culture is acknowledged as the worst enemy of women's equality. The implementation and enforcement of laws aimed at protecting women is among the challenges the country faces. otnaydur/Shutterstock

According to a report to the UN, a national network of shelters for victims opened in 2009, providing shelter for 293 women and 92 children (Mexico, 2012). Four justice centers to assist in obtaining protection or restraining orders have also been established. Despite the advances, Human Rights Watch charges that women and girls in Mexico still are not adequately protected by law against domestic violence and sexual abuse (Human Rights Watch, 2012).

Mozambique

Mozambique is a coastal country in South Africa whose independence from Portuguese rule in 1975 was followed by civil war and natural disasters. Three out of four people now live below the poverty line with limited access to basic needs such as water and health care (Department for International Development, 2012). Life expectancy is between 41 and 47 years of age (Jethá et al., 2011), and the quality of life is poor.

Based on 2003 data, polygamy is a common practice, and 43 percent of girls between 15 and 19 years of age were married, divorced, or widowed (OECD Development Centre, 2012). Despite recent reforms in family law, the status of women in Mozambique is far worse than that of their male counterparts due to family practices, marriage, and polygamy, according to the Social Institutions and Gender Index (OECD Development Centre, 2012).

Until very recently, domestic violence and marital rape were not offenses in the Republic of Mozambique. In 2009, the legislation explicitly making domestic violence and marital rape public crimes provided a penalty ranging from community service work to a prison sentence for persons convicted of the offense. The police are now empowered to act on a complaint of such offenses from any person, including the victim and third parties. The court has been empowered to issue protection orders to ban the offender from the couple's home, keep him from selling the family property, and restrict his access to their children (High Commission of the Republic of Mozambique, 2009). The law also makes it illegal to engage in sexual activity while knowingly infected with a contagious disease (OECD Development Centre, 2012).

Despite recent legislation, domestic violence continues to be a significant and widespread problem in Mozambique. More than half of women are believed to be victims of domestic violence (The Mercury Phoenix Trust, 2010). It is questionable whether laws that exist to protect women and children from rape and abuse are taken seriously by law enforcement. No arrests are known to have been made of persons who engage in sexual relations while affected with HIV/AIDS (U.S. Department of State, 2011d).

Practices that subjugate women continue to pose a threat to the equality of women in Mozambique (U.S. Department of State, 2011d). One example is the custom of the groom's family providing a *bride price* to the bride's family, usually in the form of money, livestock, or other goods. Among Muslims, the bride's family usually pays for the wedding and provides gifts. Some believe that these payments contribute to the idea that their husbands own women. Another ritual that continues in practice is called *purification*; it requires a widow to have unprotected sex with a member of her deceased husband's family. Failure to be purified is cited as the reason for more than half of widows losing their inheritance after the death of their husbands.

Noting the link between disability, domestic violence, and the spread of HIV/AIDS, community service agencies have undertaken a campaign to educate women about and raise awareness of domestic violence, along with its contributing health and economic issues. Power International is an organization that runs 21 radio clubs to combat domestic violence through education over the airways (The Mercury Phoenix Trust, 2010). Indications are that the cultural acceptance of family violence in Mozambique is beginning to change (Jethá et al., 2011). One hope is that the campaign will raise awareness sufficiently to overcome discriminatory customs and practices.

Peru

Domestic violence is a serious and long-standing problem in Peru. The 1993 Law for Protection from Family Violence was updated in 1997, but it remains a serious disappointment to both its advocates and the victims of intimate partner violence. The law safeguards women's rights, including the right to be protected from rape and spouse abuse. Spousal rape is considered a crime in Peru. Enforcement of the provisions is considered weak since few prosecutions have occurred. In 2011, a new law (008/2011-CR) made it illegal to kill a woman who is a domestic partner or immediate relative (U.S. Department of State, 2011a). If convicted, the perpetrator faces a minimum of 15 years of imprisonment for femicide. Perpetrators may be ordered to refrain from committing the acts of violence and directed to vacate their home. Penalties for domestic violence include imprisonment from one month to six years.

Reports charge that the legal system in Peru is slow to respond to complaints of domestic violence. Police and the courts are criticized for failing to take complaints seriously, excusing the violence as acts of machismo, and frequently blaming the victim. It takes an average of two to three years for a case to progress to a finding of guilty before a sentence can be imposed against the perpetrator (Immigration and Refugee Board of Canada, 2010). In 2011, there were more women killed by family violence abusers than those who were prosecuted for domestic-related offenses. A mere 35 men were sentenced during the entire year for domestic violence-related crimes, although 77 women were murdered and an additional 60 attempts to murder women occurred (U.S. Department of State, 2011a).

The WHO has ranked Peru as having one of the highest rates of physical and sexual violence by an intimate partner in the world (World Health Organization/London School of Hygiene and Tropical Medicine, 2010). Tied with Ethiopia, the prevalence rate of intimate partner violence in Peru is 70 percent. According to a 2010 report, 12 women are murdered every month by their husbands (Immigration and Refugee Board of Canada, 2010). The same report stated that between September 2008 and October 2009, 97 out of 109 homicides involved domestic violence. Approximately two out of every five women are victims of domestic violence. Between 2009 and 2012, 269 women in Peru were murdered by a current or former partner, according to news reports (Andean Air Mail & Peruvian Times, 2012). The majority of the victims are between 18 and 34 years old, with approximately 11 women killed each month.

The problems do not appear to be improving, despite large grassroots response. In Peru, volunteers to aid victims of domestic violence have come in the form of *community defenders* (CDs). These individuals are trained on the dynamics of abuse and then train others about domestic violence, work with victims, and attempt to influence policy change. Since 1999, the number of CDs has grown from 40 to 450 individuals (Thériault, 2011). Without a strong government response, the women of Peru face enormous obstacles to safety in their homes.

Philippines

The Philippine law criminalizes physical, sexual, and psychological harm against women and children from family members; yet, evidence suggests that authorities do not give these crimes a high priority. Ineffective enforcement of laws protecting women from intimate partner violence and rape is a serious problem in the Philippines. Police reports cite 9,255 cases of domestic violence during 2010, a 91 percent increase over 2009 during the same period (U.S. Department of State, 2011b).

According to human rights reports, protection of women is a complicated issue due to official corruption and high levels of political violence in the Philippines. Reports of rape and physical abuse of women in police custody are common. In some cases authorities demand extra fees from women before complaints of domestic violence can be registered; men with connections to authorities can avoid prosecution of domestic violence crimes. In 2011, police reported 8,332 complaints of domestic violence against women and children (U.S. Department of State, 2011b). Typically, the number of reports to police underestimates the amount of violence in the home. Underreporting is likely to be the case in the Philippines as well. In addition to police response, the Department of Social Welfare and Development provided services to 760 victims (U.S. Department of State, 2011b).

Nongovernmental organizations and the Philippine Commission on Women (PCW) report that they have provided police officers with gender-sensitivity training to assist them in dealing with domestic violence victims. The Philippine National Police (PNP) has control over 1,823 desks throughout the country to specifically investigate crimes against women and children (U.S. Department of State, 2011b).

Advocates for women's rights argue that the high incidence of domestic violence is linked to the government's failure to provide an avenue for women to leave abusive husbands. Except the Vatican City, Rome, the Philippines is the only country in the world where divorce is not legally permitted. Two bills filed in 2010 sought to legalize divorce—House Bill 1799 and House Bill 4368—and both measures were defeated in 2012. Women in the Philippines are left with the options of applying for a legal separation or annulment.

Republic of Iraq

During the three years Americans were involved in the war (2003–2006), upward of 223,000 Iraqis died (Iraq Family Health Survey Study Group, 2008). The high death rate has continued, and violence is the most common cause of adult death. In a country where violence is common, women are targeted for domestic violence crimes, sexual offenses, murder, and human trafficking. Reliable statistics on the scale of violence against women are difficult to obtain. The government ignores or trivializes violence against women, and the abuse is rarely reported (Ghanim, 2009).

The government favors the patriarchal system through its legal system. Following the first national election in 2005, the constitution was redrafted to explicitly state that personal and family issues are under the jurisdiction of the religious laws applicable to the community. According to Iraq's penal code, "honorable motives" is a mitigating factor in serious crimes against women, including murder (Human Rights Watch, 2011). The majority of adult males are intolerant of women's rights by supporting behavior that is considered domestic violence in most countries of the world. Over half of the Iraqi population is under the age of 19, and this generation holds strong patriarchal attitudes. Approximately 80 percent of youth believe a woman should only travel with a chaperone, and 92 percent agree that women should not get work without getting permission from her husband or a male family member (UNFPA, 2010).

Of significance is a survey that reported on the attitudes of men toward women in Iraq (Government of Iraq, 2012). The report documented that a majority of Iraqi men believe they have the right to beat their wife, to prevent her from going to a medical center, to control the type of dress code she follows, and to force a female child into marriage before she is of legal age to marry. Resources for women who suffer domestic abuses are rare. Outside of Kurdistan, there are no government-run women's shelters.

Over 80 percent of Iraqi husbands subject their wives to controlling behaviors, including insisting on knowing where they are at all times (Human Rights Watch, 2011). Over 21 percent of married Iraqi women ages 15 to 49 have suffered physical violence at the hands of their husbands; approximately 14 percent of them were pregnant at the time of the abuse (WHO/COSIT/KRSO/Ministry of Health, 2008). The WHO estimated that more than a third of married women had suffered emotional violence from their husbands (2008). The true figure for women who face sexual and domestic abuse in Iraq may be as high as 73 percent (Bayoumy & Kami, 2012).

An allegation that a woman has dishonored her family is among the reasons for honor killings in the Middle East. The UN reports that honor killings are one of Iraq's most serious human rights abuses. Honor killings are thought to be a daily occurrence in Kurdish areas of Turkey, Iraq, and Iran (Ghanim, 2009). Violence against women has only intensified in Iraq with at least 10 women killed monthly—some found in garbage dumps with bullet holes as evidence of having been shot, while others were decapitated or mutilated (UNAMI, 2008). Government reports document that 133 women were killed in Basra alone during 2007; 79 of these victims were found to have been "violating Islamic teachings" and another 47 died in honor killings (Ghanim, 2009). Attitudes of the youth mirror that of adult males. More than 60 percent of youth agree that a family member can kill a girl for profaning the family honor (UNFPA, 2010).

Documenting the actual number of honor killings is difficult because many are disguised as accidents or suicides. Evidence suggests that honor killings remain a problem in Iraq (UNAMI, 2011). A woman deemed to have violated the family honor may be given the choice to commit suicide rather than be killed by a family member (Ghanim, 2009). An Iraqi human rights ministry report stated 249 women were murdered in 2010, including for reasons of "honor crimes," although no specific number from the total women murdered was attributed to these crimes (Bayoumy & Kami, 2012).

Russian Federation

According to Human Rights Watch, a woman in Russia is killed by domestic violence every 40 minutes—approximately 12,000 deaths each year (Margolis, 2017). In 2015, the report stated, 11,756 boys and girls were victims of family violence. Still, very few services exist for victims of violence in Russia. Advocates claim that the Russian police treat incidences of family violence as amusing (Drake, 2007). The general reaction to complaints is best described by the experience of one battered woman, who, upon calling the local precinct for help, was told, "You're still alive. When we get a corpse, then we'll investigate." Intimate partner violence is not recognized by criminal law as a separate offense. Cases that do go forward for prosecution are done through a justice of the peace as opposed to the regular criminal court. This means that the woman must file charges as a private citizen, collect her own evidence, and round up witnesses (Drake, 2007).

According to a Russian news reporter, women are frequently beaten to death, shot, or thrown out of windows in Moscow (Nemtsova, 2010). The Russian government in 2017 passed what is being referred to as the "slapping law" (Weisberg, 2017). The new law decriminalizes the first reported instance of domestic assault if there is no injury that would warrant a leave of absence from work. Under the new law, an offender may be fined, held for up to 15 days in detention, or receive 120 hours of community service (Onuh, 2017). Lawmakers argue that strong domestic violence laws contradict Russian family values, constituting state interference.

There are only 40 shelters for the victims of intimate partner violence in the Russian Federation (Balmforth, 2013). NGOs do not receive government funding to aid victims of intimate partner violence, with the exception of occasional short-term small grants; they rely instead on international funding to exist.

Scotland

In Scotland, there are various types of legal orders to protect an intimate partner or ex-partner from domestic violence in his or her home, place of work, and school. A protection order, known as an "interdict," prevents someone from committing unlawful action or prohibits the person from going to specific places. Also available are non-harassment orders and exclusion orders. The process for obtaining a nonharassment order has recently been simplified through the Domestic Abuse Act of 2011. An exclusion order is a court order that suspends the right of a married person, civil partner, or cohabitee to live in the family home.

The most recent civil protection order made available in Scotland came under the Forced Marriage Bill (Scottish Government, 2011). This court order can be crafted to meet the specific victim needs by ensuring safety or by helping someone in danger of being taken out of the country for marriage. Violation of a Forced Marriage Protection Order can lead to a two-year prison sentence, a fine, or both. In 2014 a law went into effect making forced marriage a criminal act punishable by a fine or up to seven years imprisonment, or both (Scottish Government, 2014). According to news reports, there were at least 35 cases of forced marriage reported in Scotland in 2011, with experts suggesting the number of such incidents to be much higher (Taneja, 2012). Similar laws have been passed to protect both females and males from a forced marriage in other countries of the United Kingdom, namely England and Wales.

The legal language is gendered, protecting partners who are married, cohabitating, or otherwise, or are ex-partners regardless of the marital status or gender. Lesbian, gay, bisexual, and transgender (LGBT) same-gender partners receive the same protection under the law. Relief for violation of an order may include fines or imprisonment. Police have the power to arrest the perpetrator in some cases and retain discretion on exercising that power.

A domestic violence incident is reported to the police every 10 minutes in Scotland with 53,681 incidents reported in 2008–2009 (Scottish Government, 2009). There were 51,926 incidents of domestic abuse reported to the police in 2009–2010, a 4 percent decrease from the previous year (Scottish Government, 2010). Approximately 60 percent of these reported incidents involved a criminal offense; the most common crimes are a minor assault or a breach of the peace. The Scottish government has noted that approximately 15 percent of incidents involve a male victim and female perpetrator; the vast majority of intimate partner violence continues to impact female victims with male perpetrators.

Women who have experienced abuse may receive support, information, and advocacy through 44 local agencies located throughout Scotland. Shelters provide refuge for upward of 374 women and 359 children or youth on any given day in addition to the support of 839 women (Scottish Women's Aid, 2011). Allocations of government support for victim programs have doubled since 2007 ("£34m to tackle domestic violence in Scotland," 2012). Government funding is directed at meeting the needs of male victims of domestic violence through education, hotline services, and research (AMIS, 2012).

A Disclosure Scheme for Domestic Abuse (Scotland), also known as Clare's Law, was passed in 2015. Named after Clare Wood, who was strangled and set on fire by her violent former boyfriend with a record of domestic violence, its goal is to help people find out if a partner has a history of violence (BBC, 2015). Individuals in Scotland have the right to ask the police for a records check of their partner if worried that the partner may have been abusive in the past (Disclosure Scheme for Domestic Abuse Scotland, nd). The law requires persons to give their identifying information and reason for the request of the disclosure. A decision to provide information is made jointly by the police and relevant partner agencies such as social services and the prison service. If the police give relevant information, it is considered confidential. The police will consider if an immediate need for protection from harm exists.

According to Scotland's LGBT Domestic Abuse Project (2012), intimate partner violence affects one out of four LGBT individuals. In the first national project of its kind in Scotland, the LGBT Domestic Abuse Project provides training to service providers and practitioners in many areas of Scotland, in addition to raising awareness of LGBT domestic abuse since 2007. Its Web site debunks myths specific to LGBT domestic violence and supports case studies to members of the community.

Research in Scotland has debunked the notion of the "older" domestic violence victim as one who is frail and therefore vulnerable (Scott & Morton, 2008). Instead, the older victim tends to be economically dependent on her abuser; therefore, the decision to stay is based on a more complex situation compared to the younger victims. Families and medical concerns complicate decisions to leave the perpetrator.

Thailand

In 2007, Thailand passed its domestic violence legislation (Protection of Domestic Violence Victims Act, B.E. 2550 [2007], 2012). The law defines domestic violence broadly as any act intended to inflict harm or through coercion cause a person to commit a crime. Similar to the United States, domestic relationships include a spouse, former spouse, or cohabiting person (current or former), along with biological or adopted children, family members, and dependent household members. Any person can report domestic abuse in addition to the victim. Restraining orders, fines, and imprisonment are among the available remedies.

The government operates crisis centers in some state-run hospitals. Emergency hotlines, temporary shelters, and counseling services are offered through NGO-supported programs. Budget difficulties and strained resources affect the availability of services. According to the U.S. Department of State, there were 831 cases of domestic violence reported to the Ministry of Social Development and Human Security (MSDHS). The majority of perpetrators were male, and the majority of victims were female (U.S. Department of State, 2011c).

At the same time that reports circulated about an increase of family violence in Thailand, the government began offering large-scale education centers and published a manual on domestic violence law. In response to the increase in family violence and the lack of prosecutions, judges and police officers across the country have attended gender sensitivity training (Immigration and Refugee Board of Canada, 2011). Reports on the government response to the violence are largely positive, while it is acknowledged that much work is needed.

CONCLUSIONS

This chapter explains violence against women from a global perspective. Violence against women is a worldwide human rights and public health emergency. It causes mental and physical injury, exposes women and girls to diseases and forced pregnancy, increases women's vulnerability in all areas of their lives, and, in the worst cases, ends in death. The international community has adopted the definition of *violence against women* from the UN's 1995 Fourth World Conference on Women in Beijing. A common understanding of the phenomenon was reached in Beijing. With that, a major step toward identifying the issues that contribute to this world epidemic has been taken. The arduous journey toward eradicating violence against women is ongoing. The involvement of every nation is necessary to continue the efforts to educate, employ, and provide adequate health care and protection for all women. Every government must respect a woman's right to be free from gender violence in her home and elsewhere.

It is beyond the scope of this text to provide information on the status of women in every country around the world. There are constant efforts to change laws that affect women in many of the countries outlined here. Training and education of police and military officers are one of the most important steps toward enforcement of legislation that may be enacted. The United States recognizes its obligation in addressing the problem of violence against women both here and abroad. Future chapters in this text will focus on the problems of violence against women in the United States. You will learn about the problems and the approaches that have been adopted to combat it. Although women are the most frequent victims of intimate partner violence, male victims will be discussed in later chapters. A special focus on children and older adults will also be provided.

SIMPLY SCENARIO
Divorce and Domestic Violence

Cynthia was a beautiful and talented woman pursuing her dreams. With success came a whirlwind of fame, a husband, and six children. Several calls were made to seek help for the violence she suffered behind closed doors. Cynthia is not alone; millions of women around the world face the same fate at the hands of a partner. In this case, her life was unbearable, and there was no way out. Married at age 20, she was dead by the age of 38.

Poverty and economic struggles in a marriage may affect the rates at which couples will part. During the Great Depression, the rate of domestic violence went up in the United States as the divorce rate went down. When women are unable to financially care for their family, history tells us that marriage—even a bad marriage—is preferred.

There is some evidence that divorce proves a safety valve in cases of family violence. In the United States, the passing of no-fault divorce laws during the 1970s resulted in a rise in divorce rates and a decrease in domestic violence and women's suicide.

There is only one country in the world, other than the Vatican, where there is a national no-divorce policy—no possibility of divorce. An annulment is an option, but it is expensive and socially discouraged.

Where is this country? What is the difference between a divorce and an annulment? Can you find any evidence for or against the position that a divorce provides a safety valve for women?

Questions for Review

1. What are the forms of violence included in any definition of violence against women?
2. Define the term "violence against women" adopted by the Istanbul Convention.
3. Explain three forms of immigration relief established under the *Violence Against Women Act.*
4. What is the primary difference in the United States between refugees and asylum seekers?
5. Describe "Clare's Law" of Scotland.
6. How does a T visa protect victims of human trafficking?
7. What is an honor killing?
8. Define the term "femicide" and contrast it with "feticide."
9. Explain the process of "purification" found in Mozambique.
10. What is the "slapping law" of the Russian Federation?

Internet-Based Exercises

1. What can you do to combat violence against women? Learn more about V-Day and other global antiviolence projects at http://www.feminist.com. Design a campaign or educational project and present your ideas to the class. What would it take to materialize your ideas?
2. NGOs in the People's Republic of China were introduced in this chapter. An NGO represents a common global approach to combating violence against women. Can you find other NGOs that exist in other countries? To learn more about the role of an NGO, visit the Web site http://www.vitalvoices.org for the Vital Voices Global Partnership.
3. What does the AHA Foundation do? Find out at http://theahafoundation.org.

References

American Immigration Council. (2012). *Violence Against Women Act (VAWA) Provides Protections for Immigrant Women and Victims of Crime.* Retrieved from Washington, D.C.: https://exchange.americanimmigrationcouncil.org/research/violence-against-women-act-vawa-provides-protections-immigrant-women-and-victims-crime

AMIS. (2012). Abused men in Scotland. Retrieved from http://www.abusedmeninscotland.org/news.html

Amnesty International. (2005). Afghanistan women still under attack—A systematic failure to protect. Retrieved from http://www.amnesty.org/en/library/info/ASA11/007/2005

Andean Air Mail & Peruvian Times. (March 9, 2012). Peru cabinet minister says women should aim for economic independence. Retrieved from http://www.peruviantimes.com/author/admin/

Asian Centre for Human Rights. (ACHR). (2012). India's draft Universal Periodic Report-II: A case of forced marriage? Retrieved from http://www.achrweb.org/UN/HRC/UPRIndia2.pdf

Australian Government Solicitor (AGS). (2009). *Domestic violence laws in Australia.* Australia: Department of Families, Housing, Community Services and Indigenous Affairs. Retrieved from http://www.fahcsia.gov.au/sites/default/files/documents/05_2012/domestic_violence_laws_in_australia_-_june_2009.pdf

Baldwin, K. (2012). *Violence puts Mexico among worst G20 countries for women.* Retrieved from http://www.reuters.com/article/2012/06/13/us-g20-women-canada-usa-idUSBRE85C00F20120613

Balmforth, T. (2013). Russia: Brutal killing highlights lack of domestic violence law. Retrieved from http://www.stopvaw.org/russia_brutal_killing_highlights_lack_of_domestic_violence_law.html

Bayoumy, Y., & Kami, A. (2012). "Honour killing" perpetrators deserve harsher sentences, say Iraqi women. *Nationalpost.com.* Retrieved from http://news.nationalpost.com/2012/03/06/honour-killing-perpetrators-deserve-harsher-sentences-say-iraqi-women/

BBC. (2015). 'Clare's Law' domestic abuse scheme rolled out in Scotland. Retrieved 26 October 2017, from BBC News Services http://www.bbc.com/news/uk-scotland-34403806

Bookey, B. (2013). Domestic violence as a basis for asylum: An analysis of 206 case outcomes in the United States from 1994 to 2012. *Hastings Women's Law Journal, 24,* 107.

Bonewit, A. (2016). *The issue of violence against women in the European Union.* Brussels: European Parliament Retrieved from http://www.europarl.europa.eu/supporting-analyses.

Burt, L., & Batalova, J. (2014). Refugees and asylees in the United States. Retrieved from http://www.migrationpolicy.org/article/refugees-and-asylees-united-states-0

Chow, L. M. (2016). ARCG-is not the solution for domestic violence victims. *Cath. UL Rev., 66*, 161.

Colombini, M., Ali, S. H., Watts, C., & Mayhew, S. H. (2011). One stop crisis centres: A policy analysis of the Malaysian response to intimate partner violence. *Health Research Policy and Systems, 9*, 25.

Council of Europe. (2011). Council of Europe Convention on preventing and combating violence against women and domestic violence: Istanbul Convention, 11, V. 2011. Council of Europe.

Crohn, M. (2007). Domestic violence in Romania: The law, the court system. *Final Report*, p. 114. Retrieved from http://www.abanet.org/rol/publications/ee_romania_domestic_violence_final_report_0407.pdf

Cuevas, M. (2017). Michigan doctors charged in first federal genital mutilation case in US. Retrieved from http://www.cnn.com/2017/04/22/health/detroit-genital-mutilation-charges/index.html

Department for International Development. (2012). Mozambique. Retrieved from http://www.dfid.gov.uk/Mozambique

U.S. Department of Homeland Security. (2017). *Female genital mutilation or cutting (FGM/C) outreach strategy*. Retrieved from https://www.hsdl.org/?view&did=798235

Disclosure Scheme for Domestic Abuse Scotland. (nd). Retrieved from http://www.scotland.police.uk/assets/pdf/205073/257814/pdf-making-an-application-about-your-partner?view=Standard

Drake, C. (2007). A house divided: Domestic violence in the Russian Federation. Retrieved from http://www.unfpa.org/public/home/news/pid/207

Eggert, D. (2017). Michigan imposes prison term for female genital mutilation. *Associated Press*. Retrieved from http://www.kswo.com/story/35861788/michigan-imposes-prison-term-for-female-genital-mutilation

Frias, S. M. (2010). Resisting patriarchy within the state: Advocacy and family violence in Mexico. *Women's Studies International Forum, 33*(6), 542–551.

García-Moreno, C., Jansen, H., Ellsberg, M., Heise, L., & Watts, C. (2005). WHO multi-country study on women's health and domestic violence against women. Retrieved from http://www.who.int/gender/violence/who_multicountry_study/summary_report/en/

Gaytan, H. (2012). Fifty-sixth session of the Commission on the Status of Women. Retrieved from http://www.un.org/womenwatch/daw/csw/csw56/general-discussions/member-states/Mexico%20-%20E.pdf

Gentleman, A. (2008). Indian prime minister denounces abortion of females. *The New York Times*. Retrieved from http://www.nytimes.com/2008/04/29/world/asia/29india.html?_r=0

Ghanim, D. (2009). *Gender and violence in the Middle East*. Westport, CT: Praeger.

Ghani, N. (2011). WOA annual statistics 2011. Retrieved from http://wao.org.my/file/file/WAO%20Annual%20Statistic%202011.pdf

Government of Iraq. (2012). Iraq Woman Integrated Social and Health Survey (I-WISH). Retrieved from http://www.iauiraq.org/documents/1666/I-WISH%20Report%20English.pdf

Harv. L. Rev. (2015). Matter of A-R-C-G- Board of Immigration Appeals holds that Guatemalan woman fleeing domestic violence meets threshold asylum requirement. *Harvard Law Review, 128*(7), 2090.

Hasrat, M. H., & Pfefferle, A. (2012). Violence against women in Afghanistan. Retrieved from http://www.aihrc.org.af/media/files/VAW_Final%20Draft-20.12.pdf

High Commission of the Republic of Mozambique. (2009). Assembly passes bill against domestic violence. Retrieved from http://www.mozambiquehighcommission.org.uk/?s=10&grupa=1&id=124&new=ok

Human Rights Watch. (January, 2011). At the crossroads: Human rights in Iraq eight years after the US-led invasion. Retrieved from http://www.hrw.org/reports/2011/02/21/crossroads

Human Rights Watch. (January, 2012). World report 2012: Mexico. Retrieved from http://www.hrw.org/world-report-2012/mexico

Immigration and Refugee Board of Canada. (2010). Peru: Domestic violence, state protection and support services available (March 2007–2010). PER103441. FE. Retrieved from http://www.unhcr.org/refworld/docid/4e438b532.html

Immigration and Refugee Board of Canada. (2011). Thailand: Domestic violence, including state protection, support services and recourse available to victims (January 2009–December 2010). THA103653.E. Retrieved from http://www.unhcr.org/refworld/docid/4e43cb852.html

Immigration Policy Center. (2012). *Violence Against Women Act (VAWA) provides protections for immigrant women and victims of crime*. Retrieved from https://americanimmigrationcouncil.org/sites/default/files/research/vawa.pdf

Instituto Nacional de Estadística y Geografía. (2009). Comments on the proposed set of indicators to measure violence against women. Paper presented at the Meeting of the Friends of the Chair of the United Nations Statistical Commission on Statistical Indicators on Violence against Women, Aguascalientes, Mexico. Retrieved from http://unstats.un.org/unsd/demographic/meetings/vaw/docs/Paper7.pdf

Instituto Nacional de Estadística y Geografía e Informática. (INEGI). (2011). *Encuesta Nacional sobre la Dinamica de las Relaciones en los Hogares 2011*. Retrieved from http://www.inegi.org.mx/

International Institute for Population Sciences. (2007). National Family Health Survey (NFHS-3), 2005–2006. *Key Findings, 2007*. Mumbai, India: IIPS and Macro International.

Iraq Family Health Survey Study Group. (2008). Violence-related mortality in Iraq from 2002 to 2006. *The New England Journal of Medicine, 358*(5), 484–493.

Ja'afar, R., Rahim, S. Z. A., Ahmad, Z., & Ismail, Z. (2006). Violence against women: Women and health learning package. *The Network: TUFH Women and Health Task-force*. Retrieved from http://www.the-networktufh.org/sites/default/files/attachments/basic_pages/WHLP%20Violence%20Against%20Women2.pdf

Jethá, E., Lynch, C. A., Houry, D. E., Rodrigues, M. A., Chilundo, B., Sasser, S. M., & Wright, D. W. (2011). Characteristic of victims of family violence seeking care at health centers in Maputo, Mozambique. *Journal of Emergencies, Trauma, and Shock, 4*(3), 369–373.

Jha, P. (2006). Up to 10M female fetuses aborted in India in last two decades, study says. *Lancet*. Retrieved from http://www.medicalnewstoday.com/articles/36000.php

LGBT Domestic Abuse Project. (2012). Scotland's Lesbian, Gay, Bisexual and Transgender Domestic Abuse Project. Retrieved from http://www.lgbtdomesticabuse.org.uk/main.htm

Linacre, S. (2012). New in recorded crime—Victims, Australia, 2011. Retrieved from http://www.abs.gov.au/ausstats/abs@.nsf/Latestproducts/4510.0Main%20Features12011?opendocument&tabname=Summary&prodno=4510.0&issue=2011&num=&view=

Love, S. (2005). *Justice and accountability: Stop violence against women*. Dublin, Ireland: Amnesty International.

Mahapatra, D. (2008). Customary payments, gifts not dowry: SC. *Times of India*. Retrieved from http://articles.timesofindia.indiatimes.com/2008-02-01/india/27773374_1_dowry-harassment-charges-dowry-prohibition-act-judicial-discipline

Margolis, H. (2017). A slap is only the start. *Dispatches*. Retrieved from https://www.hrw.org/news/2017/02/14/slap-only-start

Mather, M., & Feldmann-Jacobs, C. (2016). Women and girls at risk of female genital mutilation/cutting in the United States. Retrieved from http://www.prb.org/Publications/Articles/2015/us-fgmc.aspx

Matter of ARCG, 26 I. & N. Dec. 388 (B.I.A., 2014).

Mexico. (2012). Mexico gaining ground in efforts to end "femicide," other violence against women, delegation tells Anti-Discrimination Committee. Retrieved from http://www.un.org/News/Press/docs/2012/wom1917.doc.htm

Musalo, K. (2014). Personal violence, public matter: Evolving standards in gender-based asylum law. *Harvard International Review, 36*(2), 45.

Myers, N. (2008). Program trains auxiliary police officers in Afghanistan. Retrieved from http://www.defenselink.mil/news/newsarticle.aspx?id=50353

National Crime Records Bureau (NCRB). (2012). Crime in India: 2011. Retrieved from http://ncrb.nic.in/CD-CII2011/Home.asp

Nemtsova, A. (2010). The predictable death of my friend. *The Daily Beast*. Retrieved from http://www.thedaily-beast.com/newsweek/2010/09/02/domestic-violence-pervades-russian-homes.html

OECD Development Centre. (2012). Mozambique. Social Institutions & Gender Index (SIGI). Retrieved from http://genderindex.org/country/mozambique

Onuh, A. (2017). Russia's slapping law: Putin reduces punishment for some acts of domestic violence. *Answers Africa*. Retrieved from https://answersafrica.com/russias-slapping-law-putin.html

Protection of Domestic Violence Victims Act, B.E. 2550 (2007). (2012). Retrieved from http://sgdatabase.unwomen.org/searchDetail.action?measureId=10675&baseHREF=country&baseHREFId=1277

Scott, M., & Morton, S. (2008). Older women and domestic violence in Scotland. Retrieved from http://www.era.lib.ed.ac.uk/handle/1842/2776

Scottish Government. (2009). Domestic abuse recorded by the police in Scotland, 2008–09. Retrieved from http://www.scotland.gov.uk/Publications/2009/11/23112407/3

Scottish Government. (2010). Domestic abuse recorded by the police in Scotland, 2009–10. Retrieved from http://www.scotland.gov.uk/Resource/Doc/330575/0107237.pdf

Scottish Government. (2011). Forced marriage law introduced. Retrieved from http://www.scotland.gov.uk/News/Releases/2011/11/25120644

Scottish Government. (2014). Anti-social Behaviour, Crime and Policing Act 2014. Retrieved from http://www.legislation.gov.uk/ukpga/2014/12/pdfs/ukpga_20140012_en.pdf

Scottish Women's Aid. (2011). Census Day 2011. Retrieved from http://www.scottishwomensaid.org.uk/publications/general-publications/duplicate-of-census-day-2011

Sinha, M. (2013). *Measuring violence against women: Statistical trends*. Ottawa, CA: Minister of Industry.

Stillwell, C. (2008). Honor killings: When the ancient and the modern collide. *San Francisco Chronicle*. Retrieved from http://www.sfgate.com/cgi-bin/article.cgi?f=/g/a/2008/01/23/cstillwell.DTL

Taneja, P. (2012). Forced marriage campaign targets mosques in Scotland. *BBC Asian Network*. Retrieved from http://www.bbc.co.uk/news/uk-scotland-17908548

The Constitution of the Islamic Republic of Afghanistan. (2004). Retrieved from http://supremecourt.gov.af/content/media/documents/constitution2004_english2412012949583255533325325.pdf

The Malaysian Bar. (August 14, 2006). Domestic violence. Retrieved from http://www.malaysianbar.org.my/domestic_violence_.html

The Mercury Phoenix Trust. (2010). Domestic violence contributes to the spread of HIV/AIDS. Retrieved from http://www.mercuryphoenixtrust.com/Content/domestic-violence-contributes-to-the-spread-of-hivaids-update-from-power-international-in-mozambique-id=1221.aspx

Thériault, A. (2011). Cusco community defenders: Planting hope to root out violence. *Andean Air Mail & Peruvian Times*. Retrieved from http://www.peruviantimes.com/17/cusco-community-defenders-planting-hope-to-root-out-violence/12769/

£34m to tackle domestic violence in Scotland. (2012). *BBC*. Retrieved from http://www.bbc.co.uk/news/uk-scotland-tayside-central-18937984

UN. (2006). In-depth study on all forms of violence against women: Report of the Secretary-General (No. A/61/122/Add.1).

UNAMI. (2008). Human rights report. Retrieved from http://www.ohchr.org/Documents/Press/UNAMIJuly-December2007EN.pdf

UNAMI. (2011). 2010 report on human rights in Iraq. Retrieved from http://www.unhcr.org/refworld/docid/4e40fc3a2.html

UNFPA. (2010). Factsheet on Iraqi youth. Retrieved from http://www.iauiraq.org/documents/387/IYD_Eng_FINAL.pdf

UNICEF. (2013). Statistics by area: Child protection. Retrieved from http://www.childinfo.org/fgmc_progress.html

U.S. Citizenship and Immigration Services. (2016). Battered spouse, children & parents. Retrieved from https://www.uscis.gov/humanitarian/battered-spouse-children-parents

U.S. Department of State. (2011a). Country reports on human rights practices for 2011: Peru. Retrieved from http://www.state.gov/j/drl/rls/hrrpt/humanrightsreport/index.htm?dlid=186536

U.S. Department of State. (2011b). 2010 human rights report: Philippines. Retrieved from http://www.state.gov/j/drl/rls/hrrpt/2010/eap/154399.htm

U.S. Department of State. (2011c). Country reports on human rights practices for 2011: Thailand. Retrieved from http://www.state.gov/j/drl/rls/hrrpt/humanrightsreport/index.htm?dlid=186310

U.S. Department of State. (2011d). Country reports on human rights practices for 2011: Mozambique. Retrieved from http://www.state.gov/j/drl/rls/hrrpt/humanrightsreport/index.htm?dlid=186224

U.S. Department of State. (2012a). Release of first United States strategy to prevent and respond to gender-based violence globally. Retrieved from http://www.state.gov/r/pa/prs/ps/2012/08/196342.htm

U.S. Department of State. (2012b). Country reports on human rights practices for 2011: Philippines. Retrieved from http://www.state.gov/j/drl/rls/hrrpt/humanrightsreport/index.htm?dlid=186301

Violence against women on the rise in Malaysia. (2009). *People's Daily Online*. Retrieved from http://english.people.com.cn/90001/90777/90851/6825095.html

Weisberg, K. (2017). Russia decriminalizes some dv. *Domestic violence report, 22*(4), 53.

Western Australia. (2013). WA strategic plan for family and domestic violence 2009–2013. Retrieved from https://www.dcp.wa.gov.au/CrisisAndEmergency/FDV/Documents/WAStrategicPlanforFamilyandDomestic Violence.pdf

WHO/COSIT/KRSO/Ministry of Health. (2008). Iraq Family Health Survey 2006/7. Retrieved from http://www.who.int/mediacentre/news/releases/2008/pr02/2008_iraq_family_health_survey_report.pdf

WHO. (2013). Eliminating violence against women in Europe: Intersectoral approaches & actions. Retrieved from http://eige.europa.eu/sites/default/files/documents/E-Fact%20Sheet%20Facts&Figures-FREI.pdf

World Health Organization (WHO). (2013). *Female genital mutilation. Fact sheet no. 241*. Geneva, CH: Author. Retrieved from http://www.who.int/mediacentre/factsheets/fs241/en/

World Health Organization/London School of Hygiene and Tropical Medicine. (2010). *Preventing intimate partner and sexual violence against women: Taking action and generating evidence*. Geneva, CH: World Health Organization.

History of Violence in the Family

CHAPTER OBJECTIVES

After reviewing this chapter, you should be able to:

1. Discuss the early social–legal history of family violence.
2. Explain the historical significance of social tolerance for family violence.
3. Describe the primary categories of family violence.
4. Explain what constitutes a domestic relationship.
5. Define the four major types of violence that occur in families.

KEY TERMS

Child abuse and neglect	Patriarchy
Elder abuse	Physical abuse
Family violence	Psychological abuse
Intimate partner violence	Sexual abuse

INTRODUCTION

There exists a hopelessness that characterizes the situation brought about by family violence. Acts of abuse toward individuals within the family have always occurred but were not considered wrong until recent times. We look to early history to get a sense of the social and legal perspectives on family relationships. As society slowly recognized and banned violence against women, there was a change in the law regarding marital relations. However, the path to protect individuals from abuse in the home is not always clear. Laws are intended to promote stability and must not be arbitrary. Domestic relationships need to be defined so that laws could be enforced in a fair and impartial way. Categories of violence need to be recognized and specific forms of violence prohibited. The term "family violence" from the legal perspective refers to specifically related individuals and includes many different forms of behaviors that will be discussed in this chapter.

EXAMPLES OF FAMILY VIOLENCE

Violence within families is a pervasive and long-standing problem, although it was not considered as such until quite recently. Even without an exact count of the numbers of victims, it certainly can be said that it affects millions of women, men, and children across the United

FIGURE 2-1 Harming or attempting to harm a member of a family or household by another member of the family or household is a crime of family violence. Image Copyright ODriscoll Imaging, 2012. O Driscoll Imaging/Shutterstock

States and around the world. It is not simply a problem for the family experiencing the violence, but as you will find out throughout this text, it is a crisis that will affect us all in some way. These people are our loved ones, neighbors, and coworkers. Who is doing these horrible things? Loved ones, parents, and children are the perpetrators, as illustrated in Figure 2-1. For example,

- A biological father on numerous occasions during visitations raped his 14-year-old daughter. Her 22-year-old sister was also his victim; she had been impregnated by her father when she was 15. The family never talked about it, but the resulting baby was a constant reminder of the physical and emotional pain caused by the rapes.
- A six-year-old girl complained that her stepbrother who lived with her was hurting her. Physical examination of the child confirmed that she had been raped. The 13-year-old boy was found guilty of rape and sodomy, which had occurred over a two-year period.
- An 11-year-old boy told his social worker that his mother's boyfriend had hit him over the head with the handle of a machete and that he was having headaches. His mother insisted that her son was not telling the truth. An investigation by the police determined that the boyfriend had repeatedly beaten the boy with a belt on at least one occasion. Another time, the man forced the child to stand in front of a door that had a poster picture of Mickey Mouse on it. He fired numerous shots from a handgun at the child, both above his head and at his feet, yelling, "You're dead; you're dead!" Afterward, the man took a razor blade and cut him on the little finger, telling him, "When you die, I am going to be the one to kill you." When a search warrant was executed on the home, the poster of Mickey Mouse was found under a mattress, and 11 bullet holes were located on the floor and in the wall.

- An older woman was reluctant to report that her grown son had been stealing her money. She was afraid because of his drug habit and believed that he might take what little she had left in life. At 70 years old, she knew there was no other way to keep from having to go into a nursing home; she had to remain self-sufficient. That meant turning her son in for larceny.
- An investigation into multiple sexual assaults on one young woman was difficult. She came forward as an adult because it had taken time for her to get away from her stepfather, who physically assaulted her as well. Unfortunately, it took her too long to break free. The assaults against her were beyond the statute of limitations; the stepfather could not be prosecuted! The case prompted the local prosecutor to submit a proposal to change the law, extending the statute of limitations in Massachusetts. Future sexual assault victims will now have 10 years after reaching majority to come forward with complaints.
- Lying in the hospital was a woman whose face was so swollen that it was barely recognizable. Her eyes were blackened, her nose was swollen to twice its size, and her lips were grotesque. It would be years after this particular incident before the woman could bring herself to testify against her husband in court for the years of wife battering. During her marriage, she had suffered broken bones, broken teeth, and a detached retina, among other injuries too numerous to mention. Because of the many times that he had kicked her on the ground and twisted her legs around the kitchen table until they snapped, she walked with a cane. Even worse, she had suffered psychological abuse that ranged from cruel to bizarre. Coming home to find the bloody head of her horse on the walkway was just another way he intimidated and kept control of her.
- A 15-year-old girl pushed her father down the stairs yet another time. She had also injured her mother in the past. It was not that the parents were old, rather just older than most parents. They were tired of fighting with their growing child and embarrassed that anyone would find out. She was the child of their dreams who had turned into a nightmare.
- A 14-year gay relationship ended in the death of the abuser from multiple stab wounds. The gay man had endured several years of physical, sexual, and emotional abuse prior to killing his abuser in self-defense. This case became the first successful use of the battered spouse defense in which the relationship involved a gay couple.

The contemporary field of family violence is the study of a social problem of enormous magnitude. Society is a collection of many groups. Patterns of behavior guide our interactions and reflect the goals of each group. We study human social behavior and interaction in sociology, psychology, and anthropology—the social sciences. They are the branches of learning that deal with the institutions and functions of human society. Family violence is studied through all of these perspectives, with each one using different approaches to examining human behavior. Sociologists study society, including patterns of human relationships and interaction. Psychologists study human behavior and mental processes. Anthropologists look at the culture and history of a group of people. You will note that the social sciences have contributed heavily to our past and present understanding of family violence issues.

The social sciences use various approaches to examine social events, and often they consider the same circumstance from different points of view. Historians, for example, trace the development of families over time. This chapter uses the historical perspective to describe the changes over time on how society has viewed family violence. There is little social historical work available that sheds light on the condition of the family in ancient and medieval times, nor is this historical account complete. So, we will examine laws from a historical perspective. These provide one way in which the society's mores can be evaluated. The legal sanctions on assault on wives inform us about the expected code of behavior by husbands. Some evidence of the expectations of wives is also provided in legal history. This brief historical account will show that family structures and social status of these members have dictated the manner in which people are treated.

The institutions of government and family are concerned with accomplishing goals within the society. The government establishes law by which the society functions. Some believe that law reflects the needs and objectives of that particular society; therefore, the laws reflect the mores of the majority. Laws regarding family violence vastly differ from society to society, as evidenced in Chapter 1. Codified into a body of law are the principles of the past and the present. Family is an important institution within the scheme of human stability. Its members follow rules of society and are bound by acceptable standards of behavior. Examining these guideposts of human behavior is one way to understand the family relations of people today.

Like people themselves, social relationships change. Awareness of the problems associated with family violence today has brought us to a point where it is a recognized indicator of a dysfunctional family. That was hardly the case throughout history. In the past, violence against intimates has been tolerated as accepted social conduct and alternatively condemned as deviant behavior. Looking at these historical examples of legally defined social relations may seem like comparing oranges and apples. Socially accepted views on property in ancient times are very different from those of today. Women were considered inferior to men, intellectually and physically. The purpose of this chapter is to provide insight into the legal developments of family relationships that in turn have shaped current socially accepted practices in families. A kernel of truth may be found in all explanations for crime, and the social–legal historical perspective is only one of many factors in a larger picture. This chapter is also designed to provide definitions of the words used in the field of family violence. Although the remaining chapters in the text will focus on family violence in the United States, it is important to understand that we are not isolated in our concerns over family violence. Family violence has existed since the beginning of recorded family history and continues to all corners of the world.

EARLY SOCIAL–LEGAL HISTORY

Domination of men over women and children has a strong historical foundation. Some experts suggest that this inequality of the sexes is the foundation for the assumption of male superiority and the foundation for intimate partner violence. By providing husbands with the right to punish wayward wives, the system gives a rationale to male brutality against women. Others advise that the social order was just that, an order to life's relations for purposes of survival.

Punishment of errant wives was in the best interest of the husband under the system of patriarchy. However, there is often a difference between the law and social practice. Isolated legal initiatives to control violence against women can be traced back as far as the Roman era when patriarchy defined the relationships between the husband

and his wife and children (Belknap, 1992). **Patriarchy** refers to a social system that recognizes the complete dominance of men over women, typically strengthened by law in addition to custom and religion. Patriarchy is recognized as the most common and enduring social system. The term "patriarchy" is used today to describe an inequity of power of men dominating women. It comes from the Greek for the patriarch, or "father as ruler." Even today, social mores reminiscent of ancient patriarchy may keep private the abuses that are legally prohibited.

The earliest known body of law, the Code of Hammurabi, appeared in the eighteenth century B.C. All matters of living were governed extensively through the code. It contains lengthy and specific arrangements between husbands and wives, usually arranged by the father of the bride. Provisions were made to allow a woman to request entry into a convent to live as a nun, and such a request could not be denied (Horne, 1998).

The Ancient World of Greece

The first written laws appeared in Athens around 621 B.C. (Rhodes, 1984). They were attributed to Dracon, a lawgiver. Regardless of how severe or small the infraction, the punishment was the same, death. Dracon felt that people guilty of small infractions of the law deserved the death penalty and that there was, after all, no greater penalty for those that had committed the more serious infractions. As a result, laws today that are cruel and harsh are sometimes referred to as Draconian. His Codes of Law, along with the Solonian Codes, had a significant influence on the courts in Athens, because rulings were based on interpretation of the law (Rhodes, 1984).

Solon, the Athenian law reformer who mitigated the Draconian laws, was appointed lawgiver in Athens around 594 B.C. When he replaced Dracon, Solon threw out all of the old laws except for the homicide law; and he created many new laws, especially in the categories of tort and family law. Solon introduced the concept that all citizens should have access to justice in the courts, redefining the nature of citizenship. Whereas formerly an individual's status had mainly been a matter of birth, now it would seem that all citizens were defined according to their economic class. This change did not affect the status of women at that time, yet it can be recognized as an essential step toward attaining political equality.

Solon's family laws were laws that regulated the behavior of men and women. He wrote laws on allowances in marriage and adoption, as well as laws concerning inheritances and supporting roles of parents. Penalties for breaking these laws were not set but were enforced by the head of the particular family. Linked to family laws were laws concerning women, whose role in Greek law was minimal. Women were controlled by men at nearly every stage of their lives. This is because they were under constant supervision by their *kyrios*, or "official guardian." Most often the *kyrios* was a girl's father, or if she were married, it was her husband. Because of this supervision, women's role in law was limited to rare court appearances, where they either presented evidence in a homicide case or were on display along with their families to try to evoke pity from the jury. The most important duties for a city-dwelling woman were to bear children—preferably male—and to run the household (Romano & White, 2002). In ancient Athens, the birthplace of democracy, women, foreigners, slaves, and children were denied the right to vote.

Back Then ...

In 753 B.C., Romulus, who is credited with the founding of Rome, formalized the first law of marriage. In part, this law "obligated both the married women, as having no other refuge, to conform themselves entirely to the temper of their husbands and the husbands to rule their wives as necessary and inseparable possessions" (O'Faolain & Martines, 1973).

The Roman Empire

According to the civil law of Rome, the male head of the family had full rights and power over his wife, children, and any descendants who sprang from him through male lineage only. This power was at one time exercised over the lives and deaths of both women and children. Women, children, and slaves were a property that could be sold or bought. Any harm committed against a woman was viewed as an offense against the father if she were unmarried or as an offense to the husband, but not to the victim.

The husband initially had the right to kill his wife if she engaged in adultery; this right was later limited to the father. Consequently, it was the male "owner" who sought vengeance or compensation for his loss. A female could not be an aggrieved party, nor was she held responsible for her actions. It was, therefore, the responsibility of the husband or father to punish the woman whose actions were injurious to others. The lack of legal standing prohibited women from appealing to the courts for relief when their punishment was excessive or without cause.

Illustrations of acceptable physical punishment by husbands against their wives are evidenced in the early Roman Empire. Although the law sometimes placed obligations on both the husband and the wife, the purpose was apparently to assure that the husband had control over his property. Early Roman law treated women and children as the property of the husband.

Under the laws of Romulus, the wife could not divorce her husband (Lefkowitz & Fant, 1992). He was granted rights of divorce when the woman had used drugs or magic, and for adultery. Other reasons were stipulated as acceptable motives for the man seeking a divorce, but he would forfeit part of his estate for doing so.

The legal punishment of errant Roman wives during the first and second centuries A.D. is recorded through the following accounts (Lefkowitz & Fant, 1992):

- Egnatius Metellus took a cudgel and beat his wife to death because she had drunk some wine. He was not charged with a crime because she had violated the laws of sobriety.
- Quintus Angistius Vetus divorced his wife after he had seen her having a private conversation with a common freedwoman in public.

The Christian Era

Christianity embraced the subordination of wives over their husbands, and Scriptures commanded women to be silent, obedient, and accepting of their husbands' authority. A passage from the New Testament, Ephesians 5:22–24, specifically states the role of a married woman according to the Church: "Wives should regard their husbands as they regard the Lord, since as Christ is head of the Church and saves the whole body, so is a husband the head of his wife; and as the Church submits to Christ, so should wives to their husbands, in everything" (The Jerusalem Bible, 1996). The notion that male supremacy was supported unconditionally by the Christian faith is further supported by the actions of Constantine the Great, the first Christian Roman emperor, later canonized as a saint. Constantine was the first emperor to order the execution of his own wife in A.D. 298.

British Common Law

Patriarchy is not the only social arrangement between married people, but it has been the dominant one in Western civilization. Under common law, women and children were no longer viewed as property, but the results were the same. The order was based on the belief that when two are joined in marriage, they become one, socially and legally. The rights of the woman are then subordinate to those of the male, unlike the woman who remains single.

Historian Laurel Thatcher Ulrich offers this comment on the legal status of women under the common law. It was authored by William Blackstone in *Commentaries on the Laws of England* and explains the concept of this patriarchal order: "By marriage, the husband and wife are one person in law; that is, the very being or legal existence of the women is suspended during the marriage, or at least is incorporated and consolidated into that of the husband; under whose wing, protection, and cover, she performs everything" (Ulrich, 1991, pg. 7).

Physical force and chastisement of one's wife is believed to have been accepted under English common law, the legal foundation in the colonies. However, evidence exists of some legal restrictions on the extent to which a wife might be chastised. Opinions of English courts in 1659 and 1674 to 1675 held that husbands' power over wives did not include beating, but was limited to admonition and confinement (Bloch, 2007). Well cited by historians of intimate partner violence, the rule of thumb referred to a common-law restriction on the size of the weapon to be used in wife chastisement. The rule came from the belief that under British common law the husband was allowed to beat his wife with a stick as long as it was no thicker than his thumb. However well cited, there is no evidence that the rule was ever evoked in America (Pleck, 1989). In fact, the rule may never have existed at all, springing from an unsubstantiated rumor (Bloch, 2007).

French Law

It was a dangerous thing to question the inferiority of women presumed by the Declaration of the Rights of Man. Olympe de Gouges wrote a Declaration of the Rights of Women in 1791 and was quickly arrested and tried for treason. On November 3, 1793,

---

Back Then ...

Corporal punishment of an errant wife was a widely accepted practice. A Christian scholar generated the Rules of Marriage in the late fifteenth century. They specified the following:

> when you see your wife commit an offense, don't rush at her with insults and violent blows .... Scold her sharply, bully and terrify her. And if this does not work ... take up a stick and beat her soundly, for it is better to punish the body and correct the soul than to damage the soul and spare the body. ... Then readily beat her, not in rage but out of charity and concern for her soul, so that the beating will redound to your merit and her good. (Davidson, 1977)

Back Then . . .

According to Lunn, the earliest case of intimate partner violence heard in the British court was in 1395. Margaret Neffield and witnesses testified that her husband attacked her with a dagger, causing several wounds and broken bones. The court was not satisfied that this constituted grounds for a judicial separation, and Mrs. Neffield was ordered to return to living with her husband (Lunn, 1991).

she was executed by the guillotine (Levy & Johnson, 1979). In the early nineteenth century, Napoleon Bonaparte formalized the civil code in France, subjugating women as legal minors for their entire lives. Under the Napoleonic Code, wives could be beaten, punched, and permanently disfigured for minor disobedience or "scolding" (Pagelow, 1984). The French code of chivalry allowed the husband to knock her to the earth, strike her in the face with his fist, and break her nose so that she would always be blemished and ashamed (Dobash & Dobash, 1978). The Napoleonic Code influenced French, Swiss, Italian, and German law (Dutton, 1998). Court relief in the form of divorce was a rare intervention for battered victims. It came only when the beatings reached the level of attempted murder.

MARITAL RELATIONS IN EARLY AMERICA

Patriarchy continued in the colonies as the ideal family structure. The British immigrants reestablished their customs of inheritance by the eldest son, called primogeniture. Land was retained within the family through a legal proscription against the sale or grant of land outside the lineage, which is referred to as entail. The absence of specific legislation on wife beating in the colonies implies a reliance on English common law to govern family relations.

English legal manuals and treatises suggested that the accepted way to deal with violent husbands under the common law was to charge them with the breach of the peace (Bloch, 2007). This necessitated the wife providing an informal testimony to the local justice of the peace or magistrate. The justice or magistrate would require her husband to post a bond or pledge to guarantee his good behavior, similar to the concept of a modern-day restraining order. Judges and magistrates in colonial times would rely on the credibility of the woman and her support of friends and family as well as their understanding of the law in making decisions on wife beating.

Puritan Restrictions

As early as 1599, Puritan ministers in England spoke out against wife beating. Bringing this objection to America, the Puritans were the first to prohibit intimate partner violence through legislation. Puritan laws provided penalties for wife beating, consisting of fines, whipping, or both. Because wife beating was considered a social problem that involved the community, enforcement included "holy watching" by neighbors. The Puritan state also intervened to discipline disobedient wives on behalf of husbands (Bloch, 2007). Puritan use of legal sanctions to maintain order within families was not a challenge to the existing patriarchal order but merely a mechanism of social control.

Back Then ...

The Massachusetts Body of Liberties, located in the Massachusetts Code of 1648, provided the following: "Everie marryed woman shall be free from bodilie correction or stripes by her husband, unlesse it be in his own defense upon her assault" (Sherman & Rogan, 1992).

The Next One Hundred Years

The American Revolution marked the turning point toward greater legal acceptance of wife beating in the United States. Reforms of the Revolution delegitimized government intervention in family affairs with the effect of weakening earlier English and colonial practices that had given legal recourse to battered women (Bloch, 2007). In instances when the offense caused death or serious bodily injury and rose to the level of a felony, wife beating was rarely brought before the courts. Between 1633 and 1802, only 12 cases of intimate partner violence were prosecuted in the Plymouth Colony (Pleck, 1989).

Some early American legislation on intimate partner violence control included corporal punishment and fines as penalties for wife beating. Some courts exacted promissory notes from perpetrators who beat their wives, with the understanding that the offender would forfeit the money if reconvicted. In 1824, the Supreme Court of Mississippi upheld the husband's right of chastisement in cases of "great emergency," saying that husbands should not be subjected to "vexatious" prosecutions for assault and battery (Dobash & Dobash, 1979). This era of nonprotection for victims of intimate partner violence lasted from the late 1770s to the 1850s. During this period, the option of abused wives to seek warrants to secure the good behavior of their husbands declined significantly. Complaints of breach of the peace changed by the end of the nineteenth century and could only involve disturbances in public places, not inside homes (Bloch, 2007).

The first case in either England or America to declare wife beating a right under the common law was the Mississippi Supreme Court case of *Bradley v. State* (1824). Calvin Bradley submitted an appeal to the higher court after being found guilty during a circuit court trial of assault and battery on his wife. The grounds for his appeal were that husbands were always exempt from indictment for assault and battery on their wives. Although the justices did not accept the argument at face value, they did maintain that a husband's susceptibility to accusation depended on whether he had been provoked by misbehavior and had responded "reasonably" against his wife. The presiding judge, Powhatan Ellis, went so far as to support the claim that a husband had a right to "beat, bruise, etc." a disobedient wife.

By 1870, wife beating had taken on an aura of social unacceptability and was once again declared illegal in most states of the United States. This change coincided with a growing concern over child maltreatment. Women were given legal standing in some isolated cases. Judges in Alabama were the first to recognize that a woman, in this case an emancipated slave, should be afforded the same legal protections as other citizens (*Fulgham v. State*, 1871).

African American Families

The West African peoples were stripped of family ties and kinship connections under slavery in Colonial America. Additionally, black women lacked the paternalist protection of the domestic sphere and were subjected to the sexual and economic desires of

More About It: *Fulgham v. State* (1871)

The defendant husband was convicted of assault and battery on his wife in a judgment of the Circuit Court of Greene (Alabama). The facts of the case were that the defendant had chastised one of his children. The wife thought the punishment excessive. The child ran, pursued by the father, and both were followed by the wife. When the wife caught up, the husband struck her on the back with a board, and she returned the blows with a switch. The blows inflicted on the wife made no permanent impression. The defendant appealed to the Alabama Supreme Court, asserting that a husband could not be convicted of battery on his wife unless he inflicted a permanent injury or used such excessive violence or cruelty as indicated malignity or vindictiveness.

In affirming the conviction of the defendant by the trial court, the court held that a rod, which may be drawn through the wedding ring, was not deemed necessary to teach the wife her duty and subjection to the husband. The husband was not allowed by law to use such a weapon, or any other, for her moderate correction. The wife was not to be considered to be the husband's slave. All stood upon the same footing before the law, as citizens of Alabama, possessing equal civil and political rights and public privileges. No special "privilege" to any rank of the people was allowed to exist in the state because the fundamental law forbade such a privilege. The court held that the husband might exercise over the wife "gentle restraint." Moreover, he may have the security of the peace against the wife, and the wife against him. The court here determined that there be no privilege for a husband to beat his wife or for her to beat him. Either could be indicted and tried in criminal court for assault and battery.

their owners. There was no legal recourse for the violence against black women during slavery. Any stability attained by kinship was transitory because neither church nor law sanctioned slave marriage. Slaves could be bought and sold; families were separated at the whim of the master.

Interracial marriage was also forbidden. Early colonial statutes made it a criminal act of marrying outside one's race or to conduct such a marriage ceremony. In Virginia, an Act Concerning Servants and Slaves, Laws of 1705, stated, "Be it enacted, … . That whatsoever English or other white man or woman, being free, shall intermarry with a Negro or mulatto man or woman, bond or free, shall by the judgment of the county court be committed to prison and there remain during the space of six months, without bail …" (Wortman, 1985). In the United States, some state laws prohibited the marriage of whites and blacks and in many states also the intermarriage of whites with Native Americans or Asians. Between 1913 and 1948, 30 out of the then 48 states enforced these laws (Loving Day, 2004). In *Loving v. Virginia* (1967), the U.S. Supreme Court unanimously ruled that miscegenation laws are unconstitutional (*Loving v. Virginia*, 1967). With this ruling, these laws were no longer in effect in the remaining 16 states that still had them.

Sharon Angella Allard maintains that the historical legal view of women ignores the significant differences that exist between white and black victims of intimate partner violence (Balos & Fellows, 1994). In her view, the women of color are excluded from legal protections due to perceptions that they are stronger than other victims of patriarchy. They have been characterized as immoral and undeserving of refuge from the sexual predators who have stalked them. Since colonial times, the black slave woman was a contradiction to the stereotypical passive white victim.

Back Then …

"Whoever is ruled by his wife, may he be the worst damned! Such men become soft, shameless, silly, unfree, and inarticulate." Further, the Church warned that to give a woman freedom was like committing suicide for a man. Disorder and destruction would be the inevitable results (Pushkareva, 1997).

During the Reconstruction period following the Civil War, the African American couple slowly was afforded the legal right to marry. South Carolina was among the first states to regulate and recognize the marriage between persons of color (in 1866). In part, the statute provided the following permissions (Wortman, 1985):

1. The relation of husband and wife among persons of color is established.
2. Those who now live as such are declared to be husband and wife.

Native American Families

Gender roles and marital customs among Native Americans were different from those in the Colonial Anglo-American patriarchal system. Most Native American cultures were matriarchal; family membership and descent were traced through the mother's side (The Colonial Williamsburg Foundation, 2013). This meant that the family name, bloodline, and inheritance came from the mother. Women controlled the land and owned the home and livestock (Feinman, 1992). The sexual division of labor in most Native societies assigned farming primarily to women and exempted men from many of the most arduous tasks. Native American men hunted and fished; these were leisurely activities to European settlers who deemed the men lazy. Early Anglo-Americans found the productivity of Indian women troubling, in part, because Native women farmed (Perdue, 1998). The matriarchal system eroded and was replaced with colonists' views of patriarchy. As the women's traditional roles were devalued, beginning around 1868, men were assigned work previously in the sphere of women. Under U.S. laws and Indian policies, women's traditional roles began to erode as the society became increasingly masculine.

Europeans neither liked nor approved of the treatment of American Indian children, on whom affection was lavished. American Indian children, unlike Europeans' children, were not punished by being spanked or beaten (The Colonial Williamsburg Foundation, 2013). Pressured to conform to Anglo norms, children were required to attend boarding schools where they were taught Anglo values. They were often beaten by teachers, thereby learning that violence was an acceptable method of reprimand and social control (Feinman, 1992). Women's political and economic roles suffered and abuse of children and women became prevalent.

One Hundred Years of Secrecy

Not long after *Fulgham*, the Supreme Court considered whether women could be prohibited from practicing law. In 1873, the Court decided in *Bradwell v. Illinois* that the laws of Illinois did not abridge any of the privileges and immunities of citizens of the United States by legislating what offices and positions should be filled by men only. The legal and social positioning of women for that period was evidenced in the concurring opinion. Concurring with the opinion of the Court, Justice Bradley said, in part, "The constitution of the family organization, which is founded in the divine ordinance, as well as the nature of things, indicates the domestic sphere as that which properly belongs to the domain and functions of womanhood . . ." So firmly fixed was this sentiment in the founders of common law that it became a maxim of that system of jurisprudence that a woman had no legal existence separate from her husband, who was regarded as her head and representative in the social state (*Bradwell v. Illinois*, 1873).

Court denials of a husband's "right" to batter his wife continued slowly. The American legal system responded to criticisms on the right of the husband to chastise his wife by physical beatings. Years of protest by temperance and women's rights advocates, along with shifting attitudes toward corporal punishment, finally discredited the law of marital chastisement. By the 1870s, judges no longer allowed the husband to claim the legal right to beat his wife. In several states, legislatures enacted statutes explicitly prohibiting wife beating. Three states even revived corporal punishment for the crime, providing that wife-beaters could be sentenced to the whipping post (Pleck, 1989). By the end of the Civil War, the legal system had rejected the doctrine of marital chastisement. In *Commonwealth v. Hugh McAfee* (1871), a Massachusetts court expressly stated that there was no law authorizing a man to beat his wife either in the Commonwealth or New York. The court went on further to say that beating or striking a wife violently with the open hand was not one of the rights conferred on a husband by marriage, even if the wife were drunk or insolent (*Commonwealth v. Hugh McAfee*, 1871). In 1882, Maryland became the first state to pass a law that made wife-beating a crime, punishable by 40 lashes or a year in jail (Davidson, 1977). Oregon passed similar legislation in 1906.

Although wife battering had become socially repugnant in the United States, it continued behind closed doors. States created innovative laws to allow the practice of battering, and women were again silenced, as portrayed in Figure 2-2. One example

FIGURE 2-2   By the 1870s, judges no longer allowed the husband to claim the legal right to beat his wife, but it continued behind closed doors. Image Copyright Oleg Golovneg, 2012. Shutterstock

Back Then ...

Acknowledging the secretive practice and justifying a husband's right to batter, the North Carolina Supreme Court held in *State v. Oliver* (1871), "If no permanent injury has been inflicted, nor malice, cruelty nor dangerous violence shown by the husband, it is better to draw the curtain, shut out the public gaze, and leave the parties to forget and forgive" (*State v. Oliver*, 1874).

was called the stitch rule. Under the regulation, a husband could only be criminally prosecuted for injuring his wife if those injuries were severe enough to require stitches. The stitch rule was overturned in 1864 (Weitzman, 2000); however, it continued as an informal factor used by police to determine whether or not to arrest in cases of intimate partner violence (Gordon, 1989). A similar statute in North Carolina referred to as the curtain rule allowed police to "interfere" with a husband's actions toward his wife only after permanent injury had been inflicted on her (Belknap, 1992).

By the beginning of the twentieth century, intimate partner violence as a legally sanctioned crime disappeared. Unfortunately, the brief reform period ended around 1914. By World War I, the concern about wife beating had faded again. Over the next half-century, the courts rarely intervened in domestic affairs, even when laws existed to prohibit the behavior. Social attention fluctuated, and no significant changes occurred concerning domestic abuse. It was not until the 1960s that violence toward intimates again became a subject of concern and an object of government interference. By this time, effective legal remedies to prevent intimate partner violence ran from seriously lacking to nonexistent. Contemporary intimate partner violence response is complicated and diverse. It provides the theme for later chapters in which family violence by gender and age will be discussed.

Wife Battering

Wife battering reemerged along with child abuse as a social issue in the 1960s. The dominant view held that marital violence was a "private affair." Intimate partner violence continued behind closed doors, although not sanctioned by law. Intervention was rare, occurring in cases where the victim had been killed or severely maimed. Forms of spousal violence prohibited by criminal law usually amounted to misdemeanors; unless police witnessed the violence, they had no powers of arrest. Most intimate partner violence assaults fell within this category. Police officers were trained to respond

More About It: The Curtain Rule

In 1864, the Supreme Court of North Carolina in *State v. Jessie Black* declared that

> a husband is responsible for the acts of his wife, and he is required to govern his household, and for that purpose the law permits him to use towards his wife such a degree of force as is necessary to control an unruly temper and make her behave herself; and unless some permanent injury be inflicted, or there be an excess of violence, or such a degree of cruelty as shows that it is inflicted to gratify his own bad passions, the law will not invade the domestic forum or go behind the curtain. It prefers to leave the parties to themselves, as the best mode of inducing them to make the matter up and live together as man and wife should. (*State v. Jessie Black*, 1864)

to the crisis of intimate partner violence by separating the parties for a "cooling-down period." It was a common practice for officers to "counsel" the parties. In extreme cases, the victim would be referred to the court to file a private complaint. The complaints were not taken seriously, however, and resulted in fewer prosecutions than for any other crime.

The lack of adequate legal remedies for the victim hindered progress, including police action. New legislation was needed to address the contemporary concerns of intimate partner violence that began to surface. A noteworthy complaint focused on the ineffective law enforcement response. The critique of the system is well founded, given that law enforcement could not legally intervene in family disputes. Isolated attempts to protect victims of abuse were contrary to the prevailing legal and social atmosphere.

Although a few examples of effective law enforcement intervention did occur, police noncompliance was a far more frequent occurrence. Faced with intimate partner violence situations, police officers often failed to affect an arrest, even when the law demanded it. During the 1970s, reformers sought changes that might ensure effective intervention. The debates centered on what type of intervention would be most appropriate, as well as the form that it might take. Civil actions against police departments and mandatory arrest of the perpetrator were tactics devised to force compliance.

WHAT IS FAMILY VIOLENCE TODAY?

Some forms of violence are criminal acts and others are not. We look to the criminal statutes to provide a legal definition. Each state and the federal government provide legal definitions, which may be slightly different from state to state or from the federal definition. The legal definition explains the relationships that are considered to be domestic and the acts that are defined as criminal. Remember that each state and the federal government determine for their jurisdiction the *act* and *relationship* for crimes of family violence. Here is an example from the state of Texas. **Family violence** is defined in the Texas Family Code (Section 71.004) as

1. an act by a member of a family or household against another member of the family or household that is intended to result in physical harm, bodily injury, assault, or sexual assault, or that is a threat that reasonably places the member in fear of imminent physical harm, bodily injury, assault, or sexual assault, but does not include defensive measures to protect oneself;
2. an abuse by a member of a family or household toward a child of the family or household; or
3. a dating violence.

Undoubtedly, the problem of family violence is noticed. People talk about it. Most individuals know or think they know, what family violence is. Daily newspapers, magazines, radio, and television report on family violence. Stories about famous people in sports, politics, and Hollywood are linked with whispers and screams of family violence. Articles appear on the Internet and in academic journals. Researchers examine the signs and symptoms of family violence. Sitting in coffee shops or boardrooms, people talk about it. Still, people laugh and tell jokes about family violence! People say that, if it is so bad, the victim ought to leave. Plain and simple: Just leave. If the victim does not leave, it cannot be that bad. Or, can it be?

FIGURE 2-3   The primary categories of family violence include intimate partner violence, child abuse, and abuse of older adults. Images Copyright Peter Bernik, ESB Professional, and Shutterstock, 2012. Used under license from Shutterstock.com

Family violence today is grouped into three major categories: intimate partner violence, child abuse, and elder abuse. Illustrated in Figure 2-3, each of these three categories of family violence will be addressed in detail throughout the text. The definitions for these three groups are listed below. Within these categories, many forms of violence may occur. Most of the forms are criminal acts; although physiological abuse is commonly present in violent situations, by itself, it usually does not constitute criminal activity.

Intimate Partner Violence

Often referred to as battering or domestic violence, **intimate partner violence** refers to violence committed within an adult intimate relationship, regardless of gender, and is part of an ongoing complex pattern of violent behavior used to gain control. Statistics bear out the fact that improved services, improved laws, and increased sanctions against abusers (including police arrest) have made a difference. As you can see in Figure 2-4, the annual rate of intimate partner victimization since 1993 has declined.

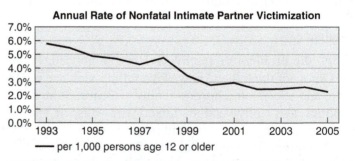

FIGURE 2-4   Nonfatal intimate partner violence has declined since 1993. The decline is attributed to increased options for victims and improved criminal justice interventions. Based on data from Catalano, 2012.

Intimate partner violence involves coercive behavior in a relationship. The control may be achieved through economic forms, such as withholding or denying access to money or other essential resources or sabotaging employment, housing, or educational opportunities. Social isolation is quite common, including the denial of communication with friends and relatives or making communication so problematic that the victim chooses to avoid it, prohibiting access to the telephone or transportation, and denying access to needed health care. Verbal and emotional forms of assault and control include intimidation, coercion, threats, or degradation. Physical and sexual assaults may occur. Individual acts do not constitute battering. Experts agree that intimate partner violence involves a continuum of behaviors ranging from making degrading remarks to cruel jokes, economic exploitation, punches and kicks, false imprisonment, sexual abuse, suffocating actions, maiming assaults, and homicide. Unchecked, domestic violence usually increases in frequency and severity. Many victims suffer all forms of abuse. Verbal and emotional abuse may be subtler than physical harm, but this does not mean that it is less destructive to victims. Many have said that the emotional scars take much longer to heal than the broken bones.

The legal definition of intimate partner violence often codified as domestic violence, may be slightly different from the social definition. That is because the law must clearly state the particular acts that are forbidden by criminal or civil law. The California Family Code defines intimate partner violence as abuse or violence that is perpetrated against any person in a legally recognized domestic relationship. It is important to note that many forms of abuse are socially unacceptable and are part of the violent relationship but do not rise to the level of criminal violations. Other domestic abuse situations constitute crimes and require law enforcement intervention. Intimate partner violence situations are often not easy to interpret laws and are always unpleasant. Sometimes it is difficult to determine accurately who has done what. The response role is not limited to law enforcement, however. Noncriminal abuse and neglect will also often come to the attention of law enforcement officers. In these situations, police officers can play a vital role by referring the apparent victim to appropriate health or social service agencies. There may be children involved who desperately need someone to intervene on their behalf.

Federal and state laws recognize that domestic relationships include partnerships where people live together but may not be legally married. Any definition that further explains intimate partner violence is necessarily general to include live-in intimates under the definition of domestic relationship. Same-sex partners and college roommates may sometimes constitute domestic partners, depending on how the state defines domestic relationships.

Child Abuse

Child abuse and neglect is defined by federal and state laws. The Child Abuse Prevention and Treatment Act (CAPTA, 2011) is the federal legislation that provides minimum standards that states must incorporate in their statutory definitions of child abuse and neglect. Any act committed against a child by a caretaker that causes death, harm, or risk of harm—physical, or sexual, or psychological—may be considered **child abuse and neglect**. The failure to provide care and protection may also be considered abuse or neglect. Federal agencies such as the Centers for Disease Control and Prevention (CDC), Children's Bureau, and Child Welfare Information Gateway are among the national resources that provide information and services on child abuse and neglect. Every state has a department devoted exclusively to the protection of children. The names for these state family services will vary by state; for example, the Department of Children & Families is the Massachusetts agency (DCF, 2013). Information on the many grassroots and nonprofit organizations that educate the public on child abuse and neglect can be found on the Internet.

There are two levels of protection for children in the United States. The first level of protection is found in civil law, defining the responsibilities of agencies that can legally interfere with family relationships and determine custody. Child protection agencies, family courts, and the juvenile justice system form the basis of civil protection for minors. Child protection agencies may include social services, foster child, and adoption organizations. Family courts investigate allegations relative to the care and custody of children. The family courts and the juvenile justice system may investigate custody arrangements and provide oversight for the well-being of a child. Child protection agencies, the police, school officials, and members of the public may petition the courts when a child is believed to be in need of services. The courts have the authority to require any number of measures designed to protect the child and may also appoint a temporary or permanent guardian due to abuse and neglect or delinquency.

The second level of protection for children in the United States comes from the criminal justice system. Individuals who abuse or neglect a child may be charged with a crime, based on the offense and the criminal statute in the state in which the abuse occurred. Children and adults may be held criminally liable for abuse and neglect against a child. Law must define the acts that constitute child abuse or neglect. The criminal penalties for violence against a child range from fines to prison sentences, depending on the severity of the abuse.

Elder Abuse

Elder abuse may involve physical, sexual, or emotional/psychological violence and neglect, abandonment, or financial exploitation. Most researchers agree on two general categories of elder abuse: domestic and institutional. Also referred to as abuse of an older adult, it refers to any of several forms of maltreatment of an older person by someone who has a special relationship with the older adult, such as a spouse, a sibling, a child, a friend, or a caregiver in the older person's home. A caregiver is one who is responsible for the elder due to a legal or contractual arrangement. Institutional abuse is any form of abuse that occurs in residential facilities for older persons, such as nursing, foster, or group homes. Perpetrators of institutional abuse are usually persons who have a legal or contractual obligation to provide elder care and protection. A significant number of cases of abuse of older adults are believed to fit into the category of self-neglect. Further, older adult abuse may involve both the purposeful or active abuse and the passive abuse that results in negligence due to ignorance or an inability to provide care. It is important that professionals who respond to elder abuse understand the legal definitions in their state. Classifications of elder abuse may be criminal or civil. Abuse may require social service intervention and mandated reporting by officials; the requirements vary greatly from state to state.

In this text, we focus on "domestic" elder abuse, perpetrated by family members or others who are known through a caregiving role in the victim's home. Abuse may have relatively little impact on the older adult, or it may threaten one's life. Physical violence ranges from a slap that knocks off an elder's glasses, to kicking and punching that might result in death. Sexual violence may include improper touching, sexual exposing, and penetration. Financial exploitation may be as straightforward as theft from the elder person's wallet, to the appropriation of one's home through forcing an older adult to sign away ownership.

FORMS OF INTIMATE PARTNER VIOLENCE

Intimate partner violence comes in many different forms. The severity of an act or the extent of harm is routinely the measuring tool used by the police to determine whether the act is criminal. The author suggests that this approach is outdated and should be changed to reflect contemporary knowledge of intimate partner violence: It is meant to hurt, intimidate, control, or place the victim in fear of the abuser. With this understanding, the physical extent of harm becomes moot. Probable cause that a crime has been committed is the standard of every other law enforcement action and therefore must continue to be applied equally when domestic crimes are being investigated.

The arrest of the perpetrator should not be considered as the punishment for domestic crimes; it is simply the legal intervention when there is evidence that a crime has been committed. This form of intervention should occur whenever the law of the state determines it to be appropriate. The courts will ultimately resolve whether the action is criminal behavior. The following examples suggest some types of violence that may be criminal conduct that is prohibited by law:

- Beating
- Pulling hair
- Shoving
- Striking
- Pulling
- Punching
- Slapping
- Kicking
- Hitting
- Choking
- Biting
- Pointing weapons
- Throwing things
- Threatening
- Harassing
- Sexual abuse
- Stalking
- Homicide

LEGAL FAMILY RELATIONSHIPS

A domestic or family relationship is typically defined by blood, marriage, relationship, and cohabitation. Specific legal definitions vary slightly from state to state. Some common legal definitions exist. These include the following:

- Persons who are or were legally married: a spouse or former spouse.
- Persons who reside together without marriage: a cohabitant or former cohabitant.
- Persons related through marriage: any person related by consanguinity or affinity within the second degree, related by blood or through marriage.

- Persons who share a child in common: where the presumption applies that the male is the biological father of the child and the female is the biological mother (whether they were ever legally married or not).
- A woman who is pregnant and the man who is presumed to be the father.
- Persons who are having or have had a substantial dating or engagement relationship.
- Biological children or stepchildren.
- Biological parents or stepparents.

The category of persons who simply reside together is controversial. Living together may be interpreted to include apartment dwellers and students who share dorm accommodations, depending on the jurisdiction. It includes persons who share a house or apartment, regardless of whether they are married. Some, but not all, states include substantial dating relationships as a category in which violence would be defined as intimate partner violence. Same-sex relationships where the persons reside as if they were married are considered to be domestic. When a crime is committed, determining the offender in a family violence situation does not depend on gender, size, or age. When the relationship is one that is legally considered to be domestic, then the crime would be a domestic violence crime. A crime may be considered intimate partner violence only when the victim-to-offender relationship is one of an intimate or dating partner, regardless of the ages of the individuals. For example, a man who hits his wife commits intimate partner violence whether he is aged 60 or 70. Crimes committed by a family member against another family member (not an intimate) are considered domestic violence and may be either child abuse or elder abuse.

DEFINITIONS OF COMMON TERMS

The primary categories in which family violence occurs are neglect, physical abuse, psychological abuse, and sexual abuse. They are the four types of abuse that can occur against any of the three primary categories of victims. As illustrated in Figure 2-5, they

FIGURE 2-5   The primary types of family violence that occur are neglect, physical abuse, psychological abuse, and sexual abuse.

frequently co-occur in situations of family violence. Each specific type of abuse is defined by federal and state law and varies from jurisdiction to jurisdiction. Researchers and practitioners may use different definitions for the following types of abuse.

Neglect

Neglect is defined as failure or refusal to provide care or services for a person when there is an obligation to do so. This form of abuse carries with it a resulting harm due to the action or inaction of the caregiver. Examples of neglect are a failure to provide necessities such as food, water, clothing, or shelter to an adult with a disability or a dependent older adult.

Signs of neglect include, but are not limited to, dehydration, malnutrition, untreated bedsores, untreated health problems or conditions, unsanitary living conditions, and abandonment.

Physical Abuse

Physical abuse is the use of force or threat of force that may result in bodily injury, physical pain, or impairment. The signs of physical abuse may be external, internal, or both. Physical injuries that are untreated in various stages of healing might indicate an approximate time of injury. External signs of physical abuse include but are not limited to, human bites, bruises, welts, marks, burns, bleeding, missing or pulled hair, ripped clothing, crying, wincing, and the appearance of a drug-induced state. Broken blood vessels or unequal pupil dilation in the eyes may indicate suffocation or strangulation. Additional signs of physical abuse may be the result of weapon use, such as from a blunt instrument, knife, or gunshot. Internal signs of physical violence include, but are not limited to, internal tissue or organ injuries, bone fractures, broken bones, bleeding, sprains, and dislocations.

Psychological Abuse

Psychological abuse is the intentional infliction of anguish, pain, or distress designed to control the victim. The verbal or nonverbal forms of psychological abuse include the infliction of emotional abuse. This type of abuse includes, but is not limited to, verbal assaults, insults, threats, frightening, intimidation, humiliation, and harassment. Except threats, this category of abuse is rarely illegal. Psychological abuse is often evidenced along with other forms of abuse. Over extended periods of time, emotional/psychological abuse may be the "force" by which other forms of abuse occur. Emotional or psychological abuse can be more damaging than physical violence.

Sexual Abuse

Sexual abuse is a nonconsensual sexual contact of any kind. Sexual contact with a person incapable of giving consent is also considered sexual abuse. A minor is presumed unable to give informed consent; therefore, sexual contact with a minor is sexual abuse. Sexual conduct includes, but is not limited to, unwanted touching, rape, sodomy, coerced nudity, and sexually explicit photographing. Force, the threat of force, or implied force may accomplish sexual abuse. Physical signs of abuse and the use of force are not always present in relationships where one person is dominant, and the power is inherent in the position rather than the person. Physical signs of sexual abuse are the exception rather than the rule. They include bruises around the breasts or genital area, venereal disease or genital infections, vaginal or anal bleeding, and clothing that is torn, stained, or bloody.

CONCLUSIONS

What we know about intimate partner violence is anything but complete. There is no easy way to abolish it, and there is no pill to take to make it better. Experts debate implications of this festering illness that breeds among us and weakens family structure. In the recent past, people routinely did not want to acknowledge that incest and sexual abuse to children even existed. It was difficult to accept that the older adults were being battered and neglected by their children. Intimate partner abuse was also readily denied. Now that these forms of abuse have been identified, the dialogue will continue.

The criminal justice community has been identified as the most logical source of protection and empowerment for the intimate partner violence victim. New legislation and public policy, which now mandate a law enforcement response, are in effect. Simultaneously, researchers and policymakers remain concerned by the pitfalls of an inadequate response by the criminal justice system to intimate partner violence. The law enforcement community is responsible for dealing with this severe problem. Educational avenues must be explored that may assist us to meet the formidable task.

The rest of the text is about meeting the challenges of protection, prosecution, and punishment for those involved in family and intimate partner violence. It will be rewarding for every person who is interested in the factors involving family violence in the United States. What do we know about it? What has been done to control family violence? How do we recognize abuses, and what actions should be taken? The purpose of this text is to bring a detailed explanation of family violence and prevention efforts to those who have been tasked by society to intervene and to those who want to become involved. Intimate partner violence includes every imaginable form of violence that can occur as long as there is a domestic relationship between perpetrator and victim. Thinking of family violence as a group of crimes linked together into a general category is helpful for remembering just what family violence is. The individual crimes that we refer to as family violence are usually crimes without being placed into the category of domestic. Defining the crimes as domestic in a legislative act allows each state to encourage law enforcement officers to enforce the laws regardless of the relationship between the people. Sometimes mandatory arrest or preferred arrest policies are included, spelling out the expectations that the particular state has about police action. Some states include inducements for full enforcement. These topics are addressed later in the text.

Once in a while, a particular crime, such as the violation of a civil domestic restraining order, becomes a crime that is specific only to intimate partner violence. An "Act to Prevent Intimate Partner Violence" is one way that the legislation in each state defines the specific crimes that will be placed into the domestic category. Further, such acts define what relationships will be considered. The relationships include all intimate partners, regardless of gender or marital status. Additionally, people who are related through marriage or blood are considered domestic partners.

The scope of family violence seems overwhelming when reading the statistics. It is important to note that not all statistics are what they appear to be. There are many reasons why a particular study or research project concludes with figures that are less than perfect. It does not matter to study the issues. It is clear that we do not know exactly the extent of intimate partner violence! Experts agree that intimate partner violence crimes are largely underreported. Skeptics suggest that the numbers are inflated. So we should expect that the figures might not be exact. What they tell us, more importantly, is that there is a problem of violence in the United States. The violence has invaded many homes. Many children are sexually and physically abused and neglected every day. We know that people are killing their children, partners, and elders. In adult intimate relationships, many people are being dominated or controlled physically, emotionally, or sexually, and even harmed financially. We have to face the horrible truth, even if we do not know the exact numbers. If you look around, you will see it.

SIMPLY SCENARIO
Man Tries to Burn Down House

Charles had been drinking heavily and argued with his ex-girlfriend. He threatened to burn down her house. A short time later, he set fire to some cardboard boxes on the porch, causing charring to the wood before she could put it out. Charles then tried to light a door on fire with a lighter before running to his truck. Charles started up his truck and starting ramming the vehicle owned by his ex-girlfriend. The ex-girlfriend indicated that she feared for her life.

Question: Is there any indication that this scenario represented an intimate partner violence situation? Explain your answer.

Questions for Review

1. Discuss the early social–legal history of family violence.
2. What is the law of Romulus?
3. Explain the historical significance of social tolerance for family violence.
4. What did Napoleon Bonaparte do to influence French law?
5. Describe and discuss Puritan law.
6. Why is the Supreme Court of Mississippi significant?
7. Explain what constitutes a domestic relationship.
8. What are the three primary categories of family violence?
9. Name at least five forms of intimate partner violence.
10. Define the four major types of violence that occur in families.

Internet-Based Exercises

1. Have you ever wondered what the domestic violence laws are in your state? Here is an online source of information that provides a drop-down box for you to find your state. Compare your state with one or more others to find the differences (if any). Go to http://www.womenslaw.org/.
2. Do you know what domestic abuse is? Go to this national site for information and definitions: http://www.thehotline.org/. Write a short essay explaining your answer.
3. The Department of Health and Human Services at the Centers for Disease Control and Prevention maintains an excellent Web site on different forms of family violence. Go to http://www.cdc.gov and get the facts on a topic of interest to you. Prepare an oral report to give in class.
4. Do an Internet search and locate the warning signs for domestic violence. Prepare a list of at least 10 red flags.

References

Balos, B., & Fellows, M. (1994). *Law and violence against women: Cases and materials on systems of oppression.* Durham, NC: Carolina Academic Press.

Belknap, J. (1992). Perceptions of woman battering. In I. L. Moyer (Ed.), *The changing roles of women in the criminal justice system* (2nd ed., pp. 181–201). Prospect Heights, IL: Waveland Press.

Bloch, R. H. (2007). The American Revolution, wife beating, and the emergent value of privacy. *Early American Studies,* October, 223–251.

Bradley v. State, 1 Walker 156 (Miss S. Ct. 1824).

Bradwell v. Illinois, 83 U.S. 130 (U.S. S. Ct. 1873).

Catalano, S. (2012). *Intimate partner violence, 1993–2010. (NCJ 239203).* Washington, D.C.: Bureau of Justice Statistics.

Child Abuse Prevention and Treatment Act of 2010 (CAPTA). (2011). Retrieved from http://www.acf.hhs.gov/programs/cb/resource/capta2010

The Colonial Williamsburg Foundation. (2013). Redefining family. Retrieved from http://www.history.org/Almanack/life/family/essay.cfm

Commonwealth v. Hugh McAfee, 108 Mass. 458 (Mass. S. Ct. 1871).

Davidson, T. (1977). *Wife beating: A recurring phenomenon throughout history.* New York, NY: Van Nostrand Reinhold.

Department of Children & Families (DCF). (2013). About the Department of Children & Families. Retrieved from http://www.mass.gov/eohhs/gov/departments/dcf/

Dobash, E., & Dobash, R. (1978). Wives: The "appropriate" victims of marital violence. *Victimology, 2,* 426–439.

Dobash, E., & Dobash, R. (1979). *Violence against wives: A case against patriarchy.* New York, NY: Free Press.

Dutton, D. G. (Ed.). (1998). *The domestic assault of Women: Psychological and criminal justice perspectives* (3rd ed.). Vancouver, BC: University of British Columbia Press.

Feinman, C. (1992). Woman battering on the Navajo Reservation. *International Review of Victimology, 2*(2), 137–146.

Fulgham v. State, 46 ALA 146-47 143 (S. Ct. Ala 1871).

Gordon, L. (1989). *Heroes of their own lives: The politics and history of family violence.* New York, NY: Penguin.

Horne, C. F. (1998). Ancient history sourcebook: Code of Hammurabi, c. 1780 BCE. Retrieved from www.fordham.edu/halsall/ancient/hamcode.html

The Jerusalem Bible. (1996). New York, NY: Doubleday.

Lefkowitz, M. R., & Fant, M. B. (1992). *Women's life in Greece & Rome. A source book in translation.* Retrieved from http://www.stoa.org/diotima/anthology/wlgr/

Levy, D., Applewhite, H., & Johnson, M. (1979). *Women in revolutionary Paris, 1785–1795.* Urbana, IL: University of Illinois Press.

Loving Day. (2004). Where were international couples illegal? Retrieved from http://lovingday.org/legal-map

Loving v. Virginia, 388 U.S. 1 (U.S. S. Ct. 1967).

Lunn, T. (1991). Til death do us part. *Social Work Today, 29*(8), 16–17.

O'Faolain, J., & Martines, L. (1973). *Not in God's image.* New York, NY: Harper & Row.

Pagelow, M. D. (1984). *Family violence.* New York, NY: Praeger.

Perdue, T. (1998). *Cherokee women: Gender and culture change, 1700–1835.* Lincoln, NE: University of Nebraska Press.

Pleck, E. (1989). Criminal approaches to family violence, 1640–1880. *Family Violence, 11,* 19–57.

Pushkareva, N. (1997). *Women in Russian history: From the tenth to the twentieth century* (E. Levin, Trans.). Armonk, NY: M. E. Sharpe.

Rhodes, H. (1984). *The Athenian court and the American court system* (Vol. II, p. 6). Retrieved from http://www.yale.edu/ynhti/curriculum/units/1984/2/84.02.08.x.html

Romano, I., & White, D. (2002). Woman's life. Retrieved from http://www.penn.museum/sites/greek_world/women.html

Sherman, L., Schmidt, J., & Rogan, D. (1992). *Policing domestic violence: Experiments and dilemmas.* New York, NY: Free Press.

State v. Jessie Black, 60 N.C. 266 (N.C. S. Ct. 1864).

State v. Oliver, 70 N. C. 44 (N.C. S. Ct. 1874).

Ulrich, L. T. (1991). *Good wives: Image and reality in the lives of women in northern New England 1650–1750.* New York, NY: Vintage Books.

Weitzman, S. (2000). *Not to people like us: Hidden abuse in upscale marriages.* New York, NY: Perseus Books.

Wortman, M. S. (1985). *Women in American law: From colonial times to the new deal* (Vol. 1). New York, NY: Holmes & Meier.

Focus on Research

CHAPTER OBJECTIVES

After reviewing this chapter, you should be able to:

1. Discuss the value of research to understanding domestic violence.
2. Describe the historical significance of the Minneapolis Domestic Violence Experiment.
3. Identify at least four major sources of data on domestic violence.
4. Differentiate between theory on domestic violence in intimate relationships as family violence versus violence against women.
5. State the eight steps to achieving *coercive control*.

KEY TERMS

Coercive control

Family violence theory

National Crime Victimization Survey

National Incident-Based Reporting System

National Intimate Partner and Sexual Violence Survey

Qualitative research

Quantitative research

Uniform Crime Reports

INTRODUCTION

Why do so many people feel free to abuse their intimate partner, their spouse, their child, or their parent? A simple answer is that we do it because we can. Most believe that the answer is not so straightforward. In fact, the answer is much more complicated and complex. Although our perceptions influence personal reality, those observations are narrow and cannot fully inform us on issues outside of our knowledge. One way in which we try to understand family violence is by measuring it. How often does it occur? What forms occur most often? What are the influences that exacerbate or contribute to family violence? Age, income, education, gender, and prevalence are some of the factors that inform us about the different types of family violence. Studies on agency response and personal responsibility help shape our organizations, direct the money available to address it, and provide theoretical avenues to understand it.

Research is important because it offers a way to reconcile our reality with experiential reality. Through scientific inquiry, we can observe and record information. Documenting research provides opportunities to replicate studies to help avoid overgeneralization, selective observation, and illogical reasoning. Replication lessens the possibility that political or personal bias will drive research results. In this chapter common research methods and specific sources of information that guide our criminal justice role in combating family violence are discussed.

HISTORICAL APPLIED RESEARCH

Crime is a social problem that may be better understood and addressed through scientific inquiry. The direction of research may be pure or applied. Pure research is conducted for the sake of knowledge whereas applied research centers around problems affecting people from a practical standpoint. Applied research is commonly used as an approach to solving criminal justice problems.

Deterrence of future family violence was a significant impetus for making a swift arrest of the perpetrator in cases of intimate partner violence. Still, problems surfaced regarding victims' reluctance to follow through with complaints of this violence. So these questions arise: Is law enforcement the appropriate agency to control intimate partner violence? If it is not, what other measures can be taken to protect victims of abuse? With many questions and few answers, the critics have debated these issues. The first national study of intimate partner violence, *Behind Closed Doors*, reported that spouses strike partners in one out of every six households (Straus, Gelles, & Steinmetz, 1980). That now-famous study on family violence found little difference in the rate of violence between husbands and wives.

The first controlled, randomized test of the effectiveness of arrest for intimate partner violence occurred in the *Minneapolis Domestic Violence Experiment* in 1980, with the results published in 1984 (Sherman & Berk, 1984). The findings of the study to assess the effects of various police responses suggest that the arrest of the perpetrator produced the least amount of repeat violence for the same victims within a six-month period (refer to Figure 3-1). Subsequent intimate partner violence was reduced by nearly 50 percent when the suspect was arrested, as opposed to other interventions, such as ordering one of the parties out of the residence or counseling the couple. Researchers made three recommendations based on the study results (Sherman & Rogan, 1992). First, that police should probably make arrests in most cases of minor

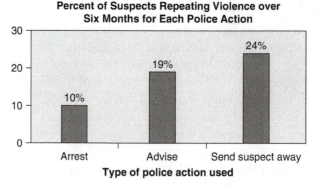

Percent of Suspects Repeating Violence over Six Months for Each Police Action

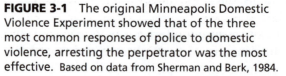

FIGURE 3-1 The original Minneapolis Domestic Violence Experiment showed that of the three most common responses of police to domestic violence, arresting the perpetrator was the most effective. Based on data from Sherman and Berk, 1984.

intimate partner violence. Second, researchers noted that the experiment should be replicated to see whether it would yield similar results in other cities with many different kinds of people. Third, that the mandatory arrest laws not be adopted, if only because they would put an end to further research and replications. However, it was only a matter of months after the results emerged before mandatory arrest procedures in instances of domestic assault were adopted across the nation (Barner & Carney, 2011).

Contributing to the use of police as a primary response to intimate partner violence was the success of civil suits brought against police departments for the failure to provide equal protection to victims of intimate partner violence. A classic example is the successful 1984 suit brought by Tracy Thurman, who was permanently disabled when Torrington, Connecticut, police failed to protect her from her estranged husband. On appeal, the court decided that failure of the police to protect a woman based on gender discrimination is a denial of equal protection under the laws, a violation of constitutional rights, and constitutes a pattern of police misconduct (*Thurman v. City of Torrington*, 1984).

The Minneapolis Domestic Violence Experiment paved the way for six replications and extensions of the experiment. Known collectively as the Spouse Assault Replication Program, the research was undertaken in a variety of U.S. police departments. The results of the replications were inconsistent; in some instances, there was no deterrent effect due to the arrest of the perpetrator. Arrest deterred only certain types of offenders, and in some cases, the arrest escalated violence (Garner, Fagan, & Maxwell, 1995). Lawrence Sherman and others involved in the Minneapolis experiment now advocate repeal of mandatory arrest policies in favor of varied responses based on the individual cases (Sherman & Rogan, 1992). Others suggest that law enforcement alone is insufficient to combat the problems of intimate partner violence (Barner & Carney, 2011), necessitating a more system-wide approach. The coordinated approach includes implementation of policies that train personnel and develop guidelines and protocols for enforcing laws related to intimate partner violence, as well as accountability measures that ensure enforcement of the law by all officers in the department. Adding to the law enforcement component are strategies to coordinate with other criminal justice agencies and victim service providers. Probation departments have instituted enhanced victim safety measurements and vigorously enforced protection orders. Prosecutors and advocates seek to keep victims better informed about their cases and the whereabouts of the perpetrators.

More About It: Minneapolis Experiment (1980)

The Minneapolis Domestic Violence Experiment is important on a number of levels; first of all, it was the first scientifically controlled test of the effects of arrest for any crime. Second, the authors considered the three most common approaches used by police in responding to domestic violence and evaluated them to see which was most effective in reducing repeat offending (Sherman & Berk, 1984). They found that arrest was the most effective of three standard methods police use to reduce domestic violence. They determined that the other police methods—attempting to counsel both parties and sending assailants away from home for several hours—were considerably less effective in deterring future violence. The preponderance of evidence in the Minneapolis study strongly suggested that the police should use arrest in most domestic violence cases. Third, it was instrumental in the enactment of mandatory arrest procedures in cases of domestic violence. The results of the Minneapolis Domestic Violence Experiment helped to change police response to domestic violence nationwide and shaped current response to intimate partner violence in America.

More About It: *Thurman v. City of Torrington* (1984)

In this case, Tracy Thurman, who had repeatedly been beaten and stalked by her husband, sued the Torrington Police for failing to protect her from abuse (*Thurman v. City of Torrington*, 1984). During the most violent beating, it took the police officer 25 minutes to arrive on the scene, and for several minutes, he failed to arrest Buck Thurman. During that time, Buck repeatedly kicked his wife on the face and neck while she lay helpless on the ground. He inflicted life-threatening injuries during the attack, including multiple stab wounds to her chest, neck, and face; fractured cervical vertebrae and damage to her spinal cord; partial paralysis below the neck; lacerations to the cheek and mouth; loss of blood; shock; scarring; severe pain; and mental anguish. The court awarded an unprecedented $2.3 million in compensatory damages against 24 police officers. The court held that Ms. Thurman had been deprived of her constitutional right of equal protection under the Fourteenth Amendment. This landmark case was instrumental in requiring police to protect battered women against assaultive husbands.

A review of the Spouse Assault Replication Program suggests that the results were flawed, indicating that arrest is the superior method of deterring future violence. All of the studies do in fact indicate that arresting deters batterers better than other police responses (Maxwell, Garner, & Fagan, 2003).

Due to the legal acknowledgment of wife abuse as an equal protection issue, a flood of legislation was enacted to address the issue. All states, the District of Columbia, and the Commonwealth of Puerto Rico have since enacted some form of legislation specific to intimate partner violence (Hamel, 2011). The first domestic abuse statutes applied only to adult married spouses of abusers, and only to women as victims. These legislative changes gave police officers the power to arrest in cases where there existed probable cause to believe that intimate partner violence had occurred, regardless of whether it was witnessed by the officer. Mandatory and preferred arrest procedures in instances of intimate partner violence have been adopted by police departments across the nation. Statutes have broadened the definitions and legislative protections; these definitions, provisions for protection, and enforcement vary widely between jurisdictions. Today's expectation of a proper police response to intimate partner violence has been shaped by legislative history.

Case in Point: No Provision for an Arrest

In 1974, a Massachusetts state trooper was sent to a domestic call at a home in his patrol area. The trooper had responded to the same house many times before. Each time the wife had accused the husband of beating her. This time, as she let the trooper in the door, she cried that her husband had hit her. Wearing only his underwear and drinking a beer, the husband yelled at his wife, "You called the police!! You called the police!! Just wait till he leaves; I'll get you good this time." To the officer, he said, "I know my rights: You can't do anything to me—now get out of my house!"

In the 1970s, there was no provision to arrest a man on an allegation of intimate partner violence when the officer did not see the beating occur, even though it appeared as though the woman had been beaten. The officer had no power of arrest. Knowing that the woman would be beaten for having made the call to the police, the trooper took action that he should not have had to take. He threw the husband out of the door into the snow on his front steps. There the trooper promptly arrested him for public drunkenness, a misdemeanor that amounted to a breach of the peace, for which the trooper did have the power of arrest.

RESEARCH METHODS

Research involves a process of learning that goes beyond the simple gathering of information or discovering facts (Leedy & Ormrod, 2013). Common goals of research are for the advancement of general knowledge or to solve specific problems. Approaches to research have become diverse in recent years, making a choice a highly personal one. Quantitative and qualitative research methods are examples of research approaches that are commonly used for criminal justice research.

In criminal justice, the tension between quantitative and qualitative research goals is stated as the conflict between the applied practitioner and the nonapplied academic (Hagan, 2011). Both quantitative and qualitative research seeks to understand social problems out of concern. While the approaches can be complementary because they look at similar issues from different perspectives, the quantitative approach has greater utility for criminal justice research. Hagan (2011) warns, however, against methodological narcissism, a fanaticism of method for method's sake. The applied research approaches of quantitative methods measure social reality by the scientific method. Paradigm shifts and new knowledge about the reality occur through pure research projects, that is, the qualitative approach.

Quantitative Research

The deductive model that uses fixed research objectives and statements, defines the terms that are relevant for the research, follows a fixed sequence of steps, and typically measures data using numbers is referred to as **quantitative research**. A survey design will provide the research with a numeric description of attitudes for the target population by studying a sample of that population. The survey is a preferred method of gathering data due to its characteristic as a scientific method, the economy of the design, and the utility of each in data collection (Creswell, 2008). Survey designs may be in the form of a self-administered questionnaire, an interview, a structured record review, or a structured observation. Interviews may be conducted in person or over the phone. A survey design may be Web-based and administered over the Internet or sent through the mail. An example of survey research is the *National Crime Victimization Survey* (NCVS), which is described later in this chapter.

Descriptive research designs are also a fundamental form of quantitative research. One type of descriptive research used in quantitative research is the observation study. It is used to describe and quantify specific phenomena by reporting frequencies, averages, and percentages of data (Leedy & Ormrod, 2013). An example of descriptive studies is the *Uniform Crime Reports* (UCR). The approach looks at the differences in one characteristic as it relates to differences in one or more other characteristics. A correlation exists when one variable increases and another decreases in a way that is somewhat predictable. Quantifying makes our observations more explicit, makes it easier to aggregate and summarize data, and opens up the possibility of statistical analysis.

The measurement of criminal justice reality is accomplished through applied research, that is, a quantitative approach. Applied research efforts search for findings that directly address criminal justice issues on matters involving the branches of the criminal justice system: law enforcement, the courts, and corrections. Applied research within the field of criminal justice is rapidly increasing (Hagan, 2011). Police departments and federal enforcement agencies have teamed up with traditional researchers in efforts to understand crime analysis issues for forecasting crime, providing investigative leads, supporting community policing, and supporting departmental planning. Intelligence analysis, operations analysis, and investigative analysis represent additional avenues for law-enforcement research efforts.

Increased attention to legal practices has resulted from the statistical measurement of court performance. Prosecutor effectiveness, judicial resolution of issues, and the cost involved in the judicial process provide examples of these research efforts. Among the concerns studied through standardized statistical measurement are sentence variations, charging accuracy, fairness in plea bargaining, and sentencing practices.

In the area of corrections, the growing prison populations during the 1980s caused alarm that was exacerbated by the lack of alternatives to incarceration (Hagan, 2011). As new programs sprang up to address this need, so did the necessity for program evaluation. For example, debates on criminal justice interventions to family violence have led to batterer intervention programs as alternatives to incarceration. Whether these programs achieve their intended goals has become a major concentration of quantitative criminal justice research.

Qualitative Research

Two elements that differentiate the qualitative method approach from the quantitative approach are the setting and the complexity (Leedy & Ormrod, 2013). The **qualitative research** approach looks at phenomena in the natural setting and incorporates the complexity of the examination into the effort. In contrast to quantitative methods, none of the qualitative research approaches relies on statistical measurements. Instead, qualitative research focuses on in-depth interviews, analysis of historical materials, and is concerned with a comprehensive account of some event or unit.

Qualitative research provides data about the characteristics of the population rather than its variables. For example, qualitative research would attempt to discover whether family violence occurs in a specific population. The population would be described by the characteristics that distinguish it, such as being Native American Indian. The researcher would discover the uniqueness of the population, background, or history of the group. Contributing factors to the phenomena would not be predetermined but discovered through the research. The qualitative approach suggests a nondirectional research effort that attempts to explore by way of a central inquiry and associated sub-questions. It attempts to provide a productive environment for understanding, discovering, and exploring phenomena. Qualitative research makes possible the discovery of subjective links between variables rather than taking the variables for granted. The information evolves by use of a methodological design that does not assume the population or the terms of the study.

Qualitative research intends to look at a single phenomenon with the recognition that the study may evolve into any examination of relationships or ideas that could not be anticipated. The evolution of design is conveyed by discovering, describing, and understanding the phenomenon under study. The outcomes are not predetermined. Even when a working definition of the phenomenon is stated in the research project, it is acknowledged as tentative and evolving. Research questions rather than objectives guide the endeavor.

Qualitative research seeks to be compassionate. It would not be unusual for the research objectives to come from the group under study. Because of this, qualitative research is considered a more humane method of research over using quantitative methods. A diversity of viewpoints and the richness or the complexities of the perspectives are among the positive aspects of the approach. It is based on awareness of cultural differences and considers alternative interpretations to individual behaviors.

SOURCES OF FAMILY VIOLENCE DATA

Data on family violence comes from many government sources, including victimization surveys, official police statistics, state and federal court statistics, and surveys of inmates in state prisons and local jails. Academics and agency professionals that conduct research provide another important source of family violence information. They suggest a significant discrepancy between official statistics and the reality of criminal behavior. Analyzed together, a picture of family violence emerges. The four primary sources of domestic violence data are the Uniform Crime Reports, the National Incident-Based Reporting System, National Intimate Partner and Sexual Violence Survey, and the National Crime Victimization Survey.

The flow of family violence in the United States is reflected in reports from all four branches of the criminal justice system: society, law enforcement, the courts, and corrections. Family crime committed against society is documented through victimization surveys. The Bureau of Justice Statistics (BJS) administers the oldest source of victimization data across America, the NCVS. The Centers for Disease Control and Prevention (CDC) also collects data from victims, through the National Intimate Partner and Sexual Violence Survey. The Federal Bureau of Investigation (FBI) collects, publishes, and archives the official data provided by state, federal, and tribal law enforcement agencies across the United States. Arrests and crimes recorded by the police are contained in the FBI databases: the *Uniform Crime Reports*, the *National Incident-Based Reporting System*, and the *Supplementary Homicide Reports*. Family violence case information in the state courts is collected by the BJS, reflected through the *State Court Processing Statistics*. For information on the correctional system, the BJS surveys all levels of facilities. An example is the *Survey of Inmates in State and Federal Correctional Facilities*. These major sources of family violence information are illustrated in Figure 3-2.

There are significant differences between the statistical programs. Concern over crime may still exist in part because we have not been counting recent crime through these traditional measurements; slowly, changes are being made to address this issue and contemporize our data collection. The sources of information for these programs are all different because they are conducted for different purposes. As evidenced, each source of data provides exciting insights into family violence.

National Intimate Partner and Sexual Violence Survey

Known as the NISVS, the **National Intimate Partner and Sexual Violence Survey** was launched in 2010 by the CDC to collect detailed information on intimate partner violence, sexual violence, and stalking victimization. The data collected about the violence experienced in the year previous to the survey and the violence perpetrated during the lifetime of the respondent. The NISVS is unique because it is the first national survey to gather data on the prevalence of intimate partner violence, sexual violence, and stalking based on the self-reported sexual orientation of the individual. Therefore,

Sources of Domestic Violence Data
Throughout the Criminal Justice System

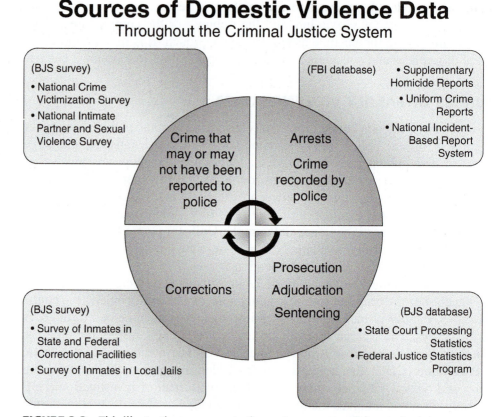

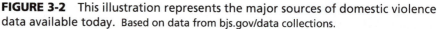

FIGURE 3-2 This illustration represents the major sources of domestic violence data available today. Based on data from bjs.gov/data collections.

NISVS is the first inclusive national survey of domestic violence victimization against both women and men; it gathers information on heterosexual, lesbian, gay, and bisexual women and men.

With the support of the National Institute of Justice and the Department of Defense, the first survey in 2010 collected information from over 16,000 adults ages 18 and older, including over 9,000 women and over 7,000 men. The first summary report published in 2011 can be found at the CDC Web site:

http://www.cdc.gov/violenceprevention/nisvs/

Reports on data collected in NISVS are continuing to become available. Very little is known about the national prevalence of domestic violence perpetration among lesbian, gay, and bisexual women and men in the United States. The void is being addressed through NISVS studies, although it is too early to have comparisons other than those between gender groups. According to NISVS, the lifetime prevalence of rape, physical violence, and stalking by an intimate partner is highest for bisexual women at over 60 percent, versus 43 percent of lesbians and 35 percent of heterosexual women (Walters, Chen, & Breiding, 2013). The study found that among men, intimate partner violence is also highest for bisexuals at 37 percent, versus 29 percent of heterosexual men and 26 percent for gay men. Heterosexual men and lesbians report mostly female perpetrators of partner violence. Males remain the most frequent offenders overall.

National Crime Victimization Survey

One of the major sources of information on criminal victimization is the **National Crime Victimization Survey**; it is conducted by the National Institute of Justice by the BJS (Bureau of Justice Statistics [BJS], 2011). Approximately 100,000 persons age 12 or older are surveyed in person or by telephone at six-month frequencies regarding characteristics, victim-offender relationships, and consequences of criminal victimization. There are 48 questions on the NCVS-1 Basic Screen Questionnaire form that establish basic descriptive data on the population. The NCVS-2 Crime Incident Report contains the 176 questions on this survey that explore but are not limited to crime victimization; victim and offender characteristics and relationships; types of harm such as damage to property or personal injury; weapons use; and police involvement. Refer to Figure 3-3 for a page from the NCVS survey. Learn more about the NCVS from this Web site:

http://www.icpsr.umich.edu/icpsrweb/NACJD/NCVS/

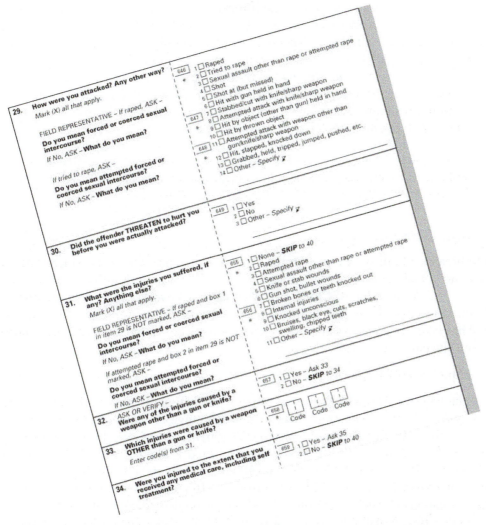

FIGURE 3-3   The NCVS is a survey of individuals and does not include official data such as police records, although individuals are asked whether they reported the crime to the police or not. Based on data from Criminal Victimization in the United States, 2006, 2008.

In 1993, the survey was redesigned to improve the questions used to discover the crime, update the survey methods, and broaden the scope of crimes measured. It now collects detailed information on the frequency and nature of the crimes of rape, sexual assault, personal robbery, aggravated and simple assault, household burglary, theft, and motor vehicle theft. It does not measure homicide or commercial crimes. The NCVS provides information about victims' age, sex, race, ethnicity, marital status, income, and educational levels. For offenders, it documents the sex, race, estimated ages, and victim-offender relationships. The experiences of victims with the criminal justice system, self-protective measures used by victims, and possible substance abuse by offenders are questions that are covered in the NCVS. The type of crimes, use of weapons, nature of the injury, and economic consequences of the victimization are part of the data that are gathered.

The NCVS gathers information from households and does not include reports of victimization against transients or visitors that may appear in police crime statistics. A significant strength of the NCVS is that information on crimes is collected to analyze whether or not those crimes were reported to law enforcement. That strength is a potential flaw because the survey is dependent on the memory of persons who may inaccurately or incompletely recall incidents that they report on the survey. According to NCVS, the total crime committed by family members and intimates increased slightly from 1.1 million in 2010 to 1.4 million in 2011(Truman & Planty, 2012). During the same period, no significant change in the rate of severe domestic violence was noted for crimes involving rape, robbery, or aggravated assault.

The two major approaches, victimization surveys and official crime data collection, show very different pictures of crime in the United States. They are thought to complement each other and may be used to provide different answers to questions about crime.

Uniform Crime Reports

Widespread concern over crime in the United States has been seen since the "lawless years" of 1921 to 1933, according to the FBI. It was during those years that the International Association of Chiefs of Police (IACP) developed the idea of collecting data on crime, which became known as the Uniform Crime Reporting Program. The IACP has taken an active role in research and policy development for law enforcement. Its Web site can be found at:

http://www.theiacp.org/

The FBI is tasked with the collection and publishing of crime statistics within the UCR system. Under this system, data on a broad range of violent and property crime known to the police are reported through the participation of over 17,000 law enforcement agencies (Federal Bureau of Investigation, n.d.). The FBI's UCR Program collects information on Part I offenses (murder, rape, robbery, assault, burglary, larceny, automobile theft, and arson) and Part II offenses (forgery, fraud, embezzlement, vandalism, weapons violations, sex offenses, drug and alcohol abuse violations, gambling, vagrancy, curfew violations, and runaways). The UCR represents the first national collection of crime data. Participation of federal, tribal, and state law enforcement agencies is voluntary. Information on the UCR may be found at:

https://ucr.fbi.gov/

Each month law enforcement reports or crime incident records are sent either directly to the FBI or to centralized state agencies, which then report to the FBI. In addition to crime counts and trends, the UCR report includes data on crimes cleared, persons arrested (age, sex, and race), law enforcement personnel killed or assaulted, and the characteristics of homicides. Information comes from police. Due in part to this effort on assessing the prevalence of crime, a downward trend in crime has become apparent.

Critics cite numerous limitations of the UCR system. First, it represents only those crimes that are reported to the police, so it does not reflect the actual number of crimes committed. The second limitation is the manner in which the crimes are reported to the FBI. When several crimes are committed in one event, for example, only the most serious is included in the UCR; the rest are not reported. Also, in the past, crimes that were not indexed in the UCR could not be included. For example, rape was defined as forced sexual intercourse with a woman by a man who is not her husband. Spousal rape was not recognized. The report of a man raped by a domestic partner would also not be included. In response to definitional problems with the UCR system, a few changes have recently been made. These changes will impact future statistics on the crimes of family and intimate partner violence, specifically rape and human trafficking.

The historical definition of rape was "the carnal knowledge of a female forcibly and against her will," which is now discontinued (FBI, 2017). The FBI approved this change to the current definition of rape: Penetration, no matter how slight, of the vagina or anus with any body part or object, or oral penetration by a sex organ of another person, without the consent of the victim. Note that the term "forcible" was removed from the definition. The new rape definition represents more than a mere change in terminology. Under the new definition, rape is not a gender-specific crime. It acknowledges multiple methods of perpetrating rape and recognizes the changing realization that force may be accomplished through a lack of consent.

A second significant change to the UCR Program is the addition of data collection on crimes of human trafficking (FBI, 2013).The last time that the UCR Program added an offense to the list of Part I crimes was in 1982. While it will take years for states to update data collections and submit these new categories to the UCR, the additions represent a dynamic change. The two added definitions are as follows:

- Human Trafficking/Commercial Sex Acts: Inducing a person by force, fraud, or coercion to participate in commercial sex acts, or in which the person induced to perform such act(s) has not attained 18 years of age.
- Human Trafficking/Involuntary Servitude: The obtaining of a person(s) through recruitment, harboring, transportation, or provision, and subjecting such persons by force, fraud, or coercion into involuntary servitude, peonage, debt bondage, or slavery (not to include commercial sex acts).

Another criticism of this source is the limited amount of information that has been gathered on the victim-offender relationship. To address these limitations, the UCR Program is currently being converted into a more comprehensive and detailed one, the National Incident-Based Reporting System (NIBRS).

National Incident-Based Reporting System

The UCR is currently being phased out and will eventually be replaced by the **National Incident-Based Reporting System** (NIBRS). The NIBRS will strengthen the official reporting of crime through detailed information regarding criminal incidents in

Group A offense categories:

Arson	Homicide Offenses
Assault Offenses	Kidnapping/Abduction
Bribery	Larceny/Theft Offenses
Burglary/Breaking &	Motor Vehicle Theft
Entering	Pornography/Obscene
Counterfeiting/Forgery	Material
Destruction/Damage/	Prostitution Offenses
Vandalism of Property	Robbery
Drug/Narcotic Offenses	Sex Offenses, Forcible
Embezzlement	Sex Offenses, Nonforcible
Extortion/Blackmail	Stolen Property Offenses
Fraud Offenses	Weapon Law Violations
Gambling Offenses	

FIGURE 3-4   The National Incident-Based Reporting System will eventually replace UCR. In the NIBRS, the offenses and arrests are reported for each occurrence within 22 offense categories called Group A offenses.

22 broad categories of offenses made up of 46 specific crimes called Group A offenses (Federal Bureau of Investigation, n.d.). For each of the offenses coming to the attention of law enforcement, specified types of facts about each crime are reported. In addition to the Group A offenses, there are 11 Group B offense categories for which only arrest data are reported. The Group A NIBRS offenses are illustrated in Figure 3-4. The NIBRS is an incident-based reporting system in which agencies collect data on each single crime occurrence. The FBI's UCR Program announced that it would transition to an NIBRS-only data collection by January 1, 2021 (FBI, 2016).

An agency can build a system to suit its own needs, including any collection/storage of information required for administration and operations, as well as to report data required by the NIBRS to the UCR Program. The NIBRS will not only provide great specificity in reporting, but it has also added a new scoring category called "crimes against society." The new category includes drug/narcotics offenses, gambling offenses, pornography/obscene material offenses, and prostitution offenses. These crimes represent society's prohibitions on engaging in certain activity. Remember, it was way back in the 1920s that the UCR was developed. There are crimes today that did not even exist at that time; for example, crimes committed using a computer! This is only one example of the update in crime that has been added. Learn more about the NIBRS from:

http://www.icpsr.umich.edu/icpsrweb/NACJD/NIBRS/

Even with the improvements in crime statistics that are being implemented through NIBRS, one major limitation remains. Because the statistics will reflect only the crimes that people are willing to report to the police, they will not accurately depict crime in some categories. For example, the findings from the National Violence Against Women (NVAW) Survey concluded that there is a difference in the prevalence of intimate partner violence among women of different racial and ethnic backgrounds, ages, and marital status (Catalano, 2012).

Today, several annual statistical publications, such as the comprehensive *Crime in the United States*, are produced from data provided by law enforcement agencies across the United States. The UCR, the NIBRS, and the Supplementary Homicide Reports are among the most important sources for information on police arrests and crime recorded by the police. Implementation of the NIBRS is an ongoing voluntary process. Slowly states are gaining the expertise and software to collect and analyze the NIBRS data. As of 2016, the FBI certified 33 state programs for NIBRS participation (IBR Resource Center, 2012). The information from those law enforcement agencies accounts for 31 percent of the U.S. population, representing 6,600 law enforcement agencies (FBI, 2016).

State Court Processing Statistics

State Court Processing Statistics (SCPS) provides data on the criminal justice processing of persons with felonies in a representative sample of counties across the country. The program tracks defendants from their being charged by the prosecutor until the disposition of their cases or for a maximum of 12 months for nonmurder cases and 24 months for murder cases. Data are obtained on demographic characteristics, arrest offense, criminal justice status at the time of arrest, prior arrests and convictions, bail and pretrial release, court appearance record, rearrest while on pretrial release, type and outcome of adjudication, and type and length of sentence.

According to an SCPS report, defendants charged with domestic violence were prosecuted, convicted, and incarcerated at rates either equal to or higher than felony defendants charged with nondomestic violence (Smith, Durose, & Langan, 2008). The report states that domestic sexual assault defendants had a higher overall conviction rate (98 percent) than nondomestic defendants (87 percent). Domestic violence in this survey includes violence among family members, intimate partners, and household cohabitants.

Federal Justice Statistics Program

Information on violations of family violence-related federal statutes that were referred to federal court comes from the *Federal Justice Statistics Program* (FJSP). The program is maintained by BJS and is constructed from data provided by the following: the Executive Office for United States Attorneys (EOUSA), the Pretrial Services Agency (PSA), the Administrative Office of the United States Courts (AO), the United States Sentencing Commission (USSC), and the Federal Bureau of Prisons (BOP) (Bureau of Justice Statistics [BJS], 2010). The federal government has jurisdiction over violent crimes between family members that occur on Indian reservations, military bases, and other federal entities. Victim-offender relationships are not available through this database; the categories of interstate travel to commit domestic violence and firearm-related domestic violence statistics are available. Information is acquired on all aspects of the federal criminal justice system, including the number of persons investigated, prosecuted, convicted, incarcerated, sentenced to probation, released pretrial, and under parole or other supervision, in addition to initial prosecution decisions, referrals to magistrates, court dispositions, sentencing outcomes, sentence length, and time served.

Survey of Inmates

The Survey of Inmates in State and Federal Correctional Facilities is made up of two distinct surveys designed by BJS to gather data on the demographic, socioeconomic, and criminal history characteristics of state and federal correctional inmates. Other variables include age, ethnicity, education, gun possession and use, lifetime drug use and alcohol use and treatment, prior incarceration record, military service, and prearrest annual income. Examining inmate survey data disputes the position that family violence offenders are a unique category of individuals whose crimes involve only violence against women. For example, a study using data from the Survey of Inmates in State and Federal Correctional Facilities concluded that domestic violence offenders rarely specialize; inmates in prison for intimate partner homicide or assault are involved in criminal behavior similar to that of other types of offenders (Felson & Lane, 2010). Their drug and alcohol abuse is like that of other violent offenders as well. Additionally, men in prison or jail for attacking women are particularly likely to have experienced sexual abuse during childhood and to have been intoxicated at the time of the incident.

SOURCE AND CITING ISSUES

The survey approach is the most frequent method used to gather information on crime in America. The largest survey attempts to measure violence against intimate partners and among families—the National Crime Victimization Survey (NCVS) and National Family Violence Survey (NFVS)—have been joined by the National Intimate Partner and Sexual Violence Survey (NISVS). Go to this site to learn more about the differences between these important surveys:

http://www.nij.gov/topics/crime/intimate-partner-violence/measuring.htm

According to estimates from the NCVS, intimate partner violence primarily involves female survivors. The definition of intimate violence includes the crimes of rape, sexual assault, robbery, aggravated assault, and simple assault. The estimated rate of nonfatal violent victimization against women age 12 or older has decreased from 13.5 victimizations per 1,000 persons age 12 or older in 1994 to 5.0 per 1,000 in 2012 (Truman & Morgan, 2014). Estimates of the extent of violence by women against men are unquestionably less than the violence committed by men against women. However, these victimized men represent a substantial amount of violence that is hardly trivial and cannot be ignored. From 2002 to 2011, a larger percentage of male (27 percent) than female (18 percent) intimate partner victimizations involved a weapon (Catalano, 2013). The NCVS and NFVS provide somewhat different views on family violence.

Contrary to the NCVS estimates, the *National Family Violence Survey* results suggest that women are more violent than men when it comes to family assaults. In minor violence (slapping, spanking, throwing something, pushing, grabbing, or shoving), the incident rates were found to be roughly equal for men and women. In severe violence (kicking, biting, hitting with a fist, hitting or trying to hit with something, beating up the other, threatening with a knife or gun, or using a knife or gun), more men were victimized than women (Straus et al., 1980).

One suggestion for the disparity on gender statistics is that information regarding minor violence may be captured more easily using one method over another. The manner in which the survey is given and the questions asked are critical in providing an accurate picture of family violence. In several studies on domestic violence, the data on assaults by women were intentionally left out of the analysis, and questions on female offenders are typically not asked. In a study that excluded samples of victims that were considered biased, such as those in domestic violence shelters, authors found high rates of violence experienced by both women and men (Desmarais, Reeves, Nicholls, Telford, & Fiebert, 2012). The authors concluded that there is a need for treatment and intervention strategies for victims of both genders. The NISVS is expected to more adequately inform us on intimate partner violence for relationships among different sexual orientation groups in the future.

Evaluating Your Source

Anyone can post information on the World Wide Web. That means that there is a lot of junk out there on the Internet. Discriminating surfers understand that information obtained through the World Wide Web must be scrutinized for its reliability and credibility. Do not believe every source discovered out there! How does one find the right information? How is the information determined to be reliable?

For choosing what information to use, first determine the purpose of the project. Ask why the information is needed. If it is to expand knowledge and gain insight from different perspectives, data use from the Internet is wide open! Take it all and do not worry. When writing an academic paper evaluate the information looking for legitimate sources to improve the chances that the information is reliable and free of bias.

Using legitimate sources increase the odds that the information will be reliable. Although some people suggest that the reputation of the author is the most important aspect to consider, this criterion is not helpful when someone is new to the field of study and unfamiliar with the experts. It is more important to consider the credibility of the publisher of the article. From where does the information originate? Look to see whether the author cited the sources of their information. News sources are notoriously inaccurate and should not be the basis of an academic paper unless the information can be verified. Government and nonprofit agencies are reliable but may have a policy agenda. Small sample studies may not be universally applicable. For help in evaluating sources, refer to the Six-Step Model illustrated in Figure 3-5. Your guide is to ask: Who? What? Where? When? Why? How? A word of caution: Do not rely on the graphics and setup of the page to decide on reliability; a Web page expert may not know anything about family violence. Be leery of old information—the field is constantly changing. Information that is not updated may not have current relevance.

APA Guidelines

The *American Psychological Association* (APA) provides a reference format style. The current style is described in the sixth edition of the *Publication Manual of the American Psychological Association*, a reference book that contains hundreds of guidelines on how to format references, statistics, tables, punctuation, and grammar. It also contains writing tips and instructions about how to format manuscripts. You can buy the manual in bookstores and online. When in doubt about which format style should be used, rely on APA style unless instructed otherwise. It is most commonly used to cite sources

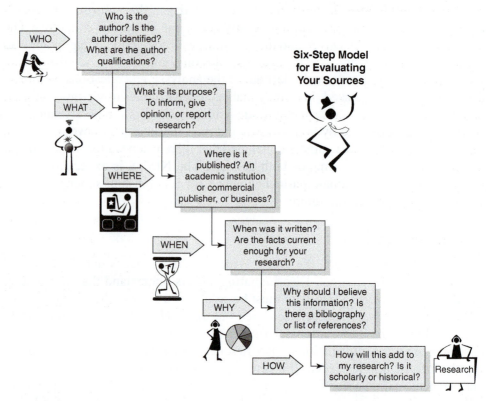

FIGURE 3-5 Scrutinize your online sources with this Six-Step Model. If you cannot answer these questions, you may want to find alternate information that is more suitable for your project.

within the social sciences. Information on APA formatting and software to accompany the book can be found here:

http://www.apastyle.org

Writing and Citing

Be sure to cite the information that is used. Most students have difficulty with citing electronic media. The OWL at Purdue has a great site on using the APA style formatting information:

https://owl.english.purdue.edu/

Citation software helps to import citations, build and organize bibliographies, and format citations for papers. It is important to cite all sources to show the reader that proper researching has been done and to avoid plagiarism. Excellent computer software packages are available to use for consistent formatting accuracy. Students may want to invest in reference management software. Finding a good one is just a matter of preference. A few ideas are EndNote, Zotero, and Mendeley. EndNote basic is a free Web version. Remember that the use of a formatting software program does not substitute for knowledge of the citation method, it makes it easier to be consistent. Do not blindly use formatting programs! The user must be able to evaluate the output.

DOMESTIC VIOLENCE THEORY

Theory drives research. Theories are the ideas that provide a framework for investigating the cause-and-effect relationship of events. Theory and research together drive policy and practice. The social sciences approach acknowledges that social interactions are not random acts. Domestic violence does not just happen; it is caused. Why does it happen? That is the question. Unfortunately, there is no consensus on why domestic violence occurs, despite hundreds of empirical studies conducted since the 1960s.

When inferences are made from individuals and applied to society at large, the study is being done on the micro level. From this perspective, an act that occurs between individuals is applied to the whole of society to form a theory. Typically, these acts involve psychological or individualist theories that are examined on the micro level of society. Most, although certainly not all, domestic abuse theories come from this view. It allows generalizations to be made about groups of people while understanding that the individual results may be different. What happens in cases of family violence is considered predictable, yet the result varies from one person to another based on intervening circumstances. The current debate in domestic violence theory comes from two diverse perspectives. The first perspective views domestic violence as family violence; the other perspective recognizes violence against women as the dominant cause of all domestic violence that occurs within the family.

FAMILY VIOLENCE PERSPECTIVE

The family violence viewpoint is the unintended consequence of the battered women's movement. **Family violence theory** acknowledges gender asymmetry and unjustified criminal violence, with a focus on reducing crimes by arresting the perpetrator and by introducing programs to reduce recidivism. In part, due to successful civil suits against police departments in the 1980s (refer back to *Thurman v. City of Torrington,* 1984) in conjunction with research on the efficacy of offender arrest, policies mandating that an arrest is made in instances of family violence have been established across the United States. System reform became the concession made by the feminist movement to receive domestic violence funding, establish shelters, and obtain services for domestic violence victims (Pope & Ferraro, 2006). Numerous theories to explain domestic violence from both perspectives have emerged and later been discredited. The important theories that remain from the family violence perspective are based on crime theory, on individual pathology and psychology, and on family-based theory. These lay the foundation for current interventions and provide a platform for future research, but are not meant to be an exhaustive list of all domestic violence theory.

Crime Theories

Crime theorists view family violence as a criminal assault that takes place within a legally defined domestic relationship. Domestic violence restraining orders and batterer treatment programs are common responses for victim protection, in addition to criminal prosecution. Throughout this book are discussions on the criminal justice responses, its variability across the country, and provisions for relief. There is the recognition that most victims are women, with each case of abuse structurally unrelated to any other. Domestic violence is a heinous crime that violates the special duty of care and concern due to the secretive nature of the crimes. This category of domestic violence theory calls for a criminal justice response but fails to explain why abuse occurs.

Contemporary crime theory on domestic violence is the foundation of the criminal justice approach. Critics of the criminal justice approach suggest that this model misrepresents the true nature of partner violence since it responds to specific acts involving injury without addressing the gendered nature of oppressive tactics. The criminal justice approach can best be described as a untended consequence of the reform movement from the violence against women proponents.

The criminal justice approach has been credited with significant achievements due to the criminalization of domestic violence. Tens of thousands of injuries and several thousand deaths have been prevented. The rate of domestic violence has declined 63 percent between 1994 and 2011 (Truman & Morgan, 2014). During the same period, the rate of violence committed by intimate partners has declined by 67 percent. Violence committed by immediate family members and relatives decreased between 49 percent and 52 percent. These statistics come from the NCVS, which defines domestic violence as rape or sexual assault, robbery, aggravated assault, or simple assault committed by an offender who is the victim's current or former spouse, boyfriend, girlfriend, parent, child, sibling, or another relative. Intimate partner violence is violence committed by the victim's current or former spouse, boyfriend, or girlfriend.

RATIONAL CHOICE THEORY   *Free* or rational choice theory states that criminal behavior is more than just a response to social pressures or upbringing—it is also a choice. According to this perspective, offenders calculate the relative costs and benefits of behavior and choose to commit family crimes. Offender choices are not necessarily rational but draw on previously established beliefs about their opportunities to commit personal violence and the likelihood of benefiting from their actions. The focus in this theory is to determine the effectiveness of interventions to decide how best to reduce the benefits of crime and increase the cost of the criminal activity.

DETERRENCE THEORY   Deterrence theory is based on the idea that punishment must be swift and sure to deter crime. The deterrent effect of punishment can be specific or general. Theorists suggest that we do not understand how useful deterrence is, and why it works or fails. They seek to update the concept with a greater understanding of community reinforcements and the role of official sanctions (National Institute of Justice, 1994).

When people are targeted in prevention efforts for a particular crime, the deterrence is considered specific. Recidivism is reduced in some instances of family violence; the reduction appears highest for those who have a more significant stake in conformity. When nonoffenders are affected by the punishment of offenders and choose not to risk apprehension, deterrence is considered general. If during an argument, a person walks away muttering, "You are not worth it," and holds himself or herself back when he or she might otherwise have swung out in anger, that is an example of the general deterrence effect. One way that experts measure the deterrent effect of the legislation is to examine the level of family crime to determine whether the rate has gone down or risen. Only recently have studies attempted to determine the effects of legal sanctions, both criminal and civil, on the recurrence of family violence.

Theories Based on Individual Pathology and Psychology

Individual-based theories ascribe family violence to psychological problems such as personality disorders, the offender's childhood experiences, or biological disposition. Studies in recent years have refuted a presumption of a personality disorder of the parent because less than 10 percent of abusive parents were found to be emotionally maladjusted. *Multiple factor theories* have sought to determine the causes of the abuse and neglect of children. The underlying psychological cause of the violence is targeted in the psychodynamic approach to therapy. A cognitive-behavioral approach is taken when the offender is taught new patterns of nonviolent thinking and behavior. If the perpetrator has difficulty in establishing healthy relationships, attempts are made to facilitate secure attachments between offenders and loved ones.

BIOCHEMICAL IMBALANCE THEORIES   Some *biochemical theories*, including glandular and hormonal imbalances, blood sugar levels, adrenaline sensitively, substance abuse, and vitamin and diet deficiencies, have been suggested as possible causes of criminal behavior (Burke, 2005). The raging hormones of women and the excess of testosterone in men have alternatively been accepted and rejected as causes of criminal behavior during this century. The most pervasive theory is a perceived link between testosterone and male aggressiveness. Burke points toward research conducted in the 1980s, which found that violent men had a significantly higher level of testosterone in their systems; however, he stated that no link has ever been definitively established between levels of testosterone and criminal behavior in men. The integration of biology with other explanations might contribute to an understanding on why some people commit domestic violence.

INDIVIDUAL PATHOLOGY AND MENTAL ILLNESS   Strong relationships between domestic violence and a variety of mental disorders have been reported. Violence perpetrators exhibit behaviors similar to persons suffering from personality disorders. From a review of the literature, Hanson (2002) characterizes individual abusers as clinically assessed problematic individuals displaying poor impulse control, aggression, fear of intimacy, emotional dependence, fear of abandonment, and impaired ego functioning. Mental health diagnoses for offenders include obsessive-compulsive, paranoid, borderline personality, passive-aggressive, narcissistic, and antisocial personalities (Hanson, 2002). Correlations between childhood abuse and neglect and other social problems have been indicated. These people are highly resistant to counseling and other forms of intervention, which is suggestive of psychopathological sickness. Court intervention with supervised therapy is the most likely option for those whose behavior can be dangerous, if not lethal.

Donald Dutton has been working with assaultive men since 1978, both as a clinician and as a researcher. He suggests that approximately 2 percent of the population would qualify as habitual woman beaters (Dutton, 2008). Also, many of his clients met the criteria for antisocial behavior; he defined them as having shallow emotional responsiveness. They are often violent with others in addition to their partners. Psychopathic batterers are frequently arrested for nonviolent crimes such as forgery, passing bad checks, or confidence rackets.

Dutton points out that his colleague Robert Hare, author of *Without Conscience: The Disturbing World of the Psychopaths Among Us* (1999), found brain abnormalities among psychopaths. Magnetic resonance imaging (MRI) brain scans performed on psychopaths lacked the considerable color patterns radiating from the brain stem to the temporal lobes that were present in healthy persons. Instead, a small amount of bright color in the stem area toward the back of the brain was the only indication of brain activity. Without evidence that psychopathy is the direct result of social or environmental factors, Hare theorizes that the condition is genetic. Recent efforts in neuroscience are exploring the biological connection which may help to understand the motivation of some domestic abusers.

Psychologist Neil Jacobson describes a subgroup of men whom he calls "vagal reactors" as psychopaths (Dutton, 2008). Approximately 20 percent of all men who perpetrate intimate partner violence and half of all antisocial personalities fall within this vagal reactors category, he maintains. These men become calm internally when engaged in heated arguments with their wives. Subjects actually showed a decline in heart rate during arguments with a spouse. The violence committed against a wife is to dominate her; it is both controlling and controlled.

Family-Based Theories

It is well accepted that no one theory adequately explains the complex nature of domestic violence, including intimate partner violence. Relatively few occurrences of family violence can be attributed to individual pathology, mental illness, or chemical imbalances. Neither do the experiences of survivors fit neatly into theoretical explanations. The theory is evolving and incomplete. Perhaps it speaks to the fact that multiple factors contribute to family violence. Sociological theories can be helpful in providing insight to family structure and the expression of violence as acceptable communication. Witnessing violence in childhood has been explored as predictive of future violence. Gender-role socialization is an enduring theory on family violence. Some of these family-based theories are particularly relevant for understanding child abuse and will be covered in greater depth later in this text.

SOCIAL–PSYCHOLOGICAL MODEL   One model has joined together major elements of feminist theory with the psychological approach. The social–psychological model is an integrated theory that brings together three general approaches to crime causation: social learning, unequal power relations, and personal choice theory. First, the model uses a broad application of social learning theory to explain that people who abuse have learned to do so through direct instruction, modeling, and reinforcement. Second, unequal power relations (real or perceived) contribute to the likelihood that abusive behaviors will be tolerated, an idea born through the feminist contribution. A third dimension is the recognition that family abuse is a personal choice: An abuser acts out with violence instead of using alternative methods of conflict resolution. According to this integrated model, social isolation creates an environment in which battering in same-sex couples can occur. In this view, family violence must be understood as both a social and a psychological phenomenon. Rather than viewing family theories as mutually exclusive of one another, their combination can enhance theories of violence.

CULTURE OF VIOLENCE THEORY   The *culture of violence theory* looks at the broad acceptance of violence in our society and concludes that its acceptance is the foundation for violence within the family. In this view, theorists point out the perverseness of violence as entertainment and the means for settling disputes at the personal and national levels. The implied approval for violence is acknowledged and legitimizes the use of violence to settle family disputes as well. This theory claims that violence occurs at all levels of society as an accepted means to resolve difficulty, arguing that a restructuring of the cultural variables of society is needed to bring change. In other words, to stop spouse abuse, it is necessary to alter men's reliance on violence as a means of resolving conflict.

GENDER-ROLE THEORY   This uncomplicated explanation for family violence blames the traditional socialization of children into gender roles (Harrison & Lynch, 2005). In this perspective, children are oriented early in life as victims or perpetrators, according to their gender. Girls are taught to be passive and yielding to the "stronger" male sex. Proponents of the gender-role theory suggest that society dictates the role of women in marriage, in child responsibilities, and toward family duties, all of which makes them vulnerable to abuse. Self-reliance and aggressiveness are male attributes that are unbecoming of women in the traditional sense.

According to gender-role theory, the expectation that girls should be physically and sexually pleasing to men makes them susceptible to sexual abuse. In relationships, girls are taught to be submissive while boys are expected to be the sexual aggressors. On the contrary, boys are taught that men must be in control at all times. They must exhibit strength and develop leadership qualities. Men are therefore socialized to believe that their position is to be protected at all costs, including by the use of violence.

The tenets of this theory are believed to contribute to sexual violence of young women in dating relationships. Emotionally immature young women socialized in their roles are vulnerable to sexual victimization through aggression and dominance of young men. Conversely, young men may respond to peer pressure to be sexually aggressive through the same model. A significant source of socialization for this model is the media. Television is blamed for depicting male and female roles in a limited and superficial characterization of male aggression and female passivity.

SOCIAL DISORGANIZATION THEORY   The *disorganization of community life* causes a lack of social control, according to this theory. Considered in part the result of high mobility, a breakdown in formal and informal controls that might otherwise mitigate family conflict encourages criminal conduct. Poverty in transitional neighborhoods is believed to contribute to the lawlessness that results. People whose emphasis is necessarily on survival may lack concern for community matters and fail to benefit from conventional sources of control such as family, school, and social service agencies.

SOCIAL LEARNING THEORIES   According to *social learning theory*, people are not born with violent tendencies. They learn them through their environment and life experiences. Deviance is learned in the same manner as normative behavior. The process of learning is through communication with others and includes motives, drives, attitudes, and rationalizations on the commission of crime. When aggressive action brings desired results, violence becomes an acceptable means to an end. The primary source of learning occurs in intimate personal groups of family and peers, according to this view.

The frequency and duration of the violence in one's environment will influence the learning experience. Because people process life events in different ways, it can be said that your perception is your reality. The manner in which a person perceives a situation from his or her viewpoint will affect their response. This becomes the reality under which the person will operate in the future and perceive similar events. This perspective provides a simplified explanation of many forms of family violence and forms the basis for numerous variations. The continuum of family violence from the social learning perspective comes from the behavior modeling theory and the intergenerational transmission theory. The equality wheel, which illustrates the components of healthy relationships, is often used in batterer treatment programs as a learning tool to help abusers in the process of becoming nonviolent.

According to social learning theory, environmental experiences are another source of influence. Children who reside in crime-prone and rough areas are more likely to act out violently. Violent television shows and movies provide a third source of modeling for children. Because violence is often portrayed as acceptable behavior, children begin to view violent acts as normal behavior, which has no consequences for the actors.

INTERGENERATIONAL TRANSMISSION THEORY   A frequently used explanation for family violence is the *intergenerational transmission theory*. Abusive behavior is handed down from generation to generation as an appropriate way to deal with conflict: Violence begets violence. This does not suggest that battering tendencies are inherited; rather, they are experienced. People who observe violence in the home as children are more likely to resort to battering in their relationships later in life. Simply put, if a child is abused, he or she learns that abuse is an acceptable, if not normal, way to achieve his or her goal. The child becomes an abusing adult—toward a spouse and often towards his or her children. A cycle of abuse occurs across generations.

VIOLENCE AGAINST WOMEN PERSPECTIVE

The battered women's movement began almost 30 years ago to challenge cultural norms from the feminist perspective. This second perspective states that domestic violence is violence against women. It is a sociopolitical struggle of equal rights with violence against women as one representation of oppression. As with other radical views that spring from a revolution, the feminist model questions the way that women have been viewed in society and the lack of economic, legal, social, and political options for women. The majority of violence against women occurs in their homes, formally a place of legal sanction for the abusers. This theory has greatly influenced the perception of family violence and criminal justice practice. The dominant theoretical analysis on family violence since the 1980s has been feminist sociopolitical theory.

Feminist Sociopolitical Theory

This feminist model has been the dominant explanation of family violence for years. The perspective considers intimate partner violence as endemic to cultures influenced by a patriarchal social structure. Patriarchy refers to a social system that recognizes the complete dominance of men over women. Custom and religion typically strengthened by law define the social standing of women as subservient to men. Patriarchy is recognized as the most common and enduring social system. Even today, social mores reminiscent of ancient patriarchy provide the reasoning for violence against women, according to this perspective. At the core of the theory is the idea that intimate partner violence is used to maintain control over women, by force, when needed.

The dynamics of an abusive relationship, according to the feminist position, include the following:

- Gender relationships are considered a fundamental component of social life. The experiences of gender are therefore emphasized. Both men and women are part of the analysis, with the greater emphasis placed on the differences within the context of society and viewed from within power relations.
- The power of men by their privileged status is the means by which women are controlled. Men are the traditional lawmakers and property owners who have excluded female participation and justified abuse to maintain power. Therefore, power and control are the key elements that establish and maintain the subordination of women in society, legitimating the positioning of the genders.
- Ending the subordination of women by changing the social structure remains the major goal of the movement. This process would include but is not limited to, equal access and protection through law.

In a more moderate form, the position is a comparison between men and women within the context of power relations. The theory does not seek to take power away from men but rather seeks to equalize it and share it between both genders. According to this view, the status of women in society is related to the frequency of wife beating. Spouse abuse is explained through the exploration of the social structure of society and the analysis of power that has historically been identified in male dominance.

Gender Inequality

Gender inequality is a complex perspective which leaves women powerless within the family unit. Economic discrimination exists through the lack of job opportunities that provide income sufficient to provide for women, thereby enforcing dependence on the male head of household. Outside the home, women may be subservient to men because of a lack of legal status, and due to custom or religion.

Some authors maintain that female family violence offenders have been considered inferior and their crimes insignificant (Vito & Holmes, 1994). Perhaps that is why there are no concise theoretical explanations that examine why some women abuse their children and lovers. Child abuse advocates point to the devaluation of children in our society. Because women are the primary offenders against children, that may in part explain the absence of research in this area. The *chivalry hypothesis* holds that women are likely to be protected by the criminal justice system and given more lenient treatment than men when they commit the same crimes (Grabe, Trager, Lear, & Rauch, 2006).

In communities where mandatory arrest policies on family violence have been rigorously applied, the number of female offenders has risen dramatically. Experts continue to debate male victimization versus the contention that female offenders are self-defending against male aggression in their relationships (Dutton & White, 2013). These researchers suggest that many women who use force were trying to get away from their abusive partners.

Coercive Control Theory

There is much discussion on the need to revitalize a woman-centered violence agenda. The most recent sociopolitical position stands on a platform of violence against women that challenges the current criminal justice approach to family violence. Referred to as

coercive control, it defines violence against women as a strategic course of gender-based abuse in which some combination of physical and sexual violence occurs.

Why do activists insist on a need for a gender-specific approach to domestic violence? According to Stark (2007), the criminal justice approach fails to address the ongoing nature and cumulative effects of domestic violence since each incident is focused on a single criminal offense. Stark and others maintain that domestic violence is violence against women and should be resolved as a chronic multifaceted oppression of women (Buzawa, Buzawa, & Stark, 2017).

There is evidence that coercive control as a form of human manipulation does exist. The term (and hence the concept of) "coercive control" comes from research conducted in 1957. In an article entitled *Communist attempts to elicit false confessions from Air Force Prisoners of War*, sociologist Albert Biderman outlines the eight Communist coercive methods for causing individual compliance through a form of brainwashing (Biderman, 1957). These tactics for achieving the goal of coercive control are illustrated in Figure 3-6. The methods used to shape compliance and undermine the resistance of the prisoner include a demonstration of omnipotence or power, which reminds that the victim's fate is in their control. Degradation, threats of violence, induced debilitation, isolation, domination, the enforcement of trivial demands, and random kindness are oppressive tactics designed to control them. These methods are very similar to what was discovered in interviewing of domestic violence victims. The Power and Control Wheel, developed by Pence and Paymar, illustrates these domestic violence experiences involving power and control in the Duluth model (Pence & Paymar, 1993).

8 Steps to Coercive Control

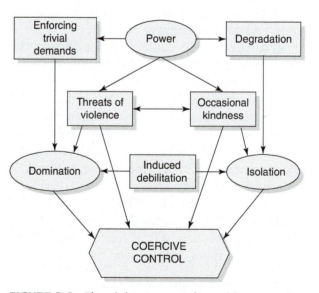

FIGURE 3-6   The eight steps used to achieve coercive control of U.S. prisoners was outlined by Biderman in 1957 as a form of torture used by the Communists. The contemporary application is made to explain violence against women by men. Adapted from Biderman (1957).

Critiques of a "one-size-fits-all" approach to domestic violence failed to acknowledge the variability of violence in family situations. Johnson applied the method of intimate terrorism to domestic violence victims as one of two types of domestic violence offenders (Johnson, 1995). Situational couple violence is acknowledged as the most common type of physical aggression in the general population. As time went on, the Johnson typology grew to recognize coercive controlling violence, situational couples violence, violent resistance, and separation-instigated violence as descriptors of violence between domestic partners. The term "intimate terrorism" had been changed to coercive controlling violence as people were reluctant to use the former in court situations. Coercive controlling violence is acknowledged in the Johnson typology as the most severe, accounting for 11 to 35 percent of cases (Kelly & Johnson, 2008).

The original *Violence Against Women Act* (VAWA, 1994) provided federal funding for domestic violence, which limited resources to help female victims of male violence only, consistent with the feminist sociopolitical approach. Refer to Chapter 1 for a discussion of the legislation. It was not until 2005, amid significant debate, that the *Act* was reauthorized to include a non-exclusivity provision to clarify that the title should not be construed to prohibit male victims from receiving services (Article Sec. 3(b)(8)). Gender exclusion is the reason that data on the victimization of men and gay, lesbian, bisexual transgender and queer individuals (GLBTQ) is incomplete. The next reauthorization of the *Act* in 2013 added a nondiscrimination provision, which ensures that service funding cannot be denied on the basis of sex; therefore, GLBTQ couples are specifically protected as well (Article Sec. 3(b)(4). Studies are ongoing to fill the gap in knowledge of these underserved populations. The debate is ongoing and still centers on the question of a gendered approach to domestic violence. The concept of coercive control is the most recent foundation for the feminist sociopolitical approach.

CONCLUSIONS

This chapter covered the common ways in which researchers gather information on family violence and the major sources of criminal justice information. An understanding of the nature and extent of family violence crime in the United States has been furthered by quantitative research. The well-known UCR and the NCVS provide examples of the usefulness of this scientific approach. Until recently, the UCR had been the most widely used evaluation of crime in the United States. Within the field of criminal justice, the quantitative method approach to research has been valuable for focusing attention on specific issues, program evaluation, and setting standards. A long-standing challenge in criminal justice research has been in determining the extent and nature of undetected crime. Victimization studies and self-report surveys, both quantitative measures, emerged to address this void that could not be filled by the UCR.

Qualitative research on family violence also provides essential information. We see increased use of qualitative studies of ethnic and cultural minorities as a means to understand minority populations. The development of culturally sensitive responses to family violence has emerged in part from this approach.

Why does family abuse occur? Two theoretical perspectives argue opposing theories about domestic violence. The dominant view is that domestic violence is a criminal offense that occurs between domestically identified men, women, and children as family violence. Numerous theories exist to explain the diverse nature of domestic violence, including psychology, individual pathology, and sociology. The opposing view is a feminist perspective that recognizes only violence against women (or children) as victims of domestic violence. Oppression and coercive control over the lives of women is the explanation for this violence.

Theorists continue to consider the complex problems involved in domestic violence and seek to develop ways to address them. Social programs and counseling methods have developed from the ideas covered here. We have gained great insight into the characteristics of family violence from the research that has developed. This chapter does not cover the specific responses to domestic violence. Subsequent chapters will address these issues.

SIMPLY SCENARIO
Conflict Resolution

Eric came out of the closet to his family while living with his two male intimate partners. The nontraditional lifestyle soon became the norm for the three men. Holiday get-togethers included extended family members. The men sought social validation through a civil ceremony that recognized the threesome relationship. For years the men lived together in harmony. As with traditional couples, they shared household expenses, vacations, meals, and daily chores around the house. After time, an escalation of violence was occurring behind closed doors. They yelled and fought frequently with each other. Typically the fighting would stop with one of the men crying and hurt from a backhand or push to the ground.

It seemed that there was never enough money to pay the bills. Fighting increased, and Eric felt he was never good enough, or deserving enough, of the love he felt for his partners. Eric was the object of verbal abuse and put-downs. He drank to drown out the noise and make himself feel better. Then it happened—he bought a baseball bat. It was the only thing he could think to do. He went home and beat up both men that he lived with ... No one reported the incident to the police.

Question: What source of official data would most likely contain information on this intimate partner crime? Do you think that responding to female victimization should exclude services to males?

Questions for Review

1. What was the Minneapolis Domestic Violence Experiment and why was it important?
2. What is the difference between quantitative research and qualitative research?
3. Describe at least four sources of domestic violence data.
4. What does the National Intimate Partner and Sexual Violence Survey tell us?
5. What is the difference between the Uniform Crime Reports (UCR) and the National Incident-Based Reporting System (NIBRS)?
6. What can be learned from the State Court Processing Statistics?
7. What does the Survey of Inmates in State and Federal Correctional Facilities tell us?
8. Explain the Six-Step Model for evaluating Internet sources.
9. What is the major premise of the family violence theories on domestic violence?
10. What is the major premise of the violence against women theory on domestic violence?

Internet-Based Exercises

1. Visit the Web site for the Office on Violence Against Women (http://www.justice.gov/ovw). This federal office administers financial and technical assistance to communities that are developing programs, policies, and practices aimed at ending domestic violence, dating violence, sexual assault, and stalking.

2. At the Bureau of Justice Statistics site (http://bjs.gov/), you will find information on victim characteristics and offender relationships. Go there and find examples of this category.
3. This chapter introduced you to the importance of research in the field of family violence. The National Criminal Justice Reference Service is the premier Internet source for research information. Go to the Web site https://www.ncjrs.gov/ and find two articles on family violence. Report your findings to the class.

4. Another significant source of research in the field of family violence can be found at the UN Women site using the Global Database on Violence Against Women. The Global Database on Violence Against Women provides easy access to comprehensive and up-to-date information on measures undertaken by United Nations member states to address all forms of violence against women. http://evaw-global-database.unwomen.org/en

References

Article Sec. 3(b)(8), Violence Against Women and Department of Justice Reauthorization Act of 2005, Act No. H.R. 3402 of 2005

Article Sec. 3(b)(4), Violence Against Women Reauthorization Act of 2013, Act No. S. 47 of 2013

Barner, J., & Carney, M. (2011). Interventions for intimate partner violence: A historical review. *Journal of Family Violence, 26*(3), 235–244.

Biderman, A. D. (1957). Communist attempts to elicit false confessions from Air Force prisoners of war. *Bulletin of the New York Academy of Medicine, 33*(9), 616.

Bureau of Justice Statistics (BJS). (2010). Data collection: Federal Justice Statistics Program (FJSP). Retrieved from http://www.bjs.gov/index.cfm?ty=dcdetail&iid=262

Bureau of Justice Statistics (BJS). (2011). Data collection: National Crime Victimization Survey (NCVS). Retrieved from http://bjs.gov/index.cfm?ty=dcdetail&iid=245

Burke, R. H. (2005). *An introduction to criminological theory*. Portland, OR: Willan Publishing.

Buzawa, E., Buzawa, C., & Stark, E. (2017). *Responding to domestic violence: The integration of criminal justice and human services*. Los Angeles, CA: Sage.

Catalano, S. (2013). *Intimate partner violence, 1993–2011.* (NCJ 243300). Washington, D.C.: Bureau of Justice Statistics.

Creswell, J. W. (2008). *Research design: Qualitative, quantitative, and mixed methods approaches* (3rd ed.). Thousand Oaks, CA: Sage.

Desmarais, S. L., Reeves, K. A., Nicholls, T. L., Telford, R. P., & Fiebert, M. S. (2012). Prevalence of physical violence in intimate relationships: Part 1. Rates of male and female victimization. *Partner Abuse, 3*(2).

Dutton, D. (2008). *The abusive personality: Violence and control in intimate relationships* (2nd ed.). New York, NY: Guilford Press.

Dutton, D., & White, K. (2013). Male victims of domestic violence. *New Male Studies: An International Journal, 2*(1), 5–17.

FBI. (2013). Human Trafficking in the Uniform Crime Reporting (UCR) Program. Washington, D.C.: Author Retrieved from https://ucr.fbi.gov/human-trafficking.

FBI. (2016). UCR Program: Criminal Justice Information Services Division. Washington, D.C.: Author Retrieved from https://ucr.fbi.gov/ucr-program-quarterly/ucr-program-quarterly-april-2016.

FBI. (2017). Uniform Crime Reporting (UCR) Program Summary Reporting System (SRS) Historical Rape Definition was Retired, Effective January 1, 2017, Washington, D.C.: Author Retrieved from https://ucr.fbi.gov/historical-rape-definition-retired.

Felson, R., & Lane, K. J. (2010). Does violence involving women and intimate partners have a special etiology? *Criminology, 48*(1), 321–328.

Garner, J., Fagan, J., & Maxwell, C. (1995). Published findings from the spouse assault replication program: A critical review. *Journal of Quantitative Criminology, 11*(1), 3–28.

Grabe, M. E., Trager, K. D., Lear, M., & Rauch, J. (2006). Gender in crime news: A case study test of the Chivalry Hypothesis. *Mass Communication and Society, 9*(2), 137–163.

Hagan, F. E. (2011). *Essentials of research methods in criminal justice and criminology* (3rd ed.). Upper Saddle River, NJ: Pearson.

Hamel, J. (2011). In dubious battle: The politics of mandatory arrest and dominant aggressor laws. *Partner Abuse, 2*(2), 224–225.

Hanson, B. (2002). Interventions for batterers. In A. Roberts (Ed.), *Handbook of domestic violence intervention strategies* (pp. 419–448). New York, NY: Oxford University Press.

Hare, R. (1999). *Without conscience: The disturbing world of the psychopaths among us*. New York, NY: Guilford Press.

Harrison, L., & Lynch, A. (2005). Social role theory and the perceived gender role orientation of athletes. *Sex Roles: A Journal of Research, 52*(3–4), 227–236.

IBR Resource Center. (2012). Status of NIBRS in the states. Retrieved from http://www.jrsa.org/ibrrc/backgroundstatus/nibrs_states.shtml

Johnson, M. P. (1995). Patriarchal terrorism and common couple violence: Two forms of violence against women. *Journal of Marriage and the Family*, 283–294.

Kelly, J. B., & Johnson, M. P. (2008). Differentiation among types of intimate partner violence: Research update and implications for interventions. *Family court review, 46*(3), 476–499.

Leedy, P., & Ormrod, J. E. (2013). *Practical research: Planning and design* (10th ed.). Upper Saddle River, NJ: Pearson.

Maxwell, C. D., Garner, J. H., & Fagan, J. A. (2003). The preventive effects of arrest on intimate partner violence: Research, policy, and theory. *Domestic Violence Report, 9*(1), 9–10.

National Institute of Justice. (1994). *Breaking the cycle: Predicting and preventing crime.* (NCJ 140541). Washington, D.C.: National Institute of Justice.

Pence, E., & Paymar, M. (1993). *Education groups for men who batter: The Duluth Model.* New York, NY: Springer Publishing Company.

Pope, L., & Ferraro, K. (2006). Bridging the Work of Social Change and Systems Reform. Retrieved from http://vawresources.org/index_files/Page705.htm

Sherman, L., & Berk, R. (1984). The Minneapolis Domestic Violence Experiment. *Police Foundation Reports* (p. 13). Washington, D.C.: Police Foundation.

Sherman, L., & Rogan, D. (1992). *Policing domestic violence: Experiments and dilemmas.* New York, NY: Free Press.

Smith, E. L., Durose, M. R., & Langan, P. R. (2008). State court processing of domestic violence cases. (NCJ 214993). Retrieved from http://bjs.ojp.usdoj.gov/content/pub/pdf/scpdvc.pdf

Stark, E. (2007). *Coercive control: The entrapment of women in personal life.* New York, NY: Oxford University Press.

Straus, M. A., Gelles, R. J., & Steinmetz, S. K. (1980). *Behind closed doors: Violence in the American family.* Garden City, NY: Anchor Press/Doubleday.

Thurman v. City of Torrington. (1984). 595 F. Supp. 1521 (D. Conn).

Truman, J., & Morgan, R. (2014). Nonfatal domestic violence, 2003–2012. Retrieved from Washington, D.C.: Bureau of Justice Statistics.

Truman, J., & Planty, M. (2012). *Criminal victimization, 2011.* (NCJ 239437). Washington, D.C.: Bureau of Justice Statistics.

VAWA 18 U.S.C., 2 § 4022, (1994).

Vito, G., & Holmes, R. (1994). *Criminology: Theory, research, and policy.* Belmont, CA: Wadsworth.

Walters, M. L., Chen, J., & Breiding, M. J. (2013). *National Intimate Partner and Sexual Violence Survey: 2010 findings on victimization by sexual orientation.* Atlanta, GA: Centers for Disease Control and Prevention.

4

Introduction to Child Abuse and Neglect

CHAPTER OBJECTIVES

After reviewing this chapter, you should be able to:

1. Discuss the history of child abuse and neglect with relevance to modern day.
2. Identify and give examples of the four primary categories of child maltreatment.
3. Examine and use major sources of child abuse data for research.
4. Explain the demographics of child abuse victims and perpetrators.
5. State the role of criminal justice in the reporting and protection of child abuse victims.

KEY TERMS

Act of commission

Act of omission

Child abuse and neglect

Endangerment standard

Harm standard

Infanticide

Mandated reporters

Safe haven laws

INTRODUCTION

Historical accounts tell us that children have always been abused and neglected by one or both parents; it is not uncommon or newly revealed. Rarely is child abuse a single physical attack or a single act of deprivation or molestation. When one form of child abuse is noted, it is generally accepted that other abuses exist in the home as well. For a child, emotional abuse includes excessive, aggressive, or unreasonable parental behavior that places demands on a child to perform beyond his or her capabilities. Sometimes emotional abuse is not what a parent does, but what a parent fails to do. Children who receive no love, no care, no support, and no guidance will carry the scars into adulthood.

Child Protective Services (CPS) is the arm of the government established to protect and provide guidance on all matters pertaining to the needs of the child, from nutrition and education to injury, instead of the parent(s). CPS may even become involved at the request of parents who need help in the care or protection of a child. Parents can ask CPS for help due to a child having a disability, if one develops substance abuse addiction, or for any other reason. This means that there is a civil side to child abuse and neglect, as well as a criminal side. When you hear about CPS, it is essential to understand that CPS protects children from family members, not strangers. When a report is filed with CPS, it will be screened out if there is no family relationship involved. If criminal wrongdoing is involved, the case will likely be forwarded to the appropriate criminal justice agency.

Until the late 1970s and early 1980s, the criminal justice professions rarely intervened in crimes against children. Allegations of child abuse were investigated only in the most severe cases or when a death obviously due to abuse had occurred. Even then, a female matron would probably be assigned to investigate—a strong message to police officers that child abuse was a "family problem" and not important enough for real police attention. With limited exceptions, the problem was referred to a social service agency for family intervention. This attitude reflected a more significant social problem: the devaluation of children and the lack of societal protections under the guise of parental rights. Every state now has legislation to prohibit crimes against children. Law enforcement officers are now active participants in the protection of children from abuse.

When acts against a child rise to the level of criminal violence, it is likely that both law enforcement and child protection services will be involved. State laws provide the avenues for law enforcement and CPS to share information and work cooperatively in the best interests of the child during an investigation. Child abuse and neglect is a form of domestic violence when it involves violence against someone in a legally recognized domestic relationship, a child, and parent relationship, for example. Violence against children is primarily committed by family members. The information in this chapter does not contain data on crimes against children if it is perpetrated by a stranger, neighbor, or another nonfamily member. Those are examples of nondomestic relationships. Since the child is unable to care for himself or herself, however, the government may become involved to protect from abuse and neglect. There is a special duty when professionals take on any role for the protection of children. Child abuse and neglect can have numerous long-term effects on a child's physical, psychological, and behavioral health. The impact can go beyond the immediate or visible harm.

As you will learn in this and the following chapters, there is an overlap between child abuse and neglect as a distinct form of violence and other forms of domestic violence. Where one form of domestic violence occurs, other forms typically occur also. It is almost impossible to separate the impact of domestic violence on children and adults. Physical, psychological, behavioral, and societal consequences may occur that last for lifetimes and perhaps generations.

There are four major forms of child abuse and neglect: physical abuse, neglect, sexual abuse, and emotional or psychological abuse. Each of these will be defined and discussed in this chapter. Recognizing the signs and symptoms of abuse and neglect is the focus of Chapter 5.

HISTORY OF CHILD MALTREATMENT

Historians agree that children have always been abused and neglected according to our contemporary standards. As far back as written accounts exist, men have owned their children, wives, animals, slaves, and other property. Children could be sent into slavery to offset a man's debt, or they might be sold outright. Physical abuse, neglect, and sexual abuse were considered socially acceptable behavior in ancient times (Hilarski, 2008).

Ancient Times

Infants were the property of their fathers and had no rights of their own. Their fathers could even kill them for some "practical" reasons. Physical deformity, questionable health, and illegitimacy were rationales for infanticide because destroying children who were bound to be a burden was viewed as promoting the general welfare of society (Colon, 2001). **Infanticide** is legally defined as the murder of a child before his or her first birthday.

The Code of Hammurabi, from the eighteenth century B.C., stated that the father had full control of his children until they were married off to someone. This right transferred to the mother in the absence of the father and even included the right to sell the children ("Hammurabi's Code of Laws," trans. 1998). During this time of history, only incest was forbidden. If incest did occur, the male perpetrator of incest was exiled with his daughter. The code also contained the attempt to protect legitimate, illegitimate, abandoned, and unborn children from harm or losing their inheritance (Colon, 2001).

Early philosophers in Greece condoned the outright killing of a newborn. Aristotle even recommended a law prohibiting crippled children to be raised. Researchers inform us of physicians' instructions to midwives during the second century outlining the duty to examine children and dispose of the unfit (Ventrell, 1998). If an infant seemed sick or had a congenital disability, it was acceptable to leave him or her on a street corner exposed to the elements to be left to die (Hilarski, 2008).

In the Roman Empire, an infant was allowed to live according to his or her potential to the family (Hilarski, 2008). This was because all children were raised to carry on the bloodline and to care for parents as they aged. Birth to age seven has historically been the age of infancy, considered the time before children had the vested right to life (Ventrell, 1998). Marriage between close relatives was allowed, although it was illegal to marry outside of one's class or ancestry.

Female children were a strain on the financial resources of a father, which was another justification for infanticide. Historically, newborn girls have been at particularly high risk for infanticide. In China, female infants were openly killed until the late 1800s, usually by drowning (Koenen & Thompson, 2008). The practice of female infanticide was evident in the 2000 Chinese census that found as many as 140 boys for every 100 girls in certain rural areas. The killing of female infants is considered no different from abortion in some parts of India (Koenen & Thompson, 2008).

Middle Ages

Under Judaism and Christianity, children's right to live was protected, regardless of the quality of life or the law. During the fourth century, the child's right to live was established through the Christian faith. The commandment "Thou shalt not kill" was linked with the practice of infanticide. A similar trend establishing the child's right to life is evidenced in the experience of the Russian Orthodox Church. Bearing children was the major task of women during the tenth century, thereby defining women's role in society. Severe penalties were prescribed for committing infanticide, terminating pregnancies, or practicing birth control. Abortion was considered similar to committing murder—and the punishment varied with the stage of pregnancy. Aborting an embryo brought five years of fasting as punishment, and seven years if the fetus were completely formed (Pushkareva, 1997).

Apart from religious practices, social restrictions against sexual relations with children differed from today's standards. Except for incest, it was permissible to loan children to guests or to hire them out for sexual use (Radbill, 1987). Pushkareva offered evidence that father–daughter incest continued to be practiced well into seventeenth-century Russia (1997). She stated that fathers had absolute authority over their daughters. Overall, child rearing was strict, and parents were encouraged to beat children frequently. Young boys and girls were also forbidden to complain about family beatings and would be flogged publicly if they brought the family business out into the open.

Early Modern Period

Chancery courts in Britain were granted control over the general welfare and property rights of children. These courts utilized the concept of *parens patriae*, meaning "father of the people." It refers to the right of the king to act in the best interests of the child, even if that means to act against the wishes of the natural parents. There is little evidence that the courts used this power to protect children from abuse or neglect. As early as 1535, the English Poor Laws allowed children identified as neglected or delinquent to be put to work or placed in poorhouses (Shoemaker & Wolfe, 2005). The provisions are not considered by history as protections, but rather as attempts to maintain strict control over children who were resistant to parental punishment.

Apprenticeship was another form used to exercise control over children. Under this system, children were removed from their homes and placed into the care of adults who would train them in various skills. Some apprenticeships were forced until the child was 21 years old. Child labor practices included working long hours, with physical punishment often leading to deformities.

English records as late as 1829 cite the cause of death for infants as including babies drowned in pits full of water, cisterns, wells, ponds, and even pans of water (Radbill, 1987). Babies were also starved by their nurses or killed by burning or scalding. A common form of death for children was overlaying or lying upon a child. This form of suffocation by carelessness accounted for 20 deaths in one English city in 1920, according to Samuel Radbill.

Children in Early America

Early attempts to protect children are questionable by contemporary standards of justice. Often, the methods of government intervention amounted to control rather than providing opportunities for relief for the child. The colonists brought the English notions of juvenile protection to the United States. Here they instituted Poor Laws and continued to practice forced apprenticeship (Dorne, 2002). The range of acceptable punishment for errant children stopped with permanent disfigurement. Early law held parents responsible for the actions of their children, giving them the authority to punish harshly. Under Stubborn Child Laws, parents were allowed to put a disobedient child to death for noncompliant behaviors. Officials today had estimated that in Colonial America as many as two-thirds of the children died before they reached age four (Hilarski, 2008). Disease, starvation, accidents, beatings, and torture are among the causes of child death in early America.

In 1838, juvenile authorities were granted unrestrained power over the lives of children through the disposition of *Ex Parte Crouse*. In this case, a Pennsylvania court ignored the father's plea for custody of his daughter. Her mother had placed the girl in a house of refuge because the child was unmanageable. A higher court denied the father's claim that parental control is exclusive, natural, and proper. This decision, which was applied only to Pennsylvania, was noticed by the other states that followed suit. The state had been given the right to restrain and protect children despite the wishes of parents. Numerous courts across the United States heard similar cases involving delinquent and dependent children in the years following; most adopted the *parens patriae* standard, allowing the unlimited authority to states to intervene in the autonomy of the family (Ventrell, 1998).

During the Victorian era, infanticide was the most covered-up crime, according to Marlene Stein Wortman (1985). Between 1861 and 1901, an annual average of 55 dead infants was found on the streets of Philadelphia, their cause of death listed as "unknown." During that same period, only one trial led to a first-degree murder verdict for the death of a child. Changes in the attitudes toward children came about slowly. Significant reform periods to protect children took place during the first half of the nineteenth century: the Refuge Movement, the Child Saver Movement, and Societies for the Prevention of Cruelty to Children.

THE REFUGE MOVEMENT   Mass migration and immigration to urban areas led to widespread homelessness and poverty during the 1800s. Citing concern for the plight of poor children, the *Society for the Prevention of Pauperism* began a movement to address the practice of children being jailed alongside adults in New York. Stemming from this humanitarian effort, New York opened its first House of Refuge in 1825 (Sanborn & Salerno, 2005). Other states soon followed New York's lead; 16 houses of refuge operated across the United States by 1860 (Ventrell, 1998). According to the New York State Education Department (n.d.), in 1857, the New York House of Refuge was heralded as the best reform school in the world.

Originally conceived as a place to protect children in need, the houses of refuge provided shelter for homeless and throwaway children and little else. With strict prison-type organization, the houses were not meant to provide therapeutic services. Delinquent and runaway children, as well as those who were neglected or incorrigible, were sent to the same institutions. Discipline was harsh, and the conditions were often met with rebellion. Many children who had been removed from their homes eventually returned to society as criminals. Critics soon charged that poverty and a cheap labor source were the reasons for removal of the children and their placement in the houses of refuge.

THE CHILD SAVER MOVEMENT   The Child Saver Movement in the United States was perhaps the most successful grassroots effort in America. The moral reformers of the day took up the cause of saving the children less fortunate due to poverty and poor parenting. This movement successfully instituted mandatory schooling and ushered in the state as an appropriate source of parenting for those unable or unwilling to manage unruly children (Platt, 1969). While some historians dispute the humanitarian aspect of this movement, its legacy became the juvenile justice system as we know it today (Ventrell, 1998). Legislation was passed in Illinois to establish jurisdiction for a special court to provide treatment and control of dependent and neglected children. It thereby authorized the creation of the first juvenile court in America; the Juvenile Court of Cook County opened in 1899.

Linda Gordon, historian and scholar, asserts that policy response to family violence emerged in the late 1870s with the "discovery" of family violence (Gordon, 1989). Social service agencies were confronted with problems of wife battering when their child welfare clients cited abuse as a significant issue. The incidence of violence was linked to alcohol abuse and poverty. Family violence was identified as a problem confined to the lower classes. The social service response to family violence was judgmental and prejudicial, with poverty determined as the common element of its clients. A lack of sufficient legal remedies existed for the family violence victim.

SOCIETIES FOR THE PREVENTION OF CRUELTY TO CHILDREN   The late 1870s witnessed a national movement to protect children who were abused or neglected. The child savers of the late nineteenth century established Societies for the Prevention of Cruelty to Children (SPCCs). Despite the fact that laws did exist in Colonial America for the protection of children from abuse, they were rarely enforced (Ventrell, 1998). Some jurisdictions protected children specifically from cruelty, and others gave deference to the right of parents to discipline unmanageable children. SPCCs grew out of early efforts to act on behalf of children who could not petition the court for help themselves. The first documented child abuse case occurred in 1871 when Henry Bergh, founder of the Society for Prevention of Cruelty to Animals, petitioned a New York court to protect eight-year-old Emily Thompson (Ventrell, 1998). According to the research of Lazoritz and Shelman, Bergh was approached by a concerned neighbor who had witnessed the frequent beatings of the child from her window (Lazoritz & Shelman, 1996). Judge Barnard took jurisdiction and found the nonbiological caretaker, Mary Ann Larkin, guilty of abuse. In 1874, Bergh intervened in the famous case of Mary Ellen, but not under the guise of animal cruelty, as is often cited (Ventrell, 1998). Henry Bergh acted as an individual petitioning the court using the Society's attorney under laws that existed at that time. Mary Ellen was removed from her abusive home and placed in foster care. Intervention on behalf of a child in need of services was formally established due to the efforts of Henry Bergh.

According to Linda Gordon (1989), the SPCC workers acted as quasi–law-enforcement officers: They conducted investigations, home searches and seizures, and threatened families with arrest for noncompliance with their directives. To further their stated mission of enforcement of existing laws against child abuse, they conscripted police officers to make arrests and to act as supervisors in their cases. The SPCCs of both New York and Boston acknowledged that sufficient laws existed at the time to protect children, yet no one had been held responsible for his or her enforcement.

Due to the increased professionalism of social workers along with police reluctance toward enforcement, the problems of child abuse were largely left with the social service agencies after 1920. Police officers did not perceive child abuse enforcement as part of their role, or else they were simply too busy with other duties to enforce child abuse statutes. The Social Security Act of 1935 somewhat improved intervention on behalf of children in need, because it mandated child welfare services for neglected or dependent children. Today, legal intervention has improved through specialized child abuse investigation units within police departments.

Child Abuse and Neglect Today

Until recently, few considered the treatment of children to be a matter of public concern. Awareness came with the coining of the phrase "battered child syndrome" in 1962 by C. Henry Kempe. Battered child syndrome refers to the repeated mistreatment or beating of a child which results in physical and psychological injuries. Although we do not know the exact numbers of children abused or neglected, private- and government-sponsored research has given us some insight into the extent of the problem. By 1967, every state and the District of Columbia had enacted laws for referring suspected cases of child abuse or neglect to a public agency.

Child Protective Services (CPS) refers to agencies that are authorized by law to act on behalf of a child when the parents are unable or unwilling to do so. In all states, these agencies are required to investigate reports of child abuse and neglect and to offer

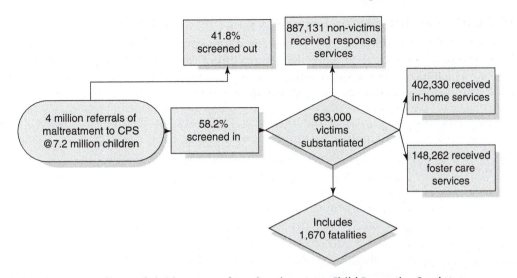

FIGURE 4-1 Millions of children are referred each year to Child Protective Services as alleged victims of abuse and neglect. Services are provided to an estimated 683,000 victims and more than 887,131 non-victims. Based on data from U.S. Department of Health and Human Services (DHHS, 2017).

services to families when maltreatment has occurred. The mandate may or may not include family preservation. All states have laws that require individual professionals such as teachers, police officers, and day care workers to report to CPS when abuse is suspected. According to the Department of Health and Human Services, these mandatory reporters make up over 60 percent of the reports of child maltreatment submitted to CPS. Over 4 million referrals of child maltreatment were received by CPS across the United States during 2015 (DHHS, 2017). More than half of the suspected abuse or neglect cases were investigated by CPS. See Figure 4-1 for an illustration of the services that were provided for the victims of abuse and neglect. Non-victims may receive referrals to other helping agencies when appropriate.

Infanticide is still a problem in contemporary society. In fact, child fatalities rose almost 6 percent between 2011 and 2015 (Children's Bureau, 2017). To address growing concerns about infant abandonment and infanticide, safe haven statutes have been passed in all 50 states and Puerto Rico (Child Welfare Information Gateway, 2017). **Safe haven laws** are also known in some states as "Baby Moses laws"; the statutes decriminalize the leaving of infants in a designated safe place so that the child becomes a ward of the state. In most states, either parent may relinquish the infant to a safe haven, while in others it is specifically required that the individual be the mother. The age that an infant can be relinquished varies according to state law; most allow the child to be left at 72 hours old to 3 months old. Most states guarantee anonymity or confidentiality to any person relinquishing an infant, unless there is evidence of child abuse or neglect.

The U.S. Department of Health and Human Services (DHHS, 2017) reports that a referral of abuse or neglect that is made to the CPS may be either screened in or screened out. The reasons behind the determination to screen out a referral may include one or more of the following:

- It did not meet the state's intake standard.
- It did not cause concern of child abuse and neglect.

- It did not contain enough information for a CPS response to occur.
- Response by another agency was deemed more appropriate.
- Children in the referral were the responsibility of another agency or jurisdiction (e.g., military installation or tribe).
- Children in the referral were older than 18 years.

An investigation is typically the response to a referral that is screened in. As the result of an investigation, a child found to have been the victim of abuse or neglect results in the case being *substantiated*. From the substantiated cases, an estimated 683,000 children were found to be victims in the United States in 2015 (DHHS, 2017).

Approximately 75 percent of child abuse victims experienced neglect, 2 percent were medically neglected, over 17 percent were physically abused, 6 percent were psychologically abused, and 8 percent were sexually abused during 2015 (DHHS, 2017). See Figure 4-2 for an illustration. Also, victims experienced such other types of maltreatment as abandonment, threats of harm to the child, and congenital drug addiction. States may code any condition that does not fall into one of the primary categories—physical abuse, neglect, medical neglect, sexual abuse, and psychological or emotional maltreatment—as "other."

It is not unusual for a victim to experience more than one form of abuse at the same time. A child who is physically or sexually abused will frequently have been subjected to emotional or psychological maltreatment and neglect. A legitimate criticism about the frequency of child abuse is that some states report more than one type of maltreatment as separate cases of abuse, which makes it difficult to determine exactly how many children are abused. These criticisms have brought attention to state reporting methods and point to the need for clear and standardized procedures. In response to the reporting criticisms, the National Incident-Based Reporting System (NIBRS) has been developed. A discussion of NIBRS is found in Chapter 3.

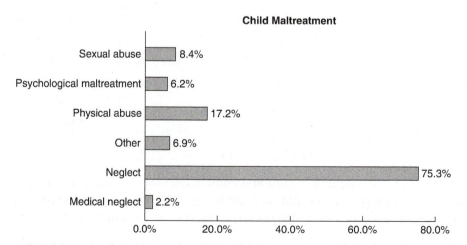

FIGURE 4-2   Neglect is overwhelmingly the most frequent type of child maltreatment. Based on data from U.S. Department of Health and Human Services (DHHS, 2017).

Back Then ...

C. Henry Kempe and colleagues raised consciousness about child abuse through their first presentation about the battered child syndrome in 1962. They were largely responsible for the shift in public attitude about child abuse and ultimately in the legal responses to it. Their contributions to our understanding of the complexities of child victimization continued through the publication of *The Battered Child* (Helfer & Kempe, 1987), which is regarded as one of the most significant works leading to professional and public awareness of child abuse and neglect (Ventrell, 1998). A major symposium on child abuse was held in response to *The Battered Child*, resulting in a recommendation for a model child abuse reporting law.

SOURCES FOR DEFINITIONS OF CHILD ABUSE

Federal law provides minimum definitional standards for child abuse and neglect. Each state is responsible for establishing its definition of maltreatment within both civil and criminal contexts. The Centers for Disease Control and Prevention suggests that consistent definitions are important to determine the incidence and trends of child maltreatment, which includes both child abuse and neglect (Leeb, Paulozzi, Melanson, Simon, & Arias, 2008). Child abuse is an **act of commission**: deliberate and intentional words or overt actions that cause harm or threat of harm to a child, regardless of the intended consequence. Child neglect is an **act of omission**: the failure to provide for a child's basic physical, emotional, or educational needs or to protect the child from harm or potential harm, regardless of the intended consequence.

Federal Sources

The CAPTA, first enacted in 1974 as Public Law 93-247, is the key federal legislation addressing child abuse and neglect (Child Welfare Information Gateway, 2016). Amended several times since then, it was most recently amended by the CAPTA Reauthorization Act of 2010 (P.L. 111-320). CAPTA provides federal funding to states in support of child abuse prevention, assessment, investigation, prosecution, and treatment activities and also provides grants to public agencies and nonprofit organizations for demonstrations and projects. The act requires states to assign an agency to receive and investigate reports of alleged child abuse and neglect. Social service agencies are most frequently designated to receive these reports; a few jurisdictions designate a police agency instead. Some state laws have expanded their reporting systems with a reciprocal reporting to a designated criminal justice agency.

Federal law specifies the minimum criteria of child abuse and neglect by identifying a set of behaviors that define abuse and neglect, although each state has its own definition. CAPTA establishes a minimum definition for child abuse, neglect, and sexual abuse, which states must incorporate into their statutory definitions to receive federal funds. Under CAPTA, **child abuse and neglect** means

- any recent act or failure to act on the part of a parent or caretaker that results in death, serious physical or emotional harm, sexual abuse, or exploitation;
- an act or failure to act that presents an imminent risk of serious harm.

The definition of child abuse and neglect refers specifically to parents and other caregivers. Statistics on crimes against children that are perpetrated by a stranger are not included in reports of child abuse and neglect or sexual abuse.

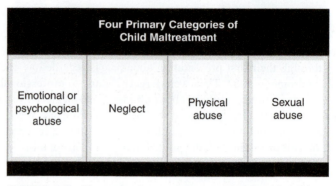

FIGURE 4-3 There are four primary categories of child maltreatment, although many subcategories exist in definitions of child abuse and neglect.

State Definitions

The policies for the protection of children from maltreatment are subject to state laws (both statutes and case law) and administrative regulations. Experts agree that although there are many subcategories of child abuse, most states recognize four primary categories. These categories are represented in Figure 4-3. Definitions of child abuse and neglect are located primarily within the following:

> mandatory reporting statutes (civil laws) that provide definitions of child maltreatment to guide the individual mandated to report suspected child abuse; criminal statutes that define the forms of child abuse and neglect that are criminally punishable; and

> juvenile court jurisdiction statutes that provide definitions of the circumstances necessary for the court to have jurisdiction over a child alleged to have been abused or neglected.

MAJOR SOURCES OF CHILD ABUSE DATA

CAPTA created the *National Center for Missing & Exploited Children* (NCMEC). Pursuant to 42 U.S.C. Sections 5771 and 5780, this nonprofit organization was established in 1984. It provides technical information on missing and exploited children, offers training programs to law enforcement professionals and social service professionals, distributes photographs and descriptions of missing children nationwide, and coordinates child protection efforts with the private sector. NCMEC also maintains a 24-hour toll-free telephone line for those who have information on missing and exploited children.

The *National Incidence Study of Child Abuse and Neglect* (*NIS*) represents a major source of information on child abuse and neglect in the United States. *NIS* conducts research every decade as a congressional mandate of the U.S. Department of Health and Human Services to periodically study and record the incidence of child abuse and neglect in America (Sedlak et al., 2010). *NIS-4*, along with its predecessor studies, provides different information than other studies because it uses more definitions than are found in CAPTA. The research includes situations in which a caregiver's behavior (either purposive acts or extreme inattention to the child's needs) caused (or clearly had the potential to cause) foreseeable and avoidable injury or impairment to the child or a worsening of an existing injury or impairment. Any of the following occurrences during the study period would meet these general definitions of abuse and neglect (Sedlak et al., 2010):

- Physical assault (including excessive corporal punishment).
- Sexual abuse or exploitation such as forcible or consensual rape, incest, intercourse, sexual molestation with or without genital contact, promoting of prostitution.
- Close confinement such as tying or binding of arms or legs, locking in a closet, or similar severe confinement.
- Any other pattern of assaultive, exploitative, or abusive treatment, such as threatened or attempted physical or sexual assault, threatened abandonment or suicide, habitual or extreme verbal abuse, or other overtly hostile, rejecting, or punitive treatment.
- Abandonment or other refusal to maintain custody, such as desertion, expulsion from home, and refusal to accept custody of a returned runaway.
- Permitting or encouraging chronic maladaptive behavior, such as truancy, delinquency, prostitution, and serious drug/alcohol abuse. "Permitted" means that the child's caregiver had reasons to be aware of the existence and seriousness of the problem (e.g., by having been informed of previous incidents), but made no reasonable attempt to prevent further occurrences.
- Refusal to allow needed treatment for a professionally diagnosed physical, educational, emotional, or behavioral problem, or failure to follow the advice of a competent professional who recommended that the caregiver obtain or provide the child with such treatment, if the child's primary caregiver was physically and financially able to do so.
- Failure to seek or unwarranted delay in seeking competent medical care for a serious injury, illness, or impairment, if the need for professional care should have been apparent to a responsible caregiver without special medical training.
- Consistent or extreme inattention to the child's physical or emotional needs, including needs for food, clothing, supervision, safety, affection, and reasonably hygienic living conditions, if the child's primary caregiver was physically and financially able to provide the needed care.
- Failure to register or enroll the child in school, as required by state law.

The *NIS* uses two definitional standards for its research on child abuse and neglect: the harm standard and the endangerment standard. The **harm standard** requires that an act of omission results in demonstrable harm in order to be classified as abuse or neglect. Its principal disadvantage is that it is so stringent that it provides a perspective that is too narrow for many purposes; it excludes even many children whom CPS substantiates or indicates as abused or neglected. Under the more stringent harm standard, one child in every 58 were found to have been abused or neglected in the United States during the *NIS-4* period (Sedlak et al., 2010). Most of the abused children experienced physical abuse (58 percent); slightly less than one-fourth were sexually abused, whereas slightly more than one-fourth were emotionally abused.

The **endangerment standard** includes all children who meet the harm standard but adds others as well. The main feature of the endangerment standard is that it counts children who are not yet harmed by abuse or neglect if a CPS investigation has substantiated their maltreatment. The endangerment standard is slightly more lenient

Been There ... Done That!

A college student once said that she could tell whether a child was abused by just looking at him or her. Having interviewed over 1,000 children who were victims and countless others who were not, I assure you that you cannot tell simply by outward appearances! Disheveled or unkempt appearances are not necessarily the signs of abuse. Not all children respond to abuse by becoming surly or openly angry; some children react to abuse by adapting—they learn how to please others and they appear overly willing to do so.

When indicators are present, they should serve as the catalyst for investigation, not as confirmation in the determination of abuse. Trained investigators, along with a team of professionals, should be consulted for abuse to be substantiated. The information presented in this text provides general guidelines to conduct child abuse investigations, which may vary between organizations and among the states. Thoroughly consider all relevant information, without bias, regarding a suspicion of abuse. The determination of abuse should not include a subjective opinion regarding the mother or father, maritial status of the parents, or indications of poverty. For example, one cannot tell whether the child in Figure 4-4 is the victim of abuse or the victim of an accident. Do not make assumptions or jump to conclusions without an investigation into the source of injury.

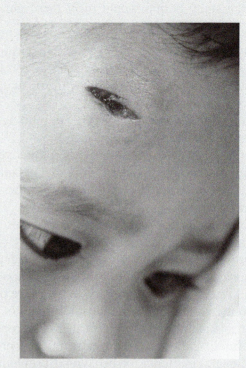

FIGURE 4-4 Victims of child abuse and neglect cannot be identified by simply viewing the child. A thorough investigation is always warranted. Manzrussali/Shutterstock.

than the harm standard in allowing a broader array of perpetrators, including adult caretakers other than parents in certain maltreatment categories and teenage caretakers as perpetrators of sexual abuse. Classifying maltreatment according to the more inclusive endangerment standard provides a very different picture of the incidence and distribution of child abuse and neglect. Nearly 3 million children experienced endangerment standard maltreatment during the *NIS-4* study year (Sedlak et al., 2010). This corresponds to one child in every 25 in the United States.

The Administration on Children, Youth and Families is the governing office of the *National Child Abuse and Neglect Data System* (NCANDS) of the Children's Bureau. National and state statistics about child maltreatment come from the data collected by child protective services agencies and reported to NCANDS. Its annual report, *Child Maltreatment*, is a valuable resource for policy makers, child welfare practitioners, researchers, students, and other concerned citizens.

The *Child Welfare Information Gateway* is a respected source of information on forensic interviewing, human trafficking, and child welfare. A service of the U.S. Department of Health and Human Services, it maintains a library database on publications and project evaluations, providing access to thousands of articles on child welfare. Also, the site includes a searchable database on statues pertaining to child protection laws for all States and territories. Resources to promote child protection, strengthen families, and support adoption are available.

The Office of Juvenile Justice and Delinquency Prevention (OJJDP) was established in 1974 under the *Juvenile Justice and Delinquency Prevention Act.* Its mission is to provide leadership and resources to prevent and respond nationally to juvenile delinquency and victimization. Countless studies and reports confronting commercial sexual exploitation and trafficking of minors to delinquency prevention are part of the OJJDP initiatives, which can be accessed on their Web site.

The *National Criminal Justice Reference Service* (NCJRS) is a federally funded online library and database that includes victim-related information in addition to juvenile justice issues. Its database contains summaries of more than 220,000 publications. Its homepage also provides links to other resources for information on topics such as sex offender registration and technology information.

The Kids Count data center, a project of the Annie E. Casey Foundation, produces a comprehensive report called the *KIDS COUNT Data Book* that assesses child well-being in the United States. Through a searchable Web site, demographic and other indicators are available on the child population for each state. Comprehensive information on child abuse and neglect is available under the topic heading of Risky Behaviors.

EMOTIONAL/PSYCHOLOGICAL ABUSE

All states and territories include emotional maltreatment as part of their definitions of abuse or neglect. It is often defined as injury to the psychological capacity or emotional stability of the child as evidenced by an observable or substantial change in behavior, emotional response, or cognition or as evidenced by anxiety, depression, withdrawal, or aggressive behavior (Child Welfare Information Gateway, 2016). Emotional or psychological abuse involves a pattern of behavior that impairs a child's emotional development and sense of well-being. More than 6 percent of substantiated child abuse cases involve emotional abuse or psychological maltreatment (DHHS, 2017). Emotional abuse occurs when a caretaker or family member belittles or ridicules a child frequently.

Emotional or psychological abuse is considered reprehensible behavior that may indicate the need for social service or therapeutic intervention, but it may not constitute criminal behavior by itself. This type of maltreatment often accompanies other forms of abuse to children and should serve as a red flag to investigators. An investigation of any form of abuse should include documentation of the emotional and psychological maltreatment in addition to other forms to show the atmosphere of abuse under which the child resides, even when the abuse does not rise to the level of criminal conduct. Emotional or psychological abuse may be considered as a factor in custody hearings when the fate of a child is dependent on the family living situation.

In its most extreme form, emotional abuse is considered criminal activity. When a caretaker or family member uses restrictive methods to place a child in confinement, such as in a room, closet, or trunk, the victim may suffer emotional abuse as a result of the action. Emotional or psychological abuse may also occur as the result of information stated on the Internet or social networks sites such as Facebook or Twitter.

Witnessing Family Violence

Witnessing family violence is a form of emotional or psychological abuse. The witnessing of domestic violence can be auditory, visual, or inferred, including cases in which the child perceives the aftermath of violence, such as physical injuries to family members or damage to property. Legal definitions of witnessing family or intimate partner violence vary somewhat from state to state. For example, in 14 states and Puerto Rico, legal language requires that the child be physically present or can see or hear the act of violence (Child Welfare Information Gateway, 2013). In contrast, Ohio law defines witnessing when intimate partner violence occurs in the vicinity of the child, within 30 feet, or within the same residential unit occupied by the child, regardless of whether the child is present in the room or can see the violent act.

Children are exposed to extremely high rates of violence in the home. More than one in nine witnessed some form of family violence in the previous year; of this number, one in 15 specifically witnessed violence between their parents (Hamby, Finkelhor, Turner, & Ormrod, 2011). Children who witness intimate partner violence are at greater risk for a numerous behavioral, social, and educational problems. These children are at increased risk for physical abuse, sibling abuse, and dating violence (Relva, Fernandes, & Mota, 2013). Children who are exposed to intimate partner violence may also be at an increased risk of being murdered (Sillito & Salari, 2011).

In one study, more than a third of adult intimate partner violence survivors reported that their children were accidentally injured during an incident, and over a quarter reported that their children were intentionally injured when the child intervened to stop abuse of others (Mbilinyi, Edleson, Hagemeister, & Beeman, 2007). Experts agree that there is a need to protect child victims who witness family violence. These victims experience multiple psychological problems and exhibit below average social and cognitive development. The effects on children who witness intimate partner violence may be more devastating than direct victimization.

Despite the evidence of harm, family violence perpetrated in the presence of a child is typically a misdemeanor offense. In 2002, the passage of U.C.A. Section 76-5-109.1 in Utah made it the first state to legislate the act of domestic violence in the presence of a child as a felony. In many states, a conviction for family violence that was committed in the presence of a child may result in harsher penalties. Approximately eight states consider an act of domestic violence committed in the presence of a child to be an "aggravating circumstance" in their sentencing guidelines. This usually results in a longer jail term, an increased fine, or both (Child Welfare Information Gateway, 2013). An additional five states provide for enhanced penalties without even using the terminology "of aggravating circumstance."

NEGLECT

The concept of neglect is based on a parental duty to provide the basic necessities for one's children because they are unable to provide for themselves. The most basic needs include food and adequate shelter. Parents are expected to seek medical attention and provide educational opportunities for their children. Caretakers are responsible for providing the appropriate supervision and nurturing to the children in their care. The failure to provide these necessities within socially acceptable standards may be considered neglectful.

According to Child Welfare Information Gateway (2016), neglect is frequently defined as the failure of a parent or other person with responsibility for the child to provide needed food, clothing, shelter, medical care, or supervision to the degree that the child's health, safety, and well-being are threatened with harm. This form of abuse carries with it a resulting harm due to the action or inaction of the caregiver.

Neglect is the most common form of abuse against children. Almost 78 percent of maltreated children were neglected by their parents or other caregivers in 2015 (DHHS, 2017). Neglect is often present when other forms of abuse occur against a child. In some states, neglect of a child would constitute a separate report to the designated child protective agency. However, neglect might not be substantiated as abuse if it were considered to be minor.

Parents have a duty to care for their children, and the law holds parents accountable for this responsibility. Children have been afforded legal protections to assure that the parent is providing the necessities of life and promoting well-being. As early as 1838, the U.S. Supreme Court ruled in *Ex Parte Crouse* that the right of the parent is not inalienable (Ex Parte Crouse, 1838). The government has the responsibility to take appropriate measures and set standards for child care to which parents are held accountable. Children may be removed from the care of the parents if the state determines that the caretaker failed to care for and protect the child. It should be noted that the extent to which children must be protected and the expanse of child rights have always been controversial in social and legal forums.

Child neglect might be a charge against a caretaker or parent for several acts or failure to act. There are six subcategories of neglect recognized in many states: abandonment, educational, emotional/psychological, medical, physical, and substance abuse. Signs of neglect include, but are not limited to, dehydration, malnutrition, untreated bedsores, untreated health problems or conditions, unsanitary living conditions, a failure to thrive, abandonment, and death. Inadequate parenting can include many different acts or omissions that might be considered neglectful.

Abandonment

A child is considered abandoned when the parent's identity or whereabouts are unknown, the child has been left alone in circumstances where he or she suffers serious harm, or the parent has failed to maintain contact with the child or provide reasonable support for a period of time. Many states and territories require professionals to report situations of child abandonment, the failure to protect a child, or the failure to provide the basics of food, clothing, and shelter. Guam, Puerto Rico, the Virgin Islands, and 19 states provide separate definitions for establishing abandonment (Child Welfare Information Gateway, 2016). Typically, abandonment is included in legal definitions as a type of neglect. The safe haven laws, described earlier in this chapter, provide the legal option for a parent(s) to relinquish the care and legal responsibility for newborns rather than abandonment.

Educational Neglect

Approximately 25 states, the District of Columbia, American Samoa, Puerto Rico, and the Virgin Islands include failure to educate the child as required by law in their definition of neglect (Child Welfare Information Gateway, 2016). At the most basic level, the education of a child includes providing behavioral limits that are age appropriate.

Been There ... Done That!

Although I was not a narcotics investigator, there were times when that unit would ask for assistance in executing warrants. I remember such a case where we "hit" an apartment with a search warrant for drugs. As I came through the door, I could not help but notice a child of about six years old sitting at the breakfast table. He would put his fingers into the bowl and pull out a cockroach, and then take a spoon full of cereal. He repeated this until he had finished eating, literally "flicking" the cockroaches across the room each time. As I searched his bedroom, the contents of each dresser drawer would appear to "move" in unison when opened to the light. When I lifted his mattress to look at that space between the mattress and box spring, thousands of cockroaches scurried to the same beat. Was this child neglect? I spoke with a social worker who reminded me that the apartment was one of approximately 150 on the block and that cockroaches are a hazard of the poverty in that neighborhood. What do you think?

All states have mandatory formal educational requirements that a child must attend school until age 16. Educational neglect includes allowing chronic truancy, failure to enroll a child of mandatory school age in school, and failure to attend to a special educational need of the child.

Emotional/Psychological Neglect

Emotional or psychological neglect includes the lack of any emotional support and love, chronic inattention to the child, or exposure to drug and alcohol abuse. It also includes the absence of supportive language such as praise or expressions of concern. Categories of emotional or psychological neglect may also include the exposure to chronic or extreme intimate partner violence and the failure to seek treatment for a child's emotional impairment, such as a suicide attempt.

Medical Neglect

Parents have the duty to seek necessary medical care for their children. Withholding of medically necessary treatment has been defined by the CAPTA as the failure to respond to a child's life-threatening condition by denial of treatment that would probably be effective in ameliorating all life-threatening conditions. Ten states additionally include a denial of mental health care as medical neglect (Child Welfare Information Gateway, 2016). Four states define medical neglect specifically to protect infants with disabilities that have life-threatening conditions to include the withholding of medical treatment or nutrition (Child Welfare Information Gateway, 2016).

An exemption from medical neglect is permitted in some states if the withholding of medical care is based on religious grounds. The CAPTA amendments of 2010 maintain provisions specifying that nothing in the act could be construed as establishing a federal requirement that a parent or legal guardian provide any medical service or treatment that is against the religious beliefs of the parent or legal guardian. Each state determines whether it will recognize this federal standard expressed by the U.S. Department of Health and Human Services. At the state level, 31 states, the District of Columbia, American Samoa, Puerto Rico, and Guam provide for a religious exemption (Child Welfare Information Gateway, 2016). However, 16 states require the court to order medical treatment for the child should the child's condition warrant intervention.

Physical Neglect

Physical neglect involves the failure to provide adequate food, clothing, shelter, hygiene, protection, or supervision. Supervision is necessary to prevent harm or to intervene when harm is occurring. Leaving a young child unattended or locking the child in a room are examples of inadequate supervision if the age and maturity of the child is insufficient to respond to problems that might occur. Young children have been known to play with matches and lighters while locked in a room, which has led to a fire and ultimate death. Parents must be sure that children who are left alone—such as latchkey kids—are reasonably able to care for themselves in case harm arises. Leaving a child in a car during extreme hot or cold weather may be considered physical neglect.

Substance Abuse

Parental substance abuse is an element of the definition of child abuse or neglect in some states (Child Welfare Information Gateway, 2016). Prenatal exposure of a child to harm due to the mother's use of an illegal drug or other substance; manufacture of a controlled substance in the presence of a child, or on the premises occupied by a child; and selling, distributing, or giving drugs or alcohol to a child are among the circumstances that might be considered abuse or neglect. An additional recognized category of physical neglect is the reckless disregard of the child's safety such as driving while intoxicated by alcohol or drugs and having a child in the car.

PHYSICAL ABUSE

Physical abuse refers to any nonaccidental physical injury to the child; this may include striking, stabbing, kicking, burning, or biting the child, or any action that results in a physical impairment or the death of the child, such as shaking or throwing. In approximately 38 states and American Samoa, Guam, the Northern Mariana Islands, Puerto Rico, and the Virgin Islands, the definition of abuse also includes acts or circumstances that threaten the child with harm or create a substantial risk of harm to the child's health or welfare (Child Welfare Information Gateway, 2016). Human trafficking, involuntary servitude, and trafficking of minors are included in the definition of child abuse in seven states.

Experts warn that some marks and bruises seen on children mimic child abuse, but may be cultural practices of the family. Cultural practices include patterns of behavior that include the actions, customs, beliefs, and values that are specific to racial, ethnic, religious, or social groups. A few examples that may result in physically hurting or leaving marks on the child, but are not defined as physical abuse include (Botash, 2013):

- *Coining*—This is a practice for treating illness by rubbing the body forcefully with a coin or other hard object.
- *Cupping*—Cupping is often used on acupuncture points in a manner similar to moxibustion. A cup in which the air in the cup has been preheated is applied to the skin, developing a vacuum. When the cup is removed, a suction mark in the shape of the cup remains.
- *Moxibustion*—This is an Asian folkloric remedy that burns the skin.

Physical disciplining of a child, such as spanking or paddling, is not considered abuse as long as it is reasonable and causes no bodily injury to the child. Severe discipline, including injurious spanking or punishment that is inappropriate to the child's age or condition, provides examples where criminal harm may occur. Specifically stated in the law of 17 states, the District of Columbia, American Samoa, and the Northern Mariana Islands, physical disciplining of a child that is reasonable and causes no bodily injury to the child is an exception to the definition of abuse (Child Welfare Information Gateway, 2016). Harm resulting from punishment, even if the harm was not intended, is abusive.

Child Fatalities

Child fatality is the death of a child by means other than natural causes as the result of a direct or an indirect injury or a condition of abuse or neglect. An estimated 1,670 children die every year in the United States from abuse or neglect, typically at the hands of one or both parents (DHHS, 2017). Caretaker risk factors associated with child deaths include domestic violence, and alcohol or drug abuse. Children under the age of one year are at the highest risk of death due to abuse and neglect. In fact, an infant is three times more likely to die from maltreatment than a one-year-old. Almost 75 percent of deaths due to abuse and neglect occur before age three. Boys are more frequently victimized than girls. African American children have the highest rate of child fatalities when population information data is considered. See Figure 4-5 for a comparison of child fatalities in 2015 by race and ethnicity.

A relatively small portion of the unnatural deaths of children results from intimate partner homicide-suicide (IPHS). From a study of 325 cases of IPHS, it was determined that children are often fatally wounded in IPHS (Sillito & Salari, 2011). At highest risk are children of suicidal parents, typically their biological father. The authors contend that while the children of IPHS die from child abuse, they are not necessarily counted as such.

Many researchers and practitioners believe that child abuse fatalities due to abuse and neglect are still underreported. Studies have estimated that 50 to 60 percent of child deaths resulting from abuse and neglect are not recorded as such (Child Welfare

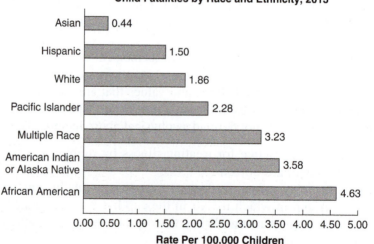

Child Fatalities by Race and Ethnicity, 2015

Race/Ethnicity	Rate Per 100,000 Children
Asian	0.44
Hispanic	1.50
White	1.86
Pacific Islander	2.28
Multiple Race	3.23
American Indian or Alaska Native	3.58
African American	4.63

FIGURE 4-5 The highest rates of child fatalities due to abuse and neglect are among the African American and Native American populations. Based on data from U.S. Department of Health and Human Services (DHHS, 2017).

Information Gateway, 2016). The issues affecting accuracy and consistency of child fatality data include the following:

- Variation in reporting requirements and in definitions of child abuse and neglect.
- Differences in death investigative systems and training.
- Lack of consistency in state child fatality review processes.
- The amount of time (as long as a year in some cases) it may take to establish abuse or neglect as the cause of death.
- Inaccurate determination of the manner and cause of death; this includes deaths labeled as accidents, sudden infant death syndrome (SIDS), or "manner undetermined" that may have been attributed to abuse or neglect if more comprehensive investigations were conducted.

Researchers also suggest that missing the link between neglect and child death is one cause of the undercounting, which may account for as much as one-half of maltreatment deaths (Brandon, Bailey, Belderson, & Larsson, 2014; Palusci & Covington, 2014). The use of child fatality review teams appears to be among the most promising current approaches to accurately count, respond to, and prevent child abuse and neglect fatalities, as well as other preventable deaths. Most states have a central office of specially trained physicians for consultation in cases of child death or to conduct an autopsy if it is warranted.

SEXUAL ABUSE

All states include sexual abuse in their definitions of child abuse. Some states refer in general terms to sexual abuse whereas others specify various acts. Sexual exploitation is an element of the definition in most jurisdictions. The CAPTA definition of child sexual abuse includes the following:

- The employment, use, persuasion, inducement, enticement, or coercion of any child to engage in, or assist any other person to engage in, any sexually explicit conduct or simulation of such conduct to produce a visual depiction of such conduct.
- The rape, and in cases of caretaker or interfamilial relationships, statutory rape, molestation, prostitution, or sexual exploitation of children, or incest with children.

Sexual abuse of children was an area of great controversy in the recent past. Experts disagreed on the prevalence of child sexual abuse, yet it then became the fastest growing form of reported child abuse. Sexual abuse of children is an issue of power and control, not love and intimacy. Unfortunately, indications are that the average age of the sexually abused child has been on a downward trend since the 1970s. Approximately 8 percent of child abuse victims are believed to have been subjected to sexual abuse (DHHS, 2017).

Child sexual abuse refers to sexual acts, sexually motivated behaviors involving children, or sexual exploitation of children. Sexual abuse includes a wide range of behaviors, such as

- oral, anal, or genital penile penetration;
- anal or genital digital or other penetration;
- genital contact with no intrusion;

- fondling a child's breasts or buttocks;
- indecent exposure;
- inadequate or inappropriate supervision of a child's voluntary sexual activities;
- use of a child in prostitution, pornography, Internet crimes, or other sexually exploitative activities.

Noncontact sexual abuse includes acts, such as

- voyeurism of the child by an adult;
- intentional exposure of a child to exhibitionism;
- exposure to pornography;
- photograph(s) of a child in a sexual manner or act;
- filming of a child engaged in a sexual manner or act;
- sexual harassment of a child;
- sexual trafficking of a child;
- employing, using, persuading, inducing, enticing, encouraging, allowing, or permitting a child to engage in or assist any other person to engage in prostitution.

CHILD ABUSE VICTIMS

Children are victimized by abuse regardless of age, gender, race, or ethnicity. This does not mean that all children are victims, but that boys and girls of various ages and cultural backgrounds are represented as victims. A child is defined as a person under the age of 18, except in those states that specify a different age.

Age and Gender

Infants and young children are the most frequent victims of neglect. As children grow older, the rate of abuse and neglect declines. Children younger than age one have the highest rates of victimization, with girls slightly more likely to be victims than boys (DHHS, 2017). The rate of victimization is inversely related to the age group of the child; refer to Figure 4-6.

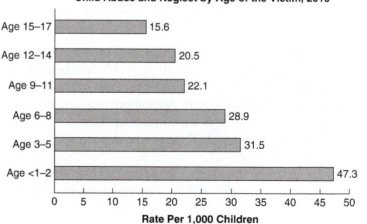

Child Abuse and Neglect by Age of the Victim, 2015

Age group	Rate Per 1,000 Children
Age 15–17	15.6
Age 12–14	20.5
Age 9–11	22.1
Age 6–8	28.9
Age 3–5	31.5
Age <1–2	47.3

FIGURE 4-6 The younger the child, the more likely he or she will be a victim of abuse and neglect. Based on data from U.S. Department of Health and Human Services (DHHS, 2017).

The percentages of child victims are similar for boys and girls. In 2015, over 48 percent of child victims were boys and 50 percent were girls (DHHS, 2017). However, the victimization rate for girls is higher at 9.6 per 1,000 girls in the population and 8.8 per 1,000 boys in the population. Official statistics reflect that girls are sexually abused more often than boys. Keep in mind that the statistics on abuse are based on cases that are reported to social service agencies; the true incidence of the sexual abuse of boys is believed to be equal to the victimization of girls.

Race and Ethnicity

According to the U.S. Department of Health and Human Services (DHHS, 2017), victimization rates vary by race and ethnicity. The majority of child abuse victims are white children (43.9 percent), followed by Hispanic (22.1 percent) and African American children (21.5 percent). These numbers do not reflect the impact of child abuse and victimization within the racial and ethnic community, since they are the percentage of the total number of victims. To develop policies that are culturally sensitive to the populations that are in need, it is helpful to look at the incidence of child abuse and neglect within the racial and ethnic group itself. When doing so, a very different picture of abuse and neglect emerges. For example, rates are highest per 100,000 children among the African American (14.5) and Native American or Alaska Native (13.8) communities. For an illustration of the rates of victimization for 2015, see Figure 4-7.

CHILD ABUSE PERPETRATORS

A perpetrator is the one who is responsible for the abuse or neglect of a child. Based on data from 51 states and 522,476 perpetrators, the Department of Health and Human Services (2017) determined that the majority of perpetrators are between the ages of 18 and 44 (83.4 percent). More than half of the offenders are women, with 45 percent men and a fraction of 1 percent are unknown. While more than half of the perpetrators maltreated one victim, it is not unusual for multiple victims to be maltreated by the same offender.

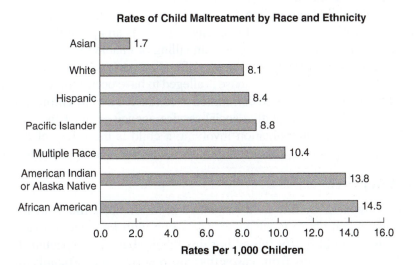

Rates of Child Maltreatment by Race and Ethnicity

Race/Ethnicity	Rate
Asian	1.7
White	8.1
Hispanic	8.4
Pacific Islander	8.8
Multiple Race	10.4
American Indian or Alaska Native	13.8
African American	14.5

Rates Per 1,000 Children

FIGURE 4-7 The highest rates of child abuse and neglect victimization are among the African American and Native American populations. Based on data from U.S. Department of Health and Human Services (DHHS, 2017).

CHILD ABUSE REPORTERS

The majority of suspected child abuse reports submitted to child protective agencies come from professionals who provide direct care or have contact with children. Examples include teachers, law enforcement officers, social services, medical and mental health personnel, child day care providers, and foster care parents. Submissions from family members, other relatives, neighbors and friends, and unrelated sources make up the remaining reports.

Mandated Reporters

Certain professionals must report cases of suspected child abuse to a designated authority within a specific time period after learning of the abuse. The individuals required by law to report suspected abuse are called **mandated reporters**. According to the Child Welfare Information Gateway, 48 states and the District of Columbia designate professions whose members are mandated by law to report child abuse and neglect (2016). These mandates differ slightly from state to state as to what agency must receive and investigate the report and the time required to accomplish the investigation.

The primary goal of agencies that investigate child abuse is to determine whether the child is in need of care and protection. The investigator must next assess the level of risk to the child in his or her present living arrangements. Protection options include the removal of the suspected offender from the home if he or she lives with the child. A parent or legal guardian of the victim should be encouraged to file for a no-contact restraining order to protect the child from further violence and threats during the investigation, whether or not the suspect resides with the child.

Though the federal government has mandated child abuse reporting within the states since 1974, it was not until the Victims of Child Abuse Act of 1990 that similar provisions were created for federal reporting laws. This act requires professionals to report on child abuse and neglect for cases arising under federal jurisdiction. Child abuse and neglect that involves any Native American as perpetrator or victim and occurs on Indian reservations must be reported to the Federal Bureau of Investigation (FBI) under the Indian Child Protection and Family Violence Prevention Act of 1996.

To prevent the child from feeling punished for having revealed abuse, removal of the child from his or her home to a safe living environment is an option that should be used only if a nonoffending parent or guardian is unwilling or unable to protect the child from the suspect. Social services to support the non-offending parent are provided according to the resources of the area in which the abuse is alleged to have occurred. An investigation to determine whether a crime has been committed is conducted by law enforcement officials and may be done either jointly with a social service agency or independently. Although the initial concern of any investigation involving a child is the safety of the child, law enforcement and social services have different mandates for investigative procedures.

Who Must Report?

Any person designated by law as a mandated reporter must file with the appropriate state agency when abuse is suspected. Any one with knowledge that child abuse may be occuring should notify the authorities when abuse is suspected. Data on the extent of child abuse comes from cases that are reported and officially investigated. Compliance with the requirements of child abuse reporting is difficult to determine and underreporting is suspected. States sometimes attach a civil or criminal penalty for the failure to report suspected abuse when it was known to a mandated reporter.

Professionals make the majority of reports of alleged child abuse and neglect. The term "professional" means that the person had contact with the alleged child maltreatment victim as part of his or her job. Typical mandated reporters include physicians, child caregivers, police officers, and teachers. Some state laws include as mandated reporters any person who has contact with children due to employment. Examples of additional individuals that may be mandated to report suspected child abuse and neglect include

- Members of the clergy
- Social workers
- School principals, guidance counselors, and other school personnel
- Nurses and other health care workers
- Counselors, therapists, and other mental health professionals
- School bus drivers
- Commercial film or photograph processors
- Probation or parole officers
- Directors, employees, and volunteers at entities that provide organized activities for children, such as camps, day camps, youth centers, and recreation centers
- Domestic violence workers

CHILD VICTIMS AND CRIMINAL LAW

State criminal codes and statutes treat children differently from adults. Crimes committed against children are specifically stated offenses, such as neglect and rape without force. The majority of states have extended the statute of limitations for child sexual abuse and other crimes against children. The statute of limitations refers to the time that is allowed by law in which a case may be prosecuted after the illegal act occurs. Limitations vary widely from state to state and among crimes. A few states have no time limitation for the prosecution of sexual offenses against children. In all states, there is no statute of limitations for the prosecution of murder.

Under the CAPTA, as amended in 2010, children are allowed to submit victim impact statements. Hand-drawn pictures and letters from child victims may be allowed in some states. Special courtroom procedures are allowed in many states. The provisions are sensitive to the needs of children in the court process and do not require special statutes in order to be implemented. Examples of criminal justice provisions that are specific to child victims and witnesses include the following:

1. Allowing the judge to close the courtroom during a child victim's testimony. The purpose of these statutes is to reduce a child's fear of testifying and to protect the child from the embarrassment of talking about his or her victimization. News reporters and others not directly associated with the case would be excluded from the courtroom.
2. Allowing leading questions to be asked of child witnesses. Trial courts have the inherent authority to allow leading questions of witnesses on direct examination. Challenges to the practice of leading witnesses can occur during trial. A few state statutes grant specific entitlement for the prosecution to ask leading questions when the victim is a child.
3. Allowing the use of anatomical dolls in child abuse trials. A few states have specified that courts may allow the use of anatomically correct dolls to aid a child's testimony.
4. Allowing the use of closed-circuit television to avoid the trauma of a child victim having to testify in front of the defendant.

There are two different systems of closed-circuit television (CCTV) used by courts in child abuse cases. The one-way CCTV allows the people in the courtroom to see the witness, but the witness cannot see any of the people in the courtroom, including the defendant. Another method is the two-way CCTV. Under a two-way system, those in the courtroom can see the witness, and the witness can see those in the courtroom. In *Maryland v. Craig* (1990), the court determined that the statute permitting child victims to testify by one-way CCTV was constitutionally permissible. Under federal law (18 U.S.C. Section 3509[b]), two-way CCTV testimony of a child victim may be allowed at the request of the child's attorney or a *guardian ad litem* (GAL). Under certain circumstances, a videotaped deposition of a child may be taken in lieu of courtroom testimony (18 U.S.C. Section 3509[b][2]).

The use of testimony other than by direct confrontation has caused considerable legal controversy. The Supreme Court's decision in *Crawford v. Washington* (2004) barred the use of "testimonial hearsay" in criminal prosecutions. Statements made by the child to a health worker or social worker during treatment may still be admissible in lieu of child testimony (Warnken, 2008). Generally, videotaped interviews by forensic teams have been found to be testimonial under the *Crawford* standard. The quandary left by *Crawford* was in the Court's failure to define the term "testimonial."

Should the perpetrator of child abuse and neglect be arrested and prosecuted criminally? The decision to arrest is made on a case-by-case basis by the investigating authority. The decision to prosecute is complicated. The district attorney makes the final decision regarding prosecution based on the following factors:

- Age of the child
- Seriousness of the offense
- Reluctance to testify
- Evidence
- Probability of successful prosecution
- Age of the perpetrator

DOMESTIC VIOLENCE AND CHILD CUSTODY

All states consider domestic violence as a factor when determining custody of children during a separation or divorce of the parents. In all cases, the safety and well-being of the child is of primary concern to the court. Reflecting the movement to advocate for children's rights over parental rights, the trend is moving in the direction of denying custody and unsupervised visitation to intimate partner offenders and child abusers. Whether the abuser has participated in intervention programs may also be a factor in determining child custody and visitation. The National Council of Juvenile and Family Court Judges recommends that zero tolerance for domestic violence be a consistent policy with supervised child visits for an abuser that has not acknowledged responsibility for past harm or if the violence continues (NCJFCJ, 2011).

The court may order an investigation when allegations of abuse surface during custody hearings. Child witnesses and expert testimony, considerations of the fitness of a parent who abuses his or her partner, and the impact of family violence on the victim's capacity to parent add to the complexity of these hearings. In many states, the court will appoint a GAL or an attorney to speak for the child. The GAL may be an attorney, a layperson, or a trained volunteer.

CRIMINAL JURISDICTION

The majority of crimes against children are investigated by local and state law enforcement. On the federal level, the Federal Bureau of Investigation (FBI), Bureau of Indian Affairs (BIA), and Department of Defense (DoD) may exercise jurisdiction. Determining criminal jurisdiction, which includes investigative and prosecutorial responsibilities, is influenced by a number of factors:

- Where the crime occurred
- The type of crime
- Statutes specifying federal, state, and tribal jurisdiction

Because the jurisdiction of federal court did not previously reach into domestic relations, the victims who resided within federal enclaves (e.g., the military, Indian reservations) were not ensured legal recourse for family violence protection until the mid-1990s. When the victim was a child, there was no clause in military or federal law authorizing the removal of the child. Abusers were subjected only to military authority, which was without family violence law. Previously, a conflict of interest existed, in that military officials represented military personnel but not the spouses or children who were being abused. Without domestic violence jurisdiction, federal installations had not adequately addressed victim needs.

The DoD recognizes that family violence is a serious problem within the military (Department of Defense, 2011). Unique problems such as deployments, reunification, and constant relocations of military families are acknowledged as contributing factors for this population. Stress and behavioral problems among children in military families have been associated with deployments. One study found that the rate of child abuse by the female parent left behind tripled when her spouse was deployed to a combat area (Gibbs, Martin, Kupper, & Johnson, 2007). Gibbs et al. (2007) also found the overall rate of child maltreatment to be 42 percent greater during deployments compared to the periods when soldiers were not deployed. The moderate or severe nature of abuse showed the greatest elevation in rate.

Indian reservations represent another area where federal protection failed to include domestic intervention and legal recourse for citizens. The Indian Child Welfare Act of 1978 was an early attempt to meet the needs of Native American children. Through this act, Congress declared its commitment to the establishment of foster or adoptive homes that would reflect the unique values of Native American culture and promote the security of Indian tribal families. Exclusive jurisdiction was recognized for Indian trial courts in proceedings that involved Indian child custody. The act also provided for full faith and credit in every state to the judicial proceedings, records, and public acts of Indian courts. The power for emergency removal of a child from Indian land was retained by state authority to prevent imminent physical damage or harm to the child.

Multijurisdictional responsibilities for investigating child abuse on Indian reservations cause confusion between law enforcement agencies on who should respond. The lack of adequate resources on some reservations has led to acquiescence to state authorities for assistance in cases of abuse; the responses have not always been culturally appropriate (Eagle, Clairmont, & Hunter, 2011). Another problem has been that the U.S. Supreme Court has ruled that tribal governments cannot prosecute non-Indians (*Oliphant v. Suquamish Indian Tribe*, 1978). This means that the perpetrators may go unpunished if they are a nonnative parent. The situation is critical for this population since reports indicate that Native Americans, Indian, and Alaskan suffer victimization at higher rates than the general population. It is generally accepted that these numbers are an underrepresentation of the actual data.

Recent federal efforts have been made to improve the reporting and investigation of child abuse and neglect on tribal lands. In 2010, the Tribal Law and Order Act (TLOA) was designed to address three overall tribal justice issues: (1) lack of federal government accountability for investigating and prosecuting crimes in Indian country, (2) lack of tribal government authority, and (3) longstanding lack of adequate and consistent funding for tribal justice systems. Jurisdictional changes that allow family violence to be prosecuted have been passed in the Violence Against Women Reauthorization Act of 2013, effective in 2015 (National Network to End Domestic Violence [NNEDV], 2013).

CONCLUSIONS

The history of child maltreatment outlines the perspective that children have been considered as property belonging to their father since ancient times. The progression to today was a slow evolution through movements to protect children from abusive treatment and neglect. Modern laws protect children from abuse and neglect at the hands of their parents and other family members. Today, the treatment of children is considered a matter of public concern. As such, legislation to protect children from criminal violence has also emerged.

Standard definitions and categories of abuse aid in the recognition of child abuse and neglect. All states recognize the four major forms of abuse, and some states have added subcategories of concern within this framework. Adhering to the federal guidelines under CAPTA provides standardization. States are free to define child abuse and neglect within their statutes and policies, but to receive federal funding the definitions used must include CAPTA categories. The primary sources of child abuse data are valuable to understand the scope of child abuse and to maintain currency on issues affecting child victims.

No profile can be drawn to describe the victims of abuse. Child abuse victims are represented in all age categories, genders, races, and ethnicities. Care needs to be taken to provide education and services for communities which have the highest rates of abuse. Some may be surprised that women are responsible for over half of the violence perpetrated against children.

Criminal jurisdiction over the plight of abused children is a fairly new phenomenon, as it was considered a civil wrongdoing under the arm of social services until recently. The courts struggle to find appropriate ways to address the legal responses to these young victims. One recent innovation is that the court will consider age-appropriate methods of court testifying. To provide continued protection in cases of the family breakdown, policies for awarding child custody do consider if domestic violence is a concern, both direct and indirect victimization.

SIMPLY SCENARIO
Mandated Reporter

As a new teacher in the Springfield Elementary School, Maryanne had her hands full. There were 40 children in her classroom. The first year was frustrating! The lack of books and supplies gave her the impression that the administration did not care about the children, many of whom were not English speaking. Maryanne overheard some girls laughing at Susan and the dirty clothes she was wearing. Taunting Susan, the girls said it was no wonder she was filthy because her mom was always high and her dad was in jail. Maryanne noticed that Susan missed more than five to seven days of school each month.

Question: What is the role of the teacher?

Questions for Review

1. What are the four major forms of child abuse and neglect?
2. Define the term "infanticide." Does it still exist today?
3. List the major movements that impacted child protection in early America.
4. Explain the difference between an act of omission and an act of commission.
5. What is the key federal legislation addressing child abuse and neglect?
6. The *National Incidence Study of Child Abuse and Neglect* uses two standards for its research on child abuse and neglect. Why does this matter?
7. Describe the typical child abuse victim.
8. Under the category of child abuse reporters, which group submits the majority of reports to child protective agencies?
9. What two Supreme Court decisions impacted child court testimony?
10. Explain the role of domestic violence in the determination of child custody during separation or divorce of parents.

Internet-Based Exercises

1. The Child Welfare Information Gateway provides an online searchable database of state statutes at http://www.childwelfare.gov/systemwide/laws_policies/state/. Go to the Web site and compare the state statutes of two different states. Write an essay on the differences you find.
2. You learned in this chapter that the National Center for Missing & Exploited Children was established in 1984. Find the Web site for this organization, and state at least five resources it provides for law enforcement.
3. Who must report suspected child abuse in the state where you live? Under what conditions must he or she make a report? Where does the report go? The answers to these questions can be found online on the Child Welfare Information Gateway at https://www.childwelfare.gov/topics/responding/reporting/. Report your findings.

References

Botash, A. (2013). Culture-based practices that may be interpreted as abuse. Retrieved from http://www.childabusemd.com/diagnosis/physical-abuse.shtml#culture

Brandon, M., Bailey, S., Belderson, P., & Larsson, B. (2014). The role of neglect in child fatality and serious injury. *Child Abuse Review, 23*(4), 235–245.

CAPTA. The Child Abuse Prevention and Treatment Act. (2010). 42 U.S.C.Chapter 67.

Child Welfare Information Gateway. (2013). *Child witnesses to domestic violence: Summary of state laws.* Washington, D.C.: U.S. Department of Health and Human Services.

Child Welfare Information Gateway. (2016). *Definitions of child abuse and neglect.* State Statutes Series. Washington, D.C.: U.S. Department of Health and Human Services.

Child Welfare Information Gateway. (2017). *Infant safe haven laws: Summary of state laws.* Washington, D.C.: U.S. Department of Health and Human Services.

Colon, A. (2001). *A history of children: A socio-cultural survey across millennia.* Westport, CT: Greenwood Press.

Crawford v. Washington, 541 U.S. 36 (2004).

Department of Defense. (2011). Domestic abuse involving DoD military and certain affiliated personnel. Retrieved from http://www.dtic.mil/whs/directives/corres/pdf/640006p.pdf

Dorne, C. (2002). *An introduction to child maltreatment in the United States: History, public policy, and research.* Monsey, NY: Criminal Justice Press.

Eagle, M. W., Clairmont, B., & Hunter, L. (2011). Responses to the co-occurrence of child maltreatment and domestic violence in Indian country: Repairing the harm and protecting children and mothers. Retrieved from http://tribal-institute.org/download/OVWGreenbookReportHVS_TD_7-18.pdf

Ex Parte Crouse, PA 11 S. Ct. Pa. (1838).

Gibbs, D., Martin, S., Kupper, L., & Johnson, R. (2007). Child maltreatment in enlisted soldiers' families during combat-related deployments. *The Journal of the American Medical Association, 298*(5), 528–535.

Gordon, L. (1989). *Heroes of their own lives: The politics and history of family violence.* New York, NY: Penguin Books.

Hamby, S., Finkelhor, D., Turner, H., & Ormrod, R. (2011). *Children's exposure to intimate partner violence and other family violence.* (NCJ 232272). Washington, D.C.: U.S. Department of Justice.

Hammurabi's Code of Laws. (1998). (L. W. King, Trans.). *Ancient history sourcebook: Code of Hammurabi, c. 1780 BCE.* Retrieved from http://www.fordham.edu/halsall/ancient/hamcode.html

Helfer, R., & Kempe, R. (Eds.). (1987). *The battered child* (4th ed.). Chicago, IL: University of Chicago Press.

Hilarski, C. (2008). Chapter 1: Historical overview. In C. Hilarski, J. S. Wodarski, & M. D. Feit (Eds.), *Handbook of social work in child and adolescent sexual abuse* (pp. 1–27). Binghamton, NY: Haworth Press.

Koenen, M. A., & Thompson, J. J. W. (2008). Filicide: Historical review and prevention of child death by parent. *Infant Mental Health Journal, 29*, 61–75.

Lazoritz, S., & Shelman, E. (1996). Before Mary Ellen. *Child Abuse & Neglect, 20*(3), 235–240.

Leeb, R., Paulozzi, L., Melanson, C., Simon, T., & Arias, I. (2008). *Child maltreatment surveillance: Uniform definitions for public health and recommended data elements.* Atlanta, GA: Centers for Disease Control and Prevention, National Center for Injury Prevention and Control.

Maryland v. Craig, 497 U.S. 836, 853 (1990).

Mbilinyi, L., Edleson, J., Hagemeister, A., & Beeman, S. (2007). What happens to children when their mothers are battered? Results from a four city anonymous telephone survey. *Journal of Family Violence, 22*(5), 309–317.

Mederos, F., & Fund, F. V. P. (2004). *Accountability and connection with abusive men: A new child protection response to increasing family safety.* Boston, MA: Massachusetts Department of Social Services, Domestic Violence Unit.

National Council of Juvenile and Family Court Judges. (NCJFCJ). (2011). Checklist to promote perpetrator accountability in dependency cases involving domestic violence. Retrieved from http://www.ncjfcj.org/sites/default/files/checklist-to-promote-accountability_0.pdf

National Network to End Domestic Violence. (NNEDV). (2013). The Violence Against Women Reauthorization Act of 2013: Safely and effectively meeting the needs of more victims. Retrieved from http://www.nnedv.org/docs/Policy/VAWAReauthorization_Summary_2013.pdf

New York State Education Department. (n.d.). New York House of Refuge. Retrieved from http://www.archives.nysed.gov/a/research/res_topics_ed_reform_history.shtml

Oliphant v. Suquamish Indian Tribe, 435 U.S. 191 (1978).

Palusci, V. J., & Covington, T. M. (2014). Child maltreatment deaths in the U.S. National Child Death Review Case Reporting System. *Child Abuse & Neglect, 38*(1), 25–36.

Platt, A. (1969). The rise of the child-saving movement: A study in social policy and correctional reform. *The ANNALS of the American Academy of Political and Social Science, 381*(1), 21–38.

Pushkareva, N. (1997). *Women in Russian history: From the tenth to the twentieth century* (E. Levin, Trans.). Armonk, NY: M. E. Sharpe.

Radbill, S. (1987). Children in a world of violence: A history of child abuse. In R. Helfer & R. Kempe (Eds.), *The battered child* (4th ed., pp. 3–22). Chicago, IL: University of Chicago Press.

Relva, I., Fernandes, O., & Mota, C. (2013). An exploration of sibling violence predictors. *Journal of Aggression, Conflict and Peace Research, 5*(1), 47–61.

Sanborn, J., & Salerno, A. (2005). *The juvenile justice system: Law and process.* Los Angeles, CA: Roxbury.

Sedlak, A. J., Mettenburg, J., Basena, M., Petta, I., McPherson, K., Greene, A., & Li, S. (2010). *Fourth National Incidence Study of Child Abuse and Neglect (NIS-4): Report to Congress.* Retrieved from http://www.acf.hhs.gov/programs/opre/resource/fourth-national-incidence-study-of-child-abuse-and-neglect-nis-4-report-to

Shoemaker, D. J., & Wolfe, T. W. (2005). *Juvenile justice: A reference handbook.* Santa Barbara, CA: ABC-CLIO.

Sillito, C., & Salari, S. (2011). Child outcomes and risk factors in U.S. homicide-suicide cases 1999–2004. *Journal of Family Violence, 26*(4), 285–297. doi: 10.1007/s10896-011-9364-6

U.S. Department of Health and Human Services (DHHS) and Administration for Children and Families, Children's Bureau. (2017). *Child maltreatment 2015.* Retrieved from http://www.acf.hhs.gov/programs/cb/research-data-technology/statistics-research/child-maltreatment.

Ventrell, M. (1998). Evolution of the dependency component of the juvenile court. *Juvenile and Family Court Journal, 49*(4).

Warnken, B. (2008). Forfeiture by wrongdoing after *Crawford v. Washington*: Maryland's approach best preserves the right to confrontation. *The University of Baltimore Law Review, 37*(203).

Wortman, M. S. (1985). *Women in American law: From colonial times to the new deal* (Vol. 1). New York, NY: Holmes & Meier.

5

Investigating Child Abuse

CHAPTER OBJECTIVES

After reviewing this chapter, you should be able to:

1. Summarize the role of law enforcement and child protective services in the assessment and response to child abuse.
2. Examine the significance of injury location and pattern on a child suspected of physical abuse.
3. Discuss family abduction and child death due to abuse.
4. Describe sexual abuse indicators and the accommodation syndrome.
5. Explain the Children's Advocacy Center model of investigation.

KEY TERMS

Family abduction	Munchausen syndrome by proxy
Feticide	Sexual assault
Filicide	Shaken baby syndrome
Incest	Sudden infant death syndrome

INTRODUCTION

Since different agencies can become involved in cases in which abuse or neglect of a child is suspected, this chapter begins with the role of professionals who are common first responders. These include emergency medical technicians, law enforcement officers, and child protective services, who are often in the position to detect child abuse due to the nature of their jobs. While the primary mission of each agency differs, they are mindful of working cooperatively in the protection of children.

The categories of child abuse that trigger a mandated reporting situation vary by state. All states include physical abuse, sexual abuse, and neglect. There are multiple forms that neglect can take, and states often differentiate and define the specific instances which are considered neglectful. For example, Iowa Code section 232.68 specifies nine categories of child abuse which includes denial of critical care, child prostitution, being in the presence of illegal drugs or a dangerous substance, bestiality in the presence of a minor, and allowing access by a registered sex offender.

The legal family relationship categories to a child when abuse is suspected vary by state. Remember from previous chapters that for abuse to be classified as domestic violence law must define these relationships. Some states broaden the definition to include anyone who is an employee or agent of any public or private facility providing care for a child, including an institution, hospital, mental health center, or shelter care facility. In some states, an adult caretaker might be held responsible for the abuse of a child if they delegated care responsibilities to an inappropriate minor caregiver such as a babysitter or other child.

Child protective services (CPS) is frequently the agency that is designated by law to receive reports of child abuse and neglect. However, some states authorize the local law enforcement agency as one who is empowered to receive initial concerns regarding child abuse. The name of a person who reports suspected abuse and neglect is typically confidential, although the protection is not absolute. The process of investigating and protecting children from physical abuse and sexual abuse is covered in depth in this chapter.

FIRST RESPONDERS TO CHILD MALTREATMENT

The role of the first responders to child maltreatment is to recognize child maltreatment, provide an initial response and investigation, and to testify in court, when appropriate. Some effects of child abuse and neglect are easily observable; detecting the signs and symptoms may require a more in-depth assessment by first responders. The physical, emotional, and behavioral effects are wide-ranging, but may also be caused by something other than maltreatment. The first person to arrive at an emergency scene is often referred to as a first responder. First responders should be able to recognize and assess any possible child abuse and neglect within the context of other situations that may occur in the home such as an accident, intimate partner violence, or substance abuse. Examples of first responders who are trained to observe child abuse indicators include EMTs, law enforcement officers, and CPS caseworkers.

EMTs

The EMTs and paramedics must determine the nature and extent of the patient's condition, give appropriate emergency care, and transport the patient to a medical facility, if necessary. First responders should recognize the limits of their particular job duties or responsibilities. For instance, EMTs would not attempt to elicit a confession, nor would law enforcement or CPS perform a medical exam. It is the role of the EMT to identify and report possible child maltreatment when it is suspected, to preserve evidence, and to testify in court when needed.

Law Enforcement Officers

Police officers often encounter situations that involve child maltreatment due to their presence and 24-hour response in the community. Police officers respond to emergencies such as domestic violence, child fatalities, or incidents of serious physical harm to a child. Law enforcement officers also may see evidence of maltreatment to a child during drug or other arrests.

The role of law enforcement is to determine if a violation of criminal law occurred, identify and apprehend the offender, file appropriate criminal charges, and remove children from their families when the child is in imminent danger. Law enforcement officers must have probable cause to believe that a crime has been committed to take legal action against a suspected perpetrator, such as an arrest. Law enforcement officers are mandated to report suspected abuse and neglect to CPS even in situations where there is a lack of probable cause for an arrest.

In some situations, police officers may conduct joint investigations of suspected child maltreatment with CPS caseworkers. A joint investigation is required when a report of child abuse or neglect indicates serious physical injury or deterioration, or sexual abuse of the child, and when there is a reason to believe action may be required to protect the child. Multidisciplinary teams may assist with investigations in some states.

CPS Case Workers

CPS is the agency legally mandated in most States to respond to reports of suspected child abuse or neglect. CPS caseworkers conduct investigations or initial assessments regarding suspected child maltreatment, assess the risk to and safety of children, and develop individualized care plans. They also provide or arrange for and coordinate services to achieve safe, permanent families for children who either have been maltreated or who are at risk of maltreatment. In most communities, CPS responds to reports of emergencies involving suspected child abuse or neglect 24 hours a day.

Social service agencies investigate to determine if evidence exists that abuse or neglect occurred, to identify the person likely to have committed the abuse or neglect and to protect the child from further abuse or neglect. These agencies make determinations regarding the safety of the child in his or her home. For child protection, a CPS caseworker does not have to meet the standard of probable cause that is needed by law enforcement. The role of a CPS worker is to report maltreatment to law enforcement if there is a suspicion that a crime has been committed per State and local statutes.

ASSESSMENT OR INVESTIGATION OF MALTREATMENT

During an assessment or investigation of suspected child abuse or neglect, the professionals involved are first concerned with whether the child is safe. If not, measures must be taken to ensure the safety of the child. Next, first responders need to ensure that all physical evidence has been obtained, preserved, or photographed. Steps should be taken to keep onlookers outside of the area if the situation involves a crime scene. Determine if there are any other possible victims through interviews and examination of the scene. If the child needs to be taken into protective custody, EMTs should call CPS or law enforcement, depending on the law in that jurisdiction. First responders should begin each case with objectivity, without jumping to conclusions before all of the facts have been assessed.

The Law Enforcement Process

The four critical steps for child abuse and neglect investigations are outlined in Figure 5-1. The first step is to collect information about the injury that led to the report for intervention, along with interviewing medical personnel who attended to the child. The investigation includes viewing the child and documenting the injury through photographs or drawings. The information in this step may come from reports filed by mandated reporters, family members, neighbors, and any other person who filed a complaint

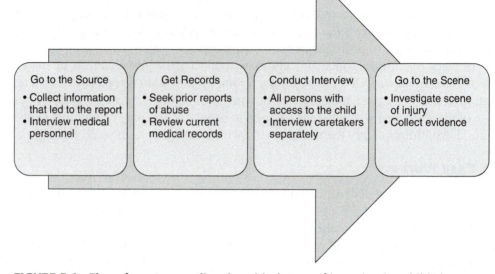

FIGURE 5-1 These four steps outline the critical steps of investigating child abuse and neglect cases.

relative to the child. Interviewing medical personnel is an important part of the fact-gathering process. These interviews are at the top of the list because the doctor or nurse may not remember the specific child days or weeks after providing medical attention.

The second step is to find out whether the child has ever been the subject of a report of abuse or neglect in the past. If the child has been abused or neglected in the past, records of the abuse or neglect should be obtained. It may be necessary to get a court order to obtain records. The third step is to interview all persons who had access to the child during the time that the current abuse or neglect is alleged to have occurred. It is important to interview the caretakers separately. The investigator is looking for the explanations of how the abuse or neglect occurred. Later, the investigator will speak with experts and compare these explanations with the injuries for a determination of whether they are consistent. When the facts do not match the explanation, a red flag should go up ... try to determine why.

The fourth step is to go to the scene of the alleged abuse or neglect, which often occurs in a person's home. Typically, the caretaker will give consent for the home to be viewed. If the caretaker does not give consent, a warrant should be sought to gain entry to the home and to conduct a search. Some cases may necessitate a search warrant to collect evidence. The investigator should look to see whether the explanation for the abuse is consistent with the location of the abuse. For example, if the caretaker said the child fell down some stairs, the investigator should document the location of the stairway and its characteristics (i.e., carpeted, wood, or cement). The collection of evidence is done in a manner consistent with legal policy and practice.

The CPS Process

No one case example can stand as typical for a protective services investigation because of the range of family situations that are reported. It is the responsibility of CPS to receive reports of child abuse and neglect and to determine whether the child is safe. When a report is made, the caseworker will talk to the person who made the report, looking to find out as much as possible about the case. Typically, a home visit is made, it might be unannounced if warranted. Conducting investigations and initial assessment regarding suspected child maltreatment involves talking to the people who live with the child including the custodial parent. The investigator takes note if there are any health hazards to the child, if there is an appropriate living space, and adequate food. CPS will talk to caretakers or school officials if needed. If maltreatment is likely to occur, CPS determines the level of risk and develops a safety plan.

Once safety is assured, the next step for CPS is to assess if the child suffered maltreatment or was threatened with harm as defined by the State reporting law. If sources of corroboration or witnesses exist, the CPS worker preserves the evidence and reports to law enforcement with names and addresses. The investigator determines if other children live in the home, and the level of risk, if any, that the situation presents to them. The case may be brought by CPS to be heard before a judge. While the actions are civil, a judge will make determinations on child custody, living arrangements, and financial obligations of the parent(s).

The focus of CPS is both on the investigation of reported maltreatment that initiates agency responsibility and on stabilizing and improving the children's own homes by helping parents to perform more responsibly regarding the care of their children. The services of CPS are involuntary, therefore intrusive and authoritative. Social workers in protective agencies must act quickly; their decision about the nature or seriousness of a complaint and the action to be taken must be based on accurate fact-finding. They cannot withdraw from the situation if the parents become uncooperative or resistant to taking help. Once protective service has been initiated, the agency can responsibly withdraw only when the level of child care in the home has improved to acceptable levels or when satisfactory care has been arranged elsewhere.

INTRODUCTION TO PHYSICAL ABUSE

Criminal prosecution of physical abuse is more common than the prosecution of emotional maltreatment. The recognition of abuse and collection of substantiating evidence become extremely important in abuse cases. The line between accident and intentional harm can be blurry, making the determination of exactly what happened difficult. The multiagency or interdisciplinary team approach is helpful in gathering information from various sources to portray an accurate picture of the abuse.

Regardless of the nature or role of the initial investigating agency, any reports and other documentation generated may become the focus of the court if prosecution proceeds. Whenever possible, obtain a written report from a medical professional on his or her opinion of the cause of injury. Medical records of the victim may be summoned, if necessary. Gathering information on the nature, type, and location of the injury is the first step toward a determination of physical abuse. This history should be collected before the victim is interviewed and then compared with the explanations. An allegation of abuse is not confirmation that a child has been victimized.

Location of Abrasions, Bruises, Lacerations, and Welts

Since bruises and cuts are often legitimate accidental injuries, the age and mobility of the child are considered along with the explanation given for the injury. Infants who are not mobile are not capable of inflicting severe injury to their bodies. In the absence of a medical condition such as brittle bone disease, such an explanation is

Been There...Done That!

Susan came into my office with a big smile on her face! A charming four-year-old, she was sparkling clean—the kind of child whose face shines. Her hair was tied in a ponytail topped with a pink ribbon, which matched her dress. Within moments of meeting, she spun around in circles to show off her frilly outfit! In an apparent effort to please me, she smiled broadly and chatted incessantly.

I already knew that there was a dark side to the life of this little girl. Months earlier, she told her mother that daddy had touched her and that he had hurt her where she pees. Frustrated by her lack of ability to protect the child, her mother fled with her and had been living in hiding ever since. A medical exam had found trauma to the vagina that "might indicate" sexual abuse. During our electronically recorded interview, Susan told me that daddy had put his pee "down there" and white stuff had come out of it. It hurt her, and she did not want to see daddy again.

not plausible. Infants who are thrown or dropped, hit or slapped, burned, or poisoned may have visible signs of injury. Any location of injury that the child is incapable of self-inflicting is cause for concern. Keep in mind that children often scratch their faces if their fingernails are not kept cut; many hospitals, for example, put mittens on newborns for this reason.

The most significant asset that an investigator can possess is the ability to remain objective and nonjudgmental when a child has suspicious injuries. Children can become injured during play; bruises, burns, and even broken bones do occur that are not due to parental abuse. Note Figure 5-2 that illustrates places on a child's body where accidental injuries commonly occur. Gather information on the location and type of injury, and speak with the caretaker about the incidents that preceded the injury. The caretaker's explanations of how the child received the injury must be consistent with the injury itself.

When an injury is caused as discipline or to inflict injury, it is an example of nonaccidental injury. If a child is punched, kicked, thrown, or shaken and sustains an injury, no matter how slight, the abuser could be held legally responsible regardless of the child's preexisting medical condition. The illustration in Figure 5-3 shows locations on the body of a child where nonaccidental injuries are commonly inflicted.

Age Dating of Bruises

Multiple bruises, abrasions, or other wounds in varying stages of healing may indicate repetitive physical assault. Age dating of bruises involves noting the color of bruising present on a victim and documenting this information using the time frame that

FIGURE 5-2 Accidental injury locations, front and back. Bruises on the walking child are usually accidental if they appear on the forehead, elbows, and stomach, and the outside of the thighs, knees, and ankles.

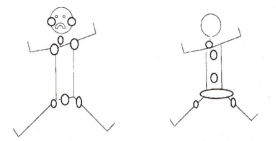

FIGURE 5-3 Nonaccidental injury locations, front and back. Bruises or fractures to a child that is suspicious for an intentional injury are located on the ears and cheeks, neck, shoulders and upper arms, genitals, and inner thighs. Bruising on locations other than bony prominences is questionable. Defense posturing can cause injuries to the outside of the lower arm. Suspicious bruising locations include the buttocks, lower back, earlobes, mouth, and neck.

follows. The investigator should note significantly different bruise colors as a possible indication of repetitive abuse. It may also be helpful to see whether the age of the bruise matches the explanation for the presenting injury because establishing a time-line of the injury is possible. Although the location can change the color somewhat, the age of a bruise is generally determined by its color:

- Bright red bruises are indicative of an injury 0 to 2 days old.
- Bluish or purple bruises are 2 to 5 days old.
- Green indicates a bruise 5 to 7 days old.
- Yellow bruises are 7 to 10 days old.
- Brown bruises are 10 to 14 days old.
- No evidence of bruising is present after 2 to 4 weeks.

Many factors influence expected bruising patterns and colors. Some people merely bruise more easily than others; bruises are harder to see on people with very dark skin, and the colors usually are seen when the bruise fades may not be apparent. How hard the person is hit and the location of the injury may alter the expected bruise colors or patterns. Persons with medical conditions, particularly leukemia, may have what appear to be severe bruises when no beating has occurred.

Been There...Done That!

During an investigation of the suspected sexual abuse of a four-year-old boy, the child drew a crude picture of an erect penis. His father was thought to have been the perpetrator. Insufficient evidence of the crime prevented my bringing criminal charges against any-one. Regardless of my suspicions that the child had been raped, probable cause to make an arrest did not exist in this case. Here is just one example of sexual abuse to a male child that would not be included in the statistics.

Whenever I arrested for a sexual abuse crime, an attempt was made to determine whether the perpetrator had been victimized as a child. Many told me "off the record" about their childhood victimization. Almost all the male perpetrators who had been sexually abused as children knew that their offenders had never been prosecuted.

Been There...Done That!

Interviewing the parent or caretaker of a child should always be done with respect. The feelings or personal opinion of the investigator should never enter into the conversation, no matter how severe the child's injuries may be. There is a distinct difference between an interview and an interrogation of the suspect. An interview is done to gather information and should not be confrontational. Keep the tone of the interview nonjudgmental to assure the compliance of the interviewee; there is always time later for an interrogation if a suspect is identified. The interview is like a conversation between two people. People are more likely to talk to you when they feel comfortable, so it is worthwhile to take the time to put the parent or caretaker at ease.

Once an accusation is made, or when the parent or caretaker feels he or she is being accused, the parent or caretaker will hesitate to answer many of your questions. The majority of parents whose children have injuries did not intend to harm the child. Some may believe that parents have the right to punish in any form they choose. In some instances, the injury may be accidental. Leave the door of communication open; you may want to speak with the parent or caretaker a second or third time during the investigation.

Take care not to accuse someone of abuse without a thorough investigation. The consequences of false allegations by authorities cannot be underestimated: Humiliation, shame, loss of job, and in some cases loss of the custody of one's children can result.

It is important for the investigator to pay close attention to the bruising to aid in estimating when the injury may have occurred. Any apparent bruising should be documented through professional photographs that do not distort the appearance of the bruises.

Patterns of Injury

Common household items are frequently used as weapons against children in abusive situations. Examples include hairbrushes, flyswatters, hangers, belts, and baseball bats. The most common dangerous weapon remains the hand. Look for the patterns of injury on the locations that have been identified as suspicious. Even if the child is unable to articulate what happened, bruise patterns on the child may help to identify and retrieve the weapon as evidence. Note the bruise on the buttocks of the child in Figure 5-4. This bruise is suspicious for abuse because it is in a location that is

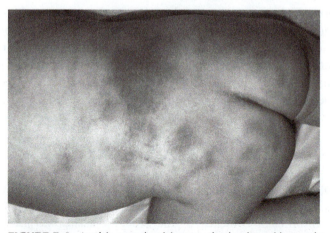

FIGURE 5-4   In this case, bruising on the back and buttocks of the child was caused by someone kicking multiple times. Notice the marks that resemble the toe and side of a shoe. A child with similar busing requires emergency medical care for possible internal injuries.   Photo Researchers, Inc./Science Source

More About It: Osteogenesis Imperfecta

The technical term for the brittle bone disease is osteogenesis imperfecta (OI). The condition is characterized by bones that break easily. There are four forms of OI, with bone fragility ranging from mild to very severe, depending on the particular type. A minor accident may result in a fracture; some fractures may even occur while an infant with the condition is being diapered, lifted, or dressed.

Child abuse is also characterized by broken bones. Consult a physician in cases of multiple fractures in multiple stages of healing, rib or spiral fractures, and when there is no adequate explanation for the trauma. In most cases, radiographic, clinical, and historical features are present and noticeable, allowing easy detection. A skin biopsy for collagen analysis in challenging cases may help to identify mild forms of OI. Because child abuse and OI have been reported together, the presence of OI does not exclude the possibility of child abuse. Infants are not capable of "falling" down, but once they begin to walk, they begin to fall. Young children who are active are more capable of hurting themselves physically.

inconsistent with an accidental injury, and it contains the identifiable footprint pattern of injury received after the child was kicked.

Other objects used to hit a child may leave a discernible pattern of a bruise that can be identified, for example, like that caused by a hairbrush, cord, or coat hanger. The doubled-over cord or coat hanger will leave a loop mark. A human bite also leaves a distinct pattern of injury that can be distinguished from animal bites by the configuration of the teeth. Toddlers bite other children in locations that are easily accessible, such as the face or extremities. If the teeth are dragged over the skin, abrasions may result. Tearing or shearing injuries are more likely to be caused by an animal.

Small oval patterns or imprints suggest an injury inflicted by being grabbed, pinched, squeezed, or slapped. These oval marks, which are characteristic of fingertips, may be found in the trunk of a child who has been shaken or around the throat if strangulation occurred. Another indication of attempted strangulation is a wrapping mark around the throat indicating that rope, cord, or wire may have been used. Tethering or tying up the child may also cause a bruise around the mouth, neck, wrists, or ankles. Wraparound or tethering or binding injuries on the neck, ankle, or wrist suggest that a child is being tied with a rope or cord.

As stated earlier, punishment taken too far is at the root of most abuse. When only minor injury is present, the investigation becomes difficult. However, the final resolution of the child abuse case should not be the result of a gut reaction. Consider the physical evidence as an outside indication of abuse; look to see whether behavioral signs and symptoms are present. Also look for other forms of abuse, such as emotional or psychological abuse, sexual abuse, or neglect. If no signs of abuse are found, the case may have to be closed.

Injuries to the Head

Infants rarely suffer head injuries that are accidental. A child riding a bicycle, roller skating, riding a dirt bike, or four-wheeling might suffer an accidental head injury. Car accidents may also be responsible for the harm to a child. Toddlers just learning to walk present a different picture; they frequently have lumps on their foreheads because of falling. See Figure 5-5 for an example of an accidental injury to a child. Close examination shows a bruise on the side of the forehead

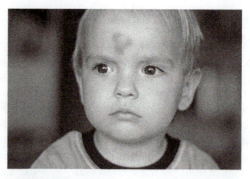

FIGURE 5-5 This bruise on the forehead is consistent with a fall taken by a young child while attempting to walk or ride a bike. Shutterstock

that could have resulted from the toddler falling. Examples of intentional injury include

- hemorrhaging beneath the scalp or when hair is missing due to being pulled;
- retinal hemorrhages, the hallmark of shaken baby syndrome and only rarely associated with some other kind of injury;
- injury from multiple slapping or hitting on the head, causing neck injury, with the child unable to turn his or her head;
- whiplash (without an automobile accident history);
- any bruising to the ear, a cause for suspicion that the child has been hit on the side of the head;
- a "cauliflower ear," similar to a boxing injury, caused when the ear is hit numerous times;
- a black or swollen eye, which can be accidental or the result of abuse (the history of the accident is essential).

Burns

Although child abuse awareness has increased significantly, intentional burn injuries often go unnoticed. An adult will experience a significant injury of the skin after 1 minute of exposure to water at 127 degrees, 30 seconds of exposure at 130 degrees, and 2 seconds of exposure at 150 degrees. A child, however, will suffer a significant burn in less time than an adult. Burn injuries account for approximately 6 percent to 20 percent of all abuse cases, and severe burns are reported in an estimated 10 percent of all children suffering physical abuse (Toon et al., 2011). Children under the age of four are at the greatest risk of being burn victims, with boys more likely to incur injury than girls.

Punishment in the form of burns may involve forcing a child under hot water, inflicting cigarette or lighter burns, or pushing/holding a child on a heating or electrical unit. In sporadic cases, children have been placed in ovens and in a microwave, which caused death. When a child has a burn that is described as accidental, the injury is

Been There...Done That!

Child Protective Services, known as the Department of Social Services in Massachusetts, called to notify me of a young child at the local hospital who was suspected of having been shaken. The child was presumed to have severe brain damage and was not expected to live through the night. The child's infant brother, who had brittle bone disease, had died on the previous day. The initial determination was that the infant had died of complications due to the OI.

An interview with the mother provided information that she and her boyfriend shared a one-bedroom apartment with the two children. In the middle of the night, the crying of the sick child, who in turn woke the other child, awakened the boyfriend. The desperate mother had carried both children into the kitchen to appease her boyfriend. She said that she stumbled over a toy in the doorway and had dropped the toddler. A search warrant executed at the apartment found there were no toys there. A dent on the side of the stove was noted in the doorway where the mother claimed to have stumbled. Her story of how the child "rolled" to the opposite side of the room was indicative of his having been thrown against the stove before coming to rest a few feet away in the opposite direction. In addition to the brain damage, the child presented with retinal hemorrhages, suggestive of shaken baby syndrome. This child became ill the next day, throwing up, and he had stopped breathing before he was rushed to the hospital. Although the toddler lived, his doctor predicted that the brain damage would prevent him from developing past his age of two.

The infant was presumed to have died immediately from the incident. It was never clear whether he was also thrown or had been mishandled, causing his brittle bones to break.

probably located on the front of the child's body. This can happen if a child pulled over a pot on the stove or a container of hot liquid. A young child might also touch or step on a heating unit, injuring the bottom of a foot or hand. A pattern of a hard object on the soft body of a child can only be made if the item is held firmly onto the skin. Note Figure 5-6 that shows a burn on the cheek of a young child. The circular shape is the result of a cigarette burn.

Heated skin will turn red (first-degree burn) and then blister (second-degree burn). The skin may become charred from flames or white from scalds in third-degree

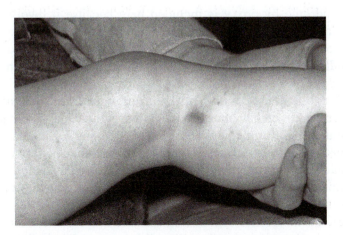

FIGURE 5-6   Close examination of the mark on the leg of this child suggests a burn that is consistent with at cigarette being held firmly against the skin. Alamy

burns caused by higher temperature and prolonged exposure. Immersion in hot water causes symmetrical patterns that are distinct from accidental burns and are common burns caused by child abuse. A person who steps into a hot bath or bumps into a pot of boiling liquid that spills on him or her will move away and jump in pain—the burns caused by this are not even across the body; splash marks result. An immersion burn occurs when a child is held or forced into the hot water. Deliberate immersion burns may be recognized by one of the following:

- An oval burn usually includes buttocks and genitals; it is caused when a child is submerged and held in hot water. The burn may not be entirely symmetrical; some areas of the body can be protected from the burn, due to the position of the arms and legs of the child.
- A glove or stocking burn results when a hand or foot is held in hot water. Hot water is a frequent cause of accidental and abusive injury. As opposed to flowing water or accidental burns, immersion burn injuries appear relatively uniform in the depth of the burn.
- A doughnut-shaped burn surrounding the buttocks indicates being forced to sit on a hot object such as an electric heater, stove, or another electrical unit. When a child is held in scalding hot bathwater, the buttocks are pressed against the bottom of the tub so forcibly that the water will not come into contact with the center of the buttocks, sparing this part of the buttocks and causing the burn injury to have a doughnut pattern.
- If a caretaker's account is that the child was left in the bathroom and told not to get into the tub, and that the caretaker then heard screaming and returned to find the child jumping up and down in the water, the absence of burns on the soles of the child's feet is evidence that the account is not valid. A child cannot jump up and down in hot water without burning the bottoms of the feet.

MUNCHAUSEN SYNDROME BY PROXY

Munchausen syndrome by proxy is included here because it involves both physical abuse and medical neglect of a child. The offender suffers from a psychological maltreatment categorized in the current *DSM IV-TR* as a factitious disorder not otherwise specified (Criddle, 2010), but many clinicians still refer to it as Munchausen syndrome by proxy.

An individual diagnosed with **Munchausen syndrome by proxy** intentionally plans and conceals his or her abusive behaviors, which may include suffocating a child or demanding painful medical tests and procedures for the child. Munchausen syndrome by proxy abuse is characterized by repeated unnecessary medical tests and procedures, which are demanded by a caretaker and cause physical injury to the child. Frequent methods of fabricating illness are lying, poisoning the child with either drugs or other substances, suffocation, specimen tampering, and chart falsification (Criddle, 2010).

To assure hospital admission for the child, case studies indicate that the parent has used a range of intentional behaviors, including an injection of urine or fecal matter into the child and administration of large amounts of laxatives. The medical procedures performed on the child or the inflicted medications may result in the child's death in severe cases (Tamay et al., 2007). The incidence of Munchausen syndrome by proxy is thought to be rare, but it may occur in as many as 2.8 per 100,000 children (Criddle, 2010).

According to Criddle (2010), the vast majority of those exhibiting Munchausen syndrome by proxy are women. Both boys and girls are victimized. It is a difficult diagnosis to make because the perpetrators believe or have convinced themselves that the child is sick, even though their behavior has caused the child's ill effects. There is an absence of motivational incentives for the behavior, and it cannot be explained by any other mental disorder.

SHAKEN BABY SYNDROME

Shaken baby syndrome (SBS) is the medical term used to describe the violent shaking of a child and the injuries that can result. SBS is a severe form of child abuse that results from abusive head trauma and inflicted traumatic brain injury. It results from the violent shaking of an infant by the shoulders, arms, or legs. According to the Centers for Disease Control and Prevention (CDC), shaken baby syndrome is the leading cause of child abuse deaths in the United States (CDC, 2013).

Children from birth to four months are at the highest risk of suffering harm from shaking because their neck muscles are underdeveloped and their brain tissue is fragile. Repeated vigorous shaking causes the brain to slam against the skull from side to side. It can cause brain damage, blindness, paralysis, seizures, and death. Most SBS victims present with retinal hemorrhages that look like broken blood vessels and small pooling of blood on the white of the eye. Learning, physical, visual, and speech disabilities are among the possible long-term consequences of shaking. Seizures, behavior disorders, cognitive impairment, and death may also occur. It is believed that one out of every four children that are violently shaken dies as a result of the abuse (CDC, 2013).

International alarm developed about the incidence of severe head injuries of children seen in emergency rooms that were not being tracked as SBS. Concern led to policy change in 2008. An International Classification for nonfatal abusive head trauma (AHT) in children under five years of age was developed by an expert panel convened at the CDC. Using the new classification code to define cases of SBS admitted to U.S. hospitals, researchers discovered more significant numbers of head injuries existed. Between 2003 and 2008 there had been an estimated 10,555 nonfatal hospitalizations of infants with abusive head trauma (Parks, Sugerman, Xu, & Coronado, 2012). The vast majority of these shaken baby cases were identified as definite/presumptive abuse.

The youngest victims of violent shaking suffer the most injuries, although the risk of abuse due to shaking is considerable for children under the age of four (CDC, 2013). The injury is highest among children under one year of age (32.3 per 100,000), with a peak in hospitalizations for children between one and three months of age (Parks et al., 2012). Boys are victims of shaking more often than girls. Hospitalization rates for children under two years of age that have been abused by being shaken are 21.9 per 100,000 for boys and 15.3 per 100,000 for girls.

According to the CDC (2013), the perpetrators of SBS are usually parents and their partners, and most often are male. Among the factors that can increase the risk of parents harming a child are being a victim of intimate partner violence, frustration with the infant's crying, poor social support, and negative childhood experiences such as abuse or neglect. A child is at risk for SBS if there has been prior abuse to the child, or if the child frequently cries and is inconsolable.

CHILD DEATH DUE TO ABUSE

Most child maltreatment deaths result from physical abuse often committed by their parents. More children under age four die from child abuse and neglect than from automobile accidents, falls, fires, drowning, suffocation, and choking on food (Hochstadt, 2006). The criminal justice community is at the center of efforts to investigate and respond to violence against children. Specialized units have been developed for investigating reports of child abuse in the courts, police departments, and social service agencies across the country.

An estimated 1,537 children in the United States die of child abuse and neglect each year. This number translates to a rate of 2.07 children per 100,000 children in the general population (U.S. Department of Health and Human Services and Administration for Children and Families, 2012). Research indicates that children ages three and younger are the most frequent victims of child fatalities. Refer to Figure 5-7 that shows children younger than one year account for 42.4 percent of fatalities, whereas children ages one to three account for 39.2 percent of fatalities. The official estimate includes only those cases that have come to the attention of authorities and were substantiated as abuse. Law-enforcement officers know that abuse is not always a precise determination and that the statistics do not include those

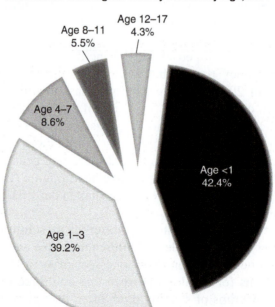

Child Abuse and Neglect Fatality Victims by Age, 2011

- Age 12–17: 4.3%
- Age 8–11: 5.5%
- Age 4–7: 8.6%
- Age <1: 42.4%
- Age 1–3: 39.2%

FIGURE 5-7 According to the U.S. Department of Health and Human Services and Administration for Children and Families (2012), children under the age of three are the most likely child abuse and neglect victims to die.

investigations where proof was lacking or when an allegation was plea-bargained to a lesser charge.

The felonious destruction of a fetus is called **feticide**, or criminal abortion. In a legal context, feticide refers to the deliberate or incidental killing of a fetus due to a criminal act, such as punching or kicking the abdomen of a pregnant woman. According to the CDC (2009), the beating of women is estimated to occur against as many as 324,000 pregnant women each year. There is no accurate number of the premature infant deaths caused by intimate partner violence against pregnant women.

The killing of an infant soon after birth up to the age of one is known as *infanticide*. Reports on infanticide often include murdered children over the age of five, which is an incorrect use of the term. However, children killed under the age of five are included as infanticide victims in the figures reported by the Bureau of Justice Statistics. The killing of a brother or sister is called fratricide. Rarer than any other family homicide, it occurs in 1.5 percent of the total criminal deaths in the United States. Relatively few sisters kill their brother, and sisters killed by a sibling are more likely to be killed by a brother rather than a sister (Cooper & Smith, 2011).

Filicide is the killing of children by parents; it is a nonlegal term that in some studies may include victims of infanticide. Children killed by their parents are the second most frequent type of family homicide (Cooper & Smith, 2011). Although all murders are tragic, a parent's killing of a child is a form of abuse that is difficult to understand. Children are unable to protect themselves against abuse and have no alternatives when confronted with lethal violence. Almost 30 percent of child abuse or neglect fatalities are perpetrated by the mother acting alone (Child Welfare Information Gateway, 2012). Most perpetrators are in their mid-20s living in highly stressful situations, including depression

More About It: Sudden Infant Death Syndrome

Sudden infant death syndrome (SIDS) is the unexplained death of a healthy infant under one year of age. SIDS is sometimes called crib death because most of these children die in their sleep. We often do not know the exact causes of child death, but some experts believe that SIDS babies are born with brain abnormalities that make them unable to awaken from sleep under certain conditions (American Lung Association, 2008). According to the American Lung Association (2008), maternal smoking during pregnancy is estimated to double the risk of SIDS.

The U.S. Department of Health and Human Services in 1992 predicted a possible decrease in the incidence of death from SIDS through precautionary measures. Formally known as the "Back to Sleep" campaign, the American Academy of Pediatrics recommended that babies be placed on their backs or sides to sleep, which significantly reduces the risk of SIDS. It is now called the "Safe to Sleep" program. This effort has been credited with a 50 percent actual reduction in SIDS deaths since 1992 (NICHD Information Resource Center, 2012).

SIDS is now the third leading cause of death among infants who are one month to one year old. In 2008, 2,250 per 100,000 live births died from SIDS (Mathews & MacDorman, 2012). Respiratory infections and low birth weight are contributing risk factors to sudden infant death syndrome. Male babies are more likely than girls to die from SIDS.

Many people believe that in SIDS-related deaths, the infants suffocated themselves because they were found with their faces pressed into the mattress. Studies have repeatedly disproved this theory. When death is caused by suffocation, it cannot immediately be attributed to SIDS; further investigation is warranted. Petechial hemorrhages, broken blood vessels in the eyes and surrounding area, will be apparent in most cases of suffocation. Investigators should be aware that SIDS is quite rare, and multiple SIDS deaths in the same family or daycare facility are immediately suspicious.

and poverty. Research suggests that fathers and mothers' boyfriends are most often the perpetrators in abuse deaths, and mothers are more often at fault in neglect fatalities.

Child Death Review Teams

More than four children per day die as the result of abuse and neglect in the United States each year. However, that number is very conservative. Research has shown that as many as 50 percent of child deaths listed as "undetermined" or "accidents" are caused by child abuse (Hochstadt, 2006). To address the concern that child abuse fatalities were not properly investigated and classified, child death review teams have been formed. In 1978, the Los Angeles County Inter-Agency Council on Child Abuse and Neglect (ICAN) formed the first child fatality review team in the United States (ICAN, 2008). The purpose of the multidisciplinary team was to share resources and information in the forensic investigation of child fatalities. Today, there are child death review teams in all 50 states, Australia, and Canada. They closely look at child deaths from various causes, often with an emphasis on reviewing child deaths involving caretaker abuse and neglect.

Benefits of the review include improved interagency case management, identification of service gaps, and systems designed to protect children. The common goal of all teams is the prevention of child death and injury. The National Center on Child Fatality Review (NCFR) provides online data sets and information on infant homicide. The online searchable database allows professionals to locate the regional resources and provides links to all 50 states. Some counties and states have extended the scope of their reviews to include fatal family violence deaths.

Death review teams are typically made up of the following representatives: a pediatrician, medical examiner, prosecuting attorney, social worker, mental health professional, police officer, nurse, educator, and paramedic. Teams may review all deaths of children under a specified age or only selected fatalities, according to the law governing them in each state. Among their goals are improved interagency communications, better intervention for surviving at-risk siblings, and improved criminal and civil prosecution.

Been There...Done That!

Having been part of the 1980s transition in policing for Massachusetts, I am still frustrated by the lack of understanding and the failure of some police departments to use traditional investigative techniques during child abuse investigations. When queried, officers with years of experience will admit to never having executed a search warrant to obtain evidence in child abuse allegations. Although this is not the case in all jurisdictions, rigor and consistency are often lacking. Some agencies have created detective divisions to investigate and follow through with the prosecution of crimes against children, but all criminal justice professionals need to be educated to recognize the signs and symptoms of child abuse. I believe the more significant problem comes from not understanding the crimes, what might constitute evidence, and how the evidence should be gathered.

What kind of information and evidence might be gathered? Everything and anything that gives credibility to the statement or medical condition of a child! The first step toward the goal of evidence gathering lies in recognition of abuse, which is the basis of this chapter. Assessing the injury or harm is done through detection (visual and medical diagnosis), along with using the medical and family history of the events leading up to the injury.

FAMILY ABDUCTION

The most common kind of child kidnapping is parental child abduction. Each year, over 200,000 children become victims of family abduction in the United States (U.S. Department of Justice, 2010). A parent may remove or keep the child from the other, seeking to gain an advantage in expected or pending child-custody proceedings or because that parent fears to lose the child in those expected or pending child-custody proceedings. A parent may refuse to return a child at the end of a visit or may flee with the child to prevent the other parent from obtaining access for a visit. Parental child abductions may be within the same city; within the state, region, or country; or they may be international. Because of the frequency of child abduction by parents, as well as by other family members, the term *family abduction* is commonly used.

Family abduction is the taking, keeping, or concealing of a child or children by a parent, another family member, or person acting on behalf of the parent or family member that deprives another individual of his or her custody or visitation rights. The three common characteristics of family abduction are concealment, the intent to deprive the child of family contact indefinitely, and flight. Family abduction places a child in isolation with a caretaker who may neglect the child regarding care, feeding, and psychological nurturing. An abduction has long-term psychological and social effects on the child and the searching parent, siblings, and extended family (U.S. Department of Justice, 2010).

Family abduction is a serious problem both in scope and in its effect. The U.S. Congress passed the Missing Children's Assistance Act of 1984 as Title IV to amend the Juvenile Justice and Delinquency Prevention Act. Through this initiative, Congress mandated a national response to the problem of missing and exploited children to be coordinated by the Office of Juvenile Justice and Delinquency Prevention (OJJDP) along with the National Center for Missing & Exploited Children. A significant source of information on parental kidnapping comes under the direction of OJJDP from the National Center for Prosecution of Child Abuse, a nonprofit agency. In 2010, law enforcement entered 531,928 records for children younger than 18 into the FBI's National Crime Information Center databases (NCIC, 2011).

In domestic parental abduction cases, fathers and mothers are equally likely to abduct their children. A mother is more likely to abduct children following the issuance of what she perceives to be an unfavorable custody decree, and father is more likely to abduct them before issuance of a family court custody order (Alanen, 2007).

All states and the District of Columbia have statutes that prohibit parental kidnapping. The majority of perpetrators are the parent of the child, yet other family members kidnap a small percentage of these victims. Family abductions can be viewed as two separate categories, according to their severity. The first type involves situations in which a family member either took a child in violation of a custody agreement or decree or, in violation of a custody order, failed to return a child at the end of a legal or agreed-upon visit. The second type involves an attempt to conceal the taking or whereabouts of the child or to prevent contact with the child; it may involve taking the child out of state. The vast majority of these child-kidnapping cases involving family occur within the context of divorce.

International Parental Abduction

The advancement and ease of travel have led to the globalization of families. In 2016, over 18.5 million passports were issued in the United States (U.S. Department of State, 2016). Legal agreements to address the transnational issues arising from the dissolution of these relationships have resulted. According to the U.S. Department of Justice, international parental kidnappings of U.S. children have been reported in countries all over the world, including Australia, Brazil, Canada, Colombia, Germany, India, Japan, Mexico, Philippines, and the United Kingdom. Most U.S. cases involve Latin America and Europe. Every year, hundreds of children are victims wrongfully removed from the United States; recovery efforts are often difficult.

The International Parental Kidnapping Crime Act of 1993 makes it a federal offense for parents to abduct children from the United States and take them to another country (18 U.S.C. § 1204). It also criminalizes keeping a child who is in the United States away from a person with parental rights to custody. Specific provisions of the act allow a battered woman with custody who is fleeing abuse from her current partner to invoke the defense that return of the children was not possible. She must, however, notify her children's father within 24 hours that the children are safe.

The global response to increased concerns of international kidnapping prompted a treaty between 98 countries who ratified or became signatories (HCCH, 2017). Known as the Hague Convention, the treaty was designed to provide a uniform legal framework in response to abuse and corruption in the international adoption system. The 1980 Convention on the Civil Aspects of International Child Abduction addressed the problem of child kidnapping. The procedures to address international child abduction cases are civil rather than criminal. Member states are expected to help quickly return abducted children to their countries of "habitual residence." It is in the child's country of habitual residence where other issues such as custody are expected to be resolved by the local criminal justice system.

The International Child Abduction Remedies Act (ICARA) enacted by Congress establishes the Hague Convention as the law of the United States concerning children less than 16 years old. The United States is among the member states who have ratified the treaty. ICARA also requires police officers to promptly enter every case of a missing child into the National Crime Information Center (NCIC) and to take any lawful action reasonably necessary to locate a child. The number of international contested child custody cases is not insignificant. In the United States, newly reported cases of abduction and access in 2015 involved 570 children, according to the U.S. Department of State.

There are two types of Hague Convention cases: return and access. In return cases, the left-behind parent with custodial rights seeks the return of his or her child to the child's country of habitual residence. In access cases, the left-behind parent seeks enforcement of visitation rights to his or her child. There are several exceptions to the mandatory return of a child to his or her habitual residence under the Hague Convention. Of note is Article 13(b) the grave risk defense, that a forced return would put the child at grave risk. Despite evidence that domestic violence is a factor in cases of international kidnapping, in Hague Convention cases there is a general hesitancy to acknowledge this as an acceptable reason for not returning a child back to another country (Goldman School of Public Policy, 2017).

SEXUAL ABUSE INTRODUCTION

Experts disagree on the prevalence of child sexual abuse, yet it was at one time the fastest growing form of reported child abuse. The numbers of sexual abuse allegations by family members peaked in 1992 and has been steadily declining for years. The number of sexual abuse cases reported to CPS between 1992 and 2000 is estimated to have declined by 40 percent (Finkelhor & Jones, 2004). This includes a particularly large decline in sexual abuse by biological fathers in intact families. There is no solid evidence on why sexual abuse reports have declined so dramatically. Increased public awareness about child sexual abuse along with aggressive prosecution and incarceration provide possible explanations. Research confirms that child sexual abuse is recognized as a significant global problem (Stoltenborgh, Van Ijzendoorn, Euser, & Bakermans-Kranenburg, 2011).

In addition to low reporting rates of child sexual abuse, the legal procedure for validating an episode is very difficult. Another possible factor contributing to lowering CPS rates is differences in substantiation requirements. Child welfare agencies use different levels of legal evidence when making decisions to substantiate child abuse and neglect. Some states use a *preponderance of evidence*, which is the highest legal standard. Others use less rigorous standards, including *credible evidence*, *reasonable evidence*, *probable cause*, and other standards. It may be impossible to compare the levels of sexual abuse from state to state due to these variations in the evidence required to substantiate the abuse.

Child sexual abuse can take place within the family, by a parent, stepparent, sibling, or another relative; or it can occur outside the home by a friend, neighbor, or child-care worker. When family members perpetrate the abuse, it usually involves multiple episodes over a period from one week to years. However, there is no "typical" victim. Sexual abuse has been known to be committed against all ages of children, even infants.

FORMS OF CHILD SEXUAL ABUSE

A **sexual assault** on a child is any forced, exploitive, or coercive sexual contact or experience with a child. Statutes typically address the issue of force, and they vary widely. Due to the usual age difference in sexual victimization and the lack of sexual maturity in a young person, force can be as minimal as instructing a child in sexual activity. The three elements to consider when sexual abuse may be occurring include the following:

1. *A significantly older person*—Five years or more is a significant difference between a child and an older person. The difference in age may indicate a coercive power differential. For example, if the child perceives that an abuser is a person in an authority position—such as a babysitter, teacher, parent, police officer, or priest—he or she is more likely to view the individual as someone that must be obeyed or believed. Sexual relationships involving power and control are always considered abusive. Remember that children may also become sexual offenders as a result of having been victimized. The younger the child perpetrator, the more likely that he or she is also a victim of sexual abuse.

2. ***A person who engages in sexual activity***—This is any act committed for the sexual gratification of the offender. We tend to think of more common forms of sexual activity concerning children. In reality, sexual activity can also include bondage, urination (referred to as "golden showers") or defecation on a child, in addition to fondling and intercourse. Cross-dressing a child or posing a child in underwear can be sexually appealing to the pedophile and should not be overlooked as sexual activity.

3. ***Activity involving someone who is legally a child***—Achieving age 18 most often defines an adult. Some states may specify a younger or older age; other states specify different ages for legally consenting participants in particular crimes. For example, a child in Massachusetts cannot consent to intercourse until age 16, yet can consent to sexual touching at age 14. The federal standard for child pornography considers a minor to be someone who has not yet achieved the age of 18.

Often, there are no physical signs of the sexual misuse of children. Forms of sexual assault include the following:

- ***Molestation***—Molestation involves indecent touching of the child or forcing the child to touch the perpetrator on the genitals or breasts.
- ***Rape***—Rape involves the insertion of any object into any orifice for sexual gratification. Penile penetration usually comes to mind; but rape also includes digital penetration into the child's vagina or anus (use of fingers) or oral penetration of breasts, penis, or vagina (use of the mouth). In fact, any object can be used for rape; common weapons include bottles, sticks, and curling irons. Any object used to penetrate a child is a weapon of rape. Rarely, there may be a visible indication that force was used in the attempt of rape.
- ***Voyeurism***—Voyeurism includes looking at the victim in various stages of undress. The victim may or may not be aware that the perpetrator is watching him or her.
- ***Exhibitionism***—When a person exhibits his or her genitalia to a child, it is known as exhibitionism.
- ***Pornography***—For the crime to be pornography, the victim does not have to be aware that the perpetrator is filming or electronically recording.
- ***Forced prostitution***—A child is always considered to be forced when he or she is engaging in prostitution at the instruction of an adult.

Incest

Incest refers to any sexual activity between persons who are so closely related that their marriage is illegal (e.g., parents and children, uncles/aunts, and nieces/nephews, etc.). If the sexual relationship is between a parent and child, the power position of the parent identifies the perpetrator. The most common type of incestuous conduct may occur between uncles and nieces, although grandfather–granddaughter incest is another frequent type of abusive relationship (Crosson-Tower, 2008). Father–daughter and father–son incest also occurs; rarer is mother–son incest.

Adult–child incest is the type that is most commonly reported, but sibling incest may be the more frequent form. Many types of sexual contact between children are not considered harmful or abnormal, but become child-on-child sexual abuse when there is coercion, lack of consent, or simply an imbalance of power or knowledge in the relationship. Childhood sibling–sibling incest is also considered to be widespread but rarely reported. The most commonly reported form of abusive sibling incest is abuse between an older brother and a younger brother or sister.

SYMPTOMS OF SEXUAL ABUSE

As stated earlier, reports of child sexual abuse have declined in recent years. Several factors may inhibit children from reporting sexual abuse. Younger children or children who have significant developmental delays may not have the communication skills to report it. Children may not recognize acts as being improper. Children and adults may also forget or repress memories, cooperate with demands for secrecy, or fear the threats and retaliation of perpetrators. Children who are related to the perpetrator may not want the perpetrator discovered and punished.

No child is prepared to cope with sexual abuse; the child who knows and cares for the abuser becomes trapped between affection and loyalty for the person and the sense that the sexual activities are wrong. Sexually abused children may develop behavior changes such as sexual acting out, excessive masturbation, and unusual interest in or avoidance of all things of a sexual nature. They may develop sleep problems or nightmares, depression, unusual aggressiveness, and suicidal behavior, and may refuse to go to school (American Academy of Child and Adolescent Psychiatry, 2008). Other possible signs of sexual abuse include headaches, aversive reactions to particular foods such as yogurt or milk, and soreness in the genitals.

Sexual and nonsexual trauma to the genital area can result in abrasion, bruising, and laceration. Tears through the hymen and anal fissures will heal over a period of weeks (Johnson, 2006). Because the child may not be taken to a physician right away, the delay of reporting may mean that the trauma has an opportunity to heal. Sexual abuse may result in a sexually transmitted disease (STD) or pregnancy. It is not unusual for the child to present with symptoms of a venereal disease. Gonorrhea, syphilis, AIDS, herpes, venereal warts, and pubic lice are examples of STDs. There are three general categories of indicators of sexual abuse. These signs include physical, behavioral, and caretaker indicators.

Physical Indicators

1. Enlarged vaginal or anal opening.
2. Bleeding or discharge from the vagina, penis, or anus.
3. Scratching or rubbing the genitals.
4. Walking with the buttocks and legs apart (as if the child has to have a bowel movement).
5. Current physical injury accompanied by signs of multiple prior injuries.

Behavioral Indicators

1. Complaining that his or her genitals hurt or were touched.
2. Acting out sexually with other children.
3. Inappropriate sexual knowledge for his or her home environment and age.
4. Being fearful or unwilling to explain the cause of any injury.
5. Regression.

More About It: Maltreatment

Keep in mind that as individuals, we have our own perspectives on how children should be raised, based on our upbringing and family history. Be careful not to impose your standards on another family! Additionally, families living in poverty will appear different due to a lack of resources and should not be accused of abuse simply because they do not live the way you do! Abuse is maltreatment, not a result of the living standards or values of other families.

Caretaker Indicators

1. Delay or failure to seek medical treatment for a child in circumstances that would warrant medical attention.
2. History is not consistent with the child's developmental level or ability to harm himself or herself.
3. Historical details change or are different from the caretaker's original version.

SEXUAL ABUSE ACCOMMODATION SYNDROME

A child who is sexually assaulted typically will not report the abuse when it first occurs. Children often do not even realize that the behavior is abusive. There is usually an *engagement phase* before the perpetrator initiates sexual contact. During this time, a relationship is being established between the victim and the offender. By the time any sexual conduct takes place, the child trusts the adult. Next is a *progression phase*: The abuser may begin with common activities that require the child to undress. Swimming is one example used to desensitize the child about removing clothing in the presence of the perpetrator. From then on, a range of sexual abuses may be attempted, ranging from indecent touching to intercourse. The final phase is *suppression*. Somehow the offender must ensure the secrecy of the events that have occurred.

Summit's characterization, referred to as the *sexual abuse accommodation syndrome*, includes five phases common to the experiences of the child who has been sexually victimized: secrecy; helplessness; entrapment and accommodation; delayed, conflicted, and unconvincing disclosure; and retraction (Summit, 1982).

Secrecy

Child sexual abuse is almost always cloaked in secrecy. Frequently, the perpetrator will warn the child not to tell anyone. Secrecy is secured in various ways, depending on the age of the child and the relationship to the perpetrator. If a child tries to tell an adult about the behavior, the attempt is usually met with disbelief and minimization. Additionally, the child abuser picks his or her victims carefully; he or she already knows the vulnerability of the child and how to guarantee silence before the abuse occurs.

Rewards and incentives for secrecy are common. For example, a young child may be bribed with toys, a bicycle, or dolls. Affection and attachment for needy youngsters is sometimes enough to win compliance. Adolescents may be permitted to use the family car; buying expensive clothing and jewelry is not uncommon. The fact that the victims are rewarded for incestual secrecy does not mean that they are being "paid" for the act. This becomes confusing when the victim is an adolescent, mainly if the child has been taught manipulative behavior through abuse. In time, the victim knows that secrecy has a price, comes to expect gifts and rewards, and may even demand them.

Shame and guilt also come as the child begins to realize what is happening to him or her. When the violator is a family member, the child may have been cajoled into the sexual activity, being told "this is normal," "everyone does this," or "this is called love." Although the child probably does not like the activity, he or she has no reason to doubt what he or she has been told. At some point, the realization that the activity is not right creeps in, regardless of what the child has been told, and the child feels guilt and shame for his or her participation.

The child victim knows that a price is being paid for the silence. Victims wonder what the cost of breaking that silence would be. Keep in mind that these are children: They do not reason as adults. They might not be able to ride the bike they love or wear that pretty dress. Often, the offender will warn the child that if he or she tells anyone, the offender will go to jail and the child will never see him or her again. To a young child, that idea is devastating. In relatively few cases, the family abuser will threaten to kill the child, other family members, or even pets. Threats do not have to be elaborate or particularly believable to adults to have a severe impact on a child. Understanding the perspective of the child is therefore essential.

A bond exists in the victim–offender relationship, even though it is deviant behavior. The child might fear to lose his or her parent's love if he or she told anyone. The victim is favored in the family—although others do not know, it is his or her secret.

Helplessness

Intrusiveness characterizes sexual assaults against children. Frequently, it occurs in their bedroom, making that place no longer safe for them. The intrusion causes anxiety and insecurity, another part of the victimization process. Children may feign sleep during the assault, even though a sibling may be in the next bed or a parent in the next room. Rarely will a child cry out. Children may feel responsible for their failure to prevent or stop the abuse.

Entrapment and Accommodation

Self-hate develops over time as the child exaggerates his or her responsibility for the abuse. "No one will believe you," victims are often told. Older children, frequently adolescents, can be blackmailed through sexually explicit photographs that the abuser states will "prove" that they consented. Remember that consent is *not* a legal issue when sex occurs between a child and an adult, but children do not know that! In most jurisdictions, a child cannot consent to sexual intercourse.

A promise not to sexually assault siblings may be involved. It is not unusual for a victim to come forward with a complaint of sexual abuse when he or she believes that the offender is breaking that promise. A child who has been victimized over time comes to accommodate his or her abuse, yet often will not tolerate it happening to a younger sibling.

Delayed, Conflicted, and Unconvincing Disclosure

Sexual abuse that is ongoing is frequently kept the secret within the family. The victim usually remains silent until he or she enters adolescence. A family fight or punishment that the teenager disagrees with may trigger disclosure. A younger sibling being targeted for abuse may also spark the victim to tell someone. Victims may tell a friend or a teacher. The reaction is usually one of disbelief and denial. If a nonoffending parent is the first told, that parent's reaction will probably affect what happens next.

Been There...Done That!

Efforts designed to provide coordination among child protective workers, the police, the medical community, and the prosecutor's office include the interdisciplinary or multiagency team approach. It is helpful to include a forensic mental health specialist or child psychologist on the team, if possible. Team members share information and discuss options for the child. In 1984, I was a member of one of the first interdisciplinary teams to investigate child abuse in Massachusetts at the Northwestern District Attorney's office under Michael Ryan. It worked like this: Once a week, the team would meet for one to two hours. The department of social services investigator would bring the week's list of child abuse allegations of serious physical or sexual abuse. The team—which included a doctor, prosecutor, mental health worker, victim witness assistant, and me, as the police representative—would discuss the cases.

We determined who would conduct the interview of the child to minimize the number of interviews. The interviewer could be any team member or a forensic interviewer. Then we discussed the cases already in the process of investigation.

In cases that the prosecutor thought were likely to go to trial, I would conduct the first interview since I typically electronically recorded these interviews with the victims. The recording would be shared with the necessary agencies, or representatives could watch through a two-way mirror as the interview was being conducted. The police would always interrogate the perpetrator and then submit a full report to the social service agency to complete the police mandate to talk with the abuser.

When present (it was difficult to have a doctor or doctor's representative attend all meetings), the physician or representative would advise on the necessity of a physical exam. He or she would explain the findings if an exam had already been done. The victim witness advocate and mental health professional would express their concerns about any mental health problems and address the victim's perceived ability to withstand the rigors of a criminal trial. We discussed the reliability of the victim and the consistency of any reports regarding the abuse. This coordinated response resulted in many child abuse cases never coming to trial, for any number of reasons that the team might bring up, including the needs of the victim. Successful prosecution of these problematic cases increased with the team approach.

Multidisciplinary teams have sprung up across the nation. Experts suggest that the team approach is the best method of investigation for child abuse cases. I agree.

Retraction

Whatever a child says about incest, he or she is likely to recant at some point. Changing the account of the abuse is problematic for criminal justice, and it must be anticipated if prosecution is to occur. The victim needs support and reassurance through a prosecution for incest. The investigation needs to seek any form of corroboration available in anticipation that the victim will, at some point, deny the abuse. If a case for sexual abuse rests solely on the word of a child (without evidence) and the truthfulness of the victim comes into question through a denial, a successful prosecution is impossible.

Been There...Done That!

At the same time that domestic violence became a criminal justice concern, women and minority officers were making their way into the ranks. Fertile ground for specialization existed, especially for officers with unique skills or education. The belief that women would be the best investigators for child abuse was a commonly held notion. One of my academy classmates was approached to take a position for child abuse investigation. Her response, it was rumored, went something like this: "I hate those little buggers. No, thank you, if I wanted to be around kids, I would have some. Don't like them, don't want them—don't make me talk to kids!" Gender alone does not qualify someone as a child abuse expert. Being a man does not exclude one from doing a great job in this field either.

CHILDREN'S ADVOCACY CENTER MODEL

From the involvement of criminal justice in the investigation and prosecution of child sexual abuse and neglect came the development of multidisciplinary response models. While there are numerous models of investigation, the Children's Advocacy Center (CAC) model of investigation has been adopted nationally and internationally as a promising approach. The CAC model is sometimes referred to as the National Children's Advocacy Center (NCAC) model. The essential components of the CAC model are built on established best practices, including the use of multidisciplinary team investigations with trained child forensic interviewers and videotaped interviews. Only specialized forensic medical examiners are involved in the investigations. Central to this model is the establishment of children's advocacy centers, which offer victim advocacy, support programs, and access to mental health treatment in addition to investigative services. Each of these components is considered critical to the success of child abuse investigations.

There are 822 CACs nationwide which serve over 324, 600 children each year (National Children's Alliance, 2017). Numerous barriers to disclosure of sexual abuse are evident; children may be re-victimized by the criminal justice system itself. The CAC model addresses these concerns by prioritizing the needs of children over bureaucratic demands through interviewing in child-friendly settings by trained forensic interviewers. Centers strive to achieve a physically and psychologically safe environment. The center location is determined to include consideration of client access and diverse cultural accessibility.

When law enforcement or CPS suspect that a child is being abused, that child is brought to the advocacy center where the child is interviewed by a trained forensic interviewer. Unlike physical abuse, child sexual abuse rarely leaves traces in the form of medical evidence. Therefore, a child's disclosure must be conducted carefully and documented. Forensic interviews are conducted in a manner that is legally sound, non-duplicative, non-leading and neutral. The CAC forensic interviewers come from a highly trained pool of professionals. Cultural competency and diversity, as well as Awareness of Trauma-Informed Care training, are core requirements for interviewers (Kenny, Vazquez, Long, & Thompson, 2017). The NCAC has established standards and accreditation for its members, offers training and certification courses, and a searchable library of child sexual abuse and related information.

Research has shown that compared to other approaches, CAC communities show significantly higher rates of coordinated investigations between law enforcement and child protective services (Cross, Jones, Walsh, Simone, & Kolko, 2007). The multidisciplinary teams coordinate intervention to reduce potential trauma to children and families and improve services while respecting the obligations of each agency (National Children's Alliance, 2017). Multidisciplinary team members with investigative responsibilities are present for the forensic interviews. Forensic interviews are routinely conducted at the CAC with active multidisciplinary team involvement. Representation includes law enforcement, child protective services, prosecution, medical, mental health, victim advocacy, and the children's advocacy center itself.

CONCLUSIONS

EMTs, law enforcement officers, and CPS caseworkers are typical first responders to cases involving child abuse and neglect. An assessment or investigation of maltreatment may involve either law enforcement or child protection services. The goals of each agency differ. CPS determines the short-term safety issues that arise from an allegation, collects evidence to substantiate the report, and makes decisions on the long-term safety of the child. Actions taken by CPS are civil and may involve going to court for a judge to make custody determinations. After the initial determination on child safety, law enforcement is tasked with determining if a crime has been committed, collecting evidence, and identifying the offender. If probable cause exists that a crime was committed, the case may proceed to criminal court. An investigation process may involve both CPS and law enforcement, often through a multidisciplinary team approach to minimize the harms associated with multiple interviews. All states have laws that protect children, providing for civil and criminal remedies.

Investigating physical abuse can be difficult since bruises and cuts can be accidental injuries as well as the consequence of abuse. Bruising, patterns of injury, and location of injury are all critical components for an investigator to consider. Even serious injuries such as broken bones can be mistaken for abuse if a child is born with a disease such as osteogenesis imperfecta. Children that are victimized by Munchausen syndrome by proxy may have undetected maltreatment due to an illness that is caused by the offending family member. Shaken baby syndrome may result in the death of the infant.

Death of a child due to maltreatment is a tragic result of abuse. Children under the age of three are at the highest risk of death due to abuse and neglect. It can be challenging to determine if a child death is the result of SIDS (sudden infant death syndrome), accidental causes, or abuse. Child death review teams have sprung up across the country with experts who are trained in the detection of abuse and neglect to assist in the investigation by making medical determinations on the cause of death. A recent concern in the area of child maltreatment comes from the problems due to family abduction—both domestic and international. In the United States, family abduction is a criminal offense. When the case involves international abduction, it may be a criminal offense, but the response to obtain the return of the child is civil under the Hague Convention.

The incidence of reported child sexual abuse cases declined steadily after 1992, despite it being recognized as a significant global problem. There is no real explanation as to why that happened, and many believe it is highly underreported. The three categories of sexual abuse indicators are physical, behavioral, and caretaker indicators. A child that is being sexually abused may not even realize due to their age and immaturity that the sexual contact is abuse. Typically, they will not report the assault when it first occurs. Summit characterized the five phases that are common to the experiences of the child who has been sexually victimized: secrecy; helplessness; entrapment and accommodation; delayed, conflicted, and unconvincing disclosure; and retraction.

The CAC model is a growing response to the investigation of child sexual abuse used in the United States and around the world. The model involves the use of multidisciplinary teams and trained child forensic interviewers. Only specialized forensic medical examiners are involved in the investigations. Central to this model is the establishment of children's advocacy centers which offer victim advocacy, support programs, and access to mental health treatment in addition to investigative services. Each of these components is considered critical to the success of child abuse investigations.

SIMPLY SCENARIO
A Burn Victim

Clare said that she was running the bathwater for her two-year-old daughter Mary when the doorbell rang. She instructed Mary to "sit and wait" until she returned. Going as fast as possible, Clare went to answer the door. Almost immediately, she heard her daughter screaming and returned to the bath to find that Mary had gotten into the tub water and was jumping up and down because it was too hot. There was a sharp line on the lower back that indicated the waterline. There was a waterline around the ankles of the child's feet that resembled a glove. There were no splash marks on the child.

Question: Is the explanation of what happened consistent with the injury?

Questions for Review

1. Who are the three most common first responders to cases involving child maltreatment?
2. State the four critical steps for child abuse and neglect investigations.
3. What is the significance of the location of the injury on a child during the assessment of child abuse?
4. What are the two types of Hague Convention cases?
5. How does a first-degree burn differ in appearance from a second- or third-degree burn?
6. What is the difference between feticide and filicide?
7. Name the six forms of sexual assault.
8. Why were Child Death Review Teams formed?
9. What are the five phases of the sexual abuse accommodation syndrome, according to Summit?
10. Explain the CAC model of investigation.

Internet-Based Exercises

1. The Child Welfare Information Gateway provides an online searchable database of state statutes at http://www.childwelfare.gov/systemwide/laws_policies/state/. From this site, search the database for the state in which you live to find the law that defines domestic violence. Compare and contrast this information with that of one or more states. Report on your findings.
2. The Children's Bureau develops the annual Child Maltreatment reports. These include data that the states submit to the National Child Abuse and Neglect Data Systems. The latest report can be found at http://www.acf.hhs.gov/programs/cb/research-data-technology/statistics-research/child-maltreatment. What can you learn about the CPS's responses to an allegation of child abuse and neglect?
3. This chapter highlighted the issue of parental kidnapping. What do you know about Amber Alert and its role in finding these missing children? Conduct an Internet search and write an essay on Amber Alert.
4. Go to the National Children's Alliance Web page at http://www.nationalchildrensalliance.org/ to research this important organization and its role with the Children's Advocacy Center Model.

References

Alanen, J. (2007). Remedies and resources to combat international family abduction. *American Journal of Family Law, 21*(2), 11–27.

American Academy of Child & Adolescent Psychiatry. (2008). Child sexual abuse. Retrieved from http://www.aacap.org/

American Lung Association. (2008). Sudden infant death syndrome fact sheet (SIDS). *Diseases—S*. Retrieved from http://www.lungusa.org

Centers for Disease Control and Prevention. (CDC). (2009). Intimate partner violence during pregnancy—A guide for clinicians. Retrieved from http://www.cdc.gov

/reproductivehealth/violence/IntimatePartnerViolence/sld001.htm

Centers for Disease Control and Prevention. (CDC). (2013). Heads up: Prevent shaken baby syndrome. Retrieved from http://www.cdc.gov/concussion/headsup/sbs.html

Child Welfare Information Gateway. (2012). *Child abuse and neglect fatalities 2010: Statistics and interventions.* Washington, D.C.: U.S. Department of Health and Human Services, Children's Bureau.

Cooper, A., & Smith, E. L. (2011). *Homicide trends in the United States, 1980–2008: Annual rates for 2009 and 2010.* Washington, D.C.: U.S. Department of Justice. Retrieved from http://bjs.gov/content/pub/pdf/htus8008.pdf

Criddle, L. (2010). Monsters in the closet: Munchausen syndrome by proxy. *Critical Care Nurse, 30*(6), 46–55.

Cross, T. P., Jones, L. M., Walsh, W. A., Simone, M., & Kolko, D. (2007). Child forensic interviewing in Children's Advocacy Centers: Empirical data on a practice model. *Child Abuse & Neglect, 31*(10), 1031–1052.

Crosson-Tower, C. (2008). *Understanding child abuse and neglect.* Boston, MA: Pearson.

Finkelhor, D., & Jones, L. (2004). *Explanations for the decline in child sexual abuse cases.* Washington, D.C.: U.S. Department of Justice, Office of Juvenile Justice and Delinquency Prevention.

Goldman School of Public Policy. (2017). The Hague Convention and domestic violence. Retrieved from https://gspp.berkeley.edu/global/the-hague-domestic-violence-project/hague-dv/hague-convention-and-domestic-violence

HCCH. (2017). Convention of 29 May 1993 on Protection of Children and Co-operation in Respect of Intercountry Adoption. Retrieved from https://www.hcch.net/en/instruments/conventions/status-table/?cid=69

Hochstadt, N. J. (2006). Child death review teams: A vital component of child protection. *Child Welfare, 85,* 653–670.

ICAN. (2008). National Center on Child Fatality Review. Retrieved from http://www.ican-ncfr.org/default2.asp

Johnson, C. F. (2006). Sexual abuse in children. *Pediatric Review, 27,* 17–27.

Kenny, M. C., Vazquez, A., Long, H., & Thompson, D. (2017). Implementation and program evaluation of trauma-informed care training across state child advocacy centers: An exploratory study. *Children and Youth Services Review, 73,* 15–23.

National Children's Alliance. (2017). Annual Report 2016: Empowering local communities to serve child victims of abuse. Retrieved from http://www.nationalchildrensalliance.org/sites/default/files/downloads/NCA-2016-Annual-Report.pdf

National Crime Information Center. (NCIC). (2011). *NCIC missing person and unidentified person statistics for 2010.* Retrieved from www.fbi.gov/about-us/cjis/ncic/ncic-missing-person-and-unidentified-person-statistics-for-2010

NICHD Information Resource Center. (2012). Safe to sleep. Retrieved from http://www.nichd.nih.gov/sids/pages/sids.aspx

Parks, S., Sugerman, D., Xu, L., & Coronado, V. (2012). Characteristics of non-fatal abusive head trauma among children in the USA, 2003–2008: Application of the CDC operational case definition to national hospital inpatient data. *Injury Prevention, 18*(6), 392–398.

Stoltenborgh, M., Van Ijzendoorn, M. H., Euser, E. M., & Bakermans-Kranenburg, M. J. (2011). A global perspective on child sexual abuse: Meta-analysis of prevalence around the world. *Child Maltreatment, 16*(2), 79–101.

Summit, R. (1982). Beyond belief: The reluctant discovery of incest. In M. Kirkpatrick (Ed.), *Women's sexual experience: Explorations of the dark continent.* New York, NY: Plenum Press.

Tamay, Z., Akcay, A., Kilic, G., Peykerli, G., Devecioglu, E., Ones, U., & Guler, N. (2007). Corrosive poisoning mimicking cicatricial pemphigoid: Munchausen by proxy. *Child: Care, Health and Development, 33,* 496–499.

Toon, M. H., Maybauer, D. M., Arceneaux, L. L., Fraser, J. F., Meyer, W., Runge, A., & Maybauer, M. O. (2011). Children with burn injuries-assessment of trauma, neglect, violence and abuse. *Journal of Injury & Violence Research, 3*(2), 98–110.

U.S. Department of Justice. (2010). The crime of family abduction: A child's and parent's perspective. Washington, D.C.: Author Retrieved from http://www.ncjrs.gov/pdffiles1/ojjdp/229933.pdf.

U.S. Department of Health and Human Services and Administration for Children and Families, Children's Bureau. (2012). *Child maltreatment 2011.* Retrieved from http://www.acf.hhs.gov/programs/cb/research-data-technology/statistics-research/child-maltreatment

U.S. Department of State. (2016). Passport statistics. Retrieved from http://travel.state.gov/content/passports/english/passports/statistics.html

Adolescent and Young Adult Victimization

CHAPTER OBJECTIVES

After reviewing this chapter, you should be able to:

1. Examine the value of resilience in contrast to vulnerability in cases of personal violence.
2. Discuss the forms of sexual offending against minors.
3. Give examples of investigative techniques and approaches when sexual exploitation and assault is involved.
4. Describe the consequences of teen and college dating violence.
5. Summarize the hazards of cyber dating abuse.

KEY TERMS

Child sex trafficking

Commercial sex act

Competency

Credibility

Dating violence

Digital dating abuse

Jane Doe reporting

Polyvictimization

INTRODUCTION

Family violence occurs at every life stage. The effects of abuse can last forever. There is an interconnectedness between the forms of violence that occur in childhood, in intimate partner relationships, and against adults both young and old. There is a stage of life rarely discussed, the tumultuous time occupied by teens and young adults.

Violence affecting youth is sometimes hidden and often goes unnoticed. These are not children and not yet fully grown individuals. Society expects adolescents to behave like adults and the laws of the United States reflect that position. We hold minors accountable as adults when they commit major crimes. Juveniles are expected to know how to respond to predators as if they understood the potential consequence of the relationship. The question is whether we adequately prepare adolescents for meeting the challenges of youthful behavior. Education on the forms of victimization that may affect this group is vital to take on the role as protectors to the coming generation. We now know that young people lack the maturity and self-discipline to conform to adult expectations. Youth are particularly vulnerable and extremely malleable.

The hidden victimization of youth occurs between childhood and adulthood in our reporting systems. Contributors to the problem in addressing adolescent harm are the inconsistency between sources of data and the lack of legitimate research on forms of violence to which juveniles are vulnerable. Some research on violence includes victimizations of females and males aged 12 and older, and crime statistics classify all as children until somewhere around age 18. The exact age of an adult varies by state law. In this chapter, when it is known, the term "girls or boys" is used to refer to a child under the age of 18. It may seem duplicitous to have a chapter devoted to minors when minors are also considered children, yet their situation is unique. When victimized, the status is legally child abuse until age 18 or later, yet offenders may be considered adults at any age.

Drawing a sharp line between children and adults is as difficult in the literature of family violence as it is in the law. This chapter addresses the void by examining the vulnerability of adolescents and young adults within the context of domestic violence. Stranger danger is not the major concern here. As with child abuse and adult violence, family, friends, and loved ones are the most frequent offenders. This chapter is devoted to issues affecting adolescents and young adults.

VIOLENCE

First, it must be stated that child abuse does not end with the onset of adolescence. Until recently, the frequency of adolescent physical and sexual victimization went unnoticed. Adolescents are thought to be capable of protecting themselves; the numbers indicate that this misconception could cause inappropriate responses to allegations of abuse by teenagers.

Violence is a form of intentional injury. Violence includes the intentional use of physical force or power whether it is threatened or actual, against any one person or a group, that either result in or may have a high likelihood of resulting in harm. Dating and family violence can have devastating effects on the health and well-being of a person throughout his or her life. There is an overlap of violence from adolescence to adulthood when adult-like decisions come from the perspective of youth.

According to the *National Intimate Partner and Sexual Violence Survey* (NISVS), individuals sexually abused as children face a higher probability of sexual victimization as an adult (Walters, Chen, & Breiding, 2013). As adults, more than 40 percent of female rape survivors report that the first completed rape occurred before their turning age 18 (Smith et al., 2017). Almost 25 percent of adult male rape victims report sexual victimization before age 18 (Smith et al., 2017). Refer to Figure 6-1 for the comparison between boys and girls. Girls and young women are more likely to be victims of rape; boys and young men are more apt to experience being forced into penetrating someone else. Where it was once thought that sexual crime victimized only girls, there is a growing awareness of the vulnerability of boys.

The effects of child abuse may affect their vulnerability through life. The proportion of women who are raped as children or adolescents and also raped as adults is more than three times higher than the percentage of women without an early rape history (Black et al., 2011). Put another way, more than one-third (35.2 percent) of the women who reported a completed rape before the age of 18 also experienced a completed rape as an adult, compared to 14.2 percent of the women who did not report rape before age 18. This information suggests that we need to consider the devastating

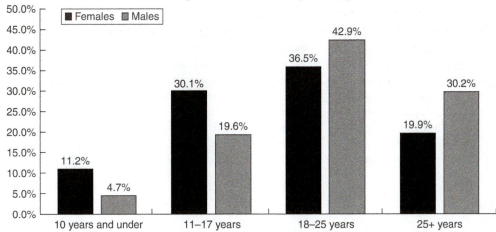

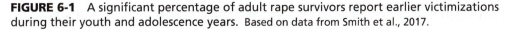

FIGURE 6-1   A significant percentage of adult rape survivors report earlier victimizations during their youth and adolescence years. Based on data from Smith et al., 2017.

effects of childhood sexual abuse as a risk factor for future victimization in shaping prevention and treatment interventions.

There is a connection between violence offending and victimization in teen dating violence and bullying. Of more than 8 percent of teens who report having bullied a classmate, almost one in five has also been a victim of dating violence (Yahner, Dank, Zweig, & Lachman, 2015). Youth who perpetrated and experienced violence were likely to have also perpetrated or experienced dating violence and cyber dating abuse.

VULNERABILITY & RESILIENCE

Due to health and safety concerns for youth who experience violence, research has looked at both the vulnerability and resilience of young people. Studies suggest that adolescents who are victims of dating violence are more likely to experience symptoms of depression and anxiety, to exhibit antisocial behaviors, and to consider suicide (Exner-Cortens, Eckenrode, & Rothman, 2013). Current prevention efforts emphasize increasing the protective factors for youth to decrease their vulnerability to violence. One in four youth reports verbal, emotional, physical, or sexual dating violence each year.

The issues that make it more likely that someone will experience violence, typically expressed as risk factors are referred to as vulnerability. Family conflict, rigid role expectations, and lack of job opportunities are examples. Alcohol, tobacco, cocaine use, driving after drinking, unhealthy weight control behaviors, and risky sexual behaviors are among the increased risks for adolescents who experience physical and sexual violence. Individuals with disabilities, mental health disorders, and LGBTI youth are among the populations with an increased vulnerability to abuse due to targeting by bullies.

Sometimes referred to as the protective factors, are the influences known to promote positive outcomes for teens. One known protective factor for youth is individual resiliency, which is the ability and skill to adapt to adversity successfully. Connectedness to family, parents, school, religion, and responsible adults are all

Been There ... Done That!

As related to me, an 11-year-old girl told her mother that she felt uncomfortable with a summer camp counselor. Being receptive to her daughter, Ellen asked the child what made her feel that way. He acts different with me and treats me special, said the child. Go on, said the mother. Ava continued to say that when the counselor goes to pick up coffee and donuts in the morning, he always takes her and no one else. On that day, he asked if he could kiss her. Ava said she said no, but did not want that to happen again.

Ellen suggested to Ava that she drop the summer camp, which was not well received. So, Ava was given the opportunity to tell the counselor that she was not his girlfriend and did not want him to be around her or try and kiss her ... while Ellen stood by for support. In an open area of the camp, Ava had the opportunity to handle the situation in a safe way! Ellen also reported the incident to the camp authorities and to the police to protect the other children whom he had access to as a camp counselor.

positive influences for adolescents. Youth with high self-esteem and social support are better prepared to protect themselves. Access to mental health services or connection to a caring adult can also promote well-being.

Disabilities

Individuals with disabilities are at significantly increased risk of violence of all forms. Among the reasons why this may occur is a reliance on caregivers, isolation, and limited transportation options. Additionally, people with disabilities experience the same types of child abuse, intimate partner violence, and older adult violence as people without disabilities. According to *Child Maltreatment 2011* (U.S. Department of Health and Human Services and Administration for Children and Families, 2012), almost 20 percent of child abuse victims have a disability or medical condition. Disabilities include emotional disturbance, visual or hearing impairment, learning disability, physical disability, behavioral problems, or another medical and mental disorders.

Among college students with disabilities, a heightened risk of experiencing intimate partner violence is also evident. Students with disabilities become targets for violence before attending college, according to research. College students with disabilities report having had experienced physical or sexual abuse before the age of 17 at rates higher than 20 percent (Findley, Plummer, & McMahon, 2016). From an analysis of the American College Health Association's (ACHA) National College Health Assessment II, one study estimated that these students are approximately twice as likely to experience intimate partner violence compared with other college students without disabilities (Scherer, Snyder, & Fisher, 2016). Depression and self-harm are among the long-term impacts on these victims of intimate partner violence. It is possible that intimate partners may view students with disabilities as being less reliable to reporting authorities or unable to resist due to mental or physical disabilities.

Research has found mental disorders to be more common in the United States than previously realized. The *National Survey on Drug Use and Health* concluded that one in four adults and one in five children has a diagnosable mental illness (Substance Abuse and Mental Health Services Administration, 2014). However, there is also a recent trend towards redefining mental disorders. Some authors state that higher estimates of mental illness in the population is entirely due to the inclusion of fourteen new disorders, including disorders specific to childhood and elderly populations (Wittchen et al., 2011). Whether increases regarding violence aimed specifically at individuals with mental illness is causal or definitional is uncertain. Refer to the data on child victims of abuse and neglect by disability type in Figure 6-2.

Sexual Orientation or Identity

Although dating violence affects people of all ages, background, and identities, LGBT youth are at a higher risk of abuse than other adolescents. Compared to heterosexual teens, research has shown that young LGB people are more likely to experience bullying and physical violence, placing them at an increased risk for suicidal thoughts and behaviors, sexual risk behavior, and substance abuse (Bouris et al., 2010). There is evidence that LGB adolescents are at greater danger of experiencing all forms of dating abuse and cyber dating abuse than their heterosexual peers (Dank, Lachman, Zweig, & Yahner, 2014). Transgender, intersex, and questioning youth are newly recognized categories which are not involved in these studies. More information is needed on the vulnerabilities of these young people.

Gay and bisexual men report sexual assault at frequencies similar to heterosexual women during their college years, approximately one in every four (Ford & Soto-Marquez, 2016). The Ford study also found that bisexual women were at the highest risk of sexual assault, almost two out of every five female college students experienced sexual assault. These rates in college are highly associated with membership rates in fraternities or sororities. Governments and non-government organizations (NGOs) in the United States estimate that lesbian, gay, bisexual, transgender, and intersex (LGBTI) youth make up to 40 percent of the adolescent homeless population at high risk of being forced into prostitution and human trafficking (U.S. Department of State, 2017a).

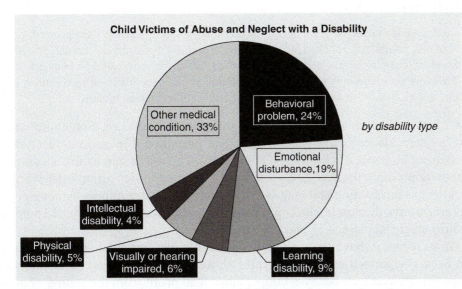

FIGURE 6-2 In 2013, almost 13 percent of children who were abused or neglected had a disability. The form of disability among that population is illustrated here. Based on data from the U.S. Department of Health and Human Services, 2015.

Research on parenting confirms that it is important for parents to have open and honest conversations about sex; to know their teen's friends and what their teen is doing, and to develop common goals with them such as being healthy and doing well in school. In a study of LGB youth who engaged in risky behaviors, authors found a notable absence of supportive and involved parents (Bouris et al., 2010). When parents are actively involved with their teen by talking and listening to them, staying involved and providing support decreases the chances that their teen will engage in risky behaviors. Based on available research, the Centers for Disease Control (CDC) suggests that for transgender youth, gay and straight alliances and family support are potential protective factors to risky behavior (CDC, 2017).

EXPLOITATION AND SEX TRAFFICKING OF MINORS

Determining how many people are being victimized by trafficking is difficult because victims are reluctant to come forward and ask for help. Even while the extent of human trafficking in the United States is unknown, it has become a major public issue and believed to involve scores of survivors. Sexual exploitation and forced labor are the most well-known forms. Trafficking can take numerous other forms including victims compelled to act like beggars, forced into sham marriages, pornography, and organ removal. Sex trafficking of youth is one of the most common types of commercial sexual exploitation. Targets of sex trafficking include girls, boys, and LGBTI youth. Commercial sexual exploitation (CSEC) is distinctly different from sex trafficking, although the terms frequently are used interchangeably, and they do overlap.

From the original statute, *Trafficking Victims Protection Act* ("TVPA," 2000)(4), A **commercial sex act** is any sex act on account of which anything of value is given to or received by any person. According to the U.S. Department of State (2017b), **child sex trafficking** occurs:

> when a child (under 18 years of age) is recruited, enticed, harbored, transported, provided, obtained, patronized, solicited, or maintained to perform a commercial sex act, proving force, fraud, or coercion is not necessary for the offense to be prosecuted as human trafficking. There are no exceptions to this rule: no cultural or socioeconomic rationalizations alter the fact that children who are exploited in prostitution are trafficking victims (p.1).

Crimes of human trafficking are of international concern. Sometimes referred to as "modern slavery," the phenomenon has prompted 158 nations to enact laws criminalizing human trafficking (UNODC, 2016). The use of minors in the commercial sex trade is prohibited under U.S. law and in most countries around the world. Sex trafficking has devastating and long-lasting consequences for minors. Among potential harms are trauma, disease (including HIV/AIDS), drug addiction, unwanted pregnancy, malnutrition, social ostracism, and even death.

Only recently have commercial sexual exploitation and sex trafficking of youth been categorized as forms of child abuse (National Research Council, 2013). The classification occurs because pimps, those who profit from the selling of a minor, can be family members, foster parents, trusted adults, or boyfriends. A commercial sexually exploited minor is someone who is under the age of 18, a victim of sex trafficking, and something of value such as money or drugs or a place to stay is traded for the sexual activity.

The actual scope of commercial sexual exploitation of minors in America is difficult to determine yet recognized as a problem of grave concern (National Research Council, 2013). Children with a history of abuse, runaways, and throwaways (children refused permission to return home) are at risk for commercial sexual exploitation. According to Kotria (2010), children are most vulnerable to victimization between the ages of 11 and 14. Research suggests that as many as 70 percent of adult women involved in prostitution were exploited as minors before age 18 (Kotria, 2010).

From what is known to date, commercial sexual exploitation victims in the U.S. are more likely to be exploited for monetary gain by family and friends (Albanese, 2013). The National Center for Missing & Exploited Children estimates that 3,083 runaways each year are likely sex trafficking victims, illustrated in Figure 6-3. Of these runaways, 86 percent (3,585) of the minors are in the care of social services or foster care when they went missing (NCMEC, 2017).

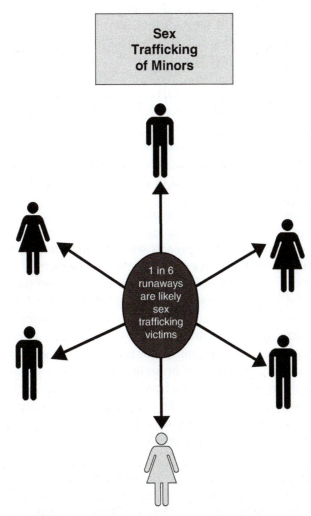

FIGURE 6-3   In 2016, 1 in 6 of the 18,500 runaways reported to the National Center for Missing & Exploited Children were likely sex trafficking victims (NCMEC, 2017).

The commercial sexual exploitation and sex trafficking of children represent the organized sexual abuse of young children and adolescents. Albanese (2013) described the organizational structure of CSEC through these three categories:

1. *Local exploitation* by one or a few adults.
2. *The citywide or regional network* involves multiple children and often other criminal activity such as drugs.
3. *National or international sex crime network* where children are trafficked and marked as goods for sale.

The first federal sex trafficking criminal statute was passed in the United States in 2000, amended in 2015 ("Trafficking Act," 2015). Under the original *Trafficking Victims Protection Act* (TVPA), all individuals under the age of 18 who trade sex for money are defined as victims of human trafficking, creating an alternative to the traditional view of prostitution when minors are involved. The downward spiral of child sexual exploitation often starts when an adult family member or friend sexually abuses a minor in his or her care. The abuse can intensify to photographing or videotaping sexual assault and distributing it through the Internet. The continuum of sexual violence and CSEC is a downward spiral, which leads to the sharing of child photos over the Internet to child pimping, and ultimately ending when the child is kidnapped and sold into prostitution and sex tourism (Albanese, 2013).

The U.S. Department of Justice (DOJ) coordinates the response to human trafficking. Multidisciplinary anti-trafficking teams are considered the best practice response. The National Human Trafficking Hotline (NHTRC) takes phone calls, online tips, and e-mails from across the country on potential human trafficking cases in the United States. In 2015, the NHTRC hotline received reports of 5,545 potential human trafficking cases in the United States, 1,630 of these cases (29.4 percent) involved minor victims (NHTRC, 2016).

Response teams include local law-enforcement agencies and victim service providers who partner with enforcement and regulatory agencies and resources. The model involves a victim-centered approach whereby the victim's wishes, safety, and well-being take priority in all matters and procedures. For victims who choose to work with law enforcement, the approach attempts to minimize re-traumatization associated with the criminal justice process by providing advocates and service providers for empowering survivors in seeing their traffickers brought to justice.

Suspected human traffickers can be sued under both state and federal law. Federal courts have jurisdiction to receive claims that arise from either state or federal violations. State courts usually hear claims brought for violations of state law. Task force partners cooperatively make decisions on how to conduct investigations and the charges that should be brought, if any. Some of the decisions made are dependent on the availability of resources, political priorities, the scope of the laws, and the agency ability to investigate and quickly obtain warrants, among other factors.

SEXUAL ASSAULTS

Sexual assaults against minors, or child sexual abuse/assault (CSA), is different from CSEC since it lacks economic gain. A common myth is that child sexual abuse is a rare event perpetrated against girls. The reality is that CSA is committed against millions of children, involving both boy and girls. The crimes of sexual assault, rape, pornography, and incest are perpetrated by men and women, strangers, along with trusted friends or family. Approximately one in 10 individuals have experienced sexual abuse before age 18 according to a broad cross-section survey (Pérez-Fuentes et al., 2013).

CPS substantiated over 61,000 cases of sexual abuse in 2011 (U.S. Department of Health and Human Services and Administration for Children and Families, 2012). Girls are more likely to be reported as sexually abused, with 12- to 15-year-olds in the most danger. It is well accepted that sexual crimes are underreported; self-reports typically report higher levels. Sexual assault of children is 75 times more common than pediatric cancer and over 160 times more common than autism in children (National Children's Advocacy Center, 2013). On a promising note, sexual violence has gone down by more than 60 percent since 1993.

Child Pornography

Most adult pornography is not criminal and is protected by the First Amendment to the Constitution as an expression of free speech. Child pornographic exploitation (CPE) is a form of child sexual exploitation which is illegal to produce or possess. According to federal law, child pornography is any visual representation of sexually explicit conduct involving minors under the age of 18 (Department of Justice [DOJ], n.d.). Federal and state laws prohibit the production, distribution, importation, reception, or possession of any image of child pornography. Sexually explicit images involving a minor do not have to be saved on a computer, they can be merely looked at for possession to occur under federal law.

There has been a recent rise in the numbers of cases involving child pornography due to recent advances in technology and Internet use, however; it is commonly believed that most child pornography crimes are undiscovered. In a study on the criminal conduct of male child pornography offenders, authors found that of the 32 percent arrested for a subsequent crime, 4 percent were charged with child contact sex offenses and 7 percent with a new child pornography offense (Eke, Seto, & Williams, 2011). Concerns are rising regarding the spread of child pornographic exploitation and the excessive brutality of violence involved in the creation of new content (Reid, 2016). Among both men and women, pornography is associated with increased sexual violence and physical aggression (Wright, Tokunaga, & Kraus, 2016).

Children whose images are uploaded to the Internet and disseminated online are victimized for their entire life through trauma and shame. There is no way of stopping the circulation and permanency of the record of abuse. Two types of pornography involve juveniles: juvenile victim pornography that includes an identifiable victim of sexual violence, and child exploitation pornography in which the child is sexually depicted, but no additional offense is involved (such as rape). Child pornographic exploitation is among the most harmful forms of cybercrime.

SEXUAL EXPLOITATION & ASSAULT INVESTIGATION

There is a growing trend for response agencies to use a trauma-informed approach with sexual assault investigations. Cities and towns that use the approach state their policy on the town or campus police department Web site. A multidisciplinary team response is a major component of the method in addition to the use of a victim-sensitive technique for interviewing.

The typical team approach includes members of law enforcement, prosecutors, mental health and health care professionals, child protective services, and religious leaders. The investigation of intimate partner and dating violence involves domestic violence response teams along with coordinated community response teams. Sexual assault response teams (SARTs) are available in some jurisdictions, offering specialized intervention services. Multidisciplinary response teams receive training on the emotional or physical pain, shock, and denial that may accompany incidents involving extreme trauma. A significant percentage of human trafficking crimes involve offenders who are known to the victim.

Some commonly recommended investigative interview approaches within the trauma-informed victim approach are the *Enhanced Cognitive Interview* (ECI) and the *Forensic Experiential Trauma Interview* (FETI). Both interview protocols involve memory enhancement and retrieval methods to increase the amount of recall. FETI has gained acceptance among the therapeutic community, social services, and for specialized law enforcement investigations involving high-risk populations.

Over half of sexual assault victims never report the crime to the police (Holderness, Moen, & Hull, 2014). The development of the *You Have Options Program* came from efforts to improve the reporting options for victims. The program is a victim-centered and offender-focused program requiring that a victim of sexual assault have three options for reporting: information only, partial investigation, and complete investigation. The victim-centered approach is vastly different from the concept of a trauma-informed investigation. Reporting is in person with the police or online and anonymous or not. The victim-centered approach is controversial because it gives the victim total control over the extent of information provided and for making an arrest, the victim must give consent. The approach is far from mainstream. Only six police departments are on the Web site as participating in the program (Currie, n.d.).

Human Rights Watch suggests that the initial contact by the first responder to a sexual assault should be brief but compassionate. The officer should address safety or medical concerns and collect just enough information to establish the elements of the crime, identify the potential suspect(s) and secure the evidence. FETI is useful when interviewing victims of sexual assault according to research (Lisak & Markel, 2016).

Identifying victims of human trafficking to provide services and protection is a daunting task for professionals. In response, the Vera Institute has developed the *Trafficking Victim Identification Tool* (TVIT) as an aid for interviewing suspected victims of trafficking (Simich, 2014). The Institute recommends that interviewers first establish trust and rapport before asking difficult questions that center on traumatic experiences of the interviewee. Victim privacy should be paramount to the interviewers. Within the context of interviewing, privacy is the victim's right to control disclosure of his or her story and personal information. A victim should not be compelled to disclose abuse. Maintaining privacy may directly reduce the chances of revictimization. Interviewers should be sensitive to the needs of trafficking victims. The TVIT tool is designed for interviewers who are familiar with the victim-centered approach, which places equal value on the well-being of the victim with that of the criminal investigation. Trafficking victims have often been held in servitude through threats of harm or fear of deportation by police and immigration authorities (Simich, 2014). The TVIT is a way to establish a safe environment where they feel protected.

Jane Doe Reporting

In cases involving recent sexual assault allegations, the victim is asked not to shower or change clothes after the attack, as it will destroy evidence. Jane Doe reporting, also known as forensic compliance, is increasingly used to encourage survivors to participate in forensic evidence testing and to receive medical care. **Jane Doe reporting** means that the victim reports the incident and is given an exam with the evidence collected anonymously. The reporter is not compelled to decide on whether or not to follow through on prosecuting, should the perpetrator be identified.

The box which holds the forensic evidence is commonly called a *Sexual Assault Evidence Kit*. Sexual Assault Nurses Examiners work within a team to conduct medical forensic examinations, treat victims for sexually transmitted infections, and address pregnancy concerns. While a kit composition may vary from state to state, a typical exam includes the collection of cut hair samples and hair combings, fluids, and documentation of bruising and marks if present. Many factors influence whether a victim chooses to follow through with the prosecution. The Jane Doe option makes it possible for care and concern for the victim without law-enforcement involvement.

Refer to the *Sexual Assault Evidence Kit* illustration in Figure 6-4 to see the typical chain of possession that is written on the box. This information assures that each professional who handles the evidence can attest to the fact that the box was handled properly, and that the evidence was not tampered with. Keeping a chain of possession is necessary to preserve the evidentiary value of the contents should the victim later choose to go forward with a prosecution. Each state has laws that limit the period a person can be prosecuted after a crime is committed, known as the statutes of limitation. For example, Minnesota statute of limitations for sex crimes is 10 years or less with exceptions for DNA evidence. Nevada is also 10 years or less, with no exceptions. These statutes of limitations will control the time that a person has available to prosecute, should they decide to at a later date.

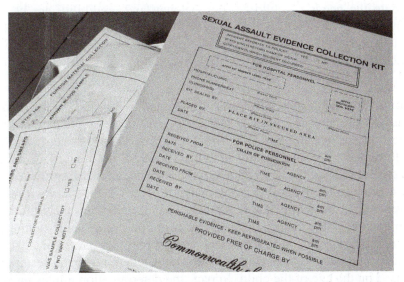

FIGURE 6-4   A forensic exam of the sexual assault victim is sometimes referred to as the "Assault Evidence Collection Kit," which is pictured here. It is simply a box that contains the materials needed for the evidence collection such as cotton swabs, envelopes, and bags. DNA may be collected and stored in the Jane Doe kit until a person chooses to have the police review the case.

More About It ... Jane Doe *Sexual Assault Evidence Kits*

A federal requirement mandates that states pay for "Jane Doe kits." As of 2009, rape victims can undergo an emergency room forensic rape exam without calling the police or making the decision about whether to press charges. Evidence will be gathered and kept on file and sealed at the time of the assault if they are unable to make the determination to call the police. This measure is meant to allow for the collection of important evidence without pressuring women or men into making a prosecution decision during the crisis. Police will be able to open the evidence only in cases in which the victim decides to go ahead with the prosecution.

Interviewing Victims

Different techniques are used for interviewing suspected victims of sexual assault. The method used for questioning often depends on the age or maturity of the young person. Taken into consideration are developmental and cognitive disabilities which may impact the interview. Our knowledge on child development, memory, and cognition has grown substantially in recent years. Considerable research has been conducted on the outcomes of child abuse investigations, resulting in protocols to improve child abuse victim statements. The Federal Bureau of Investigation (FBI) endorses the use of multidisciplinary teams with a trained forensic interviewer in cases involving young children and adolescents (Connell & Finnegan, 2010). The current best practice in most jurisdictions is to have the young person interviewed once by a skilled forensic interviewer when sexual abuse is suspected (Faller, Cordisco-Steele, & Nelson-Gardell, 2010). Children as young as three years old may have the necessary cognitive, verbal, and communication skills to be informative witnesses when properly interviewed (Hershkowitz, Lamb, Orbach, Katz, & Horowitz, 2012).

Although courts are afforded broad discretion in modifying trial practices to accommodate the needs of children, competency and credibility are usually issues that the investigator must address. State practices on how the judge may alter the trial varies by law and policy, as does the determination of competency itself. Every interview of a child is conducted in anticipation of a future legal challenge to competency and credibility.

1. **Competency** means that a person is fit to stand trial or to take the oath to tell the truth for testimony in court. A child may sometimes demonstrate competency through his or her ability to determine the difference between a truth and a lie and to understand the morality of lying. In 1974, the revised Federal Rules of Evidence abolished the competency rule for trials in federal courts. A majority of states followed the federal example when it comes to the child witness and does not require a basic competency inquiry. To determine that the child understands the meaning of the oath, however, the truth–lie competency demonstration of children to testify in court remains a common requirement (Lyon, 2011). A judge conducts competency hearings in those states where no such presumption exists or based on the age of the child. In part, the determination hinges on whether the child can recall events, separate fact from fantasy, and maintain those memories independently without being influenced by others.

2. **Credibility** refers to whether or not the child witness can be believed. Children who cannot articulate their abuse or have memory gaps or demonstrate behavioral

inconsistencies are less likely to be believed when they report abuse. For states that presume competence, juries are left to determine the credibility (believability) of the child witness. Other models decide through the competency hearing whether the testimony will be allowed. Investigators must establish credibility before submitting a case for trial, and that process can be a difficult one.

Experts suggest that asking a child to promise to tell the truth increases their honesty (Lyon, 2011). Still, children differ from adults in their ability to remember and recount events accurately. Child statements in sexual abuse cases are notoriously incomplete and fragmented; they frequently omit critical information relating to the sexual abuse acts during the first interview (Leander, 2010). It is not uncommon for children to make statements on having been abused, particularly in sexual assault cases, and then for the child to recant the statement at a later time.

Recording of Interviews

Experts are in favor of recording because it has the potential to reduce the number of interviews, has a strong visual impact, and has the potential to induce a confession when played for the offenders. Multiple victim interviews on their sexual abuse victimization may cause secondary trauma; deliberately minimizing the number of child interviews is, therefore, a common policy. In opposition to the practice of recording are concerns about the artificial setting that it produces as well as potential conflicting accounts of the molestation. The controversy includes some of the points discussed in this section:

1. Does this method provide an accurate documentation of the victim's account of the crime? It depends on the technology used as well as the skill of the interviewer. Recording only provides verification of what happens during that session. It may not record voices that are too low to be heard. Common problems resulting from human error and technology failures must be avoided.

    Professionals who routinely interview children regarding suspected abuse and neglect can attest to the fact that words alone cannot sufficiently describe the impact of abuse on a child. While revealing the details of ill-treatment, the body language, facial expressions, and physical demonstrations by the victim can be as revealing as the disclosure itself. Documenting preserves this account and freezes the abuse within the time frame of the disclosure. The child who testifies is often more mature and will present differently in the years after the abuse occurs when the case finally comes to trial.

2. How can an investigator use a recorded statement? The recording is a training tool to sharpen interviewing skills. Routinely used as a training method for forensic interviewers, an interview can be scrutinized to improve techniques and develop appropriate questions for future interviews.

    Children who divulge abuse during a recorded interview provide the investigator with a tool for interrogation that should not be overlooked. Although this point is unexamined by research, the practice is probably more frequent than suspected. Confrontation of the perpetrator should be a routine part of any child abuse investigation, and the child's statement can be part of the interrogation. Showing the recording to someone in denial breaks down barriers and may elicit a statement from the offender.

3. Is the child emotionally and psychologically ready for an interview that will likely elicit the facts of the case? Research suggests that the clear majority of children express reluctance to talk about sexual abuse during the first interview, and a portion initially deny that assault occurred at all (Leander, 2010).

The record of an interview becomes evidence given to the defense attorney. In the case of an incomplete or failed interview, the portrayal of denial may be an insurmountable hurdle to overcome for prosecution. Determining if the child is ready to give a statement is a decision made since some make full revelations of sexual abuse having occurred only after multiple interviews, while the first interview may not be a complete portrayal of the abuse (Leander, 2010).

Forensic Interviewing

Child and adolescent interviewing has grown into a specialized forensic field. The child forensic interviewer is trained to use techniques that are established by childhood development experts to create legal evidence and testimony based on the accounts of the child. Legal guidelines constrain the questioning of a child. The child forensic interviewer may be a trained police officer or civilian, depending on the resources of the community. Typical child forensic interviews include social workers, child advocates, and individuals who work for the courts. The child forensic interviewer must be comfortable communicating with young people in addition to possessing knowledge on age-appropriate questioning. Additional qualities include an individual free of bias on the issues of child abuse and knowledgeable of the court system.

Free-recall retrieval strategies and open-ended questioning are among the techniques suggested for child interviewing. An interview protocol developed by the Eunice Kennedy Shriver National Institute of Child Health and Human Development (NICHD) incorporates advanced scientific awareness about memory and children's linguistic and cognitive development (Harris, 2010). The three phases of the NICHD interview protocol are introductory, rapport building, and substantive or free recall. The introductory phase occurs when the interviewer explains to the child the expectations for the conversation. The interviewee is put to ease during the rapport-building phase. The final phase consists of the interview itself, encouraging children to engage in a narrative stream of events without the use of specific, leading, or closed-ended questions. Research has shown that the NICHD protocol adds to the substance and quality of information from child victims (Harris, 2010).

Of all domestic cases, child abuse investigations are the most time consuming and challenging. Interviewing victims is a task that requires a thorough knowledge of children's age and developmental levels. When someone uses complex words that a child does not understand, confusion and conflicting statements result. It is not acceptable to ask leading questions because they encourage the interviewee to phrase their response to please the interviewer. The legal interview required to lend credibility to the child's statement is different from the social service interview.

DATING VIOLENCE

Scholars are beginning to associate intimacy with violence, in both adult and adolescent dating relationships. Dating someone is different than being married. The two most stressful events of marriage—money management and child rearing—do not exist in the context of dating. Problems associated with having a place to live and going to work are not involved. It sounds as though dating would be free of any factors that are associated with violence. So why does it happen?

James Makepeace suggests a developmental theory based on the need for intimacy between partners as his explanation of courtship violence (Makepeace, 1997). He states that intimacy is a fundamental individual need, and its attainment is both magnified and romanticized in our culture. The frustrations that accompany that need begin early during the courtship stage. Youngsters often begin dating when they have not yet gained the maturity to handle the frustrations of intimacy and so may react in inappropriate ways. He cites jealousy as the most frequent reason for courtship violence, and hitting as a response to jealousy is often accepted by both males and females.

Life experiences that are significant in predicting intimate partner violence (IPV) among young people include the family background, such as absent, emotionally distant, or harsh parents; school difficulties; difficulties in employment; and having begun dating at an early age. Consistent with studies on adult interpersonal violence, the use of drugs and alcohol is a consistent risk factor in abuse. Neither can be used as an excuse for perpetration of violence, however. Medeiros and Straus (2006) found that risk factors related to the probability of assaulting a partner applied to both men and women, but somewhat more strongly in men. For severely assaulting a partner by punching or choking, 12 risk factors were found to be associated with an increased probability of assaulting a partner (Medeiros & Straus, 2006):

- Anger management
- Antisocial personality
- Conflict with partner
- Communication problems
- Criminal history
- Dominance
- Jealousy
- Negative attributions about the partner
- Neglect history
- Sexual abuse history
- Stressful conditions
- Violence approval

TEEN DATING VIOLENCE

Teen dating violence is a severe problem that is experienced by adolescents across racial and ethnic lines. **Dating violence** means "an act by an individual that is against another individual with whom that person has or has had a dating relationship and that is intended to result in physical harm, bodily injury, assault, or sexual assault or that is a threat that reasonably places the individual in fear of imminent physical harm, bodily injury, assault, or sexual assault, but does not include defensive measures to protect oneself" (Texas Family Code Section 71.0021). Dating violence is a form of IPV, which occurs between two people in a close relationship. The forms of dating violence can be physical, emotional, or sexual.

Years after adult victimization was recognized, scholars began to look at violence during the courtship phase. Younger individuals are particularly at risk from this form of abuse, which includes sexual assault, rape, physical assault and battery, and verbal and emotional abuse. Studies have consistently shown that dating couples are even more likely to be violent than married couples. In a nationally representative survey of adults, more than 37 percent of female rape victims reported being raped between the ages of 18 and 24 (Black et al., 2011).

Dating violence is known to happen in relationships of people who are as young as 12 years old in relationships as early as the seventh grade. Students reported mutual aggression by 66 percent of both boys and girls (Mulford & Giordano, 2008). The study discovered that girls were more likely to be the sole perpetrators and that violence was mutual in roughly half of the middle school student relationships. A recent national survey found that 9.4 percent of high school students had been hit, slapped, or physically hurt on purpose by their boyfriend or girlfriend in the year prior to the survey (Eaton et al., 2012). Extremely high rates of physical assault on dating partners have been found among university students.

The medical and social responses to victims of dating violence may differ from the available legal options. Interventions from Universities, schools, counselors, and mental health agencies will happen at any age and under any circumstance whenever a young person believes abuse has occurred and is in need of help. The initial response of helping agencies does not legally establish someone as a victim of domestic violence, however, because state law must be satisfied for standing.

Each state has the right to determine, by statute, their definition of domestic violence and the remedies afforded to its victims. Some states do not recognize dating relationships as "domestic," others specifically say that a dating relationship or a significant dating relationship constitutes a "family (domestic) relationship." The law-enforcement officer determines whether the relationship is significant (based on time and intensity), or law may also name a judge or other appointed person as making the final determination. These definitional issues are relevant to minors and when there is no marriage or child in common.

In cases of violence where a crime such as an assault has occurred, the relationship between the offender and the victim does not impact the criminal justice response. Massachusetts, for example, has two laws designed to protect individuals from others. The two laws are known as Abuse Prevention (G.L. 209A) and Harassment Prevention (G.L. 258E). While both laws were created to protect from abuse, the Abuse Prevention law protects people who are in a specific close relationship, while an individual relationship is not necessary under the Harassment Prevention Law.

Been There ... Done That

The mother of a 12-year-old reported that her daughter was being followed and harassed by a teenage boy in the neighborhood. The two had gone out for ice cream a few times, but the girl stated that he was just a friend. Apparently, the boy felt differently about the relationship. He was following her around and hiding when he was noticed. Also, she received up to 40 texts and e-mails from him each day. Recently the messages had become menacing, with suggestions that something would happen to her if she did not go out with him. The situation was frightening to the young girl. Her mother asked for a domestic violence restraining order—but the relationship did not fit the Massachusetts definition of a substantial dating relationship. Instead, she could apply to the court for a *Harassment Prevention Order*, also known as a Chapter 258E order. Under the law, the protection order could be obtained regardless of what the relationship might be.

Adolescent dating violence rates are significant, although these differ from individual studies and between states. Rates of dating violence vary from 7 percent in Vermont to 16 percent in Georgia (Office of Adolescent Health [OAH], 2013). Severe dating violence may be occurring at a rate of 1.6 percent (Hamby, Finkelhor, & Turner, 2012). Among high school students who date, 21 percent of females and 10 percent of males experience physical and or sexual dating violence according to the *2013 National Youth Risk Behavior Survey* (Vagi, Olsen, Basile, & Vivolo-Kantor, 2015). One study on teen dating violence found that significantly more males than females reported physical teen dating violence, yet female injuries were three times higher than those of the males (Hamby et al., 2012). Research strongly indicates the need to address relationship violence through education on positive relationship building among adolescents.

The *National Survey of Teen Relationships and Intimate Violence* (STRiV) is the first survey to provide a national picture of adolescent dating violence (Taylor, Mumford, & Liu, 2016). The study found that two out of three adolescents between the ages of 12 and 18 who were in a relationship in the past year had been victimized (69 percent) or perpetrated violence (63 percent). The most common type of adolescent dating abuse is psychological (over 60 percent). Both sexual assault and physical abuse victimization among students were 18 percent. There are no differences between male and female victimization rates, however, girls reported higher rates of committing physical violence according to STRiV.

Polyvictimization is closely associated with teen dating violence (Hamby et al., 2012). **Polyvictimization** refers to the co-occurrence of violence across different forms of victimization at the hands of multiple perpetrators. Physical teen dating violence is also closely linked with child maltreatment, sexual victimization, and Internet harassment. Among adult victims of rape, physical violence, and stalking by an intimate partner, 22 percent of women and 15 percent of men first experienced some form of partner violence between 11 and 17 years of age (Black et al., 2011).

Teen dating violence is related to an increase in other violence-related behaviors such as substance use, depression, posttraumatic stress, unhealthy weight control, and risky sexual behavior (Holmes & Sher, 2013). In a self-reported frequency study of suicide ideation and physical dating violence perpetration, one out of four students in high school reported having considered suicide at least once by grade 12 and almost half reported victimization by physical dating violence (Nahapetyan, Orpinas, Song, & Holland, 2014). The association between adolescent dating violence and an increase in suicidal behavior is a significant public health concern.

Legal reforms across the United States has attempted to address growing problem of teen dating violence. A significant dilemma is the lack of consistency with which the states protect minors from violence in a dating relationship. The state codes vary on whether domestic violence restraining orders are available to young victims based on age and relationship status.

According to a comprehensive review on dating violence laws in the United States, 45 states and the District of Columbia allow minors in a dating relationship access to protection orders (Break the Cycle, 2010). State laws vary as to whether minors can petition for these orders; nine states and the District of Columbia explicitly allow and nine states prohibit minors from self-petition. Fifteen states allow filing for protection orders against adolescent abusers. Five states prohibit protection orders against minors: Maryland, Missouri, Nevada, New Jersey, and Oregon. State laws on dating violence protection orders are frequently changing.

Preventing teen dating violence through school-based programs that address dating violence and other youth risk is an approach suggested by the *Centers for Disease Control* (CDC, 2016). In a strategy named *Dating Matters*, the educational focus is on 11-to 14-year-olds in high-risk urban communities to prevent dating violence (CDC, 2014). School-based and parent curricula target sixth-, seventh-, and eighth-grade students with programs designed to promote healthy relationships through coping and relationship skills and education on sexual violence. A rigorous multi-pronged assessment of the programs currently in place will assist in addressing dating violence among teens.

COLLEGE DATING VIOLENCE

Numerous studies have estimated the prevalence of intimate partner violence among samples of college students, finding that this population is at significant risk of experiencing violence. Both male and female victims of psychological and physical aggression experience increased mental health symptoms, including depression, anxiety, somatic complaints, posttraumatic stress symptoms, and increased substance use (Shorey, Cornelius, & Strauss, 2015; Shorey et al., 2011). It is well known and accepted that both men and women physically assault the other within heterosexual dating relationships during the college years, much less is known about violence among LGBTI couples. Research shows mixed results on the motivations for perpetrating physical aggression in these relationships.

The gender differences that motivate physical dating violence among college students are under scrutiny. Langhrinrichen-Rohling et al. suggested using a seven-category classification scheme for examination of IPV motivations. The categories are *power/control*, *self-defense*, *expression of negative emotion* (i.e., anger), *communication difficulties*, *retaliation*, *jealousy*, and *other* (Langhinrichsen-Rohling, McCullars, & Misra, 2012). From an analysis of articles, the authors found that violence was most frequently used as an expression of negative emotions, followed by retaliation, jealousy and communication difficulties. Some studies have adopted the scheme to find current information about dating violence among this population. Elmquist and colleagues report that communication difficulties and self-defense were the most frequently cited motives for both male and female perpetrated domestic violence at a prevalence rate of almost 30 percent (Elmquist et al., 2016). With concern that some college students may be engaging in risky sexual behaviors, the authors noted that sexual arousal was a motive in 22 percent of women's and 27 percent of men's violent episodes (under "other").

Referred to as the gender differences controversy, conflicting reports on the incidence of sexual assault among college women currently exist. In a recent study involving 21,000 students, researchers addressed the information gap on sexual assault victimization among LGB college students as well as among heterosexual students (Ford & Soto-Marquez, 2016). Consistent with numerous studies, approximately 25 percent of heterosexual women and 12 percent of men reported having experienced sexual assault during college. Gay and bisexual men reported a rate similar to heterosexual women. Bisexual women were the most vulnerable group, with two out of every five females experiencing sexual assault after four years in college. Lesbians report the lowest rate of victimization of 11 percent.

On the other hand, the National Crime Victimization Survey (NCVS) finds that the incidence of rape or sexual assault for college students aged 18 to 24 is approximately 6 percent compared to the rate of non-college attending women of the same age group at 7.5 percent (Sinozich & Langton, 2014). A heightened risk of victimization occurs with moderate to heavy alcohol use among college students. A multi-campus study found that rates of forcible rape decrease significantly after women enter college, but incapacitated sexual assaults increase sharply (Krebs, Lindquist, Warner, Fisher, & Martin, 2009). Heavy episodic drinking has the strongest association with alcohol-involved rape, more than doubling the risk of victimization (Messman-Moore, Ward, & DeNardi, 2013).

The Jeanne Clery Act

The *Jeanne Clery Act* (20 USC § 1092(f)), also known as the Campus Security Act, requires that each university report criminal offenses that occur on campus. Both public and private institutions are required to report under the federal law. Public safety on campus is responsible for reporting crimes that occur to the FBI through the Uniform Crime Reporting System.

The Cleary Act is named in memory of Jeanne Cleary, a student who was raped and murdered on campus by a fellow student in 1986. The *Campus Sexual Violence Elimination Act* (SaVE), is a 2013 amendment to the Jeanne Clery Act. SaVE requires colleges and universities participating in federal student aid to make available to students information on the scope of sexual violence on campus, guarantee victims enhanced rights, provide for standards in institutional conduct proceedings, and provide campus community-wide prevention educational programming (U.S. Department of Education, 2016).

Under SaVE, institutions must provide any student or employee who reports having been the victim of an incident of sexual violence with information on their rights. Campus police departments recommend that regardless of reporting concerns a victim should still speak with a department Sexual Assault Investigator for details of all the options available. Alternately, a victim advocate or counselor should be contacted. Recommended procedures to be followed in the event of an incident of sexual abuse include:

- The preservation of evidence for proof in criminal proceedings;
- A named person for reporting an offense;
- Assistance from campus authorities with options for reporting to local law enforcement;
- Information regarding the choice of reporting, or not, to law enforcement; and
- How to obtain no contact or harassment protection orders from a court.

Title IX Reporting

Sexual misconduct and sexual harassment are forms of sex discrimination under Title IX of the Education Amendments of 1972. Sex discrimination by colleges and universities is banned under the federal Title IX. All public and private elementary and secondary schools, colleges, and universities receiving any federal financial assistance must comply with Title IX.

Schools are committed to providing an environment that is free from harassment, discrimination, and violence. Title IX cases are investigated by the Office of Human Resources or similar appointed entity. Title IX of the Education Amendments of 1972 states: "No person in the United States shall, on the basis of sex, be excluded from participation in, be denied the benefits of, or be subjected to discrimination under any education program or activity receiving Federal financial assistance."

If a person is the victim of sexual assault on a high school or college campus, procedures for reporting have already been established. On calling the police they will be assisted in arranging for hospital treatment or attending to medical needs; they will be met privately to be interviewed and to make a statement. Officers will make every effort to maintain confidentiality and not prejudge, to assist in privately contacting counseling and other available resources within the community and on campus. Regardless of the gender of the victim or the alleged violator, reports will be taken in a nonjudgmental manner by the campus security. The report will be fully investigated, and information on options will be provided.

Date Rape

The terms acquaintance rape and date rape include unwanted sexual intercourse, oral sex, anal sex, or another sexual contact through the use of force or threat of force by casual or intimate dating partners. There is no crime called "date rape." This is a social term used to explain the context in which the crime is occurring; it brings attention to the fact that rape occurs within dating relationships. The legal term for date rape is simply rape. Studies on the prevalence of acquaintance rape have indicated shocking rates of occurrence. Unfortunately, forced sexual intercourse is a common experience among young adult women; almost one in five report having experienced forced sex at some point in their lives (Holcombe, Manlove, & Ikramullah, 2008). Forced sexual intercourse did not differ by race or level of parental education in the Holcombe et al. study (2008).

In addition to the fear and depression that are common to rape victims, adolescent survivors suffer in unique ways (Thompson & Kingree, 2010). Young people frequently feel invincible, and the personal violation of rape shatters that myth, altering their reality. The self-esteem of an ordinarily narcissistic adolescent may be damaged from an assault. Victims tend to internalize and falsely blame themselves for being with the offender in the first place. Sudden personality changes—such as a drop in school performance, withdrawal from regular school or social activities, and flagrant promiscuous behavior—are among the symptoms that adolescent rape victims display. They may engage in self-destructive behavior such as drug or alcohol abuse or develop an eating disorder such as bulimia or anorexia.

A concern now is the increasingly predatory nature of rape indicated by the use of date rape drugs by high school and college students. The most common is Rohypnol, often called "roofies" and "forget pill." According to the U.S. Drug Enforcement Administration, this illegal drug is manufactured worldwide and brought in through Mexico. Its popularity among young people is due to the drug's low cost. Placed in the drink of an unsuspecting victim, the drug is tasteless and odorless. Within 15 to 30 minutes, its effects include dizziness, drowsiness, confusion, and memory impairment. Another drug, gamma-hydroxybutyrate (GHB), is also being used to incapacitate victims in order to abuse them sexually. Its side effects are similar to those of Rohypnol. Most commonly found in liquid form, it is also colorless and odorless.

People who suspect that they have been drugged and sexually violated should have their urine and blood tested within 24 hours. All clothing and physical evidence should be kept and given to the police. It is important not to change, shower, or douche so that a hospital protocol and rape examination may be made to secure evidence of the assault.

CYBER DATING ABUSE

Using a cell phone or the Internet, **cyber dating abuse** (CDA) is a pattern of behaviors that control, pressure or threaten a dating partner. CDA is sometimes referred to as digital dating abuse. Similar rates of cyber dating abuse are experienced regardless of gender, but girls are more likely to experience negative emotional responses (Reed, Tolman, & Ward, 2017). CDA causes injury through the use of technology to inflict emotional, psychological, and sexual harm to its victims.

Studies have only recently begun to examine the extent of **digital dating abuse** and the context in which it occurs. Zweig, Dank, Yahner, and Lachman (2013) that found among high school youth, more than 26 percent of the students experienced cyber dating abuse victimization, and 11 percent reported being a perpetrator in the year before the survey. A more recent study confirmed that approximately one in four high school students annual experience CDA (Temple et al., 2016). Within the Zweig et al. sample, roughly one-quarter of youth had experienced non-sexual forms of cyber dating abuse, and 11 percent had experienced sexual forms of cyber dating abuse. Females were twice as likely as males to report being a victim of sexual digital dating abuse (Zweig et al., 2013).

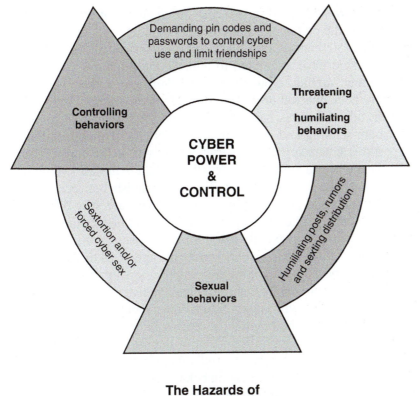

**The Hazards of
Cyber Dating Abuse**

FIGURE 6-5   Dating violence occurs online as well as in person. Known
cyber dating behaviors are illustrated here to show the similarities.

Power and control are exercised as abuse through numerous forms of controlling,
threatening or humiliating, and sexual behaviors (refer to Figure 6-5). Frequent use of
cyber controlling behaviors such as reviewing phone calls lists and reading text messages to monitor their partner's activity are indicators of an unhealthy relationship.
Threats and humiliation involve spreading of rumors, insults, or sexting images through
cyber postings, threatening e-mails, and texts. Sexual forms of abuse include forced
cybersex and sextortion. Cyber dating abuse is significantly related to actual threats
and physical violence in a dating relationship (Houck, 2016).

TEEN & YOUNG ADULT SEXTING

Sexting is a common practice among youth today, despite the damaging consequences
that can result. Sexting is defined as the production and transmission of explicit or
sexually suggestive pictures via mobile phone or other electronic devices. Sexting has
attracted much attention among the public and with researchers. The term did not exist
15 years ago, and its present scope could not have been imagined. The proliferation of
sexting has increased teen vulnerability to victimization and subjected them to criminal
prosecution. Minors engaging in sexting are in an awkward position for legal charges
of child pornography, child enticement, disseminating obscenity, and harassment.
Sexting images without permission is a tactic used by cyberbullies who torment their
victims over digital networks.

Many states have addressed the severe consequences of teen sexting by passing laws that criminalize the practice. Unless those laws include exceptions to address teen sexting, however, adolescent images that depict minors constitute child pornography. Some state lawmakers have attempted to address the dilemma through statutes that explicitly define teen sexting, typically as a misdemeanor rather than a felony. Teen sexting laws have been enacted or proposed in 32 states (Lampe, 2013). As of a 2015 report, however, only 18 states had passed statutes that addressed minors under the age of 18 for both sending and receiving sexting photos (Hinduja & Patchin, 2015). Experts suggest that lawmakers have overwhelmingly failed to consider the voluntary acts of adolescents who are publishing sexually explicit materials (Mujahid, 2011).

In some states, the criminal law fails to distinguish between juvenile images taken by consent and child pornography, although these are very different by nature. Possession of a sexually explicit image of a minor would be a crime, even if the photo were not solicited. Sending a sexually explicit picture to someone else is a crime. The crime of *child enticement* is asking a child under the age of 18 to share a nude photo of him or herself. Child pornography laws may impose harsh prison sentences for those convicted along with requirements that individuals register as sex offenders. Being on the registry of sex offenders will impact future careers and living conditions.

Of concern is whether the practice of sexting is harmful to the individuals who share sexually explicit photographs or videos of themselves. Typically, the behaviors are consensual and conducted between individuals within a romantic relationship. There is some evidence that teenage sexting behaviors are substantially associated with substance use behaviors, increased sexual behaviors, and emotional health.

Studies show that sexting among teenagers is common, although rates vary among age groups. Among minors between the ages of 12 and 18, approximately 20 percent are found to engage in sexting (Dake, Price, Maziarz, & Ward, 2012). Among older adolescents, the range is between 15 percent and 28 percent, with some studies indicating even higher rates. Larger rates of sexting (32 percent or more) are found among those over age 18. Once an image is made it can easily be shared, stored, and reproduced with or without consent of the person depicted. Teenagers who appear in sexting images face the potential risk of embarrassment and social stigma if the pictures are sent beyond the intended individual. Cyberbullying is one of the consequences of teenage sexting. Ridicule and peer abuse can continue long after the teen leaves school.

In a small sample study of sexting behaviors among college students, almost 40 percent of respondents indicated that they had sent and received sexts during the past six months (Perkins, Becker, Tehee, & Mackelprang, 2014). Individuals who engage in nude sexting had an earlier age of beginning sexual behavior, more sexual partners, and evidence of engaging in risky behavior.

An unintended consequence of engaging in sexting is an increase of cyber victimization among those who engage in the practice of sending nude or semi-nude materials. The transient nature of adolescent dating relationships adds to the likelihood of images being disseminated beyond the intended audience. A link between engaging in sexting and cyber victimization among college students is well established (Reyns, Burek, Henson, & Fisher, 2013).

A recent trend associated with teen sexting is the use of the photo for sextortion, a form of blackmailing with threats to release the photo online unless demands are met. If photos are posted on social media sites, the presence can have long-lasting implications. Universities and employers typically check applicants through social media

Been There ... Done That!

A six-year-old girl complained that her step-brother who lived with her was hurting her. Physical examination by a doctor who specialized in child sexual abuse confirmed that she had been raped. I questioned the 13-year-old boy about the allegation. At first, he denied having touched the younger child. It was only after being faced with evidence of the crime that he admitted to having had sex with his stepsister. He was arrested and tried. At trial, he was found guilty of rape and sodomy, which had occurred over a two-year period. I discovered that the perpetrator was also a victim. He provided the name of an adult who had sexually abused him. The investigation did not stop with this one victim. Sufficient probable cause was found to arrest the adult for his sexual assault crimes. The adult was tried and convicted.

sites. Prospective employers increasingly conduct background checks online to look for evidence of the applicants' good judgment and veracity. An online sexual photo, or arrest for a sex crime, will negatively impact the chance of being hired regardless of the circumstances.

STALKING

Modern stalking behaviors are complex and far-reaching. Stalking refers to a pattern of harassing or threatening tactics that are unwanted and cause fear in the victim. Beyond the familiar tactics of following and harassing, text messages, e-mails, instant messages, and Web site messages are venues for stalking behaviors. Approximately 1 in 34 women in the United States reports being stalked before the age of 18 (Smith et al., 2017). An estimated 0.8 percent of men reported having been stalked before age 18 in the United States.

Stalking behaviors among college students in dating relationships are relatively common, with men and women equally likely to be the perpetrator (Shorey et al., 2015). While less is known about the health effects of stalking, research indicates that stalking victimization by an intimate partner is associated with acute, chronic, and stress-related health problems (Walker, Cole, & Shannon, 2006).

CONCLUSIONS

As reflected in this chapter, the victimization of adolescent and young adults is complex and diverse. The actual scope of the violence against teens and young adults is lost in the reporting systems. Data involving the age range between 12 and 18 is sometimes reflected in statistics of child victimization and at other times reported through studies of adult victimization. Adding to the confusion are controversial studies on sexual violence. Much needs to be done in standardizing the way in which information is gathered and disseminated.

What is clear is that child abuse and neglect affects an individual over the course of her or his lifetime. Connections between victimization and offending are established. Vulnerability to future victimization is tied to abuse against the young. Education, family, and parental connections are vital to extend self-esteem and prepare youth to protect themselves when possible. Medical and mental health services promote healing and healthy living. For populations who are at increased risk of violence, the lessons learned on building positive relationships is essential.

Exploitation and sex trafficking of minors is a current criminal justice issue recently realized. The hidden population is difficult to count, but the targets are well documented. Children, adolescent girls and boys, and LGBTI youth are recognized to be at risk of mistreatment. The classification of commercial sexual exploitation and sex trafficking of minors as a form of child abuse is not surprising given that most offenders are family, romantic partners, and friends. Exploring the phenomenon of sexual exploitation of young people based on the structure of the organization provides clarity to a murky problem. Multidisciplinary teams are a current best practice response to investigate and prosecute instances of trafficking.

The sexual abuse of minors is a disturbing reality for boys and girls, a risk that is greater than cancer for young people. Characterized by the absence of economic gain, adolescents suffer for the pleasure of others in this category of crime mostly perpetrated by trusted adults. Physical and sexual violation of a person may be described as an occurrence that is sometimes captured by pornographic exploitation that documents the abuse in perpetuity.

Investigations of sexual exploitation and assault require empathy and understanding. Compassionate interviewing techniques are suggested in this chapter. Jane Doe reporting provides an avenue for accessing care and support without the pressure of making decisions on contacting the police. Methods to interview young people include recording with an emphasis on bolstering the competency and credibility of the victim. Teen and college dating present unique concerns and challenges along with the risk of polyvictimization.

SIMPLY SCENARIO
Consequences of Abuse

As a 15-year-old, Susan began running away from home, but was caught and returned, each time. Her parents were alarmed at the behavior problems that were surfacing. She was getting into fights at school with other girls and had been suspended on two occasions. Up and down the inside of her arms and thighs were self-inflicted burn marks from cigarettes, in addition to cuts from a razor blade. In therapy, she divulged that her brother had molested her when she was younger.

Question: Based on the information in this chapter, what are some of the questions that you would want this teenager to answer? What are the current concerns you might have? Is there any intervention that might be of benefit?

Questions for Review

1. According to the *National Intimate Partner and Sexual Violence Survey* (NISVS), how might sexual abuse of children affect adults?
2. Discuss the relationship between vulnerability to violence and resilience.
3. Discuss the difference between a commercial sex act and child sexual assault.
4. What are the two types of pornography involving juveniles?
5. Explain the prevalence of child sexual abuse as compared to pediatric cancer and autism.
6. What is the estimated percentage of unreported sexual assault victimization? How does Jane Doe reporting expect to change this?
7. Describe how competency and credibility are assessed in cases involving children.
8. What is polyvictimization and its association to teen dating violence?
9. Describe the hazards of cyber dating abuse.
10. Explain the dilemma of teen sexting practices.

Internet-Based Exercises

1. In 2014, the National Center for Injury Prevention and Control (CDC) introduced *Dating Matters* education programs in key urban areas. Conduct an Internet search to learn more about this innovative program. Evaluate and discuss this initiative in class.

2. Trafficking in persons include many different forms of violence. The U.S. Department of State maintains a Web site with quick links to information on these crimes. There you can find out about issues such as *vicarious trauma*, also known as compassion fatigue, which can affect professionals who repeatedly witness or hear about victims' experiences. Go to https://www.state.gov/j/tip/rls/fs/2017/index.htm, and research the topic that you find most interesting.

3. The Office for victims of Crime (OVC) helps lead communities throughout the country in their annual observances of National Crime Victims' Rights Week during April. https://ovc.ncjrs.gov/topic.aspx?topicid=12. Go to https://ovc.ncjrs.gov/ncvrw/ and find out what you can do to help in the effort raise awareness on crime and victimization. Discuss some options for a class project.

4. There is a lot of controversy about sexting and the way laws address this practice. Are you aware of the difference from state to state on this issue? Do you know the law in your state? Visit this Web site on state sexting laws and locate the state in which you live and compare it to the state where you go to college. Your investigation can begin with a visit to https://cyberbullying.org/state-sexting-laws.pdf. Write a short report on your findings.

References

Albanese, J. (2013). *Commercial sexual exploitation of children: What do we know and what do we do about it?*: BiblioGov.

Black, M., Basile, K., Breiding, M., Smith, S., Walters, M., Merrick, M., ... Stevens, M. (2011). *The National Intimate Partner and Sexual Violence Survey (NISVS): 2010 Summary Report*. Atlanta, GA: Centers for Disease Control and Prevention.

Bouris, A., Guilamo-Ramos, V., Pickard, A., Shiu, C., Loosier, P. S., Dittus, P., ... Waldmiller, J. M. (2010). A systematic review of parental influences on the health and well-being of lesbian, gay, and bisexual youth: Time for a new public health research and practice agenda. *The Journal of Primary Prevention, 31*(5–6), 273–309.

Break the Cycle. (2010). State law report cards: A national survey on teen dating violence laws. Retrieved from http://www.breakthecycle.org/sites/default/files/pdf/2010-Dating-Violence-State-Law-Report-Card-Full-Report.pdf

CDC. (2014). *Dating Matters: Strategies to promote healthy teen relationships*. Washington, D.C.: National Center for Injury Prevention and Control. Retrieved from https://www.cdc.gov/violenceprevention/pdf/Promote-Healthy-Teen-Relationships_2014.pdf.

CDC. (2016). *Understanding teen dating violence*. Retrieved from https://www.cdc.gov/violenceprevention/pdf/teen-dating-violence-factsheet-a.pdf.

CDC. (2017). *Protective factors for LGBT youth: Information for health and education professionals*. Retrieved from https://www.cdc.gov/healthyyouth/disparities/lgbtprotectivefactors.htm.

Connell, C. S., & Finnegan, M. J. (2010). Interviewing compliant adolescent victims. *FBI Law Enforcement Bulletin, 79*(5), 16–25.

Currie, C. (n.d.). *You Have Options Program: Sexual Assault Reporting*. Retrieved from https://www.reportingoptions.org/.

Dake, J. A., Price, J. H., Maziarz, L., & Ward, B. (2012). Prevalence and correlates of sexting behavior in adolescents. *American Journal of Sexuality Education, 7*(1), 1–15.

Dank, M., Lachman, P., Zweig, J., & Yahner, J. (2014). Dating violence experiences of lesbian, gay, bisexual, and transgender youth. *Journal of Youth and Adolescence, 43*(5), 846–857.

DOJ. (n.d.). Child Exploitation and Obscenity Section. Retrieved from http://www.justice.gov/criminal/ceos/subjectareas/childporn.html

Eke, A. W., Seto, M. C., & Williams, J. (2011). Examining the criminal history and future offending of child pornography offenders: An extended prospective follow-up study. *Law and Human Behavior, 35*(6), 466–478.

Elmquist, J., Wolford-Clevenger, C., Zapor, H., Febres, J., Shorey, R. C., Hamel, J., & Stuart, G. L. (2016). A gender comparison of motivations for physical dating violence among college students. *Journal of Interpersonal Violence, 31*(1), 186–203.

Exner-Cortens, D., Eckenrode, J., & Rothman, E. (2013). Longitudinal associations between teen dating violence victimization and adverse health outcomes. *Pediatrics, 131*(1), 71–78.

Faller, K., Cordisco-Steele, L., & Nelson-Gardell, D. (2010). Allegations of sexual abuse of a child: What to do when a single forensic interview isn't enough. *Journal of Child Sexual Abuse, 19*(5), 572–586.

Findley, P. A., Plummer, S.-B., & McMahon, S. (2016). Exploring the experiences of abuse of college students with disabilities. *Journal of Interpersonal Violence, 31*(17), 2801–2823.

Ford, J., & Soto-Marquez, J. G. (2016). Sexual assault victimization among straight, gay/lesbian, and bisexual college students. *Violence and Gender, 3*(2), 107–115.

Hamby, S., Finkelhor, D., & Turner, H. (2012). Teen dating violence: Co-occurrence with other victimizations in the National Survey of Children's Exposure to Violence (NatSCEV). *Psychology of Violence, 2*(2), 111–124

Harris, S. (2010). Toward a better way to interview child victims of sexual abuse. *National Institute of Justice Journal*, 267 (NCJ 233282).

Hershkowitz, I., Lamb, M., Orbach, Y., Katz, C., & Horowitz, D. (2012). The development of communicative and narrative skills among preschoolers: Lessons from forensic interviews about child abuse. *Child Development, 83*(2), 611–622.

Hinduja, S., & Patchin, J. (2015). *State Sexting Laws*. Retrieved from Cyberbullying Research Center: https://cyberbullying.org/state-sexting-laws.pdf.

Holcombe, E., Manlove, J., & Ikramullah, E. (2008). Forced sexual intercourse among young adult women. *Child Trends*. Retrieved from http://www.childtrends.org/files/Child_Trends-2008_09_10_FS_ForcedSex.pdf

Holderness, T., Moen, S., & Hull, C. (2014). You have options: Improving law enforcement's response to sexual assault. *The Police Chief, 81*(December), 30–33.

Holmes, K., & Sher, L. (2013). Dating violence and suicidal behavior in adolescents. In *International Journal of Adolescent Medicine and Health* (Vol. 25, pp. 257).

Houck, C. (2016). Digital-controlling behaviors among early adolescents with mental illness symptoms. *Journal of the American Academy of Child & Adolescent Psychiatry, 55*(10), S339.

Justice for Victims of Trafficking Act, § 108 Pub. L. No. Pub. L. 114-22, 129 Stat. 227, 238 Stat. (2015).

Kotria, K. (2010). Domestic minor sex trafficking in the United States. *Social Work, 55*(2), 181–187.

Krebs, C. P., Lindquist, C. H., Warner, T. D., Fisher, B. S., & Martin, S. L. (2009). College women's experiences with physically forced, alcohol-or other drug-enabled, and drug-facilitated sexual assault before and since entering college. *Journal of American College Health, 57*(6), 639–649.

Lampe, J. (2013). A victimless sex crime: The case for decriminalizing consensual teen sexting. *University of Michigan Journal of Law Reform, 46*(2), 703–736.

Langhinrichsen-Rohling, J., McCullars, A., & Misra, T. A. (2012). Motivations for men and women's intimate partner violence perpetration: A comprehensive review. *Partner Abuse, 3*(4), 429–468.

Leander, L. (2010). Police interviews with child sexual abuse victims: Patterns of reporting, avoidance and denial. *Child Abuse & Neglect, 34*, 192–205.

Lisak, D., & Markel, D. (2016). Using science to increase effectiveness of sexual assault investigations. *The Police Chief, 83*, 22–25.

Lyon, T. D. (2011). Assessing the competency of child witnesses: Best practice informed by psychology and law. In M. Lamb, D. La Rooy, L. C. Malloy, & C. Katz (Eds.), *Children's Testimony: A Handbook of Psychological Research and Forensic Practice* (pp. 69–85). Sussex, UK: Wiley-Blackwell.

Makepeace, J. M. (1997). Courtship violence as process: A developmental theory. In A. Cardarelli (Ed.), *Violence Between Intimate Partners: Patterns, Causes, and Effects* (pp. 29–47). Needham Heights, MA: Allyn & Bacon.

Medeiros, R., & Straus, M. (2006). Risk factors for physical violence between dating partners: Implications for gender-inclusive prevention and treatment of family violence. In J. Hamel & T. Nicholls (Eds.), *Family Approaches in Domestic Violence: A Practitioner's Guide to Gender-Inclusive Research and Treatment* (pp. 59–85). New York, NY: Springer.

Messman-Moore, T. L., Ward, R. M., & DeNardi, K. A. (2013). The impact of sexual enhancement alcohol expectancies and risky behavior on alcohol-involved rape among college women. *Violence Against Women, 19*(4), 449–464.

Mujahid, M. F. (2011). Romeo and Juliet-A tragedy of love by text: Why targeted penalties that offer front-end severity and backend leniency are necessary to remedy the teenage mass-sexting dilemma. *Howard Law Journal, 55*, 173.

Nahapetyan, L., Orpinas, P., Song, X., & Holland, K. (2014). Longitudinal association of suicidal ideation and physical dating violence among high school students. *Journal of Youth and Adolescence, 43*(4), 629–640.

National Children's Advocacy Center. (2013). Learn. Retrieved from http://www.nationalcac.org/we-are-you-can/wayc-learn.html

National Research Council. (2013). *Confronting Commercial Sexual Exploitation and Sex Trafficking of Minors in the United States: A Guide for Providers of Victim and Support Services*.

NCMEC. (2017). *Child sex trafficking*. Retrieved from http://www.missingkids.org/1in6.

NHTRC. (2016). *National Human Trafficking Resource Center (NHTRC) Data Breakdown: United States*

Report 1/1/2015 – 12/31/2015 Washington, D.C.: National Human Trafficking Resource Center. Retrieved from https://humantraffickinghotline.org/resources/human-trafficking-and-minors-2015.

Office of Adolescent Health [OAH]. (2013). February 2013: Crossing the Line - Teen Dating Violence. Retrieved from http://www.hhs.gov/ash/oah/news/e-updates/eupdate-feb2013.html

Pérez-Fuentes, G., Olfson, M., Villegas, L., Morcillo, C., Wang, S., & Blanco, C. (2013). Prevalence and correlates of child sexual abuse: A national study. *Comprehensive Psychiatry, 54*(1), 16–27.

Perkins, A. B., Becker, J. V., Tehee, M., & Mackelprang, E. (2014). Sexting behaviors among college students: Cause for concern? *International Journal of Sexual Health, 26*(2), 79–92.

Reed, L. A., Tolman, R. M., & Ward, L. M. (2017). Gender matters: Experiences and consequences of digital dating abuse victimization in adolescent dating relationships. *Journal of Adolescence, 59*, 79–89.

Reid, J. A. (2016). *Child pornography in the 21st Century: From child pornographic exploitation to youth sexting*. In Oxford Handbooks Online: Criminology and Criminal Justice. doi: 10.1093/oxfordhb/9780199935383.013.132.

Reyns, B. W., Burek, M. W., Henson, B., & Fisher, B. S. (2013). The unintended consequences of digital technology: Exploring the relationship between sexting and cybervictimization. *Journal of Crime and Justice, 36*(1), 1–17.

Scherer, H. L., Snyder, J. A., & Fisher, B. S. (2016). Intimate partner victimization among college students with and without disabilities: Prevalence of and relationship to emotional well-being. *Journal of Interpersonal Violence, 31*(1), 49–80.

Shorey, R., Cornelius, T., & Strauss, C. (2015). Stalking in college student dating relationships: A descriptive investigation. *Journal of Family Violence, 30*(7), 935–942.

Shorey, R. C., Sherman, A. E., Kivisto, A. J., Elkins, S. R., Rhatigan, D. L., & Moore, T. M. (2011). Gender differences in depression and anxiety among victims of intimate partner violence: The moderating effect of shame proneness. *Journal of Interpersonal Violence, 26*(9), 1834–1850.

Simich, L. (2014). *Out of the shadows: A tool for the identification of victims of human trafficking*. New York, NY: Vera Institute of Justice.

Sinozich, S., & Langton, L. (2014). *Rape and sexual assault victimization among college-age females, 1995-2013*: US Department of Justice, Office of Justice Programs, Bureau of Justice Statistics.

Smith, S., Chen, J., Basile, K., Gilbert, L., Merrick, M., Patel, N., ... Jain, A. (2017). *The National Intimate Partner and Sexual Violence Survey (NISVS): 2010-2012 State Report*. Atlanta, GA: National Center for Injury Prevention and Control, Centers for Disease Control and Prevention.

Substance Abuse and Mental Health Services Administration. (2014). *Results from the 2013 national survey on drug use and health: Mental health findings*. Rockville, MD: Substance Abuse and Mental Health Services Administration.

Taylor, B., Mumford, E., & Liu, W. (2016). *The National Survey of Teen Relationships and Intimate Violence (STRiV)*. Washington, D.C.: National Institute of Justice.

Temple, J. R., Choi, H. J., Brem, M., Wolford-Clevenger, C., Stuart, G. L., Peskin, M. F., & Elmquist, J. (2016). The temporal association between traditional and cyber dating abuse among adolescents. *Journal of Youth and Adolescence, 45*(2), 340–349.

Thompson, M. P., & Kingree, J. B. (2010). Sexual victimization, negative cognitions, and adjustment in college women. *American Journal of Health Behavior, 34*(1), 54–59.

Trafficking Victims Protection Act § 103, Pub. L. No. Pub. L. 106-386, 114 Stat. 1464, 1470 Stat. (2000).

U.S. Department of Education. (2016). *The Handbook for Campus Safety and Security Reporting: 2016 Edition*. Washington, D.C.: Author. Retrieved from https://www2.ed.gov/admins/lead/safety/handbook.pdf.

U.S. Department of Health and Human Services and Administration for Children and Families, Children's Bureau. (2012). *Child maltreatment 2011*. Retrieved from http://www.acf.hhs.gov/programs/cb/research-data-technology/statistics-research/child-maltreatment.

U.S. Department of Health and Human Services and Administration for Children and Families, Children's Bureau. (2015). *Child maltreatment 2013*. Retrieved from http://www.acf.hhs.gov/programs/cb/research-data-technology/statistics-research/child-maltreatment.

U.S. Department of State. (2017a). *The vulnerability of LGBTI individuals to human trafficking*. Washington, D.C.: Author. Retrieved from https://www.state.gov/j/tip/rls/fs/2017/index.htm

U.S. Department of State. (2017b). *What is trafficking in persons?* Washington, D.C.: Author. Retrieved from https://www.state.gov/j/tip/rls/fs/2017/index.htm

UNODC. (2016). *Global Report on Trafficking in Persons 2016*. New York, NY: United Nations Publication, Sales No. E.16.IV.6.

Vagi, K. J., Olsen, E. O. M., Basile, K. C., & Vivolo-Kantor, A. M. (2015). Teen dating violence (physical and sexual) among US high school students: Findings from the 2013 National Youth Risk Behavior Survey. *JAMA Pediatrics, 169*(5), 474–482.

Walker, R., Cole, J., & Shannon, L. (2006). *Partner stalking: How women respond, cope, and survive*: Springer Publishing Company.

Walters, M. L., Chen, J., & Breiding, M. J. (2013). *National intimate partner and sexual violence survey: 2010 findings on victimization by sexual orientation.* Atlanta, GA: Centers for Disease Control and Prevention.

Wittchen, H.-U., Jacobi, F., Rehm, J., Gustavsson, A., Svensson, M., Jönsson, B., ... Faravelli, C. (2011). The size and burden of mental disorders and other disorders of the brain in Europe 2010. *European Neuropsychopharmacology, 21*(9), 655–679.

Wright, P. J., Tokunaga, R. S., & Kraus, A. (2016). A meta analysis of pornography consumption and actual acts of sexual aggression in general population studies. *Journal of Communication, 66*(1), 183–205.

Yahner, J., Dank, M., Zweig, J., & Lachman, P. (2015). The co-occurence of physical and cyber dating violence and bullying among teens. *Journal of Interpersonal Violence, 30*(7), 1079–1089.

Zweig, J. M., Dank, M., Lachman, P., & Yahner, J. (2013). *Technology, teen dating violence and abuse, and bullying.* Washington, D.C.: Urban Institute.

7

Adolescent Perpetrators

CHAPTER OBJECTIVES

After reviewing this chapter, you should be able to:

1. Compare the major theories of family violence that pertain to adolescent offending.
2. Scrutinize the consequences of child abuse and neglect.
3. Predict why abused children may not themselves become offenders.
4. Classify acts that constitute adolescent offending patterns.
5. Apply the consequences of family violence on subsequent juvenile behaviors.

KEY TERMS

Animal abuse

Bestiality

Juvenile firesetters

Parricide

Patricide

Pedophile

Status offense

Survival sex

INTRODUCTION

Child maltreatment is a grave and pervasive health care problem in the United States with staggering costs to the individual and society. According to the Center for Disease Control and Prevention, the annual cost of child maltreatment is $124 billion (Fang, Brown, Florence, & Mercy, 2012). Abuse and neglectful child experiences negatively affect the vast majority of its survivors psychologically and biologically (Cicchetti, 2013). The lifetime economic burden of associated costs may be as high as $585 billion when the costs of child welfare and health care, productivity loss, and criminal justice are factored in (Fang et al., 2012). Children are at risk both for being victimized by family violence and for perpetrating it against others. Research and theory suggest that some forms of victimization increase the risk of juvenile criminal offending. Child maltreatment is found to be a significant predictor of adult arrest, although achieving all three developmental roles (high school graduation, employment, and marriage) dramatically reduces the risk (Allwood & Widom, 2013). This chapter will look at both the theory of child abuse and some consequences of child abuse and neglect. What is known about violence in the family and its influences on juvenile behaviors is the focus of this chapter.

FAMILY-BASED THEORY

Traditional criminological theory often appears inadequate to explain violence within the family. Multidimensional theories have surfaced to address this void. Researchers are turning to these multidimensional theories to understand the complexities of domestic violence. The *ecological model* has been identified as the best-suited framework to address the causes, consequences, and treatment formulations for abused children (Fallon et al., 2013). This model is becoming increasingly popular to explain intimate partner violence as well. The ecological model incorporates much of the research developed through the three traditional schools of criminological theory. Its framework not only helps the professional to understand the many levels that impact abuse in the family but also serves as a holistic approach to shape interventions.

The ecological model of factors associated with family violence is depicted as four circles, shown in Figure 7-1. The innermost circle represents the biological and psychological history that each brings to his or her behavior in a family. The second circle represents the context in which abuse against members of the family occurs. The third circle represents the social structures and institutions that influence family interactions, both formal and informal. The final circle is the societal level that includes cultural norms that influence behavior, the laws and policies that tolerate physical punishment of women and children, and the acceptance of violence as a means of settling interpersonal disputes.

With the expansion of theoretical approaches, however, comes confusion. Determining what does and does not work is harder than ever. The lack of consensus on the cause of family abuse causes different responses between jurisdictions. The

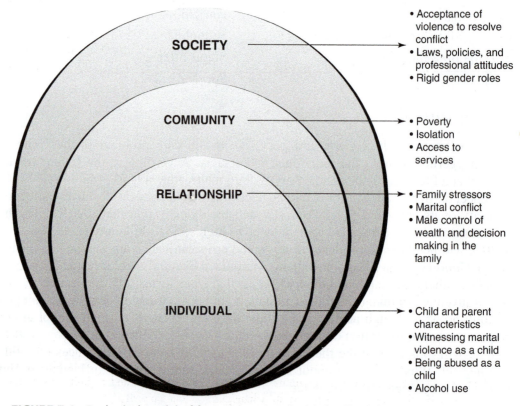

FIGURE 7-1 Ecological model of factors associated with family violence.

incongruity results in various approaches to deal with the problems. Although it is not necessary that all agree, it would be helpful to have a clearer picture of how to combat the violence that is so pervasive. Multidimensional theories do not restrict themselves to any one dominant school of thought. In this way, they retain the flexibility to consider causes and effects of family violence from a broader perspective.

Family-based theories are examples of multidimensional theories. According to family-based theories, violent behaviors are due to the family structure and family interactions rather than by an individual within the household. Some researchers question the fact that most people do not commit family violence—in fact, the majority of children do not grow up to be abusive parents. This positive approach has potential. Family systems theory and ineffective parenting are both examples of family-based theories.

Family Systems Theory

Family systems theory focuses primarily on family behavior and seeks to identify the problems that are a consequence of dysfunctional relationships among family members. An important concept in family systems theory is the interconnectedness of each member who influences the others in a predictable and recurring way. The role that each family member takes in contributing to the abuse or neglect is considered. In situations of sexual assault by an intimate partner of a parent, for example, the possibility that the nonoffending parent's reluctant intervention may appear to be tacit approval would be explored as a contributing factor in the repeated occurrence of abuse (McLaren, 2012).

Conflict within an intimate relationship is blamed on the lack of communication between the partners. Complicating the issue is the deeply intertwined mutual dependency that develops in some relationships. Self-imposed social isolation in addition to rigid expectations of loyalty and privacy make this a difficult situation for families when physical abuse is introduced as a means of control. One way for us to understand the context with which family violence occurs is to consider the family dynamics from healthy and unhealthy perspectives. Six concepts are related to the family structure in family systems theory (McCallion & Ferretti, n.d.):

- Boundaries
- Power and intimacy
- Freedom of expression
- Warmth, joy, and humor
- Organization and negotiating skills
- Value systems

Been There ... Done That!

An 11-year-old boy told his social worker that his mother's boyfriend had hit him over the head with the handle of a machete and that he was having headaches. His mother insisted that her son was not telling the truth. An investigation by the police determined that the boyfriend had repeatedly beaten the boy with a belt on at least one occasion. Another time the man forced the child to stand in front of a door that had a poster picture of Mickey Mouse on it. He fired numerous shots from a handgun at the child, both above his head and at his feet, yelling, "You're dead, you're dead!" Mom had handed the bullets to her boyfriend as he shot at the child. Afterward, the man took a razor blade and cut the child on the little finger, telling him, "When you die, I am going to be the one to kill you." When a search warrant was executed on the home, the poster of Mickey Mouse was found under a mattress, and 11 bullet holes were located on the floor and the wall.

Ineffective Parenting

Parents are the most critical factor in the development of children. Empirical findings in many studies indicate that parental behavior can either increase or decrease an adolescent's risk for delinquency and other problem behaviors. Poor monitoring, low levels of positive parent–child involvement, and coercive parenting are among the practices that are believed to affect aggression and bullying in juveniles (Connor & Barkley, 2004).

Sibling abuse may be the most frequent violence that affects children. Left without proper parental supervision, children may be victimized by overly aggressive siblings. While there is no easy explanation for sibling abuse, ineffective parenting may be a primary cause (Knafo, Jaffee, Neiderhiser, Marceau, & Reiss, 2013). Research suggests that parents may have unrealistic expectations of older siblings and leave these immature children to care for younger siblings (Relva, Fernandes, & Mota, 2013). In some cases, the parents simply do not know how to handle fighting children and fail to intervene when needed. Apathetic parents may be so wrapped up in their own problems that they fail to act appropriately when conflict arises between their children.

CONSEQUENCES OF CHILD ABUSE AND NEGLECT

Children may experience similar symptoms from abuse that adults would if they were to experience a traumatic event. For example, adults might have nightmares or constantly think about a traumatic event, or they might lose interest in doing things or avoid activities that remind them of the event. Children may have these same feelings but have not developed skills to understand and deal with such emotions. Children who have either witnessed violence in their parents or experienced abuse may learn violent behavior and may also learn to justify violent behavior as appropriate. Survivors of multiple forms of ill-treatment experience greater suicidal ideation (Thompson et al., 2012).

The majority of abuse victims do not commit family or other forms of violence as adults; however, many suffer long after the abuse ends. Victims are at higher risk for many other problems throughout their lives, including participation in violent crime as adults. Due to the added risks of victimization in domestic settings, advocates are seeking additional rights for children in custody and marital torts. Fair consideration of children in the legal system is deemed a vital intervention when assessing visitation and custody rights of parents.

Chronic physical abuse can result in long-term physical disabilities, including brain damage, hearing loss, dental problems, and eye damage. Infants who are physically abused are more likely to experience neurological alterations such as irritability, lethargy, tremors, and vomiting (OVC, 2012). In cases of shaken baby syndrome (SBS), the infant may experience seizures, permanent blindness or deafness, mental and developmental delays or retardation, coma, paralysis, and death.

Intergenerational Cycle of Violence

Although the numbers vary, child abuse studies commonly support the finding that some maltreating parents or caregivers were victims of abuse themselves as children. The intergenerational cycle of violence asserts that abused children are at high risk to become abusers in their adult intimate relationships (Siegel, 2013). While there is much evidence to support the violence-begets-violence hypothesis, experts suggest that the responses to the intergenerational transmission of violence have not kept pace with treatment options. Studies of school-age children who are raised in homes where they witness partner violence have suggested that those children are at risk of developing psychological problems. Among those problems are low self-esteem, high rates of internalizing and externalizing behavior problems, and they may show symptoms of posttraumatic stress (Siegel, 2013).

Often associated with childhood abuse, a cycle of predictable self-inflicted violence may occur in the adolescent addiction model, triggered by negative emotions such as alienation, frustration, rejection, anger, isolation, depression, or sadness. Self-inflicted violence in adolescents may be an indication of past abuse and a risk factor for future offending. Variables that are thought to affect the intergenerational cycle of violence, and consequently, the impact of family violence on children, include the following (Fritz, Slep, & O'Leary, 2012):

1. Type, degree, and frequency of violence.
2. Witnessing interparental aggression.
3. Parent-to-child aggression.
4. Stability of the home otherwise and general quality of the parent(s) aside from the violence.
5. Child's chronological and emotional age, stage of physical development, intellectual functioning at the time of the first occurrence, and relationship with each parent.

Resilience and Self-Esteem

An incorrect assumption is that all maltreated children will grow up to abuse their children later in life. Studies have indicated that this is not necessarily true. The majority of children who are victimized through domestic violence do not commit criminal acts as adults (Allwood & Widom, 2013). Research has suggested that approximately one-third of individuals who experience abuse will subject their children to maltreatment (Cicchetti, 2013). While the idea of intergenerational transmission of violence is commonly accepted, we cannot calculate who will engage in child maltreatment as an adolescent or adult. This lack of predictability has led some researchers to conclude that the intergenerational cycle of violence is overstated. What happens because of abuse is that there is simply an increased likelihood that the victim will become an abuser. On the other hand, some people who have never been victimized themselves will abuse their children. The harm to a victimized child is not universal and cannot be predicted with any certainty. Many conditions might affect the response to abuse, both as a child victim and later in life as an adult.

Been There ... Done That

One investigation of child sexual abuse proved to be a classic example of the intergenerational cycle of violence. Evidence first pointed to a 35-year-old man who had molested a group of children, including his son, daughters, nieces, and nephews. Information evolved indicating that his 75-year-old father was still molesting children in the neighborhood. The kids on the street referred to him as the "dirty old man" and warned newcomers to stay away from him. Finally, probable cause was developed regarding sexual molestation by the 15-year-old grandson. All three generations of sexual abusers were arrested.

Childhood experiences play an important part in building positive self-image and resilience. Exposure to cumulative family abuses is associated with mental health difficulties in the child's future (Miller-Lewis, Searle, Sawyer, Baghurst, & Hedley, 2013). The self-image that is characterized by self-esteem may then be more fully developed throughout adolescence. Lower self-esteem has also been associated with severe juvenile criminal offending (Imbach, Aebi, Metzke, Bessler, & Steinhausen, 2013). Resilience is the manifestation of self-esteem, thought to be one of the factors that mediate the negative effects of child abuse (Cicchetti, 2013). Cognitive resilience underscores the fact that adverse consequences are not inevitable following adversity.

Childhood resilience has been conceptualized as adaptations in a phenomenon referred to as turning. Turning refers to a significant transition in the life of a person when he or she takes on a new persona, enters into fresh relationships with new individuals, and achieves a new self-concept (Allwood & Widom, 2013). It is a method of coping that brings about change in an effort to avoid continuing the negative behavior that has been witnessed or experienced.

Forms and frequency of abuse, age, and mental condition of the child, as well as his or her personality, will all play a role in how the victim reacts to abuse. The consequences of abuse will vary according to multiple factors, including the form and severity of the abuse (Cicchetti, 2013).

1. *Characteristics of the child*—The age, emotional and cognitive development, gender, race/ethnicity, personality, and strengths or resiliency of the child all play a part in determining the effects of maltreatment.
2. *Type of trauma*—Two types of trauma are related to the severity and intensity of the abuse. Type I, referred to as acute trauma, is a single event; type II, chronic or repetitive abuse over time, is usually more difficult for the child to overcome.
3. *Type of abuse or neglect*—All forms of maltreatment to a child—physical abuse, sexual abuse, psychological/emotional abuse, and witnessing domestic violence—carry the possibility of long-term effects on the psychological and social adaptation of the victim.
4. *Co-occurrences of types of abuse and neglect*—When multiple cases of abuse occur simultaneously, the risk of maladaptive behavior is heightened as a result. Frequently, emotional/psychological abuse happens when any other form of abuse is perpetrated.
5. *Relationship*—Child relationships affect the resiliency of the victim and his or her ability to overcome adverse effects of ill-treatment. All relationships that the child has with the victimizer, the nonoffending parent, other family members, other adults, and peers will affect the consequences of abuse and neglect.

Childhood Abuse and Delinquent or Criminal Behavior

In addition to the psychological and behavioral effects that children may experience due to their exposure to domestic violence, there is concern about later criminalization. Child victims are at higher risk of becoming offenders themselves. Being abused or neglected as a child substantially increases the likelihood of arrest as a juvenile and as an adult (Allwood & Widom, 2013). The most consistent predictor of juvenile violence is childhood physical abuse victimization (Maas, Herrenkohl, & Sousa, 2008). When multiple forms of abuse and increased severity of abuse occur, it appears that the likelihood of later perpetration of violence is increased.

Harsh parenting and more severe forms of physical punishment can result in an increased likelihood of later violence for at-risk youth.

This "cycle of abuse" suggests strongly that those children who are abused or neglected, either physically or sexually, grow up to engage in criminal activity at a higher rate than those who are not abused or neglected. Both boys and girls are evidenced in the higher rates of criminal activity due to victimization. Future criminal activity may also involve their abuse of their children.

Research suggests that it is not necessarily the severity of the abuse that best predicts future delinquent behavior, but more importantly the internalizing of anger (Feiring, Miller-Johnson, & Cleland, 2007). Those children exhibiting a shame-rage type of explosive anger that is associated with sexual abuse against female victims were most at risk for delinquency. Early intervention, anger management, and peer relationships are important efforts to prevent delinquency as well as to lessen the psychological distress of victims.

Childhood Abuse and Social Consequences

Research indicates that the victimization of children has grave social consequences (Cicchetti, 2013). Among other things, ill-treatment and neglect increase the likelihood of repressed social information processing, lower performance in school, and relationship problems. Studying a cohort of 1,680 youth from the National Survey of Children's Exposure to Violence (NatSCEV), experts found that all of the victims of teen dating violence reported experiencing other forms of victimization as well (Hamby, Finkelhor, & Turner, 2012). On average, the survivors of teen dating violence reported twice as many other forms of victimization than those who had not experienced teen dating violence.

Additional social problems include difficulties with the quality of personal relationships, evidenced by intimate partner violence in adult relationships. Abused children grow up with violence and learn that it is an acceptable way to handle stress and assert their views. In particular, victimization by mother-to-child abuse appears to be a particularly consistent predictor of intimate partner violence within the adult relationships of the victim (Fritz et al., 2012).

Sexual assault victims frequently experience a decline in school grades or participation in after-school activities. Distrust of others, over compliance with authority figures, and a tendency to solve interpersonal problems with aggression are all risk factors for victims of physical abuse (OVC, 2012). Consequences of child abuse and neglect can be severe and diverse. Research points to numerous problems for the adult survivor. A significant intervention opportunity occurs with education on positive dating relationships (see Figure 7-2).

Childhood Abuse and Psychological Consequences

Child sexual abuse is thought to be associated with all childhood-onset psychiatric disorders and many adult-onset disorders. An extensive national study of 34,000 individuals confirmed that those who have experienced child sexual abuse are significantly more likely to have a mental health disorder sometime in their life (Pérez-Fuentes et al., 2013). Strong associations were evidenced for bipolar disorder, panic disorder, posttraumatic stress disorder (PTSD), attention-deficit/hyperactivity disorder (ADHD), and conduct disorder. Sexual abuse as a child has also been found to elevate maternal

FIGURE 7-2 It's everyone's responsibility to stop dating violence.
Image copyright Dragon Images, 2012. Used under license from
Shutterstock.com

depression and substance abuse (Mapp, 2006). Higher rates of suicide attempts, diagnosis of antisocial personality disorder, and alcohol abuse—regardless of age, sex, race, or criminal history—have been documented as consequences of childhood abuse (Pérez-Fuentes et al., 2013).

Shame, the desire to hide the damaged self from others, may result from childhood sexual abuse (Feiring et al., 2007). A central feature for the development of shame in childhood comes from attachment theory. Shame has been correlated with trauma in childhood, such as physical and emotional abuse, neglect, and abandonment. Shame that develops early in childhood due to an insecure attachment with one's mother is believed to be a significant factor in the progression to borderline and narcissistic personality disorders (Coleman, 2003). Borderline and narcissistic personality disorders have been noted as personality characteristics of some intimate partner offenders.

Consequences of Witnessing Family Violence

The effects of indirect abuse are a topic of concern to child advocates. What happens when children reside in a home where parental abuse occurs? Reports from abused women show that the majority of children do witness domestic violence; some see

Been There ... Done That!

A biological father on numerous occasions during visitations raped his 14-year-old daughter. Her 22-year-old sister was also his victim; she had been impregnated by her father when she was 15. The family never talked about it, but the resulting baby was a constant reminder of the physical and emotional pain caused by the rapes. The older sister reported the incident to a teacher when she found out that the father had turned to abusing her little sister. It is not uncommon for perpetrators to gain compliance from the older child through a promise not to touch the younger siblings. Do not be surprised if you come across this scenario.

their mothers being beaten and raped. They hear their parent screaming and crying; they see the effects of blood, bruises, or broken windows and furniture. More than one in four children are exposed to some form of family violence during their lifetimes, and these are not passive observers. Almost half of children who are witnesses to domestic violence either yell at the offender to stop or try to get away from the violence (Hamby, Finkelhor, Turner, & Ormrod, 2011).

There is a recognized overlap between domestic violence and child abuse. Where one form of family violence exists, experts agree, there is a likelihood that the other does as well. In homes where domestic violence occurs, somewhere between 40 percent and 50 percent may also involve child abuse (Mederos, 2004). For this reason, domestic violence is a factor when custody is being determined by the court in cases of separation or divorce of the parents. Much of the violence committed against children is direct abuse, physical and sexual abuse are forms that target children. Witnessing family violence and emotional abuse indirectly cause harm. As a child gets older and becomes a juvenile, he or she can access the courts for domestic violence restraining orders and other forms of relief when the offender is another family member, such as a parent or sibling.

Violence toward an intimate partner causes a variety of psychological problems for the children and places them at greater risk for delinquency and adult criminality. Child witnessing of family violence has been linked to a variety of problems, from aggression and hostility to depression and cognitive impairment. Although we cannot predict which children will become victims of abuse, those that reside in violent homes are at greater risk. How many children witness violence in the home? We can only speculate based on those we know who live with a mother who is being abused.

Although witnessing family violence affects children of different ages in a variety of ways, its impact is noted on children's emotional, social, neurobiological, and cognitive development (Siegel, 2013). A strong positive association has been documented between a person witnessing parental aggression and engaging in the future use of partner violence. One study revealed a 2.6 risk ratio between witnessing and perpetrating intimate partner violence (Roberts, Gilman, Fitzmaurice, Decker, & Koenen, 2010). In addition to the short-term effects, there is evidence of a long-range impact on families and society when children are exposed to violence in the home.

ADOLESCENT OFFENDING PATTERNS

It is not uncommon that an adolescent is both a victim and an offender. For example, juvenile sexual offenders account for more than one-third of all sexual offenses against minors that are known to the police; often these perpetrators were victims of sexual

Been There ... Done That

Jay was a willing suspect and confessed during my interrogation of him to having sexually abused his children and countless others. He knew that what he did was legally wrong, but professed that he "loved" the children. It was important to him that the children were not "hurt." Jay explained that more good was done for them by showing his love. He was totally unaware of the emotional, physical, and psychological effects on his victims. His actions were not benign, regardless of the claims; Jay was adjudicated as a sexually dangerous person.

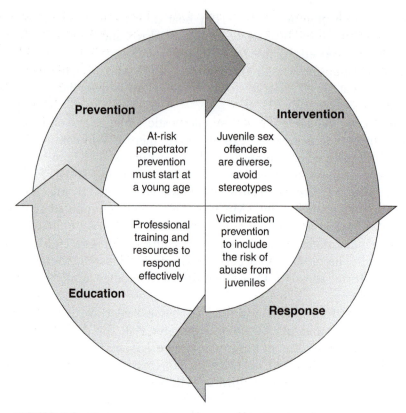

Prevention

At-risk perpetrator prevention must start at a young age

Intervention

Juvenile sex offenders are diverse, avoid stereotypes

Professional training and resources to respond effectively

Victimization prevention to include the risk of abuse from juveniles

Education

Response

FIGURE 7-3 Responses to juvenile sex offending involve a multidimensional approach. Based on data from Finkelhor et al., 2009.

abuse as well. Experts suggest that since offenders vary by age, gender, and motivation, their treatment approaches should differ (Finkelhor, Ormrod, & Chaffin, 2009). See Figure 7-3 for an illustration of multidimensional approaches to juvenile sex offending responses. Most offending adolescents do not continue to perpetrate sexual offenses as adults.

The original jurisdiction for prosecution in juvenile court depends on the state, typically with an upper age of 15, 16, or 17. In the juvenile courts, violations of criminal law are referred to as delinquency cases. In 2009, U.S. courts with juvenile jurisdiction handled more than 1.5 million delinquency cases (Adams & Addie, 2012). Another category of offenses dealt with by the juvenile courts is status offenses. A **status offense** is an act that would not be an offense if an adult committed it. Examples of status offenses include breaking curfew laws, runaway statutes, and truancy laws. The third type of juvenile case concerns juveniles who need supervision. While the name may vary somewhat, 49 jurisdictions have the Children in Need of Services (CHINS) category (National Law Center on Homelessness & Poverty and the National Network for Youth, 2012). Petitions for changes in legal custody and oversight of incorrigible youth are examples of CHINS cases. States also have laws that allow younger juveniles to be tried as adults for some specific crimes such as homicide. Being tried as an adult will depend on the legal designation by the age of the individual and the crime alleged to have been committed.

Numerous studies have found a correlation between child abuse and future juvenile delinquency. Children who are abused are nine times more likely to become involved in crime (Gold, Sullivan, & Lewis, 2011). The majority of juveniles who commit crimes are never arrested. Official statistics on juvenile delinquency underrepresents juvenile delinquent behavior. Among those who are detained and processed in the juvenile justice system, almost 90 percent in juvenile placement facilities are being held for delinquency, according to the 2014 *National Juvenile Offenders and Victims Report*. Youth between the ages of 16 and 17 make up more than 50 percent of arrests for those under the age of 18 (Sickmund & Puzzanchera, 2014).

In a 2012 landmark decision, the U.S. Supreme Court struck down laws that mandate a life sentence for convicted juvenile offenders (*Miller v. Alabama*, 2012). The Court held that mandatory life without parole for those under the age of 18 at the time of their crimes violates the Eighth Amendment's prohibition of "cruel and unusual punishments." A "judge or jury must have the opportunity to consider mitigating circumstances before imposing the harshest possible penalty for juveniles" (The Oyez Project, 2013). At the time *Miller* was decided, approximately 2,000 prisoners were serving life without parole sentences as a result of a mandatory sentencing requirement for crimes committed when they were under age 18 (National Center for Youth Law, n.d.). The laws of the federal government and 28 states that allowed mandatory life without parole sentences for juveniles are being reviewed and revised. The U.S. Supreme Court ruled in *Roper v. Simmons* (2005) that it is unconstitutional to execute an offender for crimes committed while under the age of 18.

Animal Cruelty

Animal abuse is defined as socially unacceptable behavior that intentionally causes unnecessary pain, suffering, or distress to and/or death of an animal (Ascione, 2001). Animal abuse ranges from the toddler pulling a kitten along by the tail to severe animal torture. Juvenile animal abuse typologies are illustrated in Figure 7-4. Childhood abuse of animals is predictive of violent crime offending at a later age as well as of

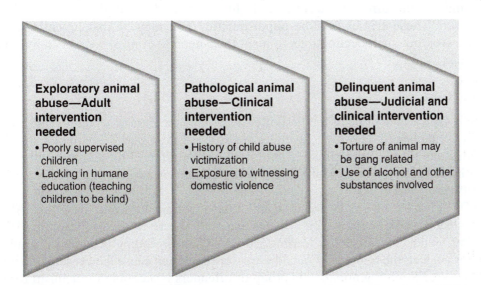

Exploratory animal abuse—Adult intervention needed
• Poorly supervised children
• Lacking in humane education (teaching children to be kind)

Pathological animal abuse—Clinical intervention needed
• History of child abuse victimization
• Exposure to witnessing domestic violence

Delinquent animal abuse—Judicial and clinical intervention needed
• Torture of animal may be gang related
• Use of alcohol and other substances involved

FIGURE 7-4 Typology of juvenile animal abusers. Based on data from Ascione, 2001.

committing property offenses, drug offenses, public disorder offenses, and exhibiting a range of antisocial problems (Sherley, 2007). Witnessing of animal abuse may be a predictor of adolescent participation in animal abuse (Gullone & Robertson, 2008).

Research suggests a connection between child abuse and neglect, domestic violence, and animal abuse. Animal abuse is more likely to occur in homes where children are abused or neglected and in homes where intimate partner violence also occurs. Animal cruelty by children may be associated with their exposure to family violence. According to the results of a Canadian study, children exposed to male-to-female family violence are significantly more likely to engage in cruelty to animals (Currie, 2006). The study found that their age and gender did not differ from children who were not cruel to animals. However, children exposed to family violence and who were cruel to animals were significantly older than nonexposed children who were cruel to animals.

Sexually abused children are more likely to be cruel to animals and to engage in bestiality as adolescents as compared to those without a history of maltreatment. **Bestiality** is human-to-animal sexual activity. Among sexually abused children, experiencing physical abuse increased animal cruelty among boys, while exposure to domestic violence increased animal cruelty among girls (Currie, 2006).

Juvenile Child-Care Offenders

Numerous studies have suggested that children are at risk for sexual abuse at the hands of child-care providers. Parents rarely consider a babysitter as a potential perpetrator of sexual assault; however, older children account for as much as 40 percent of the offenses committed in the child-care context (Moulden, Firestone, & Wexler, 2007). Most juvenile sex offenders are teenagers between the ages of 12 and 17 (Finkelhor et al., 2009). Sex offenses committed by juveniles typically occur within a home and during the afternoon or evening hours (Finkelhor et al., 2009).

In a study of child-care providers who sexually abuse children, juvenile offenders charged with supervising younger children tended to victimize four- and five-year-olds, predominately (Moulden et al., 2007). In the same study, juvenile sexual abusers were found to be more likely to offend against female victims; male and female youth offenders were equally likely to fondle and perform oral sex on the victim. These crimes may be opportunistic, or it may be that juvenile sexual abusers seek out such occupations to meet their need to control weaker individuals (Moulden et al., 2007).

Firesetting

Arson is typically not one of the first offenses that come to mind when juvenile delinquency is mentioned. However, juveniles are arrested for a greater share of arson than any other age group; approximately half of all people arrested for arson are juveniles. **Juvenile firesetters** are typically defined as children or adolescents who engage in firesetting.

There is a strong link between juvenile abuse victimization and firesetting. Abuse and neglect is a risk factor that contributes to a more severe course of firesetting (Root, MacKay, Henderson, Bove, & Warling, 2008). When firesetting occurs as a result of abuse or neglect, the removal of outside stressors can often cause the firesetting behavior to cease. Firesetting among this group of offenders is a coping mechanism for the troubled youth who have been victimized.

According to the *BushFIRE Arson Bulletin*, there is an association between juveniles who abuse animals and those who set fires ("Firesetting as a predictor of violence," 2006). In an Australian survey, firesetting was just one in a range of antisocial behaviors of children experiencing family stress, with boys demonstrating cruelty to animals as well. A typology of juvenile firesetters developed by the Salt Lake City Area Juvenile Firesetter/Arson Control and Prevention Program categorizes children into the following groups (Ascione, 2001):

- *Normal curiosity firesetters*—Age ranges from three to seven years. Children in this group often share the characteristics of poor parental supervision, a lack of fire education, and no fear of fire.
- *Plea-for-help firesetters*—Age ranges from 7 to 13 years. The group's firesetting is often symptomatic of a more deeply seated psychological disturbance.
- *Delinquent firesetters*—Age ranges from 13 years to adulthood. Firesetting may be one of a number of adolescent antisocial behaviors, including gang-related activities.

Research suggests that sexual abuse perpetrated by both males and females is a common pattern for the juvenile arsonist. The coexistence of juvenile firesetting and sexual offending has been noted. Most of the juvenile arsonists in one study were also sexual abusers (Burlin, 2007).

Intimate Partner Violence

An association between intimate partner violence (IPV) and a history of child maltreatment has long been suspected, and research results are mixed. Millett and colleagues (2013) examined public sector records such as child welfare and juvenile court reports to determine if the assumption was legitimate. Their study found that dating violence perpetration rates were higher among maltreated than control youths and higher in maltreated men than in women. For men, child abuse victimization had both direct and mediated effects on IPV perpetration through violent delinquency. For women, childhood abuse victimization did not directly or indirectly predict IPV perpetration.

In contrast, data from the *Longitudinal Study of Adolescent to Adult Health* showed that girls who experienced childhood physical abuse were up to 7 percent more likely to become perpetrators of youth violence and 10 percent more likely to be perpetrators of dating violence. Boys who experienced childhood sexual abuse were up to 12 percent more likely to commit youth violence and 17 percent more likely to commit relationship violence (Fang & Corso, 2007). The results reinforce the commonly held view that preventing child abuse may also prevent future IPV perpetration.

Murder

In all age categories, most perpetrators of homicides are male (Cooper & Smith, 2011). According to the Office of Juvenile Justice and Delinquency Prevention (OJJDP), approximately 120 juvenile females are implicated in homicides in the United States, each year (OJJDP, 2012). Juvenile offenders were involved in at least 800 murders in the United States in 2010, an estimated 8 percent of all known murder offenders. The majority of juvenile homicide perpetrators are age 16 or 17. Family members account for approximately 6 percent of the victims killed by a person under 18 years old (Cooper & Smith, 2011). Female juvenile murder offenders are more likely than male offenders to have female victims and to kill family members (Sickmund & Puzzanchera, 2014).

Parricide, the act of killing one's parent, is one form of a murder committed by juveniles. When a mother is killed by one of her children, matricide is the term used to describe this specific form of criminal homicide. **Patricide** is the act of killing one's father. Fathers are more likely than mothers to be killed by their children. From 1980 to 2008, the most frequent perpetrators of parental killings were teenage sons between the ages of 16 and 19 (Cooper & Smith, 2011).

In a review of 5,781 cases of parricide over a 24-year period from 1976 to 1999, approximately one of four offenders involved in the killings of fathers (25.4 percent) and one of six offenders who participated in the murders of mothers (17.0 percent) were under 18 years of age (Heide & Petee, 2007b). The incidents examined were those identified by the FBI as involving the killings of biological fathers or mothers and did not include stepparents. The study reported that juvenile offenders were more likely to use a firearm to kill a father when compared to adults who committed the same crime. At least half of parricide killings stem from an argument between the child and the parent (Heide & Petee, 2007a). Research suggests that parricide may be the result of escalating violence in the family where the parent, rather than the child, is the victim of abuse at the hands of the child (Walsh & Krienert, 2008).

Runaway

According to the report *Alone Without a Home*, 18 jurisdictions in the United States explicitly define the term *runaway* in their laws (National Law Center on Homelessness & Poverty and the National Network for Youth, 2012). The report cites Ohio's definition as concise: a runaway is "any child who is separated from the child's guardian and appears to be in need of emergency housing and other services" (Ohio Rev. Code Ann. §5119.64 (2011)). Approximately 1.6 million children and youth (ages 12 to 17) run away every year. Before running away, two out of five homeless youth report being beaten by a caretaker; one out of four youth have had a caretaker request sexual activity; and one out of five youth had a conflict with their parents about their sexual orientation, which caused them to leave.

Runaway youth is a status offense, which may be specifically named in the CHINS category. Police policy and laws on juvenile runaways vary from state to state. Sometimes, police use formal charges to force runaways to see social workers and court-appointed counselors. Even in a state where it is not illegal to be a runaway, police have the power to detain juveniles and often arrest them on warrants related to their runaway status. Police are allowed by law to take runaway youth into custody in 50 jurisdictions (National Law Center on Homelessness & Poverty and the National Network for Youth, 2012).

The National Runaway Safeline (NRS) (1-800-RUNAWAY) is a 24-hour toll-free hotline that receives over 100,000 calls each year from runaway youth, throwaway youth, and young people in crisis (National Runaway Safeline, n.d.). The vast majority of callers are ages 18 and younger; abuse was the identified problem in 13 percent of the calls for 2012. In partnership with Greyhound Lines, Inc., the NRS's Home Free Program has reunited over 14,000 youth with family members by providing a free bus ticket home (Benoit-Bryan, 2012). The most commonly reported significant problem in the lives of Home Free Program users in 2011 (65 percent) was a conflict with parents or guardians.

Youth victimization is highly correlated with the decision to run away from home. *The Runaway Youth Longitudinal Study* concludes that verbal abuse, physical abuse, and sexual abuse before the age of 18 are all correlated with higher runaway rates (Benoit-Bryan, 2011). The likelihood of running away from home is three times greater for respondents who were physically or verbally abused and twice as likely for sexual violence survivors as compared to those youth who were not abused. Victims of sibling abuse are also at greater risk of being arrested as juvenile runaways than those who are not abused by a sibling (Kiselica & Morrill-Richards, 2007).

Sexual Offending

Frequently, sexual offenders report that they began offending in their adolescent years. An early target may be a younger sibling. The child may abuse because he or she has learned that this is acceptable or may act out of rage due to his or her own experiences of being abused.

Juvenile offenders make up more than one-third of the sexual offenders against minors that are known to the police (Finkelhor et al., 2009). Adolescent males constitute the majority of offenders, but females constitute 7 percent of juveniles who commit sex offenses (Finkelhor et al., 2009). Most juvenile sex offenders are teenagers between the ages of 12 and 17 (Figure 7-5), according to Finkelhor et al. (2009), and approximately 16 percent are younger than age 12. Juvenile sexual offenders represent a diverse group; some target only children, whereas others assault peer and adult females. Many of these juveniles view themselves as socially inadequate, anticipate peer ridicule and rejection, and experience feelings of loneliness.

What is known about sex offenders is limited to those that have been identified through the criminal justice system. In 2007, juvenile sex offenders who were prosecuted in the state of Idaho had offended against family members in 36 percent of the cases (Office of the Governor, 2008). Although little information is available about female juvenile sexual offenders, they are represented in state prosecutions.

There is concern that exposure to online pornography increases the risk of sexual offending. An online survey with over 1,000 children found that by age 15 adolescents are more likely than not to have inadvertently seen online pornography, slightly more

Juvenile Sex Offenders WHO Victimize Minors by Gender of Offender

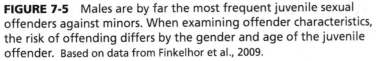

FIGURE 7-5   Males are by far the most frequent juvenile sexual offenders against minors. When examining offender characteristics, the risk of offending differs by the gender and age of the juvenile offender. Based on data from Finkelhor et al., 2009.

than half of the population (Martellozzo et al., 2016). Reactions were varied; some in the survey report were curious, shocked, and ultimately disturbed by what they saw. Researchers found that of those who viewed online pornography, 42 percent of 15- to 16- year-olds wanted to emulate what they saw. There are concerns that young people who view online pornography may indulge in risky sexual acts or may be groomed by predators for sexual abuse activities. Most of the adolescents in the Martellozzo study did not report having taken sexually explicit 'selfies,' however; 13 percent had taken topless pictures of themselves (boys and girls), and three percent had taken fully naked pictures of themselves. More than half of these children shared the self-images with others.

A particularly salient concern is whether child pornography offenders are likely to commit a sexual act involving contact with a child. One study found that men arrested for child pornography tended to re-offend in some way at a rate of about 17 percent within a two-and-a-half-year period (Seto & Eke, 2005). Juvenile victim pornography is frequently associated with a sexual or violent offense. Possession of child pornography is a valid indicator of pedophilia because it correlates positively with a self-reported sexual interest in children (Seto & Eke, 2005).

One study examined the degree to which adjudication for a sexual offense identified juveniles at increased risk for reoffending. Caldwell (2007) found in a six-year follow-up study of youths who had been arrested as juvenile sex offenders that they were no more likely to commit future sexually violent crimes or sexual homicides than nonsexual offending juveniles. Approximately 85 percent to 95 percent of young delinquents who abuse minors do not become sex offenders in adolescence or adulthood (Finkelhor et al., 2009). Consistent with other studies, juvenile sexual offenders are more likely to commit nonsexual offenses as adults than sexual offenses (2007). According to Caldwell, sex offender registration, notification, and residency restriction statutes applied to juvenile sex offenders are unlikely to benefit community safety substantially.

SURVIVAL SEX

Estimates of the number of youth who trade sex for survival vary widely. **Survival sex** involves minors under the age of 18 who have traded sex acts (including prostitution, stripping, and pornography) without overt force, fraud or coercion, to meet the basic needs of survival such as food and shelter. Most feel that their circumstances left little or no other option. In New York City alone, estimates of minors engaged in the sex trade industry range between 2,200 and 4,000 (Curtis et al., 2008; Gragg, Petta, Bernstein, Eisen, & Quinn, 2007). Results from the Gragg study found predominately female victims, yet Curtis and colleagues report that boys outnumber the girls in their sample of youth. Both studies revealed that most of the youth had prior child welfare involvement, typically ill-treatment and neglect or foster care placement. Runaways are particularly vulnerable as they become homeless.

Homelessness is at the core of youth engagement in survival sex. Studies suggest that young men are three times more likely than girls to trade sex for shelter (Dank et al., 2015). Transgender youth are highly susceptible to engaging in survival sex. In New York City, minors who are transgender have been found eight times more likely than nontransgender adolescents to trade sex for a safe place to stay (Freeman & Hamilton, 2008). Similar results are found in the central cities around the country, including Chicago, Los Angles, and New York City. Survival sex is a measure pursued by young victims who run from desperate situations of abuse.

Findings suggest that "couch surfing," which involves sexual exchange as a way to avoid homelessness or potential violence in youth shelters, is preferred by LGBTQ youth (Dank et al., 2015). Couch surfing may be relatively common among households with 13- to 17-year-olds and 18- to 25-year-olds (Curry et al., 2017). Youth over the age of 18 who engage in survival sex does not fit the U.S. federal definition of trafficking but make up 20 percent of the Curry study.

SIBLING VIOLENCE

Research has suggested that sibling abuse may be the most common form of family violence (Relva et al., 2013). Often considered a normal part of sibling rivalry, it is hard to recognize without looking at the severity and intent of an act. Sibling abuse goes beyond child play because it contains strong elements of violence. Abuse of a sibling is not an isolated act but a cycle of behavior that looks very much like IPV. The co-occurrence of child abuse and IPV increases the risk of sibling violence in the home.

No single explanation has evolved to explain sibling abuse; instead, a combination of conditions has been identified under which a child is born and conditioned into violent behavior. The abusers may perceive an imbalance between themselves and younger siblings, whom they believe are favored due to academic or social successes or by their age or gender. Frequently, the abuse of power occurs along gender lines, with males abusing females. The gender-role socialization that favors male aggressiveness and female passivity contribute to this condition. Research also suggests that abusers experience high levels of parent-to-child abuse, rendering them desensitized to violence (Relva et al., 2013).

Over half of children, ages 3 to 7, have committed severe violence against a sibling (Kiselica & Morrill-Richards, 2007). The child who is violent is often male and bigger than his siblings. The size of the child is deceiving, however, because the abuse is a way to compensate for the offender's lack of power or perceived loss of power. The child may feel jealous of siblings who appear to please the parents through better academic achievement, looks, or personality. Given the opportunity to express feelings of inadequacy, the child may direct them at the siblings.

Violence between siblings is under reported and under-documented, and its effects can be severe. Adults and children commit similar types of abuse: physical, sexual, and emotional abuse. The acts involve punching, hitting, kicking, biting, and rape. Critics have argued that most aggression between siblings should not be a big deal or considered abuse; proponents of reviewing the issue of sibling abuse contend otherwise.

Physical Abuse

One method to assert control over brothers and sisters is through the use of physical and verbal force. Left unchecked by parents, the use of force may escalate. Physical abuse by a sibling occurs when one member of the sibling pair deliberately causes physical harm to another (Kiselica & Morrill-Richards, 2007). Physical abuse by a sibling has consistently been revealed by research as the most common form of family violence in America. The most significant predictors for severe sibling violence with a weapon are animal abuse and physically assaulting school staff (Khan & Cooke, 2008).

The abuse may involve shoving, hitting, slapping, kicking, biting, pinching, and hair pulling. Severe forms of physical violence by siblings to inflict injury and pain include the use of broom handles, rubber hoses, coat hangers, hairbrushes, belts, sticks, knives, guns and rifles, broken glass, razor blades, and scissors. Some victims have reported that siblings attempted to drown them, nearly suffocated them with a pillow, or repeatedly hit them in the stomach. A twisting motion of an extremity—or the body about a fixed extremity—is needed to produce a spiral fracture. In the past, investigators were taught that all spiral fractures were a result of abuse, but this is inaccurate. As with all pediatric injuries, the investigator must determine whether the injury is consistent with the history.

Sexual Abuse

Sexual behavior between siblings that is not age appropriate, not transitory, and not motivated by developmentally appropriate curiosity is considered sibling incest (Kiselica & Morrill-Richards, 2007). A common misconception is that sexual abuse of a sibling is playful and not harmful for the younger child. Sibling abuse is thought to be more common than parental abuse. Unwanted sexual advances, sexual leers, and forcing a sibling to view pornographic material are examples of behavior that may occur in addition to intercourse. Sibling sexual abuse is more common than child–child sexual abuse; approximately 2.3 percent of women have been sexually victimized by a sibling (Kiselica & Morrill-Richards, 2007).

Actual prevalence rates of sibling sexual abuse are difficult to come by, and experts believe that such abuse is grossly underreported (Carlson, 2011). Sibling incest survivors report significantly higher anxiety, depression, hostility, adult victimization, and lower self-esteem. Relationship quality as an adult is negatively impacted by sibling sexual abuse as a child.

Emotional Abuse

Emotional sibling abuse is characterized by the constancy and intensity of the words and actions that express contempt and degradation. Serious long-term effects due to psychological abuses can occur, along with an increased risk of developing habit disorders, conduct disorders, neurotic traits, and psychoneurotic reactions in addition to attempts of suicide (Kiselica & Morrill-Richards, 2007). Emotional or psychological aggression is highly prevalent among siblings (Relva et al., 2013). Abusive acts include teasing, ridiculing, and insulting a sibling. Emotional abuse can lower self-esteem and raise anxiety in a child.

PARENT ABUSE

Studies have revealed that a significant proportion of family violence is perpetrated by a juvenile against parents or siblings. Violence against a parent, or parent abuse, is arguably the least studied form of domestic violence. Researchers suggest that parent victims feel shame at their inability to control their children; therefore, the problem is grossly underreported (Baker, 2012). The data indicate that the percentage of parent abuse has increased and is likely to continue. Reasons for the increase in reported cases may include better training that enables police to identify domestic violence, a broader definition of domestic violence that includes family members other than parents, and greater awareness of what is unacceptable behavior within a family.

Mothers are the primary target of juvenile parent violence in the household. In a study consisting of 209 families who were receiving social work services, 112 adolescents reported being violent against their parents (Biehal, 2012). Boys and girls were found equally likely to be violent among the sample of 11- to 16-year-olds. One in ten parents referred to their children "smashing up the house," "kicking in the door," or "smashing up his room." The severe violence included kicking and hitting the parent.

A strong association was found between domestic violence and parent abuse. Two-thirds of the violent adolescents had experienced abuse or had grown up in the context of domestic violence (Biehal, 2012). Those who had witnessed domestic violence were nearly three times more likely to be violent to their parents than those who had not. It is theorized that children of abused women may also identify with the perpetrator against the mother.

Experts suggest that anger directed toward the mother for the tension in the home and for having provoked the abuse from the father is partially the cause. The adolescent may also fear the father and develop an unconscious alliance with him to ward off danger from himself. Another perspective on parent abuse suggests that adolescents become violent in retaliation for child victimization. In one study, 80 percent of the youth who were violent toward parents indicated that their parents were violent toward them (Zahn et al., 2008).

PEDOPHILIA

The term **pedophile** refers to an adult who has a sustained sexual orientation toward children. The history of pedophilia can be traced from accounts in ancient Greece to modern-day priest scandals of the Catholic Church, where taking sexual advantage of young males was an accepted practice (Hughes, 2007). Attempts to legitimize the practice of boy sexual relationships involving an adult and a child are found in the North American Man/Boy Love Association (NAMBLA), the René Guyon Society, and the Childhood Sensuality Circle. The American Psychiatric Association (APA) has included pedophilia in its *Diagnostic and Statistical Manual of Mental Disorders* (DSM), since 1968. In the *DSM*, which is updated periodically, pedophilia is defined as "recurrent, intense sexually arousing fantasies, sexual urges, or behaviors that involve children, nonhuman subjects, or other non-consenting adults, or the suffering or humiliation of oneself or one's partner" (APA, 2000).

In the News: NAMGLA Takedown

On July 25, 2006, the Web site www.namgla.net was shut down by the FBI. It served an international community of online predators where thousands of graphic images of sexually abused children could be shared. At least 35 domestic subjects were identified. Also, 49 subjects in 27 foreign countries were identified. The FBI coordinated the execution of 29 search warrants and six consensual interviews in 20 different states. Results of these investigations yielded 22 confessions to possessing or distributing child pornography, as well as several arrests. Three subjects were determined to have had prior sex offenses against minors, and another three subjects were found to be in possession of narcotics. International investigations have been conducted in Ecuador, Chile, Poland, Canada, Spain, Portugal, Bulgaria, and Sweden.

Been There ... Done That!

It is not uncommon for people to possess a picture of their loved one in a wallet or a frame. In our society, we hang posters on our walls with pictures of those we find attractive. Individuals whose love object is a child will act similarly. The majority of pedophiles that I arrested carried pictures of children. Some of the photos were sexually explicit while others were not. Searching the home of a pedophile under a search warrant will frequently net sexually explicit pictures of children within his or her preferred age range and gender. In one case, the photos recovered in a search showed actual rape; in another, they depicted the way in which the offender would pose his victim in provocative positions. The Internet is increasingly the avenue where pedophiles share these photos.

According to Hughes (2007), studies indicate that the mean age of male pedophiles is 28 years and 26 years for female offenders. Pedophiles have a more frequent sex preference for their own gender as compared to adults who commit sex crimes like rape. Research suggests that pedophiles often experienced sexual abuse in childhood and frequently choose victims similar to their own age at victimization. As children, they also tended to commit sexual offenses. Although most victims of sexual abuse do not become later abusers, previous abuse—along with other factors such as cruelty to animals and intrafamily violence—increases the risk of pedophilia. Studies indicate that 75 percent to 90 percent of pedophiles were abused within their own families (Hughes, 2007).

CONCLUSIONS

At the beginning of this chapter, a distinction was made between the behaviors occurring in healthy families versus those in unhealthy households. The characterization is presented to underscore the fact that there are documented reasons for domestic violence. The implication is that interventions may be appropriate when family violence is occurring. Personal characteristics such as resilience and self-esteem may act as mediators of the effects of abuse. As mandated reporters, it is helpful to understand the reasons why it is important to make referrals outside of the justice system in some cases.

As a society, we frequently dismiss or ignore concerns about juvenile violence. New events have forced us to look again at the consequences of abuse and neglect and its effects on adolescents. It is important not to underestimate the devastating consequences that family violence has on all children, adolescents included. Survival sex is recognized as a measure pursued by young victims who run from desperate situations of abuse.

Juvenile crime is a concern that must be addressed through prevention strategies. Family violence perpetrated against siblings and parents are areas that receive little attention from researchers; however, service providers and law-enforcement officers are likely to have contact with affected individuals. Because adolescent offending patterns may be linked to victimization, a case-by-case analysis might be done to determine whether further investigation is warranted.

SIMPLY SCENARIO
Pornography

A 15-year-old girl pushed her father down the stairs yet another time. She had also injured her mother in the past. It was not that the parents were old, rather just older than most parents. They were tired of fighting with their growing child and embarrassed that anyone would find out. She was the child of their dreams who turned into a nightmare. The parents were at a loss about what to do. They did not want to tell anyone, and yet the child needed help. Eventually, she received counseling, and the abuse stopped.

Question: Based on what you have learned, what theory might account for the family dysfunction in this scenario?

Questions for Review

1. Explain the major theories of family violence that pertain to adolescent offending.
2. Discuss why children abused by family violence may not themselves become offenders.
3. Discuss the link between juveniles and firesetting.
4. What are some consequences of witnessing family violence?
5. Explain the three ways in which ineffective parenting may contribute to sibling abuse.
6. Which theory states the hypothesis that violence begets violence?
7. Describe the consequences of family violence on subsequent juvenile behaviors.
8. What is meant by "turning"?
9. What type of child abuse most consistently predicts juvenile violence?
10. What is meant by the term survival sex?

Internet-Based Exercises

1. The National Center for Juvenile Justice, which is the research division of the *National Council of Juvenile and Family Court Judges*, maintains an interactive Web site entitled **Easy Access to NIBRS: Victims of Domestic Violence, 2010.** The data are categorized by the characteristics of the victim, the offender, and the offense. Go to Skip to Main Content at http://ojjdp .gov/ojstatbb/ezanibrsdv/. Using the drop-down boxes, determine the number of aggravated assaults that have been perpetrated against a child by a sibling or stepsibling. Does this number seem high (or low) to you? Compare similar crimes against children by various offenders, and discuss this in class.
2. The National Center for Juvenile Justice also maintains a Web page on homicide. There you can find out how many juveniles murdered juvenile family members. Go to **Easy Access to the FBI's Supplementary Homicide Reports: 1980–2010** at http://ojjdp.gov/ojstatbb/ ezashr/, and conduct a comparison of two states. Report your findings to the class.
3. Learn more about shaken baby syndrome at http:// dontshake.org/. What can you do to help in the effort to prevent this deadly form of child abuse? Discuss some options with your class.
4. There is a lot that we do not know about sudden infant death syndrome. Are you aware of the complexity of this form of child death? Do you know the recommended ways to reduce the risk of it? Visit the American SIDS Institute at http://www.sids.org/index.htm. Write a short report on your findings.

References

Adams, B., & Addie, S. (2012). Delinquency cases waived to criminal court, 2009. *National Report Series.* Washington, D.C.: Office of Juvenile Justice and Delinquency Prevention.

Allwood, M. A., & Widom, C. S. (2013). Child abuse and neglect, developmental role attainment, and adult arrests. *Journal of Research in Crime & Delinquency, 50*(4), 551–578.

American Psychiatric Association (APA). (2000). *Diagnostic and statistical manual of mental disorders, DSM-IV-TR* (4th ed.). Washington, D.C.: Author.

Ascione, F. (2001). Animal abuse and youth violence. *Juvenile Justice Bulletin*. Washington, D.C.: U.S. Department of Justice.

Baker, H. (2012). Problematising the relationship between teenage boys and parent abuse: Constructions of masculinity and violence. *Social Policy and Society, 11*(2), 265–276.

Benoit-Bryan, J. (2011). The runaway youth longitudinal study. National Runaway Switchboard. Retrieved from http://www.1800runaway.org/assets/1/7/nrs_longitudinal _study_report-_final.pdf

Benoit-Bryan, J. (2012). Key statistics from the National Runaway Switchboard's Home Free Program. Retrieved from http://www.1800runaway.org/media/sourcebook/

Biehal, N. (2012). Parent abuse by young people on the edge of care: A child welfare perspective. *Social Policy and Society, 11*(2), 251–263.

Burlin, G. S. (2007). An examination of juvenile firesetting and the reasons that kids set fires. Retrieved from http:// sos.strateja-xl.com/professional-information/Articles/ Burlin_final_paper.pdf

Caldwell, M. (2007). Sexual offense adjudication and sexual recidivism among juvenile offenders. *Sexual Abuse: A Journal of Research and Treatment, 19*(2), 107–113.

Carlson, B. E. (2011). Sibling incest: Adjustment in adult women survivors. *Families in Society, 92*(1), 77–83.

Cicchetti, D. (2013). Annual research review: Resilient functioning in maltreated children—Past, present, and future perspectives. *Journal of Child Psychology and Psychiatry, 54*(4), 402–422.

Coleman, V. E. (2003). Treating the lesbian batterer: Theoretical and clinical considerations—A contemporary psychoanalytic perspective. *Journal of Aggression, Maltreatment & Trauma, 7*(1), 159–205.

Connor, D., & Barkley, R. (2004). *Aggression and antisocial behavior in children and adolescents: Research and treatment*. New York, NY: Guilford Press.

Cooper, A., & Smith, E. L. (2011). *Homicide trends in the United States, 1980–2008: Annual rates for 2009 and 2010*. (NCJ 236018). Washington, D.C.: U.S. Department of Justice. Retrieved from http://bjs.gov/content/ pub/pdf/htus8008.pdf

Currie, C. (2006). Animal cruelty by children exposed to domestic violence. *Child Abuse & Neglect, 30*(4), 425–435.

Curry, S. R., Morton, M., Matjasko, J. L., Dworsky, A., Samuels, G. M., & Schlueter, D. (2017). Youth homelessness and vulnerability: How does couch surfing fit? *American Journal of Community Psychology, 60*(1–2), 17–24.

Curtis, R., Terry, K., Dank, M., Dombrowski, K., Khan, B., Muslim, A., … Rempel, M. (2008). *The commercial sexual exploitation of children in New York City*. New York, NY: Center for Court Innovation.

Dank, M., Yahner, J., Madden, K., Banuelos, I., Yu, L., Ritchie, A., … Conner, B. (2015). *Surviving the streets of New York: Experiences of LGBTQ Youth, YMSM, and YWSW engaged in survival sex*. Washington, D.C.: Urban Institute.

Fallon, B., Ma, J., Allan, K., Pillhofer, M., Trocmé, N., & Jud, A. (2013). Opportunities for prevention and intervention with young children: Lessons from the Canadian incidence study of reported child abuse and neglect. *Child and Adolescent Psychiatry and Mental Health, 7*(1), 4.

Fang, X., Brown, D. S., Florence, C. S., & Mercy, J. A. (2012). The economic burden of child maltreatment in the United States and implications for prevention. *Child Abuse & Neglect, 36*(2), 156–165.

Fang, X., & Corso, P. S. (2007). Child maltreatment, youth violence, and intimate partner violence: Developmental relationships. *American Journal of Preventive Medicine, 33*(4), 281–290.

Feiring, C., Miller-Johnson, S., & Cleland, C. (2007). Potential pathways from stigmatization and internalizing symptoms to delinquency in sexuality abused youth. *Child Maltreatment, 12*(3), 220–232.

Finkelhor, D., Ormrod, R., & Chaffin, M. (2009). *Juveniles who commit sex offenses against minors*. (NCJ 227763). Washington, D.C.: Office of Justice Programs.

Firesetting as a predictor of violence. (2006). *BushFIRE Arson Bulletin, 36*. Retrieved from http://www.aic.gov .au/publications/currentseries/bfab/21-40/bfab036.html

Freeman, L., & Hamilton, D. (2008). *A count of homeless youth in New York City*. New York, NY: Empire State Coalition of Youth and Family Services.

Fritz, P. A. T., Slep, A. M. S., & O'Leary, K. D. (2012). Couple-level analysis of the relation between family-of-origin aggression and intimate partner violence. *Psychology of Violence, 2*(2), 139–153.

Gold, J., Sullivan, M. W., & Lewis, M. (2011). The relation between abuse and violent delinquency: The conversion of shame to blame in juvenile offenders. *Child Abuse & Neglect, 35*(7), 459–467.

Gragg, F., Petta, I., Bernstein, H., Eisen, K., & Quinn, L. (2007). *New York prevalence study of commercially sexually exploited children*. Rensselaer, NY: New York State Office of Children and Family Services.

Gullone, E., & Robertson, N. (2008). The relationship between bullying and animal abuse behaviors in adolescents: The importance of witnessing animal abuse. *Journal of Applied Developmental Psychology, 29*, 371–379.

Hamby, S., Finkelhor, D., & Turner, H. (2012). Teen dating violence: Co-occurrence with other victimizations in the National Survey of Children's Exposure to Violence (NatSCEV). *Psychology of Violence, 2*(2), 111–124.

Hamby, S., Finkelhor, D., Turner, H., & Ormrod, R. (2011). *Children's exposure to intimate partner violence and other family violence.* (NCJ 232272). Washington, D.C.: U.S. Department of Justice.

Heide, K. M., & Petee, T. A. (2007a). Parricide: An empirical analysis of 24 years of U.S. data. *Journal of Interpersonal Violence, 22*(11), 1382–1399. doi: 10.1177/0886260507305526.

Heide, K. M., & Petee, T. A. (2007b). Weapons used by juveniles and adult offenders in U.S. parricide cases. *Journal of Interpersonal Violence, 22*(11), 1400–1414. doi: 10.1177/0886260507305528.

Hughes, J. R. (2007). Review of medical reports on pedophilia. *Clinical Pediatrics, 46*, 667–682.

Imbach, D., Aebi, M., Metzke, C. W., Bessler, C., & Steinhausen, H. C. (2013). Internalizing and externalizing problems, depression, and self-esteem in non-detained male juvenile offenders. *Child and Adolescent Psychiatry and Mental Health, 7*(1), 7.

Khan, R., & Cooke, D. J. (2008). Risk factors for severe inter-sibling violence: A preliminary study of a youth forensic sample. *Journal of Interpersonal Violence, 23*(11), 1513–1530. doi: 10.1177/0886260508314312.

Kiselica, M., & Morrill-Richards, M. (2007). Sibling maltreatment: The forgotten abuse. *Journal of Counseling & Development, 85*(2), 148–162.

Knafo, A., Jaffee, S. R., Neiderhiser, J. M., Marceau, K., & Reiss, D. (2013). Four factors for the initiation of substance use by young adulthood: A 10-year follow-up twin and sibling study of marital conflict, monitoring, siblings, and peers. *Development and Psychopathology, 25*(1), 133–149.

Maas, C., Herrenkohl, T. I., & Sousa, C. (2008). Review of research on child maltreatment and violence in youth. *Trauma Violence Abuse, 9*(1), 56–67. doi: 10.1177/1524838007311105.

Mapp, S. (2006). The effects of sexual abuse as a child on the risk of mothers physically abusing their children: A path analysis using systems theory. *Child Abuse & Neglect: The International Journal, 30*(11), 1293–1310.

Martellozzo, E., Monaghan, A., Adler, J. R., Davidson, J., Leyva, R., & Horvath, M. A. (2016). … I wasn't sure it was normal to watch it…. A quantitative and qualitative examination of the impact of online pornography on the values, attitudes, beliefs and behaviors of children and young people. Retrieved from https://www.mdx.ac.uk/__data/assets/pdf_file/0021/223266/MDX-NSPCC-OCC-pornography-report.pdf

McCallion, P., & Ferretti, L. (n.d.). Family system theory: Applications for PSA casework. Retrieved from http://www.albany.edu/aging/FamilySystemsTheory.pdf

McLaren, H. J. (2012). (Un)-blaming mothers whose partners sexually abuse children: In view of heteronormative myths, pressures and authorities. *Child & Family Social Work.* doi: 10.1111/j.1365-2206.2012.00863.x.

Mederos, F. (2004). Accountability and connection with abusive men: A new child protection response to increasing family safety. Retrieved from Massachusetts Department of Social Services www.thegreenbook.info/documents/Accountability.pdf

Miller v. Alabama, 567 U.S. ____, 132 S. Ct. 2455, 183 L. Ed. 2d 407 567 (2012).

Miller-Lewis, L., Searle, A., Sawyer, M., Baghurst, P., & Hedley, D. (2013). Resource factors for mental health resilience in early childhood: An analysis with multiple methodologies. *Child and Adolescent Psychiatry and Mental Health, 7*(1), 6.

Millett, L. S., Kohl, P. L., Jonson-Reid, M., Drake, B., & Petra, M. (2013). Child maltreatment victimization and subsequent perpetration of young adult intimate partner violence: An exploration of mediating factors. *Child Maltreatment, 18*(2), 71–84.

Moulden, H. M., Firestone, P., & Wexler, A. F. (2007). Child care providers who commit sexual offences: A description of offender, offence, and victim characteristics. *International Journal of Offender Therapy and Comparative Criminology, 51*(4), 384–406. doi: 10.1177/0306624x06298465.

National Center for Youth Law. (n.d.). US Supreme Court bans mandatory life without parole for youth. Retrieved from http://www.youthlaw.org/juvenile_justice/6/us_supreme_court_bans_mandatory_life_without_parole_for_youth/

National Law Center on Homelessness & Poverty and the National Network for Youth. (2012). Alone without a home: A state-by-state review of laws affecting unaccompanied youth. Retrieved from http://monarchhousing.org/wordpress/wp-content/uploads/2012/09/AloneWithoutaHome.pdf

National Runaway Safeline. (n.d.). Retrieved from http://www.1800runaway.org/national-runaway-safeline/

Office of Juvenile Justice and Delinquency Prevention (OJJDP). (2012). Statistical briefing book: Juveniles as offenders. Retrieved from http://www.ojjdp.gov/ojstatbb/offenders/faqs.asp

Office of the Governor. (2008). *Prosecution of child sexual abuse in Idaho.* Boise, ID: Office of the Attorney General.

OVC. (2012). *Child abuse and neglect.* Online: Office for Victims of Crime Retrieved from https://www.ovcttac.gov/downloads/views/TrainingMaterials/

NVAA/Documents_NVAA2011/ResourcePapers/Color_Child%20Abuse%20Resource%20paper%202012_final%20-%20508c_9_13_2012.pdf

The Oyez Project. (2013). *Miller v. Alabama.* IIT Chicago-Kent College of Law. Retrieved from http://www.oyez.org/cases/2010-2019/2011/2011_10_9646

Pérez-Fuentes, G., Olfson, M., Villegas, L., Morcillo, C., Wang, S., & Blanco, C. (2013). Prevalence and correlates of child sexual abuse: A national study. *Comprehensive Psychiatry, 54*(1), 16–27. doi: 10.1016/j.comppsych.2012.05.010.

Relva, I., Fernandes, O., & Mota, C. (2013). An exploration of sibling violence predictors. *Journal of Aggression, Conflict and Peace Research, 5*(1), 47–61.

Roberts, A. L., Gilman, S. E., Fitzmaurice, G., Decker, M. R., & Koenen, K. C. (2010). Witness of intimate partner violence in childhood and perpetration of intimate partner violence in adulthood. *Epidemiology, 21*(6), 809–818.

Root, C., MacKay, S., Henderson, J., Bove, G. D., & Warling, D. (2008). The link between maltreatment and juvenile firesetting: Correlates and underlying mechanisms. *Child Abuse & Neglect, 32*(2), 161–176.

Roper v. Simmons, 543 U.S. 551 (2005).

Seto, M., & Eke, A. (2005). The criminal histories and later offending of child pornography offenders. *Sexual Abuse: A Journal of Research and Treatment, 17*(2), 201–210.

Sherley, M. (2007). Why doctors should care about animal cruelty. *Australian Family Physician, 36*(1), 2.

Sickmund, M., & Puzzanchera, C. (2014). *Juvenile offenders and victims: 2014 national report.* Pittsburg, PA: Office of Juvenile Justice and Delinquency Prevention.

Siegel, J. P. (2013). Breaking the links in intergenerational violence: An emotional regulation perspective. *Family Process*, 1–16. doi: 10.1111/famp.12023.

Thompson, R., Litrownik, A. J., Isbell, P., Everson, M. D., English, D. J., Dubowitz, H., ... Flaherty, E. G. (2012). Adverse experiences and suicidal ideation in adolescence: Exploring the link using the LONGSCAN samples. *Psychology of Violence, 2*(2), 211–225.

Walsh, J. A., & Krienert, J. L. (2008). A decade of child-initiated family violence: Comparative analysis of child–parent violence and parricide examining offender, victim, and event characteristics in a national sample of reported incidents, 1995–2005. *Journal of Interpersonal Violence, 28*. doi: 10.1177/0886260508323661.

Zahn, M., Brumbaugh, S., Steffensmeier, D., Field, B., Morash, M., Chesney-Lind, M., ... Kruttschnitt, C. (2008). *Girls study group: Understanding and responding to girls' delinquency.* (NCJ 218905). Washington, D.C.: Office of Juvenile Justice and Delinquency Prevention.

8

Intimate Partner Violence

CHAPTER OBJECTIVES

After reviewing this chapter, you should be able to:

1. Explain the battered women's movement along with its accomplishments.
2. Discuss the health and safety issues that affect the survivors of intimate partner violence.
3. Provide rates of intimate partner violence victimization among groups of American women.
4. Describe how intimate family violence victimization may impact males differently as compared to female survivors.
5. Describe the domestic violence green card.

KEY TERMS

Cycle of violence

Disability

Gaslighting

Economic abuse

Intimate partner violence

Learned Helplessness Theory

Marital rape

Male partner reproductive coercion

INTRODUCTION

Intimate partner violence (also called domestic violence or spouse abuse) is violence committed by a current or former spouse, opposite-sex cohabiting partner, same-sex cohabiting partner, date, or boyfriend or girlfriend. Intimate partner violence and abuse take many forms, and it is often a repeated offense. During 2005 through 2014, approximately 26 percent of intimate partner violence victims experienced repeat violent crime at the hands of their spouse, more than victims of violence by any other type of offender (Ouderkerk & Truman, 2017).

Intimate partner violence (IPV) is believed to affect 3 in 10 women and 1 in 10 men in the United States (Black et al., 2011). The *Intimate Partner Violence in the United States–2010* report indicates that women and racial or ethnic minorities are disproportionally impacted by higher lifetime rates of rape, physical violence, and stalking by an intimate partner. Significant progress has been made since the days when it was legally permitted for husbands to discipline their wives, when domestic violence was a private matter, and when it was not against the law for a man to physically assault his wife in the United States! Rates have declined substantially, but IPV remains a significant public health problem.

Millions of Americans experience IPV each year. Women and men with a lifetime history of IPV experience poor physical health in general; they are more likely to have frequent headaches, chronic pain, and difficulty sleeping. Experienced emotional and psychological abuses include verbal abuses such as calling of names, criticizing, playing mind games, humiliating the partner, and reinforcing internalized homophobia. Forms of IPV covered in this chapter include economic control, physical abuse, sexual violence, and male partner reproductive coercion.

THE BATTERED WOMEN'S MOVEMENT

Battering is an obsolete term that refers to a repetitive pattern of behavior that is intended to gain power and control over a person. Many years have passed since the beginnings of the alliance to gain equal rights and end oppression against women. Still, we find that the overwhelming majority of survivors of IPV are women. Violence against women is considered one part of the oppression that patriarchy maintains. The movement sought a social change of the cultural values that enable oppressors to control and retain the power as they have done in the past. The movement attempted to empower all women and children and to restructure and redistribute the social power. Ending physical and sexual abuse perpetrated against women and children is a significant effort in the movement, but it is essential to see it in a broader context of ending economic and sexist oppression.

The battered women's movement that began as a grassroots movement during late the 1960s (Barner & Carney, 2011) has accomplished significant victories since its inception. It is still active today:

1. The victims have been identified: They are 85 percent female and 15 percent male. The rates have remained relatively stable since 1994 (Catalano, 2012).
2. Heightened public awareness has been achieved, although the causes and consequences are still hotly debated.
3. Intervention strategies have been established through a range of services: shelters, information services, hotlines, and police response. Complaints of insufficient funds to implement additional needed services and to maintain existing ones are constant. Major organizations, including the American Medical Association and American Bar Association, have acknowledged the high number of instances of IPV against women and have sought reform to address needs. Legal reform has been accomplished in every state in the United States. Federal legislative reform has brought unprecedented change.
4. Protection and prevention efforts now include civil and criminal actions that were never before available to IPV victims.
5. Batterers' programs have become the most frequent response from the courts to cases involving IPV. Education is occurring at this level on television and in classrooms across the country.

One unintended consequence of the battered women's movement has been increased awareness of violence committed against lesbian and gay partners and males. Violence in dating relationships was discovered as well. Feminist organizations are responsible for having brought the issue to the forefront, where it can no longer be

FIGURE 8-1   Intimate partner violence rates declined in the United States by 64 percent from 1993 to 2010. The victimization rate went from 9.8 victimizations per 1,000 persons age 12 or older to 3.6 per 1,000.   Based on data from Catalano, 2012.

ignored. Credit must be given to the dedicated women and men who pioneered efforts to understand the dynamics of spousal abuse and to protect those victims of violence.

IPV is now recognized as a significant social problem. Having identified the problem, people then seek ways to do away with it. Federal and state funding has been established for research, protection, and education on IPV. The legislation was passed to provide necessary protection for the victims. Criminology, victimology, and family violence courses are offered in colleges and universities to address the issues and discuss solutions. We have taken enormous strides toward understanding the various ways in which we survive IPV.

The rate of IPV varies by year and collection method. Research confirms that great strides have been made in the battle against IPV. Fewer people are victimized than ever before (refer to Figure 8-1). From 1993 to 2010, IPV rates have dropped in the United States by 64 percent (Catalano, 2012). According to the *National Intimate Partner and Sexual Violence Survey* (NISVS), nearly one in three heterosexual women and one in four heterosexual men have experienced rape, physical violence, and stalking by an intimate partner in their lifetime (Walters, Chen, & Breiding, 2013).

THE CYCLE OF VIOLENCE

Research focusing on the dynamics of IPV has resulted in several ways of understanding the interactions between the offender and the victim. One of the first conceptualizations is the **cycle of violence**. The theorist most often cited for application of the transmission of violence theory to family abuse is Lenore Walker. In *The Battered Woman*, she described three separate phases of an abuse cycle represented in a pattern that is repeated time and again in an abusive relationship (Walker, 1979). Phase I, *tension building*, is characterized by poor communication and minor incidents of abuse. In this phase, the woman is compliant and attempts to minimize problems in the relationship. The man feels an increased tension and takes more control through dominance, causing the victim to withdraw. During phase II, *acute battering*, the offender who is highly abusive evidences a loss of control. The woman suffers stress and injury. Phase III is often referred to as the *honeymoon phase*, when kindness and loving behavior emanate from the contrite offender. As the tension drops between the perpetrator and the victim, a renewed love is experienced.

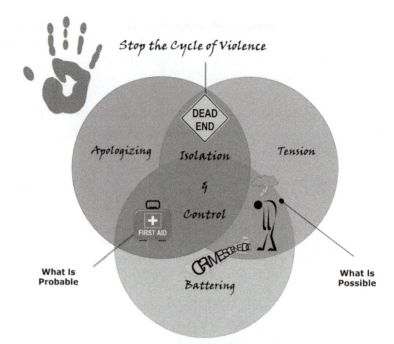

FIGURE 8-2 The cycle of violence was first introduced in 1979 as a theory by Lenore Walker (1995) to explain the manipulation that may occur in abusive relationships. This is an updated version of the cycle. It helps to understand why women sometimes stay in violent relationships. While they may hate the violence, they love the offender.

He is often apologetic and attentive to his partner. She at first has mixed feelings and then feels guilty and responsible for the outburst. He continues to manipulate the relationship through promises of change. It is not unusual during the final phase for the offender to shower gifts and flowers on the woman. The cycle usually repeats itself, however, and the violence is believed to escalate over time. Figure 8-2 illustrates this continual nature of the cycle of violence as envisioned by Lenore Walker.

The concept of *learned helplessness* was developed to explain the psychological response to repeated violence. In suggesting this alternative, Lenore Walker made clear that the most popular explanation in 1978 was that abused women were believed to be masochistic (Walker, 1995). Refuting the assumption that women sought out men who would fill their need to be beaten, she claimed another psychological rationale. Employing the social learning perspective, Walker theorized in the **learned helplessness theory** that

Been There...Done That!

Off-duty one night, I came out of the restaurant to find a man on the ground in the parking lot. He was screaming in pain. A woman was kicking him over and over while he winced and tried to roll away from her sharp high heels. I pulled her away and yelled for someone to call the police. The officer that arrived seemed to know both the man and the woman. He told the woman to go on home.

Confused, I asked whether he was going to arrest her for assault. It was a vicious attack! He said no; Fred was drunk. He would be so embarrassed in the morning...was I missing something?

women accept their powerlessness in IPV situations due to gender-role socialization that induces a false belief that they cannot escape from the situation. The feeling of powerlessness may be reinforced by the "happy family" cultural stereotype as well, she suggested. Victim isolation from friends, family, and other victims allows the reality of the situation to be minimized while victims accept responsibility for the violent incidents. In this explanation, IPV produces a psychological paralysis that maintains the victim's status of being victimized. Economic and social factors contribute to the victimization and its continuance in this view.

Intimate partner abuse is not a single explosive incident of hitting; it is the building of tensions that contribute to the ever-existing nature of the abusive relationship. Victim denials and accommodation of the offender add to the victimization, which is psychological and emotional as well as physical or sexual.

HEALTH AND SAFETY ISSUES

A recent trend in the study of IPV is toward changing the characterization of the victim to that of a survivor. Kathleen Ferraro typifies this movement. Citing the Campbell study of 1994, she clarifies the incredible obstacles that are overcome by almost half of abused women who are ultimately successful in leaving their abusers (Ferraro, 1997). Her discussion of stages of engagement and disengagement offers insight into the intimacy characteristics of marital relationships and the difficulties of dealing with dependent men who threaten, harass, and often assault women as they try to leave. An adaptation of Ferraro's theory illustrates that the final desperate attempt to get away may lead to homicide. The four stages leading to homicide begin with an initial attraction whereby the woman feels that the social isolation she is experiencing is mutual affection. Next, when a physical assault occurs, it is met with disbelief. Then, if the intensity or severity of violence increases, her survival depends on successfully leaving the offender. The final phase occurs if the woman cannot get away. She suffers from horror, depression, and posttraumatic stress syndrome. A close fight may lead to a kill or be killed scenario.

The survivors of IPV face numerous challenges. It is widely accepted that the economic stability of an individual suffers from abuse. It is harder to maintain a job while abuse is occurring. Compared to women who are not victimized, those experiencing IPV have significantly less stable employment, which relates to lower job benefits (Adams, Tolman, Bybee, Sullivan, & Kennedy, 2012). Additionally, the survivor who is raising one or more children is likely to have lower income. In 2010, almost 3 million children, representing 3.9 percent of all children, lived in a household in which at least one person over age 12 had experienced one or more nonfatal violent victimizations during the year (Truman & Smith, 2012). For those children living in violent homes, the lower the income, the more likely that there was IPV. Researchers Truman and Smith (2012) found that as the annual income of families with children goes up, the extent of victimization goes down.

Homelessness

Due to the strong link between domestic violence and homelessness and the pervasiveness of housing discrimination against victims of domestic violence, the Violence Against Women Act of 2005 (VAWA) prohibits public housing agencies from denying public housing or Section 8 housing voucher assistance to applicants that have been victims of domestic violence or stalking (Bernardi, 2007). Shelters and other domestic violence service providers are not required to provide identifying information that could be used to track and locate victims to the Homeless Management Information Systems (HMIS). HMIS is a program designed to track homeless individuals' use of services and programs. This landmark legislation protects survivors of domestic violence living in public and assisted housing from discrimination and unjust evictions.

According to the National Network to End Domestic Violence (NNEDV), the Violence Against Woman Act of 2013 expands the protections to individuals in all federally subsidized housing programs, explicitly protecting victims of sexual assault, and creates emergency housing transfer options (NNEDV, 2013). While IPV is acknowledged to occur at every income level, poor women fleeing IPV are more susceptible to homelessness. Intimate partner survivors who live in poverty are often forced to choose between abusive relationships and homelessness.

Long waiting lists for assisted housing and the lack of affordable housing still force many women and their children to choose between abuse at home and life on the streets. Survivors of domestic violence may also encounter difficulty finding suitable housing due to bias and discrimination. An estimated 16 percent of homeless adults across the nation are victims of domestic violence (U.S. Conference of Mayors, 2012). The figure varies from state to state. In North Carolina, for example, 45 percent of its homeless are domestic violence survivors. Of women who experience IPV in their lifetime, 2.4 percent need housing services. For men who have been victimized by IPV, approximately 0.4 percent needs housing services (Black et al., 2011).

Injury and Trauma

The American Medical Association declared in 1992 that physical and sexual violence against women had reached epidemic proportions and recommended that physicians routinely screen all women patients for intimate partner abuse. Reports indicate that abused women have higher levels of health care use when compared with those with no history of abuse. Of those who have ever been victimized by IPV, one in seven women and one in 25 men were injured as a result (Walters et al., 2013). Women are the more frequently injured when intimate violence occurs; however, when men are injured, they typically require medical attention as a result of the violence (see Figure 8-3).

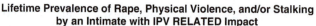

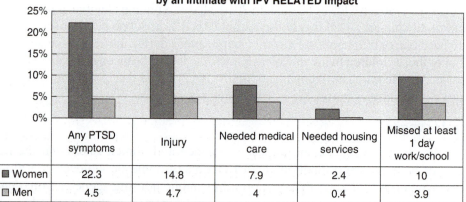

Lifetime Prevalence of Rape, Physical Violence, and/or Stalking by an Intimate with IPV RELATED Impact

	Any PTSD symptoms	Injury	Needed medical care	Needed housing services	Missed at least 1 day work/school
■ Women	22.3	14.8	7.9	2.4	10
□ Men	4.5	4.7	4	0.4	3.9

FIGURE 8-3 Intimate partner violence affects the medical well-being of those impacted. It costs in medical care, need for housing, and lost work for women and men. Based on data from Black et al., 2011.

Research on the physical injuries directly caused by abuse informs us on this crucial matter. The consequences of IPV go beyond the more apparent physical injuries. IPV is associated with a broad range of lingering adverse physical health problems. These effects include arthritis, chronic neck or back pain, migraines, stammering, visual impairment, sexually transmitted infections, chronic pelvic pain, peptic ulcers, irritable bowel disease, and other digestive problems.

Anxiety, depression, or other emotional health issues are among the psychological injuries suffered from IPV. Researchers identified over half a million Californians victimized by IPV who reported serious psychological distress as a result of victimization (Zahnd, Aydin, Grant, & Holtby, 2011). About 25 percent of these survivors needed mental health services, and approximately 7 percent reported weekly binge drinking. The fear exists that some victims may turn to alcohol to cope with or mask their pain. Interventions and services for survivors need to be aware that both males and females who suffer IPV trauma may be similarly affected. The effects may be severe and long-lasting. Survivors of physical or sexual abuse are likely to experience significant levels of posttraumatic stress syndrome decades later (Cook, Dinnen, & O'Donnell, 2011).

Quality of Life Issues

The majority of violence against women consists of pushing, slapping, grabbing, and shoving. Considered less than severe, these forms of violence typically do not require medical attention. However, a survivor's quality of life is severely affected by all forms of IPV. Women that have experienced intimate partner rape, physical violence, or stalking during their lifetime report being negatively impacted by the violence in one or more ways. Research has suggested that IPV puts women at an increased risk for poverty, divorce, and unemployment (Gillum, 2009). Approximately 25 percent become fearful or concerned for their safety; many experience posttraumatic stress disorder (PTSD) symptoms (Black et al., 2011). According to the National Intimate Partner and Sexual Violence Survey, more than one in seven victims are injured as a result of IPV. Approximately 1 in 10 survivors miss work or school as a result of the incident.

Male survivors, who report having been kicked, bitten, punched, and choked, face ridicule due to stereotypical ideas of violent behavior and the expectation that men can protect themselves. These IPV survivors are met with disbelief when seeking protection from a female partner. Research suggests that this population suffers from fear for their safety, experiences significant psychological effects requiring counseling, and may need medical care for injuries (Dutton & White, 2013).

Hotlines and Shelters

The first hotline for battered women started in St. Paul, Minnesota, in 1971. Since then, national and local hotlines have been established to provide callers with crisis intervention, details on local resources, and information about IPV. The National Domestic Violence Hotline is toll-free, confidential, and anonymous in all 50 states, Puerto Rico, Guam, and the Virgin Islands. Since its inception in 1996, the hotline has answered more than 3 million phone calls from the survivors of IPV, their family members, and their friends from all over the world (National Domestic Violence Hotline, 2013). This nonprofit agency receives over 23,000 calls each month through it operations 24 hours a day, 365 days a year, in more than 170 different languages through interpreter services, with a TTY line available for the deaf, deaf-blind, and hard of hearing.

Individuals who call domestic violence hotlines are looking for a variety of information and support from advocates. Making the call may be a difficult but crucial first step in self-protection. It may be the opportunity to be believed and have one's fears validated. Calls originate from abusers, survivors, and friends or family. Of paramount importance to the advocate is the safety of the person who is calling. Typically, the caller receives help-seeking strategy options and self-protection ideas. Experts suggest that IPV survivors who are remaining in the situation develop a safety plan for the future. These plans vary depending on the severity of the abuse, the living circumstances of the survivor, and the presence of children in the home.

There are many variations to the safety plan. Figure 8-4 shows some of the critical steps for any person experiencing IPV who elects to stay in the relationship. A safety plan addresses the need for a victim to think about the risks within the relationship that pose a danger and to prepare for a safe exit. Typically, a safety plan involves putting together items that would be easy to grab in the event of having to leave in a hurry. Critical documents, medications, and clothing are examples of things that are placed together in an easy to reach place. The planning process emphasizes teaching strategies to children when they hear or witness domestic violence, such as calling the police.

Recent years have seen emerging services for male, gay, and lesbian survivors of IPV. The Domestic Abuse Helpline for Men and Women (DAHMW) provides a rare example of an agency providing nongendered support to survivors of IPV. Part of its mission statement is the stated commitment to ALL victims of domestic violence (DAHMW, 2013).

Over 5,000 shelters and service programs exist today. Due to the magnitude of the problem of IPV, however, shelters are inadequate to meet the needs of all survivors. In many areas, shelters turn away four women (and their children) for every woman they can accept. Women with adolescent male children are frequently denied access to shelters, due to possible disruptions and the fear that their presence produces. Lesbians, gay men, and male victims are also denied refuge in traditional safe houses.

Adequate resources for those who qualify are insufficient to meet the demands of IPV survivors. Each year the NNEDV surveys hotlines and shelters across the nation to assess the impact of services to the survivors of domestic violence. Its survey conducted on September 12, 2012, reported that more than 22,000 adults and children served on that survey day found refuge in shelters, while more than 23,000 adults received advocacy through nonresidential services (NNEDV, 2012). On that one day, four women were killed by their abusers in the United States.

ECONOMIC CONTROL

Economic abuse occurs when the abuser makes or tries to make the victim financially reliant. Economic control creates financial dependency; it may include keeping the partner from getting a job, getting the partner fired from a job, making the partner ask for money, or taking the money that he or she has earned. Threats of violence include making a partner afraid by using looks or gestures, destroying personal property, hurting pets, displaying weapons, threatening to leave, threatening to take the children,

Personalized Safety Plan

Step 1. Safety during violence.

I can use the following options:

a. If I decide to leave, I will _____.
b. I can keep a bag ready and put it _____ so
   I can leave quickly.
c. I can tell _____ about the violence
   and have them call the police when violence erupts.
d. I can teach my children to use the telephone to call 9-1-1.
e. I will use this code word _____ for
   my children, friends, or family to call for help.
f. If I have to leave my home, I will go _____.
   (Be prepared even if you think you will never have to leave.)
g. When an argument erupts, I will move to a safer room such as

   _____.
h. I can teach these strategies to my children: _____.
i. I will use my instincts, intuition, and judgment. I will protect myself and my children
   until we are out of danger.

Step 2. Safety when getting ready to leave.

I can use the following strategies:

a. I will leave money and an extra set of keys with _____.
b. I will keep important documents and keys at _____.
c. I will open a savings account by this date _____ to increase
   my independence.
d. Other things I can do to increase my independence are _____.
e. The domestic violence hotline is _____.
f. The shelter's hotline is _____.
g. I will keep change for phone calls with me at ALL times. I know that if I use a
   telephone credit card, that the following month the telephone bill will tell the
   offender who I called after I left. I will keep this information confidential by using
   a prepaid phone card, using a friend's telephone card, calling collect, or using
   change.
h. I will check with _____ and _____
   to know who will let me stay with them or who will lend me money.
i. I can leave extra clothes with _____.
j. I will review my safety plan every _____
   (time frame) in order to plan the safest route.
k. I will review the plan with _____
   (a friend, counselor or advocate).
l. I will rehearse the escape plan and practice it with my children.

FIGURE 8-4   A positive step toward becoming a survivor of domestic violence is taking
charge of one's life. For protection of one's self and one's children, a personalized safety
plan is recommended. Here is an example of a questions commonly included in a Personal
Safety Plan.

threatening to commit suicide, and threatening to reveal homosexuality to the community, employer, or family.

EMOTIONAL ABUSE

Emotional abuse is the use of verbal and non-verbal communication that is meant to manipulate and control another person, causing harm to that person mentally or emotionally. It is well accepted that where domestic violence occurs in any form, it is often accompanied by emotional abuse as well. Victims may experience trauma from emotional abuse, including panic attacks and trouble sleeping. The abuse may cause victims to have low self-esteem and difficulty in trusting others. Stress that victims feel can lead to eating disorders and depression.

From a literature review of 300 studies on intimate partner, authors Carney and Barner (2012) found prevalence rates of emotional abuse are high, averaging around 80 percent. Approximately 40 percent of women and 32 percent of men reported verbal abuse or emotional abuse from a partner in response to an aggravating circumstance.

A common technique of emotional abusers is to obtain control through gaslighting. **Gaslighting** is a form of manipulation used against a partner to convince them they are wrong, it involves twisting of information or giving false information with the intent of making victims doubt their own memory, perception, and sanity. Individuals who are gaslighted feel that they are constantly wrong in what they say to their partner and are confused and defensive since their word is constantly questioned.

PHYSICAL VIOLENCE

Physical abuse behaviors may include punching, shoving, slapping, biting, kicking, using a weapon against a partner, throwing items, pulling hair, and restraining the partner. Severe physical violence by an intimate partner (including acts such as being hit with something hard, being kicked or beaten, or being burned on purpose) was experienced by an estimated 22 percent of women and 14 percent of men during their lifetimes (Breiding et al., 2014). During the 12 months before the *National Intimate Partner and Sexual Violence Survey* (NISVS) in 2010, an estimated 2 percent of women and men reported having experienced severe physical violence by an intimate partner. Physical abuse may also include denying someone medical treatment, or necessary medication may also include forcing drug or alcohol use on a person.

More About It...Gaslighting

Gaslighting is a term that comes from a 1938 play *Gaslight* by the British novelist Patrick Hamilton. The play, which has been made into numerous movies, portrays a husband psychologically taunting his wife by telling her she is forgetful. He turns down the (gas)lights, moves furniture, and removes pictures while accusing her of having made the changes. The wife becomes increasingly nervous and confused. When she protests to having moved anything, he threatens to have her "committed" since she is acting crazy and going out of her mind. This mental taunting is a common form of emotional abuse that has been recognized by the adoption of the term *gaslighting* to explain the process.

SEXUAL VIOLENCE

Sexual violence is an all-encompassing, non-legal term. Legal definitions of sexual abuse crimes vary from state to state. Behaviors may include forcing a partner to perform sexual acts, telling the partner that she or he asked for the abuse (in sadomasochism), reproductive coercion, and rape. Sexual assault takes the form of attempted rape, fondling or unwanted sexual touching, being forced to perform sexual acts such as oral sex, or penetrating the perpetrator's body. Physical symptoms may include broken bones, black eyes, bloody noses, and knife wounds that occur during the sexual violence. Miscarriages, stillbirths, bladder infections, infertility, and the potential contraction of sexually transmitted diseases including HIV are specific gynecological consequences of intimate partner rape. While rates of sexual violence have declined over 60 percent in the last 20 years, hundreds of Americans are affected every day (Truman & Langton, 2015).

Rape

Rape is non-consensual intercourse forbidden by statute (due to age or infirmity) or committed by physical force, threat, or other duress. Although the exact definition varies from state to state, rape is a crime against a female or male in every state in the United States, Puerto Rico, Guam, the District of Columbia, and under Federal law.

Approximately 1 in 10 women (9.4 percent) have been raped by an intimate partner in their lifetime (Black et al., 2011). Survivors of rape often experience changes in their overall health. Sleep disorders such as insomnia or eating disorders may occur following rape or sexual assault. Some women experience nightmares and flashbacks. Others encounter body aches, headaches, and fatigue. PTSD is the most common disorder seen in victims of rape or sexual assault. Rape victims sometimes experience anxiety, depression, self-injury, and suicide attempts, as well as other emotional disorders. They sometimes try to cope with their feelings by indulging in alcohol or drugs. The physical effects of rape may include injuries to the vaginal and anal areas, lacerations, soreness, bruising, torn muscles, fatigue, and vomiting.

An estimated 1.7 percent of men have been raped during their lifetimes, and over 23 percent of men experienced other forms of sexual violence during their lifetimes, including being made to penetrate, sexual coercion, unwanted sexual contact, and non-contact unwanted sexual experiences (Breiding et al., 2014). The prevalence of men who experienced these other forms of sexual violence victimization in the 12 months preceding the survey was estimated at 5 percent. Male victims of rape had predominantly male perpetrators, but sexual coercion and being made to penetrate were predominantly by women. Unwanted sexual contact and unwanted sexual experiences were a mix of males and female offenders against men.

Marital Rape

Rape in a marriage is a prevalent form of intimate partner sexual violence. **Marital rape** is any unwanted intercourse or penetration (vaginal, anal, or oral) obtained by force, the threat of force, or when the marital partner is unable to consent. Until the 1970s, most states did not consider marital rape a crime. It was not until 1993 that marital rape became a crime in all 50 states under at least one section of the sexual offense code. Because rape occurs in relationships that are characterized by other forms of violence, experts argue that it is an extension of IPV. Researchers who have documented the relationship between marital rape and other forms of IPV suggest that advocates recognize and validate coerced sex in marriages (Basile, 2008).

Most women do not report the marital rape to traditional sources; therefore, it is difficult to determine the actual prevalence. A few states retain parts of the age-old marital exemption for rape (AEquitas, 2012). For example, the punishment prescribed for spousal rape may be lighter than for other types of rape, and the standard of evidence required in convicting may be higher. In some states, the reporting period is shorter for marital rape than for stranger rape. The Prosecutors' Resource on Violence Against Women (AEquitas, 2012) cautions attorneys that some states' rape laws simply removed the language that exempted spouses from prosecution for rape, leaving language intact that could make it difficult to prosecute marital rape; others allow marriage as a defense to sexual assault crimes.

Male Partner Reproductive Coercion

Concerns about the reproductive health of women in the context of IPV in the United States has recently surfaced. The term **male partner reproductive coercion** refers to the behaviors used to pressure or coerce a woman into becoming pregnant or into continuing or ending a pregnancy against her will through intimidation, threats, or acts of violence (Miller & Silverman, 2010). Authors maintain that unintended pregnancy is common, disproportionately affects younger women, and is two to three times more likely to be associated with IPV. Male attempts to promote pregnancy comes through verbal pressure and threats, direct interference with contraception, and threats related to pregnancy continuation or termination. The coercive tactics of male partner reproductive coercion are summed up as:

- Pregnancy coercion
- Birth-control sabotage
- Control of pregnancy outcomes

Among the 9 percent of women who experience reproductive coercion, almost one-third report being victims of IPV (Clark, Allen, Goyal, Raker, & Gottlieb, 2014). Miller and Silverman (2010) acknowledge that women may also attempt to become pregnant or control the outcome of a pregnancy without their partner's knowledge. Little is known about the phenomenon of female partner reproductive coercion.

VIOLENCE AGAINST WOMEN

More than 12 million women and men are the victims of rape, physical violence, or stalking by an intimate partner in the United States each year (Black et al., 2011). Women are the most frequent victims of IPV. A woman who has survived IPV is typical of any woman encountered in public, but the danger for her is in her own home. She comes from every walk of life, age, race, ethnicity, and social class. Violence against women in intimate partner relationships has reached epidemic proportions in the United States and is considered a major social problem. IPV is the leading cause of injury and death to American women, causing more harm than vehicular accidents, rapes, and muggings combined.

Accepted is the fact that violence against women is underreported. It is estimated that only 49 percent of IPV against women is reported to the police (Catalano, Smith, Snyder, & Rand, 2009). However, the majority of women who experience IPV disclose their victimization to someone, typically a friend or family member. As many as 21 percent tell a nurse or doctor about their abuse (Black et al., 2011). The costs associated with IPV exceed US$8.3 billion each year (Bonomi, Anderson, Rivara, & Thompson, 2009).

Although lower-income levels are one predictor of IPV, the picture of intimate partner victims as being impoverished and uneducated women is inaccurate. Many professional women have partners who victimize them. Working women, military women, and those earning more money than their abusers are all at risk. According to the National Violence Against Women Survey data, the majority of heterosexual IPV victims are females who were physically assaulted by an intimate male partner (Walters et al., 2013).

All too often, the question "Why do women stay in violent relationships?" is answered with a victim-blaming attitude. The fact is that women do leave their abusers. It just is not up to society to determine when or whether a particular woman should stay.

Female victims of abuse often hear that they must like or need such abuse, or they would leave. Others may be told that they are one of the many "women who love too much" or who have "low self-esteem." No one enjoys being beaten, no matter her emotional state or self-image. A woman's reasons for staying are more complex than can be explained by a statement about her strength of character. In many cases, it is dangerous for a woman to leave her abuser. If the abuser has all of the economic and social control, leaving can cause the woman additional problems. Leaving could mean living in fear and losing child custody, losing financial support, and experiencing harassment at work. Survivors experience shame, embarrassment, and isolation. Here are some of the many reasons why a survivor may not leave an abusive situation immediately:

- She realistically fears that the offender will become more violent and maybe even use deadly force if she attempts to leave.
- Her friends and family may not support her leaving.
- She knows the difficulties of single parenting in reduced financial circumstances.
- There is a mix of fun, love, and hope along with the manipulation, intimidation, and fear.
- She may not know about or have access to safety and support.
- She may have been socialized to believe that she is responsible for making her marriage work. Failure to maintain the marriage then equals failure as a woman.
- She may have become isolated from friends and families, either by the jealous and possessive abuser or to hide signs of the abuse from the outside world.
- The isolation of an abused woman contributes to a sense that there is nowhere to turn.
- She may have rationalized her abuser's behavior by blaming stress, alcohol, problems at work, unemployment, or other factors.
- She may have been taught that her identity and worth are contingent upon getting and keeping a man.

African American Women

Overall, African American women experience IPV at a slightly elevated rate compared to white females, at a rate of 7.8 per 1,000 females age 12 or older (Catalano, 2012). Some research suggests that women of color in America experience four sexual assaults per 1,000 in the population (Restoration, 2008).

Racial and ethnic experiences of IPV may differ, according to experts. Some research has suggested that mainstream domestic violence services fall short in meeting the needs of African American IPV survivors (Gillum, 2009). Culturally sensitive options should be considered in the future. Fear of perpetuating negative stereotypes of black men is a source of pressure not to report an abuser. Abusers often manipulate their partners to gain control. In African American IPV, religion and claims of discrimination may be used to justify abuse or elicit empathy.

Poverty, unemployment, and intergenerational violence all contribute to the continuance of IPV. To better understand and predict IPV risk factors in the lives of urban African American women, researchers surveyed 180 adolescent females using cluster analysis of their experiences with violence (Kennedy, Bybee, Kulkarni, & Archer, 2012). Extremely high rates of witnessing IPV within the families were noted (85 percent), and almost 50 percent had seen an adult severely injured as a result of domestic violence. The sample of low-income urban women of color provided evidence that family physical abuse may be relatively common among female adolescents similarly situated.

Native American Indian and Alaska Native Women

AIAN refers to those living in the United States that are of Native American Indian and Alaska Native origin who maintain tribal identity and community affiliation. For the 2010 U.S. Census, 5,220,579 individuals self-identified as AIAN (Norris & Jones, 2012). The federal government has jurisdiction over felony crimes on tribal lands and therefore responsibility for the safety of AIAN women and men. AIAN women experience violent victimization at a higher rate than any other U.S. population. AIAN women were significantly more likely than white women, African American women, or mixed-race women to report that they had been sexually assaulted or stalked.

The first nationally representative sample of AIAN women was included in the *National Intimate Partner and Sexual Violence Survey in 2010*. More than half of AIAN women have experienced physical violence by an intimate partner during their lifetime and 1 in 12 report victimization annually (Rosay, 2016). Compared to non-Hispanic white-only women, AIAN women are 1.6 times more often to have experienced physical violence by intimate partners and 1.7 times as likely to have experienced severe physical violence by intimate partners.

High rates of violence among AIAN families are associated with poverty, alcohol use, and significant cultural stresses in life. One study found that 45 percent of the female respondents experienced a physical assault since the age of 18 and that intimate partners perpetrated the vast majority of these assaults (Yuan, Koss, Polacca, & Goldman, 2006). These findings are consistent with earlier studies among AIAN populations documenting as high as 50 percent of women experiencing IPV, with 39 percent reporting severe physical abuse. Current rates are no different. Four out of every ten Native American Indian and Alaska Native women report having been the victim of rape, physical violence, and stalking by an intimate partner in their lifetime (Black et al., 2011).

Been There...Done That!

Alice knew that her husband did not like her to have friends over to the house. He made it quite clear. However, she was a self-employed woman who was confident about herself and the friends that meant so much to her. During the early years of their marriage, she continued to invite the friends. Over time, she drifted away from them—it became too difficult, she stated. She thought she was going mad and could not face them with the confusion that she felt. She could not remember doing things that she had apparently done or did not even know how to do. For example, the plates were kept in the cupboard to the right of the sink. Then they were on the left side. They had always been there, said her spouse. The clothes she wore were in her bedroom closet, or were they kept in the hall closet? Dog food was always in the cellar—why was it in the garage? Years later, she realized that she was not going crazy at all—it was her husband who had tried to convince her otherwise. He frequently moved things and insisted that she was "losing it." He said he loved her; she had believed him.

There is a shortage of culturally appropriate support services for Alaska Native women. For example, the Arctic Women in Crisis center in Barrow, Alaska, is the only safe shelter within 500 miles (Amnesty International, 2007). The services it offers range from crisis housing to promoting Inupiat values with advice for fathers to nurture nonviolent sons. In 2010, the state of Alaska conducted its first survey on domestic violence. The key results estimated that almost half of the adult women in Alaska had experienced IPV in their lifetime, with approximately 10 percent acknowledging IPV in the previous year (Rivera & Morton, 2011). The same report discovered that over one-third of adult women in Alaska had experienced sexual assault in their lifetime, with over 4 percent have survived sexual violence in the previous year. A strong commitment is being made to address these high violence rates within the Alaskan population.

Asian Women

It is estimated that one-fifth of Asian or Pacific Islander women have been the victim of rape, physical violence, and stalking by an intimate partner in their lifetime (Black et al., 2011). The rate of physical assault was lower than that reported by any other racial or ethnic group. The low level for Asian and Pacific Islander women may be attributed to underreporting. Experts acknowledge that it is hard to determine the prevalence of IPV in Asian communities due to sociocultural factors among differing ethnic Asian groups. Evidence suggests that the prevalence of IVP in Asian communities may, in fact, be higher for some ethnic groups than others (Yoshihama, Ramakrishnan, Hammock, & Khaliq, 2012).

One study of IPV against Asian American women found extremely high levels of violence. More than 95 percent of Filipinas and Indian/Pakistani women reported having experienced IPV victimization in their lifetime (Yoshihama, Bybee, Dabby, & Blazevski, 2010). Rigid gender norms, parallel abuse by in-laws, and abuse related to conflicts over dowry come from hierarchical and patriarchal family structures and practices.

Help-seeking barriers among the study group include the notion of shame, and lack of social support, which the authors suggest is particularly relevant to Asian survivors of IPV. Unlike previous research, the study found that more than 50 percent of those victimized by IPV had called the police for help at least once (Yoshihama et al., 2010). Asian women living in the United States may have unique experiences of IPV. Indeed, significant cross-cultural differences among and within Asian populations have been noted by research. Limited knowledge of the language and laws protecting women may make it difficult for these survivors to assess options when they are victimized.

Caucasian Women

The rate of IPV against white females age 12 or older is 6.2 per 1,000 (Catalano, 2012). This figure represents a decrease of IPV against this population of 60 percent since 1993, but a rise of over 14 percent since 2005. These percentages represent the great strides that have been made in addressing intimate violence in the United States, as well as the need to continue committing resources and education to this social problem.

It is not yet time to rejoice over the declining rates of IPV in the United States. More than one-third of white, non-Hispanic women still report having been the victim of rape, physical violence, and stalking by an intimate partner in their lifetime (Black et al., 2011). More than 18 percent of Caucasian women experienced being raped in their lifetime (Black et al., 2011).

Aggressive police action, including mandatory arrest policies, has become a mainstream response. Therapy involving couples is strongly discouraged in this model because it encourages the victim to discuss openly issues that may later be used against her by the offender. The terms *educational* and *psychoeducational* are associated with interventions based on this perspective.

Women with Disabilities

Approximately 18 percent of the U.S. population age 12 or older has some form of a disability (Brault, 2012). Intimate partners were the offenders for 13 percent of nonfatal violence against persons with disabilities in 2010, roughly similar to the rate for individuals without disabilities (Harrell, 2011). Traditional forms of IPV are not broad enough to inform on the types of abuse that women with disabilities might experience. Denial of access to telephones, destruction of adaptive equipment, and medication manipulation are only a few of the coercive tactics used against this population. The prevalence rates of IPV from studies is so pronounced that their use is limited for forming policy or response. For example, researchers documented from a literature review that the prevalence of any IPV among women with disabilities ranged from 26 percent to 90 percent for lifetime; 4.9 percent to 29.1 percent for

More About It…Disability in the United States

The National Crime Victimization Survey defines **disability** as a sensory, physical, mental, or emotional condition lasting six months or longer and causing difficulty in activities of daily living (Harrell, 2011). The classifications of disability are based on six personal limitations and conditions:

- Deafness or severe hearing difficulty
- Blindness or serious difficulty seeing, even with glasses

- Cognitive difficulties that include serious difficulty in decision making, concentrating, or remembering due to a physical, mental, or emotional condition
- Difficulty walking or climbing stairs
- Limitation in the ability to care for oneself by dressing or bathing
- Inability to live independently due to a physical, mental, or emotional condition

the past 5 years; and 2 percent to 70 percent for the previous year (Hughes, Lund, Gabrielli, Powers, & Curry, 2011).

In some studies, when compared to females without disabilities, women with disabilities experienced more lifetime, five years, and past year physical and sexual IPV (Hughes et al., 2011). Women with a disability are at risk for experiencing rape, sexual coercion, and non-contact unwanted sexual experiences at increased rates as compared with those without a disability (Basile, Breiding, & Smith, 2016).

Hispanic Women

There are over 50 million individuals of Hispanic or Latino origin living in the United States, according to the 2010 Census (Ennis, Rios-Vargas, & Albert, 2011). Accounting for 16 percent of the population, the rate is estimated to rise to 25 percent by 2050. The terms *Hispanic* and *Latino* are often used interchangeably. As with other ethnic groups, Hispanic people come from diverse cultural backgrounds. The National Crime Victimization Survey data report a slightly larger decline in the rate of IPV compared to that of other ethnic groups from 1993 to 2010 (Catalano, 2012). Refer to Figure 8-5.

A study on the lifetime prevalence rates of IPV among adult Latina women in a national sample suggests that half have been victimized at least once in their lives; more than 66 percent have experienced significant revictimization (Cuevas, Sabina, & Milloshi, 2012). Another study puts the prevalence rate lower, stating that more than one-third of Hispanic women in the United States have been the victim of rape, physical violence, and stalking by an intimate in their lifetime (Black et al., 2011). Confinement, violence, and withholding money constitute the Latina abusive control patterns found in one study (Burke, Oomen, & Rager, 2009). In this research, the fear of being reported to immigration authorities or deportation was found as an emergent theme, along with language barriers. Researchers suggest that providing services and outreach to Latina women may be difficult because they may not be aware of protective orders or resources available and are hesitant to use shelters. Culturally, Latina women are more likely to be tolerant of IPV due to their belief in a strong maternal role of marianismo (Burke et al., 2009).

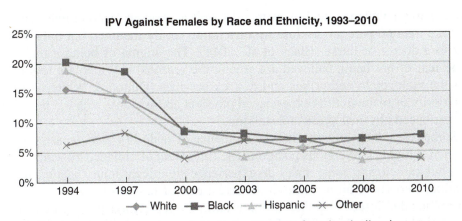

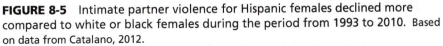

FIGURE 8-5 Intimate partner violence for Hispanic females declined more compared to white or black females during the period from 1993 to 2010. Based on data from Catalano, 2012.

Been There...Done That!

The relationship was over—moving out was the next step. Debbie explained that she had returned home one day to an ominous setting that convinced her that moving day had come! He had "set up" the house to appear as though he had committed suicide, she stated. The gun drawer was left open, with an empty holster and an open box of ammunition. The house alarm was not set. All indications were that he was somewhere in the house, possibly dead or dying, maybe lying in wait for her. She did an intense search through every closet, behind every door, and throughout the cellar, before she realized he was not there at all. Then another fear set in: He would be back, and he had a loaded weapon on him! What would happen then?

The Military and Violence Against Women

The Defense Department's Family Advocacy Program report for 2011 reflects two categories of IPV survivor: spouse (currently married) and intimate partner (not married, which included former spouses) (DOD, 2011). Of these two, the majority of abuse was against a spouse, with IPV having occurred in about 1 percent of the military family population. The vast majority of violence against an intimate was physical, almost 90 percent of IPV. Males were the perpetrators in about two-thirds of cases, with females offending in about one-third of IPV. The victim was equally likely to be a civilian versus an active-duty member. In about two-thirds of spouse abuse cases, the offender was an active-duty member.

If the abuser is a military service member, IPV situations are handled on two separate tracks: the military justice system and the family advocacy system. These are two independent systems. Family advocacy is an identification, intervention, and treatment program, not a punishment system. It is possible that the Family Advocacy Program substantiates a case in which there is insufficient evidence to allow punishment under military law. There is no right to confidentiality under the family advocacy system. Based on the committee's recommendation, a commander determines whether treatment, disciplinary action, or discharge from the military is an appropriate response.

VIOLENCE AGAINST MEN

Intimate partner violence victimizes men as well as women. Among male victims of IPV, more than 60 percent disclose to a friend or family member, but only 6 percent report to a doctor or nurse (Black et al., 2011). The stigma of being a male victim and the fear of not being believed are among the reasons why men are less likely to report the violence to authorities and to seek services (Dutton & White, 2013). The vast majority of male victims experienced physical abuse alone, with 6.3 percent having experienced physical abuse and stalking.

Some researchers suggest that the incidence of male IPV may be as high as that of women, a highly contentious position. The full extent of violence by women against men is not known, and some males do experience significant injury as a result of victimization. Reports of an increase in the arrest rate of females for IPV are explained as an unintended effect of police training and new legislation that seeks to identify the "primary aggressor" in cases of family violence. Almost all (99.5 percent) of heterosexual men who experience rape, physical violence, and stalking by an intimate partner report that the perpetrators were female (Walters et al., 2013).

Been There...Done That!

A call came into the barracks one night. The man on the other end of the line was pleading for a trooper to be sent; he gave the address. In the midst of explaining that his girlfriend would not let him leave, there came a loud noise and screaming. It was my first domestic violence call. Arriving at the house, I found the man had been struck over the head with the phone while he was calling...that was the noise I had heard. There was blood everywhere! The ambulance was called and he received numerous stitches for his injury. He was attempting to move out of the house he shared with his girlfriend. The anger and rage were more than he wanted to live with. It had been a difficult decision to move out. Now he had medical bills and nowhere to go.

Some suggest that research on IPV has purposely and systematically been biased (Dutton & White, 2013). These researchers refer to the gender paradigm wherein studies reinforced the political notions with numerous studies on male perpetrators and female victims exclusively. These studies have traditionally been samples from women's shelters. The Violence Against Women Act (VAWA) in the past only funded programs concerned with the protection of women. That gap has been closed with the passage of the Violence Against Women Act of 2013 (NNEDV, 2013). The VAWA renewal bill includes antidiscrimination provisions to ensure equal access to critical services, funding, and research, regardless of race, gender, or sexual orientation.

Even though a model has not been forthcoming, four factors stand out as leading to husband abuse:

- Ineffective communication between spouses contributes to abuse.
- Struggle over control and power in the relationship or perception of lesser power.
- Husband abuse is evidenced as a form of social disorganization. A lack of adequate financial resources and social bonds leaves a relationship vulnerable to IPV. The higher the family stress, the higher the likelihood of family violence. Inadequate financial resources do not necessarily suggest poverty; life stresses seem to produce an increase in wife beating and husband beating in all income brackets.
- The decision by a woman to slap, hit, push, or punch a husband or boyfriend is made with the knowledge that the likelihood of apprehension or social censure is slim. These forms of violence against men appear acceptable and are perpetuated by the media. In one national survey concerning heterosexual relationships, 24 percent of individuals reported having engaged in violent relationships. In fact, 71 percent of the instigators in nonreciprocal partner violence were women (Arehart-Treichel, 2007).

Approximately one in four men report having been slapped, pushed, or shoved by an intimate partner in their lifetime, with almost one in seven reporting having experienced severe physical violence by an intimate partner (Black et al., 2011). Refer to Figure 8-6 for a comparison between male and female IPV, according to the *National Intimate Partner and Sexual Violence Survey*. In the same survey (Black et al., 2011), male victims reported that about half of stalking perpetrators are male offenders. The majority of offenders of unwanted sexual experiences against men are male. Females are predominately the offenders against men in all other forms of IPV.

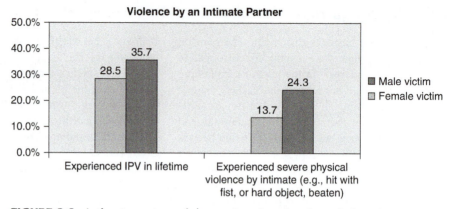

FIGURE 8-6 Intimate partner violence. Based on data from Black et al., 2011.

The following nine socialization factors make it more difficult for male survivors to achieve recovery:

1. *Treatment*—Men are not as likely as women to seek treatment. The failure to seek help is due to a reluctance to see oneself as a victim—which is a female-associated persona.
2. *Minimization*—Males are reluctant to disclose sexual abuse for fear that it will not be seen as a victimization experience. If the victim is a self-identified gay, the abuse may be seen as the result of sexual choice.
3. *Shame*—The male victim typically focuses on why he failed to protect himself.
4. *Masculine identity*—The male survivor may overcompensate for the anxiety surrounding his inability to protect himself by using macho behaviors to project a strong male image. For the heterosexual male, fears that he will be "branded" as gay will plague him.
5. *Male intimacy*—Intense anxiety or anger is produced in settings with other males, which might create intimacy. The victim typically will avoid relationships with other males, to avoid appearing weak or needy.
6. *Sexual identity*—A male that has been sexually assaulted may assume that his failure to protect himself equates with passivity, wrongly considered a female trait. Because the majority of perpetrators are also male, the self-perception of arousal or physical pleasure from a same-sex assault can lead to the false assumption of homosexuality.
7. *Power and control dynamics*—Low self-esteem is related to having been victimized sexually. It may result in an exaggerated effort to control others.
8. *Externalization*—Victimizing others sexually is one way that victims externalize their feelings. Isolation surrounding his victimization and patriarchal values place the victim at risk for offending against others.
9. *Compulsive behaviors*—Some male survivors mask their emotional anxiety and pain through compulsive behaviors. These may include alcohol and substance abuse, or rigid, repetitive behavior patterns.

Prevalence Rate of Violence Against Men

Estimates of intimate partner and sexual violence against American Indian and Alaska men are typically based on local and small samples that do not accurately represent the native population in the United States. According to Black et al. (2011), almost half of Native American Indian or Alaska Native men have experienced rape, physical violence, or stalking by an intimate partner during their lifetime.

The *National Intimate Partner and Sexual Violence Survey* is the first nationally representative sample to measure violence in this population. During their lives, more than 43 percent of Native American and Alaska Native men have experienced physical abuse by an intimate partner (Rosay, 2016). Annually, almost 6 percent experience physical violence by an intimate partner.

Forty percent of Black non-Hispanic men and 39 percent of multiracial non-Hispanic men report rape, physical violence, or stalking by an intimate partner (Black et al., 2011). Approximately 28 percent of white non-Hispanic men experienced rape, physical violence, or stalking forms of IPV (Black et al., 2011).

Men with Disabilities

As stated earlier in this chapter, individuals with one or more disability make up a significant portion of the U.S. noninstitutionalized population over age 12, estimated to be over 56 million (Brault, 2012). Most of the research investigating the association between personal violence and disability status have excluded men, and much of what is known at this point comes from small sample studies netting a range of prevalence estimations. According to a literature review of existing studies, the occurrence of any IPV against men with disabilities ranged from 28.7 percent to 86.7 percent for a lifetime; 24.9 percent for the past five years; and 36.7 percent annually (Hughes et al., 2011).

Mitra and Mouradian (2014) found that men with disabilities were more likely to report lifetime IPV than men without disabilities and, among those reporting any lifetime IPV, men with disabilities were more likely to report past-year IPV than both nondisabled men and women. The Bureau of Justice Statistics, however, determined that IPV against men with disabilities is similar to rates committed against those without disabilities (Harrell, 2017).

One study found that men with disabilities were more likely to experience past-year sexual violence than men or women without disabilities, but less likely to be victimized than women with disabilities (Mitra, Mouradian, & Diamond, 2011). More than half of a sample of men with physical or cognitive disabilities indicated that they had been sexually victimized since acquiring their disability (Powers et al., 2008). Compared with persons without a disability, men are at increased risk for being made to penetrate a perpetrator (Basile et al., 2016). Further research is needed related to the characteristics of perpetrators and the occurrence of IPV among the population of men with disabilities.

DOMESTIC VIOLENCE GREEN CARD

The green card is a permanent resident status document obtained when a family member or employer sponsors an immigrant's application to live in the United States on a permanent or long-term basis. If a person is residing in the United States and is a victim of domestic violence, she or he can self-petition for a domestic violence green card, under a provision of the VAWA without the knowledge of the abuser (U.S. Citizenship and Immigration Services, 2016). Refer to Chapter 1 for additional information on protections for immigrants suffering from domestic violence. If the abuse occurred in the United States and the abuser is an employee of the U.S. government or a member of the uniformed services, a victim can still file for a green card even if she no longer lives in the United States.

There must be a qualifying relationship between the abuser and victim for a person to request a domestic violence green card. Relationship requirements for application include the following:

- The victim is married to the abuser who is a U.S. citizen;
- The victim is a child of a U.S. citizen, and the applicant is the non-abusing parent and spouse to the abuser;
- The victim is the parent of an abusive son or daughter who is a U.S. citizen;
- If the victim is an unmarried child under age 21 who has been abused by a parent who is a U.S. citizen.

Additional criteria are involved to be eligible for permanent residency due to domestic violence. Factors considered in granting of the domestic violence green card include the severity or cruelty of the abuse, having resided with the perpetrator and being a person of good moral character.

CONCLUSIONS

Intimate partners who are abused by their intimates often experience a broad pattern of abuse that can include intimidation, isolation from other sources of support, economic dependency, threats, abuse or threatened abuse of the children, emotional violence, sexual abuse, physical violence, and reproductive coercion. These are tools that abusers use to maintain power and control over their victim.

Survivors of IPV come from all racial and ethnic backgrounds. As you can see in this chapter, ours is a diverse country. Although most of the victims of IPV are women, men are also victimized. Injury and consequences appear to be more significant for females than for males. There are less male victims than female. However, the men who are victimized are no less important just because there are fewer of them. All violence perpetrated against an intimate partner must be critically assessed so that appropriate response occurs.

The health and safety concerns of women who survive violence in an intimate relationship are predicated on research that documents the possibility of severe injury. The physical injury due to abuse of women is a significant social problem. The costs of IPV are felt by all of the society through lost productivity and compensation to victims. Women and men with disabilities are particularly vulnerable to abuse from an intimate partner. Homelessness has also been defined as a problem related to domestic violence.

For female and male victims of physical or sexual abuse, the psychological effects can be devastating. Numerous mental and emotional problems associated with victimization at the hands of an intimate point to the need for increased sensitivity to all victims of abuse. Gender has been the primary victim characteristic in the past, but this does not mean that men do not experience forms of domestic violence or that women do not commit it.

SIMPLY SCENARIO
Why Some Women Choose to Stay…for a While

Cindy fell deeply in love with Jim and they married; it was her second marriage. She had two children by her first husband and one more since she and Jim married. They own their own home and both hold professional jobs. Shortly after the birth of their daughter, things started getting tense. Cindy felt like she was walking on eggshells because Jim would get angry about the most insignificant things. One day he flew into a rage and hit her; he pulled her across the room by her hair. Afterward he was so sorry, he promised to change. He bought her a gift. Things got really good, like when they had first met—it was great! About 10 months later, he started getting cranky again …. Question: What theory best describes this scenario? What will likely happen next?

Questions for Review

1. Define IPV.
2. Where was the first hotline and shelter for abused women?
3. What is the relevance of the battered women's movement to the responses toward IPV today?
4. Against what group does most IPV occur?
5. What are the three cycles of violence according to Lenore Walking?
6. Explain the coercive tactics of male partner reproductive coercion.
7. What is gaslighting?
8. Where does IPV occur more often and why?
9. Describe physical and sexual abuse behaviors.
10. What factors may make it more difficult for men to overcome victimization?

Internet-Based Exercises

1. What can you do to prevent violence against women and girls? For ideas, go to the United Nations Equity for Gender Equality and the Empowerment of Women Web site. Visit http://www.endvawnow.org/en/.
2. The National Sexual Violence Resource Center serves as the nation's primary information and resource center regarding all aspects of sexual violence. Providing national leadership, consultation and technical assistance the NSVRC works to address the causes and impact of sexual violence. Located online at http://www.nsvrc.org/ the NSVRC maintains a searchable library on sexual assault topics. Search their resources and prepare a day of education at your school by sharing what you have learned.
3. The U.S. Department of Health and Human Services maintains a Web site with information and resources for healthy, violence-free living. Prepare a written or oral report to share your findings with the class. Visit http://www.womenshealth.gov/violence-against-women/, and research a topic of interest.
4. What are the signs of domestic violence against men? Help for men who are being abused can be found at https://www.helpguide.org/articles/abuse/help-for-men-who-are-being-abused.htm is one site to begin your research. Start a conversation in class about what you find.

References

Adams, A. E., Tolman, R. M., Bybee, D., Sullivan, C. M., & Kennedy, A. C. (2012). The impact of intimate partner violence on low-income women's economic well-being: The mediating role of job stability. *Violence Against Women, 18*(12), 1345–1367.

AEquitas: The Prosecutors' Resource on Violence Against Women. (2012). *Rape and sexual assault analyses and laws: Current as of July 2012*. Washington, D.C.: Pennsylvania Coalition Against Rape.

Amnesty International. (2007). *Maze of Injustice: The failure to protect Indigenous women from sexual violence in the USA*. New York, NY: Author.

Arehart-Treichel, J. (2007). Men shouldn't be overlooked as victims of partner violence. *Psychiatric News, 42*(15), 31.

Barner, J., & Carney, M. (2011). Interventions for intimate partner violence: A historical review. *Journal of Family Violence, 26*(3), 235–244. doi: 10.1007/s10896-011-9359-3.

Basile, K. C. (2008). Histories of violent victimization among women who reported unwanted sex in marriages and intimate relationships. *Violence Against Women, 14*, 29–52.

Basile, K. C., Breiding, M. J., & Smith, S. G. (2016). Disability and risk of recent sexual violence in the United States. *American Journal of Public Health (ajph), 2016*(106), 928–933.

Bernardi, R. A. (2007). The Violence Against Women and Department of Justice Reauthorization Act of 2005: Applicability to HUD programs. Washington, D.C.: Department of Housing and Urban Development. Retrieved from http://portal.hud.gov/hudportal/documents/huddoc?id=vawa.pdf

Black, M., Basile, K., Breiding, M., Smith, S., Walters, M., Merrick, M.,…Stevens, M. (2011). *National Intimate Partner and Sexual Violence Survey (NISVS): 2010 Summary Report*. Atlanta, GA: Centers for Disease Control and Prevention.

Bonomi, A., Anderson, M., Rivara, F., & Thompson, R. (2009). Health care utilization and costs associated with physical and non-physical intimate partner violence. *Health Research and Educational Trust, 44*, 1052–1067.

Brault, M. (2012). *Americans with disabilities: 2010*. Washington, D.C.: US Census Bureau.

Breiding, M. J., Smith, S. G., Basile, K. C., Walters, M. L., Chen, J., & Merrick, M. T. (2014). Prevalence and characteristics of sexual violence, stalking, and intimate partner violence victimization—National Intimate Partner and Sexual Violence Survey, United States, 2011. *Morbidity and Mortality Weekly Report, 63*(8), 1.

Burke, S. C., Oomen, J. S., & Rager, R. C. (2009). Latina women's experiences with intimate partner violence: A grounded theory approach. *Family Prevention and Health Practice, 1*(8). Retrieved from http://www.futureswithoutviolence.org/health/ejournal/category/issue-8/

Carney, M., & Barner, J. (2012). Prevalence of partner abuse: Rates of emotional abuse and control. *Partner Abuse, 3*(3), 286–335.

Catalano, S. (2012). *Intimate partner violence, 1993–2010*. (NCJ 239203). Washington, D.C.: Bureau of Justice Statistics.

Catalano, S., Smith, E., Snyder, H., & Rand, M. (2009). *Female victims of violence*. (NCJ 228356). Washington, D.C.: Bureau of Justice Statistics. Retrieved from http://bjs.gov/content/pub/pdf/fvv.pdf

Clark, L., Allen, R., Goyal, V., Raker, C., & Gottlieb, A. (2014). Reproductive coercion and co-occurring intimate partner violence in obstetrics and gynecology patients. *American Journal of Obstetrics and Gynecology, 210*(1), 42-e1.

Cook, J. M., Dinnen, S., & O'Donnell, C. (2011). Older women survivors of physical and sexual violence: A systematic review of the quantitative literature. *Journal of Women's Health, 20*(7), 1075–1081.

Cuevas, C. A., Sabina, C., & Milloshi, R. (2012). Interpersonal victimization among a national sample of Latino women. *Violence Against Women, 18*(4), 377–403.

DAHMW. (2013). The Domestic Abuse Helpline for Men and Women. Retrieved from http://dahmw.org/

Department of Defense (DOD). (2011). Family advocacy program domestic abuse (DA) data FY11 report. Retrieved from http://www.militaryonesource.mil/12038/Project%20Documents/Reports/FAP_FY11_Briefing_Slides.pdf

Dutton, D., & White, K. (2013). Male victims of domestic violence. *New Male Studies: An International Journal, 2*(1), 5–17.

Ennis, S. R., Rios-Vargas, M., & Albert, N. G. (2011). The Hispanic population: 2010. *2010 Census Briefs*. Retrieved from http://www.census.gov/prod/cen2010/briefs/c2010br-04.pdf

Ferraro, K. (1997). Battered women: Strategies for survival. In A. P. Cardarelli (Ed.), *Violence between intimate partners: Patterns, causes, and effects* (pp. 124–140). Needham Heights, MA: Allyn & Bacon.

Gillum, T. L. (2009). Improving services to African American survivors of IPV: From the voices of recipients of culturally specific services. *Violence Against Women, 15*(1), 57–80.

Harrell, E. (2011). *Crime against persons with disabilities, 2008–2010—Statistical tables*. (NCJ 235777). Washington, D.C.: U.S. Department of Justice.

Harrell, E. (2017). *Crime against persons with disabilities, 2009–2013—Statistical tables*. (NCJ 250632). Washington, D.C.: U.S. Department of Justice.

Hughes, R. B., Lund, E. M., Gabrielli, J., Powers, L. E., & Curry, M. A. (2011). Prevalence of interpersonal violence against community-living adults with disabilities: A literature review. *Rehabilitation Psychology, 56*(4), 302–319.

Kennedy, A. C., Bybee, D., Kulkarni, S. J., & Archer, G. (2012). Sexual victimization and family violence among urban African American adolescent women:

Do violence cluster profiles predict partner violence victimization and sex trade exposure? *Violence Against Women, 18*(11), 1319–1338.

Miller, E., & Silverman, J. G. (2010). Reproductive coercion and partner violence: Implications for clinical assessment of unintended pregnancy. *Expert Review of Obstetrics & Gynecology, 5*(5), 511–515.

Mitra, M., & Mouradian, V. E. (2014). Intimate partner violence in the relationships of men with disabilities in the United States: Relative prevalence and health correlates. *Journal of Interpersonal Violence, 29*(17), 3150–3166.

Mitra, M., Mouradian, V. E., & Diamond, M. (2011). Sexual violence victimization against men with disabilities. *American Journal of Preventive Medicine, 41*(5), 494–497.

National Domestic Violence Hotline. (2013). Get educated: Violence Against Women Act (VAWA). Retrieved from http://www.thehotline.org/get-educated/violence-against-women-act-vawa/

National Network to End Domestic Violence (NNEDV). (2012). *Domestic violence counts 2012: A 24-hour census of domestic violence shelters and services.* Washington, D.C.: Author.

National Network to End Domestic Violence (NNEDV). (2013). The Violence Against Women Reauthorization Act of 2013: Safely and effectively meeting the needs of more victims. Retrieved from http://www.nnedv.org/docs/Policy/VAWAReauthorization_Summary_2013.pdf

Norris, T., & Jones, N. A. (2012). *The American Indian and Alaska Native population: 2010.* Washington, D.C.: U.S. Census Bureau.

Ouderkerk, B., & Truman, J. (2017). *Repeat violent victimization, 2005-14.* Washington, D.C.: U.S. Department of Justice.

Powers, L. E., Saxton, M., Curry, M. A., Powers, J. L., McNeff, E., & Oschwald, M. (2008). End the silence: A survey of abuse against men with disabilities. *Journal of Rehabilitation, 74*(4), 41–53.

Restoration. (2008). Statistics of shame: An SOS to policy makers. In J. Agtuca & T. Henry (Eds.), *Restoration of Native Sovereignty* (Vol. VIII, pp. 10–12). Rapid City, SD: National Resource Center to End Violence Against Native Women.

Rivera, M., & Morton, L. (2011). Results of the 2010 Alaska victimization survey. Paper presented at the Domestic Violence and Sexual Assault Training Conference, Anchorage, AK.

Rosay, A. B. (2016). Violence against American Indian and Alaska Native women and men: 2010 findings from the National intimate partner and sexual violence survey.

Truman, J., & Langton, L. (2015). *National crime victimization survey, 2010–2014.* (NCJ 248973). Washington, D.C.: Bureau of Justice Statistics.

Truman, J. L., & Smith, E. L. (2012). *Prevalence of violent crime among households with children, 1993–2010.* (NCJ 238799). Washington, D.C.: Bureau of Justice Statistics.

U.S. Citizenship and Immigration Services. (2016). *Battered spouse, children & parents.* Retrieved from https://www.uscis.gov/humanitarian/battered-spouse-children-parents

U.S. Conference of Mayors. (2012). *Status report on hunger & homelessness.* Washington, D.C.: Author.

Walker, L. (1979). *The battered woman.* New York, NY: Springer.

Walker, L. (1995). Battered women and learned helplessness. In J. Makepeace (Ed.), *Family violence: Readings in the social sciences and professions* (pp. 243–251). New York, NY: McGraw-Hill.

Walters, M. L., Chen, J., & Breiding, M. J. (2013). *National Intimate Partner and Sexual Violence Survey: 2010 findings on victimization by sexual orientation.* Atlanta, GA: Centers for Disease Control and Prevention.

Yoshihama, M., Bybee, D., Dabby, C., & Blazevski, J. (2010). Lifecourse experiences of intimate partner violence and help-seeking among Filipina, Indian, and Pakistani women: Implications for justice system responses. Retrieved from https://www.ncjrs.gov/pdffiles1/nij/grants/236174.pdf

Yoshihama, M., Ramakrishnan, A., Hammock, A. C., & Khaliq, M. (2012). Intimate partner violence prevention program in an Asian immigrant community: Integrating theories, data, and community. *Violence Against Women, 18*(7), 763–783.

Yuan, N., Koss, M., Polacca, M., & Goldman, D. (2006). Risk factors for physical assault and rape among six Native American tribes. *Journal of Interpersonal Violence, 21*(12), 1566–1590.

Zahnd, E., Aydin, M., Grant, D., & Holtby, S. (2011). *The link between intimate partner violence, substance abuse and mental health in California Health Policy Brief.* Los Angeles, CA: UCLA Center for Health Policy Research.

LGBTI Partner Abuse

CHAPTER OBJECTIVES

After reviewing this chapter, you should be able to:

1. Compare examples of violence occurring in LGBTI relationships that are unique to the population.
2. Recognize why an understanding of intimate partner violence in the LGBTI community is vital.
3. Restate theoretical explanations for abuse in the LGBTI community.
4. Explain the problems for the LGBTI community in accessing criminal justice interventions.
5. Describe how the Full Faith and Credit requirement impacts violence in LGBTI relationships.

KEY TERMS

Gay	Intersex
Homophobia	Outing
Lesbian	Primary aggressor
LGBTI	Transgender

INTRODUCTION

Lesbian, gay, bisexual, transgendered, and intersex (LGBTI) populations are particularly vulnerable to the harms of marginalization and devaluation in our society. As a result, the strides that have been made for female victims of intimate partner violence within heterosexual relationships have not translated into social service and policy responses for persons who are victimized by a same-sex intimate partner. An unwillingness to acknowledge intimate partner violence has come from within the community as well as from outsiders.

In the United States, same-sex relationships fall into the category of intimate partnerships. LGBTI couples constitute a relationship with a legal status and protection that varies widely from state to state. The variability is similar to the ambiguity surrounding any dating relationship, however. As with opposite-sex couples, in the absence of marriage, the state law determines the status of the intimate or dating relationship under domestic violence law. Rapid changes in the legality of same-gender couples have occurred with states scurrying to keep up with necessary revisions.

The issue of same-sex marriage was settled in 2015 when the U.S. Supreme Court ruled in *Obergefell v. Hodges*, 576 US __(2015) that same-sex couples have the right to get married under the Equal Protection Clause of the 14th Amendment. Same-sex marriage refers to a legally recognized marriage between two spouses of the same gender. Same-sex spouses have the same rights and benefits as any legally married couple. The legal recognition of marriage brings with it the same domestic violence law status for same-sex couples as with opposite-sex couples.

We do not know the exact number of people who live in the United States that identify as LGBTI. The 2010 and 2000 Census data must be viewed with caution. Errors have been identified in the data on same-sex individuals and households by the U.S. Census Bureau, resulting in an overestimation of the population (O'Connell & Feliz, 2011). The revised estimates suggest that approximately 646,464 same-sex individuals are residing in about 6 percent of the households in the United States (Lofquist, Lugaila, O'Connell, & Feliz, 2012).

The current estimate on households is that there are approximately 56 million opposite-sex couple households and about 400,000 same-sex married couple households. Changes to the census for 2020 are expected to count same-sex couples, since marriage has gained legal acceptance. Among the changes will be an acceptance of stated relationships of those who report as same-sex married couples and will include same-sex unmarried partners (Ortman, 2017). Parent identification will be gender neutral as either parent 1 or parent 2 rather than mother and father.

The LGBTI community is as diverse as the nation itself; it is made up of individuals from every ethnic and racial background residing in the United States. See Figure 9-1, which illustrates the ethnicity/race of the persons who survived LGBTI intimate partner violence and called for services in 2006 (National Resource Center on Domestic Violence [NRCDV], 2007).

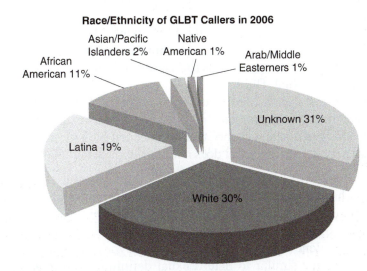

Race/Ethnicity of GLBT Callers in 2006

FIGURE 9-1 The majority of callers who utilize the LGBTQ domestic violence hotline are white, yet diverse ethnic and racial backgrounds are also represented in the population. Based on data from the National Resource Center on Domestic Violence (NRCDV), 2007.

Been There...Done That!

The call came in that a woman was being held at gunpoint in her home by her female roommate. Marilyn was a middle-aged professional woman in a 10-year relationship. The reality that her lesbian partner was leaving did not sink in until Betty came home to pack her belongings, bringing her new companion for support. Marilyn burst into the room waving a gun. Stating that she could not stand it any longer, she threatened to kill herself and maybe take someone with her. Fortunately, the two women were able to get out of the house and call the police.

After hours of negotiation, the STOP team was able to remove Marilyn to safety without anyone being hurt. Finally, she threw the weapon down. She was arrested and transported to the station. Remember to classify these same-sex situations under domestic abuse calls so that resources can be allocated to respond appropriately in the future.

DEFINITIONS

Investigators expect that the perpetrator of intimate partner violence will be larger and stronger than the victim, which is not necessarily the reality. Myths of sexual identity portray fighting between men as normal aggressive behavior and abuse between two women as nonexistent. These and other myths need to be confronted. Issues in alternative relationships force us to reconsider the identities of survivors of intimate partner abuse. Numerous terms have already been used in the introduction that may or may not be familiar to students. To understand the material in this chapter, these definitions are provided:

- *LGBTI*—is an acronym for lesbian, gay, bisexual, transgendered (or trans), and intersex individuals. LGBTI is a demographic category, similar to race/ethnicity, sex, disability, and so on. It is used for scores of people who have major characteristics in common, although they are certainly not "the same."
- *Lesbian*—is an individual who identifies as a woman and whose sexual orientation is primarily to other women.
- *Gay*—refers to a person who identifies as a man and whose sexual orientation is mainly to other men.
- *Bisexual*—men and women identify as bisexual+ because they feel attraction to people of multiple genders. Relationship history does not define a bisexual+ person's identity. Alternative words to describe their identities under the bisexual+ umbrella are pansexual, fluid, and queer.
- *Transgender*—is a term used to describe a group of individuals whose gender identity, and how it is expressed, is different from the sex assigned at birth.
- *Intersex*—this is a social category that reflects real biological variation in which a person has a sexual anatomy that does not fit the typical definition of male or female.

The lack of uniform definitions of same-sex domestic abuse makes it difficult to compare research on abuse and violence in nontraditional relationships. When "Q" appears in the acronym after LGBT it may refer to the term "queer" or "questioning." Early recognition of same-sex IPV came on the heels of the movement that documented domestic violence against women. Early categories of same-sex intimate partner violence were very similar to heterosexual definitions. Over time, there was an understanding among experts that shared characteristics of abuse did not translate to similar victimization. This understanding moved our definitions away from specific features toward the general understanding we have today. For example, lesbian intimate partner violence (IPV) consists of a pattern of violent or coercive behaviors that are committed by a lesbian against her lesbian partner to control the partner's thoughts, beliefs, or conduct. Lesbian IPV may be physical, sexual, emotional, economic, or identity abuse, which is used to maintain or punish the intimate lesbian partner for resisting the perpetrator's control. This approach to defining bisexual and lesbians partner abuse differentiates it from heterosexual partner abuse.

Similarly, IPV against a gay man refers specifically to him. For example, gay male IPV refers to any unwanted physical force, psychological abuse, or material or property damage inflicted by one man on another (National Coalition of Anti-Violence Programs [NCAVP], 2012). The abuse consists of a pattern of violent behaviors to control the partner's thoughts, beliefs, or conduct.

Another definition attempts to illustrate the similarity between opposite gender intimate partner abuse and gay violence. The National Center for Injury Prevention and Control suggests that the patterns of ill-treatment recognizable in all relationship abuse should be defined similarly to facilitate the collection of data and comparison. For this reason, a definition that is inclusive of all victims has been recommended by the CDC (Breiding, Basile, Smith, Black, & Mahendra, 2015):

> Intimate partner violence includes physical violence, sexual violence, stalking and psychological aggression (including coercive tactics) by a current or former intimate partner (i.e., spouse, boyfriend/girlfriend, dating partner, or ongoing sexual partner) (pg.11).

PREVALENCE OF ABUSE

Experts who argue on the incidence of LGBTI intimate partner violence (IPV) agree that domestic violence is a serious social problem regardless of sexual or gender identity. Most of the reports on IPV come from small sample groups or convenience samples from the LGBTI community; therefore, the prevalence figures must be viewed with caution. We do not know exactly how much LGBTI IPV exists, in part because of the hidden nature of LGBTI relationships. These studies are relevant because they provide some idea of the magnitude of the problem, though they are most likely underestimating the real prevalence.

One of the first attempts to compile statistics on domestic abuse within the LGBTI community comes from the New York Gay and Lesbian Anti-Violence Project report. The National Coalition of Anti-Violence Programs'(NCAVP's) annual report, *Lesbian, Gay, Bisexual, Transgender, Queer and HIV-Affected Intimate Partner Violence Report 2011*, showed an adjusted 18.3 percent increase in reporting of LGBTI IPV nationwide compared to the previous year (NCAVP, 2012). Note that NCAVP adds "H" to the acronym LGBTI to be inclusive of all individuals who experience IPV. Of concern relative to this report was the increased lethality of the violence. The report documents that the highest number of IPV homicides ever recorded by NCAVP occurred in 2011: The 19 deaths (12 men and 7 women) represent more than three times the documented homicides from 2010. We do not know whether this increase represents an actual increase in the violence, or whether the relationship of the offender to the victim in same-sex violence is being more documented.

Cited from early research is that IPV occurs at approximately the same rate (12 percent to 33 percent) in LGBTI relationships as it does in heterosexual relationships (National Task Force to End Sexual and Domestic Violence Against Women [NTF], 2011). However, there is a lack of consensus on the actual prevalence of IPV in LGBTI partnerships; few studies have compared sexual minority data to that of heterosexual relationships. Using data from the 2007 *California Health Interview Survey*, researchers found significant differences by sexual orientation for IPV (Zahnd, Grant,

Aydin, Chia, & Padilla-Frausto, 2010). Results from this study suggest that sexual minorities are almost twice as likely to experience IPV as compared to heterosexual adults; rates of occurrence compared to 16.7 percent for heterosexual adults versus 40.6 percent for bisexuals and 27.9 percent for gay or lesbian adults.

In contrast, Goldberg and Meyer (2012) looked at the same data and found that only gay men had higher incidence rates of lifetime and one-year IPV; their odds of IPV occurring were 2.5 higher than those of heterosexual men. Additionally, IPV against WSW (women having sex with women), according to Goldberg and Meyer (2012), was almost entirely perpetrated by men (97 percent) against women in bisexual relationships. Additional research is needed to clarify this discrepancy.

Another significant report on partner abuse within the LGBTI community comes from the *Los Angeles Gay & Lesbian Center* data, which accounted for 48.8 percent of total survivors reporting to NCAVP (2012). While still a substantial contribution to the data, this represents a 66 percent decrease in reporting from 2010 as the result of funding cuts to the agency. Budget cuts and constrained revenue sources may impact the services and response to those who seek help. When positions are cut that would provide services, it has a large impact on the agency.

According to NCAVP (2012), the majority of IPV survivors nationwide identified themselves as white; Latina/o survivors represent the second largest number of survivors at 36 percent of the total. People of color under age 30 were more likely to experience IPV injuries, physical violence, and threats and intimidation. The NCAVP member organizations exemplify the fact that IPV affects all races and ethnic backgrounds, regardless of sexual identity.

As the baby boomer generation grows older, the number of adults ages 65 and over across the nation will double. Noting that the 1.5 million lesbian, gay, and bisexual adults ages 65 and older in California will likely increase to 3 million by 2030, researchers are examining the health issues of the older gay community (Wallace, Cochran, Durazo, & Ford, 2011). Aging LGBTI adults were found to be more likely to suffer some chronic conditions as they age, as compared to heterosexual men and women, despite similar access to health care. Aging gay and bisexual men suffered more from hypertension, diabetes, psychological distress symptoms, and fair/poor health status overall compared to heterosexual men. Aging lesbians were found to have a greater risk of experiencing psychological distress symptoms and physical disability as compared to the group of similarly situated heterosexual women. The authors noted that the lesbian, gay, and bisexual populations have higher rates of mental health distress than the general population due to stigma and discrimination, which are chronic social stressors for the population. A lack of this research is an examination of the participants' history of IPV and its role in their psychological distress.

Gay Male Survivors

Intimate partner abuse is a leading health problem facing gay men today, along with drug addiction and AIDS. An additional challenge for these same-sex survivors is the silence about same-sex violence and the risk of a homophobic response. Male gay survivors of physical abuse must overcome the social barriers that prevent others from seeing their abuse as legitimate. These factors contribute to the tendency for gay and bisexual men not to report intimate partner abuse. Gay men and bisexual men are likely to deny or minimize the abuse that is perpetrated against them. Among the LGBTI resources, gay men made up the largest IPV group of survivors (38.7 percent of help seekers) in 2011(NCAVP, 2012).

Homophobia and internalized homophobia present unique risk factors specific to LGBTI survivors. Homophobic attacks may occur by individuals targeting LGBTI persons and can be evidenced as a form of abuse in gay IPV. In a rare look at homophobia, Dunn (2012) interviewed 25 gay men that had suffered vicious attacks in the United Kingdom, where it is estimated that at least 75 percent of such crimes go unreported to the police authorities. This research found that gay male victimhood was incompatible with a masculine gay identity, which proved to be an impediment to psychological healing. For gay men, the shame and devaluation through pervasive homophobia and other abusive experiences were frequently triggers for the onset of posttraumatic stress disorder, anger, depression, and fear.

The *National Violence Against Women (NVAW) Survey* is the only national survey on IPV that does not exclude same-sex respondents, and as such it is very valuable to understand how this issue affects the LGBTI community. Analyzing data from the survey, Messinger (2011) concluded that being a gay man is a significant predictor of IPV victimization. Gay men were approximately twice as likely to be victimized by IPV as compared to heterosexual males or females, with verbal and controlling behaviors having the strongest effect. Although the survey does not ask respondents about their sexual identity, it does ask whether they have ever lived with a same-sex partner. It also asks whether they have a history of intimate partner victimization by a same-sex cohabiting partner.

Another study included a sample of white gay men between the ages of 18 and 71, comparing relationship satisfaction to the level of victimization or perpetration of IPV. Over one-third of respondents reported experiencing emotional violence from a male partner, almost one-quarter of the interviewees reported experiencing physical abuse, and one-tenth reported experiencing sexual assault at the hands of their intimate partner (Stephenson, Rentsch, Salazar, & Sullivan, 2011). Not surprising, these IPV survivors also reported lower relationship satisfaction, common coping strategies, and couple efficacy than men who did not experience relationship violence. The prevalence of violence in this study was roughly similar to that of other studies; the unique nature of this examination rested on the position that the gay male relationship status could be mutually beneficial and positive.

Being bisexual, according to the Messinger study (2011), was also a significant predictor of IPV. Bisexual respondents were found more likely to be victimized by IPV as compared to all other groups of individuals. Many of the bisexual men experienced verbal or controlling IPV in both same-sex and opposite-sex relationships. Bisexual men who experienced sexual IPV were all victimized by men.

McKenry, Serovich, Mason, and Mosack (2006) provide an example where researchers hypothesized gay IPV to be a function of disempowerment. Among other variables, the authors considered self-esteem and internalized homophobia, educational level, and socioeconomic status as influences of physically violent behavior among gay and lesbian intimate partners. While supporting the general thesis, they concluded that lower self-esteem, educational level, and socioeconomic status contribute to gay partner violence but not to lesbian partner violence.

Not unlike heterosexual survivors, gay survivors of IPV may stay in marital discord and abusive relationships for reasons that are similar. Fear of losing contact with their children may inhibit fathers from leaving abusive relationships; women most often receive physical custody of children. It is also wrong to assume that the male has the financial ability to care for his family as well as himself adequately; financial instability may be a factor in remaining in an abusive relationship. Electing to end an abusive relationship may be a tough decision for a gay man.

Lesbian Survivors

The cycle of abuse that represents cyclical and repetitive changes in behavior experienced in an abusive relationship is often used to explain lesbian IPV as well as opposite gender IPV. According to the NCAVP (2012), lesbian (31.3 percent) survivors were the second most represented sexual orientations reported among total LGBTI survivors. Bisexual women, according to Messinger (2011), are more likely to experience all forms of IPV compared to bisexual men. They are also more liable to be abused by verbal, controlling, and physical IPV. All of the bisexual women studied from data in the *NVAW Survey* who were victimized sexually, were victimized by men.

The prevalence of IPV in the lesbian community remains largely hidden, and its prevalence still is hotly debated. Stereotypical ideas that women are passive and that only men perpetrate IPV may still be inhibiting acknowledgment of the abuse that occurs. In a study that revealed that some form of IPV had victimized half of the lesbian participants, its author found survivor stories of indifference and denial (Walters, 2009). The lesbian community itself clings to ideal notions of a utopian existence that fails to acknowledge lesbian IPV that is occurring. This reluctance to discuss lesbian IPV within the community is harmful to its victims, further isolating and rejecting those who have experienced violence and abuse.

We know that women in lesbian relationships may experience all forms of IPV to varying degrees. Analyzing data from the *NVAW Survey*, Messinger (2011) concluded that being a lesbian is a significant predictor of IPV victimization. Lesbians were approximately twice as likely to be victimized by IPV as compared to heterosexual males or females, with verbal and controlling behaviors having the strongest effect. Controlling for sexual orientation, the study found that the sex of the victim does not have a relationship with IPV victimization. In other words, women (regardless of their sexual orientation) are more likely to experience physical and sexual IPV and equally likely to experience verbal and controlling IPV, as compared to men.

Significant barriers exist that influence the decision for a lesbian to leave her abuser; many do leave multiple times before doing so successfully. Looking at issues that affect the woman's decision to stay with her domestic abuser, researchers have stated that social support is one of the most critical factors (Yamawaki, Ochoa-Shipp, Pulsipher, Harlos, & Swindler, 2012). Authors suggest that the extent of social support is often rooted in myths about IPV, the relationship with the abuser, and the sex of the survivor. These issues pose complicated situations for the lesbian intimate partner survivor. First, society is resistant to acknowledge IPV in the lesbian community (Hassouneh & Gloss, 2008). This reluctance comes from within the community as well as from without. Domestic violence response over the past 30 years has been predicated on the belief that women are not violent and do not abuse in relationships. While this attitude is slowly changing, Walters (2009) noted that the willingness to concede female perpetration comes most often from the older and more mature lesbians. Second, the relationship of a lesbian to her abuser is very much influenced by her lesbian identity in the community. Leaving an abuser may also mean leaving the limited support for her lesbian identity. Last, her gender greatly affects the ability to be independent and self-supporting. Women do not have the same earning capacity as men; leaving the relationship may not be economically feasible for the survivor.

FORMS OF ABUSE

Same-sex IPV is similar to opposite sex IPV in many ways. Regardless of the sexual orientation of the individuals, the forms of IPV are inclusive of physical, sexual, emotional, and economic abuses. Same-sex IPV is also different because identity abuse is unique to the LGBTI community. It should be noted that a one-time assault may be considered a criminal act; however, it would not be regarded as IPV unless it was ongoing as part of a pattern to control the victim. Some IPV is severe and includes the threat or use of a gun and knife, strangulation, being hit with an object, and kicking (Messinger, 2011).

In a groundbreaking nationwide study on lesbian IPV, Renzetti (1992) classified the 100 participants into three types of abusive lesbian relationships: situational, chronic, and emotional or psychological. In cases of situational relationships, abuse is experienced only once or twice as a result of a crisis. This type of abusive relationship was found to be extremely rare, occurring in 8 percent of the abusive lesbian relationships (Renzetti, 1992). Often consisting of low-level violence from both parties, situational abuse differs from other types because there is a lack of desire to control the partner.

Chronic lesbian IPV represents the category of violence that typically escalates in its severity over time. Chronic violent lesbian relationships are characterized by two or more occurrences of physical abuse that demonstrate the increasingly destructive

FIGURE 9-2 Physical abuse is a common form of intimate partner violence noted in any population of survivors. Image copyright Nicholas Piccillo, 2012. Used under license from Shutterstock.com.

behavior. This form of lesbian partner violence is consistent with heterosexual women battering. It is not uncommon for victims to also experience emotional abuse in chronic relationships. Consistent with studies on heterosexual partner violence, a vast majority of lesbian participants (87 percent) in the 1992 Renzetti study reported experiencing both physical and psychological abuse.

Emotional abuse consists of verbal or mental tactics rather than physical violence. Though emotional abuse is typically a component seen in chronic IPV, it may not constitute criminal behavior. Emotional abuse includes verbal abuse such as calling names, criticizing, playing mind games, humiliating the partner, and reinforcing internalized homophobia.

The cycle of violence represents the way that violence develops and is perpetuated in an abusive relationship. Similar to intimate heterosexual violence, research suggests that the frequency and severity of bisexual and lesbian violence increase over time (Renzetti, 1992).

Physical Abuse

Physical abuse that invokes fear of the abuser and causes the victim to modify his or her behavior in response to the assault or potential assault is physical abuse (Dunn, 2012). Hitting, beating, pushing, slapping, kicking, pulling hair, biting, punching, burning, and arm-twisting are examples of abusive physical assaults that may also rise to the level of criminal behavior. Throwing objects, punching walls or doors, and locking the partner out of the home are examples of abusive behaviors that constitute the pattern of abuse. Harming children or pets in the house to control the partner comes under the category of physical violence. Any of these actions should constitute a red flag to the victim. These are high-risk behaviors that cannot be ignored; victims should seek outside assistance from a trustworthy agency or person in these circumstances. The possibility of intimate partner homicide is a genuine risk in violent partnerships.

Sexual Abuse

Sexual partner abuse includes any forced behavior intended to demean or humiliate the partner and instigates feelings of shame or vulnerability (Dunn, 2012). Demeaning remarks about the partner's appearance or background, berating the partner, and withholding sex as a punishment are abusive. Some forms of sexual abuse constitute criminal behavior. Examples include non-consensual intercourse and forcing non-consensual sexual actions on the partner. It is clear that sexual IPV is perpetrated in LGBTI relationships; the extent and severity of sexual violence within these relationships are less certain.

Emotional/Psychological Abuse

Making repeated hurtful exchanges with disregard for the partner's feelings, which are meant to control the victim, is an abuse of the relationship. Intimacy is not an invitation for exploitation. Studies have indicated that emotional or psychological abuse is present in all relationships in which other forms of partner violence occur. Social isolation and manipulation are forms of emotional abuse often used as tactics to set up the relationship for further controlling behaviors. While it is often difficult to explain emotional or psychological abuse, one way to envision it is a lack of respect. Actions and words that you would not use in public or against a stranger are suspect when used against an intimate partner. In today's society, use of electronic monitoring of an intimate partner is a form of emotional or psychological abuse. A controlling partner may oversee the phone and text messages of the partner or demand that the partner instantly respond to messages that are sent to him or her. Be very wary of attempts to monitor activity under the guise of affection.

Economic Abuse

Economic or financial abuse is the use or misuse of financial or other monetary resources of the partnership. Controlling a person's employment by trying to get him or her fired, making excessive calls to work, or creating scenes are examples of efforts to monitor the victim's financial situation and force dependence. Refusing to work, yet contributing to the relationship expenses, is a further example of economic abuse and control. Using the partner's identity, credit cards, checks, or money without permission is financial abuse that may rise to the level of criminal behavior.

Identity Abuse

Unique to same-sex partnerships is identity abuse, which consists of the threat of "outing" and exposure to homophobia (Messinger, 2011). **Outing** is the act of exposing someone as LGBTI. Concealment of the identity is a frequent method of coping with anticipated rejection by society. Telling family, boss, or neighbors about a victim's identity may jeopardize individual personal relationships, and sometimes the person's job is put in jeopardy. Threatening to "out" someone is a manipulative form of emotional abuse; it can cause anxiety and increase the individual's isolation.

Individuals who abuse their partner, regardless of sexual identity, seek ways to expose or humiliate the person's perceived weaknesses. With gay male and lesbian individuals, there is a unique vulnerability due to internalized homophobia. **Homophobia** refers to the condemnation, loathing, fear, societal disdain, and religious rejection of all things gay. Homophobia makes use of stereotypes that stigmatize LGBTI individuals. Experiencing internalized homophobia means that the individual feels the rejection and disdain of some members of society deeply. LGBTI survivors may experience internalized homophobia as the cause of minority stress or posttraumatic stress syndrome (Messinger, 2011). Exploitation of these negative feelings by a partner would constitute abusive behavior.

Been There... Done That!

Jack came to the District Attorney's office with a complaint that his car had been stolen. I was assigned to the investigation. His explanation of how his Mercedes was taken did not sound plausible. After a period of talking with him, he admitted that he had picked up a male prostitute in the city and brought him home for the evening. In the morning, the car was gone and he found a note demanding $5,000 in cash for its return. It got complicated; he was married but living apart from his wife, who knew he was gay. However, he had concealed his sexual identity for many years in fear that he might lose his job. He felt violated and was angry at the man who was exploiting him.

Jack made a difficult choice. To proceed with the extortion investigation and retrieve his car, he had to be willing to testify as to the circumstances of the case. He would have to "out" himself in the community where he worked. The investigation and subsequent sting were successful. The offender was arrested and charged with extortion and automobile theft. Jack testified against him in court, and the perpetrator was found guilty.

THEORETICAL EXPLANATIONS

Humiliation, constant criticism, jealous accusations, and controlling involvement with family and friends are forms of abuse that make up the pattern of ill-treatment in LGBTI relationships. A statistically significant predictive relationship between internalized homophobia and the number of acts of physical violence and sexual coercion has been documented (Gosselin, 2008). Education may also be a factor in abusive relationships; participants with less than a college education were found to be more than twice as likely to commit physically violent or sexually coercive acts as those with advanced or graduate degrees. Class differentials, jealousy, and poor communication skills may all contribute to partner abuse regardless of sexual orientation (Gosselin, 2008).

Studies indicate a robust relationship between alcohol and drugs and IPV in opposite gender relationships (Zahnd et al., 2010). A similar association has been discovered between alcohol use and IPV in LGBTI relationships. Aggression has also been linked with the use of psychoactive drugs such as barbiturates, amphetamines, opiates, phencyclidine, cocaine, and alcohol–cocaine combinations (Stalans & Ritchie, 2008). It should be noted that these associations do not imply that alcohol or drug abuse causes partner violence. Underlying causes that trigger substance abuse may also contribute to the violence against an intimate partner.

Psychological causes contributing to IPV have received the attention researchers (Stuart, Moore, Hellmuth, Ramsey, & Kahler, 2006). Perpetrators of IPV may demonstrate poor impulse control, aggression, fear of intimacy, emotional dependence, fear of abandonment, and impaired ego functioning. Mental health diagnoses for batterers range from obsessive-compulsive, paranoid, borderline personality, passive-aggressive, narcissistic, and antisocial. Correlations between childhood abuse and neglect and other social problems have been indicated.

Feminist Approach

The dominant theoretical explanation for family abuse since the 1970s has been the feminist sociopolitical theory. Research on domestic violence indicates an unwillingness to acknowledge that some women may be violent in domestic relationships, and studies on relationship abuse have purposefully excluded female perpetrators (Hassouneh & Gloss, 2008). This approach has hampered the recognition of partner abuse in LGBTI relationships. Some experts of relationship abuse continue to support the feminist position as viable for explaining LGBTI abuse, whereas others are highly critical of the gendered feminist theory.

The feminist approach is often used to describe the context of violence within LGBTI relationships as well as heterosexual relationships. Applying the feminist approach to explain lesbian partner abuse has included a two-prong analysis of the abuse. First is that an understanding of lesbian abuse requires an integrated analysis of oppression. An integrated analysis of oppression means that abuse perpetration is influenced by numerous sources of oppression that exist within the lives of gay and bisexual survivors (Hassouneh & Gloss, 2008). Oppression from society may cause stress in a relationship and lowered self-esteem for some individuals.

Depending on the coping mechanisms of the individual, the use of alcohol, drugs, and self-destructive behaviors may lead to the possibility of relationship violence. Binge drinking as a way to cope with recent victimization has been noted in the research. Almost 1 in 10 IPV victims reported daily to weekly binge drinking (Zahnd et al., 2010). Authors of the study suggested that since a strong connection between adult victimization and substance use is substantiated, health care screening of women and men substance abusers for recent IPV is warranted.

In the pro-feminist approach, the female is the victim, and the male is the offender. This general standard of feminist ideology has affected policing in two unintended ways. One consequence is that recent years have seen an increase in the percentage of women arrested for domestic abuse (Durfee, 2012). A second consequence is that it has complicated the response strategies when the victim is male or when violence involves same-sex partners (Durfee, 2012).

Psychological Model

The psychological model suggests that the feminist approach is inadequate to fully explain same-sex partner abuse since both men and women can be perpetrators. In this gender-neutral approach, partner abuse is considered learned behavior and ill-treatment is the choice of the aggressor. With little chance of being held accountable for abusive actions, the offenders engage in the blatantly criminal behavior. The psychological model suggests that a strong message to all persons in society must be made. Equal enforcement of the laws and punishment of offenders is the method to control partner abuse in same-sex relationships. Victims must be provided equal legal protections regardless of gender or sexual orientation. The psychological model is widely based on the characteristics of both the offender and the survivor to investigate the principal cause of violence. Self-control and self-esteem, mental illness, and criminal behavior proclivity constitute the elements of the psychological approach (Walters, 2009).

Social–Psychological Model

The social–psychological model argues that the feminist theory and the psychological approach both fall short of providing tools for intervention. It recognizes the socio-political context of homophobia and internalized homophobia, which create the environment that supports relationship abuse. Personal characteristics may also influence the choice to use abuse in relationships. The primary focus is on the institution of family (including dyads). A dyad refers to two individuals in an ongoing committed relationship. This model investigates stressors specifically related to the families and how these stressors result in violence between partners. Such stressors could include socioeconomic status, race, sexuality, income, education, beliefs regarding traditional gender roles, and religion.

Internalized Homophobia

Internalized homophobia has been linked to IPV as an important variable explaining the severity and occurrence of partner violence in same-sex relationships (Gosselin, 2008). Internalized homophobia refers to the internalized stress due to homophobia, which consists of condemnation, loathing, fear, societal disdain, and religious rejection of all things gay and of those who practice it. It is sometimes called internalized homo-negativity by clinicians; this term refers to LGBTI internalization of negative societal and environmental attitudes against this population.

Internalized homophobia is exhibited differently throughout the life of LGBTI individuals. A person can struggle to reconcile his or her feelings with the stigmatized view of having a nontraditional sexual identity in models of sexual identity development. Internalized homophobia may also continue long after the individual reconciles

FIGURE 9-3 This lesbian couple will face the same marital relationship challenges as heterosexual couples. Image copyright Anton Gvozdikov, 2012. Used under license from Shutterstock.com.

his or her sexual orientation. In its most overt form, internalized homophobia results in a hatred of oneself and a self-belief that homosexuality is a "sickness." Shame, negative feelings about self-worth, and negative feelings about other LGBTI people are among the messages that are reinforced through internalized homophobia.

Beyond the standard definition of internalized homophobia, there is a wide variation on how mental health practitioners and researchers conceptualize, define, and operationalize the term. Typically, it involves a shared knowledge about society's condemnation of sexual minorities and shame of being associated with being LGBTI. In a study on same-sex lesbian relationships and the use of violence, results indicated that internalized homophobia might be a significant predictor of the use of physical and sexual abuse (Gosselin, 2008).

Numerous psychological problems may stem from internalized homophobia. Psychological characteristics associated with internalized homophobia include low self-esteem, self-hatred, self-doubt, and belief in one's inferiority (Ross & Rosser, 1996). Additional associated characteristics are an acceptance of popular myths about homosexuality, the belief that others will reject one by one's sexuality, and self-imposed limits on one's aspirations (Ross & Rosser, 1996).

PERPETRATORS IN GAY MALE RELATIONSHIPS

A study on the association of relationship satisfaction to perpetrating or experiencing IPV among a group of gay men found that those who reported greater satisfaction with their relationship, and who shared lifestyle choices were less likely to report IPV (Stephenson et al., 2011). At the same time, its authors discovered high levels of IPV among the sample of gay men, with more than 33 percent of men perpetrating emotional violence, 20 percent perpetrating physical violence, and 9 percent perpetrating sexual abuse against their intimate partner. This study reinforced the idea of shared values and goals as integral to relationship satisfaction and the absence of IPV.

One theoretical perspective predicts that assaultive men would be violent across relationships and that their responses are based on the triggering situations. Research has suggested that gay abusers may see the chance to abuse; and without strong communication or anger management skills, their frustrations turn to violence as a tactic to control, making abusive behavior their choice (Chong, Mak, & Kwong, 2013). Effective IPV-specific anger management therapy is an appropriate way to respond to this type of offender.

Substance abuse is a risk factor that has consistently been identified in IPV for all perpetrator categories and was significantly related to physical abuse in LGBTI IPV (Chong et al., 2013). The same study concluded that power imbalance in the relationship, as evidenced by the dominance of one partner in the relationship, was associated with LGBTI IPV. Coercion, jealousy, criticism, isolating of the victim, lying and humiliation are noted as typical controlling behaviors (Messinger, 2011).

PERPETRATORS IN LESBIAN RELATIONSHIPS

While many similarities exist between intimate violence perpetrators, some significant differences do exist. Dynamics of lesbian intimate partner abuse may also include HIV-related abuse, heterosexism, and homophobia/biphobia. The gender-based theory that is typically used to explain male domestic abuse offending dynamics may also apply to understanding lesbian offenders. Domestic violence is seen clearly as a pattern of behaviors designed to control another; and women, as well as men, are capable of physical, sexual, emotional, verbal, and economic abuse and other controlling behaviors (Messinger, 2011).

The lesbian community may also internalize the utopian myth, which is that lesbian relationships are egalitarian, loving, and passionate, but never violent (Hassouneh & Gloss, 2008). As such, due to an unwillingness to give up their expectations of the lesbian relationship or to expose the reality to others for fear of fueling the hatred against them, lesbian victims may deny their victimization.

CRIMINAL JUSTICE INTERVENTIONS

Criminal justice interventions for IPV vary based on the severity of the incident and whether or not the act is a crime. Certain emotional or psychological abuses may not be criminal, even though they may be considered abusive and can cause mental anguish, loss of self-esteem, or loss of self-respect. The criminal justice system is reactive rather than proactive. It reacts through police action and by court intervention when an act rises to the level of violating criminal law. There is an added layer of variability when the parties are same-sex individuals due to differences in state law. For an act to be legally considered domestic violence, the individuals must fall within the state's definition of a domestic relationship. Each state has the legal right to determine what constitutes a domestic relationship. State law can be broad enough so that a same-sex relationship dating relationships are included. It may specifically include or exclude same-sex relationships, or it may be silent on the issue.

Having the legal status as "domestic" assures civil protections that are not available to other individuals, such as strangers, neighbors, or friends. An example would be the domestic civil violence restraining/protection order. An individual petitioning for a domestic violence restraining/protection order first has to meet the definition of being in a domestic relationship to qualify for the order.

Been There…Done That!

It was a difficult decision for Jane to "come out" to her family. In her forties, she had decided that it was time to live life the way that she had chosen. Free to move in with her lesbian partner, Jane felt at peace. She quit her job and went to work in the shop that her partner owned and managed. The "honeymoon" did not last long—yelling, and screaming were followed by objects being thrown at her by her partner. It was confusing to Jane. This was not supposed to happen in a lesbian relationship. Shame followed. How could she explain to her mother and friends that this was not the perfect relation-ship? On top of that, Jane's whole world now revolved around the friends she and her partner shared in the lesbian community. Within a year, life became intolerable. She began to experience physical beatings as well as sexual coercion. If she left, she would have to quit her job also. Jane had no way to support herself anymore, no place to live, and no friends to lean on. It took another year to break free. It was many years before the break was clean and the back and forth had finally ended. Jane studied and was recertified for her old job…which did not seem so bad a place anymore.

Criminal justice professionals recognize that regardless of whether the relation-ship is legally domestic or not, there is a responsibility to serve and protect all indi-viduals. Domestic violence issues among same-sex partners may appear to differ from those in opposite gender relationships, necessitating nonjudgmental approaches. There is some evidence that gay and lesbian survivors are accessing the criminal justice pro-tections available at higher rates than in the past. According to the statistics of the NCAVP report (2012), a substantially higher number of victims of same-sex partner-ship abuse called the police for support. In 2011, 45.7 percent of survivors called the police, compared to 2010, when only 28.0 percent of survivors called the law enforce-ment for help.

FACTORS IN REPORTING TO THE POLICE

Historically, victim advocates have charged law-enforcement officers with failure to meet the needs of domestic violence survivors. Changes in the law and societal responses, along with the education of police officers, have improved the situation somewhat. Research, since the 1970s, has consistently documented the failures and biases of police officers toward women in general and same-sex persons in par-ticular (Pattavina, Hirschel, Buzawa, Faggiani, & Bentley, 2007). Much discussion has centered on the idea that police response to incidents is affected by the gender and lifestyle of the parties as well as being reflective of general societal attitudes (Perez, Johnson, & Wright, 2012). In the study by Pattavina et al. (2007) examining the differences in the police response to opposite gender and same-sex couples, no substantial differences in police response were found to support differential arrest treatment based on the victim's sex. The authors did question that mandatory arrest policies appear to increase the likelihood of arrest more for female same-sex cou-ples than for male same-sex couples. More research is needed to determine the locus for this finding.

Victim cooperation is necessary at every critical stage of the criminal justice pro-cess, including the filing of a police report by the crime victim. The factors influenc-ing the decision not to call the police for help are still not understood. Fear of police hostility due to the same-sex nature of the partner crime has been assumed to impact the reporting practices of LGBTQ victims (NCAVP, 2012). Some experts suggest that fear of retaliation, cultural barriers, emotional trauma, or stress may play a role in the failure to report (Zahnd et al., 2010). Lesbians fear to report domestic abuse due to the double victimization that is likely to occur. Women are expected to be nonviolent in this culture that attributes violence primarily to males. Accusations of abuse by a female toward another female may be met with disbelief. Males are expected to protect themselves and may feel shame and be met with disbelief at having been victimized (Dunn, 2012). It seems that only slightly more than half of victims report talking about their violent victimization; we can assume most of this reporting is not to the police. Women are only slightly more likely to have discussed the incident with someone, compared with men in the Zahnd (2010) study.

A pervasive fear that exists with same-sex IPV reporting also involves elements of shame or humiliation due to stigmas that are attached to these lifestyle choices. Stereotypical responses by police can be devastating to the victims. One of the most pervasive lesbian stereotypes, that of mutual abuse, puts victims of IPV at risk for further victimization (Hassouneh & Gloss, 2008). Unlike IPV, mutual abuse is when both people in the IPV relationship are equally responsible as perpetrator and victim. Police arrested survivors or both individuals in 28.4 percent of the same-sex incidents, a slight increase from 2010 (21.9 percent) (NCAVP, 2012). Advocates are rightly concerned that police officers may tend to label lesbian partner violence as a mutual fight rather than as IPV if the victim made any attempt to defend herself against her attacker. The consequences to the victim when a mutual abuse assessment is made range from humiliation or taunting to her being arrested. As illustrated in Figure 9-4, the victim's fear of being arrested is not unfounded; the majority of dual arrests occur when IPV involves a same-sex couple.

Conceding that violence perpetrated by a same-sex partner can be confusing to law-enforcement officers; a new paradigm needs to occur. Traditionally, police officers have looked at gender and physical size when determining who is at fault in a domestic dispute. A more precise picture of who is in need of protection must be developed in same-sex violence. Neither stature nor gender points out the aggressive person in the relationship. Experts have acknowledged this dilemma and offer direction on how to proceed for a determination called primary aggressor. A **primary aggressor** is an individual in a domestic dispute who is the most significant or principal aggressor. Here is

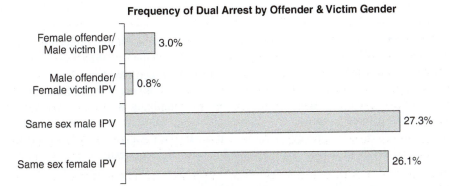

FIGURE 9-4 Dual arrests occur with greater frequency when same sex partners are involved. Based on data from Hirschel et al., 2007.

an example of the New York law regarding arrest and primary aggressor determination (Coleman, 2009):

> When an officer has reasonable cause to believe that more than one family or household member has committed an act of domestic violence, the officer is not required to arrest each person. In these circumstances, the officer must try to identify and arrest the primary physical aggressor after considering: (1) the comparative extent of any injuries inflicted by and between the parties, (2) whether any person is threatening or has threatened future harm against another party or another family or household member, (3) whether any person has a prior history of domestic violence that the officer can reasonably ascertain, and (4) whether any person acted defensively to protect himself or herself from injury. The officer must evaluate each complaint separately to determine who is the primary physical aggressor.
>
> Nothing in the statute requires the arrest of any person when the officer reasonably believes the person's conduct is justifiable under New York's self-defense law (Crim. Proc. Law § 140.10(4)).

A research finding confirms that the police are equally likely to resolve heterosexual and same-sex IPV through an arrest (Hirschel, 2008). However, researchers also found that the police are substantially more likely to arrest both parties in a same-sex case (Hirschel, Buzawa, Pattavina, Faggiani, & Reuland, 2007). In female same-sex cases, 26.1 percent resulted in a dual arrest, compared to 0.8 percent of the cases with male offenders and female victims. For cases that involved male same-sex partners, the arrest of both of the involved parties was 27.3 percent, compared to 3.0 percent of the cases with female offenders and male victims.

Deciding to contact the police is complicated; some issues have been noted that impact that decision. Factors include past experiences with the police, the presence of injury, and the use of a weapon (Walters, 2009). Regardless of gender or sexual preference, evidence suggests that most IPV survivors do not tell anyone about their abuse, even their friends (Zahnd et al., 2010). Reporting prevalence itself is very low, with a somewhat higher reporting of victimization by lesbians versus gay men. LGBTI women are more likely to report experiencing physical violence and more likely to have police classify their incident as a domestic violence case, according to the NCAVP report (2012). This may be due to the accepted stereotype that women are victims and men are perpetrators of abuse.

More About It: Full Faith and Credit

Police have a duty to enforce domestic violence restraining orders that were issued from another state under the Violence Against Women Act (VAWA), passed by Congress as part of the Violent Crime Control and Law Enforcement Act of 1994. The act contains the provision for interstate enforcement of protection orders (Title II of VAWA), which is referred to as full faith and credit. It establishes that states must recognize and enforce protection orders issued by foreign states or tribal courts. Expressly forbidden is providing full faith and credit in instances where cross or counter-petitions have been filed.

Any victim with a valid court order continues to receive protection until the expiration of that order, regardless of which state she or he has entered and regardless of the issuing state. VAWA does not require that a victim register the foreign protection order in the enforcing state to validate it. Whenever a state fails to provide for full faith and credit, the federal VAWA standards apply. Given this, many states have adopted their procedures for complying with the VAWA requirement. According to the Full Faith and Credit provision of the VAWA, if a same-sex survivor of IPV successfully obtains a domestic violence restraining order in his or her state, that protection order is enforceable in every state in the United States.

LEGAL ISSUES

Though same-sex IPV appears to mirror opposite IPV in both type and prevalence, its victims receive fewer legal protections. LGBTI IPV may be a criminal offense that evokes neither civil nor criminal protections for the victim unless the definition recognition of "domestic" is attained. When same-sex individuals are legally married, their "domestic" status is assured. Additionally, support services are often unavailable to LGBTI survivors. Few shelters exist for LGBTI individuals, and few hotlines are available for support. The available resources are insufficient to meet the needs of LGBTI survivors. In 2011, 61.6 percent of LGBTI survivors who sought shelter reported having been denied, as compared to 44.6 percent in 2010 (NCAVP, 2012).

LGBTI survivors face challenges in obtaining protection from the courts. For example, the civil protection order available to opposite gender domestic abuse victims in every state in the United States may be complicated for same-sex victims to obtain, unless the couple is married. In 2011, the majority of survivors who sought orders of protection (78.1 percent) did receive them; however, almost 60 percent of survivors did not attempt to obtain an order of protection (NCAVP, 2012). The lack of legal remedies leaves the victims vulnerable to further abuse.

The Violence Against Woman Act (VAWA) was renewed in February 2013. VAWA has become the first piece of federal legislation that includes non-discrimination provisions on the basis of sexual orientation and gender identity. The LGBTI population was recognized as deserving of federal recognition and protection, despite misconceptions regarding its inclusion (NTF, 2011). The VAWA renewal bill includes antidiscrimination provisions to ensure that LGBTI victims of violence have equal access to critical services. Service providers across the country identified LGBTI victims as an underserved group.

CONCLUSIONS

This chapter focused on partner abuse in gay and lesbian abusive relationships. New terminology was introduced and concepts were clarified. It should be noted that there are many similarities between the abuse that occurs within heterosexual relationships and opposite gender relationships. From the available literature, we can see that the prevalence of abuse is similar. As should be expected, LGBTI individuals are not a homogeneous group. Within the different sexual identities, people come from diverse ethnic and racial backgrounds. Individual perspectives originate from the homes in which they grew up and the experiences that they bring into the relationship.

A difference in background and experience suggests different perspectives on what constitutes a good relationship. It can be expected that rates of violence differ among various cultural backgrounds, as is the case in all partnerships. The forms of abuse are similar to those used in opposite violence. Unique to LGBTI relationships, however, are the forms of identity abuse and the effects of homophobia and internalized homophobia. The threat of outing is also specific to these relationships.

The trend of a recent decline in IPV has been noted, which is also similar to the rate of IPV among heterosexual partnerships. It should be expected, however, that the LGBTI prevalence rates may appear higher in future years as the social climate changes relative to coming out in society. Hostility toward LGBTI individuals is believed to victimize LGBTI abuse survivors further.

Law and prejudices limit criminal justice interventions and services. While police officers are called to respond to incidents of IPV among same-sex couples, the arrest rates are low, according to some reports. Increased training for police officers has been suggested as a way to overcome barriers. One promising approach for this population has been the requirement that police officers make arrests based on the primary aggressor determination.

SIMPLY SCENARIO
Full Faith and Credit

Brian obtained a protection order against his same-sex offender, Tom. The provisions of the court order requiring that Tom must refrain from abusing, threatening, or attempting to harm Brian in any way. Further, Tom is ordered not to contact Brian or come near his residence.

Brian decided to move to another state to start a new life without fear. He has learned that Tom is looking for him, and he wonders what to do.

Question: Is Brian's protection order enforceable in his new home state?

Questions for Review

1. Define lesbian IPV.
2. Why is the NVAW Survey an important source of data on same-sex IPV?
3. Describe forms of violence experienced in gay and lesbian abusive relationships.
4. What is same-sex partner identity abuse?
5. Explain the major tenets of the psychological model that are used to explain IPV.
6. Define and discuss gay male IPV.
7. Describe the social–psychological model and its utility in explaining IPV.
8. Explain factors that may inhibit gay men from reporting IPV.
9. How prevalent is lesbian same-sex IPV?
10. What are the three categories of lesbian violence identified by Renzetti?

Internet-Based Exercises

1. The Safehouse Progressive Alliance for Nonviolence has published its second edition of *LGBTQ Safe Relationships Handbook* (2008). A copy is available at http://www.safehousealliance.org/get-support/lgbtq-support/. View this booklet online for insight into the issues surrounding IPV in the community. According to the handbook, are protection orders available in the state of Colorado? Explain the pros and cons of accessing the legal system.
2. National Coalition of Anti-Violence Programs (NCAVP) is the first national organization dedicated to reducing violence and its impacts on LGBT individuals in the United States. The NCAVP annual report updates the status of IPV in the gay community. Go to its Web site at http://ncavp.org/about/default.aspx, and view the most recent annual report. Write a short paper outlining the changes noted from the previous year.
3. The Centers for Disease Control and Prevention (CDC) provide the oversight for the National Intimate Partner and Sexual Violence Survey (NISVS). The Web site offers an enormous amount of information regarding IPV and same-sex couples, Go to https://www.cdc.gov/violenceprevention/nisvs/index.html. Prepare a report that compares IPV by sexual orientation.

References

Breiding, M., Basile, K., Smith, S., Black, M., & Mahendra, R. (2015). *Intimate partner violence surveillance uniform definitions and recommended data elements*. Atlanta, GA: Centers for Disease Control and Prevention.

Chong, E., Mak, W., & Kwong, M. (2013). Risk and protective factors of same-sex intimate partner violence in Hong Kong. *Journal of Interpersonal Violence, 28*(7), 1476–1497.

Coleman, S. (2009). Domestic violence primary aggressor laws. *OLR Research Report.* Retrieved from http://www.cga.ct.gov/2009/rpt/2009-R-0460.htm

Delaware.gov. (2012). Delaware civil unions: The Civil Union and Equality Act. Retrieved from http://www.delaware.gov/CivilUnions/

Dunn, P. (2012). Men as victims: "Victim" identities, gay identities, and masculinities. *Journal of Interpersonal Violence, 27*(17), 3442–3467.

Durfee, A. (2012). Situational ambiguity and gendered patterns of arrest for intimate partner violence. *Violence Against Women, 18*(1), 64–84.

Goldberg, N. G., & Meyer, I. H. (2012). Sexual orientation disparities in history of intimate partner violence: Results from the California Health Interview Survey. *Journal of Interpersonal Violence.* Retrieved from http://www.escholarship.org/uc/item/3m58w6n7

Gosselin, D. K. (2008). *Internalized homophobia, self-esteem, education, income, and the use of partner violence in a group of self-identified bisexual and lesbian women* (Unpublished doctoral dissertation). Minneapolis, MN: Capella University.

Greenwood, G., Relf, M., Huang, B., Pollack, L., Canchola, J., & Catania, J. (2002). Battering victimization among a probability-based sample of men who have sex with men. *American Journal of Public Health, 92*(12), 1964–1967.

Hassouneh, D., & Gloss, N. (2008). The influence of gender role stereotyping on women's experiences of female same-sex intimate partner violence. *Violence Against Women, 14*(3), 15.

Hirschel, D. (2008). Domestic violence cases: What research shows about arrest and dual arrest. *National Institute of Justice ePub.* Retrieved from http://www.ojp.usdoj.gov/nij/publications/dv-dual-arrest-222679/welcome.htm

Hirschel, D., Buzawa, E., Pattavina, A., Faggiani, D., & Reuland, M. (2007). *Explaining the prevalence, context, and consequences of dual arrest in intimate partner cases.* (NCJ 218355). Washington, D.C.: U.S. Department of Justice.

Lofquist, D., Lugaila, T., O'Connell, M., & Feliz, S. (2012). Households and families 2010 Census briefs. Retrieved from http://www.census.gov/prod/cen2010/briefs/c2010br14.pdf

McKenry, P., Serovich, J., Mason, T., & Mosack, K. (2006). Perpetration of gay and lesbian partner violence: A disempowerment perspective. *Journal of Family Violence, 21*, 233–243.

Messinger, A. M. (2011). Invisible victims: Same-sex IPV in the National Violence Against Women Survey. *Journal of Interpersonal Violence, 26*(11), 2228–2243.

National Coalition of Anti-Violence Programs (NCAVP). (2008). Lesbian, gay, bisexual and transgender domestic violence in the United States in 2007. Retrieved from http://www.ncavp.org/publications/default.aspx

National Coalition of Anti-Violence Programs (NCAVP). (2012). Lesbian, gay, bisexual, transgender, queer and HIV-affected intimate partner violence 2011. New York City Anti-Violence Project. Retrieved from http://laglc.convio.net/site/DocServer/2011_IPV_REPORT_Final.pdf?docID=16421

National Conference of State Legislators (NCSL). (2013). Defining marriage: Defense of Marriage Acts and same-sex marriage laws. Retrieved from http://www.ncsl.org/issues-research/human-services/same-sex-marriage-overview.aspx

National Resource Center on Domestic Violence (NRCDV). (2007). Lesbian, gay, bisexual and trans (LGBT) communities and domestic violence: Information and resources. *LGBT Communities and Domestic Violence: Information & Resources Statistics.* Harrisburg, PA: Author.

National Task Force to End Sexual and Domestic Violence Against Women (NTF). (2011). LGBTQ provisions of S. 1925: Myths vs. facts. Retrieved from http://4vawa.org/pages/lgbtq-provisions-of-s-1925-myths-vs-facts

O'Connell, M., & Feliz, S. (2011). Same-sex couple household statistics from the 2010 Census. SEHSD Working Paper Number 2011-2. Retrieved from http://www.census.gov/hhes/samesex/

Ortman, J. (2017). *Changes to the Household Relationship Data in the Current Population Survey.* Washington, D.C.: US Census Bureau Retrieved from https://www.census.gov/library/working-papers/2017/demo/SEHSD-WP2017-40.html

Pattavina, A., Hirschel, D., Buzawa, E., Faggiani, D., & Bentley, H. (2007). A comparison of the police response to heterosexual versus same-sex intimate partner violence. *Violence Against Women, 13*(4), 374.

Perez, S., Johnson, D. M., & Wright, C. V. (2012). The attenuating effect of empowerment on IPV-related PTSD symptoms in battered women living in domestic violence shelters. *Violence Against Women, 18*(1), 102–117.

Renzetti, C. (Ed.). (1992). *Violent betrayal: Partner abuse in lesbian relationships.* Newbury Park, CA: Sage Publications.

Ross, M., & Rosser, B. R. S. (1996). Measurement and correlates of internalized homophobia: A factor analytic study. *Journal of Clinical Psychology, 52*(1).

Stalans, L., & Ritchie, J. (2008). Relationship of substance use/abuse with psychological and physical intimate partner violence: Variations across living situations. *Journal of Family Violence, 23*(1), 9–24.

Stephenson, R., Rentsch, C., Salazar, L. F., & Sullivan, P. S. (2011). Dyadic characteristics and intimate partner violence among men who have sex with men. *Western Journal of Emergency Medicine, 12*(3), 324.

Stuart, G. L., Moore, T. M., Hellmuth, J. C., Ramsey, S. E., & Kahler, C. W. (2006). Reasons for intimate partner violence perpetration among arrested women. *Violence Against Women, 12*(7), 609–621.

Wallace, S. P., Cochran, S. D., Durazo, E. M., & Ford, C. L. (2011). *The health of aging lesbian, gay and bisexual adults in California health policy brief.* Los Angeles: UCLA Center for Health Policy Research.

Walters, M. L. (2009). Invisible at every turn an examination of lesbian intimate partner violence. *Sociology Dissertations.*

Paper 42. Retrieved from http://digitalarchive.gsu.edu/sociology_diss/42/

Yamawaki, N., Ochoa-Shipp, M., Pulsipher, C., Harlos, A., & Swindler, S. (2012). Perceptions of domestic violence: The effects of domestic violence myths, victim's relationship with her abuser, and the decision to return to her abuser. *Journal of Interpersonal Violence, 27*(16), 3195–3212.

Zahnd, E., Grant, D., Aydin, M. J., Chia, J., & Padilla-Frausto, I. (2010). *Nearly four million California adults are victims of intimate partner violence health policy brief.* Los Angeles: UCLA Center for Health Policy Research.

10

Abuse in Later Life

CHAPTER OBJECTIVES

After reviewing this chapter, you should be able to:

1. Discuss various categories of elder abuse.
2. Give examples of forms of violence against older adults that are unique to the population.
3. Discuss the differences in civil versus criminal action in cases of abuse against older adults.
4. Explain the problems for the elder community in accessing criminal justice interventions.
5. Describe mandated reporting on abuse against older adults.

KEY TERMS

Abandonment

Dementia

Elder abuse

Financial exploitation

Institutional abuse

Ombudsman

Self-neglect

Undue influence

INTRODUCTION

According to official crime statistics, older adults are the least likely to become victims of violent crime in the United States. Property crime, not personal violence, typically provides the highest percentage of crime against persons age 65 or older (Bureau of Justice Statistics [BJS], 2012). Retirement can be a peaceful age, a time to sit back and reminisce about the accomplishments of a more active period in life. Increased leisure time becomes available for activities that were not possible in younger years. For some, however, growing old can become a time of increased fears due to vulnerability.

Until the last quarter of the twentieth century, abuse of older adults remained a private matter. Statistics have not been available for intimate partner crime among older adults. This lack of information is increasingly being seen as critical. It is a problem that will continue to grow as we experience rapidly aging populations. In 1900, the over-65 age group accounted for just 4 percent of the population. The 65+ population stood at 40.4 million in 2010, and the U.S. Census Bureau predicts that by 2030, the population over age 65 will reach over 72.1 million people (Administration on Aging, 2011). By 2050, senior citizens will outnumber children ages 14 and under for the first time in history. The aging population of America is noteworthy since individuals require additional care and support as they grow older. Issues of vulnerability and dependency become more urgent in light of these demographic changes.

Compared to other forms of family violence, the response to abuse against older adults is in its infancy. Some experts suggest that we are way behind the curve in our responses to family crimes against older adults (McNamee & Murphy, 2006). Some credit the report entitled "Battered Parents" with bringing the idea of abuse against older adults to contemporary study (American Psychiatric Association, 1979). Much later, the work of researchers Finkelhor and Pillemer first looked at its prevalence and characteristics (Finkelhor & Pillemer, 1988).

This area of family violence is unlike any other; a "Just the facts, ma'am" approach will not work. Policing violence against older adults for the upcoming generation will involve intellect and patience on the part of police officers. Strength and aloofness must be replaced with confidence and compassion when responding to this population. Some consider this approach to be a departure from traditional police work; it is. Now, the job of law enforcement means incorporation of appropriate responses to reports from older Americans so that it becomes the tradition of good police work in the future.

The environment under which abuse against older adults occurs provides some insight into the condition of older adults as well as their ability to protect themselves. Knowledge of that environment is essential to assure that everything that can be done for the elderly is put into motion. In each setting, the rights of the victim must be fully protected. Adult protective services are available in every state and in the District of Columbia to assist in the protection of older adults against abuse; these agencies act alone or in conjunction with law enforcement.

DEFINITIONS

What constitutes an older adult? A major problem in defining the older adult is in determining when one becomes an older adult! The obvious youngest age comes from the AARP, which considers an older adult to be age 50 or older. Abuse victims in later life include persons who have attained the age of 50 (National Clearinghouse on Abuse in Later Life, 2013). The National Center on Elder Abuse refers to older adults as ages 60 and above (Government Accountability Office [GAO], 2012). The Bureau of Justice

Back Then ...

Early references to abuse against older adults in Britain coined such phrases as *granny battering, granny bashing*, and *granny abuse*, according to the authors of *Elder Abuse in Perspective* (Biggs, Phillipson, & Kingston, 1995). These terms conjure up images of the little old white-haired lady, someone frail and considered incompetent. Now the stereotypical older adult is anything but typical, and current research cautions against identifying elders as one age group of 65 and beyond. Their health and functional abilities have greatly improved with innovations in medical technology. Increased income, educational attainment, and access to support services provide many older adults with improved standards of care (Teaster, Dugar, Mendiono, Abner, & Cecil, 2006).

Early retirement programs have brought people ages 50 to 55 into the category of senior citizens.

Qualifying membership into the American Association of Retired Persons (AARP) is age 50. The spouse of an AARP member is admitted at any age. Because the category of senior citizen has expanded along with the life expectancy, social investigation may necessitate more specifically defined categories of older adults. Although states have the flexibility to define older adults by law, they do not differentiate between categories such as early old age or advanced old age. The ability or lack of ability to protect oneself is of little consequence when applying legal protections to the older adult. It does, however, make prosecutions more difficult. Social intervention can and often does differentiate between those who are able and those who require additional consideration. The term *granny bashing* is no longer applicable to describe older adult victimization.

Statistics differentiates between adult and older adult crime victims at age 65 (BJS, 2012). Typically, older adult abuse is defined to include individuals who are 60 or 65 years and older. All states and the federal government have laws that protect older adults from abuse; the definition of who qualifies for this protection varies by state. It is important to know how the law in your state defines the age for legal protections as an older adult. Abuse statistics vary between studies, in part due to differing definitions of what constitutes abuse against older adults.

Defining the abuse is important for the older adult population because the perceptions of victim advocates or other professionals may determine how the case is handled. Advocates suggest that these categories overlap and require a coordinated response among adult protective services (APS), law enforcement, and domestic violence agencies. In each case involving an older adult, this question should be asked: Is this a case of elder abuse, domestic violence, or abuse later in life? For a legally abusive situation to exist, the action against the elder must have been intentional, and it must cause harm or the risk of harm to the older adult. An abusive situation may also exist if the elder is dependent on a caregiver and that caregiver fails to provide the necessities or protection from harm to the elder. Examples of necessities include food and medication. The term *abuse* is defined in the Older Americans Act Amendments (2006) as follows:

1. The term abuse means the willful
   A. infliction of injury, unreasonable confinement, intimidation, or cruel punishment with resulting physical harm, pain, or mental anguish; or
   B. deprivation by a person, including a caregiver, of goods or services that are necessary to avoid physical harm, mental anguish, or mental illness.

Once a point of contention, experts now agree that intimate partner violence, which is often called domestic violence, has both a legal and a behavior meaning.

More About It: APS

APS are the service providers to older adults and people with disabilities who are in danger of being mistreated or neglected, or are unable to protect themselves and have no one to assist them. All states have an APS program. The duties of APS include receiving reports of older adult abuse, neglect, or exploitation; investigating these reports; assessing risk; and developing and implanting case plans, service monitoring, and evaluation. APS may also provide or arrange for medical, social, economic, legal, housing, law enforcement, or other protective emergency or supportive services. In most states, APS is the first responder for allegations of abuse or neglect against an older adult. APS as an agency is situated in different departments and organizations as determined by each state. There is no national consistency, however. APS may be part of a social services department or contracted to a private, nonprofit agency; eligibility may be based on age (50, 60, or 65), incapacity, or vulnerability.

The professionals who investigate the case are trained to deal with the older adult in a sensitive and caring manner. The resolution will depend on what is in the best interests of the older adult. It may mean that other agencies will be involved to assist with the care, meals might be delivered, and medical needs may be met. Contacting APS is not an accusation or indictment against someone; instead it is a positive move toward protecting a vulnerable adult. Getting involved may be exactly what is needed! Neglect and abuse are conditions of social concern, not private family problems. Reducing the isolation of the older adult, introducing better nutrition, and monitoring medications are all ways to help older adults to feel less vulnerable and more able to help themselves.

APS may involve other agencies such as domestic violence response agencies or law enforcement if the situation warrants the coordinated response.

While the legal definitions vary from state to state, *domestic violence* is often defined as a pattern of coercive controls that one person exercises over another. Studies have documented that much of the abuse that occurs in older adults couples does consist of intimate partner violence.

PREVALENCE

In addition to the problems of definition, the private nature of elder abuse makes it difficult to determine the exact numbers of individuals who are affected. Studies provide approximations, but these are considered to be very low because of underreporting. It is estimated that 2.1 million older adults are victimized by physical, psychological, and other forms of abuse and neglect every year, yet only one out of every six cases is reported to the authorities (American Psychological Association [APA], 2012). This translates to one older American being victimized every 2.7 minutes (The National Center for Victims of Crime, 2008). Estimates are that one in every 20 persons over the age of 60 experiences financial abuse (Acierno, Hernandez-Tejada, Muzzy, & Steve, 2009). Estimates are that one in every ten older adults experiences abuse and neglect each year.

As the most rigorous national study of state-level APS, the *2011 Survey of State Adult Protective Services* offers significant insights into the problem of abuse directed at older adults. In 2009, the APS investigated 292,000 cases of alleged abuse based on the estimates from 33 states (Government Accountability Office [GAO], 2011). The survey found that approximately 14.1 percent of noninstitutionalized older adults had experienced physical, psychological, or sexual abuse; neglect; or financial exploitation (GAO, 2011).

Due to the changing elder demographics, it is estimated that the number of investigations of elder abuse may increase by 50 percent by 2030. The Bureau of Justice Statistics has noted that while violence against elders is the lowest among the more elderly population, the occurrence of violence is on the rise. From 2014 and 2015 the violent victimization rate for individuals age 65 and older experienced an increase from 3.1 victimizations per 1,000 to 5.2 per 1,000, despite declines among other age groups (Truman & Morgan, 2016).

CATEGORIES OF ABUSE

In most states, definitions of elder maltreatment fall within these three categories:

- Family or domestic elder abuse
- Institutional elder abuse
- Self-neglect or self-abuse

Family abuse against older adults refers to several forms of maltreatment by someone who has a special relationship with the older person, such as a spouse, a sibling, a child, a friend, or a caregiver. The abuse typically occurs in the home of the older adult or the home of a caregiver. This category of abuse includes intimate partner violence.

Abuse of an older adult who lives in a long-term care facility such as a nursing home or residential care facility is termed **institutional abuse**. The forms of abuse remain the same regardless of the environment. For example, physical abuse may occur in a domestic abuse situation or an institutional setting. Perpetrators are more likely to be persons who have a legal or contractual obligation to provide care and protection to the older adult.

Self-neglect is characterized as the behavior of an older adult that threatens his or her health or safety. It involves the failure to provide himself or herself with adequate food, water, clothing, shelter, personal hygiene, medication, and safety precautions.

The category of abuse does influence which responding agency is most appropriate. An ombudsman, health care services, or APS would most likely respond to allegations of institutional abuse and self-abuse because the majority of complaints would not be criminal. Police would be more involved in the investigation of physical or sexual violence in domestic settings (alone or in conjunction with APS) but may also become involved in severe institutional abuses. Domestic violence services such as shelters, hotlines, and advocates also are essential responders to intimate partner violence for the older adult. It is necessary for all agencies that are charged with responsibility to contact each other and work together to resolve conflicts and protect the older adult victims.

In any category of abuse, the maltreatment may be either active or passive. This refers to the difference between intentional abuse of the older adult (active) and benign neglect (passive), which also could be unintentional. Intervention may be necessary for the protection of the older adult in either case, and determination would have to be made as to whether the action or inaction of the caregiver was involved. Social services are provided to older adults on a consent basis. If older adults refuse services, they may be enrolled in an elder-at-risk program and offered whatever services are appropriate.

FAMILY ABUSE

Intimate partner violence constitutes a significant number of cases of abuse against adults over the age of 50. Although the incidence of spouse abuse in older couples is significantly less than that in younger couples, many of the risk factors present in abusive couple relationships are the same. In one study, almost 40 percent of the older battered women also reported severe sexual abuse by an intimate partner (Bonomi et al., 2007). In a sample of older women that had a lifetime partner, over 25 percent reported ongoing domestic violence (Bonomi et al., 2007).

The Department of Justice recently acknowledged that no large-scale effort exists to track elder abuse in the United States (BJS, 2012). National Incident-Based Reporting System (NIBRS) data from the state of Michigan was used to provide some of the lacking information. In a special report of its findings, approximately half of elders targeted by violent crime known to the police were victimized by a family member. The most frequent offender was the child of the victim (BJS, 2012).

More About It: Elder-at-Risk Program

The elder-at-risk program is a short-term, program-focused, goal-oriented crisis intervention. Offered to self-neglecting and self-abusing older adults ages 60 and older, it is strictly voluntary. Usually, its clients have demonstrated a reluctance to accept interventions by more traditional efforts. The programs provide nontraditional services for those older adults seriously in need.

FIGURE 10-1   The overlapping of violence against older adults and domestic violence can cause confusion on how to categorize violence against older adults. When investigating concerns of abuse against an older adult, it may be helpful to utilize domestic violence interventions available in your stage when the perpetrator is an intimate partner. Image copyright Andy Dean Photography, 2012. Used under license from Shutterstock.com.

During a domestic crime, an older person is more likely to be seriously hurt and may even die from the abuse. Several patterns of family violence exist among older adults. Intimate partner violence among older adults may be the result of an abusive relationship that has existed over the life of the couple. Stress, caregiving, and age-related issues may trigger intimate partner violence later in life. An individual who was abused by an intimate partner may be battered by his or her adult children later in life.

In about 90 percent of cases, perpetrators of abuse in later life are family members (National Council on Aging [NCOA], 2013). The most probable source of violence is adult children, spouses or partners, friends, and other caregivers. Abusers of older adults are both women and men. Research on which family member constitutes the most frequent offender is conflicting. In some studies, intimate partners were found more likely than adult children to abuse older adults emotionally, and adult children were more likely than intimate partners to abuse older adults physically and financially (Acierno et al., 2009). Studies have consistently found the adult child to be the more frequent perpetrator of abuse against an older adult. Refer to Figure 10-2 (Teaster et al., 2006).

INSTITUTIONAL ABUSE

Older adults enter long-term care facilities when they become limited in the ability to care for themselves in some way. An older adult may have become ill or injured and may need this form of temporary assistance until he or she can care for himself or herself. It is false to assume that going into a nursing home is permanent. Approximately 30 percent of older adults return to their own homes or to assisted-living situations after a recuperative stay in a nursing home.

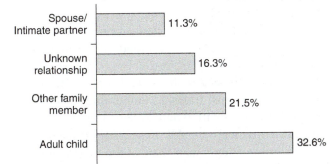

Perpetrators of Abuse Against Older Adults

Spouse/Intimate partner — 11.3%
Unknown relationship — 16.3%
Other family member — 21.5%
Adult child — 32.6%

FIGURE 10-2 The most frequent perpetrator of abuse against an older adult is his or her own adult child. Based on data from Teaster et al., 2006.

There are two categories of long-term care facilities in the United States: nursing homes and residential care facilities. According to the National Ombudsman Reporting System, there are approximately 17,000 licensed nursing homes in the United States that house 3.2 million people, mostly older adults (National Center on Elder Abuse [NCEA], 2012). Residential care facilities are the fastest growing form of alternative senior living. This category includes assisted-living facilities, personal care homes, domiciliary care homes, adult congregate living facilities, adult care homes, and shelter care homes. Over 50,000 residential care facilities are home to more than 900,000 people (Hawes & Kimbell, 2010). Residents of long-term care facilities are predominately female (two out of three) with six out of seven being age 65 or older (NCEA, 2012). The vulnerable adults in these institutional settings, according to reports of severe and widespread maltreatment of residents, are thought to be at higher risk for abuse and neglect than older persons who live at home. It should be noted, however, that most elder abuse and neglect occurs in elders' homes, not in institutional settings where only 5 percent of older Americans live (APA, 2012).

Both state and federal statutes regulate and monitor nursing homes in the United States. The responsibility for the protection of residents, however, rests principally with the states. Residential care facilities are not regulated by the federal government, and unlicensed facilities are a growing problem (Hawes & Kimbell, 2010). Obtaining a clear picture of maltreatment of the older adult is difficult in part due to the various agencies and definitions that are involved. In some states, as many as seven different agencies may investigate complaints of institutional abuse. Primarily, the state long-term care ombudsman's office and adult protective service agencies handle these allegations; however, law enforcement or state health department officials might be charged with the task.

What we do know is that nursing home residents can be vulnerable to abuse because of low staff-to-resident ratios, poor working conditions and wages, and inadequate supervision, to name a few of the problems. Approximately 25 percent to 30 percent of complaints on long-term care facilities involve allegations of physical abuse, and 7 percent of complaints are of sexual abuse (National Center on Elder Abuse [NCEA], 2012). Neglect and financial exploitation make up another 30 percent of complaints (NCEA, 2012). In any case of suspected abuse, it is critical that documentation begins at the onset of an investigation. Once the facility records abuse, it may become admissible in a criminal court, and therefore all records should be stored correctly and with limited access allowed to the professional staff of the facility.

Claiming that no national system exists to monitor abuses, Hawes and Kimbell (2010) found significant evidence of widespread abuse in long-term care facilities. They cite sexual abuse cases ranging from touching to rape committed by staff, residents, and family members. Physical abuse was found to be perpetrated by staff and mentally impaired residents against frail and vulnerable residents. Drug diversion was also noted to be a significant problem, whereby staff might steal medication and falsify drug records or substitute medications. All these issues caused a great deal of pain and suffering to the older adult residents who were at the mercy of their abusers.

These authors assert that preventive measures and oversight of personnel are lacking in long-term care facilities. The requirements of criminal background checks and use of registries that list those workers who have histories of abuse or neglect are not consistent from state to state; some use them whereas others do not. Even when preventive efforts are made, they are not useful in addressing universally inadequate training and staffing levels (Hawes & Kimbell, 2010).

Current controversies surrounding institutional abuse and neglect involve the character of long-term care facilities. In a society that is ambivalent about institutional residential settings, there is little consensus on the nursing or adult foster home. Some authors suggest that such institutions themselves are oppressive, due to the invasion of personal privacy and forced dependency, a setting that by its very nature abuses residents (Hawes & Kimbell, 2010). Others disagree with this perspective while citing the need for increased awareness that institutional abuse is a category of family violence that deserves attention and concern. Investigations require knowledge of state and federal regulations concerning nursing and foster homes.

More About It: Dementia

The term **dementia** comes from Latin for "madness" or "senseless." We use the word to describe the deterioration of intellectual faculties such as memory, concentration, and judgment. Many conditions can cause dementia. It may be related to depression, drug interaction, thyroid imbalances, and other problems. Emotional disturbance and personality changes are indicative of this brain disorder or disease. Some diseases that can cause dementia include Parkinson's, Creutzfeldt–Jakob, Huntington's, and multi-infarct or vascular disease, caused by multiple strokes (Alzheimer's Association, 2012). The most common form of dementia among older people is *Alzheimer's disease*, which initially involves the parts of the brain that control thought, memory, and language.

Alois Alzheimer (1864 to 1915), a German neurologist, first diagnosed Alzheimer's disease, the most common form of dementia, in 1906. Over 5.1 million Americans have Alzheimer's disease, and experts estimate that 14 million will be affected by the middle of the next century if a cure is not found (Alzheimer's Association, 2012). The disease usually begins after age 60, and risk goes up with age. During the middle stages of Alzheimer's disease some individuals experience confusion which may result in frustration and irritability. Patients also experience restlessness, causing some to pace or wander and get lost. It is not uncommon for the police to be called when an older adult with Alzheimer's disease is discovered to be wandering.

Dementia is included as a new category of neurocognitive disorders in the DSM-5 (APA, 2015). The nine neurocognitive disorders are characterized by damage to the brain which can affect memory, thinking, or reasoning. Symptoms of a major neurocognitive disorder include evidence of significant cognitive decline from a previous level of performance in one or more cognitive areas such as learning, memory, language, perceptual-motor or social cognition.

More About It: Ombudsman

An **ombudsman** is an advocate for residents of nursing homes, board and care homes, and assisted-living facilities. Federal legislation has provided the standards for the care of older adults through the Older Americans Act of 1965. An amendment in 1987 provided for the creation of a long-term care ombudsman's office to act as the agency for nursing home certification and licensure. The amendments of 1987 and 1992 included services to prevent abuse of older people. Bringing together the long-term care ombudsman program with programs for the prevention of abuse, neglect, and exploitation, as well as state elder rights and legal assistance development programs, the act calls for a coordination and linkage within each state. It establishes a requirement that each state agency on aging provide a person who will investigate and resolve complaints made by or on behalf of older persons who are residents of long-term care facilities.

The ombudsman is responsible for investigating complaints and providing or arranging appropriate resolutions for complaints. He or she might become a reporter of abuse that is discovered and provide information to criminal justice or health department agencies. An ombudsman may be a paid staff member or a trained volunteer. In addition to being an impartial fact finder, the ombudsman is an advocate for improving the quality of life for nursing home residents.

Misuse of Restraints

Nursing home reforms included in the Omnibus Budget Reconciliation Act of 1987 (OBRA 1987, Pub Law No. 100-203) specified that nursing home residents had the "right to be free from verbal, sexual, physical, and mental abuse, corporal punishment, and involuntary seclusion" (42 CFR Ch. IV [10-1-97 Edition] §483.13 [b]). Under this federal regulation, improper use of physical or chemical restraints in long-term care facilities has been added to the list of abusive actions (Hawes & Kimbell, 2010). Although misuse of restraints is usually associated with institutional settings, this practice may also be identified in an abusive home. It involves the chemical or physical control of an older adult beyond a physician's order or outside accepted medical practice.

Restraints (cloth bindings on chairs or beds) may be used in nursing homes under only two conditions:

1. A person is confused and unable to comprehend or remember that by moving about, he or she may harm himself or herself or someone else, or
2. A person is unable to maintain his or her position because of a severe physical handicap such as paralysis.

Restraints are used only for a resident's safety; they are never to be used without a physician's order and even then only for the span of time absolutely necessary. A restraint used for the convenience of the caretaker is never acceptable. Used in anger or for punishment, a restraint constitutes abuse. Caretakers at home may not be familiar with state laws on abuse and need to be educated about the limited acceptable use of restraints. Educating the caretaker on alternative methods may be helpful. If the restraints are used as a punishment or for the purpose of inflicting pain, particularly if the practice is an ongoing or repetitive action, prosecution may be a feasible option. The misuse of restraints can cause physical injuries such as rope burns. In suspected cases, look for rope burns on the extremities, neck, or torso that result from being tied up or restrained for long periods of time. Although some patients themselves may not think that the use of restraints is improper, their use does not allow the person to be able to flee in the case of fire or other emergency.

SELF-NEGLECT AND SELF-ABUSE

Self-neglect in later life refers to the inability or failure of an older adult to adequately care for his or her own needs. Self-neglect is the most common form of older adult mistreatment and must be differentiated from abuse caused by another person. Approximately half of adult protective services caseloads involve self-neglect (Jackson & Hafemeister, 2011). Self-neglect and self-abuse are included as a separate form of violence because they do require APS intervention. This type of abuse may accompany other forms of abuse for which there are criminal consequences. The differences are important, and an investigation of neglect must include the consideration that abuse may be in part or wholly self-inflicted.

Generally, noninstitutionalized self-neglectors struggle with a mental and/or physical impairment. Service needs for this population can be substantial. Recognition of this form of abuse by law enforcement is crucial to making the appropriate referrals to APS that can provide suitable intervention. Self-abuse is not a criminal violation, and necessary emergency intervention should come from the adult protective service agency. Signs of self-neglect may include the following:

- Lacking food or basic utilities
- Refusing medications
- Hoarding animals and/or trash
- Unsafe living conditions or vermin-infested living space
- Inability to manage finances (frequently borrowing money, giving away money and property, not paying bills)
- Disorientation, incoherence
- Alcohol or drug dependence

FORMS OF ABUSE

The forms of abuse and neglect described in this chapter should sound familiar to you by now, because they exist in other categories of family violence. The Centers for Disease Control defines **elder abuse** as an "intentional act or failure to act by a caregiver or another person in a relationship involving an expectation of trust that causes or creates a serious risk of harm to an older adult" (Hall, Karch, & Crosby, 2016, pg. 28). Elder abuse can also take the form of financial exploitation, intentional/unintentional neglect by the caregiver, or abandonment. The lack of consensus on definitions still hampers efforts to investigate, research, and document cases of abuse against older adults. Some authors do not include self-neglect as a category of abuse. Sexual abuse has rarely been documented in the past, so some classifications consider sexual abuse as a subgroup of physical abuse. Refer to Figure 10-3 to see the forms of abuse documented against older adults and their prevalence rates. Every year, an estimated 4 million older Americans are victims of physical, psychological, or other forms of abuse and neglect (APA, 2012). Just as with other victims of abuse, it is not unusual for an older adult to have more than one injury or different forms of abuse and/or neglect. Physical abuse may be the tool to accomplish financial exploitation, and vice versa. Determining the cause of injury begins with ruling out the obvious and looking toward possible explanations that are nonabusive. If the older person is mentally incompetent, his or her patterns of behavior should be observed to assure that the person is not self-neglecting.

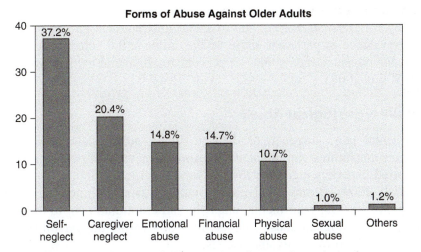

FIGURE 10-3 All forms of abuse and neglect are investigated to determine the proper intervention strategy. Self-neglect occurs so frequently, however, that it is an important category to differentiate from abuse caused by others. Based on data from Teaster et al., 2006.

When abusive conditions seem likely, the ability of older adults to protect themselves against abuse must be assessed. Older adults may be dependent on others for their care, which is a factor contributing to their vulnerability. A greater need of some older adults for assistance in accomplishing everyday activities is associated with verbal abusiveness and economic exploitation (Acierno et al., 2010).

Physical Abuse

To be clear, physical abuse against an older adult involves inflicting or threatening to inflict physical pain or injury on a vulnerable older adult, or depriving that person of a basic need. It includes battering, assault, and inappropriate restraint. Physical abuses range from slapping or shoving to restraining with ropes or chains. When a caregiver or other person uses enough force to cause injury or unnecessary pain, the behavior might be regarded as abusive, even if the harm was not intentional. Hitting, beating, pushing, kicking, burning, or biting constitutes acts of physical abuse. Over- or under-medicating the older adult, depriving him or her of food, or exposing the person to severe weather may be abusive.

Bruises and rope or gag marks, which are indications that the older adult has been tied or taped, should make investigators highly suspicious of abuse against older adults. Slapping an older adult is an example of physical abuse. Injuries that are not consistent with the explanation given for their cause are a red flag that should cause an investigator to look deeper into the situation. Does the older adult have a history of similar injuries or hospitalizations? Do people in the household give varying accounts of how the older adult was injured? However, injuries due to falls or accidents may not be caused by abusive conditions. Observing the behavior of the older adult may help to clarify the situation if abuse is suspected. Presence of fear, agitation, contradictory statements, or refusal to talk openly should alert officers to a potential abuse situation. These conditions are not confirmation of abuse but should be further investigated.

In 2008, a nationally representative random sample assessed 3,000 individuals ages 57 to 85 for physical, verbal, and financial mistreatment having occurred in the past year. Prevalence of past year abuse was as follows: 9.0 percent for verbal abuse, 0.2 percent for physical abuse, and 3.5 percent for financial exploitation (Laumann, Leitsch, & Waite, 2008).

Emotional/Psychological Abuse

Inflicting mental pain, anguish, or distress on an older adult through verbal or nonverbal acts constitutes emotional abuse. Approximately 4.6 percent of adults over age 60 reported experiencing some form of emotional mistreatment in the year prior (Acierno et al., 2009). It may involve name-calling, using intimidating and threatening language, or causing fear, mental anguish, and emotional pain to the older adult. Emotional or psychological abuse can also include treating the person as a child and isolating him or her from family and friends.

Providing care for an infirmed or impaired person that results in unintentional injury or neglect is in the category of passive abuse and necessitates social intervention. Caregiver stress is not the most common cause of abuse against older adults, as many have previously assumed, but it may be a factor in some cases. A caregiver's emotional and psychological problems or drug or alcohol addictions are all indications that the caregiver may not be capable of providing adequate care to an older adult.

Psychological and emotional abuse is the willful infliction of mental or emotional anguish by threat, humiliation, intimidation, or other abusive conduct. The forms of psychological and emotional abuse are the most difficult to identify. Isolation, name-calling, and being treated like a child by a caretaker, as cited above, are examples of recognizable conditions. Usually, there is a lack of evidence to support claims of these as abuse. If an older adult is suffering from another type of abuse, it is not unusual for psychological and emotional abuse to be taking place also. Documenting signs of psychological and emotional abuse in conjunction with other more visible forms of abuse will not only provide an accurate statement of the general living conditions that are indicators of abuse but also strengthen the case against the suspect.

Additionally, the investigation may find the older adult to be in need of services. A referral to the local elder protection agency is warranted when the complainant seems confused or unable to distinguish between reality and fantasy. It is appropriate to contact a caregiver or protection agency when a person is displaying inappropriate behaviors.

Sexual Abuse

Practitioners and researchers acknowledge that estimates on sexual abuse against older adults represent only the most obvious cases, and this is a serious underestimate of this type of abuse (Burgess, 2006). Age can no longer be considered a protection against sexual abuse. Nonconsensual sexual contact of any kind is sexual abuse. Reports indicate that older victims are less likely to report sexual abuse than are younger victims. It can range from sexual exhibition to inappropriate touching, photographing the person in suggestive poses, and forcing the older person to look at pornography. Sexual abuse may involve rape, sodomy, or coerced nudity.

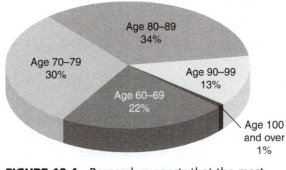

Sexual Assault Victim by Age Group

FIGURE 10-4   Research suggests that the most frequent sexual abuse victimization of older adults occurs against 80- to 89-year-olds. Based on data from Burgess, 2006.

Of the 284 cases of sexual abuse in the Burgess (2006) study, the majority of victims (70 percent) resided in domicile locations. Institutional locations accounted for 58 older adults (23.2 percent), and assaults occurred in 12 (4.8 percent) locations other than a home or institution. The characteristics of the victims by age group are illustrated in Figure 10-4. The majority of victims were women (93 percent). The National Institute of Justice estimates that over 0.6 percent of Americans reported forced sexual intercourse or sexual assault after age 60 (Acierno, Hernandez-Tejada, Muzzy, & Steve, 2009).

Research on sexual abuse against older adults is emerging slowly. We know that it is happening because the professionals in the field are identifying cases. Sexual maltreatment may be "covert" or "overt," as described in one major study from Massachusetts (Ramsey-Klawsnik, 1991). The author describes covert sexual abuse as a sexualized relationship. It involves sexual interest, jokes, comments, and harassment of the victim or discussion of sexual activity in front of the victim. Overt sexual abuse is any unwanted or forced sexual conduct with an older adult. Overt sexual abuse can be any form of sexual activity, including but not limited to kissing and fondling, oral-genital contact, penetration of the vagina or anus, voyeurism, and exhibitionism.

It may be surprising to know that many sexual assaults against the older adult are witnessed by a third party. In one study, 39.4 percent of cases of sexual victimization against an older adult was witnessed (Burgess, 2006). Victims of sexual abuse are not spared because of infirmity. A majority of sexual abuse offenders against the older adult do not live with the victim (Amstadter et al., 2010).

Sexual assault victims share the same or similar symptoms regardless of their age or gender. The following signs are suspicious for sexual abuse, although their presence does not verify that abuse to the older adult is occurring and may be indicative of other problems.

Physical Indicators

1. An injury such as bruising, bleeding, or pain in the genitals, rectum, mouth, and breasts should be investigated thoroughly. Urinary incontinence would complicate the diagnosis for abuse if the older adult were not cleaned and cared for properly. Redness of the genital area could be caused by poor hygiene.

2. When bruising or pain is evidenced along with the injury to the face, neck, cheek, abdomen, thighs, or buttocks, the patterns of bruising might be suggestive of grab marks or the use of restraints.
3. Evidence of torn, stained, or bloody underwear is highly indicative that sexual abuse is occurring.

Behavioral Indicators

1. Intense fear, anxiety, and mistrust of one person—along with other indicators of sexual maltreatment—are signs of sexual abuse.
2. The victim of sexual abuse may offer a "coded" disclosure to someone that he or she trusts. The older adult may give hints about the sexual abuse, described as "testing of the waters" (Burgess, 2006). This may include statements about a dislike for a particular caregiver or a reluctance to be bathed by that person.
3. Depression without other explanation or cause may indicate sexual abuse.
4. Self-destructive behavior or suicide attempts without a history of mental illness or underlying medical causes may indicate sexual abuse.

SEXUALLY TRANSMITTED DISEASES   Presence of a sexually transmitted disease (STD) if the older adult is not engaged in consensual sexual activity and does not have a prior record of an STD is cause for concern when present with other indicators, such as fear, apprehension, or neglect. Some STDs are related to poor hygiene and would not indicate abuse, so caution is recommended. Examples of STDs that could be caused by poor hygiene or sexual abuse include *Trichomonas vaginalis* (vaginitis) and bacterial vaginosis (Hammerschlag, 1996). Herpes and herpes simplex might be self-infected in the genital area if the person was previously infected with mouth sores. Severe and untreated infections may be indicative of neglect rather than abuse.

Financial Exploitation

Financial exploitation is defined as illegally taking, misuse, or concealment of funds, property, or assets of a vulnerable older adult.

Financial exploitation is also known as fiduciary abuse, financial abuse, economic abuse, and financial mistreatment. It covers a broad range of conduct that is difficult to define and to prove. The determination is often subjective and rarely is it possible to prove criminal knowledge of incompetence and intent. Although prosecution of the perpetrator has been rare, it is possible in some cases. A civil lawsuit, to recover misappropriated property, is also an option for the victim. As the phenomenon of exploitation becomes better understood, its indicators will increasingly be recognized and effective intervention more commonplace. This form of violence to the older adult could be called the invisible tragedy; without the external signs of abuse, it has often been unrecognized and its effects minimized.

Prevalence of financial exploitation is exceptionally high. According to recent research, one in 20 older adults reported some form of perceived financial mistreatment by family members occurring at least one time in the recent past (Acierno et al., 2009). Financial exploitation by family members and by strangers was increased among the more physically disabled adults. Losing financial resources can be especially worrisome to a person who is of an age when he or she cannot replenish them. Anguish about the lack of adequate resources and confusion over financial arrangements can be devastating. Loss of property rights to one's home may mean institutional commitment or dependence when the older adult would have otherwise been able to care for himself or herself. Financial abuse does not always occur in isolation and may be accompanied by physical abuse, neglect, homicide, and other crimes. Approximately 5.2 percent of elder abuse cases investigated by adult protective services involve financial exploitation (Acierno et al., 2010).

Because the banking industry has a stake in protecting its clients, educational efforts should be aimed at bank personnel in addition to protective service agencies and law enforcement. This model, which includes the banking business in efforts to combat financial exploitation, is exemplified in the Bank Reporting Project (Attorney General, 2013). Its design includes a sample protocol for reporting and responding to financial exploitation by bank personnel in addition to consumer education. A collaboration of agencies and organizations provides the resources and training to banks, which participate on a volunteer basis in training their personnel on the warning signs associated with financial exploitation. Along with the training, each bank designates a person to raise awareness among its staff and to develop bank protocols for addressing concerns and community outreach.

Experts have described financial exploitation as an epidemic with society-wide repercussions. A 2010 study estimated that financial exploitation cost older adults at least $2.9 billion in that year alone (MetLife, 2011). Perpetrators may be strangers who inundate older adults with mail, telephone, or Internet scams (51 percent of cases); family members, friends, or neighbors (34 percent of cases); those with fiduciary responsibilities, such as financial advisers or legal guardians (12 percent of cases); or those perpetrating Medicare fraud (4 percent of cases). Older adults are particularly vulnerable to financial exploitation because, as research has shown, financial decision-making ability decreases with age. The money lost in these cases is rarely recovered for the older adults, with the potential to undermine their ability to support themselves.

Police officers have found themselves inundated with investigations involving multifaceted misappropriation of property through powers of attorney, quitclaim deeds, wills, and living trusts. In response to these crimes, fiduciary abuse specialist teams, or multidisciplinary FASTs, have been developed to meet the investigative need. Typical professionals included on these teams are law-enforcement personnel, mental health professionals, consultants with expertise in financial matters, bank personnel, realtors, real estate attorneys, insurance brokers, and Medicaid fraud investigators (MetLife, 2011). A rapid response FAST team exists to respond to imminent danger and in cases of emergency in some jurisdictions. According to Nerenberg (2003), examples of financial abuse that has been evidenced are as follows:

- Home equity loan scams
- Misuse of "protective" legal instruments such as powers of attorney and trusts
- Confidence crimes
- Identity theft
- Investment scams
- Telemarketing fraud
- Homicide for profit

Neglect

Neglect is the refusal or failure by those responsible for providing food, shelter, health care, or protection for a vulnerable older adult. Signs that the older person may be suffering from neglect include some of the following:

- Sunken eyes or loss of weight
- Extreme thirst
- Bedsores

Neglect occurs when a caregiver is unable or unwilling to provide the necessary care for an older adult for whom he or she is responsible. Some neglect may be due by caretakers who are too young or inexperienced to take care of an older person who has special needs. Sometimes, the person responsible for elder care is handicapped by a mental or physical disability and is unable to handle the difficult chores of caring for an older adult. Neglect can occur even when there is no willful desire to inflict physical or emotional distress on the older person. Symptoms of neglect include the following:

1. *Overmedication or denial of medication*—Overmedication may be used to keep an older adult "quiet" or might be due to ignorance and carelessness on the part of the caretaker. Either way, it can be unsafe to the person, and intervention is necessary. Overmedication could be a life-threatening situation for the older adult. Deliberate overmedication is a form of an improper use of restraint. In some instances, a lack or perceived lack of financial resources could cause the withdrawal or denial of health services. Medical attention for the older adult should be sought to determine the condition and provide necessary medications. Withdrawing a person without medicational supervision can also create a life-threatening situation. The denial of needed medication is hazardous to the health and well-being of someone.

2. *Untreated injuries and illnesses*—These may alert the responder to neglect or abuse. Although it is not life-threatening to be denied eyeglasses, dentures, or hearing aids, this would constitute a lower standard of life for the older adult and is neglectful.

3. *Denial of adequate food*—The older adult may become malnourished or dehydrated as a result of being deprived of food. If he or she is living alone, the investigator should look into the refrigerator and cupboards to confirm suspicions that food is not being supplied or made available to the older adult.

4. *Lack of proper hygiene*—If the older person smells of old urine or is caked with feces, he or she is not being cleaned properly. Other signs of neglect include matted, dirty, or uncut hair, bodily crevices caked with dirt, or overgrown finger/toenails. The presence of a serious rash, bedsores, urine burns, or impetigo is also suggestive of neglect.

The neglected older adult's environment may also provide clues that abuse is occurring. Evidence suggestive of neglect includes the following:

- An excessively cluttered or dirty home
- Lack of heat, running water, electricity, or air-conditioning in extremely hot climates
- Infestation by cockroaches or rodents

Abandonment

Abandonment is the intentional and permanent desertion of an older adult in any place (such as a hospital, nursing facility, shopping center, or public location) or leaving the person without the means or ability to obtain necessary food, clothing, shelter, health care, or financial support (Stiegel & Klem, 2007). Risk factors for abandonment include the following:

- Absence of available significant others or peers
- Advanced age
- Cognitive impairment
- Decreased health status
- Depression
- Functional impairment
- Impaired psychosocial health
- Inadequate personal resources
- Physical impairment

If a special relationship exists between a caretaker and the older adult, the caretaker can be held legally responsible for a failure to act on that duty of care in some states. California is one state among six that have adopted criminal abandonment legislation, making it a felony to cause or permit a dependent older adult to suffer harm. In 1995, the California Supreme Court put that law to the test. It tried family members for "abandonment" after the death of 67-year-old Robert Heitzman, Sr. His "body was found in his bedroom on a mattress covered with feces and rotted through with urine." Two sons who lived with the older adult were found guilty of Section 368(a) of the California Penal Code. Upon appeal, the California Supreme Court held that the statute was not unconstitutional or vague—yet a duty to care for an older adult, through a special relationship, must be present for legal liability to attach. A daughter who did not live full time with her father was not found guilty.

THE VICTIMS OF ABUSE AGAINST OLDER ADULTS

All states and the District of Columbia have passed legislation to protect the vulnerable older adult population because of the impairments associated with old age. In some states, those laws will apply to other categories of vulnerable adults, such as those with

---

More About It: *People v. Heitzman*, 886 P.2d 1229 (Calif. 1994)

Sixty-seven-year-old Robert Heitzman resided in the home of his grown son, Richard Heitzman, Sr., along with another grown son, Jerry Heitzman, and Richard's three sons. On December 3, 1990, police were summoned to the house, where they discovered Robert dead in his bedroom. His body lay on a mattress that was rotted through from constant wetness, exposing the metal springs. The stench of urine and feces filled not only Robert's bedroom but the entire house as well. His bathroom was filthy, and the bathtub contained fetid green-colored water that appeared to have been there for some time.

Police learned that Jerry Heitzman was primarily responsible for his father's care, rendering caretaking services in exchange for room and board. Jerry admitted that he had withheld all food and liquids from his father for the three days preceding his death on December 3. Jerry explained that he was expecting company for dinner on Sunday, December 2, and did not want his father, who no longer had control over his bowels and bladder, to defecate or urinate because it would further cause the house to smell.

disabilities, as well. Every state has laws that mandate police to intervene in situations of domestic violence, regardless of the age of the victim or perpetrator. Federal law protects elder victims on federal enclaves and plays an important role in funding programs and developing a policy for the prevention of and response to elder mistreatment. Some of the risk factors associated with the abuse of older Americans pertain to demographics, including age, gender, and ethnicity. Elder abuse victimization occurs against approximately 10 percent of the older adult population (Lachs & Pillemer, 2015).

Age

A baby born in 1900 was expected to live an average of 47.3 years. In the United States, this figure rose to an average of 77.8 years in 2005 (Kung, Hoyert, Xu, & Murphy, 2008), with 65-year-olds in 2010 expecting an additional 18.8 years of life, according to the Administration on Aging (2011). This trend in life expectancy changes the face of Americans from visions of the young to the wrinkles of the old. If there were such a thing as a "typical" victim of elder violence, she would be 80 years old, frail, and dependent on others for her care. Substantiated reports show that persons ages 80 and older suffer the greatest share of abuse (42.8 percent), as illustrated in Figure 10-5 (Teaster et al., 2006).

Gender

According to the Administration on Aging (2011), 17.5 million men and 23.0 million women were ages 55 and over in 2010, meaning a sex ratio of 100 men per 132 women nationally. Women and men age differently, and female life expectancy has long exceeded male life expectancy. This trend is expected to continue with a narrowing of the gap between the number of women and men. By 2050, the ratio of women to men is expected to be 55 percent to 45 percent of the population (Vincent & Velkoff, 2010). Experts suggest that changing sex ratios may have implications on the social and economic well-being of the older population.

During their older years, men and women are equally likely to become victims of physical abuse (Amstadter et al., 2010). Women are more likely than men to live with the perpetrators of physical abuse (80 percent versus 47 percent) and for a relative to

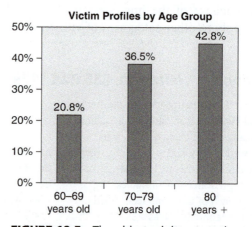

FIGURE 10-5   The oldest adults are at the greatest risk of abuse and neglect. Based on data from Teaster et al., 2006.

be the offender in almost equal proportions. According to the Administration on Aging (2011), 40 percent of older women in 2010 were widows; and almost half of women ages 75 and older lived alone. Older men are more likely to be married than older women: 72 percent of men versus 42 percent of women.

Almost all older victims of adult sexual assault are women (93.5 percent), although men have been victimized also (Teaster et al., 2006). In the Teaster study, the reports of sexual abuse came through many persons who had access to the older adult, with one-third coming from the older adults themselves. In more than half of the cases, physical trauma was observed. Some of the victims were diagnosed with STDs as a result of the abuse. Severe physical abuse and evidence of forcible restraint were found in about 20 percent of the cases.

Ethnicity

By the year 2050, the older adult minority populations will have increased substantially, from 14 percent in 1985 to approximately 42 percent of the entire population (Vincent & Velkoff, 2010). *A Profile on Older Americans* (Administration on Aging, 2011) sheds light on the changing face of race and ethnicity in the United States. Minority populations are believed to be increasing at a faster rate than the white population. In 2010, 20 percent of persons ages 65 and older were minorities. More than 8 percent were African Americans; persons of Hispanic origin (who may be of any race) represented almost 7 percent of the older population. More than 3 percent were Asians or Pacific Islanders, and less than 1 percent were American Indians or Native Alaskans. In addition, 0.8 percent of persons over age 65 identified themselves as being of two or more races. The majority (77 percent) of victims in substantiated cases are white (Teaster et al., 2006).

VULNERABILITY AND UNDUE INFLUENCE

Older people and their families worry about crime. Though older people are less likely to be victims of crime than teenagers and young adults, the number of crimes against older people is hard to ignore. Each year hundreds of thousands of older persons are abused, neglected, and exploited by family members and others. Many victims are people who are older, frail, and vulnerable and cannot help themselves. Some may depend on others to meet their most basic needs. People ages 80 and older, and women of all ages, are at greater risk. Older adults who are dependent on others for basic care are particularly vulnerable.

Some of the reasons why people may not seek help for the older adult are as follows:

- Uncertainty about whom to talk to
- Uncertainty about what can be done
- Fear of not being believed
- Fear of getting involved

As people age, it is normal to experience some decline in certain mental functions, particularly memory. Pronounced decline may signal illness or disease, which may be treatable. Poor nutrition, depression, and medication interactions may be factors that contribute to the older adult's vulnerability to undue influence. **Undue influence** occurs when people use their role with the older adult to exploit the trust,

Been There ... Done That!

Phyllis lived alone and had been widowed for many years. She had only one child and no one else to turn to for help. What could she do? she wondered. She loved her son, but she did not have much money and was afraid that he was going to take it all. Her son had been taking money out of her purse after she had cashed her Social Security check. He had a drug problem, she confided, and she was afraid to confront him about the missing money.

She did not know exactly how much money had been taken, or when the stealing had begun. She had never seen her son go into the purse; it must have happened while she slept. No, Phyllis did not want to press criminal charges against her son. Phyllis wanted me to make her son stop taking her money—that's all. Hardly the job for a supercop, I thought. This was not really what I expected to be doing in the major crime bureau! It was easy, though; a little time spent with Phyllis to assess the problem made the choices clear.

First, I spoke to Phyllis about a security alarm for her house—it might make her feel more comfortable knowing that she had the ability to decide who would enter her home while she slept. We discussed having her checks sent by direct deposit to her bank so that she would not have large amounts of cash in her home. Finally, I told her about APS, the social service agency that could help her to make those things happen. The agency could check up on her and provide a place to call if she had further problems. A small thing, right? Phyllis sent a letter of thanks to the district attorney, which did not hurt me a bit. It has since occurred to me that I had the opportunity to make a difference, a small one to be sure, but it might have made her life a little better. All it cost was my time, and I was already being paid for that! Although the lack of evidence made prosecution impossible, we found an acceptable alternative.

dependency, and fear of others. This deceptive use of power is used to gain control over the decision making of the vulnerable adult. Vulnerability to undue influence is not related to the person's intelligence, but cognitive impairment may make the manipulation easier to accomplish.

CONSEQUENCES OF ABUSE AGAINST OLDER ADULTS

The severe emotional distress experienced by older persons as a result of mistreatment has been well documented. It is important to note that older adults die disproportionately of suicide (Suicide Awareness Voices of Education [SAVE], 2013); reporting an individual as being in need of services may save his or her life. If a person is considered a risk to himself or herself or others, regardless of age, either law enforcement or social service agencies may seek assistance from the civil or family court. Even abuse that is not defined by state law as a crime against older adults may be addressed by using provisions of the mental health, social service, or penal code.

Rates of depression are higher in abused older adults as compared to nonabused persons. Social supports have had a positive effect on the level of psychological distress in victims, indicating that victims benefit more from the social supports they receive. Older adult victims of sexual assault are confronted with the psychic trauma of victimization as well as possible physical injuries that can pose significant health threats due to the victim's age and physical well-being (Burgess, 2006). To many older victims, rape is the worst form of lost dignity. Shame may be exacerbated by misplaced feelings of self-blame and guilt. There may be profound shame in discussing the crime or participating in a medical exam with law enforcement and medical personnel. There may be feelings of embarrassment that family members and neighbors will find out or that the media may somehow access and release the information to the community.

CIVIL VERSUS CRIMINAL ACTION

Should the perpetrator be charged criminally? The determination on civil versus criminal action for abuse against older adults is extremely complex. Criminal prosecution is rarely presumed, as with other adult domestic crimes. Neither is the decision made with purely protective concerns, as with child abuse cases. The older adult victim is assumed to have an interest in protecting family relationships because of some dependence on the perpetrator. Often, the relationship is of value to an increasingly isolated older adult, and threats of abandonment or commitment to an institution make the older adult reluctant to follow through with criminal court proceedings. Institutional settings often prefer to handle their own "problems" and historically do not pursue criminal avenues for redress. An institutionalized resident is already limited in ability and may be severely disabled, further complicating determinations in an abusive situation.

Examples of civil actions include assault and battery for physical abuse, false imprisonment when excessive restraints have been used, negligence for mismanagement of funds, and restraining orders against perpetrators of abuse. Although this approach could serve to free assets or provide compensation to the victim, he or she must be competent and able to pay the costs of litigation.

Criminal actions include assault and battery for physical abuse, burglary or extortion for financial abuse, and specific crimes against older adults with enhanced penalties. Some states have a caretaker statute that makes it a specific crime to omit care to a dependent or vulnerable person. The advantage to criminal prosecution is the possibility of court-mandated counseling or removal from the victim's presence. Criminal prosecution may serve as a deterrent to future abuse. However, the older adult may refuse to press charges due to a fear of retaliation or may change his or her mind and drop all charges. It is not uncommon for an older adult to be ashamed or embarrassed to admit that his or her family member is abusive. Statutory definitions of older adult abuse can be confusing.

Prosecution attorneys make the final decision on criminal complaints and must consider the status of each person as well as the severity of the abuse. In some cases, adult protective services seek custody of the older adult who is unable physically or mentally to make determinations for his or her best interests. Although criminal statutes do not differentiate by age category and ability to self-protect, the choice between civil intervention and criminal prosecution may involve that differentiation.

Been There ... Done That!

A report came into the barracks of theft from an older adult. When responding to the call, I found the man extremely agitated as he described his wallet being stolen. His fear of being victimized was real, but the account of how it happened did not sound plausible. After careful consideration of his narration and interviewing of the suspect, I doubted that the wallet had been taken. We slowly retraced his steps throughout the day. Actually walking the property where he had been, I found the wallet lying on the ground in the barn. He was embarrassed to find that it had been dropped, not stolen.

Complaints from senior citizens should never simply be dismissed. If possible, they should be resolved. Older adults' fear of victimization is high even though the actual incidence may be low. Failure to be sensitive to fears will leave the person in emotional turmoil, if not psychological pain. Although frivolous complaints may occur from time to time, we have no way of determining whether the abuse is occurring without an investigation. A case solved is a case solved, regardless of the complaint!

The frequency of neglectful behavior and its duration, intensity, severity, and consequences are all taken into account when making a determination as to abuse against older adults and neglect having occurred. It is not a simple decision that can be made haphazardly. Controversy exists between the child abuse model and spousal abuse model, both of which have been applied to address the needs of the older adult victim. The child abuse model uses language similar to child abuse protective statutes and takes a stronger view of victims as unable to protect themselves. Conversely, the spousal abuse model assumes older adults to be victimized yet legally independent adults. Some researchers claim that the family violence paradigm is not suitable for these cases because cases of neglect are forms of inadequate care, not violence. Concerned about the civil rights of older adults, professionals disagree on this area of government interference. Because many APSs have modeled legislation after child abuse statutes, this raises questions on freedom of choice. Some suggest that the government-defined level of care denies older adults' basic constitutional rights.

MANDATED REPORTING

Forty-five states, the District of Columbia, Puerto Rico, and the Virgin Islands have mandatory reporting laws under which physicians, nurses, social workers, and others designated by the state are legally required to report suspected abuse against older adults to adult protective services (Stiegel & Klem, 2007). A *mandatory reporter* is a person required by law to report allegations and suspicions of abuse against an older adult. The remaining states have voluntary reporting laws or are mandated to report to the police if a crime against an older adult is suspected. Those who are required by law to report suspected abuse or neglect vary by states. In some states, everyone is considered to be a mandated reporter of suspected abuse; in other states, the individuals who are required to report are specifically named by profession.

A mandated reporter is required to report when he or she saw abuse taking place or when there is a reasonable belief that it is occurring. It is tough to identify abuse in some instances, because many older adults are reluctant to tell and because many physical and mental difficulties that older adults suffer from have results that can easily be mistaken for some forms of abuse. When reports are based on a good faith belief that abuse is occurring, the trend in most states is to grant immunity from legal sanctions for reporting situations that are found not abusive on investigation.

States that have mandated reporters seem to create a duty to report for almost all professionals with whom the older adults come into contact. If a mandated reporter believes that abuse is possible but fails to report it, there may be criminal repercussions. For failing to report abuse, for example, a reporter can be found to have committed a misdemeanor in some states. However, most states do not take such aggressive action against this omission.

MULTIDISCIPLINARY TEAM RESPONSE

The criminal justice community has been slow in responding to the needs of older adults. Prosecutions of abuse against older adults have been rare in the past. Significant changes have been seen in the past few decades along with new criminal justice system responses. Challenging the traditional response that older adults did not want help from the criminal justice system, alternative approaches that include aggressive prosecution are evolving.

Multidisciplinary teams are forming nationwide as the best approach to prevent abuse against older adults (National Center for the Prevention of Elder Abuse, 2008).

Although the makeup of multidisciplinary teams varies from state to state, the teams share common prevention goals. For the victims, the enhanced autonomy and improved access to service options are evident. Professionals share information as well as the needs and approaches of the protective services, the criminal justice system, victim witness assistance programs, and aging services. Additionally, the approach acts as a support system for the various professionals who are concerned with abuse against older adults, providing an environment for sharing frustrations and the uncertainty that these cases might bring. For the communities, the team approach acts to identify gaps in services and ultimately provide an improved system response. Since various agencies have conflicting goals and perspectives on how cases of abuse should be handled, the team approach offers a forum for balancing their different goals. The team approach aids in case resolution through to be in the best interest of the older adult based on a consensus of the team members.

POLICE RESPONSE

Law enforcement is encouraged to use a multidisciplinary approach to investigations of abuse against older adults. Overlapping responsibilities of multiple state agencies, including long-term ombudsmen, APSs, department of social services, and law enforcement, make this category of abuse particularly amenable to agency cooperation. As mentioned earlier, the call for services from all agencies is expected to increase dramatically in future years.

The National Elder Mistreatment Study provides reporting information that can shape the policy and response of police for elder abuse and neglect (Amstadter et al., 2010). Underreporting of abuse to the police is a problem which needs to be addressed. Police are only notified in about 25 percent of incidents of physical abuse and less than 20 percent of sexual victimization. Interestingly, older men are more likely to report sexual abuse to the police than older women (28.8 percent versus 19.6 percent).

Due to the dependence that an older adult may have on an abusive caretaker, the Police Executive Research Forum (PERF) recommends a modified police response to this category of domestic violence. Arrest and removal of the perpetrator may cause more harm than good. Research suggests that mandatory arrest policies in cases involving an older adult may sometimes lead to further violence. Each situation must be evaluated with flexibility as part of the standard operating procedure. Knowledge of the resources in the jurisdiction will make assisting the domestic violence victim more humane as well and efficient. Examples of standard operating procedures in cases of suspected abuse against an older adult include an assessment on alternative emergency care along with a protocol with that agency for a quick response.

Because abuse against older adults and neglect is a new area of intervention for the criminal justice community, it is imperative to consider the duties and responsibilities that are in place to direct law enforcement action. Police officer liability is a factor that must be taken into account. If the state has a mandated arrest policy for domestic abuse that does not specifically exclude older adults, then that law must be enforced. If probable cause to believe a crime has been committed does exist, officers must consider already existing domestic violence law in their state. If the state has a more liberal policy involving discretionary action, officers can consider the entire situation before

More About It: Triad

The National Association of Triads (NATI) is a partnership of three organizations: law enforcement, older adults, and community groups. The triad model includes state and local efforts that survey the needs and concerns of older citizens, expand crime prevention programming, and provide reassurance programs to local seniors. Increasing public awareness and decreasing victimization against older people are the guiding principles. A senior advisory counsel called SALT is established for each chapter to integrate the triad activities and tailor them to fit a community's particular needs.

Providing law-enforcement services for older adults means accepting that this group of citizens is not incompetent. Understanding the unique character and needs of the people in every age category allows dignity and life choices. Sometimes older adults will make decisions in a manner that is perceived as inappropriate. Their concerns and considerations are simply different. When age or illness overcomes an older adult's ability, interventions become more complex and crucial. Institutional abuse is included because of the caretaker status that nursing homes undertake on behalf of the older adult.

taking any action. Depending on the severity of the abuse and the likelihood of repeated assaults, an arrest, further investigation, or referrals are all options to consider.

In neglectful situations, it may be more difficult to determine an appropriate course of action. Any investigation is primarily concerned with the safety of the victim. Determine if the victim is able to protect himself or herself from further abuse or neglect. Make appropriate referrals and contact social services to intervene when the situation does not rise to the level of criminal conduct.

Community policing is another attempt to remedy this problem and to combat the excessive fear that plagues many older citizens. The AARP, the International Association of Chiefs of Police (IACP), and the National Sheriffs' Association (NSA) signed an agreement in 1988 to work together to reduce crime and to improve law-enforcement services for older adults. Referred to as *triad*, they are community-based programs that involve law enforcement, concerned citizens, and advisory boards that are being formed across the United States to improve education and police response to this population of citizens (National Association of Triads [NATI], 2008).

CONCLUSIONS

As a society, we are faced with many challenges in the upcoming years. The older population is exploding along with a need for services. Among the population where law enforcement has been recently become involved, the need for continued self-education and policy assessment is imperative. Community triad programs demonstrate the commitment of this generation of law-enforcement personnel to protecting our older citizens. Fiduciary investigation units, such as the LAPD's FAST, provide an example of a police department's response to the unique problems that older adults face. Contemporary police officers can expect to work with these issues throughout their careers.

The characteristics of physical and sexual abuse of older adults are similar to other forms of family violence. The signs and symptoms are nearly the same; injury is still a primary indicator of criminal abuse. The possible extent of injury for the older adult can be higher than for other populations, however, due to infirmity and old age. The emotional and psychological harm of abuse can be devastating when severe abuse occurs. Elders may become more vulnerable to neglect as they age. A complicating factor in cases of abuse occurs during later stages of life due to the dependency to caretakers that develop. As individuals become more isolated they also become more vulnerable to abusive situations. Social services play a vital role in providing care and protection for older adults.

Change in abilities and dependencies leave this population susceptible to abuse in ways that do not apply to other age groups. Due to the vulnerability of older adults, legislation has been enacted that will guide enforcement action for the future. Financial exploitation, the invisible abuse, should be a growing area of specialization for law enforcement in the future. Compassion and empathy will go a long way toward preserving the dignity of seniors in the United States.

SIMPLY SCENARIO
Concern for the Elderly

Mary is a 71-year-old widow who lives alone in her own home. Joanne, a granddaughter who lives in another state, came to visit after not having seen Mary for over a year. Joanne noticed that there was no food in the house and that Mary looked frail and did not recognize her.

Question: What form(s) of abuse does this describe?

Questions for Review

1. What is the APS and what are some of its duties?
2. What is meant by late onset cases of abuse?
3. What are the responsibilities of an ombudsman?
4. What are the signs of possible emotional or psychological abuse against older adults?
5. Describe some symptoms for neglect against older adults.
6. What are some of the reasons people may not seek help for the abuse against older adults?
7. Describe some of the consequences of abuse against older adults.
8. What is the controversy that exists between the child abuse model and the spousal abuse model, in relation to how they are used to address the needs of the older victim?
9. How does the multidisciplinary approach work as a response to abuse against the older adult?
10. What does it mean to be a mandatory reporter of abuse against an older adult?

Internet-Based Exercises

1. The American Bar Association, Commission on Law and Aging, maintains a Web site with information on law and practices relating to abuse against older Americans. Go to http://www.americanbar.org/groups /law_aging/resources.html, and write a short report on the legal issues related to elder abuse.
2. Information about the National Long-Term Care Ombudsman Resource Center can be found at this Web site: http://www.ltcombudsman.org/. Go to the map of the United States, and find the office in the state where you reside. Prepare a presentation on the information on older adults and aging that you find at this Web site.
3. The National Committee for the Prevention of Elder Abuse (NCPEA) maintains a Web site that features many resources to help understand the complexities of abuse and neglect committed against an older adult. Visit http://www.preventelderabuse.org/index .html, and find information on recognizing the signs of abuse.
4. The National Center on Elder Abuse (NCEA) works to improve the national response to elder abuse and exploitation. They have published the first ever report from the National Adult Maltreatment Center in 2017. Go to https://ncea.acl.gov/ and report on your findings.

References

Acierno, R., Hernandez-Tejada, M., Muzzy, W., & Steve, K. (2009). The National Elder Mistreatment Study. Retrieved from https://www.ncjrs.gov/pdffiles1/nij/grants/226456.pdf

Acierno, R., Hernandez, M. A., Amstadter, A. B., Resnick, H. S., Steve, K., Muzzy, W., & Kilpatrick, D. G. (2010). Prevalence and correlates of emotional, physical, sexual, and financial abuse and potential neglect in the United States: The National Elder Mistreatment Study. *American Journal of Public Health, 100*(2), 292–297.

Administration on Aging. (2011). A profile of older Americans: 2011. Retrieved from http://www.aoa.gov/AoA-Root/Aging_Statistics/Profile/2011/docs/2011profile.pdf

Alzheimer's Association. (2012). Alzheimer's caregivers: Behavioral vs. cognitive challenges. Retrieved from http://www.alzfdn.org/Surveys/Alzheimer%27s%20Caregivers%20Study%20090612.pdf

American Psychiatric Association. (1979). Battered parents—A new syndrome. *American Journal of Psychiatry, 136*(10), 1288–1291.

American Psychological Association. (APA). (2012). Elder abuse and neglect: In search of solutions. Retrieved from http://www.apa.org/pi/aging/eldabuse.html

Amstadter, A. B., Cisler, J. M., McCauley, J. L., Hernandez, M. A., Muzzy, W., & Acierno, R. (2010). Do incident and perpetrator characteristics of elder mistreatment differ by gender of the victim? Results from The National Elder Mistreatment Study. *Journal of Elder Abuse & Neglect, 23*(1), 43–57.

APA. (2015). *Understanding mental disorders: Your guide to DSM-5.* Washington, D.C.: American Psychiatric Publishing.

Attorney General. (2013). Massachusetts Bank Reporting Project. Retrieved from http://www.mass.gov/ago/consumer-resources/consumer-information/resources-for-elders/bank-reporting-project.html

Biggs, S., Phillipson, C., & Kingston, P. (Eds.). (1995). *Elder abuse in perspective.* Bristol, PA: Open University Press.

Bonomi, A., Anderson, M., Reid, R., Carrell, D., Fishman, P., Rivara, F., & Thompson, S. (2007). Intimate partner violence in older women. *The Gerontologist, 47*(1), 34–41.

Bureau of Justice Statistics. (BJS). (2012). Violent crime against the elderly reported by law enforcement in Michigan, 2005–2009. *Special Report: National Incident-Based Reporting System.* Washington, D.C.: Department of Justice.

Burgess, A. (2006). *Elderly victims of sexual abuse and their offenders.* Washington, D.C.: U.S. Department of Justice.

Finkelhor, D., & Pillemer, K. (1988). Elder abuse: Its relationship to other forms of domestic violence. In G. Hotaling, D. Finkelhor, J. Kirkpatrick, & M. Straus (Eds.), *Family abuse and its consequences: New directions in research* (pp. 244–254). Newbury Park, CA: Sage.

Government Accountability Office (GAO). (2011). Elder justice: Stronger federal leadership could enhance national response to elder abuse. Retrieved from http://www.gao.gov/assets/320/316224.pdf

Government Accountability Office (GAO). (2012). Elder justice: National strategy needed to effectively combat elder financial exploitation. Retrieved from http://www.gao.gov/assets/660/650074.pdf

Hall, J., Karch, D., & Crosby, A. (2016). *Elder abuse surveillance: Uniform definitions and recommended core data elements* Atlanta, GA: Centers for Disease Control and Prevention.

Hammerschlag, M. R. (1996). *Portable guides to investigating child abuse.* Washington, D.C.: U.S. Department of Justice.

Hawes, C., & Kimbell, A. M. (2010). Detecting, addressing and preventing elder abuse in residential care facilities. Retrieved from https://www.ncjrs.gov/pdffiles1/nij/grants/229299.pdf

Jackson, S. L., & Hafemeister, T. L. (2011). Financial abuse of elderly people vs. other forms of elder abuse: Assessing their dynamics, risk factors, and society's response. Retrieved from https://www.ncjrs.gov/pdffiles1/nij/grants/233613.pdf

Kung, H.-C., Hoyert, D., Xu, J., & Murphy, S. (2008). Deaths: Final data for 2005. *National Vital Statistics Reports, 56*(10), 121.

Lachs, M. S., & Pillemer, K. A. (2015). Elder abuse. *New England Journal of Medicine, 373*(20), 1947–1956.

Laumann, E. O., Leitsch, S. A., & Waite, L. J. (2008). Elder mistreatment in the United States: Prevalence estimates from a nationally representative study. *The Journals of Gerontology. Series B, Psychological Sciences and Social Sciences, 63*(4), S248–S254.

McNamee, C., & Murphy, M. (2006). Elder abuse in the United States. *National Institute of Justice Journal,* (255), 16–20.

MetLife. (2011). The MetLife study of elder financial abuse: Crimes of occasion, desperation, and predation against America's elders. Retrieved from https://www.metlife.com/mmi/research/elder-financial-abuse.html#key_findings

National Association of Triads (NATI). (2008). Communities working to keep seniors safe. Retrieved from http://www.nationaltriad.org/index.htm

National Center for the Prevention of Elder Abuse. (2008). Multidisciplinary teams. Retrieved from http://www.preventelderabuse.org/elderabuse/communities/mdt.html

The National Center for Victims of Crime. (2008). Crime clock. Retrieved from http://ovc.ncjrs.gov/gallery/posters/pdfs/Crime_Clock.pdf

National Center on Elder Abuse (NCEA). (2012). Abuse of residents of long term care facilities. *Research Brief*. Retrieved from http://www.ncea.aoa.gov /Resources/Publication/docs/LTCF_ResearchBrief_web508.pdf

National Clearinghouse on Abuse in Later Life. (2013). Information: What is abuse in later life? Retrieved from http://www.ncall.us/information/landing

National Council on Aging (NCOA). (2013). Elder abuse fact sheet. Retrieved from http://www.ncoa.org/public-policy-action/health-care-reform/elder-justice/elder-abuse-fact-sheet.html

Nerenberg, L. (2003). *Elder abuse prevention teams: A new generation*. Washington, D.C.: National Center on Elder Abuse.

Older Americans Act Amendments. (2006). Pub. Law No. 109–365. Retrieved from http://www.gpo.gov/fdsys /pkg/PLAW-109publ365/html/PLAW-109publ365.htm

Ramsey-Klawsnik, H. (1991). Elder sexual abuse: Preliminary findings. *Journal of Elder Abuse & Neglect, 3*(3), 73–89.

Stiegel, L., & Klem, E. (2007). Reporting requirements: Provisions and citations in adult protective services laws, by state. Retrieved from http://www.americanbar.org/content/dam/aba/migrated/aging/docs/MandatoryReportingProvisionsChart.authcheckdam.pdf

Suicide Awareness Voices of Education (SAVE). (2013). Suicide facts. Retrieved from http://www.save.org/index.cfm?fuseaction=home.viewPage&page_id=705D5DF4-055B-F1EC-3F66462866FCB4E6

Teaster, P., Dugar, T., Mendiono, M., Abner, E., & Cecil, K. (2006). *The 2004 survey of state adult protective services: Abuse of adults 60 years of age and older*. Lexington, KY: The University of Kentucky.

Truman, J., & Morgan, R. (2016). *Criminal victimization, 2015*. Bureau of Justice Statistics.

Vincent, G., & Velkoff, V. (2010). The next four decades, The older population in the United States: 2010 to 2050. *Current Population Reports*. Washington, D.C.: U.S. Census Bureau.

11

Adult Perpetrators

CHAPTER OBJECTIVES

After reviewing this chapter, you should be able to:

1. Identify the characteristics of IPV offenders.
2. Give examples of intimate violence typologies, and explain how they may help criminal justice professionals better protect the survivors.
3. Discuss the policy recommended by the International Association of Chiefs of Police in dealing with police officer batterers.
4. Explain the criminal justice interventions on military installations.
5. Discuss pet abuse in the context of family violence.

KEY TERMS

Antisocial batterer

Dysphoric or borderline offender

Exploder offender

Family-only offender

Generally violent or antisocial offender

High-risk offender

Sociopathic batterer

Tyrannical offender

INTRODUCTION

This chapter is about intimate partner violence (IPV) offenders. As a society, we have come a long way in recognizing and responding to IPV. Since 1993, the rate of nonfatal IPV has declined. Advocates claim that the decline is due to improved services for battered women, such as hotlines and shelters. The criminalization of IPV has also played a large role. Criminal justice professionals point to the increased involvement of law enforcement and the courts, which have provided sanctions for IPV. We must also credit education of the public. IPV is recognized as a significant health risk to society; as such, it cannot be ignored. As you have seen in the previous chapters, we have learned a lot about IPV and its survivors.

In this chapter, you will learn about the perpetrators of IPV. Descriptions of the offenders and the risks that they pose are the focus. Controlling tactics and methods of intimidation are part of the IPV cycle. All professionals need to be sensitized to all forms of family violence, regardless of preexisting notions about gender and perpetration. Increasingly, more female and male victims report the abuse to the police than they did in the 1990s (Durose et al., 2005). Researchers are also finding that a significant number of family violence survivors go directly to courts for civil orders of protection, bypassing the police (Klein, 2009). In some jurisdictions, more family violence is reported to the courts than to police departments.

ABUSER CHARACTERISTICS

The theories on the causes of family violence still do not tell us much about the individual batterer. What type of person commits violence in an intimate partner relationship? What behaviors indicate an abusive partner? Studies show a strong relationship between alcohol and/or drugs and IPV committed by men against women (Thompson & Kingree, 2006). Aggression has also been linked with psychoactive drugs such as barbiturates, amphetamines, opiates, phencyclidine, cocaine, and alcohol–cocaine combinations (Fagan, 1990).

From a review of the literature, Hanson (2002) characterizes individual batterers as clinically assessed problematic individuals displaying poor impulse control, aggression, fear of intimacy, emotional dependence, fear of abandonment, and impaired ego functioning. Mental health diagnoses for batterers range from obsessive–compulsive, paranoid, borderline personality, passive–aggressive, narcissistic, to antisocial (Hanson, 2002).

Significant controversy exists as to whether it is possible to predict future violent behavior as a means of protecting family violence survivors. The Spousal Assault Risk Assessment Guide (SARA) is one tool that has been developed to help determine whether an offender is at risk for future offending by classifying individuals into high- and low-risk categories (Dutton & Kropp, 2000). Used extensively by criminal justice professionals, it has been tested and found to illustrate good predictive validity of offender recidivism (Wong, 2008). The 20-question interview is not a controlled psychological test; therefore, it can be used by practitioners with some training (Dutton & Kropp, 2000). Community responses and multidisciplinary teams are becoming involved in the protection of survivors to a greater degree through high-risk offender assessment.

Legislation passed in recent years has included strong measures allowing police officers to arrest offenders and the courts to issue protective orders. We have learned that not all abusers are men, that not all men are abusers, and that there are degrees of seriousness in domestic violence cases. In other words, not all family violence is the same. We are moving into the phase in which different approaches may be considered to respond to different offenders, based on their risk of offending, motivations, and the population that they target. The profile of a domestic abuser as a serial recidivist is emerging. New measures will address this concept of family violence. New York is one of the first states that are raising the bar in holding serial domestic perpetrators more accountable. As of 2013, enhanced penalties are in place through an Aggravated Family Offense law, which allows law enforcement to prosecute family abusers as felons in certain situations (New York S 240.75).

The most frequent form of family violence is simple assault, and approximately three-quarters of the incidents occur in or near the victim's residence (Durose et al., 2005). Violence committed against a boyfriend or girlfriend is most likely to result in a conviction, with sentencing to a state or federal prison or in a local jail. Refer to Figure 11-1.

Gender and Age

Most offenders of IPV are men who perpetrate against women, but some women also offend. The NCVS provides information on the prevalence of the crime committed, the relationship between the victim and the offender, and the demographics of both

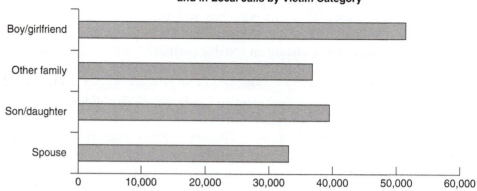

Convicted Family Violence Offenders in State and Federal Prisons and in Local Jails by Victim Category

FIGURE 11-1 Convicted family violence offenders that are sentenced to jail or prison are most likely to have committed violence against a boyfriend or girlfriend. Based on data from Durose et al., 2005.

(Durose et al., 2005). Analysis of this source tells us that men are the overwhelming majority of offenders of IPV and women are the primary victims (Figure 11-2). Violent crimes against a spouse, approximately 86 percent of the offenders are men; against a boyfriend or girlfriend, 82 percent of the perpetrators are men, according to the NCVS. Female offenders, while comprising smaller percentages of perpetrators, add up to significant numbers. Almost 80 percent of family violence offenders are white (Durose et al., 2005).

Those who offend in intimate partner relationships can be found in all age groups, although general patterns have been identified from two major sources. According to Klein, most studies find that perpetrators tend to be between the ages of 18 and 35 with a median age of about 33 years (Klein, 2008). The NCVS reports that most intimate

FIGURE 11-2 The majority of family violence offenders are white males, ages 30 and older. Image copyright Artem Furman. Used under license from Shutterstock.com.

partner abuse offenders (73 percent) are age 30 or older. Those who abuse in a dating relationship tend to be younger; about one-half of the offenders are between the ages of 18 and 29.

Descriptions of the Offender

The following descriptors have developed from studies on the battering male. Although illustrating the characteristics of an abusive man, they are applicable to either gender of offender. These behaviors have been attributed to the perpetrators in heterosexual, homosexual, and lesbian relationships; elder and child battering; and to female offenders.

CONTROLLING BEHAVIORS   A tendency for the abuser to dominate the victim has been noted in the various forms of IPV. Sometimes, the control is due to jealousy; the perpetrator often seeks control over the victim's time, dress, and behavior. Controlling behaviors show contempt and a general lack of respect for the partner.

Insulting behavior and put-downs are techniques used to attack the confidence of the victim and to ensure future dominance. Calling a partner a "bitch" or similar derogatory terms devalues the person. An abuser may refer to the other as a "pig," "lousy housekeeper," "bad mother," or "lousy father." The use of derogatory language in addressing one's partner may start as the intimates develop a familiarity with each other. Such a pattern is not legally prohibited. It signifies emotional abuse, however, which often accompanies physical battering. Name-calling and insulting language have indirect effects on IPV by facilitating conflict between intimate partners (Stalans & Ritchie, 2008).

FEAR AND INTIMIDATION   Fear and intimidation is achieved through violence or the perception of impending violence. Victims of repetitive abuse recall a particular "look" from the offender that serves as a warning signal of an explosion that is about to occur. A raised fist or hand in a threatening gesture serves the same purpose.

Firearm use or display in or around the house or at pets is a severe form of intimidation. It is the ultimate display of power. Even the presentation of a weapon raises the level of acceptable violence that is difficult to decrease. Any direct or indirect threat that involves a gun or other weapon should not be taken lightly because of the desperation it signifies.

ANIMAL CRUELTY   Adults who perpetrate IPV often abuse the victims' pet(s) as a means to control and intimidate the survivor. One of the first empirical analyses of the prevalence of animal maltreatment in a small sample of battered women in shelters found that 71 percent of women who reported current or past pet ownership reported that their partner had threatened and/or actually hurt or killed one or more of their pets (Ascione, 1998). Fifty-seven percent of the reports involved actual rather than threatened harm to pets.

MANIPULATION   Abusers have been characterized as the masters of manipulation. After an abusive attack, it is not unusual for the offender to beg for forgiveness. Gifts and flowers may accompany the statements that he or she will never "do it" again. Another destructive behavior is the unrealistic demand for proof of love or loyalty that is characteristic of abusive dating relationships. Coercion into sexual relations as a condition of a continued relationship can be extremely dangerous for the victim during a dating relationship.

EXCESSIVE RULE MAKING When a partner makes rules that the other must follow, it signifies an unequal relationship based on dominance. One way to recognize this pattern is to notice when a penalty or punishment is attached to the failure to fulfill expectations. A healthy request does not begin with the phrase "you had better...," and it is not followed with the statement "or else...." Taking back a gift or present because "you are not a good girl" indicates an anticipation of rule following by the abuser. It implies that some form of punishment will result for unfulfilled expectations.

ISOLATION Demands for constant attention to the exclusion of friends and family are one form of isolating the victim. Although it may be attractive in the beginning of a relationship, it becomes a form of isolation when the abuser insists on being the sole focus of the victim's life. Extreme forms include demands that the victim must not work or denial of transportation to leave the home. These accomplish economic and physical isolation that cuts the victim off from resources or protection from abuse. The choice to reside in isolated areas of the country may stem from a batterer's calculated decision. Control tactics include removing the phone receiver (when the batterer goes to work), disabling or destroying motor vehicles to limit the victim's mobility, closely monitoring the odometer reading on motor vehicles, and locking the thermostat in the winter (as a form of torture).

The victims of IPV who reside in rural areas face unique isolation issues. Geographic isolation increases vulnerability and places these rural victims at a disadvantage to obtaining services (Eastman, Bunch, Williams, & Carawan, 2007). A general lack of available services and long distances are identified barriers, causing frustration to victims who are living in secluded areas. Research also suggests that vast differences exist between the processes of protective orders in rural areas versus urban areas. In some counties of Kentucky, for example, the nonservice rate of restraining orders is as high as 91 percent (Logan, Shannon, & Walker, 2005). By not being able to serve the abuser, the order of protection cannot be enforced and is of little value. Regardless of federal regulations prohibiting states from receiving Violence Against Women funds if fees are imposed for restraining orders, researchers found that some women in rural areas are being charged for delivery (Logan et al., 2005). The service fee and doubts about whether the order will even be served constitute critical barriers to the safety of rural victims.

Styles of Violence

The majority of domestic violence offenders that come to the attention of criminal justice or court authorities have a prior criminal history for nonviolent and violent offenses against males as well as females (Klein, 2009). Perpetrators of family violence commit crimes of a domestic or nondomestic nature. From the perspective of offenders themselves, two violent styles used by men against women have been identified: the tyrannical offender and the explosive offender. The **tyrannical offender** is one who feels justified in using aggression, intimidation, verbal abuse, and physical assault to control and dominate the partner. The **exploder offender** is one who experiences the violence in a sudden and explosive manner, typically in response to criticism or challenge by the partner.

Both offender groups use violence as a method of response to intolerable emotions of anxiety or anger, and they are unable to understand the violence in terms of its impact on their partner. The characteristics of tyrannical offending versus exploder offending are described below (James, Seddon, & Brown, 2002):

Tyrannical Offender Characteristics

- Knows what he is doing and intends to frighten, intimidate, and punish his partner
- Sees his violence as a justified or understandable response to frustration and anger
- Tends to minimize his violence by admitting to having committed verbal abuse
- Describes his partner as being submissive and careful around him

Exploder Offender Characteristics

- Uses the violence to get distance from his partner and to silence her
- Usually acknowledges that he has used violence but blames his partner for provoking him

The **sociopathic batterer** is the type of offender who is likely to have a diagnosable personality disorder or a problem with substance abuse. Threats to kill or commit more violence are associated with this type of offender, along with a tendency to make sexual demands after committing the violence. These batterers are not apologetic and sometimes use religious beliefs to justify the violence. The most dangerous group of offenders is that of the antisocial batterers. The **antisocial batterer** is an individual with a diagnosable mental illness or personality disorder, a substance abuse problem, and is more likely to have a criminal record.

High-Risk Offenders

Most researchers agree that intimate partner battering is a pattern of behavior that follows somewhat predictable stages. In severe cases, the **high-risk offender** is one who beats his partner as frequently as 60 times per year. In contrast, the offender that is not high risk typically commits battering approximately five times per year (Straus, 1993). The length of time in each battering stage can vary from hours to weeks.

Education groups for men who batter frequently use the *power and control wheel* developed by the Duluth model to illustrate the elements of a battering relationship. At the core of the cycle is the element of power and control—all abusive actions committed by the batterer are viewed as the means to dominate and control the partner. Each cog in the wheel represents a form of behavior that in total makes up the abusive conduct. This wheel represents the feminist idea of the battering relationship.

Straus suggests two criteria to help identify high-risk offender cases (Straus, 1993): *Criterion A*—That the suspect initiated three or more instances of violence in the preceding year. *Criterion B*—That the suspect threatened a partner with a weapon in hand or verbally threatened to kill the partner. There are numerous red-flag indicators that assist in identifying high-risk offender cases. Examples include situations in which severe injury is inflicted on the victim that requires medical treatment (regardless of whether it was obtained) or injury that was caused to a child. The offender may be a high risk to seriously batter if he was physically abused as a child or witnessed severe violence between his parents. Typically, a high-risk offender is extremely domineering and feels justified in hitting or physically forcing sex on a partner. We now recognize that killing or injuring a pet and threats to kill or injure a pet are signs of a high-risk offender.

Straus (1993) questions the appropriateness of applying criminal justice sanctions to all family disputes. Acknowledging that the police and courts are not equipped to understand the unique circumstances of each family that can lead to violence, he argues that they also cannot be expected to determine what might be in the best interest of the victim, the offender, or the family. In addition, numerous reports have indicated that in approximately half of the cases, women are the first to commit a physical assault. If men are arrested for "only" slapping their wives a few times, should not women receive equal treatment? "If even half of the intimate partner assaults came to the attention of the police, the courts would have to deal with literally millions of such incidents and would be overwhelmed" (Straus, 1993).

A promising development toward managing high-risk offenders and reducing domestic-related homicide has come from a model developed by the Jeanne Geiger Crisis Center of Newburyport, Massachusetts. Its nationally acclaimed team approach focuses on early risk assessment of domestic offenders, a case-specific response, and offender monitoring (Jeanne Geiger Crisis Center, 2012). The center claims that from the 106 high-risk offenders screened in over a period of six years, no homicides have resulted.

THE ROLE OF ALCOHOL AND DRUG USE

Studies have long linked drug and alcohol abuse with male-perpetrated IPV. The link between female offending and substance abuse is less clear. Some evidence exists suggesting that males are also at an increased risk of victimization by an intimate partner due to substance abuse (Schneider, Burnette, Ilgen, & Timko, 2009). Drug and alcohol use are not the cause of violence, but there is a significant relationship between excessive drinking and drug use with violence against intimate partners. The association is contributory rather than causal. Substance abuse increases the risk of IPV occurring. Studies have shown that substance abuse also increases the severity of injury to the victim.

The NCVS asks victims to indicate whether they thought the offender was drinking or on drugs at the time of the criminal incident. In response, victims stated that more than 40 percent of spousal offenders were under the influence of alcohol or drugs at the time of the incident (Durose et al., 2005). The survey also found the rate of intoxication to be similar for offenders who abused their boyfriend or girlfriend (41.4 percent).

Illicit drug use is strongly associated with IPV. Relationship conflict, including insults and psychological abuse, is further escalated by the use/abuse of marijuana in groups of offenders who have already experienced high levels of stress (Stalans & Ritchie, 2008). Stimulant and sedative abuse also increases the likelihood of committing IPV, according to the Stalans study (2008). Insulting behavior inherent in psychological abuse and drug use may be significant predictors of IPV occurrence.

Along with IPV, alcohol abuse presents a major public health problem in the United States. In a study concerning the role of alcohol use in IPV outcomes, authors point out that more than 7 percent of the population, approximately 14 million Americans, meets the diagnostic criteria for alcoholism (Thompson & Kingree, 2006). Their research found that there are gender differences in alcohol use and the risk of injury. For women, past frequency of abuse and fear of life endangerment were predictive of injury risk by their male partner. Women were more likely to report victimization to the police when they had been victimized six or more times and feared life endangerment. Nonwhite women were more likely to report the incident to the police than white women. For a man abused by a female intimate partner, her use of a weapon and fear of life endangerment were predictive of injury risk. Men were more likely to report victimization when the female partners were drinking while the men were not drinking. Victim use of alcohol did not increase the risk of injury in this study.

Substance Abuse and Male Offenders

Men have been found to be 3.1 times more likely than women to have used alcohol or drugs prior to their arrest for IPV (Simmons & Lehmann, 2007). Severe drinking problems increase the risk for violent victimization of women in intimate partner relationships, including the risk of homicide (Sharps, Campbell, Campbell, Gary, & Webster, 2003).

Researchers have recommended that future responses to IPV should include

1. Testing assailants at the time of arrest for alcohol or other drug intoxication,
2. Detoxifying arrested drug- or alcohol-dependent assailants prior to release from jail,
3. Assessing children who directly witness IPV to determine whether psychological treatment is needed, and
4. Allowing intimate partner assault victims to swear out arrest warrants at the scene.

Experts agree that substance abuse problems and IPV overlap and that they often co-occur. However, substance abuse and IPV are different problems, and they require different interventions. There are multiple causes for both substance abuse and IPV; little evidence suggests that one problem causes the other.

Substance Abuse and Female Offenders

Research consistently indicates that a large portion of women in treatment for substance-related diagnoses use violence within their relationship. Additionally, male victims of IPV report that their female abusers often have a history of alcohol and/or drug abuse (Hines, Brown, & Dunning, 2007). According to the limited literature on female domestic violence offenders, some conclude that women may have more in common with male domestic violence offenders than was previously thought (Carney, Buttell, & Dutton, 2007).

Although most of the literature on domestic violence offending has focused on men as perpetrators, research on female perpetration is slowly emerging. Some research suggests that women are similar to men in terms of their use of violence in inflicting severe injuries on their partner, use of violence against nonintimates, and usage of alcohol and/or drugs at the time of their arrest (Busch & Rosenberg, 2004). A definite link between substance abuse and female perpetration has been established in a study on the arrests of women who commit IPV wherein almost half of the court-referred women met the criteria for being problem drinkers (Stuart, Moore, Ramsey, & Kahler, 2004). In another study (Simmons & Lehmann, 2007), researchers concluded that women arrested on domestic violence charges are at an increased risk of being substance abusers.

It has become increasingly clear that women use violence against men in intimate partner relationships. Substance abuse is consistently found to be a significant factor in perpetration. IPV batterers' treatment programs continue as the primary policy response to these crimes. Some suggest that the need for substance-related treatment of women arrested for IPV is not significant (Simmons & Lehmann, 2007). Others argue that the models based on male-perpetrated violence are in desperate need of adaptation to meet the unique needs of females who offend (Bair-Merritt et al., 2010). Studies on the characteristics of female IPV offenders continue to surface and inform on the role of substance abuse in this population of offenders.

Substance Abuse and Older Adults

Substance abuse is also linked to domestic violence against older adults. In all forms of elder mistreatment, family members are the perpetrators in more than half the cases. Researchers that conducted the 2009 *National Elder Mistreatment Study* documented the role of substance abuse in older adult victimization (Acierno, Hernandez-Tejada, Muzzy, & Steve, 2009). They found that one-fifth of the known offenders have been identified as abusing substances around the time of their emotional mistreatment of older adults. Perpetrators of physical assault are even more likely to have been abusing substances at the time of assault; 50 percent had a substance abuse problem at the time of the abuse. Where the perpetrator was known in cases of sexual abuse against an older adult, over 28 percent had substance abuse problems. Relative to homicide of older adults by a caregiver, Karch and Nunn (2011) found substance abuse to be among the characteristics of the perpetrators.

Having family members who have substance abuse problems is also identified as likely to increase the risk of elder financial abuse (Jackson & Hafemeister, 2011). If the substance abuse of the adult child increases, the offender may become more violent in general or in the demand for the elder's assets. Researchers that conducted the *National Elder Mistreatment Study* discovered that financial exploitation by family members was unexpectedly common, occurring in over 5 percent of respondents (Acierno et al., 2009). Older adults and those who need assistance with activities of daily living are considered most at risk.

THE ROLE OF ANIMAL CRUELTY

As far back as 1991, Murray Straus included previous animal cruelty as an assessment criterion for predicting future lethal violence against women (Dutton & Kropp, 2000). There is renewed interest in the link between IPV and animal abuse. Violence against pets is considered to be a predictor of adult violence in children (Figure 11-3). The threat of violence against a pet is a strong predictor of violence against the intimate partner. Since the seminal study of Ascione (1998), researchers have continued to find evidence of a link between animal cruelty and IPV. Findings from one study indicate that batterers who also abuse their pet use more forms of violence and demonstrate greater use of controlling behaviors than batterers who do not abuse their pets (Simmons & Lehmann, 2007). A substantial relationship has been found between specific controlling behaviors and cruelty to pets. In other research, authors found that severe physical violence was a significant predictor of animal abuse (Ascione et al., 2007). The study found that women in domestic violence shelters were almost 11 times more likely to report that their partner had hurt or killed their pets compared with a group of women who had not experienced IPV.

Pet abuse has been shown to influence the decision of abused women to seek safety. Abusers harm pets to punish the victim for leaving or to coerce him or her to

FIGURE 11-3 When a child abuses an animal, it is a red flag as a risk factor for the child offending as an adult. The link between animal abuse and IPV is so strong that many states now include the protection of animals as a category in domestic violence restraining orders. Image copyright imageegami. Used under license from Shutterstock.com.

return. According to cruelty connections, history is full of high-profile examples of the dangerous connection between perpetrating violence and animal abuse (http://pet-abuse.com, 2008). For example, Luke Woodham, age 16, killed his mother in Pearl, Mississippi, in 1997. He tortured animals before embarking on shooting sprees where he also killed two students and wounded six others. Luke described how he and an accomplice beat his dog, Sparkle, and then set it on fire and threw it in a pond. "I'll never forget the sound of her breaking under my might. I hit her so hard I knocked the fur off her neck … it was true beauty," he wrote (Mendoza, 2002).

If a batterer assaults or mutilates pets, he is more likely to kill a partner (Meuer, Seymour, & Wallace, 2002). The killing of a pet is meant to convey the message, "You could be next." For the many victims of IPV, there is no such thing as an idle threat. A commentary entitled *Domestic Violence and Animal Abuse: The Deadly Connection* reported on a study of 111 battered women who sought shelter; almost half stated that their current or former male partners had threatened or abused their animals (Cohen & Keweller, 2000). Cited was an example where a man, whose wife went to a shelter, sent her a picture of him using gardening shears to chop off the ears of his wife's dog. After receiving the photo, the wife told the shelter counselor she had to go home to save the lives of her dog and other animals. Abusers harm animals to punish their wives for leaving and for real or imagined injustices. Common types of cruelty include torture, shooting, stabbing, drowning, burning, and bone breaking.

As a result of the research surrounding the connection between animal violence and violence against humans, 47 states, the District of Columbia, Guam, Puerto Rico, and the Virgin Islands have enacted laws making certain types of animal cruelty a felony offense (Addington & Randour, 2012). Since Maine became the first state to include the protection of animals in cases of domestic violence in 2006, it has been joined by an additional 21 states, the District of Columbia, and Puerto Rico (Wisch, 2012). These states provide animal protection through domestic violence protection orders. No data for instances of animal cruelty are currently collected at the federal level through the UCR or NIBRS. However, 18 states do receive animal cruelty data, and the classification is being considered (Addington & Randour, 2012).

POLICE OFFICER OFFENDERS

Of particular concern to professionals is the abuser who is legitimately carrying a firearm for work, business, or pleasure. Acts of IPV by a police officer against a partner are estimated to be at least as common as acts committed by the general population. Limited research indicates the possibility of higher incident rates of IPV among law-enforcement professionals. In the few large-scale studies that have been conducted, the rate of physical abuse was approximately 7 percent to 8 percent, in contrast to 10 percent in the general population (Erwin, Gershon, Tiburzi, & Lin, 2005). One study reported higher rates: Between 20 percent and 40 percent of police families experience family violence. The International Association of Chiefs of Police (IACP) takes the position that the problem exists at a serious level and deserves careful attention regardless of estimated occurrences.

Research also indicates that documentation of such incidents by departments varies dramatically, with some incidents reported in great detail, others handled through informal actions, and still others undocumented in any way. Departmental positions on police officer IPV also differ significantly: Some departments have clear "zero tolerance" positions, other departments have less-defined positions, and still others have no articulated position at all (Lonsway & Conis, 2003). The exact prevalence of police officer battering is unknown.

In cooperation with the Office on Violence Against Women, IACP worked to develop a comprehensive policy response for reports of police battering. The IACP 2003 policy on *Domestic Violence by Police Officers* establishes the policy and procedures for handling IPV committed by police officers. It recognizes that federal law prohibits police officers convicted of qualifying misdemeanor IPV crimes from possessing firearms and states that officers found guilty of an IPV crime through criminal proceedings shall be terminated (IACP, 2003).

Authoritarianism—physical and psychological domination—is recognized as a component of the policing job, which may create occupational stress for the individual while off duty. The tragic case in 2003 when Chief David Brame of the Tacoma Police Department shot himself and his wife, Crystal, in front of their two children brought media attention to the problem. On June 13, 2012, Officer Kevin Ambrose of the Springfield Police Department responded to a domestic violence call in the city and was shot and killed by Shawn Bryan, a Rikers Island corrections officer. After the incident, Officer Bryan killed himself. Such tragedies have left many wondering whether something more could have been done to prevent these incidents.

Researchers have examined how police officer stress might affect the likelihood of becoming a domestic violence offender. Potential risk factors causing occupational stress that have been identified are shift rotation and weekend work, exposure to danger on the job, and the presence of weapons in the home (Wetendorf, 2006). Officers may also experience emotional exhaustion and burnout rising to the level of posttraumatic stress disorder (PTSD). Recent research suggests that police officers may experience PTSD at higher levels than the general population, rendering them up to four times more likely to engage in domestic violence against an intimate or family member (Oehme, Donnelly, & Martin, 2012).

To better understand the frequency and type of IPV filed against police officers, researchers looked at 106 reports filed with a department's Internal Investigation Division from 1992 to 1998 (Erwin et al., 2005). The majority of the case reports involved middle-aged male patrol officers, with an average age of 34. Most (70 percent) were from a racial/ethnic minority group and had been on the job for an average of eight years. Most of the police officers had been assigned to high-crime precincts. Most perpetrators were men (83 percent), and the remaining cases involved women police officer perpetrators. The majority of the accused officers were suspended immediately with a small portion arrested. The vast majority (92 percent) of cases were dropped for lack of testimony, lack of physical evidence, and conflicting testimony.

Anderson and Lo (2010) reanalyzed over 1,000 questionnaires from full-time police participants in the Baltimore Police Stress and Domestic Violence study of 1997–1999. The majority of participants were white (65 percent) males (86 percent). While 9 percent of the officers admitted to using force against an intimate partner, African American male and female officers were most likely to have offended. Female officers were 60 percent more likely to use aggression against their partners as compared to the male officers. Clearly, further research is needed to look into this phenomenon.

Consistent with research regarding risk factors for abusing among the general population, there is a strong association between perpetration of domestic violence and alcohol abuse among police officers (Oehme et al., 2012). Officers who reported hazardous drinking or dependent drinking patterns were four to eight times more likely to use physical violence in an intimate or family relationship as those without alcohol risk factors. Hazardous drinking is a pattern of alcohol consumption that produces physical and psychological health consequences, typically with four or more days of drinking per week. Dependent drinking is when an individual needs alcohol to function or feel good. Both patterns produce risk factors that require intervention study (Oehme et al., 2012).

Been There ... Done That!

A frequent complaint is that IPV perpetrated by police officers is not taken seriously when the victim complains. In one case, both the victim and the perpetrator were police officers. The male batterer had "backhanded" the female police officer's nine-year-old daughter, giving her a black eye. During an argument over the woman's smoking behavior, the perpetrator repeatedly beat her on the head. The relationship was characterized by extreme jealously and controlling behaviors. Embarrassment and the belief that no one would believe her kept the woman from reporting the abuse.

He stalked her when she left the house for any reason. The perpetrator interfered with her work on numerous occasions. These behaviors included him unplugging the phone when she was on call to more overt efforts of storming into her workplace, falsely accusing her of being unfaithful. The relationship nearly became deadly when she left him ... she held him off at gunpoint and got into her car. In this case, there was unofficial support from the department. She was hidden in a drug safe house for weeks until he had calmed down.

MILITARY PERSONNEL

Over 3.6 million persons make up the United States military forces and civilian ranks (Department of Defense, 2010). IPV committed by military personnel is challenging due to the unique nature of the military services. First is the problem of jurisdiction. Many families live outside of military installations. According to a RAND study on domestic-violence-related arrest requirements, any family or IPV incident that occurs off the military installation is under the jurisdiction of local civilian authorities (Hickman & Davis, 2003). In fact, civilian authorities may also be the first responders and may even have jurisdiction over incidents that occur on installations. The process for civilian arrest and protection order violation arrest varies greatly by state. The Department of Defense has taken a strong proactive position against family and IPV. The military process for domestic violence prevention is outlined in Figure 11-4.

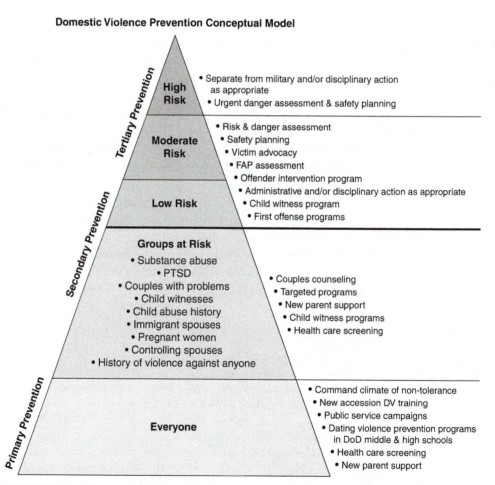

FIGURE 11-4 The Department of Defense has outlined its Domestic Violence Prevention Conceptual Model by intervention to targeted at-risk groups of military personnel. Based on data from the Department of Defense, 2003.

Military Offenders

Military-related victims fail to report for reasons similar to those of other victims of IPV. They experience shame, isolation, and financial concerns. The demographics of the military personnel present additional challenges that may amplify these issues. For example, members must move every three years, isolating the victim, who is unable to build a support system from friends and family. Because of the frequent moves, a spouse may be unable to obtain employment in all but low-level jobs, making financial concerns difficult to address.

Most active-duty military personnel are men (85.6 percent), many are young (under 25 years old), and many are married with children. Refer to Figure 11-5 (Department of Defense, 2010). In FY 2005, the abuser was typified as an active-duty member in 63 percent of the cases and a civilian spouse of an active duty member in the remaining 37 percent of cases (Erwin & Beals, 2007). The report reflected that 45 percent of the victims were active-duty members and the remaining victims were civilian spouses. There were 11 IPV fatalities in FY 2005. During the same year, intimate partner victims who obtained services self-reported physical abuse in 77 percent of the cases, 23 percent entailed emotional or verbal abuse only, and 6 percent involved sexual abuse.

In a study on family abuse by army soldiers, results showed that the majority of substantiated family violence offenders were intimate partner offenders who had not committed child abuse (61 percent), followed by child offenders who had not committed intimate partner abuse (27 percent), and finally those who had committed both spouse and child offenses (12 percent) (Martin et al., 2007). The types of abuse they perpetrated (neglect of children, emotional abuse, physical abuse, and sexual abuse), their experiences of being a spouse abuse victim, and sociodemographic characteristics differed among the offenders. Twelve percent of all intimate partner abusers committed multiple offenses, and 10 percent of all child abusers committed multiple child abuse incidents.

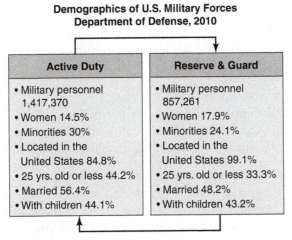

Demographics of U.S. Military Forces
Department of Defense, 2010

Active Duty	Reserve & Guard
• Military personnel 1,417,370	• Military personnel 857,261
• Women 14.5%	• Women 17.9%
• Minorities 30%	• Minorities 24.1%
• Located in the United States 84.8%	• Located in the United States 99.1%
• 25 yrs. old or less 44.2%	• 25 yrs. old or less 33.3%
• Married 56.4%	• Married 48.2%
• With children 44.1%	• With children 43.2%

FIGURE 11-5 The Department of Defense has taken positive steps toward addressing family violence within the military. As noted by these demographics, members are mostly young married men, many of whom have children. Based on data from the Department of Defense, 2010.

Reporting Options

In the past, all military personnel, except chaplains, were required to report any suspected domestic violence, regardless of how the suspicion arose or whether the victim wanted this information to be communicated to the command and others (Erwin et al., 2005). The person notified of the IPV was the perpetrator's boss. Therefore, victims were reluctant to report incidents of abuse for fear of negative career consequences. Confidentiality was not granted to victim advocates, social workers, therapists, or physicians. A new policy was signed into effect in August 2007 that attempted to balance the competing interests of holding abusers accountable for their actions and protecting victims and their children (Department of Defense, 2011). This Department of Defense policy has established two different reporting options for victims of intimate partner abuse: restricted reporting and unrestricted reporting.

Restricted Reporting

- Does not initiate the investigative process. Neither law enforcement nor the command is notified with personal identifiable information.
- Allows the victim of IPV to confidentially disclose to the victim advocate, the victim advocate supervisor, health care providers, or chaplains.
- The limitation to restricted reporting is that the offender is NOT held accountable and thus may continue to be abusive.
- The victim is not eligible to receive a military protective order and may still continue to have contact with the offender.
- If the assessment reveals a "high risk" for future injury or death, a restricted report may not be granted.
- If the victim discloses the abuse to someone other than the specified individuals, these actions may alert the command or law enforcement and may initiate an investigation and the report will become unrestricted.

The benefits of restricted reporting are that the victims are able to obtain medical treatment for their injuries, advocacy, and counseling. It provides the victims with some personal space and time to consider their options. The victims are able to control the release and management of their personal information. It may increase the victims' trust in the system. It may also encourage other victims to come forward.

Unrestricted Reporting

- Military policy favors unrestricted reporting.
- Command and investigative services are notified.
- Allows the victim to receive medical treatment, a forensic examination, advocacy services, clinical counseling, pastoral counseling, and protective services.

The benefits of unrestricted reporting are that the victim receives medical treatment, advocacy, and counseling. It also ensures the widest range of rights and protections for the victim, including military and civilian protective orders, commander support, and separation from the offender. A full investigation offers the opportunity to hold the offenders accountable for their actions (crime scene, witness interviews, and suspect interrogation). Among its limitations is that it cannot be changed to a restricted report once the decision is made and the investigation started. The victim may consider the investigative process intrusive because information about the domestic abuse incident will be in the public domain. It requires the victim to face the offender in court. In addition, the investigation

More About It: The 1996 Lautenberg Amendment

The victim of IPV whose abuser is in the military may hesitate to report abuse because of the impact it could have on the spouse's career. Criminal conviction of even a misdemeanor involving domestic violence can end a service member's military career. The Domestic Violence Amendment to the Gun Control Act of 1968 (1996 Lautenberg Amendment), AR 600-20, 4-23, makes it unlawful for anyone who has been convicted of a misdemeanor of domestic violence to possess firearms. The law applies equally to all, including law-enforcement officers and military personnel. Conviction means that the abuser will lose his or her right to carry a firearm. This amendment applies to all soldiers throughout the world, including those in hostile fire areas.

and court proceedings may be lengthy, without any guarantee that the offender will be convicted in either a court-martial or a civilian court. The reporting of IPV has the likelihood of negatively impacting the future career of the abuser.

ABUSIVE MEN

According to government studies that use arrest as a criterion, the majority of IPV perpetrators are men. They often have low self-esteem and are overly dependent on the victim. Most are extremely jealous and possessive. Almost always the abuser blames others for his actions and denies or minimizes the effects of his violence on his victims. Abusers often present a very different posture in public than they do in the privacy of their own homes. Although they may be charming on the outside, they can terrorize their partner behind closed doors. Risk factors for IPV include these individual factors:

- Aggressive and hostile personality
- Antisocial personality
- Depression
- Emotional dependency
- Insecurity
- Low impulse control
- Low empathy
- Low income
- Narcissism
- Poor communication and social skills
- Prior history of being physically abusive

Experts caution against a one-size-fits-all description of the male batterer, however. In a review of the different types of men who abuse their spouses, colleagues Holtzworth-Monroe and Stuart categorize three types of violent men, illustrated in Figure 11-6 (Holtzworth-Monroe & Stuart, 1994):

1. *Family-only offenders*—The perpetrators in this category may have a history of exposure to aggression in their family of origin. They rank as less deviant than the other two categories of men in areas of impulsivity, substance abuse, and criminal behavior. These men report low levels of anger, depression, and jealousy and are the least likely to have been severely abused as children. They claim the most satisfaction in their relationships, the least marital conflict, and the least psychological abuse. Their violence is associated with alcohol about half the time.

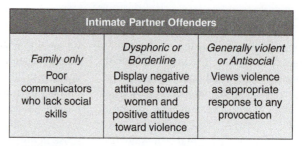

Intimate Partner Offenders		
Family only	*Dysphoric or Borderline*	*Generally violent or Antisocial*
Poor communicators who lack social skills	Display negative attitudes toward women and positive attitudes toward violence	Views violence as appropriate response to any provocation

FIGURE 11-6 One of the most respected typologies of violent men reveals three categories of intimate partner abuser. Based on data from Holtzworth-Monroe & Stuart, 1994.

2. *Dysphoric or borderline offenders*—These men are believed to have had a history of child abuse and parental rejection. Delinquent behavior has been an early indicator of problems for these men. They are marked by negative attitudes toward women and positive attitudes toward violence, coupled with low remorse. In addition, this group has a high dependency on their partners and poor social and communication skills. They are generally psychologically distressed. They do not engage in violence outside the home.

3. *Generally violent or antisocial offenders*—The batterer in this category is the most aggressive. He is profoundly deficient in communication and social skills. This abuser has developed antisocial behavior and views violence as an appropriate response to any provocation, due to his socialization. The majority of these offenders have been severely abused as children, yet they report low levels of depression and anger. Their lower level of anger may reflect an attitude of "I don't get mad; I get even." Their violence is usually associated with alcohol, and they report the most frequent severe violence. Their attitudes about sex roles are more rigid than those of family-only offenders.

Robert J. White and Edward W. Gondolf classified battering men by personality types with the intent to recommend treatment approaches for each type (White & Gondolf, 2000). They found three levels of personality pathology that they characterized as low, moderate, and severe personality dysfunction. They also found that most batterers fell into one of two groups that cut across the personality types: narcissistic (overly focused on themselves) and avoidant/depressive. The researchers argued that most batterers did not suffer from severe personality dysfunction and were therefore good candidates for cognitive-behavioral group therapy. This treatment could help the batterers with self-image problems as well as provide feedback to correct distorted thinking about relationships. Men with more severe personality problems (as much as 15 percent of batterers) would need additional attention within the group and possibly individualized psychological treatment.

Some researchers argue that IPV consists of separate types of violence with unique characteristics and outcomes (Johnson, 2006). Johnson and Ferraro identified two categories of IPV: "intimate terrorism" and "common-couple violence" (Johnson & Ferraro, 2000). Intimate terrorism refers to partner violence where one person is violent and controlling over the other. It typically involves serious injury and has a higher frequency of events than common-couple violence. With common-couple violence,

Been There ... Done That!

Experts tell us that in homes where abuse occurs, there is likely to be more than one form. In this case, Thomas had been extremely violent against his wife. The violence was physical and emotional. Thomas also hit his stepdaughter, who ran away from home when she was 15. Years later, she told her mother that Thomas had been sexually abusing her when she was younger. This is the co-occurrence of violence that often happens in homes where batterers reside.

Been There ... Done That!

The marital relationship of Frank and Martha was described by witnesses as mutually combative. Frank was a police officer. His wife called the station to report that during an argument, he had held a gun to the head of their child. Officers who responded confiscated all of his weapons and arrested him for assault and battery with a dangerous weapon. He was suspended without pay and denied access to any guns pending a full investigation. Ultimately, he was fired.

neither person is controlling and there is a low frequency of violence. Johnson further suggested that survey research more frequently captures gender symmetry data that typify common-couple violence, while intimate terrorism is usually demonstrated by agency data (police agencies, courts, hospitals, and shelters).

Male Perpetrators of Marital Rape

Marital rape refers to any unwanted intercourse or penetration (vaginal, anal, or oral) obtained by force, threat of force, or when the wife is unable to consent. Most studies have included couples who are legally married, separated, divorced, or cohabitating. Determining the extent of marital rape is complicated by the fact that while rape is prohibited by law in all states, 26 states still provide exemptions to husbands for prosecution (Lemon, 2005). Studies have indicated that marital rape has long-term and severe consequences for women and that it is usually accompanied by other forms of violence. As many as 1 in 10 wives may have been sexually assaulted by their spouses at least once. Rape in marriage is an extremely prevalent form of sexual violence. Risk of coerced sex is high when women attempt to leave or are separated from their abusers (Tjaden & Thoennes, 2006).

Sexual offenders who perpetrate in intimate partner relationships can readily be compared with stranger rapists. No personality or physical characteristics make them stand out from others. They are not identified through their social status, occupation, race, or ethnic group. Rapists may be motivated by power or anger. Those who commit the crime of rape do so with purpose. It may be to confirm their own manhood or to express their manhood to the victims, as in the power rapist category. Anger rapists are considered extremely dangerous, because they may obtain pleasure from inflicting pain and seek to degrade their victims.

In one of the first books to address marital rape, authors graphically point out that rape is not a trivial family quarrel over sex, with the man getting his way (Finkelhor & Yllo, 1985). It is a brutally forced act, designed to humiliate and harm the woman. In the authors' study on the topic, one-fourth of the wives spoke of forced anal intercourse; one-fifth stated that they were forced to perform oral sex; almost one-fourth of the women were raped in the presence of others, usually their children; and the majority reported brutal vaginal intercourse. Battered women have reported that abusive male partners have forced them to have unprotected sex, sometimes for the purposes of conception (Raj et al., 2006).

Male Perpetrators of Dating Violence

Men who have a family history of observing or experiencing abuse are more likely to inflict abuse, violence, and sexual aggression on their partner during the courtship years. As the consumption of alcohol by either the victim or the perpetrator increases, the rate of serious injuries associated with dating violence also increases. Studies have found the following factors to be associated with sexual assault perpetration: the male having sexually aggressive peers; heavy alcohol or drug use; the male's acceptance of dating violence; the male's assumption of key roles in dating, such as initiating the date, being the driver, and paying dating expenses; miscommunication about sex; previous sexual intimacy with the victim; interpersonal violence; traditional sex roles; adversarial attitudes about relationships; and rape myths.

Unlike the picture presented for physical dating violence, sexual aggression is almost exclusively perpetrated by men. Experts agree that the crime is grossly underreported. A number of studies indicate that both men and women often share the belief that women are responsible for both stimulating and satisfying men's sexual urges, a factor that might contribute to a victim's unwillingness to view the event as criminal. Cultural pressures on young men lead them to insist on sexual relations, using whatever psychological or physical force that is necessary.

Overall, 19 percent of undergraduate women and 6 percent of men report experiencing attempted or completed sexual assault since entering college, according to *The Campus Sexual Assault (CSA) Study* (Krebs, Lindquist, Warner, Fisher, & Martin, 2007). It finds that violence against women and sexual assault on college campuses is prevalent, yet less than 13 percent of sexual assaults or attempted sexual assaults on college campuses are reported to the police. Most of the sexually assaulted women knew the person who victimized them. For completed and attempted rapes, nearly 90 percent of the victims knew the offender, who was usually a classmate, friend, ex-boyfriend, or acquaintance.

ABUSIVE WOMEN

Research shows that women perpetrate violence in intimate partner relationships at rates equal to or greater than those of men. These findings raise many questions about the prevalence and severity of violence committed by women in their intimate partner relationships. Studies have revealed that male-to-female violence is more harmful than female-to-male violence. Female victims of IPV are more likely than men to be injured, to require medical attention, and to take time off from work as a result of injury (Archer, 2002).

Female-perpetrated IPV is a highly controversial topic. Advocates and practitioners claim that women who use force in their intimate partner relationships are victims of violence who respond through self-defense and retaliatory use of force (Larance, 2006). In support of the claim that women use violence as self-defense, studies suggest that women's IPV is generally not as frequent or severe as that of their partners (Weston, Temple, & Marshall, 2005).

There are very few studies on the characteristics of women who are violent toward an intimate partner. One study found that women who were arrested for IPV against their male partners had higher rates of mental disorders than women in the general population (Stuart, Moore, Gordon, Ramsey, & Kahler, 2006). In the sample that had been court referred to domestic violence intervention programs, the women revealed high rates of posttraumatic stress disorder, depression, generalized anxiety disorder, panic disorder, substance use disorders, borderline personality disorder, and antisocial personality disorder. These women also had significant levels of violence victimizations. The authors concluded that the female offenders were suffering from symptoms consistent with being victims rather than perpetrators.

On the other side of the debate, certain researchers claim that there is a tendency to dismiss male victimization by women because there is less of it (Dutton & Nicholls, 2005). Government studies consistently find that sizable numbers of male victims exist. Conflict studies produce roughly equal perpetration rates by men and women. Dutton and Nicholls (2005) argue that society has a responsibility of protecting all victims, regardless of the gender of the offender or victim.

Female Perpetrators of Physical Dating Violence

Major studies on dating violence find that women are both victims and perpetrators of physical dating violence at the same rate as or a higher rate than men (Medeiros & Straus, 2006). This does not mean that couples engage in mutual combat, but that either person in the relationship may instigate violence at one time or another as a response to situations, regardless of gender. In support of this conclusion, Medeiros and Straus (2006) report overwhelming research evidence confirming that women assault male partners at a slightly higher rate than men assault female partners. Straus and Ramirez found that women self-reported physical assaults against their partner at a rate of 32 percent versus 29 percent for males (Straus & Ramirez, 2007).

The consequences for personal violence differ significantly between the sexes, however. Typically, women are injured more frequently and severely when they are victimized by violence.

OFFENDERS AGAINST OLDER ADULTS

Abuse of older adults is complex. Elder abuse is a reportable condition in all states, although its definition varies from state to state. When the offender is a family member, it constitutes domestic or family abuse, a subset of older adult abuse. If the perpetrator is the spouse or live-in partner of the victim, it is also family violence and, more specifically, is called intimate partner abuse. Remember that there is an overlapping of the forms of violence against older adults that may require multiple agency reporting.

Current data on the prevalence and forms of abuse against older adults suggest that the most frequent perpetrators of domestic violence against an older adult include the victim's child, intimate partner, and grandchild. Daughters-in-law and sons-in-law also perpetrate in significant numbers. In New York City, almost half of such incidents reported to authorities involve a suspect who was the victim's child (Fernandez-Lanier, 2010). An intimate partner offended in approximately 25 percent of cases across the State of New York. In a self-report study on violence against older adults in New York, the most common perpetrator was the intimate partner (Lifespan of Greater Rochester, Cornell University, & New York City Department for the Aging, 2011).

Consistent with earlier research, the New York study (2010) found that the majority of offenders against older adults are male. An exception was that when the victim was a parent, the offender was equally either male or female. Female grandchildren were suspects in approximately 4 out of 10 cases. Ages of the perpetrators vary by the type of domestic relationship. The median age of the intimate partner offender was

67 years of age, with most suspects over age 65. Adult children of the victim had a median age of 41 years.

Some studies suggest that the most common reasons for abuse in later life are power and control dynamics that are similar to those experienced by younger battered women. The abuser feels a sense of entitlement to use various forms of abuse to gain and maintain power and control over the victim, using a pattern of coercive tactics. Isolation; intimidation and threats; withholding food, medication, and sleep; and physical and sexual abuse are common tactics of abuse. The common notion that caregiver stress and the victim's level of dependency are factors leading to the abuse of older adults is losing credibility (Brandl, 2004).

The 2009 *National Elder Mistreatment Study* adds significantly to the available information on abuse against older adults (Acierno et al., 2009). Gender was not found to be a significant predictor of any form of abuse. Those between the ages of 60 and 70, referred to as the "younger old," are at an increased risk of physical and emotional abuse, according to the researchers. Slightly over 40 percent of emotional abuse perpetrators were family members of the older adult; this consisted of current intimate or ex-partners (25 percent) and adult children or grandchildren (18 percent). Surprisingly, the risk of emotional abuse was three times greater for those below age 70 than for those over age 70.

There can be little doubt that violence against older adults is domestic violence. Acierno et al. (2009) found that 76 percent of physical abuse against older adults was perpetrated by family members. They suggested that prevention efforts should borrow heavily from domestic violence research with younger adults. Almost 60 percent of the perpetrators of physical assault were intimate partners of the older adult. What is unknown from these figures is whether the IPV is a continuation of violence from younger years (intimate partner abuse grown old). Other possibilities are that IPV is a consequence of one partner being more abled than the other. Further study is needed to examine the physical violence perpetrated against older adults.

Financial abuses are crimes specific to the aging population. Perpetrators are largely family members but may also be acquaintances or strangers. What these offenders have in common is the use of undue influence to deceive the older adult to gain control of the decision making of their victim. Undue influence occurs when people use their role and power to exploit the trust, dependency, and fear of others (Brandl, Heisler, & Stiegel, 2006). Prevalence of financial exploitation is extremely high, with one in 20 older adults indicating some form of perceived financial mistreatment by a family member having occurred at least once in the recent past (Acierno et al., 2009).

Offender Characteristics

Holly Ramsey-Klawsnik (2000) has proposed a typology of five categories of older adult offenders, along with their offender characteristics. She suggests that offenders may be adults caring for older adults who feel guilty when they are unable to care for the person, and so they strike out. Other offenders simply do not realize that what they are doing could be considered improper, such as overmedicating or using restraints improperly. The final three categories are not well-meaning individuals that are caring for the elder; instead, they may be bullies, may enjoy harming a vulnerable person, or are exploiting the elder financially.

From the 2009 *National Elder Mistreatment Study*, the following conclusions emerged:

1. Abuse of older adults is primarily domestic violence perpetrated by intimate partners, children, grandchildren, and other family members.
2. A significant number of abusers suffer from impairments such as substance abuse, high unemployment, and increased likelihood of mental health problems.
3. Abusers tend to be dependent on their victims rather than the common belief to the contrary.
4. Perpetrators of violence against older adults are socially isolated, with fewer than three friends in about half of all the cases in which perpetrators were known.
5. Financial dependency of adult children may be a key reason to abuse.
6. Majority of the perpetrators are men.

Perpetrators of Sexual Abuse Against Older Adults

In her groundbreaking study involving 284 cases of older sexual abuse victims, Burgess (2006) studied the characteristics of 230 offenders (refer to Figure 11-7). Offenders ranged in age from 13 to 90 years, with the largest group between 30 and 39 years old (27 percent of offenders). Approximately one-quarter of the perpetrators were strangers to the victim, and the remaining were related or known to the victim. The largest group of sexual offenders comprised a family member, including a spouse or partner to the victim. In 10 percent of cases, the offender was an unrelated care provider.

Less than 1 percent of cases involve sexual abuse against an older adult (Acierno et al., 2009). This is believed to be an underestimation of the problem. The 2009 *National Elder Mistreatment Study* found that 16 percent of older adult domestic violence victims reported their sexual mistreatment to the police. In more than half of the cases, perpetrators were family members. Intimate partners and spouses account for approximately 40 percent of the reported sexual abuse, with an additional 10 percent of offenders found in various family relationships. Researchers found that older adults appear to be more likely to report sexual victimization than younger adults (Acierno et al., 2009). However, more than 85 percent of older adults who are sexually abused

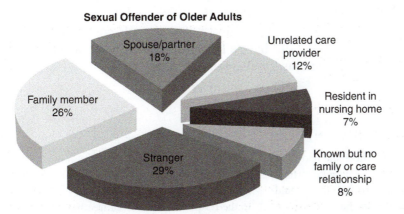

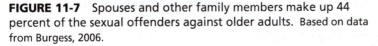

FIGURE 11-7   Spouses and other family members make up 44 percent of the sexual offenders against older adults. Based on data from Burgess, 2006.

do not report the event to police or other authorities. Sexual violence against older adults is best described as a form of domestic violence.

Abuse Against Older Adults Treatment Program

Domestic violence against an older adult family member has unique issues when compared to abuses against younger persons. Court referrals to batterer treatment programs are generally the most frequent criminal sanction for batterers. Program development has expanded to include services for holding older adult perpetrators accountable. Stop Elder Abuse and Mistreatment (S.E.A.M.) is one example of a psychoeducational program for abusers of older adults (Mason, 2003). It is a 12-week educational and rehabilitative program that not only teaches abusers to recognize unacceptable behaviors but also teaches them alternative acceptable behaviors. It is not mental health, psychiatric, or substance abuse counseling but a court-referred abuser program. Using the curriculum created by Lifespan, it has been attended by physical abusers, financial exploiters, sexual abusers, and verbal abusers. Both genders in the age range of 19 to 76 have taken part in this program. Lifespan is a nonprofit agency located in Rochester, New York.

CONCLUSIONS

Adult perpetrators of heterosexual IPV are predominately men. The increase in arrests of women offenders in recent years has caused advocates and researchers to rethink the characteristics of the intimate partner abuser, however. The abuse of men by women is controversial. This has led to a closer look at different styles of violence and at different categories, such as high-risk offenders. The one-size-fits-all abuser no longer fits. Alcohol and drug use is definitely linked to abuse by both male and female offenders and may also play a role in the abuse of older adults.

This chapter looked at offenders in military and paramilitary organizations. Because police officers and military officers legally carry weapons as a requirement of their work, advocates are rightly concerned about abuse from these populations. The Department of Defense has structured responses to IPV. It has added confidentiality to cases involving military spouses.

Offenders are young and old, men and women. Physical abuse in dating relationships appears to be perpetrated by both genders, while sexual abuse is committed almost exclusively by men. Abuse against older adults is committed by both genders, including sexual abuse. We still have a lot to learn about abuse and the abusers to provide appropriate interventions for everyone affected.

SIMPLY SCENARIO
Police Officers Who Batter

Jill recently moved in with the police officer she had been dating. Because of his shift work and demanding overtime schedule, he bought her a cell phone so that they could keep in touch during the day. One day, she had gone shopping and forgot to turn the phone on. When Al came home, he was furious and started accusing her of cheating on him. He was yelling and throwing things around the house. Jill was very angry and yelled back at him, demanding that he leave her house. Al responded by pushing her down; then he started to kick her repeatedly. When Al left, Jill went to the hospital and received treatment for broken ribs. She was frightened; after all, he was a police officer!

Question: What is the policy recommended by the International Association of Chiefs of Police?

Questions for Review

1. What were some of Hanson's characteristics and mental health diagnoses for individual batterers?
2. Describe the excessive rule-making descriptor of intimate partner abusers.
3. In what ways do departmental positions on police officer IPV significantly differ?
4. What did the 2003 IACP policy on domestic violence by police officers establish?
5. Who are family-only offenders?
6. What is the difference between common-couple violence and intimate terrorism?
7. What is the general age and gender description of intimate partner abusers?
8. Who are high-risk offenders? How does Straus suggest they be identified?
9. What category of crimes is specific to the older adult?
10. Explain the perpetrator characteristics of sexual abuse against the older adult.

Internet-Based Exercises

1. The National Center on Domestic and Sexual Violence maintains a Web site on the military response to allegations of family violence involving members of the military. Go to http://www.ncdsv.org/ncd_militaryresponse.html Based on what you read, are civilian protective orders enforceable on a military installation?
2. Many studies have documented the link between animal cruelty and perpetrating violence against children, intimate partners, and older adults. Visit http://www.pet-abuse.com/, and view its statistics. Do you agree in legislation that would require individuals convicted of animal abuse crimes to register with a public database?
3. Domestic violence by police officers is a difficult category of crime to document and respond to. Visit the policy statement of the IACP. Explain the procedures that IACP recommends for handling police officer–perpetrated domestic violence. Go to http://www.theiacp.org/, and type in the search "domestic violence by police officers."
4. The Family Justice Center Alliance of California is a valuable resource for family violence intervention and prevention. Visit https://www.familyjusticecenter.org/?s=risk+assessment for information on offender risk assessment and a variety of other topics. Write a report on an intervention that you find interesting.

References

Acierno, R., Hernandez-Tejada, M., Muzzy, W., & Steve, K. (2009). The National Elder Mistreatment Study. Retrieved from https://www.ncjrs.gov/pdffiles1/nij/grants/226456.pdf

Addington, L. A., & Randour, M. L. (2012). *Animal cruelty crime statistics: Findings from a survey of State Uniform Crime Reporting programs.* Washington, D.C.: Animal Welfare Institute.

Anderson, A. S., & Lo, C. C. (2010). Intimate partner violence within law enforcement families. *Journal of Interpersonal Violence.* Retrieved from http://jiv.sagepub.com/content/early/2010/06/03/0886260510368156

Archer, J. (2002). Sex differences in aggression between heterosexual partners: A meta-analytic review. *Psychological Bulletin, 126,* 651–680.

Ascione, F. (1998). Battered women's reports of their partners' and their children's cruelty to animals. *Journal of Emotional Abuse, 1*(1), 119–133.

Ascione, F., Weber, C., Thompson, T., Heath, J., Maruyama, M., & Hayashi, K. (2007). Battered pets and domestic violence: Animal abuse reported by women experiencing intimate violence and by nonabused women. *Violence Against Women, 13*(4), 354–373.

Bair-Merritt, M. H., Crowne, S. S., Thompson, D. A., Sibinga, E., Trent, M., & Campbell, J. (2010). Why do women use intimate partner violence? A systematic review of women's motivations. *Trauma Violence Abuse, 11*(4), 178–189.

Brandl, B. (2004). *Assessing for abuse in later life.* Madison, WI: National Clearinghouse on Abuse in Later Life.

Brandl, B., Heisler, C., & Stiegel, L. (2006). *Undue influence: The criminal justice response.* Omaha, NE: YWCA.

Burgess, A. (2006). *Elderly victims of sexual abuse and their offenders.* Washington, D.C.: U.S. Department of Justice.

Busch, A., & Rosenberg, M. (2004). Comparing women and men arrested for domestic violence: A preliminary report. *Journal of Family Violence, 19*, 49–58.

Carney, M., Buttell, F., & Dutton, D. (2007). Women who perpetrate intimate partner violence: A review of the literature with recommendations for treatment. *Aggression and Violent Behavior, 12*, 108–115.

Cohen, M., & Keweller, C. (2000). Domestic violence and animal abuse: The deadly connection. Retrieved from http://www.gevha.com/prensa/articles/39-articles/190-domestic-violence-and-animal-abuse-the-deadly-connection

Department of Defense. (2003). Principle elements of strategic plan for most effectively addressing domestic violence matters within the Department of Defense. Retrieved from http://www.ncdsv.org/images/revstrategicplan.pdf

Department of Defense. (2010). Demographics 2010: Profile of the military community. Retrieved from http://www.ncdsv.org/images/DOD_Demographics ProfileOfTheMilitaryCommunity_2010.pdf

Department of Defense. (2011). Domestic abuse involving DoD military and certain affiliated personnel. Retrieved from http://www.dtic.mil/whs/directives/corres/pdf/640006p.pdf

Durose, M., Harlow, C. W., Langan, P., Motivans, M., Rantala, R., & Smith, E. (2005). *Family violence statistics.* (NCJ 207846). Washington, D.C.: U.S. Department of Justice.

Dutton, D., & Kropp, R. (2000). A review of domestic violence risk instruments. *Trauma, Violence, & Abuse, 1*(2), 171–181.

Dutton, D., & Nicholls, T. (2005). The gender paradigm in domestic violence research and theory: Part 1. The conflict of theory and data. *Aggression and Violent Behavior, 10*(6), 680–714.

Eastman, B. J., Bunch, S. G., Williams, H., & Carawan, L. W. (2007). Exploring the perceptions of domestic violence service providers in rural localities. *Violence Against Women, 13*(7), 700–716.

Erwin, M., Gershon, R., Tiburzi, M., & Lin, S. (2005). Reports of intimate partner violence made against police officers. *Journal of Family Violence, 20*(1), 13–19.

Erwin, P., & Beals, J. (2007). Understanding the military response to domestic violence: Tools for civilian advocates. Retrieved from http://www.bwjp.org/files/bwjp/articles/BWJP_Military_Part1.pdf

Fagan, J. (1990). Intoxication and aggression. In M. Tonry & J. Q. Wilson (Eds.), *Drugs and crime* (pp. 241–320). Chicago, IL: University of Chicago Press.

Fernandez-Lanier, A. (2010). *2008 domestic incident reports involving elderly victims.* New York, NY: NYS Division of Criminal Justice Services.

Finkelhor, D., & Yllo, K. (Eds.). (1985). *License to rape: Sexual abuse of wives.* New York, NY: Holt, Rinehart, and Winston.

Hanson, B. (2002). Interventions for batterers. In A. Roberts (Ed.), *Handbook of domestic violence intervention strategies* (pp. 419–448). New York, NY: Oxford University Press.

Hickman, L., & Davis, L. (2003). *Formalizing collaboration: Establishing domestic violence memorandums of understanding between military installations and civilian communities.* Arlington, VA: RAND.

Hines, D., Brown, J., & Dunning, E. (2007). Characteristics of callers to the domestic abuse helpline for men. *Journal of Family Violence, 22*(2), 63–72.

Holtzworth-Monroe, A., & Stuart, G. (1994). Typologies of male batterers: Three subtypes and the differences among them. *Psychological Bulletin, 116*(3), 476–497.

Jackson, S. L., & Hafemeister, T. L. (2011). Financial abuse of elderly people vs. other forms of elder abuse: Assessing their dynamics, risk factors, and society's response. Retrieved from https://www.ncjrs.gov/pdffiles1/nij/grants/233613.pdf

James, K., Seddon, B., & Brown, J. (2002). "Using it or losing it": Men's construction of their violence towards female partners. *Australian Domestic & Family Violence Clearinghouse, 1*, 1–20.

Jeanne Geiger Crisis Center. (2012). The Domestic Violence High Risk Team Network (DVHRTN). Retrieved from http://www.jeannegeigercrisiscenter.org/dvhrtn_impact.html

Johnson, M. (2006). Conflict and control: Gender symmetry and asymmetry in domestic violence. *Violence Against Women, 12*(11), 1003–1018.

Johnson, M., & Ferraro, K. (2000). Research on domestic violence in the 1990's: Making distinctions. *Journal of Marriage and the Family, 62*, 948–963.

Karch, D., & Nunn, K. C. (2011). Characteristics of elderly and other vulnerable adult victims of homicide by a caregiver: National Violent Death Reporting System—17 U.S. states, 2003–2007. *Journal of Interpersonal Violence, 26*(1), 137–157.

Klein, A. (2008). *Practical implications of current domestic violence research. Part II: Prosecution.* Washington, D.C.: National Institute of Justice.

Klein, A. (2009). Practical implications of current domestic violence research: For law enforcement, prosecutors, and judges. *Special Report.* Washington, D.C.: National Institute of Justice.

Krebs, C. P., Lindquist, C. H., Warner, T. D., Fisher, B. S., & Martin, S. L. (2007). The Campus Sexual Assault (CSA) Study final report. Retrieved from https://www.ncjrs.gov/pdffiles1/nij/grants/221153.pdf

Larance, L. Y. (2006). Serving women who use force in their intimate heterosexual relationships: An extended view. *Violence Against Women, 12*(7), 622–640. doi: 10.1177/1077801206290240

Lemon, N. (2005). *Domestic violence law* (2nd ed.). St. Paul, MN: West Group.

Lifespan of Greater Rochester, Cornell University, & New York City Department for the Aging. (2011). *Under the radar: New York State Elder Abuse Prevalence Study.* New York, NY: Author.

Logan, T., Shannon, L., & Walker, R. (2005). Protective orders in rural and urban areas: A multiple perspective study. *Violence Against Women, 11*(7), 876–911.

Lonsway, K., & Conis, P. (2003). Officer domestic violence. *Law and Order, 51*(10), 133–140.

Martin, S., Gibbs, D., Johnson, R., Rentz, E. D., Clinton-Sherrod, M., & Hardison, J. (2007). Spouse abuse and child abuse by army soldiers. *Journal of Family Violence, 22*, 587–595.

Mason, A. (2003). S.E.A.M., Stop Elder Abuse and Mistreatment: A psycho-educational program for abusers of the elderly. *Domestic Violence Report, 8*(6), 87–88.

Medeiros, R., & Straus, M. (2006). Risk factors for physical violence between dating partners: Implications for gender-inclusive prevention and treatment of family violence. In J. Hamel & T. Nicholls (Eds.), *Family approaches in domestic violence: A practitioner's guide to gender-inclusive research and treatment* (pp. 59–85). New York, NY: Springer.

Mendoza, A. (2002). *Teenage rampage: The worldwide youth crime phenomenon.* Colchester, Essex, UK: Virgin Publishing.

Meuer, T., Seymour, A., & Wallace, H. (2002). *Domestic violence.* Washington, D.C.: Office for Victims of Crime.

Oehme, K., Donnelly, E. A., & Martin, A. (2012). Alcohol abuse, PTSD, and officer-committed domestic violence. *Policing, 6*(4), 418–430.

Pet-abuse.com. (2008). Cruelty connections. Retrieved from http://www.pet-abuse.com/pages/abuse_connection.php

Raj, A., Santana, C., Marche, A. L., Amaro, H., Cranston, K., & Silverman, J. (2006). Perpetration of intimate partner violence associated with sexual risk behaviors among young adult men. *American Journal of Public Health, 96*(10), 1873–1878. doi: 10.2105/ajph.2005.081554

Ramsey-Klawsnik, H. (2000). Elder-abuse offenders: A typology. *Journal of the American Society on Aging, XXIV*(11), 17–22.

Schneider, R., Burnette, M. L., Ilgen, M. A., & Timko, C. (2009). Prevalence and correlates of intimate partner violence victimization among men and women entering substance use disorder treatment. *Violence and Victims, 24*(6), 744–756.

Sharps, P., Campbell, J., Campbell, D., Gary, F., & Webster, D. (2003). Risky mix: Drinking, drug use, and homicide. *National Institute of Justice Journal, 250*, 8–13.

Simmons, C., & Lehmann, P. (2007). Exploring the link between pet abuse and controlling behaviors in violence relationships. *Journal of Interpersonal Violence, 22*(9), 1211–1222.

Stalans, L., & Ritchie, J. (2008). Relationship of substance use/abuse with psychological and physical intimate partner violence: Variations across living situations. *Journal of Family Violence, 23*(1), 9–24.

Straus, M. (1993). Identifying offenders in criminal justice research on domestic assault. *American Behavioral Scientist, 36*(5), 587–599.

Straus, M., & Ramirez, I. L. (2007). Gender symmetry in prevalence, severity, and chronicity of physical aggression against dating partners by university students in Mexico and USA. *Journal of Aggressive Behavior, 33*(4), 281–290.

Stuart, G., Moore, T., Gordon, K., Ramsey, S., & Kahler, C. (2006). Psychopathology in women arrested for domestic violence. *Journal of Interpersonal Violence, 21*(3), 376–389. doi: 10.1177/0886260505282888

Stuart, G., Moore, T., Ramsey, S., & Kahler, C. (2004). Hazardous drinking and relationship violence perpetration and victimization in women arrested for domestic violence. *Journal of Studies in Alcohol, 65*(1), 46–53.

Thompson, M., & Kingree, J. B. (2006). The roles of victim and perpetrator alcohol use in intimate partner violence outcomes. *Journal of Interpersonal Violence, 21*(2), 163–177.

Tjaden, P., & Thoennes, N. (2006). *Extent, nature, and consequences of rape victimization: Findings from the National Violence Against Women Survey.* Washington, D.C.: U.S. Department of Justice.

Weston, R., Temple, J., & Marshall, L. (2005). Gender symmetry and asymmetry in violent relationships: Patterns of mutuality among racially diverse women. *Sex Roles: A Journal of Research, 53*(7), 553–571.

Wetendorf, D. (2006). *Police domestic violence: A handbook for victims.* Retrieved from http://www.abuseofpower.info/Book_Index.htm

White, R. J., & Gondolf, E. W. (2000). Implications of personality profiles for batterer treatment. *Journal of Interpersonal Violence, 15*(5), 467–488.

Wisch, R. F. (2012). Domestic violence and pets: List of states that include pets in protection orders. Retrieved from http://www.animallaw.info/articles/ovusdomesticviolencelaws.htm

Wong, T. (2008). *Spousal Assault Risk Assessment (SARA) validation study, State of Hawaii, 2004–2007.* Honolulu, HI: Department of the Attorney General.

12

The Police Response
to Intimate Partner Violence

CHAPTER OBJECTIVES

After reviewing this chapter, you should be able to:

1. Translate empirical findings in police research into professional police arrest practices for intimate partner violence and use of probable cause.
2. Explain the difference between proarrest and mandatory arrest policies.
3. Discuss the implications of dual arrest and its effects for future criminal justice practices.
4. Identify the major concepts and provisions for domestic violence orders of protection.
5. Explain practical approaches to interviewing in cases of intimate partner violence.

KEY TERMS

Dual arrest

Full faith and credit

Mandatory arrest

Primary aggressor

Proarrest

Probable cause

Rapport

Risk assessment

INTRODUCTION

What is the police role in response to intimate partner violence (IPV)? Increased demands for enforcement of criminal justice statutes in IPV and the creation of legislation to address newly recognized forms have not settled the debate regarding the role of the police officer. If anything, they have fueled the controversy over appropriate intervention strategies for intimate partner disputes. A lack of consensus has resulted in practices that vary widely from state to state. Without a clear direction on how to handle these complex problems, police officers will often respond inappropriately. At one time, a call regarding IPV was considered the most dangerous police call. Although that is no longer true, it certainly is a frequent call that police respond to. In fact, IPV is the most frequent violence that police officers encounter.

How dangerous are domestic violence calls to the police officers who respond? Looking at the years between 1996 and 2009, 771 police officers were murdered in the line of duty (Meyer & Carroll, 2011). Over that 14-year period, 106 officers were identified as having been murdered when responding to a domestic violence call—14 percent of the total. Over half of those slain officers were ambushed before having contact with the suspect. This finding has led the authors to call for more research regarding the context of murders of officers in domestic violence situations, so that training and policy may be developed to enhance officer safety.

How do the police get involved in these cases? In this chapter, arrest policies are examined in addition to alternative resources for police to consider. Civil protection codes and mental health codes appear to complicate the police response at first glance, but ultimately they are tools for officers to use in resolving the conflict. The determination of probable cause is critical to any police action that may involve an arrest; therefore, the officer must collect evidence and interrogate suspects. Included in this section is information on the primary and dominant aggressor determination. Also discussed are the constitutional constraints that police officers must work within to gather information and evidence.

CRIMINALIZATION OF INTIMATE PARTNER VIOLENCE

Police have the duty to respond to reports of domestic disputes. Early research has documented the relationship of family crisis to crime. In Marvin Wolfgang's 1958 study, 65 percent of 500 homicide victims were found to be relatives, close friends, paramours, or partners of the principal offender (Zahn, 1991). Only 12 percent were complete strangers. The realization that family crime could be deadly was born. The criminal justice community, under attack for being lax with perpetrators of family violence, began searching for a way to deal with IPV that was consistent with criminal enforcement policy. In what was called the *family crisis model*, police officers were trained to negotiate with the parties and refer them to social services agencies in this mediation process.

By the early 1980s, the effectiveness of the family crisis model was in question. James Q. Wilson suggested that a study be conducted using various police responses to domestic violence. The issue was whether the use of criminal penalties should replace the peacekeeping efforts. Because the offenders in cases of spousal abuse were rarely arrested, advocates claimed that police officers were not treating violence against intimates as legitimate crimes. Studies were undertaken to test empirically whether arrests deterred subsequent violence better than less formal alternatives. The most important research efforts addressing this question were six experiments known collectively as the National Institute of Justice's *Spouse Assault Replication Program* (SARP). These experiments, conducted in the field, were carried out between 1981 and 1991 by six police departments and research teams.

The *Minneapolis Domestic Violence Experiment* (MDVE) was the first experiment. The study design called for officers in the Minneapolis Police Department to carry out one of three responses when they had probable cause to believe that a

More About It: The Family Crisis Model

The family crisis model was developed from the classical study undertaken by Morton Bard in 1968 (Bard, 1969). Realizing that family disturbances constituted a significant aspect of police work, the project tested an intensive training period for officers who would respond in the "family crisis car." The month-long course was followed by weekly in-service training sessions. In an attempt to reduce injury to police officers who were dispatched, a mental health strategy of intervention was employed. At the same time, the participating officers also received generalized calls—rejection of an exclusively specialized role was a key goal. Emphasis was placed on the establishment of police agency relationships with other agencies in the helping system. Bard reported that the method did reduce injuries suffered by enforcers, and the community's attitude toward the police showed a marked improvement.

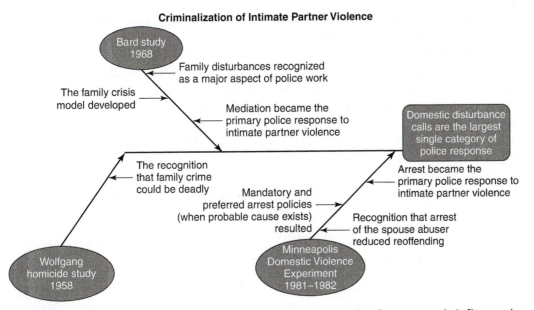

Criminalization of Intimate Partner Violence

FIGURE 12-1   The criminalization of intimate partner violence has been strongly influenced by research.

misdemeanor assault had occurred between cohabitants or spouses: (1) arrest the suspect, (2) order one party out of the residence, or (3) advise the couple at the scene on how to solve their problems. The researchers reported that when the suspect was arrested, there were statistically significant reductions in the number of reoffenses in the official records of all the cases and the cases with victim interviews.

Many departments that were desperate for an answer that would suggest action to solve the complex problem welcomed the idea that police should arrest for crimes of IPV. Social science researchers first reported preliminary results of the MDVE in an article that appeared in *The New York Times* in 1984. Ten days after the initial report, the same paper reported that Police Commissioner Ward had issued new orders requiring police officers to make arrests for domestic violence, citing the experiment as among the reasons for the new rules. A rush to establish mandatory and proarrest procedures resulted, which was a total departure from the mediation approach that was prevalent. The arrest of the perpetrator, when probable cause exists, emerged as the preferred response in most jurisdictions. The criminalization of domestic violence had begun. Note the timeline for the criminalization of IPV in Figure 12-1.

THE ROLE OF POLICE

Domestic disturbance cases require a substantial portion of law-enforcement resources. They are now the largest single category of police response. Domestic-violence–related calls to the police account for between 15 percent and more than 50 percent of all calls (Klein, 2008). In Charlotte, North Carolina, police respond to approximately 30,000 domestic disturbance calls each year, almost 60 percent of all calls for assistance (Friday, Lord, Exum, & Hartman, 2006). The level of response from police varies from town to town.

The role of police officers in responding to IPV is a challenging one. The dichotomy of the legalistic response and expectations that police officers meet social service needs of victims can cause role conflict and increased stress for the officers (Balenovich, Grossi, & Hughes, 2008). Police officers are increasingly being required by law and policy to arrest in cases of domestic violence, which is a legalistic approach. On the other hand, police officers may be required to take on a social service role such as mediating between both parties or counseling the suspect (Townsend, Hunt, Kuck, & Baxter, 2006). Researchers have examined police officer attitudes toward domestic violence and identified three different police response roles (Balenovich et al., 2008). Response roles depend on the orientation of the individual police officer. One category believes in following the letter of the law for enforcement, the next takes on the social service role, and the final category combines the two approaches as an investigator. Authors suggest that the integrated investigator is the role that police should aspire to because it is the most effective at fully resolving domestic violence incidents.

The Effect of Arrest on Intimate Partner Violence

The body of research that is known collectively as the SARP fueled rather than quieted the debate on the effectiveness of arrest in cases of domestic violence. With the Minneapolis Domestic Violence Experiment conducted first, five additional replication experiments were conducted in Omaha, Charlotte, Milwaukee, Miami, and Colorado Springs in the early 1990s. These five jurisdictions used a diverse set of incidents and a variety of outcome measures; consequently, they reported that the use of arrest was only occasionally associated with statistically significant reductions in subsequent repeat offending. The results of the experiments varied by measures used and by the jurisdiction studied.

In July 2001, a new analysis of the five replication studies reported that a consistent set of measures of repeat offending and appropriate statistical analyses for the combination of data had been developed and the studies reanalyzed (Maxwell, Garner, & Fagan, 2003). The findings of the research by Maxwell et al. provide evidence supporting the argument that arresting male batterers may, independent of other criminal justice sanctions and individual processes, reduce subsequent IPV. Specifically, arrest is associated with reduced recidivism regardless of the jurisdiction. Authors also found that regardless of arrest, some abusers will continue to abuse yet more than half will not re-offend. Whether or not the police officer makes an arrest depends on his or her understanding of the law and perspective on domestic violence.

Been There ... Done That!

A former student dropped by my office to say hello. He was halfway through the police academy and was proud that he had been selected to tutor other recruits who were having difficulty with the academic portion of the training. Of course, I asked how much time was being dedicated to domestic disputes, because it will ultimately be the most frequent type of call for the graduates. "Four hours," he responded, adding that the instructor tried to cram into that time frame what my student had been exposed to during a semester course.

The academy class was told that the law requires an arrest for violation of protection orders and that it was preferred that they arrest in all dispute cases. Failure to make an arrest leaves the officer personally liable. Drill instructors repeatedly shouted, "What do we do at a domestic disturbance?" "We arrest everyone and let the courts sort it out," was the expected reply shouted in response. The academy is teaching police recruits to arrest victims, I thought in horror. Why is this still happening?

POLICE OFFICER TRAINING

Training police officers on domestic violence response is an imperative that cannot be overlooked. Close to three-quarters of police departments require specialized domestic violence training for officers, and 63 percent require the training be received during both in-service and recruit training (Townsend et al., 2006). Training time varies with departments. Academies that offer domestic violence training will frequently provide between two or three days and one week of instruction for recruit and special unit training. Townsend et al. (2006) documented the topics typically covered in domestic violence training in their study involving 368 police departments. Less than 70 percent of police officers are being trained in domestic violence definitions, law, or policy. See Figure 12-2 for an illustration of sample training topics and the percentage of police departments that offer the topics during domestic violence training of police recruits.

The focus of IPV training is an important issue rarely discussed. Developing sensitivity to family violence issues does not ensure a successful prosecution. There is a need for increased training on the collection of evidence-based prosecution standards. Research suggests that the way to increase successful prosecutions of IPV cases is to train police officers in methods of evidence collection (Friday et al., 2006). Research also suggests that domestic violence arrest decisions are influenced more by an officer's assessment of the legal variables involved than by his or her attitude (Klein, 2009).

Experts know that training is an important part of the proper implementation of domestic violence law and policy. Some state law-enforcement training academies and police agencies now offer increased training and specific policies for identifying predominant aggressors (Crager, Cousin, & Hardy, 2003). Examples include the California Commission on Peace Officer Standards, the San Diego Police Department, the Washington State Criminal Justice Training Commission, and the Colorado Springs Police Department. State police academies in Delaware, Maryland, Louisiana, Tennessee, and Texas also provide specific training on the identification of a predominant domestic aggressor. It is accepted that without extensive, adequate training, police will not implement IPV laws properly.

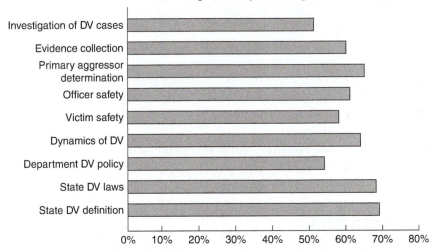

FIGURE 12-2   According to one study, less than 70 percent of police department training includes domestic violence definitions or state laws. Based on data from Townsend et al., 2006.

Specialized Domestic Violence Response Units

Promising results occur in cases that officers investigate as though the victim will not be available to testify at trial, a typical approach of the specialized domestic violence response unit. To do this, the patrol officers participate in specialized evidence collection training on an ongoing basis. The training includes victim case studies from actual incident responses and the specific responsibilities the officers have in making domestic violence arrests, treating the cases like stranger assault. Training includes mandatory arrest and primary aggressor decision making and detailed case preparation. Also, a lethality or dangerousness assessment tool is used to identify the victims who are at the greatest risk but have not received the level of attention warranted.

In a study on the law-enforcement response to domestic violence calls, its authors report that most police departments' written policies include procedures regarding the arrest decisions (95 percent), handling of violations of protection orders (89 percent), and conducting on-scene investigations (75 percent) (Townsend et al., 2006). The majority of departments also require that victims are interviewed separately from the suspect, and that information about shelter and other services is provided. Few departments have established specialized domestic violence units, approximately 11 percent, according to the Townsend report (2006). The departments with specialized units had greater success with subsequent prosecution. The victims handled by regular patrols declined to prosecute at a rate of 30 percent, compared with only 8 percent of victims who were handled by the specialized unit declining. In Mecklenburg County, North Carolina, for example, the specialized unit collected evidence in 61.8 percent of its cases, compared with only 12.5 percent collected by patrol officers.

One report on the law-enforcement response to IPV addressed the question on the effectiveness of domestic violence units (Klein, 2008). It stated that specialized domestic violence units, emphasizing repeat victim contact and evidence gathering, significantly increase the likelihood of prosecution, conviction, and sentencing. Specialized domestic violence officers are trained to make more extensive inquiries, including asking whether there are weapons involved. Klein (2008) noted the following:

1. *Specialized domestic violence units influence prosecution and conviction of abuse suspects*—Specialized units are more likely to collect evidence to turn over to prosecutors. Victims are more likely to testify against their abuser.
2. *Specialized domestic violence units influence victim behavior*—When specialized police response occurs, victims are more likely to leave their abusers sooner than those who receive traditional police response.
3. *Specialized domestic violence units do reduce subsequent abuse*—Victims self-report lower incidences of subsequent abuse and are more likely to report re-abuse when it does occur.
4. *Specialized domestic violence units increase victim satisfaction*—The most appreciated service police officers can deliver to the greatest number of victims is arresting their abusers.

ARREST PROCEDURES

The mandate to police officers is far from clear. While each state has laws that provide police officers with the power to arrest in cases of domestic assault, the conditions under which the officer may arrest vary greatly. For example, Michigan Statute

Section 776.22(3)(i) states the following: *In most circumstances, an officer should arrest and take an individual into custody if the officer has probable cause to believe the individual is committing or has committed domestic violence and his or her actions constitute a crime.* Note the term *should*—this can be interpreted as either a proarrest stance or that arrest is at the officer's discretion. Laws are constantly changing with respect to arrest procedures; generally, policies are classified into three categories:

- Mandatory arrest
- Proarrest
- Arrest is at the officer's discretion

As you can see from the map in Figure 12-3, many states have adopted proarrest and mandated arrest policies. The third situation in cases involving IPV is that the state has not limited police officer discretion on whether or not to make an arrest. Mandatory arrest laws for at least some assault and battery domestic violence cases exist in 20 states and Washington, DC, proarrest provisions exist in 9 states, and arrest is discretionary in 21 states (American Bar Association, 2007). Laws may also state the circumstances in which police officers can make an arrest, in cases of felonies, within a specified time after the incident, or when a specific relationship exists between the perpetrator and the victim. A city or town may require more of the police than the state law requires. For example, a state law may say that arrest is preferred in domestic violence cases, but a city or town may choose to make domestic assaults a mandatory arrest situation.

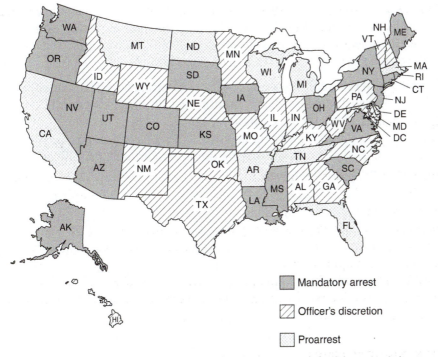

Domestic Violence Arrest Policies

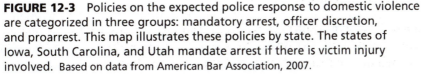

FIGURE 12-3 Policies on the expected police response to domestic violence are categorized in three groups: mandatory arrest, officer discretion, and proarrest. This map illustrates these policies by state. The states of Iowa, South Carolina, and Utah mandate arrest if there is victim injury involved. Based on data from American Bar Association, 2007.

More About It: Abuse Prevention Law

Each state specifies the responsibilities of police within its abuse prevention law. Excerpts from the Massachusetts General Laws Ch. 209A, Section 6, Abuse Prevention Law, show some of the specific procedures that are required when a Massachusetts police officer responds to a domestic abuse scene, beyond arrest requirements. Section 6—Powers of police:

> Whenever any law officer has reason to believe that a family or household member has been abused or is in danger of being abused, such officer shall use all reasonable means to prevent further abuse. The officer shall take, but not be limited to the following action:
>
> a. remain on the scene of where said abuse occurred or was in danger of occurring as long as the officer has reason to believe that at least one of the parties involved would be in immediate physical danger without the presence of a law officer. This shall include, but not be limited to remaining in the dwelling for a reasonable period of time;
>
> b. give such person immediate and adequate notice of his or her rights. Such notice shall consist of handing said person a copy of the statement which follows below and reading the same to said person. Where said person's native language is not English, the statement shall be then provided in said person's native language whenever possible.

The statement that follows within the Massachusetts law spells out the rights of the person with respect to domestic violence protection.

Proarrest and Mandatory Arrest Policies

As stated in the preceding section, the conditions under which police departments apply the arrest policy required by law do vary greatly. Domestic violence-related arrest policies are stated in the laws of each state. Policies also have been legislated in federal, military, and tribal laws. These laws do change frequently, so look closely at the domestic violence statute in your state to determine how police must respond. What do the terms *mandatory arrest* and *proarrest* mean?

- **Mandatory arrest** requires a police officer to arrest a person without a warrant, based on a probable cause determination that an offense occurred and that the accused person committed the offense.
- **Proarrest** laws give authority for an arrest without a warrant as the preferred, but not required, action in cases involving domestic partners. An officer who fails to make the arrest may be required to file a written incident report justifying why no arrest was made.

There have been increases in raw arrest numbers since the passage of mandatory and proarrest domestic violence laws. Researchers found that the odds of arrest in intimate partner cases increase by 97 percent compared to states with discretionary arrest laws (Hirschel, Buzawa, Pattavina, Faggiani, & Reuland, 2007). For states with proarrest statutes, the odds of arrest compared to states with discretionary arrest statutes are even higher—approximately 177 percent. According to Hirschel et al. (2007), an explanation for the increase in domestic violence arrests is that definitions have been expanded in all states to include a broader range of domestic relationships. Alternatively, it may in part be due to an increase in arrests of women.

Recent years have seen a substantial increase in the number of women arrested for domestic violence. In California between 1991 and 1996, the rate of female arrests rose 156 percent (Durfee, 2012). During the same period, arrests of men in California rose approximately 21 percent. Arrests of women for domestic violence have risen in other states as well. New Hampshire and Vermont provide examples with less dramatic increases. Some have attributed this trend of female arrest to mandatory arrest policies, in which police are required to arrest if there is probable cause that a person has committed domestic violence (Hirschel et al., 2007). In a gender analysis of arrest in cases of domestic violence, Durfee (2012) concluded that mandatory arrest policies appear to be working. In those states that mandate police to make an arrest, there are the highest rates for arrest in all categories—for male arrest (7 percent), female arrest (5 percent), and dual arrest (43 percent). Overall, men are being arrested at only slightly higher rates than women.

One of the unexpected consequences of the criminalization of domestic violence has been an increase in the number of cases in which both parties involved in IPV are arrested. When both parties in domestic violence–related assault are arrested, it is called a **dual arrest**. Both the courts and the legislature discourage the practice of making dual arrests because it fails to protect and further victimizes the individual who is not the batterer. Same-sex relationships are particularly vulnerable to dual arrests, because the police may have difficulty in determining the primary aggressor.

An analysis of NIBRS data for the year 2000 indicates that police officers make more arrests when there is a domestic relationship between the victim and the offender, compared to cases in which such a relationship does not exist (Hirschel, 2008). Figure 12-4 provides an illustration of the rate of arrest for each category of relationship. In calls where the offender and the victim were intimate partners, an arrest is made in 48.0 percent of cases of intimidation, simple assault, and aggravated assault. When some other domestic relationship exists between the victim and the offender, the arrest rate is slightly less, at 43.0 percent. Stranger and nondomestic relationship cases have lower arrest rates, 34.5 percent and 28.1 percent, respectively. As noted in Chapter 8, however, if the intimate relationship is between same-sex partners, the chance of the police arresting both persons is higher than in cases involving heterosexual couples. Primary aggressor laws were passed to address dual arrest situations in IPV.

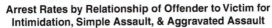

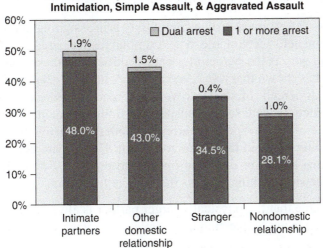

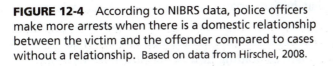

FIGURE 12-4   According to NIBRS data, police officers make more arrests when there is a domestic relationship between the victim and the offender compared to cases without a relationship. Based on data from Hirschel, 2008.

Primary Aggressor Determination

In response to increasing numbers of dual arrest in domestic violence incidents, states began to pass "primary aggressor," "predominant aggressor," or "dominant aggressor" provisions. At least 24 states have laws that contain a special aggressor designation (Hirschel & Buzawa, 2002). The **primary aggressor** in IPV is the person who is responsible for the perpetuation of the violence, not necessarily who initiated it in one particular incident. A primary aggressor determination should not include who started verbal arguments because verbal provocation is not a justifiable cause for assaultive behavior.

Primary aggressor laws offer guidance to police officers in determining who is the victim and who is the offender, using standards other than gender or size of the individuals involved. There is a general trend to direct police officers to avoid dual arrests. In a study on dual arrest in cases of IPV, more than 44 percent of surveyed agencies in states without primary aggressor laws had department policies that mandate police officers to identify primary aggressors along with specific instructions on how to make that identification (Hirschel et al., 2007). Figure 12-5 is a diagram that describes the decision-making process for the primary aggressor determination.

Questions that the police officer considers in making the primary aggressor determination include the following—Who in this relationship poses the most danger to the other? Who is at most risk of future harm? For situations that appear to be mutual combative, the police officer can look for three elements of self-defense that may be helpful in making the primary aggressor determination:

- Did one person using force have a reasonable belief that he or she was at risk of bodily harm? The risk is reasonable if based on prior incidents, when a recent escalation in violence has occurred, or when a specific threat was made to the self-defender that caused the defense posture.
- Was the risk of harm actual or imminent?
- Was the force used reasonably necessary to prevent or stop the infliction of bodily harm? For example, a person small in stature may use a weapon to prevent the abuser from inflicting bodily harm.

The challenge for the criminal justice community is in assigning blame. One party must be responsible and held accountable in the criminal justice paradigm. Determining who is the victim and who is the perpetrator can be difficult in these complex crime situations. Research has shown that role reversal occurs in some relationships. In Charlotte, for example, 19.8 percent of suspects were recorded in future events as victims, and 17.8 percent of victims were seen as suspects in future incidents (Friday et al., 2006).

Some police officers respond by arresting both the man and woman in the domestic violence dispute to avoid having to sort it out. Experts are beginning to acknowledge this dilemma and offer direction on how to proceed. Some common criteria to involve in the decision-making process include the following:

- Do not assume that the physically larger partner is always the primary aggressor. Care must be taken to question the couple and any witnesses closely before making an arrest.
- Be aware that bruises may take hours to appear, whereas signs of defensive violence, such as scratching or biting, are immediate. Question the partners separately and determine how the visible marks were made and why. Did the victim bite the arm that was holding him or her down, for example?

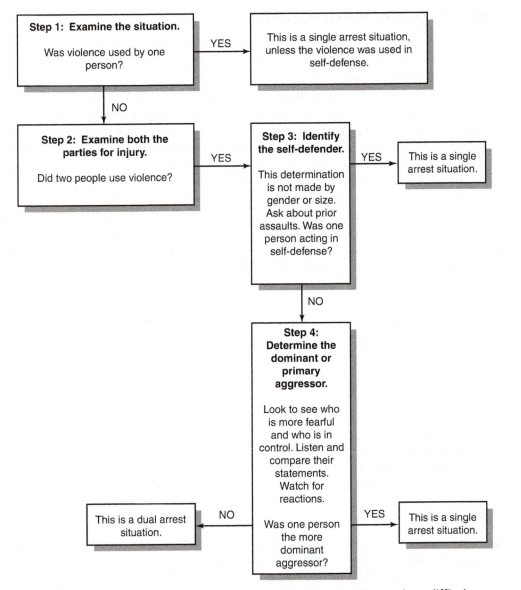

FIGURE 12-5   The dominant or primary aggressor determination can be a difficult decision for police officers. This chart shows the decision-making process that may be used to make the primary aggressor determination.

- Determine whether there has been a history of abuse. Batterers tend to recommit their offenses. It is more likely that the perpetrator of violence in the past has perpetrated again. Ask whether there has been a recent escalation in the violence and why.
- Victims may feel free to express their anger about the violence to police. Anger or the expression of anger should not be mistaken for primary aggressive behavior.
- Do not allow yourself to be provoked into arresting both partners. An angry victim's conduct is not a justification for arrest. Failure to "shut up" is not criminal behavior and does not indicate who the batterer is.
- Determine who the initial aggressor was. When signs of injury are exhibited by both parties, consider the possibility of self-defense and examine the relative level of injury or force involved.

HOW DO POLICE GET INVOLVED?

The majority of calls for service are domestic disturbance calls resulting from citizen complaints. These reports of domestic violence are crisis situations in which the violence is still likely to be occurring. Most reports will be from telephone calls. The caller may be angry, confused, or injured due to abuse at the time of the call. It may be a child who is frantic because a parent is being beaten up in the next room. It may also be a neighbor or someone else who is fearful of the noises from a fight next door. The dispatcher or desk officer should gather as much information as possible to prepare the officers who are responding. If possible, the caller should be kept on the phone until help arrives to provide updates on what is occurring.

Traditionally, officers were dispatched to domestic calls without having enough information to be prepared. Knowledge is power, and in this case knowledge of the situation can prevent anxiety and result in a better response. The following are the basic questions asked by the person taking the report and dispatching it to the officers. If the abuse is occurring at the time, any change in the level of violence is important to convey to the responding officer.

- Who is the caller?
- What is the caller's telephone number?
- Where is the location of the abuse?
- Is anyone hurt?
- Are any weapons involved (guns, knives, clubs, sticks, etc.)?
- Are there guns in the house?
- Who are the parties involved?
- What is happening?
- Is either party drunk or high on drugs?
- Is there a restraining or protection order in effect?
- Are there children in the house?

At the Scene

The officer must be aware constantly; the violence does not necessarily stop when the police arrive. The officer must look and listen. The level of anger is likely to remain high after the officer intervenes and separates the people involved. Most domestic disturbance calls involve misdemeanor crimes or civil violations. Offering aid to the victim and disarming an assailant are the priorities for officers who first arrive at the scene. In Charlotte, North Carolina, approximately one-half of the victims received bruising or more serious injury during domestic–violence–related assaults in 2003 (Friday et al., 2006). Refer to Figure 12-6 to see the types of injury recorded in Charlotte, North Carolina.

1. The first responsibility of the responding officer(s) is to determine whether emergency medical care is needed. How the injured are taken to the hospital is dictated by police department policy. For some jurisdictions, the police and the emergency medical transportation are the same. In others, officers are required to transport victims to the nearest hospital in their cruiser. Some departments are forbidden by policy from transporting victims, and the officers would call for an ambulance. The major reason behind calling for an ambulance is that officers may not be able to render lifesaving care to a victim during transportation.

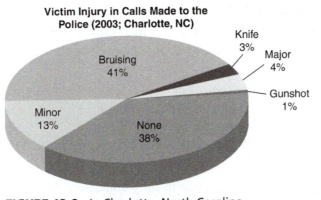

FIGURE 12-6 In Charlotte, North Carolina, approximately 8 percent of the domestic violence calls to the police involved major injury or the use of weapons. Based on data from Friday et al., 2006.

2. When it is safe to do so, and after the injured person has received emergency medical attention if needed, the officer will investigate to determine who the perpetrator is and who the victim is. Determining the primary aggressor is sometimes the most challenging part of the effort to resolve any domestic dispute. Spouses and cohabiting adults talk to police the most during a dispute—that usually changes after the emergency is over.

3. The next step is to assess the level of risk for injury to the victim. Questions for cohabiting couples and those in dating relationships should be specific. Many states require officers to request initially that a firearm or weapon be placed temporarily in their custody. Without compliance, the officers may have the right to search for and take custody of a firearm or weapon to alleviate the threat of severe violence that it poses. The weapon might be returned after a check to determine that it is lawfully possessed. Unless the officer is required by law to return the weapon immediately, it is within his or her discretion to make the return at a later date. If the weapons cannot be seized legally, a judge may order the defendant to surrender guns, his or her license to carry them, and his or her firearm identification card during the pending of an order or criminal prosecution.

4. The final step is to collect evidence. Three types of evidence can be gathered: real (or tangible) evidence, documentary evidence, and testimonial evidence. The first form of evidence, real or tangible evidence, is physical. Things that you can acquire, such as a fingerprint or a bullet, are examples. The second type of evidence is documentary, something that is recorded, such as financial statements or 911 tapes. By themselves, these items are not evidentiary but may have significance after a crime has been committed. The third type of evidence is testimonial; both interviews and interrogations come under this heading. The majority of court-introduced evidence, approximately 80 percent, is testimonial.

TO ARREST OR NOT TO ARREST: THAT IS THE QUESTION!

How do police officers decide to arrest? Does the act committed fall within the definition of a felony or a misdemeanor? Does the offense constitute a crime that carries with it the power of arrest? Is there a proarrest or mandated arrest response that would limit the discretion at the scene? In other words, officers need to know what must be done and then what can be done, in response to the violence encountered in their jurisdiction. Here are five questions that police officers must consider when making the decision:

1. Does the action constitute a crime?
2. Is there probable cause that a crime was committed?
3. Is the crime a misdemeanor or a felony?
4. Does the officer have the warrantless power of arrest for that crime?
5. Is there an outstanding protection order that has been violated?

Review copies of the state's penal code to fully understand laws explicitly intended to address domestic violence offenses. If the call involves an older adult or a child, specific legislation may offer protection in addition to the criminal codes with which the officers are more familiar. The use of protective custody may be helpful when misconduct fails to reach the level of a crime and the police officer has the legal power to use this option. Factors that appear to increase the likelihood of arrest are victim injury and the presence of minors (Hirschel et al., 2007).

Civil Protection Codes

Although it varies from state to state, a large number of states make it a criminal offense to violate a restraining order. When there is probable cause to believe that there has been a violation of a restraining order, police are mandated to make an arrest in at least 33 states (Hirschel et al., 2007). See Figure 12-7 for an illustration of the states that mandate arrest for protection order violations. Violation of a civil restraining,

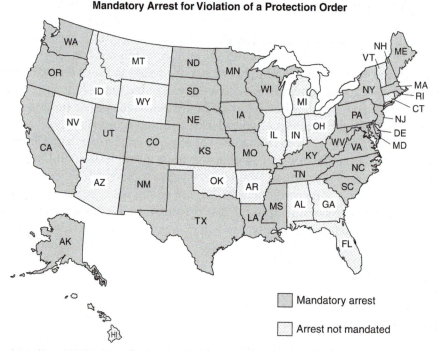

Mandatory Arrest for Violation of a Protection Order

☐ Mandatory arrest

☐ Arrest not mandated

FIGURE 12-7   In the majority of states, violation of a court-ordered domestic violence protection order involves a mandatory arrest situation. Based on data from Hirschel et al., 2007.

no-contact, or protection order is a separate crime in these states, apart from the ongoing abuse. Usually, it is a misdemeanor, with the power of arrest given by statute.

Mental Health Codes

In some instances, it may be necessary to remove suspects and to hold them involuntarily for evaluation at a mental health facility. Emergency procedures for overnight commitment are specific to each state, with particular amounts of time allowed before a court hearing. Officers should become familiar with state mental health provisions for involuntary commitments and evaluations.

Use of Available Resources

In addition to any legal requirements that might exist for reporting abuse to another agency, response to domestic violence can be simplified by using local and state resources whenever possible. Networking and developing the sources for extralegal intervention are beneficial to both the victim and the officers. If the crime involves an elderly victim, contact the local elder services or adult protective services for assistance and future follow-up. If an arrest is anticipated in a home where children would be left unattended, contact the local department of social services or child protective agency and request that it take custody.

Victim-witness programs exist in every state and are helpful in advising domestic violence victims of their rights and procedures to obtain civil restraining orders. Local crisis centers are valuable in offering emergency shelter for the victim. Referrals of battered women to other agencies have been used as an avoidance tactic. That is not the suggestion here. A coordinated system approach to domestic violence response includes utilizing alternative services in addition to traditional policing.

WHAT ABOUT PROBABLE CAUSE?

Probable cause is a standard of proof that must be satisfied for any search or seizure to occur. An arrest is legally defined as a seizure and therefore falls under the same requirement for probable cause as a search. The probable cause requirement is stated in the Fourth Amendment to the U.S. Constitution and state constitutions: "The right of the people to be secure in their persons, houses, papers, and effects, against unreasonable searches and seizures, shall not be violated, and no Warrants shall issue, but upon probable cause."

An officer has the task of determining whether probable cause exists to believe that a crime has been committed and that an arrest is warranted. Sources for determining probable cause include the following:

- Collective knowledge doctrine
- Knowledge about the suspect
- Suspect's behavior to police
- Reliable hearsay
- Observations of the police

The U.S. Supreme Court explicitly defined the probable cause requirement in *Gerstein v. Pugh* (1975), while referring to past instances of definition: "Probable cause to arrest exists when the facts and circumstances known to the officer are sufficient to warrant a reasonably prudent person in believing that the suspect has committed or is committing a crime" (*Beck v. Ohio*, 1964). The standard is universal; both federal and state laws require meeting this level of proof to justify depriving persons of their liberty under the Fourth and Fourteenth Amendments to the Constitution. Additional states' constitutional provisions echo the requirement.

Exact requirements for the level of information to rise above mere suspicion without reaching the adjudication standard of proof beyond a reasonable doubt are clarified through both state and federal case law and legislation.

> Probable cause to arrest [in Massachusetts] must exist at the moment of arrest. Facts and circumstances, which come to an officer's attention after a person has been taken into custody, may not be used retroactively to justify the arrest. However, an officer need not make the arrest as soon as probable cause arises. Unlike probable cause to search, which is of limited duration, once probable cause to arrest is formed, it will continue to exist for an indefinite period, at least if no intervening exculpatory facts come to light. (Commonwealth of Massachusetts, 1996)

When an arrest is not possible due to the lack of probable cause, additional options for police officers may be available. Many agencies give police officers the ability to seize weapons used by the suspect, separate parties, seize weapons in the home, and remove one party (Townsend et al., 2006). Examples of other options include the issuance of a citation or an appearance ticket or asking one party to leave.

SEARCH AND SEIZURE

The probable cause requirement attaches to searches as well as seizures conducted by government officials. Strict adherence to federal and state constitutional guidelines is imperative to obtain evidence that will withstand the scrutiny of the court. Therefore, it is best to conduct a search with a warrant whenever time permits. The use of searching with a valid warrant is beneficial in domestic cases and should be considered to validate the statements of victims. Its use should not be limited to investigations of fatalities; tangible evidence speaks louder than words.

Searching without a warrant is per se unreasonable. Some exceptions to the warrant requirement do exist, however. Places that are not covered by the Fourth Amendment protection that can be searched without a warrant include common areas, entranceways, public places, semipublic places, open fields, and driveways. An open field or driveway that is posted "no trespassing" does not invoke constitutional protection. An officer may commit a trespass and be held separately accountable for that crime but still search without violating the warrant requirement.

Exceptions to the Warrant Requirement

Some of the relevant exceptions to the warrant requirement are presented below, but this is not an exhaustive list.

CONSENT SEARCH   This form of exception is scrutinized more than others and must be used judiciously. Consent must be given freely and voluntarily, not as a mere acquiescence to legal authority or under intimidation. Although officers may mention the possibility of getting a warrant, they cannot demand, trick, or force cooperation. Consent to enter a home is not equivalent to a search consent, and even if consent is given it may be revoked at any time. The person providing consent can do so only for areas that are commonly used. People who live together cannot give consent to search in areas that are private and used exclusively by the other person. A person who has a locked desk, a separate closet, or a private room may have an expectation of privacy and must be the one to offer consent for searching those areas. Because domestic violence usually occurs in a place where there is a joint ownership or residence, this distinction is quite important.

EXIGENT CIRCUMSTANCE AND DOMESTIC VIOLENCE   Police routinely enter homes for domestic calls and may investigate under this exception to the warrant requirement. This allows for a sweep to be conducted searching for weapons and injured people. It does not authorize a protracted and general search of the entire home.

SEARCH INCIDENT TO A LAWFUL ARREST   A person who is legally under arrest may be searched. The body and areas within the immediate control of the arrested person are included. The purpose is to allow an officer to seize weapons, and the search is used for his or her protection. It is not a general search of a house or vehicle where the person is found to look for evidence. The scope and intensity of the search are limited.

PLAIN-VIEW SEIZURE   Articles in plain view in public places or where the police have a legitimate right to be present, which are readily apparent as contraband or as the fruits or instrumentality of a crime, can be seized. This is not considered a search, and no warrant is required. To justify the plain-view seizure, the officer cannot move items to find identifying serial numbers to confirm that the item is in fact contraband. The key point is that the contraband must be readily apparent, such as drugs, instruments of the crime, or weapons. Plain-view observation can occur where no expectation of privacy exists, such as public bathrooms (not stalls), open fields, public airspace, or a private driveway. Using enhancements, such as binoculars, to view suspected contraband is acceptable. Techniques to improve hearing cannot be used where persons have a reasonable expectation of privacy, such as telephone lines in some states.

The plain-view doctrine justifies the seizure of items that are not anticipated during a search under a warrant. A search warrant executed for evidence of domestic violence, for example, may lead to the discovery of illegal drugs. The drugs may be seized without applying for a new warrant. In some jurisdictions, the seizure must bear a relationship to the crime under investigation, however, or a new warrant is required.

What Police Look For

A checklist is helpful to remind the investigator of the responsibilities at the scene. Refer to Figure 12-8. This checklist can be adapted and changed to fit the needs and specific responsibilities in any jurisdiction. Evidence of the crime can be seized whenever possible. This includes, but is not limited to, weapons that were used during the crime. If the abuse allegations involve physical abuse and injury, the following evidence must be preserved:

1. Further evidence of the assault, such as bloodstained articles and clothes, should be secured at the scene and placed in paper bags (not plastic).
2. Photographs of the damage to property can be taken. Such damage may include smashed windows in the house or car, bullet holes, and knife slashes.

DOMESTIC VIOLENCE INVESTIGATION CHECKLIST

Victim Information

Name: _____

Noted date of birth
Noted location upon arrival
Administered first aid, noted if
    medical treatment was sought
Noted time dispatched, arrived,
    and when victim spoke
Recorded excited utterances
Described demeanor
Height and weight noted
Described physical condition
Noted complaints of injuries
Described injuries in detail (size,
    location, color)
Noted relationship to suspect
Detailed description of incident
Recorded history of abuse
Recorded history of court orders
Explained rights
Provided written copy of rights
Recorded temporary address/phone
    (Do <u>NOT</u> include in report!)
Advised of suspect's right to bail

Does this case also involve:

Child abuse   report filed
Elder abuse   report filed
Disabled abuse   report filed

Witness Information

Identified reporting party
Interviewed reporting party
Documented names, DOBs, addresses,
    and phone numbers of all witnesses
Interviewed all witnesses, separately
Listed names and DOBs of children
    present
Recorded names of emergency
    personnel
Identified treating physician
Identified desk officer/dispatcher

Suspect Information

Name: _____

Noted date of birth
Noted location upon arrival
Administered first aid, noted if
    medical treatment was sought
Noted when suspect first spoke
Recorded excited utterances
Described demeanor
Height and weight noted
Described physical condition
Noted complaints of injury
Described injuries in detail (size,
    location, color)
Temporary address noted (if vacate
    order exists)
Noted existence of any restraining
    orders

Following Miranda, when applicable

Asked if she/he wanted to make
    a statement
Noted whether suspect knew of
    and/or understood restraining
    order
Detailed description of incident
Noted history of abuse in any
    relationship

Evidence

Photographed/described crime scene
Took full body picture of suspect
Took full body picture of victim
Photographed victim's injuries
Photographed suspect's injuries
Seized items thrown or broken
Seized firearms for safety
Seized firearms under surrender
    order
Requested medical records
Requested 911 tape

FIGURE 12-8 Domestic violence investigation checklist.

3. Photographs of the injury to the victim should also be taken, but these are normally taken at the police department or hospital. Bruising on the victim may not be immediately apparent, so it is important to follow up with the victim in the days following an assault.

4. Photographs of the location can be substituted for a sketch to document where the assault took place and to portray property damage as the result of the assault.

5. If the assault took place in multiple rooms/locations, each location should be documented for damage and any evidence seized.

INTERVIEWING

The best method of interviewing is to separate the parties and question them individually after a brief cooling-down period. The interviews should be conducted outside the hearing range of the other, with equal levels of respect afforded to each. For crimes involving intimate partners, the process may be a long one. Sufficient time to assess the situation involves skillful interviewing and the desire to be thorough. There is no quick resolution of a domestic dispute.

The three basic phases of the interview process are preparation, establishment of the psychological content, and the actual questioning. Obtaining information from the dispatcher or from officers on the scene satisfies the preparation stage. If the interview is staged at the convenience of the officer rather than as a result of crisis intervention, additional preparation would include contacting agencies that have previously been involved. Record checks and witness interviews would also be considered part of the necessary preparation.

The second phase contains the extremely important element of rapport, which describes the relationship established between the interviewer and the interviewee. This relationship can be constructed or destroyed within seconds if the responder shows distaste, distrust, or condemnation of the person who is confronted. Showing obvious bias such as asking the woman what she did to provoke an attack, or assuming that a blood-soaked man was the abuser, breaks down rapport and inhibits information that would benefit the officer and facilitate a resolution. Victim cooperation is consistently tied to officer attitudes. Look at the evidence and question both parties without prejudice. If a victim does not believe that he or she will get fair treatment from the officer, the person will not bother to try. If victims do not give information it may be difficult for the case to proceed.

The third phase is the actual questioning. In addition to questions about the incident under investigation, a risk assessment must be made to determine the level of danger the batterer presents. The following key points constitute a **risk assessment**:

1. Does the suspect believe the victim is attempting to end the relationship? This is when the majority of killings take place. The most dangerous period for the victim is when the batterer realizes that this time the victim is really going through with the breakup.

2. Does the suspect possess weapons? This question must be asked in all situations. Guns, knives, *nunchaku*, and any other weapons should be confiscated, if possible, even if they have not been used against the victim. If they have been used before, the danger for the victim is much higher. Threats to use a weapon, even if they were not carried out, are just as dangerous as a display of the weapon.

3. Does the suspect abuse alcohol or drugs? The batterer who is also a substance abuser is at increased risk of committing a dangerous or lethal assault.

4. Were threats made? Threats to kill the victim and the children and/or to commit suicide must be taken seriously. Batterers do not commonly kill themselves without first attempting to kill at least one family member.

5. Has the suspect committed any previous sexual assaults against the victim? Previous sexual assaults are indicators that the batterer is almost twice as likely to commit a dangerous act of violence against the victim.

6. Has the suspect been following the victim? Stalking, reading the victim's mail, listening in on phone calls, or other acts of surveillance should be considered an implied threat.

7. What are the frequency and severity of the violence? The best predictor of future violence is past violence. Frequent violence (two or three times per month or more) or severe violence (requiring hospitalization) places the victim in a high-risk category.

8. Is the batterer depressed or suffering from mental health problems? Some mental health problems are linked to increased propensity to commit a lethal assault. Look for delusional fears and for severe depression.

Interviewing the Older Adult Victim

Empowering the elderly victim is helpful to both the victim and the officer. Communicating respect by referring to the victim by his or her title—Miss, Mrs., Mr., or Dr., for example—can be helpful during the rapport-building portion of the interview. At all times, the dignity of the elder person should be maintained. The interviewer should go slowly and use language that is easily understood but not patronizing.

According to the Police Executive Research Forum, the following guidelines are suggested for interviews with older adults (Nerenberg, 1993).

- Investigations should be coordinated with adult protective services personnel or the ombudsman when possible to avoid multiple interviews.
- Joint interviews with public health nurses or others treating medical conditions may assist agencies when appropriate.
- Interviewers should attempt to establish **rapport** with the person being interviewed.
- Whenever possible, interviewers should use audio and video technology.
- Officers should respect the confidentiality of all parties whenever possible.
- To prevent contamination or collusion, interviewers should avoid disclosure of case information to all parties involved in the alleged offense.
- Interviewers should ask general, nonleading questions.
- Officers should ask all witnesses to identify others who have relevant information and to provide their contact information. Interviewers will need to identify the victim's doctor, conservator, attorney, social worker, and any agencies that provide service to the victim.

INTERROGATION OF SUSPECTS

A suspect's confession presents the most injurious evidence of a crime. Properly conducted in accordance with legal requirements to ensure voluntariness, an admission provides the best evidence. Supreme Court Justice Byron White wrote, "The defendant's own confession is probably the most probative and damaging evidence that can be admitted against him" (*Bruton v. United States*, 1968).

VICTIM PROTECTIONS

Protection from an IPV offender is found in various forms, including criminal law (with legal sanctions) and criminal or civil protection orders (some provisions may include criminal/legal sanctions). Police officers have the responsibility to enforce domestic violence law and the provisions of a protection order. In cases of domestic violence, there is an additional need to seize any weapons belonging to a person who is the subject of a domestic violence restraining order.

Been There ... Done That!

The years that Alice was married to William can only be described as a reign of terror. Her daughter Deborah moved out of the house at an early age to escape the frequent rape and other physical assaults that she had endured at the hands of her stepfather. I knew of the sexual assaults because of the investigation later prompted by the adult Deborah. It was a frustrating experience—most of the incidents had been committed past the statute of limitations for Massachusetts. So heinous were the crimes, however, that Assistant District Attorney Anger, who was handling the case, filed new legislation to extend the period under which crimes against children could be prosecuted across the state. Little was known about the conditions under which the abuse had occurred.

Then, the call from Deborah came: Would I do her a favor and come to the hospital to document her mother's injuries? The face that I photographed was so swollen, blackened, and bloody that one would swear she had barely survived a fatal car accident. It was not the first time that William had beat her bloody, and it would not be the last. Prosecution did occur, but the system was not equipped to offer any protection or advice.

Approximately 10 years later, I met Alice again. She has difficulty looking at me; the detached retina in one eye is a permanent condition, due to the numerous blows to her face. Hunched over, she finds it difficult to stand erect; hard objects that were used to beat her across the back took their toll. She walks with a cane; her legs had suffered many breaks. I remembered her telling how William would beat her to the ground and twist her legs backward around the kitchen table.

She now works as an advocate for battered women and felt able to tell me more of what had happened. Worse than the beating was the loss of her daughter, she related. She was still bitter about her inability to protect herself or her child, and their relationship was strained. Living in an isolated area of the state, she took solace in caring for her animals. Her precious dogs were found dead from gunshots from time to time. Anything of joy to her was broken over the years, including her spirit. My intervention was the first of many that were necessary for her to leave the situation. She had little strength left after the ordeal. What had changed? The criminal justice response had changed. Once restraining orders were made available, she used that option. She could report the events to the police, even though it had taken years for anyone to listen. She survived, barely.

Orders of Protection

To deter abusive and intimidating acts, civil and criminal courts have the authority to issue restraining orders. As explained earlier, police officers have the responsibility to enforce protection orders. Referred to as restraining orders, injunctions, or protective orders, these court orders restrict or prohibit one individual's behavior in order to protect another. They generally include provisions restraining contact; prohibiting abuse, intimidation, or harassment; and prohibiting the possession of firearms. Protection provisions may include financial resources for costs incurred due to partner violence and temporary custody of minor children.

Gun Control

The system for assuring proper gun ownership is partially achieved through the *National Instant Criminal Background Check System* (NICS), which is a national database that contains records on individuals who are disqualified from possessing a firearm under state or federal laws. These records include an individual's name, sex, race, other personal descriptive data, date of birth, state of residence, and sometimes a unique identifying number. This information is maintained so that gun dealers may determine whether the sale of a firearm to a prospective purchaser would violate federal or state law. The purpose of the NICS check is to ensure timely transfer of firearms to law-abiding citizens while denying those transfers to persons who are prohibited from receiving firearms under the Brady Handgun Violence Prevention Act.

POSSESSION OF FIREARM WHILE SUBJECT TO ORDER OF PROTECTION. 18 U.S.C. §922(G)(8) The Protective Order Gun Ban, passed in 1994, prohibits any person against whom there is a restraining or protective order for domestic violence from possessing a gun. The protection order must have been issued following an evidentiary hearing for which the defendant had notice and an opportunity to appear. The protection order must also include a specific finding that the defendant represents a credible threat to the physical safety of the victim or must include an explicit prohibition against the use of force that would reasonably be expected to cause injury.

POSSESSION OF FIREARM AFTER CONVICTION OF MISDEMEANOR CRIME OF DOMESTIC VIOLENCE. 18 U.S.C. §922(G)(9) A 1996 law, known as the Lautenberg Amendment, prohibits anyone convicted of a misdemeanor crime of domestic violence or child abuse from purchasing or possessing a gun. This prohibition applies to persons convicted of such misdemeanors at any time, even if the conviction occurred prior to the new law's effective date. The official use exemption does not apply to Sections 922(d)(9) and 922(g)(9). This means that law-enforcement officers or military personnel who have been convicted of a qualifying domestic violence misdemeanor will not be able to possess or receive firearms for any purpose, including the performance of official duties.

A misdemeanor crime of domestic violence is defined in the act as an offense that (1) is a misdemeanor under federal or state law and (2) has, as an element, the use or attempted use of physical force, or the threatened use of a deadly weapon, committed by a current or former spouse, parent, or guardian of the victim; by a person with whom the victim shares a child in common; by a person who is cohabiting with or has cohabited with the victim as a spouse, parent, or guardian; or by a person similarly situated to a spouse, parent, or guardian of the victim. Application of this legislation is retroactive. It prohibits people convicted of domestic violence offenses from purchasing a weapon or ammunition even if the offense occurred before the legislation became effective, regardless of whether a weapon was used during a domestic assault.

Specific concerns about the extent of domestic violence among police officer families prompted the legislative change that did not exempt them from the gun ban. The act was purposefully amended to prohibit all law-enforcement officers and government employees convicted of domestic violence offenses—misdemeanor or felony—from carrying, owning, or possession of guns for any purpose. This provision, known as the Lautenberg Amendment to Public Law 104-208, has caused considerable controversy among law-enforcement officers. Police officers without the ability to carry a weapon in the performance of their duties might lose their jobs.

More About It: National Instant Criminal Background Check

As of December 1998, the Federal Bureau of Investigation began the new NICS. Within 14 days, the system had processed 372,565 background checks on people who sought to purchase firearms. There were 3,348 gun sales denied to those attempting to purchase weapons in violation of federal law during that period. Domestic violence offenders have lost the right to purchase weapons and ammunition, along with fugitives, the mentally ill, those dishonorably discharged from the military, illegal aliens, drug users, and those under domestic violence restraining orders.

The NICS eliminates the need for the waiting or "cooling-off" period that had been required under the Brady Act. Sarah Brady, wife of James Brady, for whom the gun control law is named, expressed concern over the removal of that safeguard.

Apart from the federal initiative, numerous state and local police departments have instituted policies that conform to the Lautenberg gun ban. Recent state law also reflects the trend in nonexemption for police officers who batter a child or spouse. A clear trend has emerged that will include, not excuse, police officers who commit family violence crimes.

INTIMATE PARTNER VIOLENCE ACROSS STATE LINES

Interstate domestic violence and interstate violation of protection orders are two newer federal offenses. This code section applies if a batterer travels across state lines to reach the victim and also if the victim was induced to travel across state lines to come to the batterer. The law is gender neutral; it applies to both male and female victims and their intimate partners. In 1995, the first successful federal prosecution for interstate domestic violence took place in the Southern District of West Virginia (Lehrman, 1997). Christopher Bailey battered his wife into a coma in their West Virginia home and then drove through Ohio and Kentucky for several days, abusing her throughout. Despite a bleeding head wound, she was confined to the trunk of the car. Several days later, he took her to a hospital in Kentucky. Because of the delay in treatment, Sonya Bailey is now in a permanent vegetative state. Bailey was convicted of kidnapping and interstate domestic violence and is now serving a life sentence. On May 2, 1997, the Fourth Circuit affirmed Bailey's conviction in *United States v. Bailey*, 112 F.3d 758 (4th Cir. 1997).

Paving the way for the nationwide reciprocal enforcement of protection orders, the National Stalker and Domestic Violence Reduction Act, 28 U.S.C. Section 534 (1997), authorizes civil restraining and abuse protection orders to be entered in all National Crime Information Center databases. Since the authorization in 1997, only 19 states have begun to enter their data, less than 5 percent of the estimated 2 million eligible orders (Office for Victims of Crime, 2002). Without participation in the database, the effective nationwide enforcement of existing orders remains doubtful. Without enforcement of the protection order, the database represents a false sense of security to the victim. Indications are that enforcement practices across the nation are inconsistent; less than one-quarter of the states have either established a streamlined method of verifying protection orders or operated a statewide registry (Office for Victims of Crime, 2002).

More About It: Full Faith and Credit

The wording found in Massachusetts General Laws Ch. 209A, Section 3.3G is representative of the full faith and credit requirement:

A protective order issued in another jurisdiction shall be given full faith and credit in the Commonwealth. Therefore, officers shall make a warrantless arrest of any person the officer witnesses or has probable cause to believe has violated an emergency, temporary or permanent vacate, refrain from abuse, stay away, or no-contact order or judgment issued by another jurisdiction.

In assessing probable cause, an officer may presume the validity of the protection order issued by another jurisdiction when the officer has been provided with: (A) a copy of the order, by any source and (B) a statement by the victim that such order remains in effect. Victims who move from an issuing jurisdiction should be aware that their order has force in another county or state. They should be prepared to carry the actual order with them at all times if they fear continuing abuse.

Full Faith and Credit

Police officers are required to enforce protection orders from other states under the Violence Against Women Act (VAWA). Passed by Congress in 1994 and reauthorized in 2000 and 2008, the VAWA provides comprehensive efforts to address IPV, sexual assault, and stalking. VAWA includes the provision for the nationwide enforcement of civil and criminal protection orders. Known as **full faith and credit**, the mandate means that a state must enforce another state's protection order, even when the enforcing state would not issue such an order itself. States have implemented this provision by including the language of full faith and credit in their own statutes and codes on domestic violence prevention.

New provisions prohibit states and tribes from requiring notification (to the perpetrator) of the registration of an out-of-state or tribal protection order unless the victim requests the notification. Furthermore, the victim cannot be required to register and/or file the order in the new state as a prerequisite for enforcing out-of-state or tribal orders of protection. While not required, some states have provisions for the registration of out-of-state protection orders. Registering an out-of-state order puts the protection order on file with a new jurisdiction for the purpose of expediting police response in the case of an emergency.

MYTH AND REALITY

When police are confronted with stranger violence, the victim is readily apparent. That is not the case with intimate partner offenses. Common myths prevail with expectations that the victim and the perpetrator can be identified easily. Myths about the reliability of the witness are common. Here are some of these misconceptions.

Victims: Myth and Reality

- *Myth:* The victim of domestic violence is the passive one in the relationship.
- *Reality:* The couple may appear to be mutually combative at the time of intervention. They may both lash out at anyone trying to help them. To determine who the primary aggressor is, it is necessary to defuse the anger and interview both parties without prejudice. There is no proper way for a victim to act. Victims may be either passive or aggressive. Victims often appear defensive. Determining who threw the first blow and why is one way to attach responsibility.
- *Myth:* The police will find the victim more likable than the perpetrator.
- *Reality:* Often, the victims of abuse will be interviewed when they are in crisis. Frustrations, anger, fear, and shame are just some of the emotions that they might be experiencing. The mix of emotions may cause the victim to yell and scream at the person attempting to intervene. It is conceivable that the victim will be the least "likable" of the people in a domestic violence situation. An objective interview will not be based on the sympathies of the interviewer toward any party.
- *Myth:* The woman is always the victim.
- *Reality:* Domestic abuse victims can be of either gender and any age. The victim is the injured party—most often that is the woman, but not always. Determining the harm can be complex and at times goes beyond a simple physical assault.

Injury may be due to defense posturing. The police officer is guided by legislation that dictates the manner and extent of law-enforcement action in domestic violence. Your state may not recognize same-sex domestic violence or marital rape. Policy and law must guide the officer.

Perpetrators: Myth and Reality

- *Myth:* Perpetrators of domestic violence are mean and nasty people.
- *Reality:* For the "family-only" type of abuser (Rucinski, 1998), the face that is presented to the outside world is of charm and humor. These offenders are often skilled in control and manipulation. They may control themselves and attempt to manipulate officials as well. This perpetrator is just as likely to be the more calm and sweet-tempered of the two when faced with police officers. Alternatively, an aggressive abuser will be more apt to remain violent during intervention (Rucinski, 1998).
- *Myth:* Abusers are lowlifes and uneducated people.
- *Reality:* The perpetrator may be the pillar of the community and have a high level of education. Such abusers will attempt to explain away their behaviors, often in front of a passive victim. Abusers know that it is in their best interest to befriend the interviewer, and they do tend to act in their best interest.
- *Myth:* "She asked for it."
- *Reality:* The perpetrator may feel justified in using physical force due to a precipitating event. This does not excuse or justify violence other than for self-defense. It is a crime to use physical violence against another, regardless of the personal relationship that exists.

CONCLUSIONS

Since the 1960s, the trend toward proactive policing for crimes of IPV has followed other examples. Moving from nonintervention to mediation to arrest, the criminalization of domestic violence has been achieved, and it is up to the policy makers to ensure the passage of legislation that will allow legitimate police action. Preconceived notions of drama and excitement drown out the reality that IPV is the most frequent call for many jurisdictions; although oddly, it has rarely appeared in the profiles of what police do. Often, departments fail to validate this large portion of duty through training or proper incentives.

Police officers have been given warrantless arrest powers in all states for domestic-related offenses. Policies dictate the requirements for arresting and the alternatives that may be used to protect intimate partner victims. In addition to the power of arrest for domestic-related assaults, many states also mandate arrest for violations of civil protection orders.

Evidence collection, including interviewing and interrogation, is an important aspect of IPV investigation. Laws of search and seizure and exemptions to the warrant requirement are tools that police officers may use during an investigation. Treating these crimes as other important crimes, an investigation checklist is helpful to consult. Assisting victims in their protection involves providing information and assuring firearm control. Police officers now have the additional requirement of enforcing civil and criminal protection orders in each state, regardless of their origin.

SIMPLY SCENARIO
The Role of the Police

On Tuesday night, Officer Jones was working the evening shift and received a call of an ongoing fight at 50 Spring Street in his city. On his arrival, he heard a woman yelling and screaming obscenities. He entered the house and found the woman standing over a man who was obviously drunk. "She hit me," said the drunk. The woman yelled louder, calling him names and pointing to her head, "Just look at this!"

Question: What is the goal of the police officer in this situation? Be sure to include the myths and reality of IPV.

Questions for Review

1. What did researchers conclude about the effectiveness of arrest in cases of domestic disturbance cases from the MDVE?
2. What kind of training do specialized domestic violence response units go through? Why is it important?
3. What is the difference between proarrest and mandatory arrest?
4. What are the three basic phases of the interviewing process? Briefly explain each of them.
5. For situations that appear to be mutually combative, the police officer can look for three elements of self-defense that may be helpful in the primary aggressor determination. Explain.
6. The five replication studies cast doubt on the effectiveness of arresting the batterer in cases of domestic violence. What did the reanalysis of these studies by Maxwell et al. conclude?
7. What is the term used to describe when both parties in a domestic situation are arrested? Why is this practice discouraged?
8. Is violation of a civil restraining order a crime?
9. What is the definition of probable cause that was stated in *Gerstein v. Pugh* (1975)?
10. Explain the Lautenberg Amendment and its effect on military and law-enforcement officers.

Internet-Based Exercises

1. Womenslaw.org is a nonprofit Web site that offers legal advice to victims of domestic violence. Included in its Web site is a searchable database on domestic violence statutes in every state. Go to http://www.womenslaw.org/, and find the domestic violence code for your state and report your findings.
2. There are many myths surrounding intimate partner violence. Conduct an Internet search and identify at least five myths in addition to the ones listed in this text.
3. The International Association of Chiefs of Police's Violence Against Women Project has posted important information on the police response to domestic violence. Go to its Web site and conduct some research. Find the training guidebook for police officers to explain federal laws for the interstate enforcement of protective orders: *Protecting Victims of Domestic Violence: A Law Enforcement Officer's Guide to Enforcing Orders of Protection Nationwide.* Summarize in a report what you think is the most important information from this guidebook. Start your search at http://www.theiacp.org.
4. The Police Executive Research Forum conducted a survey on police practices in response to cases involving domestic violence. What are your reactions to this debate on police response? Read the report and discuss the findings with your class. View this report at http://www.policeforum.org/assets/docs/Subject_to_Debate/Debate2015/debate_2015_janfeb.pdf

References

American Bar Association. (2007). Domestic violence arrest policies by state. Retrieved from http://www .abanet.org/domviol/docs/Domestic_Violence_Arrest_ Policies_by_State_11_07.pdf

Balenovich, J., Grossi, E., & Hughes, T. (2008). Toward a balanced approach: Defining police roles in responding to domestic violence. *American Journal of Criminal Justice, 33*, 19–31.

Bard, M. (1969). Family intervention police teams as a community mental health resource. *Journal of Criminal Law, Criminology and Police Science, 60*(2), 247–250.

Beck v. Ohio, 379 U.S. 89 (1964).

Bruton v. United States, 391 U.S. 123 (1968).

Commonwealth of Massachusetts. (1996). *Police training program.* Middlesex County, MA: Office of the District Attorney.

Crager, M., Cousin, M., & Hardy, T. (2003). Victim-defendants: An emerging challenge in responding to domestic violence in Seattle and the King County region. *Minnesota Center Against Violence and Abuse.* Retrieved from http://www.mincava.umn .edu/documents/victimdefendant/victimdefendant .html#id2636079

Durfee, A. (2012). Situational ambiguity and gendered patterns of arrest for intimate partner violence. *Violence Against Women, 18*(1), 64–84.

Friday, P., Lord, V., Exum, M. L., & Hartman, J. (2006). *Evaluating the impact of a specialized domestic violence police unit.* Washington, D.C.: U.S. Department of Justice.

Gerstein v. Pugh, 420 U.S. 103 (1975).

Hirschel, D. (2008). Domestic violence cases: What research shows about arrest and dual arrest. *National Institute of Justice ePub.* Retrieved from http://www.ojp.usdoj.gov /nij/publications/dv-dual-arrest-222679/welcome.htm

Hirschel, D., & Buzawa, E. (2002). Understanding the context of dual arrest with directions for future research. *Violence Against Women, 8*(12), 1449–1473.

Hirschel, D., Buzawa, E., Pattavina, A., Faggiani, D., & Reuland, M. (2007). *Explaining the prevalence, context, and consequences of dual arrest in intimate partner cases.* (NCJ 218355). Washington, D.C.: U.S. Department of Justice.

Klein, A. (2008). *Practical implications of current domestic violence research. Part I: Law enforcement.* Washington, D.C.: National Institute of Justice.

Klein, A. (2009). Practical implications of current domestic violence research: For law enforcement, prosecutors, and judges. *Special Report.* Washington, D.C.: National Institute of Justice.

Lehrman, F. L. (1997). *Domestic violence practice and procedure.* Washington, D.C.: West Group.

Maxwell, C. D., Garner, J. H., & Fagan, J. A. (2003). The preventive effects of arrest on intimate partner violence: Research, policy, and theory. *Domestic Violence Report, 9*(1), 9–10.

Meyer, S., & Carroll, R. (2011). When officers die: Understanding deadly domestic violence calls for service. *The Police Chief, 78*(5), 24–27.

Nerenberg, L. (1993). *Improving the police response to domestic elder abuse.* Washington, D.C.: Police Executive Research Forum.

Office for Victims of Crime. (2002). Enforcement of protection orders. *OVC Legal Series.* Washington, D.C.: U.S. Department of Justice.

Rucinski, C. (1998). Transitions: Responding to the needs of domestic violence victims. *FBI Law Enforcement Bulletin, 67*(4), 15–18.

Townsend, M., Hunt, D., Kuck, S., & Baxter, C. (2006). *Law enforcement response to domestic violence calls for service, final report.* (NCJ 215915). Rockville, MD: National Institute of Justice.

Zahn, M. (1991). Wolfgang model: Lessons for homicide research in the 1990's. *Journal of Crime and Justice, 14*(2), 17–30.

13

Stalking and Homicide

CHAPTER OBJECTIVES

After reviewing this chapter, you should be able to:

1. Discuss forms of stalking behavior and common stalking offender characteristics.
2. Put stalking crimes in the context of the issuance of protection orders.
3. Explain the legal categories of homicide in relation to intimate partner violence.
4. Identify the relevance of the circle of death for homicide investigators.
5. Summarize the strategies of a murder investigation.

KEY TERMS

Cyberharassment

Cyberstalking

Excusable homicide

Familicide

Homicide

Murder

Stalking

Uxoricide

INTRODUCTION

Stalking is not a new behavior. We have referred to it as harassment, annoyance, and now we know it to be a domestic violence crime. **Stalking** is a pattern of repeated and unwanted attention, harassment, contact, or any other course of conduct directed at a specific person that would cause a reasonable person to feel fear. Pioneering legislative action in California coined the term *stalking* and defined a set of behaviors that constitute this deviant conduct, which is now prohibited by law. Unprecedented interest in all aspects of stalking has followed. Since that time, anti-stalking legislation has been passed in every state and the District of Columbia.

The relationship between homicide and domestic violence has always been assumed but not acknowledged. Statistics on homicides in the United States have been collected from police reports for many years, but only recently have we documented the relationship between the perpetrator and the victim. **Homicide** is defined as the killing of a human being by the act, procurement, or omission of another human being. The term *homicide* is neutral and a necessary component to what most people think of as murder. Intentionally causing death to another may be a homicide, but not necessarily murder. In this chapter, we explore stalking and homicide, the relationship between stalking and homicide, and their association to intimate partner violence.

STALKING

Celebrity accounts of the terror of being stalked heightened public awareness during the 1980s. Actresses Theresa Saldana, Jodie Foster, and Madonna are among those who were stalked. Mark David Chapman stalked and killed famous Beatle John Lennon. Margaret Ray, who had stalked David Letterman since 1988, committed suicide in 1998. Ms. Ray also stalked astronaut Story Musgrave for approximately four years before her death. Those who stalk go to great lengths to get noticed by their victims. They may do bizarre things to gain attention. Theresa Saldana's assailant, who had obtained her address through a private detective, stabbed her; John Hinckley Jr. shot President Reagan to impress Jodie Foster; Margaret Ray, claiming to be the wife of David Letterman, repeatedly broke into his house and stole his car. When her stalker killed Rebecca Shaeffer in 1989, California responded as the first state to pass anti-stalking laws (Cal. Penal Code §646.9). Subsequent research showed that stalking of strangers, whether public or private figures, is less common than stalking of known persons. Once thought to be a crime committed only against celebrities and politicians, stalking became known as the crime of the 1990s.

In addition to the fear generated by stalking behaviors, it is estimated that stalkers are violent toward their victims 25 percent to 35 percent of the time. Domestic violence stalking is the most common type of stalking and the most dangerous to its victims. The groups most likely to be violent are those that have had an intimate relationship with the victim (Catalano, 2012). Research has been done on the identifying features and motivation of perpetrators and their relationships to their victims. The first national study to determine its prevalence was undertaken in the National Violence Against Women (NVAW) Survey (Tjaden & Thoennes, 1998). Using a definition of stalking that requires the victim to feel a high level of fear, the NVAW Survey found that it was more prevalent than had previously been thought. Eight percent of women and 2 percent of men surveyed said they had been stalked at some time in their lives. Estimating that approximately 1 million women and 371,000 men are stalked annually in the United States, the report concluded that stalking should be considered a major criminal justice and public health concern. Stalking is so common that it is sometimes stated as a separate category of domestic violence.

The largest study on stalking, the Supplemental Victimization Survey (SVS), estimated that over 3 million victims had been stalked during a one-year period (Catalano, 2012). Victimization occurred at a rate of 1.5 percent per 1,000 persons age 18 or over. Victims reported being stalked over a period of months or years, and 11 percent said they had been stalked for five years or more. Stalking may have entered the public consciousness through highly publicized cases, but it affects many people every day. It is a gender-neutral crime that is perpetrated by both men and women; it crosses all racial, social, religious, ethnic, and economic lines. Like all crimes, it can be perpetrated by strangers or by offenders known to the victim. When the victim and offender are in a legally recognized domestic relationship such as marriage, cohabitation, intimacy, or dating, the crime is also categorized as one of intimate partner violence.

WHAT IS STALKING?

Stalking is a distinctive form of criminal activity because it is a pattern of behavior that is intended to cause harm or to instill fear in a person. Following or harassing someone typically characterizes the offense. It is different from the majority of crimes because it consists of a series of actions rather than a single act. When the events are viewed individually, they may not constitute illegal behavior. For example, sending flowers, sending love notes, and telephoning someone are perfectly legal activities. When the repetitive actions of the perpetrator instill significant fear of bodily harm or cause injury to the person, such actions then constitute a pattern of behavior that is legally prohibited. The intent is, therefore, an important element of stalking, but it is not the stalker's motives or the context in which the stalking occurs that should be considered when the crime is charged. Attempts to force the victim to comply with the desires of the offender by the use of threats or intimidation can turn the scenario into a nightmare. If the conduct of the pursuing person is seriously threatening, it should be charged as stalking, regardless of the defendant's motivations or relationship to the victim.

For NVAW, only those victims who reported being very frightened or those who feared bodily harm were counted as stalking victims. The survey used the following questions to screen for stalking victimization: Not including bill collectors, telephone solicitors, or other salespeople, has anyone, male or female, ever

- Followed or spied on you?
- Sent you unsolicited letters or written correspondence?
- Made unsolicited phone calls to you?
- Stood outside your home, school, or workplace?
- Showed up at places where you were, even though he or she had no business being there?
- Left unwanted items for you to find?
- Tried to communicate with you in other ways against your will?
- Vandalized your property or destroyed something you loved?

Stalking Behaviors

The motivations of a stalker are varied. Offenders routinely attempt to intimidate and control their victims. Some attempt to scare their targets. Others may have a fanaticized love interest. A significant factor is the stalker's desire to keep the victim within a personal relationship since more than half of the stalkers begin before the intimate relationship has ended. Violence appears to occur in 30 percent to 50 percent of stalking cases with severe violence noted in approximately 6 percent of the cases (Rosenfeld, 2004). Weapons are used to harm or threaten in one out of five cases (Mohandie, Meloy, McGowan, & William, 2006). The most consistent indicator of violence is threats and a previous intimate relationship between the victim and the offender. Substance abuse history is predictive of an increased rate of violence among stalking offenders.

There is no template for the actions of a stalker. The behavior appears to be closely related to intimate partner violence. Research confirms that many stalkers have had a previous intimate relationship with their target. The prevalence of this relationship ranges from 50 percent of cases (Mohandie et al., 2006) to a high of 90 percent of cases (Melton, 2007). More than half of stalkers had a precipitating event before the beginning of their stalking behavior, most often the breakup of a relationship or

More About It: Stalking with Technology

There is a frightening increase in the use of technology for stalking. Some abusers install a Global Positioning System (GPS) in the car of an intimate to stalk that person (Silverstein, 2005). In 2000, a Colorado man, while under a stay-away protection order from his estranged wife, installed a GPS under the hood of her car. Gathering information on her activities, he admitted that the intent was to frighten her and to make sure that she knew that wherever she went, he could and would find her. ... A Wisconsin man in 2003 sent over 100 e-mails to his ex-girlfriend stating that he would get nasty. He would show up at random in places where she did not expect him. A search of her car netted a hidden GPS. ... In 2004, a New York man installed a GPS in his wife's car after she had begun divorce proceedings against him. Using his parent's computer, he would download information from the device. He also rewired her home security system so that the alarm would go off at random intervals.

Stories like these become more common as obsession and technology join forces. Cellular telephone, wireless video cameras, and other digitally based devices are increasing the arsenal of would-be stalkers. Experts from the national Safety Net Project suggest educating survivors and advocates about how abusers are using technology. Safety Net has trained over 12,000 advocates, police officers, and prosecutors on the use of this technology for improved investigation and prosecution of persons who use these technological devices to stalk their victims (Southworth, Dawson, Fraser, & Tucker, 2005).

rejection. Once the stalking begins, the pattern of contact varies. Approximately two-thirds of stalkers pursue their victims at least once a week, but many pursue them daily. Stalking behaviors typically involve more than one means of approach. In the study by Mohandie et al. (2006), 78 percent of the subjects used more than one form of contact. The eight most frequent forms of contact were approaching the target in person, telephoning, taking part in surveillance, sending letters/cards/fax, burglarizing, sending packages or gifts, using a third party to contact, and stalking over cyberspace. The manner in which the offender pursues the victim and the rate of occurrence of the stalking are illustrated in Figure 13-1.

Stalking behaviors often include assaulting the victim, violating protective orders, sexually assaulting the victim, vandalizing the victim's property, burglarizing the victim's home or otherwise stealing from the victim, threatening the victim, and killing

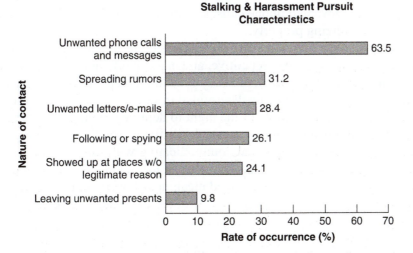

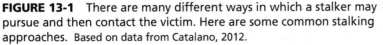

FIGURE 13-1   There are many different ways in which a stalker may pursue and then contact the victim. Here are some common stalking approaches.   Based on data from Catalano, 2012.

the victim's pet. Common elements in the crime of stalking include following the victims, harassing them, and threatening them. The act of threatening may constitute a separate criminal offense. The actions are not only multiple events that taken together indicate a single pattern of conduct, but they must also cause fear and be intentional or willful to satisfy legal definitions of stalking.

FOLLOWING   The most common stalking behavior is following the victim. Stalkers may stand outside a person's home. Still, the crime is more complicated than merely following or spying on someone. It is done for a specific purpose, although each stalker is different and the range of behaviors is equally unpredictable. Achieving a victim's reaction is routinely the objective of the stalker. The stalker's motivations determine what reaction is the desired one.

Often, the offender will alert the victim to ensure that he or she is aware of the presence or intent of the perpetrator. The purpose here is to control and intimidate the victim. For example, a note or telephone message may be sent mentioning places that the victim frequents, stores in which he or she shops, and where he or she works or resides. These actions by the stalkers, therefore, ensure that they get their victims' attention and make them aware that they are being followed or spied upon. A stalker may or may not initiate conversation if seen in the act of stalking by the victim. Following the victim is meant to cause fear on the part of the victim and bolster the self-esteem of the assailant.

HARASSMENT   It is difficult to list all forms of harassment that are possible. Harassment is the knowing and willful pattern of conduct or series of acts over a period of time directed at a specific person, which seriously alarm or annoy the person. A reasonable person would be expected to suffer substantial emotional distress as a result of harassment.

The behavior of a coworker who consistently stands uncomfortably close to the victim in conjunction with other acts may rise to the level of harassment. A stalker who breaks into (by key or force) the victim's home and leaves evidence that someone was in the house is also guilty of a form of harassment. Typical examples of stalking behaviors include making unwanted phone calls, sending unwanted letters, leaving items for the victim, and vandalizing property.

Women report receiving harassing phone calls more frequently than do male victims. The calls may be excessive, repetitive, and made at odd hours of the day or night. They may be hang-up calls or involve heavy breathing. Depending on the pattern and type of the calling, a purpose may be determined in some instances. For example, calls may frequently come in the middle of the night to deprive the victim of sleep.

A stalker frequently attempts to contact the victim by sending or leaving unwanted items or letters. Numerous attempts at communicating with the victim routinely contain veiled threats. It is imperative that the item be looked at carefully not only for its physical properties but also for its intended meaning. Flowers or a gift may be sent on an anniversary or date of significance to reaffirm the existence of a relationship that in reality no longer exists.

THREATS   The legal requirement of a credible threat against the victim can be the most challenging element to establish. Not all statutes require the existence of a credible threat, however, so it is essential to know the law in your state. The threat does not

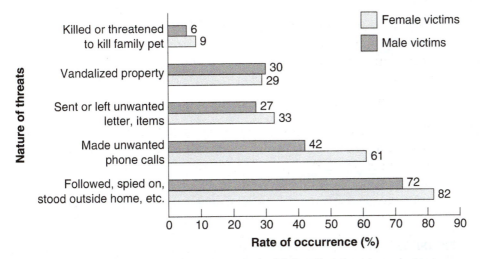

FIGURE 13-2 Common behaviors may contain thinly veiled threats against a stalking victim. Here are five common stalking behaviors and the difference in which they are used against a male versus a female victim. Based on data from NIJ, 1998.

need to be written or verbal to instill fear; delivering a dead animal to the doorstep or pointing a finger at someone as if it were a gun are examples of threats. Some states require additional conduct after a threat has been made; others specify that the threat must be one causing fear of serious harm. Common, threatening behaviors are illustrated in Figure 13-2.

This requirement might seem like an impossible obstacle to overcome. Among college women who reported having been stalked, the prevalence rate of 13 percent fell to only 1.96 percent due to the lack of a threat of harm (Fisher, Cullen, & Turner, 2000). Overall, 60 percent of victims (male and female) are overtly threatened by their stalkers (Mohandie et al., 2006). Prior acts of violence against a person by the stalker may be admitted to prove that the threats were intended to instill fear of death or severe injury. A person who has been victimized previously in a partner relationship, who then receives a veiled threat from the former partner, may react with the level of fear required to satisfy the elements of the crime, even though the "threat" at hand was not itself serious.

Thinly veiled threats are much more common than overt threats; these may rise to the level of credible threat in the face of a past or current abusive relationship. It ultimately falls on the court to determine whether the action will satisfy the requirement of creating fear. Threats come in unusual packages that may have meaning to the stalker and the victim alone. Asking the victim why she or he feels threatened can enlighten others. Ripped, torn, or mutilated objects that are sent signify anger and are meant to scare the victim. They may include dolls, photographs, or broken statues, to name a few. Sending black roses or a game called "Hangman" can be threatening if the victim is afraid of the stalker or believes that the gift signifies a step closer to fulfilling an earlier threat to hurt him or her. Killing or threatening to kill a family pet indicates a hazardous situation for the victim. Should this occur, safety precautions should be taken, and the victim should be considered to be in imminent personal danger.

Stalking behaviors may also involve the use of technology (see Figure 13-3). The term **cyberstalking** has been used to describe a variety of behaviors (a) that involve repeated threats and/or harassment, (b) that involve the use of electronic mail or other

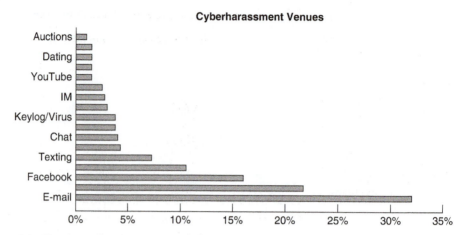

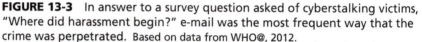

FIGURE 13-3   In answer to a survey question asked of cyberstalking victims, "Where did harassment begin?" e-mail was the most frequent way that the crime was perpetrated. Based on data from WHO@, 2012.

computer-based communication, and (c) that would make a reasonable person afraid or concerned for his or her safety (Southworth, Finn, Dawson, Fraser, & Tucker, 2007). The use of phones, bombarding victims with instant messages, photographing with hidden cameras, and the use of Global Positioning Systems are tools sometimes used by the stalker. Wiretapping, identity theft, and video voyeurism are terms used to describe technology-based stalking. **Cyberharassment** includes behaviors associated with cyberstalking yet is different from cyberstalking because it is defined as not involving a credible threat. Other forms of computer and telecommunication-based harassment and cyberstalking include the following:

- Sending e-mail that threatens, insults, or harasses;
- Monitoring e-mail communication either directly or through sniffer programs;
- Disrupting e-mail by flooding a victim's e-mail box with unwanted mail or by sending a virus;
- Using the victim's e-mail identity to send false messages to others or to purchase goods and services;
- Using the Internet to seek and compile a victim's personal information for use in harassment.

VICTIMS OF STALKING

Anyone, male or female, can become the victim of a stalker. The person targeted for this crime has not done anything to provoke the behavior of the offender. Approximately 1.5 percent of the population aged 18 and older experience being stalked (Catalano, 2012). The crimes often go undetected, however. When domestic violence is committed along with stalking behaviors, police are more likely to focus on what is perceived to be the more significant crimes. Examining victim characteristics is part of the attempt to understand the stalker and of the phenomena that occur. According to Mohandie et al. (2006), four out of five victims of stalking are female. Men were stalked in approximately 20 percent of the total cases surveyed. Males and females are equally likely to experience harassment (Catalano, 2012). The end of an intimate relationship is closely associated with personal violence in stalking cases.

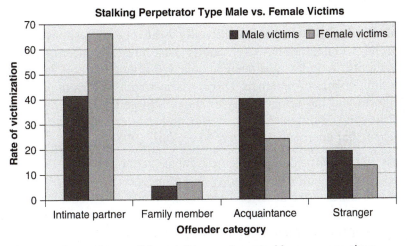

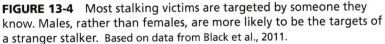

FIGURE 13-4   Most stalking victims are targeted by someone they know. Males, rather than females, are more likely to be the targets of a stranger stalker. Based on data from Black et al., 2011.

Young adults are the primary targets of stalkers; over half are between the ages of 18 and 29. Many victims know their stalker; see Figure 13-4. Among college women stalked on campus, 80 percent knew their stalker (Fisher et al., 2000). Women ages 55 and older are more likely than men of the same age to be stalked. For older women, stalking often occurs as part of intimate partner violence in later life (Jasinski, 2003). The SVS found only 9.7 percent of stalking was by strangers. The largest group of stalkers (39.3 percent) consisted of current or former intimates or family members, and the remaining 36.1 percent, acquaintances (Catalano, 2012). Further, the survey suggests that intimate victims were more likely to experience fear or actions that would cause a reasonable person to feel fear than nonintimate or stranger victims subject to the same conduct.

Safety Precautions for Stalking Victims

Doreen Orion, author of *I Know You Really Love Me*, suggests that stalking victims must acknowledge being a target of this crime and take extra safety precautions (Orion, 1998). She proposes the following commonsense approaches for persons who suspect that they may be targeted by a stalker. Ways to reduce the feeling of vulnerability include getting a dog or putting in a house alarm. It may be useful for someone that is concerned with being stalked to screen telephone calls through an answering machine or cell phone. When going shopping or to work, always park in an open, well-lit lot. It is essential to keep a journal of suspicious activities; the small actions that are often considered legal actions become more apparent as stalking when the behaviors are grouped in a pattern. Investigators and court personnel will need a complete picture of the stalking behaviors to advise appropriate strategies for keeping safe.

It is important that the stalking victim attempt to assess the probability of impending danger. When emotions run high, it may be helpful to allow common sense to replace fear. Contrary to popular belief, the majority of stalking incidents begin before an intimate relationship has actually ended. Be aware of the possibility that the violent domestic relationship may also include stalking.

Threat Assessment

The role of criminal justice has traditionally been one of response, not of prevention. This trend is changing, however, and is most notable concerning violent crimes. Proactive policing includes advanced knowledge about the population that is most likely to commit crimes of violence. Threat assessment is a current project for stalking of public figures and has applicability to stalkers in general. The Secret Service provided the following findings of the histories and personal characteristics of attackers and their near-lethal approaches (Fein & Vossekuil, 1998):

- Almost half had attended college or graduate school.
- They often had histories of mobility and transience.
- About two-thirds were described as socially isolated.
- Few had histories of arrests for violent crimes or for crimes that involved weapons.
- Many had histories of harassing other people.
- Most had histories of explosive, angry behavior, but only half had histories of physically violent behavior.
- Many had histories of serious depression or despair.
- Many were known to have attempted suicide or to have considered suicide at some point before their attack or near-lethal approach.

This information suggests that stalkers are typically intelligent, have violent or deviant pasts, and suffer from emotional and behavior disorders. Revenge and the need for vindication may motivate them.

PERPETRATORS OF STALKING

Although stalking is described as a gender-neutral crime, the majority of perpetrators are male (Schell, 2003). There is no single profile of a stalker; instead, stalkers are categorized by their relationship to the victim and within broad categories according to their behaviors. The one trait all stalkers share is that they suffer from a personality or mental disorder, if not both. Despite their demographic diversity, data show that some characteristics are more common among stalkers than others (Mohandie et al., 2006):

- Eighty-six percent are male, and 14 percent are female.
- More than half are Caucasian. Hispanic, African American, Asian, Native American, and Middle Eastern stalkers are also represented.
- Almost half of stalkers are single.
- Most are heterosexual.
- Approximately one-third had prior histories of adult violent criminal behavior.

Characteristics of Perpetrators

A progression that is similar to what occurs in other intimate partner violence is also apparent in stalking. If the stalker is spurned, he or she may escalate the behavior to intimidation. In rare instances, the episodes of stalking become a persistent pattern of behavior that turns threatening and violent. The majority of stalkers are not mentally ill, although their behavior is not normal or appropriate. Stalking can be lethal in domestic violence; studies suggest that the majority of women who were murdered by a current or former intimate partner had been stalked in the months before the murder (Mechanic, Weaver, & Resick, 2008).

One approach taken to understand stalkers has been a categorization based on prior relationship to the victims. Mohandie et al. (2006) suggest that a previous relationship stalker may be either an intimate stalker or an acquaintance stalker. Within the intimate category, a history of domestic violence exists in about half of the cases. Acquaintances are those who are known to the victim casually through work, as neighbors, or through friendship.

RELATIONSHIP OR SIMPLE OBSESSIONAL STALKERS The most common and best-known type of stalker is the *relationship or simple obsessional stalker*. The perpetrator and victim typically have a previous relationship that could include marriage, friendship, or that of coworkers. Most stalkers in cases of intimate partner and dating relationships are simple obsessional stalkers. The use of *simple* as a descriptor refers to the fact that this is a common type of stalker, not that the issue is simple or that the victim is not at risk. Simple obsession is the most likely category of stalking to result in murder. Thirty percent of all female homicides were committed by intimate partners. Victims of intimate partner violence run a 75 percent higher risk of being murdered by their partners (Seymour et al., 2002). "If I can't have you, nobody will" has become all too common a refrain in cases that escalate to violence. Many of these cases end with the murder of the victim followed by the suicide of the stalker.

People in this category are more frequently those who batter. It should not be a surprise that their characteristics resemble those of the intimate partner violence offender; they are, in general, as follows:

- Emotionally immature
- Socially incompetent
- Unable to maintain relationships
- Overly jealous
- Insecure
- Low in self-esteem

LOVE OBSESSIONAL STALKERS Stalkers in this group develop a love obsession or fixation, generally targeting celebrities and politicians. There is no personal relationship between the victim and offender; therefore, the target might also be a casual acquaintance. These stalkers tend to be persistent in their pursuit of their victims. They fantasize about the victim being their love partner and may go to drastic means to get attention. Their bizarre attempts may be lethal to the victim because the stalker does not care whether the attention is negative or positive.

Unlike stalkers suffering from erotomania, love obsessional stalkers do not believe that their targets love them. They may believe that they are destined to be with their victims and only need to try harder to convince them. These stalkers often invent detailed fantasies of nonexistent relationships.

EROTOMANIA The term *erotomania* is usually associated with a stalker who has severe mental problems, including delusions. The perpetrator may believe that the victim knows and loves him or her. These stalkers expect the target to play the role the stalker has determined, and when threats or intimidation do not work, they may resort to violence. This type of stalker may continue to pursue the victim for long periods of time, up to 8 or 10 years. Though relatively rare (constituting less than 10 percent of all cases), cases of erotomanic stalking often draw public attention because the target is usually a public figure or celebrity (Seymour et al., 2002). Like love obsession stalkers, erotomaniacs attempt to garner self-esteem and status by associating themselves with well-known individuals who hold high social status. Although the behavior of many erotomaniacs never escalates to violence, or even to threats of violence, the irrationality that accompanies their mental illness presents particularly unpredictable threats to victims.

VENGEANCE AND TERRORISM STALKER   The fourth stalking category is very different from the others. Vengeance and terrorist stalkers seek to change the behavior of their victims without intending to have a personal relationship with the victim. The vengeance stalkers may only seek to punish their victims for some wrong they perceive the victim has done to them. This is typified by the person who stalks an employer after being fired. The terrorist stalker has a political agenda and uses the threat of force to keep the target from engaging in a particular activity. Prosecutions of cases in this category have included antiabortionists who stalk doctors who perform abortions.

STALKING LAWS

In response to the murder of actress Rebecca Schaeffer, in 1990 California became the first state to pass an anti-stalking law (California Penal Code §646.9). In a short period, all 50 states, the District of Columbia, Puerto Rico, and the Virgin Islands have followed suit, and federal legislation also exists. Stalking is classified as a felony for the first offense in 14 states, 35 others make it a felony with aggravating circumstances or on the second offense. In Maryland, stalking is always a misdemeanor. Aggravating factors may include violation of a court order or condition of probation; a victim under age 16; possession of a deadly weapon; or targeting the same victim as on prior occasions. Some state laws require only that prosecutors show that the victim suffered emotional distress, whereas others require that the victim experience fear of death or serious bodily harm for the elements of stalking to be satisfied.

Since stalking is a relatively new criminal offense, the laws can be confusing. Broadly written statutes in some states have caused difficulty for criminal justice implementation and resulted in constitutional challenges. Typically, statutes define stalking as willful, malicious, and repeated following and harassment of another person. Many states further require that the perpetrator make a threat of violence that is credible. Stalking behaviors that do not involve a credible threat are defined as harassment. New York's laws use the terms *menacing* (Chapter 353) and *aggravated harassment* (NY Penal Law Code, Section 240.30), yet both provisions refer to stalking behaviors. Nine states—Alaska, Connecticut, Florida, Iowa, Louisiana, Michigan, Minnesota, New Mexico, and Vermont—permit enhanced penalties in stalking cases involving victims who are minors.

On July 25, 1996, the United States Senate passed the Interstate Stalking Punishment and Prevention Act of 1996 (Title 18 U.S.C. Section 2261), making it a federal crime to cross state lines to injure or harass another person. The act was signed by President Clinton two months later. Under the act, the victim must be in reasonable fear of the death of, or serious bodily injury to, himself or herself or to a member of his or her immediate family. The definition of *victim* includes any person who is stalked, not only intimate partner victims. Punishment includes up to 5 years in prison for stalking, up to 10 years in prison for stalking with a dangerous weapon or if serious bodily injury occurs, up to 20 years if permanent disfigurement or a life-threatening injury occurs, and life in prison if death results from the stalking. The act also makes a restraining order issued in one state enforceable in other states.

ARREST WITHOUT A WARRANT   The majority of states classify stalking as a felony, particularly if it is a second offense or when aggravating circumstances exist. Examples of aggravating circumstances include the violation of a restraining order, and when "stay-away" is a condition of a court-ordered release. Maryland alone classifies stalking as a misdemeanor in all circumstances (Klein, Salomon, Huntington, Dubois, & Lang, 2009). The power to arrest without a warrant for a felony is based on probable cause, and no warrant is required.

In some states, stalking may be either a felony or a misdemeanor, depending on the seriousness of the action, the use of a weapon, or the type of resulting injury. When states classify stalking as a misdemeanor, police may be expressly authorized to arrest without a warrant, regardless of any existing personal relationship between stalker and victim. If stalking is perpetrated against an intimate or another legally recognized domestic individual, no warrant is necessary if sufficient probable cause exists. Police are authorized in 49 states to arrest, without a warrant, a person suspected of committing misdemeanor domestic violence, including stalking.

STALKING PROTECTION ORDERS   According to the Stalking Resource Center, the District of Columbia and 38 states have statutes establishing a civil order specific for the protection of stalking victims (Stalking Resource Center, 2007). Violation of a stalking protection order is typically a misdemeanor criminal offense that carries with it the possibility of some amount of incarceration and fines. Georgia and Virginia do not specify whether the violation of their protection order is civil or criminal contempt. New York stands alone by not stating any penalty for violation of the stalking protection order. Look at the map in Figure 13-5; it shows penalties for violation of civil stalking protection orders, by state.

CIVIL HARASSMENT   Victims who experience behaviors associated with stalking may not experience a credible threat or feel the level of fear required by some stalking laws. States have responded by enacting laws explicitly defining harassment as a lesser crime that does not rise to the threshold of stalking victimization. In general, civil harassment is abuse, threats of abuse, stalking, sexual assault, or severe harassment by someone you have not dated and do NOT have a close family relationship with, such as a neighbor, a roommate, or a friend (that you have never dated).

Harassment may also be considered a separate crime under civil harassment provisions if the abuse is perpetrated by a person that is not explicitly identified by law as being in a domestic relationship with the victim. So, for example, if the harassment offender is an uncle or aunt, a niece or nephew, or a cousin, the protection may come from civil harassment provisions and NOT from domestic violence laws.

The civil harassment laws state that "harassment" is

- Unlawful violence, such as assault or battery or stalking, OR
- A credible threat of violence, AND
- The violence or threats seriously scare, annoy, or harass someone and there is no valid reason for them.

Stalking Protection Orders by State

FIGURE 13-5 The majority of states provide stalking victims with civil orders of protection. Violation of a stalking order of protection, in most states, would constitute a criminal offense. Based on data from the Stalking Resource Center, 2007.

The credible threat of violence means intentionally saying something or acting in a way that would make a reasonable person afraid for his or her safety or the safety of his or her family. A credible threat of violence includes following or stalking someone, making harassing calls, or sending harassing messages (by phone, mail, or e-mail) over a period of time (even if it is a short time).

Cyberstalking

There is no one comprehensive federal law that addresses all of the issues concerning cyberstalking and cyberharassment. Instead, protections are found piecemeal in different laws. The lack of comprehensive legislation leaves some gaps in protection. For example, under 18 U.S.C. 875(c), it is a federal crime, punishable by up to five years in prison and a fine of up to $250,000, to transmit any communication in interstate or foreign commerce containing a threat to injure the person of another. Thus, this section of the statute includes threats transmitted in interstate or foreign commerce via the telephone, e-mail, beepers, or the Internet. Without a credible threat, this statute is not applicable. Posting messages on a bulletin board or in a chat room is not explicitly included in this provision either.

Cyberstalking behaviors that do not include an actual threat are typically referred to as cyberharassment. Such behaviors include a pattern of conduct intended to harass or annoy another. If a telephone or telecommunication device is used to annoy, abuse, or threaten any person, federal law 47 U.S.C. 233 may be applicable. However, this law requires that the person not reveal his or her name. Federal law needs updating to meet the challenges of interstate cyberstalking and cyberharassment.

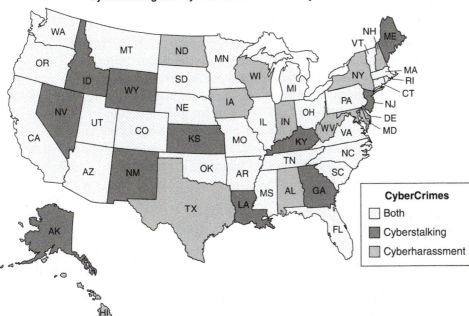

Cyberstalking and Cyberharassment Laws by State

CyberCrimes
- Both
- Cyberstalking
- Cyberharassment

FIGURE 13-6   All 50 states of the United States have passed laws that prohibit either cyberstalking or cyberharassment, or both. Based on data from the National Conference of State Legislatures, 2012.

State laws on virtual anti-stalking vary widely. All states have some provision that prohibits either cyberstalking or cyberharassment, or both. Refer to Figure 13-6. According to the National Conference of State Legislatures (2012), the Massachusetts law does not explicitly specify "electronic" or "Internet" but rather "by any action, method, device or means," which is interpreted to include cybercrimes. Four states—Alaska, Michigan, Oklahoma, and Wyoming—specifically prohibit stalking through electronic means such as e-mail. These statutes present enormous difficulty for law enforcement in identifying perpetrators, determining the jurisdiction of the crime, and satisfying necessary elements of the crime of stalking. They may be unenforceable or fall to a constitutional challenge on vagueness. Still, they represent the states' attempt to include all possible modes of victim harassment. Michigan has a law that makes it illegal to post a message through the use of the Internet without the victim's consent. Nevada goes further and charges a person with stalking if he or she uses the Internet or e-mail to "publish, display, or distribute information in a manner that substantially increases the risk of harm or violence to the victim." Cyberstalking provisions may be most helpful when considered in harassment cases or in addition to other acts that together satisfy the elements of state stalking statutes. The difficulty in legislating against personal cybercrimes may be due to the complex nature of the offenses and the various methods used to perpetrate these crimes.

INVESTIGATIVE STRATEGIES

Half of all victims reported their stalking to the police, according to the NVAW Survey (Tjaden & Thoennes, 1998). Some suggested that the police did not take them seriously; approximately half were satisfied with the response. We understand the importance of taking these cases seriously. The following are a few key points to consider in an investigation into the complaint of stalking.

ASSESSING THE VICTIM'S CREDIBILITY   Assessing the victim's credibility is accomplished by observing the conduct of the victim during the investigation. This is important because there are instances of perpetrators who report themselves as being the victim. How articulate is the victim? What are the motivations for reporting this stalking crime? What did he or she do to reach out for assistance, and was it at an appropriate time? What are the mental health and criminal background of the reporter? Determine whether the statements made are consistent with the injuries or documentation provided. Has this victim reported being a victim of other domestic–violence–related crimes?

FALSE VICTIMIZATION SYNDROME   Professionals have long recognized that a small percentage of violent crimes reported appear to be false allegations. Those who suffer from Munchausen syndrome and Munchausen syndrome by proxy provide examples of individuals with recognized disorders who make false claims. False victimization syndrome is believed to be involved in an estimated 2 percent of stalking complaints that are encountered by law enforcement (Mohandie, Hatcher, & Raymond, 1998). Although this appears to be an insignificant number, even one case that involves a false complaint causes many problems for police officers who want to protect the victim from this horrible crime. It is imperative that suspected false complaints be thoroughly investigated and all attempts to find the perpetrator exhausted before concluding that it is a fantasy crime. Gently confronting the victim may be necessary at some point. Mohandie and colleagues further suggest that mental health intervention should be considered for the benefit of the victim and a determination made about whether charges of perjury or filing a false police report will be pursued in the future (Mohandie et al., 1998).

In a study on the characteristics of false stalking victimization, five distinct categories were investigated (Sheridan & Blaauw, 2004):

1. Stalkers that claim to be victims themselves;
2. Persons with severe mental disorders and persecutory or erotomanic delusions that include stalking;
3. Previously stalked persons who have become hypersensitive to perfectly innocent actions of others because of fear of recurrence;
4. Fictitious victims that seek gratification of dependency needs through adopting victim status;
5. Malingerers that consciously fabricate or exaggerate claims of victimization for understandable external incentives, such as financial rewards.

Their results indicated that the majority of false stalking reports are made by persons who are delusional (Sheridan & Blaauw, 2004). The next largest group of false reports was made by factitious victims, followed by reports of false revictimization.

ASSESSING THE OFFENDER'S CONDUCT   Does the offender have a mental health or criminal background? What is the employment record of the offender? Has this offender committed prior intimate partner violence, or are there outstanding restraining orders against him or her? The answers to these questions help the investigator to

Been There ... Done That!

For three years, the police responded to fearful complaints from a woman who was being stalked. Since stalking victims frequently endure stalking for years, this was not unusual. She produced letters that had been written to her and mailed from various locations by the unknown assailant. Often, they included graphic descriptions of his sexual prowess. He described her in detail in the accounts of bizarre sex play and professed love. She received flowers at her place of business and her home. Countless hang-up calls had been made to her house. She came to the police station twice with bruises and cuts to her arms and face that were the result of confrontations with the assailant. A beautiful 25-year-old woman, she was a perfect target for this sick predator, thought the officers!

However, for the police officers involved, it was a frustrating experience. They were unable to identify the perpetrator and, from the onset, they were concerned for her safety. Responding quickly to her home each time she called, they even put a tap on her telephone line and put surveillance on her house. Their efforts were to no avail. The only contact occurred when there were no witnesses.

As time went by, the officers began to suspect that she was fabricating the "evidence" of the crime. They noticed that she would request specific officers that she liked. She was always freshly made-up and unusually well dressed when they arrived. Her demeanor would often change from extremely fearful to gleeful. Still, they were hesitant to ignore her complaints, because there had been physical assaults.

Asked to consult and offer advice to the other officers, I reviewed the evidence. The tone of the letters suggested to me that they had been written by a woman rather than a man. The acts that were graphically described contained too much detail. They were impossible from a physical standpoint. Rather than intimidating, they seemed to be erotic stories that were meant to be so. Pictures of her injuries appeared suspicious also. The facial injuries were minor, with superficial cuts on her cheeks, but not across her nose. The bruising from being hit looked more like makeup than what one might expect from an attack by an assailant. The facts did not match the evidence.

The "victim" was not pleased when she was told that the local officers would no longer respond to her calls and that a female police officer had been assigned to help her. When I met with her, my gut reaction was precisely what the other officers felt—that she was making up the whole thing. Eventually, I confronted her, and she confessed that there was no stalker. She even smiled broadly when I told her she had impressive imagination and complimented her writing ability!

determine whether the victim's perception of a threat is accurate. Some victims may tend to underestimate the potential harm in a stalking situation.

It is essential to document any history of problems, conflicts, and mental health problems in a suspected stalking situation. Recognizing that there is a difference between making a threat known as "venting anger" and actually "posing" a threat, law-enforcement professionals should evaluate the possibility of violent action through the suspect's history. The task of the investigator is to gather information about the suspect's thinking. Interviewing the suspect may be beneficial because it allows him or her to relate the suspect's story to a third party. This then allows the investigator an opportunity to communicate that the subject's behavior is unwelcome, unacceptable, and must cease.

GATHERING PHYSICAL EVIDENCE Investigating a complaint of stalking requires full and often lengthy documentation of the actions, which then presents an accurate portrayal of the stalking. Victims should be aware of the need to save any tangible evidence of harassment, such as photos of vandalism or injuries, answering machine messages, or written notes; this kind of evidence is necessary to form probable cause that the crime of stalking has been committed. Keeping a journal or diary is another method of gathering additional valuable information.

Victims should be encouraged to obtain a search warrant or summons for the telephone records of the offender if the communications are by telephone. They should also be encouraged to install "caller ID" to track the calls. If e-mail is the medium used, investigators should trace the address to the suspect and consider intercepting all e-mail messages designated for the victim.

DOCUMENTING PREVIOUS LAW-ENFORCEMENT RESPONSE   Investigators should obtain actual reports on prior incidents of violence. They should read the statements and determine whether they reflect the present situation accurately.

INTERVIEWING THIRD PARTIES   Investigators should talk to family members of the victim, neighbors, and coworkers to assess the level of danger that may exist. They should determine the reasons the victim has come forward at that particular time. What has happened to explain the escalation or change in the behavior of the stalker? Should the police consider this an ongoing stalking that places the victim at risk to probable danger, or is the victim in imminent danger? What can be done to protect this person?

CONSIDERING CIRCUMSTANTIAL EVIDENCE   Anything can be considered circumstantial evidence. Does the stalker have access to the types of messages that have been sent to the victim? For example, if the notes are sent through e-mail, does the stalker have access to a computer? Where? Do not overlook any correspondence, pattern of behavior, or gift that may have significance to the victim or the offender.

ASSISTING THE VICTIM IN OBTAINING A RESTRAINING OR NO-CONTACT ORDER
Although the investigation is ongoing, the victim should be directed to obtain a restraining or no-contact order, if possible. Be aware that this may give the victim a false sense of security, however. One-fourth of the women in the NVAW Study (Tjaden & Thoennes, 1998) obtained a restraining order, and the assailant later violated the vast majority of these. Victims who believe that the stalker will persist, regardless of a court order, must be taken seriously. A restraining or no-contact order does not replace day-to-day efforts to reduce vulnerability. The victim cannot let his or her guard down by thinking that the piece of paper is itself full protection.

Because all states have arrest provisions for violation of restraining or stay-away orders, such orders do permit a faster police response. For the stalker who is rational and can control his or her behavior to avoid legal consequences, these orders offer the best way to make the person accountable. Restraining orders are ineffective, however, if the stalker has little regard for the consequences of the stalking behavior and is obsessed with harming or harassing the victim.

Police officers should attempt to assess the level of threat that the perpetrator poses to the victim. Stalkers are not easily deterred and tend to be obsessive. Therefore, current sanctions, including court orders, may not necessarily make an impact. It is not unusual for an offender to stop or begin stalking again before an anniversary, following a stressful event, or at any number of precipitating triggers that renew the stalker's interest in the victim. Using a multidisciplinary approach is an important option to ensure that victims receive consistent professional support services. Community resources that may be necessary to address stalking include domestic violence shelters, mental health treatment providers, housing associations, schools and colleges, faith-based programs, neighborhood watch organizations, and victim advocacy organizations. Additionally, officers should suggest that victims take further safety precautions and make contact with a local victim assistance unit to develop a safety plan.

CATEGORIES OF HOMICIDE

The nature of intimate relationships provides both the intensity and the opportunity for hostile aggression and even murder. Stalking behaviors by former intimate partners have been closely linked as a risk factor for both murder and attempted murder. *Homicide* is a more general term, referring to the killing of a human being, whether or not it is a criminal act. Three general categories are recognized to describe the forms of homicide: *justifiable*, *excusable*, and *felonious*. All three categories relate to intimate partner violence.

Justifiable Homicide

Justifiable homicide is killing without evil or criminal intent, for which there can be no blame, such as that done in self-defense to protect oneself or to protect another or shooting by a law-enforcement officer in fulfilling his or her duty. Carrying out the death sentence of an inmate and killing during combat are other examples of homicides where death is intentional but not criminal. These are killings completed as part of a person's duty. Justifiable homicide is viewed by society as appropriate behavior, even though death resulted. It is self-defense when the person committing the homicide is not at fault. In determining whether a defendant acted in self-defense, a trier of facts considers issues such as (1) whether the defendant reasonably feared that he or she needed to use force to defend himself or herself; (2) whether the threat to the defendant was imminent; (3) whether the defendant met the threat with excessive force; and (4) whether the defendant had a duty to retreat.

Excusable Homicide

A homicide committed accidentally or with sufficient provocation while doing some lawful activity is termed **excusable homicide**. For example, if someone is physically attacked in a parking garage and kills the attacker while defending himself, that would be excusable homicide if the attack victim did not use a dangerous weapon or kill cruelly or unusually. Examples of an excusable defense include temporary insanity and diminished capacity. Excusable homicide is often treated as another form of justifiable homicide; both pardon the defendant from criminal liability. A person who commits homicide that is excusable must be released from responsibility for the death through the determination of a court, after an investigation by the state's prosecutor, and in rare cases through clemency. Excusable homicide is perceived by society to be wrong but is tolerated because of the person's state of mind.

Psychiatrists and psychologists frequently testify in both criminal and civil courts on the mental health of persons accused of major crimes, including murder. It is not uncommon for evidence that relates to the person's state of mind to be presented in an attempt to show a diminished responsibility for the offender who committed a crime. The best-known defense is insanity. As the behavioral sciences advance, other mental health disorders, such as multiple personality disorder, postpartum psychosis, and diminished capacity, have also been recognized. One highly publicized and controversial defense specific to intimate partner violence is the battered women's syndrome.

THE BATTERED WOMEN'S SYNDROME   An example of excusable homicide is the defense referred to as the battered women's syndrome. Proponents suggest that the continuum of violence in battering relationships excuses the woman who kills her intimate assailant. Some argue that battered women who kill their oppressors should be considered legally justified, not merely excused from the act. Opponents are divided about whether battered women's syndrome is a valid defense or a claim by someone trying to escape a murder conviction. As in any defense that is raised on behalf of the defendant, some instances of it may be legitimate applications of the concept and others are not. There is always the possibility that any defense will be used illegitimately.

The battered women's syndrome is based on the theory of learned helplessness and the cycle of abuse. According to these theories, the battered victim begins to believe that she or he cannot influence or escape the abuser's violence. One unusual reaction, when faced with the "reality," is to resort to the only perceived option, that is, to kill the abuser. It is considered self-defense even though the victim may not have been in imminent danger of death or great bodily harm at the exact time that the killing occurred.

The primary source of evidence comes from expert testimony on the battered spouse syndrome. Early attempts to introduce the syndrome through psychiatrists met with several objections, including lack of its acceptance as scientific knowledge. Expert witness testimonies explaining the psychological state of the battered woman are allowed in a majority of states and the District of Columbia. There are four general characteristics of the syndrome:

1. The woman believes that the violence is her fault.
2. The woman cannot place the responsibility for the violence elsewhere.
3. The woman fears for her life and her children's lives.
4. The woman has an irrational belief that the abuser is omnipresent and omniscient.

Expert testimony on battering and its effects are introduced as a defense in cases in which a woman has killed her assailant intimate. The defense has been used successfully in at least one same-sex partner homicide (Vickers, 1996). Robert McEwan was arrested in Perth, Western Australia, and charged with the murder of his gay partner of 14 years. The defense was accepted, and a plea of guilty to the lesser charge of manslaughter was recorded. Controversy over the term *battered women's syndrome* has surfaced in recent years, in part, because the term ignores male victims of domestic violence (Smith, 2005). The national trend is to abandon the term in favor of using *battering and its effects* instead. Current research suggests that each person reacts to domestic violence victimization in ways that are dependent on multiple psychological and practical circumstances. According to some experts, use of the term *battered women's syndrome* is therefore not an appropriate foundation for expert testimony (Dutton, 2009).

CLEMENCY   Clemency is a general term for the power of an executive to intervene in the sentencing of a criminal defendant to prevent injustice from occurring. It is a relief imparted after the justice system has run its course. Clemency provisions exist in every judicial system in the world except China's. The U.S. Constitution gives the president the power to grant clemency for federal death row inmates. In 30 states, the governor can make clemency decisions directly or exercise this power in conjunction with an advisory board (Death Penalty Information Center, 2013). Also, boards in five states make clemency decisions. There are 33 states with the death penalty and 17 without a death penalty. When a state changes its death penalty law, it also chooses whether or not to make that change retroactive.

As the defense of battered spouse syndrome became increasingly admissible, a clemency movement also began. Requests to state governors for the release of those women who had been convicted of murdering or assaulting an intimate partner began in the early 1990s. Ohio Governor Celeste and Maryland Governor Schaefer granted clemency to 25 women who were incarcerated for killing or assaulting abusive husbands or boyfriends (Schneider, 2007). Other states' governors have since followed the lead. Most of those released had been denied the opportunity to offer evidence on battered women's syndrome. Media attention to the clemency action fuels the controversy for this justification, which is likely to continue.

Felonious Homicide

The wrongful killing of a human being is criminal behavior; it is referred to as a felonious homicide. Murder, manslaughter, or negligent homicides are categories of death with varying degrees of culpability. The term **murder** refers to the killing of any human being by another with malice aforethought. Most states provide different degrees of culpability that are designated by the criminal statute itself, often referred to as a non-negligent homicide. Murder is considered the most serious crime in our society. The penalties reflect this belief: Murder can be punished by life imprisonment or by death. There is no statute of limitations on murder; a person can be tried in a court of law at any time that sufficient proof exists to do so, regardless of how many years have elapsed since the offense.

INTIMATE PARTNER HOMICIDE

According to the Bureau of Justice Statistics, the most frequent victims of family homicides are spouses or ex-spouses (Fox & Zawitz, 2007). This category of family killing is known as *intimate partner homicide*, the killing of a spouse, ex-spouse, boyfriend, or girlfriend. There is an undeniable link between intimate partner homicide, stalking, and intimate partner violence. More than half of femicide victims and 71 percent of attempted femicide victims had been assaulted by their intimate partner before having been murdered. *Femicide* is the killing of a woman by her relative, friend, or lover. The prevalence of stalking by intimate partners has been documented as high as 67 percent for femicide victims and 71 percent for attempted femicide victims (Farlane et al., 1999).

Since men commit approximately 90 percent of all murders in the United States, it is not surprising that they also commit the majority of intimate partner murders. Men have the physical attributes to overcome their female partners if they choose to. Coupled with the psychological and social explanations for battering, there appears to be a higher willingness to engage in violent encounters to maintain power and control in intimate relationships. For every age group, female murder victims are substantially more likely than male victims to have been killed by an intimate partner.

Of great concern and controversy is whether the criminal justice system can protect women from intimate partner homicide. According to one study, before they were killed by their stalkers, 54 percent of femicide victims had reported the stalking to the police (Farlane et al., 1999). Approximately 46 percent of attempted femicide victims had also had reported the stalking to the police.

INTIMATE PARTNER HOMICIDE VICTIMS

Intimate partner homicide victims make up approximately 11 percent of all murders nationwide (Fox & Zawitz, 2007). In cases of intimate partner homicide recorded since 1976, women are the overwhelming majority of victims. In 2005, for example, 22 percent of victims were men and 78 percent were women; see Figure 13-7. Many studies have found that separation through actual leaving or the start of legal procedures is a common catalyst for intimate partner homicide. The most dangerous time is between three months and one year after separation.

The good news is that the homicide rate of intimates has declined since 1975 (Fox & Zawitz, 2007). Between 1976 and 2005, the number of white women killed by intimate partners rose in the mid-1980s, then declined after 1993, reaching the lowest recorded in 2002. The number fluctuated slightly after 2002. The most pronounced decline has been in the number of black men killed by intimate partners, which has dropped by 83 percent. The number of white men murdered by an intimate partner fell by 61 percent from 1976 to 2005. The number of black women killed by intimate

Intimate Partner Homicide by Gender of Victim

Male (22%)

Female (78%)

FIGURE 13-7 According to the FBI Supplementary Homicide Reports, women are the majority of victims in cases of intimate partner homicide. Image copyright Fabiana Ponzi. Used under license from Shutterstock.com.

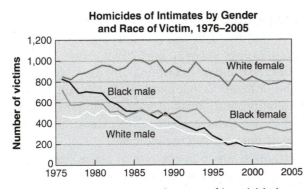

FIGURE 13-8 Since 1975, the rate of homicide by an intimate partner has gone down significantly for males and African American females. Based on data from Fox and Zawitz, 2007.

partners has also declined substantially, by 52 percent. When intimate homicide was broken down by gender and race, the most significant difference was noted among black perpetrators. Refer to Figure 13-8 to see the decline in intimate partner homicide by gender and race.

This welcome decline in intimate partner homicide has been studied, and explanations are being offered to account for this downward trend. Advocates claim that domestic violence hotlines, legal advocacy, and shelter interventions have been successful in lowering the rate of domestic homicide. As services to female victims of domestic violence increased during the years of 1976 to 1996, the rate of intimate partner homicide decreased (Duggan, Nagin, & Rosenfeld, 2003). Great strides have been made in response to intimate partner violence in all segments of society, including the criminal justice system, social services, healthcare, and public opinion.

Risk Factors in Homicide

Several studies have looked at the risk factors and death rituals associated with spousal homicide to understand why it happens. The most significant risk factor for intimate partner homicide, regardless of which partner is killed, is the recorded history of intimate partner violence against the female partner (Campbell, Glass, Sharps, Laughon, & Bloom, 2007). The availability of guns has been a frequently noted factor contributing to all forms of homicide, including intimate partner violence. Despite a decline in gun use, firearms are still common weapons used in the intimate homicide. According to the FBI Supplementary Homicide Reports, over two-thirds of spouse and ex-spouse victims were killed by guns (Fox & Zawitz, 2007). Boyfriends were more likely to be killed with knives than any other group of intimates; girlfriends were more likely to be killed by force than another group of intimates.

According to the Campbell study, a combination of factors increases the likelihood of intimate partner homicide involving an abusive man who kills his female partner, rather than one single factor (Campbell et al., 2003). The research suggests that the risk of intimate partner homicide is increased fourfold if the abuser is unemployed. The Danger Assessment study found that women who were threatened or assaulted with a gun were 20 times more likely than other women to be murdered. Women whose partners threatened to kill them were 15 times more likely than other women to be killed (Campbell et al., 2003).

A batterer's unemployment, access to guns, and threats of deadly violence are among the strongest predictors of femicide. Other demographic and relationship risk factors include an age difference between the partners when the abuser was older; mental illness; and illicit drug use and prior criminal involvement, which also increased the risk of homicide to the intimate female partner (Campbell, Webster, & Glass, 2009). After extensive consultation and constant validity support, coinvestigator Campbell developed the Danger Assessment instrument to assess the likelihood of lethality or near lethality in a case of intimate partner violence.

The term *death ritual* refers to the pattern of abuse that may lead to homicide. It begins when the abuser talks about weapons, then display weapons, then brandishes weapons. This occurs while he or she is making threats to the victim. The offender may take the partner to a secluded area and threaten to kill him or her there if the partner ever tries to leave. The more these rituals are acted out, the more likely it is that the abuser will carry out his or her threats.

INTIMATE PARTNER HOMICIDE DEFENDANTS

Few studies have examined the differences in criminal justice processing of intimate partner homicide defendants. In one such comparison of cases in Philadelphia, during the period from 1995 to 2000, significant differences were found in court outcomes (Auerhahn, 2007). Female intimate partner defendants are found more likely to have been convicted of lesser grades of homicide and sanctioned less severely than their male counterparts. Male intimate partner homicide defendants are treated more harshly than female defendants and are more severely sanctioned than male defendants convicted of nonintimate partner homicide. The author concluded that the results confirmed the realities that the majority of female-perpetrated intimate partner homicide is defensive and occurs within the context of a history of domestic abuse. It appears as though female defendants are not being convicted as frequently as male defendants, and they are receiving substantially fewer prison terms than do husbands who kill. A possible explanation is the high rate of victim provocation noted in these cases, which may justify the battered women's syndrome defense. A small percentage of spouse murders are not prosecuted; typically the perpetrators are victims of intimate partner violence who killed their abusers in self-defense.

HOMICIDE-SUICIDE

Until recently, the United States did not have a system capable of tracking suicide-homicide events. The National Violent Death Reporting System (NVDRS) was established to fill that need. What little we know about these tragic events is that the majority of homicide-suicides occur within intimate partner relationships. Approximately 2 percent of all homicides in the United States are classified as cases of murder-suicide. Usually, the husband kills his wife or intimate partner, and within minutes or hours commits suicide. For cases involving homicide-suicide, perpetrators were twice as likely to have a current or former spousal relationship compared to individuals in cases of homicide without suicide. Shooting is the most frequent method of killing. Among men who killed their intimate female partner with a firearm, homicide-suicide was the norm (Barber et al., 2008). Most of the deaths were preceded by breakups initiated by the victim, jealousy, or arguments.

In a study of 17 states within the United States participating in the National Violent Death Reporting System, authors identified 408 homicide-suicide deaths that had occurred between 2003 and 2005 (Logan et al., 2008). Over half of the male homicide-suicide perpetrators versus 26 percent of other male suicide decedents had prior intimate partner conflicts. Most incidents were

- Committed with a firearm (88.2 percent)
- Perpetrated by men (91.4 percent)
- Perpetrated by men who were over the age of 19 (97.6 percent)
- Perpetrated by men who were white (77 percent)

Familicide

A rare form of lethal domestic violence, **familicide** is defined as a multiple-victim homicide incident in which the killer's spouse or ex-spouse and one or more children are slain. One study found that while familicide itself is rare, in approximately one-quarter of parent homicide-suicide cases, one or more children were also killed (Sillito & Salari, 2011). The study also found that the vast majority of children killed in familicide—almost 90 percent—were biological children of the perpetrator. An unexpected outcome of the Sillito and Salari (2011) study was that more children were killed from marriages that were intact than from relationships that were estranged. The authors suggested that marital breakup of violent relationships may affect child survival.

Researchers Wilson and Daly used information from Canada, England, and Wales to examine the phenomenon of familicide (Wilson & Daly, 1996). They found that the majority (93 percent to 96 percent) of familicide incidents were perpetrated by men. The child victims are almost equally divided between sons and daughters. The recording of pertinent data in Chicago between 1965 and 1989 allowed analysis for familicide in that city. Of the 15 familicides during the 25-year period, one was committed by a female.

Additionally, Wilson and Daly reported that suicide is particularly prevalent in familicide cases. Interviews showed that perpetrators (some who had failed at their suicide attempt) were often despondent at the time of killing their family. Experiencing a recent devastating experience of personal and financial failure and dwelling on the probable shame to the wife and children are seen as justifications for taking all their lives. Sorrow rather than anger appears to be the motivating factor for these killings.

GAY AND LESBIAN PARTNER HOMICIDE

Information on homicides committed by same-sex intimate partners is slowly evolving. Relationship information is typically not included in these cases. It is believed that intimate partner violence within the gay and lesbian communities mirror intimate partner violence in the heterosexual community. In 2007, the National Coalition of Anti-Violence Programs (NCAVP) documented five murders of individuals in the context of actual or suspected same-sex intimate partner violence (NCAVP, 2008). The organizations that belong to the NCAVP are among the few organizations that do collect information on same-sex intimate partner violence deaths that are known to them. These numbers may reflect only the tip of the iceberg. In one study, an increased risk of homicide in domestic LGB relationships was noted when there was a significant disparity between the partners' ages or when the offender had an arrest history for a violent offense (Block & Christakos, 1996).

In an analysis of 50,000 homicides, evidence suggests that the intimate homicide rate among gay and lesbian couples is higher than that of heterosexual couples (Mize & Shackelford, 2008). Lesbians in the study killed partners at a higher rate than heterosexual women did: over 9 per million per year versus 7.97 per million per year. Gay partners killed intimate partners at a higher rate than did intimate heterosexual partners also. Clear theoretical explanations for these differences have not been furthered. Future research in this area is warranted.

HOMICIDE IN LATER LIFE

When the murder of an older adult is committed by a family member, the spouse of the person over age 80 is the perpetrator in almost 40 percent of cases, followed by a son in 33 percent of deaths (Karch & Nunn, 2011). In their study on the characteristics of elderly homicides by caretakers from data collected in the National Violent Death Reporting System, the authors found the following in the 50- to 79-year-old group where the killer could be identified:

- Husbands are the most common killers, in 30.9 percent of deaths.
- This is followed closely by wives being the killers in 17.2 percent of deaths.
- Sons perpetrate homicide in 13.8 percent of cases.
- Daughters offend in 10.3 percent of homicides.
- In 10 percent of deaths, the caregivers were nonintimate roommates.

Firearms, intentional neglect, poisoning, suffocation, and the use of blunt instruments are common mechanisms of injury for the homicide of older adults. Homicide by a caretaker is evidenced by different types of incidents and motivations, including financial gain and drug use. Typically, the deaths occur in the victim's home. Authors point out that of the 15,000 homicide deaths in 2005, a total of 2,531 were ages 50 and above (Karch & Nunn, 2011). It is unknown how many homicide deaths in the older adult population were perpetrated by caregivers or domestic partners.

Cohen reports that older adults have homicide-suicide rates that are twice as high as those for younger adults (Cohen, Llorente, & Eisdorfer, 1998). Older adult homicide-suicide rates represent approximately 1,000 deaths per year, which means that nearly 20 older Americans die each week in a homicide-suicide. Contrary to popular belief, the majority of these episodes do not represent mercy killings or acts of love, the authors maintain. Instead, these are acts of desperation and depression among older adults. A Florida study found that persons ages 55 and over had homicide-suicide rates almost twice that of persons under age 55; the majority (75 percent) involve a husband who kills his wife before killing himself (Malphurs, Eisdorfer, & Cohen, 2001). A husband who kills his wife and then commits suicide is the most frequent characterization of elder homicide followed by suicide (Salari, 2007).

At least three types of spousal homicide-suicide involving older couples have been identified (Cohen et al., 1998):

1. *Dependent-protective*—About half of the episodes involving older adult homicide-suicide are classified as dependent-protective. In this category, the couple has been married for a long time and are highly dependent on each other. The man fears losing control of his ability to care for or protect his wife due to a real or perceived change in his health.

2. *Aggressive*—Occurring in about 30 percent of older adult homicide-suicide cases, the aggressive type involves marital conflict or intimate partner violence within the relationship. This type is more common in young-old couples, ages 55 to 65 years. The perpetrator is usually much older than the victim. Pending or actual separation, issuance of a restraining order, and threatening behavior are common precipitants.

3. *Symbiotic*—An extreme interdependency characterizes the relationship in cases of the symbiotic type, involving about 20 percent of couples in which homicide-suicide occurs. One or both of the individuals are extremely sick, leading the husband to a mercy killing. The male perpetrator is often the dominant personality, and the female victim is often submissive.

INVESTIGATIVE STRATEGIES

Since 1976, more than 64,500 men and women have been murdered by those with whom they share an intimate relationship (Fox & Zawitz, 2007). The implication of a domestic relationship is far more significant for female murder victims than for male murder victims, however. Men are most often the perpetrators and the victims in homicides, and they are nine times more likely than women to commit murder; both male and female offenders are more likely to target male than female victims.

Approximately half of homicide victims know their assailants, either as intimates, family members, or acquaintances. The expectation of privacy that may exist due to a domestic relationship underscores the need for a search warrant in homicide investigations. Evidence seized without a warrant may otherwise fall prey to the exclusionary rule. The exclusionary rule excludes the use of evidence to prove a person's guilt when it has been seized in violation of the offender's constitutional rights.

Guidelines have been established to assist police officers and to ensure that the rights inherent under the *Mincey v. Arizona* (1978) decision are protected. An example of a mere evidence search warrant affidavit and application that is consistent with the *Mincey* requirements is provided in Figure 13-9. The information contained in an affidavit must be particular to the crime committed, give the exact location of the evidence, and detail exactly what the officer seeks to seize.

The homicide investigation begins with an examination of the area immediately surrounding the body. Clues within the circle of death aid in the primary first step of determining whether the death is due to homicide, suicide, or attributable to natural causes. See Figure 13-10 for the illustration of the circle of death. Without visible signs of a theft-, gang-, or drug-related murder, the investigator looks from the intimate relations outward toward the strangers. The search to identify the perpetrator of the murder also begins in the circle immediately surrounding the victim. Likely suspects are considered from the core intimates outward. A core intimate refers to the husband, wife, boyfriend, or girlfriend of the victim. If the person slain is a woman, the probability that the suspect is someone other than a stranger is increased substantially because women are most likely to be killed by someone they know.

The collection of evidence also begins within the circle and moves outward. The victim tells a story: The place where the body is found, its gender, injury, and even the positioning of the body speak to the circumstances surrounding the death. Some police departments employ specialists who are called immediately to work on evidence collection; some departments train their police officers to do this step. Whether or not

* This is a Mere Evidence Search Warrant Affidavit and Application pursuant to
Mincey v. Arizona (1978) 437 U.S. 385.

A.)   Blood, semen, saliva, physiological fluids and secretions, hair fibers, fingerprints, palm prints, footprints, shoeprints, weapons and firearms including pistols, rifles, revolvers, shotguns, hatchets, axes, cutting instruments and cutting tools, blunt force instruments, projectiles, ammunition, bullet casings and fragments; dirt, dust and soil, paint samples, glass and plastic fragments, marks of tools used to gain access to locked premises or containers, and items containing traces of any of the above mentioned articles.

B.)   Constitutes evidence of an offense, or that a particular person participated in the commission of an offense, to wit: **Murder**

C.)   **Description of the location of the place to be searched goes here.**

D.)   **(The following paragraphs should be added to the wording of the Search Warrant application at the end of the Affidavit).**

1.   That the affiant _____ , is a regular member of the _____ Police Department and has been a member for the past _____ years. That I am presently assigned to the Detective Division's Major Crime Squad Scene processing Unit and have been so assigned for the past _____ years. That I have investigated and processed numerous serious and violent crimes, including murder, and have received specialized training and experience in the collection of physical evidence, crime scene processing and the investigation of such cases. That I have personal knowledge of the facts and circumstances hereinafter related as a result of my own investigative efforts and those of brother officers who have reported their findings to me.

(One of the two affiants should be a member of the crime scene processing unit. The second affiant should be an investigator and should include his customary paragraph of introduction.)

2.   That the affiants do believe that the offense herein before stated was committed at the location to be searched in that: (Specify circumstances indicating commission of the offenses at the place to be searched: include information as to when the crime was first reported, what first officer on the scene observed, a description of the scene, etc. This information may require several paragraphs.)

3.   That the affiants have personal knowledge, based on their experience and training, that crimes of violence involve a struggle, a break, the use of weapons and other instrumentality, and/or the element of unpredictability. That the person or persons participating in the commission of a violent offense is in contact with physical surroundings in a forceful or otherwise detectable manner. That there is often an attempt to alter, destroy, remove, clean up or cover up evidence of a crime. That traces may be left in the form of blood, semen, saliva, physiological fluids and secretions, hair, fibers, fingerprints, palm prints, footprints, shoeprints, weapons and firearms including pistols, rifles, revolvers, shotguns, hatchets, axes, cutting instruments and cutting tools, blunt force instruments, projectiles, ammunition, bullet casings and fragments; dirt, dust and soil, paint samples, glass and plastic fragments, marks of tools used to gain access to locked premises or containers, and items containing traces of any of the above mentioned articles. That many of the above items are minute and microscopic, thus requiring additional specialized examination by forensic laboratory techniques.

4.   That the affiants have personal knowledge based upon their experience and training, that crime scene, such as described above, will contain physical evidence, herein before itemized, which will aid in establishing the identity of the perpetrator (s), the circumstances under which the crime was committed, and/or which in general will assist in the discovery of the pertinent facts; and that such evidence requires a systematic search to located, seize, record and process.

5.   That based on the foregoing facts and information, the affiants have probable cause to believe and do believe that evidence of the MURDER will be found within and upon (specify the place to be searched).

FIGURE 13-9   Here is a sample Mincey warrant application for the collection of mere evidence related to a homicide. Notice that sections A–C describe the things to be seized and the places to be searched within the homicide scene. Section D provides information that a police officer would include in the affidavit, which attaches to the search warrant application. Mincey v. Arizona (1978).

forensic specialists are called by the police depends on the severity of the crime, the apparent signs of the cause of death, and the policy in the jurisdiction of the crime. Experts in ballistics, hair and fiber analysis, DNA analysis, fingerprint analysis, and photography are among the more common forensic specialists involved in the initial

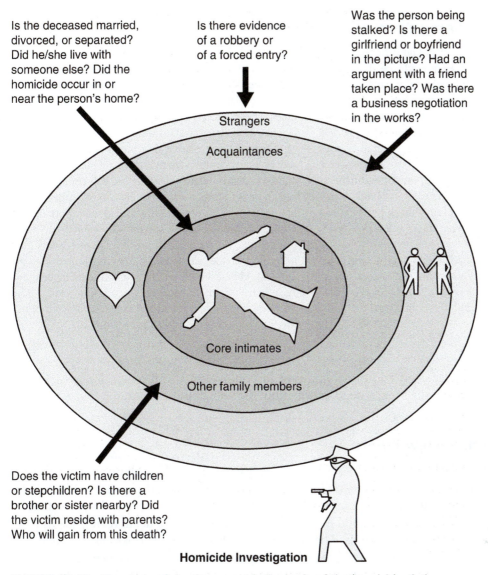

Is the deceased married, divorced, or separated? Did he/she live with someone else? Did the homicide occur in or near the person's home?

Is there evidence of a robbery or of a forced entry?

Was the person being stalked? Is there a girlfriend or boyfriend in the picture? Had an argument with a friend taken place? Was there a business negotiation in the works?

Strangers

Acquaintances

Core intimates

Other family members

Does the victim have children or stepchildren? Is there a brother or sister nearby? Did the victim reside with parents? Who will gain from this death?

Homicide Investigation

FIGURE 13-10 The circle of death surrounds the body of the homicide victim. Intimate partners are at the core of the investigation and should quickly be excluded as potential perpetrators before other relationships to the victim are considered.

murder investigation, in addition to law enforcement. As more is learned about the death, others may be called in to assist the primary investigators.

If the victim has been shot or otherwise physically wounded, the cause of death may appear self-evident but cannot be considered conclusive until a forensic medical autopsy has been performed. Police officers work closely with a medical examiner, sometimes called a coroner, to determine the cause of death. If the person died under the care of a physician for a known fatal illness, an autopsy might not be necessary. For violent or sudden deaths that were not witnessed by another person, an autopsy is often a standard procedure. Confirmation of a sexual assault may be necessary and is considered regardless of the age or gender of the deceased. The coroner is a medical doctor

More About It: The *Mincey* Warrant Requirement

A common misconception is that police officers do not need a warrant to search and seize evidence if they are investigating a homicide. Although many exceptions to the Fourth Amendment warrant requirement do exist, the warrantless search of a dwelling is not allowed just because it is the scene of a homicide. In *Mincey v. Arizona* (1978), the U.S. Supreme Court expressly stated that an exception to the warrant requirement was inconsistent with both the Fourth and the Fourteenth Amendment to the United States Constitution. The case involved an undercover police officer who was killed during a drug buy at Mincey's apartment. Following the murder, police officers secured the scene and then conducted a four-day search of the apartment. They subsequently seized hundreds of items. The Court held that the exhaustive search of the apartment of Mincey was unreasonable and a violation of his privacy, even though the police were lawfully in the apartment.

Without a warrant, a police officer may be on the premises legally to conduct an "emergency" response, such as a search for other victims and the killer. Hot pursuit and imminent danger to people are examples of recognized emergencies. The possibility of evidence destruction is considered an exigent circumstance. The officers may search only for evidence establishing the circumstances of death or circumstances relevant to motive, intent, or knowledge.

A person can waive his or her rights to Fourth Amendment protection and consent to a search of his or her property. This consent must be given before the commencement of the search and must be made freely and intelligently by the person or a proper third party. Consent searching is the most frequently challenged exception and should be used judicially in a homicide investigation. A search warrant is necessary, according to the *Mincey* decision, for a homicide crime scene investigation, in the absence of other recognized exceptions.

who has received additional training in conducting the forensic autopsy. Officially pronouncing the victim dead and naming the cause of death are the responsibilities of the coroner.

Death Review Teams

In 1978, the Los Angeles County Inter-Agency Council on Child Abuse and Neglect (ICAN) formed the first child fatality review team in the United States (Langstaff & Sleeper, 2001). The purpose of the multidisciplinary team was to share resources and information in the forensic investigation of child fatalities. Today there are child death review teams in all 50 states, Australia, and Canada. They review child deaths from various causes, often with an emphasis on reviewing child deaths involving caretaker abuse and or neglect.

The first review team to investigate older adult deaths (EDIRT) was formed in Sacramento, California, in 2000 (Nerenberg, 2003). Its purpose was to assist in the identification and prosecution of older adult abuse-related deaths and to enhance medical professionals' skill in making the cause of death determinations. Forensic investigations may prove helpful in evaluating suicide-homicides in long-term care facilities. Similar teams are being formed nationwide to address the complex forensic needs of investigating senior adult fatalities. Typical members of these multidisciplinary efforts include coroners, medical examiners, mental health professionals, law-enforcement personnel, and prosecutors, based on the needs of the particular locality.

CONCLUSIONS

This chapter began with an introduction to the crime of stalking. This crime is considered gender neutral because it affects both female and male victims, although the majority of victims are women. A major difference between stalking and other crimes is that stalking consists of a series of actions rather than a single act. It may involve activities that are otherwise legal if not committed within the context of other criminal behavior. Extreme fear is often felt by those victimized in this manner.

Following or harassing the victim constitutes a significant element of the crime. The actions are purposeful, and a specific person is targeted for the unwanted attention. A stalker can be anyone: a former intimate or acquaintance or a perfect stranger. Every report should be taken seriously, as the behavior is known to turn violent in approximately one-fourth of cases. An important note relative to the role of law enforcement is the changing role of the police officer to involve prevention in addition to crime response. This means that a threat assessment should be conducted to learn whether the victim is in imminent danger. Strong associations between intimate partner violence stalking and intimate partner homicide have been established.

Recent statistics suggest that the homicide rate of intimate partners has declined and is most pronounced in the number of men killed by an intimate partner. This may be due to the increased information, services, and options that are available to victims of abuse. The suicide-murder situation involving older adults is a category that should be watched in the future. Since the rates for this category appear to be double as compared to those for younger adults, we can expect these rates to rise with the increased aging population in the United States.

The circle of death is used to illustrate the investigative strategy when a victim of homicide is discovered. The family and friends of the victim are eliminated as suspects through this method. The evidence is also located in the area surrounding the body. For these reasons, the crime scene must be protected, and a search conducted that protects the legal rights of domestic killers. A search warrant should be sought whenever possible, due to the possibility of a relationship between the victim and the killer.

SIMPLY SCENARIO
Stalking and Homicide Risk

Your friend tells you in confidence that she thinks that her ex-boyfriend is following her. She describes seeing him in various places around campus, but he does not attend the same college that she does. Recently she has been receiving hang-up calls in the middle of the night. Her ex-boyfriend's car was parked outside the bar the night before when she went out with friends. The whole thing is making her feel kind of creepy. She states that they had broken up two months before because he was so jealous. He had an explosive temper but had never hit her.

Questions: What type of stalker does this typify? Should she contact the police?

Questions for Review

1. Explain the foundational theory of the battered women's syndrome.
2. What is erotomania?
3. What actions are used to satisfy the element of threat required for stalking?
4. What is the purpose of the offender ensuring his or her presence and intent toward the potential victim?
5. Name some characteristics common among stalkers.
6. Explain the phrase "stalking with technology."
7. What is the statistical link between femicide, intimate partner assault, and stalking?
8. Which category of intimate partner homicide victim has shown the biggest increase since 1976?
9. Name some known risk factors associated with intimate partner homicide. Which is the most significant?
10. Explain the three types of spousal homicide-suicide involving older couples.

Internet-Based Exercises

1. How much do you know about stalking? What is the anti-stalking law in your state? Look at the Stalking Resource Center, which provides links to the stalking laws in all 50 states. You can find this site at the following: http://www.victimsofcrime.org/our-programs/stalking-resource-center. Compare and contrast the laws of two different states.

2. Stalking laws also exist in Military and Tribal codes. You will find these laws here: http://www.victimsofcrime.org/our-programs/stalking-resource-center/stalking-laws. Write a short report comparing protection on these federal enclaves.

3. The Bureau of Justice Statistics provides statistical information on many topics, including intimate partner homicide. Visit it at http://bjs.ojp.usdoj.gov/content/homicide/intimates.cfm, and report your findings of gun use and intimate partner homicide.

4. The National Criminal Justice Reference Service is an online library housing information on criminal justice publications and resources. Find the collection on Internet Safety. Go to https://www.ncjrs.gov/internetsafety/cyber.html to learn more on cyber-stalking.

References

Auerhahn, K. (2007). Adjudication outcomes in intimate and non-intimate homicides. *Homicide Studies, 11*(3), 213–230.

Barber, C., Azrael, D., Hemenway, D., Olson, L., Nie, C., Schaechter, J., & Walsh, S. (2008). Suicides and suicide attempts following homicide: Victim–suspect relationship, weapon, type, and presence of antidepressant. *Homicide Studies, 12*(3), 285–297.

Black, M., Basile, K., Breiding, M., Smith, S., Walters, M., Merrick, M., ... Stevens, M. (2011). *The National Intimate Partner and Sexual Violence Survey (NISVS): 2010 summary report.* Atlanta, GA: Centers for Disease Control and Prevention.

Block, C. R., & Christakos, A. (1996). Chicago intimate partner homicide: Patterns and trends across three decades. In *National Institute of Justice Research Report.* Washington, D.C.: U.S. Department of Justice.

Campbell, J., Glass, N., Sharps, P., Laughon, K., & Bloom, T. (2007). Intimate partner homicide: Review and implications of research and policy. *Trauma Violence Abuse, 8*(3), 246–269.

Campbell, J., Webster, D., & Glass, N. (2009). The Danger Assessment: Validation of a lethality risk assessment instrument for intimate partner femicide. *Journal of Interpersonal Violence, 24*(4), 653–674.

Campbell, J., Webster, D., Koziol-McLain, J., Block, C. R., Campbell, C., Curry, M., ... Wilt, W. (2003). Assessing risk factors for intimate partner homicide. (NCJ 196547). *National Institute of Justice Journal*, (250), 14–19.

Catalano, S. (2012). *Stalking victims in the United States—Revised special report.* Washington, D.C.: U.S. Department of Justice.

Cohen, D., Llorente, M., & Eisdorfer, C. (1998). Homicide-suicide in older persons. *American Journal of Psychiatry, 155*(3), 390–396.

Death Penalty Information Center. (2013). Clemency. Retrieved from http://www.deathpenaltyinfo.org/article.php?did=126&scid=13#process

Duggan, L., Nagin, D., & Rosenfeld, R. (2003). Do domestic violence services save lives? *National Institute of Justice Journal*, (250), 25–29.

Dutton, M. A. (2009). *Update of the "battered woman syndrome" critique.* Harrisburg, PA: VAWnet, a project of the National Resource Center on Domestic Violence/Pennsylvania Coalition Against Domestic Violence. Retrieved from http://www.vawnet.org/Assoc_Files_VAWnet/AR_BWSCritique.pdf

Farlane, J., Campbell, J., Wilt, S., Sachs, C., Ulrich, Y., & Xu, X. (1999). Stalking and intimate partner femicide. *Homicide Studies, 3*(4), 300–316.

Fein, R. A., & Vossekuil, B. (1998). *Protective intelligence threat assessment investigations: A guide for state and local law enforcement officials.* Washington, D.C.: U.S. Department of Justice.

Fisher, B. S., Cullen, F. T., & Turner, M. (2000). *The sexual victimization of college women.* Washington, D.C.: National Institute of Justice.

Fox, J., & Zawitz, M. (2007). Homicide trends in the United States. Retrieved from http://bjs.gov/index.cfm?ty=pbdetail&iid=966

Jasinski, J. (2003). Police involvement in incidents of physical assault: Analysis of the redesigned National Crime Victimization Survey. *Journal of Family Violence, 18*(3), 143–150.

Karch, D., & Nunn, K. C. (2011). Characteristics of elderly and other vulnerable adult victims of homicide by a caregiver: National Violent Death Reporting System—17 U.S. states, 2003–2007. *Journal of Interpersonal Violence, 26*(1), 137–157.

Klein, A., Salomon, A., Huntington, N., Dubois, J., & Lang, D. (2009). A statewide study of stalking and its criminal justice response. Retrieved from https://www.ncjrs.gov/pdffiles1/nij/grants/228354.pdf

Langstaff, J., & Sleeper, T. (2001). *The National Center on Child Fatality Review*. Washington, D.C.: U.S. Department of Justice.

Logan, J., Hill, H. A., Black, M. L., Crosby, A. E., Karch, D. L., Barnes, J. D., & Lubell, K. M. (2008). Characteristics of perpetrators in homicide-followed-by-suicide incidents: National Violent Death Reporting System—17 U.S. states, 2003–2005. *American Journal of Epidemiology, 168*(9), 1056–1064. doi: 10.1093/aje/kwn213

Malphurs, J., Eisdorfer, C., & Cohen, D. (2001). A comparison of antecedents of homicide-suicide and suicide in older married men. *American Journal of Geriatric Psychiatry, 9*(1), 49–57.

Mechanic, M. B., Weaver, T. L., & Resick, P. A. (2008). Risk factors for physical injury among help-seeking battered women: An exploration of multiple abuse dimensions. *Violence Against Women, 14*(10), 1148–1165.

Melton, H. C. (2007). Predicting the occurrence of stalking in relationships characterized by domestic violence. *Journal of Interpersonal Violence, 22*(1), 3–25.

Mincey v. Arizona, 437 U.S. 385 (1978).

Mize, K. D., & Shackelford, T. K. (2008). Intimate partner homicide methods in heterosexual, gay, and lesbian relationships. *Violence and Victims, 23*(1), 98–114.

Mohandie, K., Hatcher, C., & Raymond, D. (1998). False victimization syndromes in stalking. In R. Meloy (Ed.), *The psychology of stalking: Clinical and forensic perspectives* (pp. 225–256). New York, NY: Academic Press.

Mohandie, K., Meloy, J. R., McGowan, M. G., & Williams, J. (2006). The RECON typology of stalking: Reliability and validity based upon a large sample of North American stalkers. *Journal of Forensic Science, 51*(1), 147–155.

National Coalition of Anti-Violence Programs (NCAVP). (2008). Lesbian, gay, bisexual and transgender domestic violence in the United States in 2007. Retrieved from http://www.ncavp.org/publications/default.aspx

National Conference of State Legislatures. (2012). State cyberstalking and cyberharassment laws. Retrieved from http://www.ncsl.org/issues-research/telecom/cyberstalking-and-cyberharassment-laws.aspx

National Institute of Justice (NIJ). (1998). *Stalking and domestic violence: The third annual report to Congress under the Violence Against Women Act.* (NCJ 172204). Washington, D.C.: U.S. Department of Justice.

Nerenberg, L. (1993). *Improving the police response to domestic elder abuse*. Washington, D.C.: Police Executive Research Forum.

Orion, D. (1998). *I know you really love me: A psychiatrist's account of stalking and obsessive love*. New York, NY: Dell.

Rosenfeld, B. (2004). Violence risk factors in stalking and obsessional harassment: A review and preliminary meta-analysis. *Criminal Justice and Behavior, 31*(1), 9–36.

Salari, S. (2007). Patterns of intimate partner homicide-suicide in later life: Strategies for prevention. *Clinical Interventions in Aging, 2*, 441–452.

Schell, B. H. (2003). Prevalence of sexual harassment, stalking, and False Victimization Syndrome (FVS) cases and related human resource management policies in a cross-section of Canadian companies from January 1995 through January 2000. *Journal of Family Violence, 18*(6), 351–360.

Schneider, R. Z. (2007). Clemency for battered women. In N. A. Jackson (Ed.), *Encyclopedia of domestic violence* (Vol. 1, pp. 77–83). New York, NY: Routledge.

Seymour, A., Murray, M., Sigmon, J., Hook, M., Edmunds, C., Gadboury, M., & Coleman, G. (2002). *National Victim Assistance Academy textbook*. Washington, D.C.: Office for Victims of Crime.

Sheridan, L., & Blaauw, E. (2004). Characteristics of false stalking reports. *Criminal Justice and Behavior, 31*(1), 55–72.

Sillito, C., & Salari, S. (2011). Child outcomes and risk factors in U.S. homicide-suicide cases, 1999–2004. *Journal of Family Violence, 26*(4), 285–297.

Silverstein, L. (2005). The double edged sword: An examination of the Global Positioning System, Enhanced 911, and the Internet and their relationships to the lives of domestic violence victims and their abusers. *Buffalo Women's Law Journal, 13*(97), 30.

Smith, E. (2005). Amicus Brief, *People v. Cornell Brown*. In N. Lemon (Ed.), *Domestic violence law* (2nd ed., pp. 870–873). St. Paul, MN: West Group.

Southworth, C., Dawson, S., Fraser, C., & Tucker, S. (2005). A high-tech twist on abuse: Technology, intimate partner stalking, and advocacy. *Violence Against Women online resources*. Retrieved from http://www.mincava.umn.edu/documents/commissioned/stalkingandtech/stalkingandtech.html

Southworth, C., Finn, J., Dawson, S., Fraser, C., & Tucker, S. (2007). Intimate partner violence, technology, and stalking. *Violence Against Women, 13*(8), 842–856.

Stalking Resource Center. (2007). Stalking protection orders. Retrieved from http://www.victimsofcrime.org

/our-programs/stalking-resource-center/stalking-laws/stalking-protection-orders

Tjaden, P., & Thoennes, N. (1998). *Prevalence, incidence, and consequences of violence against women: Findings from the National Violence Against Women Survey.* (NCJ 172837). Washington, D.C.: National Institute of Justice.

Vickers, L. (1996). The second closet: Domestic violence in lesbian and gay relationships: A Western Australian perspective. *Murdoch University Electronic Journal of Law, 3*(4). Retrieved from http://www.murdoch.edu.au/elaw/issues/v3n4/vickers.html

Wilson, M., & Daly, M. (1996). Familicide: Uxoricide plus filicide? In National Institute of Justice (Ed.), *Research Report.* Washington, D.C.: U.S. Department of Justice.

Working to Halt Online Abuse (WHO@). (2012). 2011 cyberstalking statistics. Retrieved from http://www.haltabuse.org

The Court Response to Intimate Partner Violence

CHAPTER OBJECTIVES

After reviewing this chapter, you should be able to:

1. Explain, through examples, the protections and resources available to domestic violence survivors.
2. Provide examples of trends and factors that have inspired court reform in cases of family violence.
3. Identify the relevance of the integrated domestic violence court model.
4. Describe domestic violence protection orders along with examples of available remedies allowed by the states.
5. Restate the elements of a protection order petition with the forms of relief available.

KEY TERMS

Concurrent jurisdiction

Domestic violence court

Driver's Privacy Protection Act

Integrated domestic violence court

Jurisdiction

Lautenberg Gun Ban

Petition

Pro se

INTRODUCTION

It is necessary to understand the complexity of the U.S. court system and the positioning of domestic violence legislation. With the recent criminalization of domestic violence, the lines between criminal and civil actions are blurring. Protection and relief from domestic violence are both criminal and civil. Domestic law is located in both federal and state court statutes.

Orders of protection originate in the court system and are sometimes protections under civil law rather than criminal law. This chapter discusses what is needed to obtain an order of protection and the forms of relief that may be available to the applicant. If charges are brought against the domestic-related person for an offense, the victim may also be involved with the criminal court system. Additionally, if there are children in the relationship or marriage is being dissolved the victim may be involved with family court or civil court. Working with different courts can be confusing to the individual seeking legal assistance, and sometimes services overlap. States have responded to the disorder with specialized courts which respond to all matters related to domestic violence. Domestic violence and integrated specialized courts in many jurisdictions attempt to streamline and standardize responses to family violence to enhance victim safety and provide clarity to the process of protection. Prosecution staff has also become specialized, with a vigorous response through enhanced training and multidisciplinary teams.

Persons who are charged in court with crimes involving a family member may receive any number of punishments if found guilty. Depending on the severity of the offense, the punishments range from probation to prison time. The most frequent response to intimate partner violence in the court is the requirement that the offender attends an offender treatment program. Offender treatment programs will be explained later in this chapter. The protection order and offender treatment programs are two initiatives that make up the most significant changes in court procedure for cases involving family violence.

Many specialists are involved with providing victim services. These include advocates who may be indirectly involved with the court system insofar as they help with victim support and issues of safety when the survivor accesses the court system. Some advocates may be directly employed by the court and serve primarily to streamline access and coordinate services while dealing with safety issues.

ADVOCATE ROLES

Fear is the leading reason expressed by survivors for opposing prosecution. First is fear of the abuser, followed by fear of testifying in court. Protection efforts are concerned with reducing these two fears by increasing survivor safety and empowerment. Advocates assist intimate partner violence survivors with overcoming the obstacle of fear by providing information and support. Increased protection and assistance for survivors who access the court system is evidenced through a number of initiatives across the country that are the combined efforts of government and civilian organizations. Domestic violence advocates may assist survivors in applying for these protections and resources. Here are just a few examples.

- *Victim services.* In this category are hotlines, support groups, and counseling resources. The first rape crisis center was opened in 1971; by 1976, over 400 programs for battered women and rape survivors existed. Support groups for lesbians first emerged in Seattle in 1985. Hotlines are available 24 hours a day, 7 days a week, in every state. The National Domestic Violence Hotline provides information and referrals in English and Spanish with access to over 170 different languages.
- *Victim shelters.* The first battered women's shelter in the United States opened in St. Paul, Minnesota, in 1974. Since then, the need for emergency shelters has been proven. The establishment of shelters for battered women has been supported partly through legislative funding. For those able to use this emergency measure, it provides a temporary safe haven from abuse. Only a handful of shelters exist for battered heterosexual or homosexual men.
- *Weapons confiscation and gun ban.* The **Lautenberg Gun Ban** was passed in 1996 as part of the Omnibus Spending Bill. It prohibits anyone convicted of a domestic violence misdemeanor or felony crime from owning or carrying a gun. Under its provisions, officers are obligated to seize the guns and gun permits from all persons convicted of misdemeanor domestic violence.

Domestic Violence Advocates

Victim assistance programs are located in law-enforcement and prosecutors' offices. Staffed with a mixture of full-time, part-time, and volunteer workers, these state-run programs receive funding from various sources, including the federal government. The services that are offered vary widely, as does the training that staff members receive. Advocates provide information about legal rights and the criminal justice process. Assistance in applying for state victim compensation aid and referrals to social service agencies are also key services.

A domestic violence advocate is an individual with experience and training related to domestic violence and crime victims' advocacy. He or she may be required to attend court hearings in support of victims, assist in the filing of forms for a domestic violence restraining order, and respond to the hospital or law-enforcement referrals to provide advocacy. Domestic violence advocates provide legal advocacy services such as notification of court dates and accompaniment to court hearings; education regarding the court system and domestic violence; assistance with obtaining of protective orders; and liaison with prosecutors, probation officers, and court personnel, as well as safety planning. Safety planning is an important component in empowering victims. Victims are educated as to the purpose of safety plans. Due to increased demands for advocate services, some jurisdictions have difficulty in arranging for assistance in filing abuse complaints. Volunteers and paid professionals from battered women's shelters may supplement the advocate services with their staff. College internship programs can arrange for appropriate undergraduate and graduate students to provide services on a voluntary basis.

COURT ADVOCACY   The courts are an intimidating place for survivors of crime. The forms necessary to request a civil or criminal protection or restraining order are confusing. On top of that, many survivors cannot afford to hire an attorney to help with the process. The victim/witness assistance program was developed to address these needs. Typically referred to as an advocate, the victim/witness advocate works for the victim, not the court. The victim/witness assistant may or may not be a specialist in domestic violence. However, he or she is experienced in the court process. Fines collected from those who are convicted of criminal acts pay their salaries. These men and women are located in most courthouses across the nation. Advocates provide a variety of victim-related services. They will instruct the survivor or witness on the procedure itself, telling the person when he or she is required for court appearances. Frequently accompanying victims into court, advocates also track the cases and provide updates for the survivors.

Victim Privacy Protections

The survivor of intimate partner violence can request that his or her name, telephone number, and address not be made part of the public record when filing for a court order of protection. Keeping personal information out of the public record is referred to as *protection order confidentiality*. Confidentiality from the courts is standard procedure for those who fear for their safety.

A concerted effort is being made at the federal level to offer protection to victims of intimate partner violence who fear that personal information will be made available to an abuser or stalker. The ***Driver's Privacy Protection Act*** (18 U.S. 123 § 2721), which became effective on September 13, 1997, is one example. Under this act, personal information from the driver's license can be disclosed only to specific categories of requesters. Personal information is defined as any information including a person's name, address, and driver's license number. Redisclosure of personal information from Registry of Motor Vehicles records to an authorized person will remain on record and retained for five years.

Another measure to protect victims from being located by an abuser is the policy change announced by the Social Security Administration that allows a victim to change her or his social security number (Social Security Administration, 2006). Since employers, banks, credit card companies, health care providers, and many other organizations use these numbers routinely, it has been almost impossible for a domestic violence victim to change their identity. For those who flee from an abuser, the difficulty in obtaining a new social security number was once an insurmountable problem. Now, a person fleeing an abuser may change his or her name and apply for a social security number to secure a new identity. The rules for doing so require a victim to provide proof of current abuse by merely presenting a protection order or statements by law-enforcement officers or other knowledgeable persons.

State-operated *Address Confidentiality Programs* (ACPs) provide victims of domestic violence with a legal substitute address to prevent their perpetrators from using public records to track them down. According to the National Network to End Domestic Violence, 28 states operate ACPs (NNEDV, 2013). Refer to Figure 14-1 for an illustration of those states that operate an ACP and those that do not. There are a few circumstances in which the actual address may be disclosed; for example, to law-enforcement officials; to government officials; and to other third parties under a court order. These exceptions are defined by law in those states that allow address confidentiality. To register for the program, many states require that the application be made through a domestic violence shelter, a law-enforcement officer, a certified advocate group, or a victim assistance program.

Victims of domestic violence and sexual assault may request that their names and addresses be kept confidential on specific public lists under *Voter Registration Confidentiality Programs*, which operate in 13 states (National Coalition Against

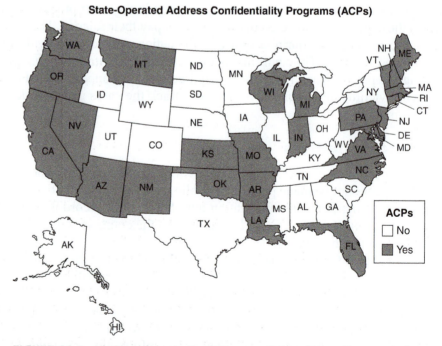

State-Operated Address Confidentiality Programs (ACPs)

FIGURE 14-1 Victims of domestic violence and sexual assault may ask that their addresses be kept confidential on certain public lists. Over half of the states operate Address Confidentiality Programs (ACPs). Based on data from NNEDV, 2013.

Domestic Violence [NCADV], 2007). A police chief or other designated law-enforcement officer must supply the victim with an affidavit stating that the person qualifies for having his or her name omitted from annual street lists and the annual register of voters. The victim completes the affidavit, and it is submitted on his or her behalf. Having confidentiality options allows victims to participate in the voting process without fearing that their vital information will be accessible to their attackers.

THE ROLE OF THE COURTS

The prosecution of domestic violence cases is no longer exceptional or rare, although the prevalence of prosecution varies from one jurisdiction to another. From an analysis of 120 studies, Klein (2008) reports that the average arrest prosecution rate was 63.8 percent. Jurisdictions with specialized domestic violence prosecution programs typically have the highest rates; a court in San Diego documented that 70 percent of cases brought by the police were prosecuted.

Not all cases filed by prosecutors go to trial. Just as in any other type of case, a large number of domestic violence prosecutions are disposed of through plea bargains and sentencing negotiations. Numerous studies have found that convictions can be consistently obtained. Victims often express ambivalence about the prosecutions and sentencing of their abusers; however, in interviews after trial, a majority support prosecution, especially mandatory referral to offender programs (Klein, 2008).

The prosecution of intimate partner violence has been dealt a blow in recent Supreme Court decisions. The impact of the *Crawford* decision (*Crawford v. Washington*, 2004), along with the *Davis* and *Hammon* decision (*Davis v. Washington*, *Hammon v. Indiana*, 2006), on domestic violence cases is still being debated. The *Crawford* decision held that testimonial hearsay is admissible only when the prosecution shows that the declarant is unavailable *and* that there was a prior opportunity to cross-examine the declarant (White, 2008). The issue left unresolved by *Crawford* is, what is "testimonial"? The holding in *Davis* and *Hammon* decided that statements *are* testimonial and therefore trigger the *Crawford* analysis (unavailability plus prior opportunity for cross-examination) if:

- Circumstances indicate that there was no ongoing emergency during the statement
- The primary purpose of the interrogation is to aid prosecution

Statements are *nontestimonial* when made during a police interrogation under the circumstances objectively indicating that the primary purpose of the interrogation is to enable the police to meet an ongoing emergency. According to White (2008), a prosecutor must show evidence that the defendant's actions caused the witness or victim to be unavailable. The forfeiture hearing can scrutinize any evidence, including that of prior abuse, testimony from friends, family advocates, prior records, or evidence of dropped charges.

The question of required intent was clarified in the *Giles* decision (*Giles v. California*, 2008). The Supreme Court held that the theory of forfeiture by wrongdoing is not an exception to the Sixth Amendment's confrontation requirement. The defendant must have intended to prevent a witness from testifying for his or her or statement to be allowed without the opportunity for cross-examination. The Court did state that acts of domestic violence are often intended to dissuade a victim from resorting to outside help. Future cases may consider the intent of the defendant based on prior abuse or threats of abuse intended to dissuade a victim from resorting to outside help.

More About It: *Crawford v. Washington* (2004)

Michael Crawford was on trial for the assault and attempted murder of a man he claimed had tried to rape his wife, Sylvia. The controversy in the case concerned the introduction into evidence of a tape-recorded statement taken by police during an interrogation of Sylvia that was being used as evidence against her husband at his trial. The tape recording was admissible as "reliable" evidence and therefore an exception to the requirement that the declarant testifies to the statement for its use as testimonial evidence. Sylvia did not testify because of the state marital privilege, which prohibits a spouse from testifying without the other spouse's consent. Michael was found guilty of assault and appealed because use of the recordings made to police by Sylvia violated his Sixth Amendment right to confront witnesses against him.

The case went through appeals in the State of Washington, where the conviction was reversed and then reinstated before it was heard by the Supreme Court. The Supreme Court held that the Confrontation Clause of the Sixth Amendment guaranteed Michael the right to confront the witness used against him. The Court reasoned that Michael also had the right of marital privilege and that he did not waive his right to Confrontation by invoking that privilege. The Court changed the decades-long practice of admitting specific hearsay evidence through a test of reliability. It is the "reliable" hearsay exception to testimonial evidence that has changed with this case.

The impact of this decision is far-reaching, and its implications still unclear. Testimonial evidence of intrafamily matters, recanting spouses, evidence from 911 calls that are recorded, and other everyday hearsay situations are now in a state of flux because the U.S. Supreme Court has changed its interpretation of the Confrontation Clause. The Court specifically declined to define the key concept of "testimonial hearsay."

The major impact of these cases is an increased pressure for victims to testify in criminal proceedings against their offenders, for police officers to collect evidence differently, and for prosecutors to try cases more effectively (White, 2008). Evidence collection, including interviewing and interrogating, will take on an increased importance for the prosecution of intimate partner violence. Statements made by the victim to third parties are nontestimonial and therefore admissible at trial (Klein, 2008). Children may prove to be potential witnesses. Also, the presence of children during a domestic assault may allow prosecutors to file additional charges against abusers for endangering the welfare of a child, even if the charges against the primary victim cannot proceed.

Prosecution Outcomes

While experts agree that the prosecution climate has changed in light of recent Supreme Court cases, it is helpful to consider the characteristics of successful prosecutions. A Bureau of Justice Statistics (BJS) study was conducted to examine how domestic violence cases were handled by the justice system. Persons charged with domestic or nondomestic violence were tracked in court records from May 2002, when charges were filed, through final court disposition (Smith, Durose, & Langan, 2008). In the majority of the cases, 7 in 10 charges were aggravated assault or sexual assault. One-third of these felony assault charges were classified as domestic violence. The domestic violence definition included violence between family members, intimate partners, and household cohabitants.

Among defendants charged with aggravated assault, case-processing outcomes for domestic violence were the same as or more serious than the outcomes for nondomestic violence cases (see Figure 14-2). Domestic violence defendants were slightly more likely to be convicted and given longer sentences than nondomestic violence defendants. The study also found that for cases involving domestic violence aggravated assaults, defendants were less likely to be granted pretrial release as compared to

More About It: *Giles v. California* (2008)

On September 29, 2002, Dwayne Giles shot his ex-girlfriend, Brenda Avie. No one saw the actual shooting, but someone inside the house had heard Avie yell, "Granny" several times, followed by a series of gunshots. Giles's niece and grandmother ran outside and saw Giles standing near Avie with a gun in his hands. Avie, who was not carrying a weapon, had been shot six times.

At trial, Giles testified that he had acted in self-defense against his ex-girlfriend, who he knew had once shot a man; that he had seen her threaten people with a knife; and that she had vandalized his home and car on prior occasions. A police officer testified that he had responded three weeks earlier to a disturbance call when Giles had punched Avie and threatened to kill her with a knife. Giles was convicted of first-degree murder.

The Supreme Court again held that the Confrontation Clause of the Sixth Amendment guaranteed the defendant the right to confront the witness used against him—he did not forfeit this constitutional right by his alleged wrongdoing. Testimony from the police officer could not be introduced at trial without showing that the wrongdoing by Giles was designed to keep Avie from testifying against him in court.

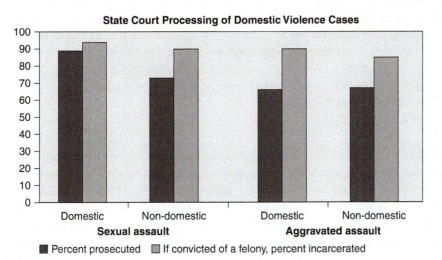

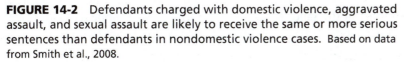

FIGURE 14-2 Defendants charged with domestic violence, aggravated assault, and sexual assault are likely to receive the same or more serious sentences than defendants in nondomestic violence cases. Based on data from Smith et al., 2008.

nondomestic violence aggravated assault cases. Of those granted pretrial release, courts were also more likely to issue a protection order against domestic violence aggravated assault defendants. About 15 percent of the domestic violence sexual assault defendants received sentences longer than 10 years, whereas none of the nondomestic violence sexual assault defendants had a sentence that long.

Specialized Prosecution Units

Research confirms that specialized units are key to successful intimate partner violence prosecution (Chaiken, Boland, Maltz, Martin, & Targonski, 2005). Greater interagency collaboration between prosecutors, social service providers, victim advocates, and victims is one major benefit of the organization of specialized prosecution units. Included in the units are attorneys and victim witness coordinators with special training and skills in obtaining evidence and prosecuting sexual predators and offenders who batter. The creation of cross-agency response teams involves an advocate and police or probation officer or nurse examiner who train together and meet with a victim at a designated facility immediately after an intimate partner violence assault has been reported. Specialized prosecution units are associated with expedited domestic violence dockets, which reduces victim vulnerability to threats and chances of reconciling with the abuser pending trial (Klein, 2008).

Does Prosecution of Offenders Deter Re-Abuse?

According to Klein, simply prosecuting without regard to the specific risk offenders pose, unlike arresting intimate violence offenders, does not deter further criminal abuse (Klein, 2008). Studies on whether or not prosecution deters future violence have netted conflicting results. Klein (2008) reports that a large study of those who were prosecuted and convicted in three states found that offenders who were prosecuted and convicted were more likely to be rearrested than offenders who were not convicted. Conversely, some studies have found that prosecution can reduce subsequent arrests and violence.

The key to deterrence may not be whether the case is prosecuted or not, but rather the disposition imposed. Those who receive more intrusive sentences, including jail, work release, electronic monitoring, and probation, show significantly reduced rearrest rates for intimate partner violence compared with those who received less intrusive sentences of fines or suspended sentences without probation (Klein, 2008). Other studies have shown conflicting results.

COURT JURISDICTION

A network of courts across the United States makes up the judicial system. The scope and authority of each court is called its **jurisdiction**. The constitutional or statutory parameters within which judicial power may be exercised limit the court to a geographical area and specific subject matter. One group of courts in the system maintains federal jurisdiction: It tries crimes and hears controversies that have occurred anywhere in the nation where a federal law is alleged to have been violated. The U.S. Supreme Court is the highest court in the land. It has the authority to hear appeals from lower federal courts. It also hears appeals from the highest state courts when there is a question about the U.S. Constitution. As illustrated in Figure 14-3, the federal court system is made up of the U.S. Supreme Court, the U.S. Court of Appeals, and the U.S. District Courts.

Within each state are one or more federal judicial districts, within each of which is a U.S. District Court. There is also a U.S. District Court in the District of Columbia. These are the trial courts with general jurisdiction over cases involving federal law violations, crimes committed on federal property, and disputes between citizens of different states. General jurisdiction refers to the court's authority to hear any case put before it that does not belong exclusively to another court. The authority to consider a case in the first instance, and to try it and pass judgment on the law and facts, begins in these courts of original jurisdiction.

District Court is also the name given to lower courts of the states and the Commonwealth of Puerto Rico. These general jurisdiction courts are sometimes called superior or circuit courts. State courts of general jurisdiction have the authority to try all cases, both civil and criminal. When a court is given limited original jurisdiction, it may, for example, hear only misdemeanor cases. Lower courts may then bind over felony cases to the higher court. Large urban areas commonly have divisions

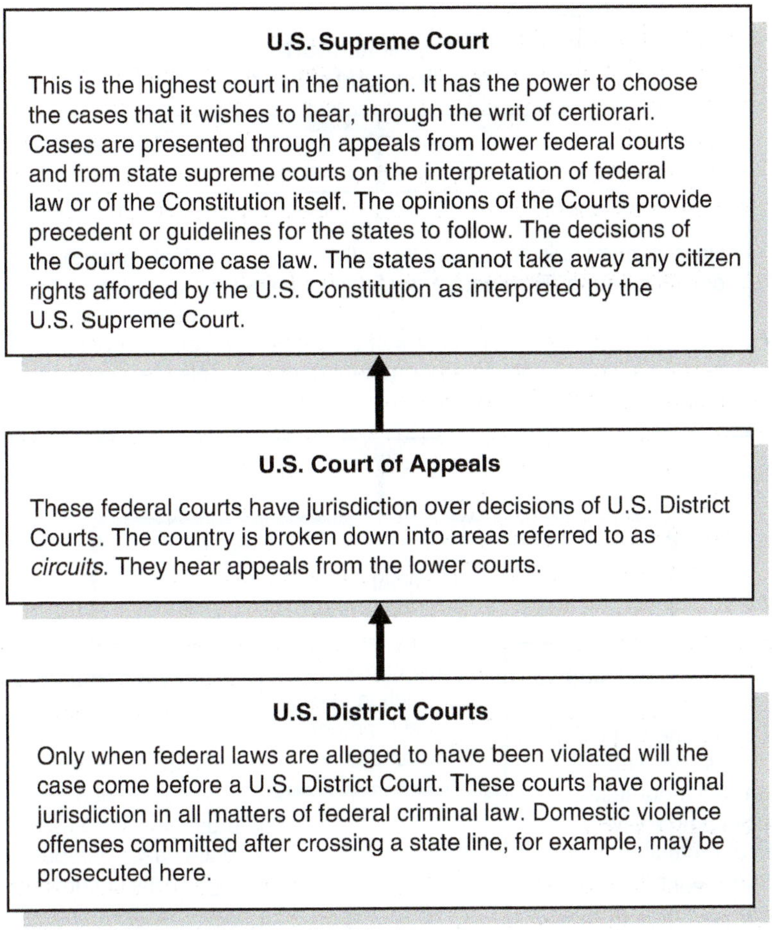

U.S. Supreme Court

This is the highest court in the nation. It has the power to choose the cases that it wishes to hear, through the writ of certiorari. Cases are presented through appeals from lower federal courts and from state supreme courts on the interpretation of federal law or of the Constitution itself. The opinions of the Courts provide precedent or guidelines for the states to follow. The decisions of the Court become case law. The states cannot take away any citizen rights afforded by the U.S. Constitution as interpreted by the U.S. Supreme Court.

U.S. Court of Appeals

These federal courts have jurisdiction over decisions of U.S. District Courts. The country is broken down into areas referred to as *circuits*. They hear appeals from the lower courts.

U.S. District Courts

Only when federal laws are alleged to have been violated will the case come before a U.S. District Court. These courts have original jurisdiction in all matters of federal criminal law. Domestic violence offenses committed after crossing a state line, for example, may be prosecuted here.

FIGURE 14-3   Pictured is an abbreviated view of the federal court system. The trial courts on the federal level are the U.S. District Courts.

that specialize in different kinds of cases, such as juvenile or family matters. Refer to Figure 14-4 for an illustration of the typical state process. Court functions are similar from state to state, but the names used for the courts differ widely. Use this figure as a guide to understanding the function of each court. Research the names of the courts in your jurisdiction to determine those that have an equivalent role.

Codes governing domestic relations belong in a body of law that is called the civil law. Contrasted with criminal law, these codes are concerned with civil or private rights and remedies. Family and probate courts typically have jurisdiction over divorce, custody, and guardianships. In some states, these courts have a limited jurisdiction in civil and criminal domestic violence cases. Those with appellate jurisdiction review the judgments of these lower courts. Laws prohibiting domestic violence are within the subject matter of original jurisdiction courts. For example, a district or lower court has original jurisdiction to hear the facts and pass judgment on violations of criminal law.

Federal versus State Jurisdiction

Until recently, domestic violence was not within federal jurisdiction. Early attempts to criminalize domestic violence at the federal level failed to pass. In 1906, the U.S. Congress defeated a bill to impose whipping of wife beaters (Pleck, 1989). It was not

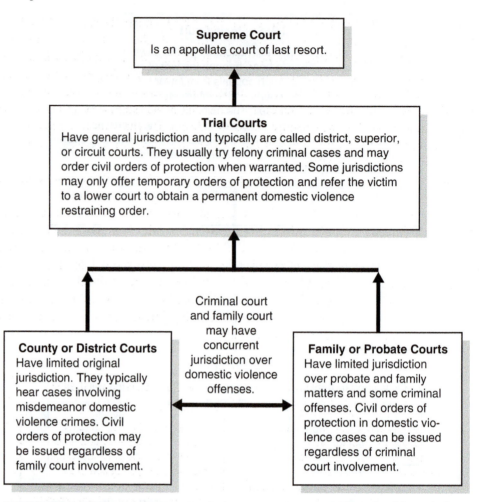

FIGURE 14-4 This represents the typical state court process. There is wide variation among state court systems.

until the 1970s that federal domestic violence legislation was again proposed. In 1978 and again in 1979, two federal efforts that would have provided federal grants to states to be used for spouse abuse shelters also failed. Since family relations were under the exclusive jurisdiction of state courts, there was no protection against domestic violence committed on federal property. Even in the absence of domestic violence laws, crimes against the person might have been prosecuted if the acts came to the attention of the police. However, domestic violence protection orders were not available for families living on military bases or tribal reservations. Over a decade later, domestic violence legislation was again considered by federal lawmakers.

In 1984, the Family Violence Prevention and Services Act (Title 42, Chapter 110) was enacted by Congress to provide services for victims and public education for family violence prevention. The act continues to provide federal funding to help states provide shelters, education, research, and crime victim compensation for domestic violence victims. The Victims of Crime Act of 1984 (VOCA) is another primary funding source for victims, including family violence survivors. The Crime Victims Fund, which was established by the VOCA, receives millions of dollars annually from criminal fines, forfeited bail bonds, penalties, and special assessments collected by the U.S. offices, courts, and prisons (Office for Victims of Crime, 2006). Under the USA PATRIOT Act of 2001, the deposit of donations from private entities into the fund was also authorized.

Domestic violence continued to be under the exclusive criminal jurisdiction of the states until the 1990s. The Violence Against Women Act (VAWA) of 1990 introduced legislation that called for the federal prosecution of a person who travels across state lines and intentionally injures or sexually abuses his or her spouse or intimate partner. Defeated initially, the bill was reintroduced in subsequent years until some provisions were incorporated into the Violent Crime Control and Law Enforcement Act of 1994, referred to as Title IV of VAWA.

The states continue to legislate and control criminal and civil actions relative to domestic violence for the majority of cases. Federal legislation is not meant to take away the jurisdiction of the states in these matters. Refer to Figure 14-5 for an illustration of significant differences between the state and the federal jurisdiction in the handling of domestic violence cases. Instead, federal legislation is a body of law that represents a joint effort between the federal and state governments to close the loopholes and provide more comprehensive protection for victims of family violence, as in the case of offenders who cross state lines. The likelihood of escaping responsibility for having committed domestic crime due to differing jurisdictions is now diminished due to the possibility of federal prosecution.

State Court Jurisdiction   **Federal Court Jurisdiction**

Domestic violence offenses have traditionally been state crimes. State statutes and civil codes protect citizens within their jurisdiction.

New federal offenses make it unlawful to cross a state line to commit domestic violence crimes or to violate a protection order. Federal statutes prohibit domestic violence crimes on federal property.

The full faith and credit provision of VAWA requires that foreign orders of protection be recognized and enforced in every state as if they had originated in the jurisdiction of the offense. Some states have responded with their own statutes to implement the requirement; others rely on the federal mandate.

Federal statutes may be used when

1. An interstate crime makes it difficult for local law enforcement to gather evidence.

2. Penalties for domestic violence, because of old statutes or early parole, don't fit the crime.

3. Release of the defendant on bond is an issue.

4. The offense occurs on federal property, such as tribal lands or military installations.

5. A civil rights violation that is gender motivated is alleged.

FIGURE 14-5   Federal versus state court jurisdiction in cases involving domestic violence.

Civil versus Criminal Court in the State System

The allegation of a criminal law violation can be tried in a court of general jurisdiction at the state level. Some states issue criminal protection orders. Provisions for civil protection orders when a domestic relationship exists are found in the state codes. An overlap of criminal law and civil law is inherent in family violence cases. Traditionally, family courts of limited jurisdiction have handled relationship issues. For this reason, a person can obtain a civil order of protection in a family or probate court in addition to filing a petition for protection in the lower criminal courts. Moreover, some criminal offenses have been added to the jurisdiction of family court through state statutes. This is called **concurrent jurisdiction**, which occurs when different courts are each authorized to deal with the same subject matter within a similar geographical area. Look at Figure 14-6 for the steps that are used in resolving concurrent jurisdiction.

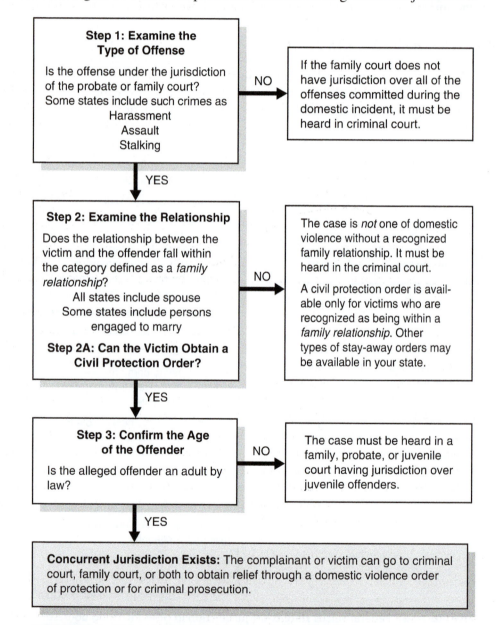

Step 1: Examine the Type of Offense

Is the offense under the jurisdiction of the probate or family court? Some states include such crimes as
Harassment
Assault
Stalking

NO → If the family court does not have jurisdiction over all of the offenses committed during the domestic incident, it must be heard in criminal court.

YES ↓

Step 2: Examine the Relationship

Does the relationship between the victim and the offender fall within the category defined as a *family relationship*?
All states include spouse
Some states include persons engaged to marry

Step 2A: Can the Victim Obtain a Civil Protection Order?

NO → The case is *not* one of domestic violence without a recognized family relationship. It must be heard in the criminal court.

A civil protection order is available only for victims who are recognized as being within a *family relationship*. Other types of stay-away orders may be available in your state.

YES ↓

Step 3: Confirm the Age of the Offender

Is the alleged offender an adult by law?

NO → The case must be heard in a family, probate, or juvenile court having jurisdiction over juvenile offenders.

YES ↓

Concurrent Jurisdiction Exists: The complainant or victim can go to criminal court, family court, or both to obtain relief through a domestic violence order of protection or for criminal prosecution.

FIGURE 14-6 Three steps to resolving concurrent jurisdiction. Based on data from the Capital District Women's Bar Association Legal Project, 1998.

No clear guidelines on whether an offense belongs in the family or criminal court can be given due to the numerous variations from state to state. Significant points that lead to the decision of whether a case belongs in the family court or a criminal court include the following:

- Type of offense
- Relationship of the victim to the offender
- Age of the perpetrator.

The victim chooses to file in civil court; the prosecutor makes the choice in criminal court. Making that choice in domestic violence cases do not exclude the possibility of dealing with both criminal and civil courts at the same time. For example, a person may file criminal charges in a trial court and obtain a civil restraining order in the family court.

THE ROLE OF THE JUDGE

The role of the judge in cases concerning domestic or intimate partner violence is characterized by the court jurisdiction where the judge resides. A judge that sits in a criminal court will hear domestic violence-related crimes in addition to nondomestic violence–related crimes. The power to hear cases varies and victim needs sometimes overlap between courts.

The role that the judge plays in the issuance of civil domestic violence restraining orders cannot be underestimated. It is the judge who can help ensure the likelihood of success of protection by his or her attitude and demeanor during the hearing. It is also essential that judges have a working knowledge of the VAWA so that they can impart information to both the victim and the perpetrator. At the time an order is issued, the judge should inform both parties orally and in writing that the protection order is valid in all 50 states, the District of Columbia, tribal lands, and all U.S. territories. The judge should advise the victim to secure a certified copy of the order if it is not certified at the time of its issuance and to carry a copy at all times.

The judge is responsible for informing the victim that there is a National Domestic Violence Hotline (1-800-799-SAFE[7233]) that can help provide information about the jurisdiction to which the victim may be moving. This number could also provide information about the nearest shelter and the telephone number of the nearest domestic violence advocate. The judge should advise that a violation of the order in a state or tribe that has given full faith and credit to the order may result in federal penalties, including fines and long-term imprisonment, in addition to any state or tribal remedies available. The judge should also inform the perpetrator that it is a federal violation to purchase, receive, or possess a firearm or ammunition once subject to the order of protection. The trial judges who conduct domestic violence hearings should not only assert strong leadership qualities to ensure that their orders will be obeyed in their jurisdictions, but also provide information to victims and perpetrators about the provisions and consequences of the VAWA.

Specialized Domestic Violence Courts

In specialized courts, judges have greater available resources and staff who are trained in domestic violence issues. In 1966, the first domestic violence court opened in Brooklyn, New York. It was designed to increase victims' safety and hold defendants accountable. The court was staffed by judges and established extensive partnerships with criminal justice and social service agencies. The Department of Probation dedicated several officers from the "intensive supervision program" to work on the intimate partner violence cases. For the past several years, the probation violation rates at the specialized court have been nearly half the violation rate typical of this probation population. The successes of the program have led to it being replicated and adapted to other courts. Today, there are nearly 300 courts nationwide that have unique processing mechanisms for domestic violence cases (Center for Court Innovation, 2008).

The term **domestic violence court** refers to those courts that assign judicial officers to hear a special domestic violence calendar, regardless of whether they hear those cases exclusively (Herman, 2004). Such courts have developed along with the realization that noninjury cases of domestic violence cases are often upstaged by "more serious crimes," regardless of the potential for escalation into high injury or homicide. These courts vary in their scope of jurisdiction, structure, and processes. Many domestic violence courts have jurisdiction over the issuance of civil protection orders, but a few also have jurisdiction over criminal domestic violence cases (Herman, 2004). The opposite is also true: Other domestic violence courts have jurisdiction over criminal cases but not overprotection orders. Still, other variations also exist.

Specialized courts have emerged slowly over the past several years. The reluctance for judicial participation in part is due to the concern that their position of neutrality would be compromised by procedures favoring one side of the community over another (Keilitz, 2000). The development of other court specializations, such as drug courts and balanced justice initiatives, has contributed to the overcoming of such barriers. Domestic violence courts have emerged for the following reasons:

1. There has been a substantial increase in the number of domestic violence cases seen in the court system, despite the drop in domestic violence rates.
2. There is an increasing awareness that specialized services and responses are needed.
3. When left in traditional courts, those with low injury or noninjury cases tend to be upstaged by more serious crimes, regardless of the potential violence attached to these offenses.

Studies suggest that intervention has the potential to contribute to the victim's empowerment and satisfaction with the legal system. This therapeutic approach to jurisprudence seems to have contributed to the "one-stop shopping" concept for domestic violence victims, a coordination of services approach (Shelton, 2007). The primary focus of the courts is on victim protection rather than the traditional concern for perpetrator rehabilitation. Some significant benefits of domestic violence courts cited by advocates include:

- Advocacy services
- Enhanced coordination of cases
- Greater understanding by judges of the dynamics
- Improved offender compliance with orders.

Integrated Domestic Violence Courts

The most innovative model to address intimate partner violence is called the **integrated domestic violence court**, or **IDV court**. Under the integrated model, one judge handles criminal domestic violence cases and related family issues, including custody, visitation, and civil protection orders, in addition to matrimonial issues. This approach is taken when the court seeks to handle all related cases about a single family where

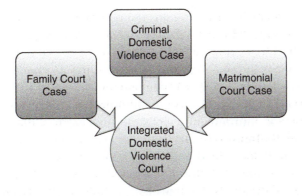

FIGURE 14-7 To be eligible for IDV court, a case must have both a criminal matter and either a civil or a family court matter—including divorce, custody, and protective orders. All matters may be heard in one court. Victim protection, offender accountability, and improved processing are among the reasons why this innovative approach is successful.

the underlying issue is intimate partner violence. Dade County, Florida, and Baltimore, Maryland, have established integrated domestic violence courts. The goal of this approach is to streamline and centralize the court processes, eliminate contradictory orders, and improve victim safety. Understanding that one domestic dispute may trigger actions in civil, criminal, and the family court at the same time, the IDV court handles criminal charges, motions for divorce, civil protection orders, child custody matters, and visitation disputes in the same court session.

Along with 30 specialized domestic violence courts, New York announced the creation of the first integrated domestic violence courts in 2001 (Cecala & Walsh, 2006). This was seen as necessary due to the large scale of domestic violence problems within the state. In New York City alone, over 20 percent of all criminal cases are domestic assaults (Shelton, 2007). See Figure 14-7 for an illustration of the model. More than three-quarters of the residents of New York State live in counties served by these courts. Dedicated to the "one family–one judge" model, IDV courts are designed as an alternative coordinated response in those situations where domestic violence victims have pending cases in multiple courts. Instead of appearing in family court, criminal court, and matrimonial court, this option allows the victims to consolidate all matters into one court. Providing greater consistency and informed judicial decision making, the use of the integrated domestic violence court also reduces the number of court visits. More than 137,000 cases have already been heard in the 42 IDV courts in New York alone (Shelton, 2007).

CIVIL PROTECTION ORDERS

The most significant legislative change for protection against domestic violence is the civil protection order. Until recent times, the use of protective orders was restricted to protect crime victims and witnesses from harassment by defendants. In 1976, Pennsylvania became the first state to enact laws that allowed survivors of intimate partner violence to obtain civil orders of protection (National Council of Juvenile and Family Court Judges [NCJFCJ], 2005). Civil protection orders are now available to adults in every state and the District of Columbia. These orders are referred to as restraining orders since they intend to restrain the perpetrator from further abusive behavior and to grant relief.

Women are the most common individuals who seek orders of protection. The civil restraining order is an essential tool in identifying and protecting domestic violence victims. More victims report intimate partner violence to civil courts than to the police (Klein, 2008). To qualify for this type of order, an abuse must have occurred that places the victim in fear of imminent serious physical harm. Violation of a civil protection order is a criminal offense, usually a misdemeanor, and carries some penalty.

Civil protection orders are domestic relations restraining orders in which the court has issued a protection or restraining order designed to limit or eliminate contact between two or more individuals. Civil protection orders differ from nondomestic relations restraining orders (which are civil cases) in that civil protection orders apply to individuals who are in a domestic relationship.

For an order to be valid, a magistrate, a clerk, or a judge authorized to issue such orders must sign it. It contains the name of the person who is under the order as well as the name of the complainant or victim. An attempt to serve the order on the offender must be made. In some cases, the offender cannot be located. Failure to accept service of the order does not invalidate its provisions. In some jurisdictions, provisions exist to obtain an emergency judicial order when the court is not in session. Referred to as the emergency judicial response system in Massachusetts, it places a judge on call to be reached by telephone when one is not available through the court. The judge can issue a temporary protection order over the phone and instruct the police officer to take protective measures. The victim must then go to the court on the next business day to obtain the order in writing.

Obtaining the order may prove challenging and burdensome to the person in distress. It requires an excessive amount of paperwork, upward of six pages, in addition to testifying in front of a judge on the necessity of the order. Even if the survivor is aware of her right to obtain a protection order, misconceptions on how to obtain one without legal counsel persist. Economic and cultural barriers may be factors.

As with any court order, the civil protection order restricts or instructs only one person to conform to the provisions of it. This is frequently misunderstood. For example, an order that directs Barney to stay away from Betty means that Barney alone is responsible for maintaining the distance between himself and the subject. If Betty calls Barney and invites him over to dinner, she is not in violation, because the order is not directed at her. However, if Barney accepts, and comes to dinner when he is under order to stay away, he is in violation of a court order and alone must face the consequences. The invitation does not render the protective order void. In many states, Barney is subject to arrest for his actions—but not Betty! Violation of some of the provisions contained in a civil protection order may be a criminal offense. The order remains valid until it expires or the judge changes it, no matter what Betty does!

Criminal and civil family violence laws vary from state to state. For civil protection orders, each state has passed legislation describing the portions of the order that are enforced through criminal action. Stated also are the criminal penalties that apply for violations of the protection order. For example, in Massachusetts, a restraining order may contain instructions to the offender to stay away from the victim. It may also include rules for the visitation of minor children and provide for temporary child support. If the offender violates the stay-away order, he or she is subject to a mandated arrest. However, violations of child support and custody arrangements stated in the protection order are not criminal offenses. In some states, if the victim encourages the offender to violate the protection order, then she or he may be charged with a criminal offense. Since there are many variations possible, it is important that students consult the Domestic Violence and Family Law in the state in which they reside.

Protection Order Criteria

To obtain a civil protection order, the victim must meet the following criteria:

1. The victim and abuser must be related family or household members as defined by the specific state code. In all states, this includes people who were or had been legally married. Although marriage is a factor, relationships may include same-sex or live-in partners. The defined domestic relationships might be so broad as to include persons who had substantial dating relationships in the past. The intensity of the relationship rather than the length is significant. Know your state code!

2. Abusive or threatening behavior that is prohibited by criminal statutes or domestic violence protection acts must have been perpetrated against the victim who is filing for the protection or against a child that the adult is responsible for protecting. Any act that is illegal, such as an assault where the relationship is domestic, is prohibited. Specific examples of prohibited behavior include attempting or causing physical harm, forced sexual relations, stalking, or threatening the victim.

3. The victim must make a written application for the order of protection. The application is called a **petition**. The forms are available at the court and sometimes at police departments or shelters for battered women. It must include the name and address of the person seeking the protection (called the plaintiff); the name and address of the accused (the defendant); and the specific behavior that occurred, along with the date(s) of violence for which the petitioner seeks relief. Provisions exist to protect the victims of abuse through confidentiality of their residence, school, employment, and child-care information.

4. The petition must be filed before a state or federal court with jurisdiction over the subject matter where the abuse occurred or where the victim is likely to be at risk. In most states, the victim appears before a probate or family court judge. A few, however, specify concurrent jurisdiction with the district court. Most of the states provide 24-hour access to the courts to obtain a protection order. Sometimes, police officers may file the petition for the victim over the telephone when the court is not in session; the judge then issues a verbal order of protection. Sometimes called the emergency judicial response system, it is activated when an officer telephones an on-call judge during evening or weekend hours.

Elements of a Petition

Many states allow the victim to proceed *pro se* when requesting a civil order of protection against domestic violence. The term **pro se** means that the victim can go into court without the assistance of a lawyer and represent or himself or herself. The victim of abuse must go to a court where he or she lives or where the abuse occurred to fill out the form requesting a civil protection order. Typical information that is asked for in a request for protection includes, but is not limited to, the following:

- The name, address, phone number, and description of the victim
- The name, address (if known), and description of the defendant (perpetrator of the offense/s)

- The age of the victim, or name of the adult who is filing for the victim if she or he is a minor
- Any knowledge of weapons that the defendant may possess
- Any knowledge of prior or pending court action involving the victim and defendant
- The forms of relief requested.

The majority of states provide temporary custody of minor children under the prevention of abuse order. These states will also include questions regarding any minor children that the parties may have in common. It is not unusual for a court to require a sworn affidavit about the circumstances of the abuse in addition to the completed form. When victims need help to fill out the forms, it is usually available from a clerk of court or a victim witness advocate. Some jurisdictions provide assistance from battered women shelters or police departments.

Forms of Available Relief

The provisions contained in a protection order are referred to as "relief." Violation of a civil protection order may be a misdemeanor offense, a felony offense, or contempt of court. All protection orders authorize some form of relief for the survivor of domestic violence. Commonly, they restrain the defendant from committing future acts of violence, grant exclusive possession of the victim's residence to the victim and evict the perpetrator, award temporary custody of common children, and provide child and spousal support along with stay-away or no-contact orders. Two or more court hearings may be required for the order of protection. Typically, one court hearing is needed to issue the temporary order and another to issue the permanent order. Some jurisdictions mandate the defendant to forfeit property such as weapons, keys to a joint residence, checkbooks, and automobiles. A recent addition to the list of remedies included in a restraining order is an order to stay away from the pets belonging to the victim. Refer to Figure 14-8 to see which states have this provision. Common forms of relief include, but are not limited to, these examples:

1. *Restraining orders.* All states have the restraining order provision as a general form of relief.
2. *Exclusive use of a residence or eviction of a perpetrator from the victim's household.* All states have some form of this provision. Some states provide for the defendant to continue to make payments for the home or apartment that the defendant and victim once shared even though the perpetrator has been evicted under a prevention order.
3. *Custody or visitation.* Most states acknowledge the risk to children due to domestic violence. Those that address custody or visitation in the restraining order will specify the parent who will be granted custody. Protection orders are not meant to supersede probate and family court orders for custody and are usually temporary, pending a separate hearing to consider the best interests of the child. Arizona, Indiana, Nebraska, Oklahoma, Virginia, and Wisconsin do not address visitation or custody in the protection order. In such cases, a custody hearing may still take place apart from the protection order, through a family or probate court.
4. *Payment of child or spousal support.* Many states now authorize the payment of child or spousal support to be determined in the protection order.

Relationships — Remedies — Violation Penalty — Length of Order

Civil Protection Orders	Spouse or Former Spouse	Pregnant or Child in Common	Stepparent or Stepchildren	Parents & Children	Present or Former Household Member *opposite sex only	Related by Blood	Adult Dating Relationship	Teen Dating Relationship	Related by Marriage *current in-laws only	other	Vacate Joint Residence	Restraining/No Contact	Custody	Child Support	Counseling	Possession of Firearm Prohibited or *Optional	Animal Protection	Misdemeanor	Felony	Contempt	Six Months or less	One Year	Two Years or More *Judge decides length
Alabama	x	x		x	x	x					x	x	x	x				x		x			x
Alaska	x	x		x	x	x	x		x	x	x	x	x	x	x	*x		x					x
Arizona	x	x		x	x	x			*x	x	x	x	x			*x		x		x		x	
Arkansas	x	x		x	x	x	x				x	x	x	x				x		x			*x
California	x	x		x	x	x	x	x		x	x	x	x	x	x	x	x	x					*x
Colorado	x	x		x	x	x	x				x	x	x	x				x	x	x			x
Connecticut	x	x		x	x	x	x	x	x	x	x	x	x					x		x	x	x	
Delaware	x		x	*x	x	x	x	x	x	x	x	x	x	x	x	*x		x		x		x	
D. C.	x	x		x	x	x	x				x	x	x	x	x	x		x		x		x	
Florida	x	x		x	x	x	x				x	x	x	x	x	x	x	x					*x
Georgia	x	x	x	x	x						x	x	x	x	x	x		x		x		x	
Hawaii	x	x		x	x	x					x	x	x			x		x		x			x
Idaho	x	x		x	x	x	x	x	x	x	x	x	x			x		x		x		x	
Illinois	x	x	x	x	x	x	x	x	x	x	x	x	x	x	x	*x	x	x		x			x
Indiana	x	x		x		x	x	x	x	x	x		x			*x		x			x		
Iowa	x	x		x	x	x	x		x	x	x	x	x	x							x	x	
Kansas	x	x		x	x	x					x	x	x	x	x			x		x		x	
Kentucky	x	x	x	x	x	x					x	x	x	x	x			x		x			x
Louisiana	x	x	x	x	x		x	x		x	x	x	x	x				x		x	x		
Maine	x	x		x	x	x	x		x	x	x	x	x	x	x	*x	x		x	x			x
Maryland	x	x	x	x	x	x			x	x	x	x	x	x	x	*x		x		x	x		
Massachusetts	x	x		x	x	x	x	x	x		x	x	x	x	x	x	x	x		x		x	
Michigan	x	x	x	x	x		x	x			x							x	x	x		x	
Minnesota	x	x		x	x	x	x			x	x	x	x	x				x		x			x
Mississippi	x	x		x	x	x	x			x	x	x	x					x		x			x
Missouri	x	x			x	x	x				x	x	x	x	x			x	x			x	

FIGURE 14-8   Civil protection orders vary from state to state due to differing domestic violence relationship definitions and remedies. Here is a state-by-state analysis that includes the typical length of the order and the violation penalty. Based on data from Lehrman, 1997; Hart, 1992; DeJong & Burgess-Proctor, 2006; Arkow, 2007; and American Bar Association, 2008.

Civil Protection Orders	Relationships										Remedies							Violation Penalty			Length of Order		
	Spouse or Former Spouse	Pregnant or Child in Common	Stepparent or Stepchildren	Parents & Children	Present or Former Household Member *opposite sex only	Related by Blood	Adult Dating Relationship	Teen Dating Relationship	Related by Marriage *current in-laws only	other	Vacate Joint Residence	Restraining/No Contact	Custody	Child Support	Counseling	Possession of Firearm Prohibited or *Optional	Animal Protection	Misdemeanor	Felony	Contempt	Six Months or less	One Year	Two Years or More
Montana	X	X	X	X	X	X	X		X	X	X	X	X	X	X	X		X				X	
Nebraska	X	X		X	X	X	X		X		X	X						X				X	
Nevada	X	X		X	X	X	X	X	X	X	X	X	X	X	X	X	X	X				X	
New Hampshire	X			X	X	X	X	X			X	X	X	X	X	X		X			X	X	
New Jersey	X	X			X		X	X			X	X	X	X	X	*X	X	X		x		indefinite	
New Mexico	X	X	X	X		X	X		X	X	X	X	X					X			X	X	
New York	X	X		X		X	X		X		X	X	X	X	X	*X	X	X					X
North Carolina	X	X		X	X	X	X		X		X	X	X	X	X	*X		X				X	
North Dakota	X	X		X	X	X	X		X	X	X	X	X	X	X	*X		X	X	X		not stated	
Ohio	X	X	X	X	X	X			X	X	X	X	X	X	X	X		X				X	X
Oklahoma	X	X	X	X	X	X	X	X	X	X	X	X			X			X					X
Oregon	X	X		X	X	X	X		X	X	X	X	X			*X		X				X	
Pennsylvania	X	X		X	X	X	X		X	X	X	X	X	X	X	*X	X	X					X
Rhode Island	X	X	X	X	X	X	X	X	X	X	X	X			X			X	X	X			X
South Carolina	X	X		X	X*	X					X	X	X	X	X			X			*X	X	
South Dakota	X	X		X	X	X	X	X	X	X	X	X	X	X	X			X					X
Tennessee	X	X		X	X	X	X	X	X	X	X	X	X	X	X		X			X		X	
Texas	X	X		X	X	X	X		X	X	X	X	X	X	X	X		X	X	X		X	X
Utah	X	X		X	X						X	X	X	X	X		X			X	X		
Vermont	X	X			X	X	X	X			X	X	X	X	X			X				X	not stated
Virginia	X	X	X	X	X	X			X	X	X	X	X	X	X			X	X	X			X
Washington	X	X	X	X	X	X	X	X	X		X	X			X			X	X	X	X	X	
West Virginia	X	X	X	X	X	X	X	X	X	X	X	X	X	X	X	*X		X			X	X	
Wisconsin	X	X		X	X	X	X					X	X	X		X	X				X	X	
Wyoming	X	X		X	X					X	X	X	X	X	X			X				X	

FIGURE 14-8 *continued*

Been There ... Done That!

Penny recounted coming home in the near dark one evening to find the severed head of her horse in the walkway. She recoiled in horror, asking herself, "Why would he do such a horrible thing?" Many years later, Walter still shoots at trees around the perimeter of her country home that he has been restricted from entering through a permanent court order. Some states specify the period of time for a restraining order. A permanent protection order is rare and may only be available in extreme cases.

Each state provides different lengths of time that the order is valid after a court order is issued, ranging from three months to over two years. Additionally, only the person who is named as the defendant on a protection order can be held liable for its violation. Every provision must be adhered to for the defendant to be in compliance with the order. If one part of the order is violated, the order itself is violated. It is not necessary that abuse recur for a violation to take place.

Limitations of Protection Orders

Professionals warn that obtaining a protection or stay-away order has its limitations and should not replace taking safety precautions. Although orders do provide immediate relief for the victims of domestic violence, they may only be a temporary measure. Citing frequent revictimization within two years of the restraining order, some experts suggest that they offer a false sense of security (Klein, 2008).

A frequent concern in the criminal justice community is that of victims who obtain a temporary restraining order and do not return to make the order permanent. One study specifically addressed this problem, citing that 40 percent of victims failed to return for permanent protection orders (Harrell & Smith, 1998). The authors concluded that the majority of women who sought protection orders had serious complaints of abuse, yet chose not to return for the permanent order. Their reasons included these explanations:

- Their abusers had stopped bothering them.
- Their abusers exerted pressure on them to drop their complaints.
- They feared retaliation if they persisted in their complaints.
- They had encountered problems in getting temporary orders served on the abusers, a prerequisite to the hearing for a permanent order.

Research strongly suggests that civil restraining orders decrease the risk of physical violence by the abuser but may increase the risk of psychological abuse when only a temporary order is obtained. Having a permanent protection order in effect has been associated with an 80 percent reduction in police-related physical violence, according to one study (Holt, Kernic, Lumley, Wolf, & Rivara, 2002). In a subsequent study, women with protection orders were less likely to be contacted by the abuser, to experience injury or weapons threats, and to receive abuse-related medical care as compared to those who did not have protection orders (Holt, 2004). Researchers concluded that permanent protection orders might be more powerful deterrents to prevent re-abuses than previously believed.

Enforcement of Restraining Orders

Criminal sanctions are typically used as the method to enforce protective orders. State laws vary on which charge might be brought against the person who violates a domestic violence restraining order. The person who violates the order might be charged with a misdemeanor, a felony, or contempt of court. In some states, a combination of these options applies, depending on the original offense for which the order was entered or the number of times that it was violated. In Utah, for example, a protective order violation can be a misdemeanor or a felony, depending on the classification of the initial crime.

Violation of a protective order might be treated as a new offense in some states. Other related penalties may apply for violations of a protective order, including bail forfeiture, probation revocation, and incarceration.

A few states require a violator to serve a minimum term of confinement. Typically, mandatory confinement occurs after multiple violations of an order, ranging from a 24-hour imprisonment to seven consecutive days (Office for Victims of Crime, 2006). Mandated counseling and electronic monitoring are examples of additional sanctions for violation of protection orders. If a person violates a provision of a protection order, that violation is often a criminal offense. However, use of the courts to enforce violations of protection orders is rare.

OFFENDER INTERVENTION PROGRAMS

Mandating offenders to attend an offender treatment program is the most common court response to intimate partner violence, whether their cases were diverted or the defendants were probated or even jailed (Klein, 2008). About 90 percent of these intervention programs are based on the power and control feminist model, discussed in Chapter 10 (Austin & Dankwort, 1998). Three major models of domestic violence intervention programs used today are outlined in Figure 14-9. The focus on standardizing offender programs developed during the mid-1980s as a response to interventions that were deemed by political activists as distancing the problem from its intended focus on the oppression of women and of concerns that rehabilitation might overshadow the safety issues for victims. By 1997, 45 states had developed, or were in the process of developing, standards for offender intervention programs.

Arguing that standardizing intimate partner violence intervention infringes on their right to practice according to their professional training, some professionals in the mental health and legal communities strongly criticize proscribing practice in the absence of empirical evidence to support particular interventions. The debate on the efficacy of traditional offender treatment programs is ongoing.

Specialized Offender Intervention

The trend toward specialized offender treatment programs came with the recognition that the offender's socioeconomic status, racial or ethnic identity, country of origin, and sexual orientation can affect intervention. In response to concerns regarding diversity, culturally competent interventions were developed to draw on the strength of the offender's family or community social systems (Healey, Smith, & O'Sullivan, 1998). Programs for men of African descent, recent Asian immigrants, and non-English-speaking Latinos who speak Spanish are examples of culturally based intervention programs.

Recognizing ethnic and racial differences in curriculum planning is central to the specialized approach. African American groups enable men to focus on what they did instead of on social injustice or racism; Asian programs counter the social acceptability of private violence, and the concept of machismo is challenged in strategies used with

Duluth Curriculum: Based on feminist theory; issues of power and control as primary targets.

Program structure: 2 or 3 sessions on each of eight themes: nonviolence; non-threatening behavior; respect; support and trust; honesty and accountability; sexual respect; partnership; negotiation and fairness.

EMERGE: Blend of feminist educational approach with more in-depth and intensive group work.

Program structure: 48-week program divided into two stages: 8 weeks of orientation and 40 weeks of group work. About one-third of the batterers require additional time in the program.

Orientation topics include: Defining domestic violence; negative vs. positive "self talk"; effects of violence on women; psychological, sexual and economic abuse; abusive vs. respectful communication; effects of partner abuse on children.

Groups meet weekly for 2 hours. Sessions typically include:
1. A short check-in to recount any conflicts during the week; a long check-in for new members to detail the last abusive episode and focus on batterer responsibility
2. Longer discussions concerning issues raised during check-in that focuses on alternatives to violence
3. Development of individualized goals based on current and past abuse

The AMEND Model: Blend of feminist educational approach with more in-depth and intensive group work.

Program structure: Variable—from 36 weeks to 5 years for the most difficult cases. AMEND takes a "multimodal" approach centered on group therapy, but it may also include some individual counseling or couples work.

Approach: AMEND's philosophy has seven tenets:
1. Belief in the feminist "power and control" theory of battering is central.
2. Intervention with batterers cannot be value-neutral—violence is a crime.
3. Counseling aims to teach behavior change to stop violence and abuse and addresses the psychological features of the batterer's problem.
4. Violence and abuse are choices, and the victims are not responsible for the violence.
5. Ending violence is a long-term process, from 1 to 5 years.
6. Ending violence is complex and requires "multimodal" intervention.
7. Treatment of batterers requires special skills and training.

FIGURE 14-9   The three major intervention programs are the Duluth curriculum, EMERGE, and the AMEND model. Based on data from Healey et al., 1998.

Latino groups. Despite well-intentioned approaches, several studies have found that the type of offender program has made no difference regarding re-abuses, including the culturally focused programs (Klein, 2008).

PROGRAM PROCEDURES FOR MALE PERPETRATORS

Offender programs typically consist of five stages: intake and assessment, orientation, victim orientation, program, and ending the program.

Intake and Assessment

The intake interview may take place at the courthouse after the perpetrator has been seen by a probation officer. In some jurisdictions, a representative from the program attends the civil court hearings. After the judge has issued an order, the staff member will meet with the perpetrator and explain the program. In some jurisdictions, it is the responsibility of the offender to initiate the contact and arrange for the assessment interview. During the intake process, the interviewer seeks information on the pattern and severity of the abuse toward current and past partners, children, and others. Not all offenders are accepted at this stage. Much depends on whether the offender has substance abuse or mental illness problems that might make a different program that can address those needs more suitable for him or her. Many programs will not admit a person who denies being violent or appears likely to disrupt the group.

Orientation

During the orientation session, the new clients meet and are told the rules and goals of the program. One purpose of the orientation is to establish a rapport between the participants and the counselors. Since a majority of clients are court ordered to attend the session, this is an effort to reduce their defensiveness. It is important to find out as much as possible about the abuse that was perpetrated so that effective intervention can occur. Counselors meet one-on-one in addition to holding a group meeting in order to assess how the program can best benefit each person.

Victim Orientation

Many programs offer an opportunity for the person who was battered to meet with the staff. Some states require that partners be notified at various points of intervention. The purpose of meeting with the victims is threefold. First, it allows a counselor the opportunity to explain the program goals and philosophy. Second, it is an opportunity to get the victim's assessment of the abuse in the relationship. Third, safety issues and protection options can be discussed so that the battered person is aware of the resources available if services are needed. Shelter locations and orders for protection are among the topics that may be discussed.

Program

Education on power and control issues and the development of critical-thinking skills are emphasized to help offenders understand and change their behavior. Anger management skills training in a group setting is a common component of offenders' programs, although anger management is not the core of the approach. Some programs offer in-depth counseling that is designed to force the offender to accept responsibility for his or her actions. Others focus on the relationship between the offender and the victim to promote respect and positive behavior.

The group sessions may involve role-playing based on personal experiences to teach appropriate ways to deal with family situations that offenders find frustrating. They may discuss situations that have caused men or women to batter and apply alternatives to violence. Videos and stories about abuse from the victim's perspective are designed to sensitize the perpetrators about the effects of abuse on their partners.

Ending the Program

A client may be terminated before completion of the program for a number of reasons. Among them is revocation of probation, alcohol and drug abuse, disrupting the sessions, failure to take responsibility for abusive acts, and not attending group sessions regularly. Successful completion of the program may involve an exit project, such as a letter on how the client was affected by the process. Some programs offer follow-ups at specified time periods after a client has been discharged from the program.

PROGRAM PROCEDURES FOR FEMALE PERPETRATORS

Researchers are in disagreement on the existence of women as offenders. Clinicians, on the other hand, have had to face increasing numbers of women in need of treatment. Numbers of women arrested for domestic violence have grown in recent years, despite the decline in the rates of intimate violence. Typically, the response to these offenders is a feminized version of the male intervention. The strategies are inconsistent and, in many parts of the United States, nonexistent.

The Domestic Abuse Project (DAP) put together the first published manual specifically intended to address the problems and behaviors of women offenders (Domestic Abuse Project, 1998). Its approach emphasizes the need for facilitators connected to the gay, lesbian, bisexual, and transgender communities. Providing guidelines for the treatment of women who batter, the program philosophy is grounded in the belief that violent behavior is learned and that it is a chosen behavior. The DAP's Women Who Abuse program is a four-step process consisting of a thorough intake assignment with referral options for the survivors, assessment follow-up sessions, a psychoeducational therapy group, and individualized therapy.

INTAKE ASSESSMENT A major focus in this stage is the assessment of offender readiness to change her abusive behavior. A thorough screening is included to ensure that the referred woman is not a self-defending victim.

INDIVIDUAL SESSIONS In preparation for group sessions, this stage is used to build rapport with the client and assist the women in the difficult process of acknowledging their abusive behavior and developing a self-control plan.

EDUCATION COMPONENT During a 20-week period, approximately 16 educational topics are covered. Examples include sessions on shame versus responsibility, communication skills, anger management, costs and payoffs of being violent, and the effects of violence on children.

INDIVIDUALIZED TREATMENT This final section of the program focuses on the development of the self-control plan. Central are the cues of escalation before violence and plans for avoiding violence. Stress management and prevention are the desired outcomes.

CAN PROGRAM INTERVENTIONS STOP OFFENDING?

Referral to offender treatment programs is fast becoming the usual procedure for the courts. How well do these programs work at lowering recidivism? Over 35 evaluations of offender programs have yielded inconsistent results, according to Klein (2008).

At best, a modest treatment effect with a minimal reduction in recidivism has been noted, while most studies indicate no positive effects at all. The author concluded that offender programs, by themselves, are not likely to protect most victims or new intimate partners from further harm from higher-risk abusers.

The length of the program (26 weeks compared to 8 weeks) has been the one component that may make a difference in deterring re-abuse. Anger management programs are not the same as offender intervention programs. Anger management programs typically are of shorter length than offender programs. Anger management programs do not address the issues that are specific to intimate partner and family violence. Certified offender intervention programs include many of the following characteristics (Massachusetts Department of Public Health, 2008):

- They work with perpetrators of intimate partner violence.
- They are at least 80 hours in length.
- They have staff that is trained in domestic violence and offender intervention.
- They must attempt to contact victims and survivors.
- They must screen clients for substance abuse.
- They must undergo annual review by the Department of Public Health.

Court-referred offenders traditionally have high rates of noncompletion, which may contribute to their ineffectiveness. Probation studies find technical violations ranging from 34 percent to 61 percent (Klein, 2008). Abusers who complete the programs are less likely to re-abuse compared with those who fail to attend, are noncompliant or drop out of the offender treatment programs.

CONCLUSIONS

Although many individuals are actively involved in victim protections, the key players in the domestic violence courts are the advocates, prosecutors, and judges. Court systems exist on both the federal and state levels, although their jurisdiction varies greatly. This can be very confusing to the person seeking assistance, and services may overlap. Specialized prosecution units and specialized domestic violence courts are among the recent responses to maximize victim safety and offender accountability.

Unprecedented efforts are noted in government agencies that deal with personal information. It appears that there is a concerted effort to allow privacy of information in the Registry of Motor Vehicles and the Social Security Administration for victims of abuse. States are more proactive than ever before to assure privacy to those who have been abused.

Victim relief may come from a criminal or civil court. Civil protection orders can be a useful emergency measure to assist these victims with or without criminal prosecution. They may be obtained in either civil or criminal courts. Although the remedies available vary from state to state, in general, they provide significant relief to victims of violence. Most recently, some states have added animals to the list of what is protected under a restraining order.

The most common court response to intimate partner violence is that the offender is mandated to a state-approved offender treatment program. Research calls into question the effectiveness of such programs, although noncompletion may be contributing to their ineffectiveness.

SIMPLY SCENARIO

James punched Janice in the stomach during a particularly bad fight. He threatened to kill her, and she believed that he would. Terrified that he would make good on this threat, she called the police. James left before the police arrived. Relieved that James had left, Janice did not pursue a restraining order against him. A week later, Janice was shot, and the police believed that James was the killer. James was arrested for her murder.

Question: Can Officer Smith testify in the trial of James that Janice told him she thought James would kill her? Explain your answer. What options do the police have in this situation?

Questions for Review

1. Explain at least three victim privacy protections.
2. Summarize the role of the domestic violence victim advocate.
3. What was the exception to the Sixth Amendment Confrontation Clause that was struck down by the Supreme Court in *Crawford* (2004)?
4. What did the Supreme Court conclude in the *Giles* (2008) decision?
5. From a comparison of court outcomes for those charged with aggravated assault, is there any difference when the assault was perpetrated by a family member, intimate partner, or cohabitant?
6. Does prosecution of domestic violence offenders deter future abuse?
7. What is jurisdiction and how is it determined?
8. When did domestic violence first come under federal jurisdiction?
9. What does the term *domestic violence court* mean?
10. Explain the integrated domestic violence (IDV) court model.

Internet-Based Exercises

1. The American Bar Association has posted a chart that lists a state-by-state analysis of Domestic Violence Civil Protection Orders at https://www.americanbar.org/content/dam/aba/administrative/domestic_violence1/Charts/2016%20CPO%20Availability%20Chart.authcheckdam.pdf. Visit this site and find your state on the list. Compare the *Definition of Abuser* from your state with that of others. Report on the similarities and differences.
2. Here is a video from findlaw.com that explains the stages of a typical criminal case. View this video and write a short paper outlining these typical stages. http://link.brightcove.com/services/link/bcpid1569843954/bctid1578615932.
3. The National Institute of Justice (NIJ) offers a wealth of information on all topics concerned with criminal justice. From its homepage, research the topic Specialized Domestic Violence Courts. Report on what you have learned. https://nij.gov/topics/courts/domestic-violence-courts/Pages/welcome.aspx.
4. Conduct an Internet search using Google Scholar on "domestic violence offender treatment." Using only the articles published since 2016 write a review on the status of offender treatment options.

References

American Bar Association. (2009). Domestic violence civil protection orders (CPOs) by state. Retrieved from http://www.americanbar.org/content/dam/aba/migrated/domviol/pdfs/dv_cpo_chart.authcheckdam.pdf

Arkow, P. (2007). Expanding domestic violence protective orders to include companion animals. Retrieved from https://www.americanbar.org/newsletter/publications/cdv_enewsletter_home/expertArkow.html

Austin, J., & Dankwort, J. (1998). *A review of standards for batterer intervention programs.* Washington, D.C.: National Resource Center on Domestic Violence.

Capital District Women's Bar Association Legal Project. (1998). *Representing victims of domestic violence in family court.* Albany, NY: Domestic Violence Legal Connection, Albany Law School.

Cecala, S., & Walsh, M. (2006). *New York State's response to domestic violence: Systems and services making a difference* (Vol. 2008). New York, NY: New York State Office for the Prevention of Domestic Violence.

Center for Court Innovation. (2008). Domestic violence. Retrieved from http://www.courtinnovation.org/index .cfm?fuseaction=page.viewPage&pageID=512&docum entTopicID=23

Chaiken, M., Boland, B., Maltz, M., Martin, S., & Targonski, J. (2005, July). Prosecutors' programs ease victim anxieties. *National Institute of Justice Journal, (252)*, 30–32.

Crawford v. Washington, 124 S. Ct. 1354 (2004).

Davis v. Washington, Hammon v. Indiana, 547 U.S. 813 (2006).

DeJong, C., & Burgess-Proctor, A. (2006). A summary of personal protection order statutes in the United States. *Violence Against Women, 12*(1): 68–88.

Domestic Abuse Project. (Ed.). (1998). *Women who abuse in intimate relationships.* Minneapolis, MN: Author.

Giles v. California, 128 S. Ct. 2678 (2008).

Harrell, A., & Smith, B. (1998). *Effects of restraining orders on domestic violence victims.* (NCJ 171666). Washington, D.C.: National Institute of Justice.

Hart, B. (1992). *State codes on domestic violence: Analysis, commentary and recommendations.* Darby, PA: Diane Publishing.

Healey, K., Smith, C., & O'Sullivan, C. (1998). *Batterer programs: What criminal justice agencies need to know.* (NCJ 171683). Washington, D.C.: U.S. Department of Justice.

Herman, M. (2004). Domestic violence courts: Organization and procedure varies. *Family Violence Forum, 3*(2), 8.

Holt, V. (2004). Civil protection orders and subsequent intimate partner violence and injury. (NCJ 199722). Retrieved from https://www.ncjrs.gov/pdffiles1/nij /199722.pdf

Holt, V., Kernic, M., Lumley, T., Wolf, M., & Rivara, F. (2002). Civil protection orders and risk of subsequent police-reported violence. *The Journal of the American Medical Association, 288*(5), 589–594.

Keilitz, S. (2000). *Specialization of domestic violence case management in the courts: A national survey.* Washington, D.C.: National Center for State Courts.

Klein, A. (2008). *Practical implications of current domestic violence research. Part II: Prosecution.* Washington, D.C.: National Institute of Justice.

Lehrman, F. (1997). *Domestic violence practice and procedure.* Washington, D.C.: West Group.

Massachusetts Department of Public Health. (2008). Massachusetts certified batterer intervention programs. Retrieved from http://www.mass.gov/eohhs/docs/dph /com-health/violence/bip-brochure.pdf

National Coalition Against Domestic Violence (NCADV). (2007). Address confidentiality programs. Retrieved from http://www.ncadv.org/files/ACPPrograms.pdf

National Council of Juvenile and Family Court Judges (NCJFCJ). (2005). A guide for effective issuance & enforcement of protection orders. Washington, D.C.: Author. Retrieved from http://www.vaw.umn.edu/docu-ments/burgundybook/Burgundy_Book_FINAL.pdf

National Network to End Domestic Violence (NNEDV). (2013). Voter confidentiality programs. Retrieved from http://www.nnedv.org/resources/voter-privacy.html

Office for Victims of Crime. (2006). Enforcement of protection orders. *OVC Legal Series #4 Bulletin.* (NCJ 189190). Washington, D.C.: U.S. Department of Justice.

Pleck, E. (1989). Criminal approaches to family violence. *Crime and Justice, 11*, 19–57.

Shelton, D. (2007). *The current state of domestic violence courts in the United States, 2007.* Williamsburg, VA: National Center for State Courts.

Smith, E. L., Durose, M. R., & Langan, P. A. (2008). *State court processing of domestic violence cases.* Washington, D.C.: Bureau of Justice Statistics.

Social Security Administration. (2006). *New numbers for domestic violence victims.* Washington, D.C.: Author.

White, J. (2008). *A roundtable on the impact of* Crawford *on prosecution of domestic violence.* Washington, D.C.: Center for Education on Violence Against Women.

INDEX